Reader's Choice

Essays for Thinking, Reading, and Writing

Seventh Canadian Edition

Reader's Choice

Essays for Thinking, Reading, and Writing

KIM FLACHMANN
California State University, Bakersfield

MICHAEL FLACHMANN
California State University, Bakersfield

ALEXANDRA MACLENNAN
George Brown College

JAMIE ZEPPA
Seneca College

PEARSON

Toronto

Vice-President, Editorial Director: Gary Bennett
Editor-in-Chief: Michelle Sartor
Acquisitions Editor: David S. Le Gallais
Marketing Manager: Jennifer Sutton
Supervising Developmental Editor: Suzanne Schaan
Developmental Editor: Rachel Stuckey
Project Manager: Lesley Deugo
Manufacturing Manager: Susan Johnson
Production Editor: Caroline Winter
Copy Editor: Caroline Winter
Proofreader: Barbara Kamienski
Compositor: Cenveo Publisher Services
Permissions Researcher: The Editing Company
Art Director: Julia Hall
Cover Designer: Miguel Acevedo
Cover Image: Clockwise from top left: Getty Images/The Image Bank/Jan Stromme; Getty Images/Photodisc/Mark Lund; Getty Images/Vetta/Ozgur Donmaz; Getty Images/PhotoLibrary/ARUNAS KLUPSAS

Credits and acknowledgments for material borrowed from other sources and reproduced, with permission, in this textbook appear on the appropriate page within the text or on page 532.

10 17

Library and Archives Canada Cataloguing in Publication

Reader's choice : essays for thinking, reading, and writing / Kim Flachmann . . . [et al.]. — 7th Canadian ed.

Includes bibliographical references and index.

ISBN 978-0-205-03241-9

1. College readers. 2. English language—Rhetoric—Textbooks.

I. Flachmann, Kim

PE1417.R42 2013 808′.0427 C2011-906541-X

ISBN 978-0-205-03241-9

RHETORICAL CONTENTS

Preface xix

INTRODUCTION: Thinking, Reading, and Writing 1

What Exactly Is Critical Thinking? 2

LINDA ELDER *Looking to the Future with a Critical Eye: A Message for High School Graduates* 5

BRIAN DENIS EGAN *The Role of Critical Thinking in Effective Decision Making* 9

HOWARD GABENNESCH *Critical Thinking: What Is It Good For? (In Fact, What Is It?)* 12

My Definition of Critical Thinking 14

What Do I Need to Know About Reading and Writing Critically? 15

Reading Critically 15
Preparing to Read 16
Reading 19

LEWIS THOMAS *To Err Is Human* 21
Rereading 24

Writing Critically 28
Preparing to Write 28
Writing 34
Rewriting 37

Conclusion 39

Reading and Writing Inventories 40

Reading Inventory 41
Preparing to Read 41
Reading 41
Rereading 41

Writing Inventory 42
Preparing to Write 42
Writing 42
Rewriting 42

CHAPTER 1

DESCRIPTION: *Exploring Through the Senses* 43

Defining *Description* 43

Thinking Critically Through Description 45

Reading and Writing Descriptive Essays 46
Reading Descriptive Essays 46
Writing Descriptive Essays 48

Student Essay: Description at Work 51

Some Final Thoughts on Description 53

Description in Review 54
Reading Descriptive Essays 54
Writing Descriptive Essays 54

TOMSON HIGHWAY *What a Certain Visionary Once Said* 55
In this descriptive essay, Tomson Highway paints a vibrant picture of the landscape, climate, and wildlife of the Canadian North.

JEAN YOON *Halmonee* 59
Actor and writer Jean Yoon creates a vivid portrait of her grandmother, in both life and in death.

EDITH IGLAUER *Red Smile* 67
The idea of a first appointment with a psychiatrist makes Edith Iglauer anxious in the first place, and then a grooming ritual results in red teeth.

JOE FIORITO *Night Shift on the Main* 73
What is it like to work a night shift at The Main in Montreal? Joe Fiorito's description appeals to the full range of senses.

LISA MOORE *Between the North Bridge and the King George IV Bridge* 79
At the Edinburgh Fringe Festival, Canadian novelist Lisa Moore eavesdrops on travellers and observes street performers, including the fire-juggling Super Scott.

CHAPTER 2

NARRATION: *Telling a Story* 83

Defining *Narration* 83

Thinking Critically Through Narration 85

Reading and Writing Narrative Essays 86
Reading Narrative Essays 86
Writing Narrative Essays 88

Student Essay: Narration at Work 90

Some Final Thoughts on Narration 92

Narration in Review 93
Reading Narrative Essays 93
Writing Narrative Essays 93

STEVEN HEIGHTON *Elegy in Stone* *94*
The author, who is a poet, short-story writer, and novelist, recounts the moving experience of visiting Vimy Ridge. Heighton's visit leads to reflections on Canada's participation in WWI and the essential nature of Canada and Canadians.

K'NAAN *Between the Highs and the Lows, Life Happens* 102
Award-winning musician and rap artist K'naan claims his childhood dream was to become an eye doctor, not an artist. In this essay, he reflects on his journey from war-torn Somalia to Toronto and the role that poetry and music played in leading him safely out of a turbulent adolescence.

ANIK SEE *Borderland* 107
In this essay, Anik See relates the story of trying to cross the Canadian–U.S. border and her resulting confrontation with the border officials when they deny her entry.

MATT COHEN *Zada's Hanukkah Legacy* 112
As an adult, Matt Cohen reflects on past Hanukkah celebrations with his grandparents and the important lessons he learned.

JOWI TAYLOR *"Beginning" from* Six String Nation 120
Broadcaster and writer Jowi Taylor wanted to build a special guitar and hoped it would be ready for the 1995 October referendum in Quebec. After all, how long could it possibly take to put together a guitar using material from every province and territory of Canada?

JENN LAMOTHE *Giving Up the Fight* 125
Usually we are encouraged not to give up, but freelance writer Jenn Lamothe believes that sometimes giving up the fight is the right thing to do.

CHAPTER 3

EXAMPLE: *Illustrating Ideas* 129

Defining *Example* 129

Thinking Critically Through Examples 131

Reading and Writing Example Essays 131
Reading Example Essays 132
Writing Example Essays 133

Student Essay: Examples at Work 135

Some Final Thoughts on Examples 137

Example in Review 138
Reading Example Essays 138
Writing Example Essays 138

ANITA RAU BADAMI *My Canada* 139
What constitutes your Canada? In this essay from the *Imperial Oil Review*, Anita Rau Badami uses a multitude of examples to make her Canada come alive and to explain why it is now her home.

RYAN McNUTT *The Music We Hate: Joanna Newsom* 148
Ryan McNutt can't stand the music of Joanna Newsom! In this essay, he explores what he dislikes about her harp-inspired compositions and why.

KATRINA ONSTAD *John Lennon, Michael Jackson: Do Celebrities Die Anymore?* 152
In this essay, Katrina Onstad discusses the ownership of a dead celebrity's image and the various reasons advertisers might want to splice images of Fred Astaire into a commercial for a vacuum cleaner.

BARBARA KINGSOLVER *Life Without Go-Go Boots* 157
What fashion item was essential to you when growing up? Barbara Kingsolver discusses the role of fashion in her life.

NAOMI KLEIN *Co-opting Dissent* 164
No Logo author Naomi Klein is well known for her frequently dissenting positions on various issues. In this essay, she uses multiple examples to show how companies respond to dissent by attempting to co-opt it.

STEPHEN OSBORNE *The Lost Art of Waving* 169
In this meditative essay, Stephen Osborne opens up the simplest of gestures, the goodbye wave, to uncover a lost world of meaning.

CHAPTER 4

PROCESS ANALYSIS: *Explaining Step by Step* 175

Defining *Process Analysis* 175

Thinking Critically Through Process Analysis 177

Reading and Writing Process Analysis Essays 178
Reading Process Analysis Essays 178
Writing Process Analysis Essays 180

Student Essay: Process Analysis at Work 182

Some Final Thoughts on Process Analysis 183

Process Analysis in Review 184
Reading Process Analysis Essays 184
Writing Process Analysis Essays 184

MALCOLM GLADWELL *Is the Belgian Coca-Cola Hysteria the Real Thing?* 185
The author of *The Tipping Point* focuses his attention on the phenomenon of mass hysteria and the case of the smelly Belgian Coca-Cola.

STANLEY COREN *Dogs and Monsters* 190
What's all the fuss about genetic engineering? Scientist, author, professor, and television host Stanley Coren walks us through the history of dog breeding.

MAUREEN LITTLEJOHN *You Are a Contract Painkiller* 196
Canadians consume almost one billion Aspirin or ASA tablets each year. In this essay, Maureen Littlejohn considers exactly how ASA works and traces its history in medicine.

DAKSHANA BASCARAMURTY *My Parents Killed Santa (and Nobody Cared)* 200
Growing up in a Hindu family in Toronto, Dakshana Bascaramurty convinces her parents to celebrate Christmas with all the traditional trimmings. Her parents do their best to accommodate her wishes, until they move to Winnipeg and forget the tree.

NICK PAUMGARTEN *Master of Play* 205
Do you remember the first video game you ever played? In this article, Nick Paumgarten describes how Nintendo transformed itself from a company that manufactured playing cards out of crushed mulberry bark to a video game company that changed the way we play.

ADAM GOODHEART *How to Mummify a Pharaoh* 212
American historian Adam Goodheart outlines the steps in the lost art of mummification for the readers of *Civilization*, the magazine of the U.S Library of Congress.

CHAPTER 5

DIVISION/CLASSIFICATION: *Finding Categories* 216

Defining *Division/Classification* 216

Thinking Critically Through Division/Classification 218

Reading and Writing Division/Classification Essays 219
Reading Division/Classification Essays 219
Writing Division/Classification Essays 221

Student Essay: Division/Classification at Work 223

Some Final Thoughts on Division/Classification 224

Division/Classification in Review 225
Reading Division/Classification Essays 225
Writing Division/Classification Essays 225

ALISON GILLMOR *Repress Yourself* 226
Television shows are increasingly populated with emotionally reserved characters defying the edict to "express themselves." This essay outlines the role of prime-time television in repopularizing the values of privacy, modesty, discretion, and restraint.

WILL BRAUN *Seven Criteria for the Adoption of New Technology* 237
When Will Braun was wondering whether to buy a car, he consulted a farmer, a sociologist, an Amish bishop, and a seven-question test to help him decide.

FAITH MOOSANG *Nancy Drew Knows It's Hard* 246
In this satirical piece, Faith Moosang considers whether the techniques of sleuth Nancy Drew can help identify and catch "perps" in our crime- and terror-obsessed world.

DANIEL J. LEVITIN *The Music of My Mind: A Neuroscientist Examines the Recipe for Listening Ecstasy* 250
Why do we like the music we do? Musician and neuroscientist Daniel J. Levitin categorizes the musical techniques that appeal to listeners' brains.

ALEX BOYD *In Defense of Graffiti* 256
In an essay originally published on the *Bookninja* website, Alex Boyd uses classification as a strategy to examine the role of graffiti and defend its value.

CHAPTER 6
COMPARISON/CONTRAST: *Discovering Similarities and Differences* 262

Defining *Comparison/Contrast* 262

Thinking Critically Through Comparison/Contrast 264

Reading and Writing Comparison/Contrast Essays 264
Reading Comparison/Contrast Essays 265
Writing Comparison/Contrast Essays 266

Student Essay: Comparison/Contrast at Work 271

Some Final Thoughts on Comparison/Contrast 272

Comparison/Contrast in Review 273
Reading Comparison/Contrast Essays 273
Writing Comparison/Contrast Essays 273

MONTE HUMMEL *A Passion for the Environment: Two Accounts* 274
The former president of the World Wildlife Fund Canada explains the roots of his passion for the environment in this essay from the *Queen's Quarterly*.

MICHAEL McKINLEY *Opera Night in Canada* 278
According to Michael McKinley, hockey and opera may have a lot more in common than you realize.

IRSHAD MANJI *Status Anxiety? Consider Socrates and the Sewer Saviour* 284
What do Facebook, Socrates, and an animated rat have in common? Irshad Manji traces the connections among them as she explores how we might liberate ourselves from our overwhelming desire to be accepted.

CHRISTOPHER DeWOLF *Montrealers, Cherish Your Clotheslines* 289
Do you hang your clothes out to dry? In this essay from *Spacing Montreal*, Christopher DeWolf compares attitudes toward clotheslines in different Canadian cities.

JENNIE PUNTER *Crime and Punishment in a Foreign Land* 293
In this essay, the author compares two foreign-language films about crime: the original Swedish version of *The Girl with the Dragon Tattoo* and the Argentinean thriller *The Secret In Their Eyes*. She argues that, unlike many Hollywood crime dramas, these films are made "for grown-ups."

CHAPTER 7

DEFINITION: *Limiting the Frame of Reference* 301

Defining *Definition* 301

Thinking Critically Through Definition 302

Reading and Writing Definition Essays 303
Reading Definition Essays 303
Writing Definition Essays 305

Student Essay: Definition at Work 306

Some Final Thoughts on Definition 308

Definition in Review 309
Reading Definition Essays 309
Writing Definition Essays 309

DREW HAYDEN TAYLOR *Pretty Like a White Boy: The Adventures of a Blue-Eyed Ojibway* 310
Like Kermit the Frog, Drew Hayden Taylor doesn't always find it easy to live with the way that he looks. In this essay he discusses the difficulties of not "looking the part."

JUNE CALLWOOD *Forgiveness* 318
"Forgiveness is hard work," June Callwood tells us, but in this "age of anger," it is worth striving for.

DOUGLAS GLOVER *On Winning and Responsibility* 325
Looking at various types of victory, Glover shows us that winning is never as clear or as simple as the victors would like it to be, and reminds us of another, more constructive use of the word "winning."

CYNARA GEISSLER *Fat Acceptance: A Basic Primer* 330
"A lot of time, effort and capital has been invested in making us believe that fat is a dirty word," Cynara Geissler writes. In this essay, she explores body image, self-acceptance and the real meaning of health.

SIMON BLACK *The Search for Mandela's Gun* 335
How do you define *terrorism?* How is a terrorist different from a freedom fighter? In this column from *Pound*, an urban music magazine, Simon Black explores the spectrum of perspectives on violence for political ends.

LAWRENCE HILL *Don't Call Me That Word* 339
Lawrence Hill makes a powerful argument against a single word on the basis of the hateful racist sentiments it carries.

CHAPTER 8

CAUSE/EFFECT: *Tracing Reasons and Results* 344

Defining *Cause/Effect* 345

Thinking Critically Through Cause/Effect 347

Reading and Writing Cause/Effect Essays 348
Reading Cause/Effect Essays 349
Writing Cause/Effect Essays 350

Student Essay: Cause/Effect at Work 352

Some Final Thoughts on Cause/Effect 354

Cause/Effect in Review 355
Reading Cause/Effect Essays 355
Writing Cause/Effect Essays 355

STEPHEN KING *Why We Crave Horror Movies* 356
Seen any good movies lately? Best-selling author Stephen King explains why we are so fascinated with movies that appeal to our darker instincts.

PETER NICHOLSON *Information-Rich and Attention-Poor* 362
Peter Nicholson examines the effect of technology on attention and memory. What are we losing as our devices acquire more memory and speed and generate ever-increasing amounts of information?

JOHN MOORE *Sporting Life* 370
In this essay, which won a Western Magazine Award, John Moore explores the appeal of X-treme sports, adventure tourism, and eco-tourism in an increasingly urbanized world.

CARMEN EVEREST WAHL *Gluten Intolerance: Why Are More People Suffering Than Ever Before?* 384

Intolerance to gluten, the protein in wheat, seems to be growing. Carmen Everest Wahl considers possible causes for the increase and explores gluten-free options and opportunities.

JEANNIE GUY *Newfoundland Cooking* 391
Monday night: leftovers. Tuesday night: boiled dinner. Wednesday: fish, brewis, and scruncheons. In this essay, Jeannie Guy remembers home cooking in her Newfoundland community and explains why Thursday was the only day they might get a "modern, foreign kind of food for supper like pork chops."

EVELYN LAU *More and More* 397
What is an addiction? What causes someone to become an addict? Evelyn Lau explores her addictive behaviour that begins with the consumption of sweets in her childhood.

CHAPTER 9

ARGUMENT/PERSUASION: *Inciting People to Thought or Action* 407

Defining *Argument/Persuasion* 408

Thinking Critically Through Argument/Persuasion 410

Reading and Writing Persuasive Essays 411
Reading Persuasive Essays 411
Writing Persuasive Essays 413

Student Essay: Argument/Persuasion at Work 417

Some Final Thoughts on Argument/Persuasion 419

Argument/Persuasion in Review 420
Reading Persuasive Essays 420
Writing Persuasive Essays 420

ARLENE PERLY RAE, IRSHAD MANJI, and ANNA PORTER
A Call to Arms on Anti-Semitism 421
Three writers—one Jewish, one Muslim, and one Christian—have come together to write this essay advocating that Canada take a leading role in fighting anti-Semitism.

JUDY REBICK *The Culture of Overwork* 426
Judy Rebick argues against the growing culture of overwork and prescribes action to counter this unhealthy trend.

DANIEL FRICKER AND LARS KUSHNER *Anti-Gay Bullying* 431

Daniel Fricker and Lars Kushner call for an end to the bullying of gay, lesbian, and transgendered youth and explore innovative solutions to the problem, including the It Gets Better project.

JANICE GROSS STEIN *Whisper, Echo and Voice* 437
When Canada speaks, does the world listen? How can Canada ensure a strong voice in world affairs? Janice Gross Stein argues for Canada's capacity to make a difference on global issues and the steps we must take to do it.

RUSSELL SMITH *Potty-Mouthed and Proud of It* 443
Why are taboo words taboo? *Globe and Mail* columnist Russell Smith explores the nature of profanity.

SHEEMA KHAN *Hijabs: Don't Kick Up a Fuss* 448
Soccer mom Sheema Khan discusses the controversy in Quebec over the religious symbol of the hijab on the soccer field.

RAFE MAIR *Raise the Driving Age* 452
In this essay from online magazine *The Tyee*, Rafe Mair argues that the driving age should be raised to 19.

ADAM GOPNIK *Shootings* 457
Using the example of the 2007 Virginia Tech mass shootings, Gopnik makes a case for gun control focused on handguns.

OPPOSING VIEWPOINTS *Hockey Violence* 462
In this pair of essays, Aaron Wherry and Laura Robinson present their views on violence in hockey.

AARON WHERRY *Violently Happy: Why the NHL Needs to Make Hockey Safe Again for Those Who Appreciate Bloodshed* 463

LAURA ROBINSON *Sports Breeds Real-Life Violence* 467

CHAPTER 10

DOCUMENTED ESSAYS: *Reading and Writing from Sources* 471

Defining *Documented Essays* 471

Documented Essay Reference Chart 473

Reading Documented Essays 473

Reading Documented Essays in Review 476
Reading Documented Essays 476

BARBARA EHRENREICH *The Ecstasy of War* 477

Do men and women possess a natural "warrior instinct" that enables them to kill their enemies during battle? Not so, claims Barbara Ehrenreich, though many social and cultural rituals help transform ordinary people into effective soldiers.

LAWRENCE NORTON *Facilitated Communication & the Power of Belief: How* Time *Magazine Got It Wrong* 486

In this documented essay, Lawrence Norton explores the flawed research regarding facilitated communication and the cost of uncritically accepting what we want to believe is true.

Preparing to Write Documented Essays 493

Finding Sources 495
Sources That Are Relevant, Reliable, and Recent 495
Consulting Interdisciplinary Databases, Subject-Specific Indexes, and Electronic Journal Collections 496

Avoiding Plagiarism 499
Types of Material 499
Acknowledging Sources 500
Direct Quotation, Paraphrase, and Summary 501
When to Quote? When to Paraphrase? 503

Staying Organized 503
Taking Notes on Sources 503
Making a Working Outline 505

Writing Documented Essays 505
Writing the Introduction 506
Writing the Supporting Paragraphs 506
Introducing Sources 507
Using Sources 508
Documenting Sources 509
Documentation Format 509
Writing the Conclusion 509
Creating the Title 510

Revising and Editing a Documented Essay 510
Revising 511

Student Essay: Documentation at Work 511

Writing Documented Essays in Review 517
Writing Documented Essays 517

CHAPTER 11

ESSAYS ON THINKING, READING, AND WRITING 518

MARGUERITE ANDERSEN *Passion for Language* 519

NATALIE GOLDBERG *The Rules of Writing Practice* 520

BENOIT VIROLE *Harry Potter's Cauldron: The Power of Myth and the Rebirth of the Sacred* 524

RYAN BIGGE *Speak English, Dammit: Why Has Jargon Become the Language of Business?* 530

Credits 532

Index of Authors and Titles 535

ESSAYS ON THINKING, READING, AND WRITING

[illegible]

PREFACE

Accurate thinking is the beginning and fountain of writing.

—Horace

Reader's Choice is based on the assumption that lucid writing follows lucid thinking, whereas poor writing is almost inevitably the product of foggy, irrational thought processes. As a result, our primary purpose in this book, as in previous editions of *Reader's Choice*, is to help students think more clearly and logically—both in their minds and on paper.

Furthermore, we believe that college and university students should be able to think, read, and write on three increasingly difficult levels:

1. *Literal*, characterized by a basic understanding of words and their meanings;
2. *Interpretive*, consisting of a knowledge of linear connections between ideas and an ability to make valid inferences based on those ideas; and
3. *Critical*, the highest level, distinguished by the systematic investigation of complex ideas and by the analysis of their relationship to the world around us.

To demonstrate this vital interrelationship between reader and writer, this text provides prose models that are intended to inspire students' thinking and writing. Although studying rhetorical strategies is certainly not the only way to approach writing, it is a productive means of helping students become better writers. These essays are intended to encourage students to improve their writing through a partnership with some of the best examples of professional prose available today. Just as musicians and athletes richly benefit from studying the techniques of the foremost people in their fields, students will, we hope, grow in spirit and language use from their collaborative work with the writers in this collection.

How the Text Is Organized

Each chapter of *Reader's Choice* begins with an explanation of a single rhetorical technique. These explanations are divided into six sections that move from the effect of this technique on our daily lives to its integral role in the writing process. Also, in each introduction we include a student essay featuring each particular rhetorical strategy under discussion. The essay is highlighted by annotations and underlining to illustrate how to write that type of essay and to help bridge the gap between student writing and the professional selections that follow.

The essays that follow each chapter introduction are selected from a wide variety of contemporary authors. Of course, "pure" rhetorical types rarely exist, and when they do, the result often seems artificial. Therefore, although each essay in this collection focuses on a single rhetorical mode as its primary strategy, other strategies are always simultaneously at work. These selections concentrate on one primary technique at a time in much the same way a well-arranged photograph highlights a certain visual detail, though many other elements function in the background to make the picture an organic whole.

In introducing each reading selection, we offer some material to focus attention onto a particular writer and topic before the essay is read. This "prereading" segment begins with biographical information about the author and ends with a number of questions to whet the reader's appetite for the essay that follows. This section is intended to help readers discover interesting relationships among ideas in their reading and then anticipate various ways of thinking about and analyzing the essay. The prereading questions forecast not only the content of the essay, but also the questions and writing assignments that follow.

The questions after each reading selection are designed as guides for thinking about the essay. These questions are at the heart of the relationship represented in this book among thinking, reading, and writing. They are divided into four interrelated sections that move readers smoothly from a literal understanding of what they have just read, to interpretation, and finally to analysis.

After students have studied the different techniques at work in a reading selection, a specific essay assignment provides an opportunity to practise all these skills in unison and encourages the discovery of even more secrets about the intricate and exciting details of effective communication. In the Ideas for Discussion/Writing section, three possible essay topics are preceded by Preparing to Write questions to help readers generate new ideas. Most of the discussion/writing topics specify a purpose (a definite reason for writing the essay) and an audience (an identifiable person or group of people who should be addressed in the essay) to help students focus their work as precisely as possible. The word *essay* (which comes from the Old French *essai*, meaning a "try" or an "attempt") is an appropriate label for these writing assignments, because they all ask students to wrestle with an idea or a problem and then try to give shape to their conclusions in some effective manner. Such "exercises" can be equated with the development of athletic ability: The essay itself demonstrates that students can put together all the various skills they have learned; it proves that you can actually play the "sport" of writing.

What Is New

We have made a number of changes in the seventh edition of *Reader's Choice* that reflect the responses of reviewers from colleges and universities all over Canada.

- *Emphasis on critical thinking.*

Three new readings are now included in the Introduction to help students discover their own definition of critical thinking and begin to understand the book's primary objective of improving their ability to think critically.

- *Nineteen new essays.*

We have added new pieces by Lisa Moore, K'naan, and Katrina Onstad, among others, and introduced new topics such as Facebook and status anxiety, fat acceptance, anti-gay bullying, the appeal of crime thrillers, and the development of classic video games. The selections in the seventh edition offer a diversity of perspectives that truly reflect the mosaic of the Canadian classroom, from "My Parents Killed Santa," about Dakshana Bascaramurty's efforts to persuade her Hindu parents to celebrate Christmas, to Jennie Guy's "Newfoundland Cooking."

- *Expanded chapter on documented essays.*

The expanded chapter on documented essays contains new information on writing a research essay, including finding reliable, relevant, and recent sources; incorporating quotes and paraphrases; and documenting sources. This new writing section uses Barbara Ehrenreich's "The Ecstasy of War" as a starting point for student research, culminating in a student essay that responds to one of the Ideas for Discussion/Writing questions.

- *Reading and writing checklists for each rhetorical mode.*

We have maintained the reading and writing checklists from the sixth edition but compiled them at the end of each chapter introduction in a more visually appealing format.

- *Access to* MyCanadianCompLab

An *access code* packaged with every new copy of the text gives you access to *MyCanadianCompLab. MyCanadianCompLab* empowers student writers and facilitates writing instruction by integrating a composing space and ePortfolio with proven resources and tools, such as practice exercises, diagnostics, and multimedia assets. Instructors can create, deliver, and track assignments online, then use the gradebook to assess student and class progress.

Supplements

- *MyCanadianCompLab*

Instructors adopting the seventh edition of *Reader's Choice* will also receive access to *MyCanadianCompLab*, Pearson Canada's comprehensive online resource for composition at **www.mycanadiancomplab.ca**. *MyCanadianCompLab* features guidelines, tutorials, and exercises for writing, grammar, and research, including material on avoiding plagiarism and evaluating resources. Students can use *MyCanadianCompLab* on their own or in connection with classroom assignments. The revised Instructor's Manual that accompanies the seventh edition of *Reader's Choice* provides helpful suggestions for using *MyCanadianCompLab* in conjunction with the text. Contact your local Pearson Education sales representative for more information on bringing the advantages of *MyCanadianCompLab* to your students.

- *Instructor's Manual*

An updated Instructor's Manual accompanies the seventh edition of the text with classroom resources and strategies, vocabulary and comprehension quizzes for each of the reading selections, discussion of theoretical approaches to the teaching of composition, and techniques for responding to student writing.

The Instructor's Manual also offers guidance on using the diagnostic quizzes found on the *MyCanadianCompLab* site to assess student progress, and suggestions for integrating the exercise material on rhetorical modes with classroom teaching strategies.

- Reading and Writing from Sources

Reading and Writing from Sources is a new instructor's supplement that includes information on MLA, APA, and Chicago documentation styles. With tips for taking good research notes and using interdisciplinary databases, this resource includes some additional material on revision and uses a student essay as an example.

Instructors can download the Instructor's Manual and *Reading and Writing from Sources* from a password-protected location on Pearson Canada's online catalogue (**www.pearsoncanada.ca/highered**). Simply search for the text, and then click on the Resources tab. Contact your local sales representative for further information.

- *Pearson's Technology Specialists*

Pearson's Technology Specialists work with faculty and campus course designers to ensure that Pearson technology products, assessment tools, and online course materials are tailored to meet your specific needs. This highly qualified team is dedicated to helping schools take full advantage of a wide range of educational resources, by assisting in the integration of a variety of instructional materials and media formats. Your local Pearson Canada sales representative can provide you with more details on this service program.

Kim Flachmann
Michael Flachmann
Alexandra MacLennan
Jamie Zeppa

Acknowledgments

A number of people who helped in the preparation of this edition of *Reader's Choice* deserve acknowledgment. At Pearson Canada, for their guidance, patience, and support, we would like to thank David Le Gallais, acquisitions editor; Kathleen McGill, sponsoring editor; Rachel Stuckey, developmental editor; Lesley Deugo, project manager; and Caroline Winter, production and copy editor.

We would like to thank all the reviewers for their feedback, especially

Karen Budra	*Langara College*
Greg Chan	*Kwantlen Polytechnic University*
Roger Fowler	*University of Ottawa*
Rosemary Hoey	*Carleton University*
Stefanie Ketley	*Fanshawe College*
Cecilia Martell	*Kwantlen Polytechnic University*
Trevor Tucker	*University of Ottawa*

Finally, thank you to our colleagues and students for their ongoing support and their feedback and advice about *Reader's Choice.*

Alexandra MacLennan & Jamie Zeppa

INTRODUCTION

Thinking, Reading, and Writing

Have you ever had trouble expressing your thoughts? If so, you're not alone. Many people have this difficulty—especially when they are asked to write their thoughts down. The good news is that this "ailment" can be cured. We've learned over the years that the more clearly students think about the world around them, the more easily they can express their ideas through written and spoken language. As a result, this textbook intends to improve your writing by helping you think clearly, logically, and critically about a range of ideas and issues. You will learn to reason, read, and write in increasingly complex ways, moving steadily from a simple, literal understanding of topics to interpretation and analysis.

Part of becoming a better writer involves understanding that reading and writing are companion activities that engage people in the creation of thought and meaning—either as readers interpreting a text or as writers constructing one. Clear thinking, then, is the pivotal point that joins these two efforts. The traditional rhetorical strategies are presented in this text as thinking techniques that you can use in other academic tasks. Inspired by the well-crafted prose models in this text and guided by the reading questions, you can raise the level of your thinking skills while improving your reading and writing abilities on three progressively sophisticated levels:

1. *The literal level* is the foundation of all human understanding; it entails knowing the meanings of words—individually and in relation to one another. In order to comprehend the sentence "You must exercise your brain to reach your full mental potential" on the literal level, for example, a person would have to know the definitions of all the words in the sentence and understand the way those words work together to make meaning.

2. *Interpretation* requires the ability to make associations between details, draw inferences from pieces of information, and reach conclusions about the material. An interpretive understanding of the sample sentence in level 1 might be translated into the following thoughts: "Exercising the brain sounds a bit like exercising the body. I wonder if there is any correlation between the two. If the brain must be exercised, it is probably made up of muscles, much as the body is." None of these particular "thoughts" is made explicit in the sentence, but each is suggested in one way or another.

3. *Thinking, reading, and writing critically,* the most sophisticated form of rational abilities, involves a mental activity that is crucial for successful academic and professional work. A critical analysis of our sample sentence might proceed in the following way: "This sentence is talking to me. It actually addresses me with the word *you.* I wonder what *my* mental potential is. Will I be able to reach it? Will I know when I attain it? What kind of exercise is meant here? I wonder if there are limitations to this development. Maybe psychologists have done studies on this." Students who can take an idea apart like this and understand its various components more thoroughly after reassembling them are rewarded intrinsically with a clearer knowledge of life's complexities and the ability to generate creative, useful ideas. They are also rewarded extrinsically with good grades and are more likely to earn responsible jobs with higher pay, because they are able to apply a greater understanding of the world to their professional and personal lives.

In this textbook, you will learn to think critically by reading essays written by intelligent, interesting authors and by writing your own essays on a variety of topics. The next several pages offer guidelines for approaching the thinking, reading, and writing assignments in this book. These suggestions should also be useful to you in your other courses.

What Exactly Is Critical Thinking?

Recent psychological studies have shown that "thinking" and "feeling" are complementary operations. All of us have feelings that are automatic and instinctive. To feel pride after winning first place at a track meet, for example, or to feel anger at a spiteful friend is not behaviour we have to study and master; such emotions come naturally to human beings. Thinking, on the other hand, is much less spontaneous than feeling; research suggests that study and practice are required for sustained mental development.

Thinking critically involves grappling with the ideas and issues in your immediate environment and in the world at large. It does not necessarily entail finding fault, which you might naturally associate with the word *critical*, but rather suggests continually questioning and analyzing the world around you. Thinking critically is one of the highest forms of mental activity that human beings engage in; it is the source of success at school and in our professional and personal lives. Fortunately, all of us can learn how to think more critically.

Critical thinking means taking apart an issue, idea, or problem; examining its various parts; and reassembling the topic with a fuller understanding of its intricacies. Implied in this explanation is the ability to see the topic from one or more new perspectives. Using your mind in this way will help you find solutions to difficult problems, design creative plans of action, and ultimately live a life consistent with your opinions on important issues.

Since critical or analytical thinking is one of the highest forms of mental activity, it requires a great deal of concentration and practice. Once you have actually felt how your mind works at this level, however, you will find that recreating the experience is somewhat like riding a bicycle: You will be able to do it naturally, easily, and skilfully whenever you want to. Our initial goal, then, is to help you think critically when you are required to do so in school, on the job, or in any other area of your life.

Rhetorical strategies are presented in this text as different ways of thinking and processing information. As you move through the following chapters, we will ask you to isolate each rhetorical mode—much like isolating your abs, quads, and biceps in a weight-training workout—so that you can concentrate on these thinking patterns one at a time. Looking closely at rhetorical modes helps us discover our own patterns of thought. This in turn lets us improve our reading and writing abilities. Thinking critically helps us discover fresh insights into old ideas, generate new thoughts, and see connections between related issues. It is an energizing mental activity that puts us in control of our lives and our environment rather than leaving us at the mercy of our surroundings.

Each chapter introduction provides exercises designed to help you focus on a particular pattern of thought. When you practise each rhetorical pattern, you should be aware of building on your previous thinking skills. As the book progresses, the rhetorical modes become more complex and require a higher degree of concentration and effort. Throughout the book, therefore, you should keep in mind that ultimately you want to let these skills accumulate into a well-developed ability to process the world around you—including reading, writing, seeing, and feeling—on the most advanced analytical level you can master.

Below we offer three essays, each from a different perspective, to help you define critical thinking for yourself. This will allow you to use this skill more effectively than if we were able to provide you with a single definition. After reading these selections, you will be asked to generate your own definition of critical thinking.

As you read these essays, consider the following questions:

1. What are the main features of critical thinking?
2. What is the relationship between critical thinking and personal success?
3. What is the role of critical thinking in our society?

As you read, we will occasionally interrupt your thinking with other questions, and we encourage you to record your thoughts on paper to help you move toward your own definition of critical thinking.

LINDA ELDER

Looking to the Future with a Critical Eye: A Message for High School Graduates

Graduation from high school is an exciting time. Finally you will be able to live your own life, make your own decisions, do exactly what you want. At last!

So the good news is that you now are free to make your own choices. The bad news is that, in this highly complex world, it is all too easy to make decisions, which might lead you in a direction you may regret. With every decision that you make, there are choices you accept and choices you reject. With every one you accept, you consequently turn your back on others. How will you know whether you are making the right choices, or the best ones?

> What is the author trying to accomplish in this introduction?
> Is this an accurate statement about choices?

The best way to face all problems and decisions in your life is with a critical view. By this I do not mean that you should improve your ability to criticize (most of us know how to do that all too well). Rather I mean that you should think critically about the problems and opportunities that face you. In other words, you will have to make lots and lots of decisions in your life, from deciding whether to pursue a college degree to choosing a spouse and having children (or deciding not to); and you will want to do the best reasoning that you possibly can with respect to those decisions. In other words, you will want to make decisions that result in positive consequences. But to do this, you must understand some very basic things about your mind.

The human mind, without discipline and rigor, is prone to shoddy thinking. Oddly enough, very often it would rather not have to "think." Instead it is frequently impulsive, preferring to go with its first response to a situation or problem rather than probing into the complexities of issues. However, although it is non-reflective by nature, it is fully capable of transforming and improving the way it operates. This fact is a mystery to most people because such thinking involves intellectual discipline; and in our culture disciplined thinking is, for the most part, neither understood nor valued.

But we can learn to take charge of our thinking, to monitor and assess the moves our mind makes if we see the value in doing it and are willing to consistently practice it. Despite the fact that becoming highly skilled at good reasoning involves a long, slow process, the basic intellectual moves that the mind must make to do so are accessible to you. By learning these moves, you can learn to approach any subject in college, any course you take with a critical eye. You can learn to ask important questions and can, in essence, take charge of your thinking so that you are not simply "doing what the teacher says to get the grade," but continually asking yourself how the content of your college classes relates to the issues in your life in a meaningful way. In other words, you can use the information you learn in school to do better reasoning if you learn to approach the content in your classes through good reasoning.

> How can thinking critically give you more control over your life?

To illustrate what I mean, while introducing you to some of the most basic moves the mind must make if it is to do good reasoning, I will focus on an everyday problem that you might face in your life. However, to make the most of your education, you should apply the same ideas to and be able to make the same intellectual moves in all of your classes and your studies.

Fundamental Critical Thinking Moves

If I am thinking critically, or reasoning well, about a problem in my life or in my coursework, I will begin by determining the precise question I am trying to answer. To a large extent, the quality of my reasoning about any problem will be determined by how well I am able to frame the question that ultimately drives my thinking. Let's say, for example, I am planning to purchase an automobile. My reasoning will be very different if I begin with the question "What type of car do I want to buy?" than if I begin with the question "Given my limited available finances and my plans to save money for college, what is the best car purchase I can make?" The first question is unclear, and thus can be interpreted in a number of ways. It does not help to direct my thinking along a clear path. Furthermore, the way the question is put implies that I can "have" any car I "want." On the other hand, the second question is much more precise, and because it narrows the possibilities (due to my limited finances), it serves as a much better guide for my thinking.

What does asking questions have to do with critical thinking?

The next step in the process of thinking through a problem is to ask: what is my purpose in answering this question? My purpose works hand in hand with my question to guide my thinking. Let us say that my purpose is to purchase a car that is dependable, safe, and inexpensive, which I will use primarily to drive to college each day. Now I have a clear question and a clear purpose, which together tell me the type of information I must have to answer the question. Now, obviously I will ultimately have to make a decision between this car or that, so that the process of thinking critically about an issue does not tell me exactly which car to purchase. Rather, it guides me to the best possible choices.

So now I know that I need to gather information about dependability, safety, and cost. Perhaps I should begin by reading consumer reports for information related to all three of these. I will then need to shop around to find the best buy for the money. If I am considering purchasing a used car, I should look at the car's maintenance records to see if it has been well cared for (to help determine potential reliability). If I will have a long distance to drive each day, I should consider purchasing only a car that will be reliable traveling long distances. In that case perhaps I should only consider cars that have very low mileage. I might look at any statistics I can gather from automobile companies about the safety of their vehicles.

Once I have gathered the information I need, I will be aware that there is usually more than one way to interpret it. I want to consider only ACCURATE or LOGICAL interpretations of information. Statistics are often presented in ways that are misleading, or result in our interpreting information incorrectly. Automobile companies exist for one reason, and that is to make money. Therefore I will guard against simply believing the information they present (and their interpretation of the information) without wondering if there is possibly some other way to interpret it. If I am told, for example, that a particular car is the safest car in the industry (interpretation), based on the fact that fewer people are known to have accidents in this car than in any other car (information), I will question why the accident rate for this car is so low. Perhaps it is that the average person who purchases this type of car is more likely to be a safer driver (perhaps because she is older and more highly educated), rather than that the car itself is safer than other cars on the market.

> What does interpretation have to do with critical thinking?

Furthermore, when I am gathering information I want to make sure I am only considering information that is RELEVANT to the question I am focused on. Therefore I avoid gathering information about cars that are out of my price range, that I know to be unsafe, and that I am relatively certain are undependable. I determine what information is relevant by keeping my question and purpose in clear view.

To summarize, when making a decision or solving a problem, you should begin with a CLEAR, PRECISE question and purpose that directly relate to the problem. Then you should gather only ACCURATE information, which is RELEVANT to the particular problem you are trying to solve. You should figure out if there are alternate ways to interpret a piece of information, continually questioning the way others interpret information or present "facts."

If you learn to ask these questions as a habit of mind, the decisions you make will be much better, and the consequences more positive than if you respond to problems in an undisciplined, non-reflective, impulsive way. If you learn to ask these questions, you will be able to approach the content of your courses through reasoning rather than through memorization. Thus, in class, at any given point, you should be able to ask yourself, "What is the key question right now? What information do I need to address the question? How can I make sure the information is relevant and accurate? Is there another way to interpret the information than the instructor or textbook is presenting? How does this content relate to my life in a significant way?"

If you are really interested in becoming a critical thinker, you should understand that developing your mind involves a deliberate, disciplined, committed process, but that its benefits far outweigh its costs.

> In one sentence, summarize Linda Elder's definition of critical thinking.

BRIAN DENIS EGAN

The Role of Critical Thinking in Effective Decision Making

What Is Critical Thinking?

Critical thinking is the art of raising what is subconscious in our reasoning to the level of conscious recognition. It is the art of taking control of our thinking processes so as to understand the pathway and inputs that our thinking employs.

Critical thinkers understand the mechanics of reasoning (thinking). They use this understanding to manage the unconscious influences that contribute to their decision-making processes.

By taking charge of the thinking process, critical thinkers develop an understanding of what they do *not* know about a particular subject, and make better decisions as a result.

> How are critical thinking and decision making related?

Who Needs Critical Thinking?

The study of critical thinking is the study of reasoning. Implicit in this study is the recognition that in order to become better thinkers, it is necessary to practice and develop our thinking skills, just like any other skill set.

Advocates of critical thinking believe that critical thinking is a philosophical perspective that can help anyone to become more successful. The logic behind this belief is that everyone can benefit from becoming a better thinker and, as a result, have greater control over their thinking processes. In the business world, a critical thinking approach to problem solving improves the quality of analysis, resulting in a more balanced, reasoned decision-making process.

Premise

To become a critical thinker is to become an effective critic of your own thinking. This involves an analysis of the inputs (information, assumptions, and biases) that form part of your reasoning, as well as the outputs (decisions, assumptions, and biases) that result from your reasoning. As part of your development as a critical thinker you learn to gauge and measure the outputs of other people's thinking (which are your inputs), and as a consequence develop improved decision-making skills.

> According to Egan, how can you become a "critic of your own thinking"?

Are You a Critical Thinker?

Most people, particularly anyone with higher education, consider themselves to be critical thinkers. Unfortunately, quality thinking does not come naturally to most people (maybe to no one) and our education system does not fill the gap.

Critical thinking is the discipline of making sure that you use the best thinking that you are capable of in every situation. To become a skilled critical thinker it is necessary to understand thought processes and to use that understanding to structure your analysis of anything and everything, in a balanced way.

What are the symptoms of being a critical thinker? The indicator that someone is practicing critical thinking (to some degree) is that they continually question their own and other people's assumptions, reasons, motivations, and outlook. This questioning must not focus on generating mere contradiction but rather on the discovery of context, reasoning, and point of view. Critical thinkers ask questions to answer questions and seek reason and logic as the foundation for understanding.

> Why are questions important to critical thinking?

[. . .]

Developing as a Critical Thinker

Becoming a skilled thinker requires practice. Everyone 'practices' thinking, but the question is whether he or she is practicing good or bad habits. The mere act of thinking does not ensure that one is becoming an increasingly skilled thinker over time.

Bad habits are easy to learn and difficult to break. To develop as a critical thinker, you must understand and then practice the necessary thinking skills. To determine whether or not you are improving, you must judge your performance against a meaningful set of quality standards.

Give an example of what you think the author is saying here.

It is much the same as the way one would advance in the development of any set of skills, in any sport or activity. Improvement comes from guided skill set development—instruction, practice, criticism, and more practice.

Imagine trying to learn skills any other way. Would you ever become an excellent soccer player without being told what to practice or how to measure improvement? Would any parent launch a child's soccer career by leaving them in a field without any idea of what the rules of the game were, the nature of the activities, or the level of performance of other players? Of course not, but this is exactly how thinking skills are developed.

The average person, because of their routine mental activity (being conscious), presumes to become a skilled thinker by virtue of random chance – just like learning to play soccer by being left on a field with a ball. Thinking, like every other skill set, requires instruction in both the attributes (skills involved) and measures of success (quality measures).

When do you know you are a critical thinker?

HOWARD GABENNESCH

Critical Thinking: What Is It Good For? (In Fact, What Is It?)

Is critical thinking worth the costs? Consider for a moment how costly uncritical thinking can be. Stephen Jay Gould (1997, x, xii) calls attention to two precious human potentials that together constitute "the most powerful joint instrument for good that our planet has ever known":

> Only two possible escapes can save us from the organized mayhem of our dark potentialities—the side of human nature that has given us crusades, witch hunts, enslavements, and holocausts. Moral decency provides one necessary ingredient, but not nearly enough. The second foundation must come from the rational side of our mentality. For, unless we rigorously use human reason, . . . we will lose out to the frightening forces of irrationality, romanticism, uncompromising "true" belief, and the apparent resulting inevitability of mob action . . . Skepticism is the agent of reason against organized irrationalism—and is therefore one of the keys to human social and civic decency.

Explain this quotation.
What is the purpose of starting this essay with a quotation?

According to this striking claim, critical thinking is one of the most important resources a society could develop. This is because bad things do not emanate only from bad people. Bad things can also occur because of the mistaken thinking of decent people. Even when a bad idea originates with a psychopath, the real danger occurs when it is accepted by the gullible and condoned by the sincere who have little more than a child's understanding of what intellectual due process entails.

It is likely that an important link exists between critical thinking, broadly defined, and democracy itself. The American jurist Learned Hand (1952, 190) described this connection as follows:

> Liberty lies in the hearts of men and women; when it dies there, no constitution, no law, no court can save it. . . . The spirit of liberty is

> the spirit which is not too sure that it is right; the spirit of liberty is the spirit which seeks to understand the minds of other men and women; the spirit of liberty is the spirit which weighs their interest alongside its own without bias.

So by cultivating genuine critical thinking, we strengthen the crucial underpinnings of democracy (Kuhn 2003). People who are careful about the truth are less likely to be fooled by the ideologies that justify illiberal practices or promise simple solutions. Moreover, such people are more likely to recognize the value of intellectual and ideological diversity—they understand that the truth comes in pieces and is unlikely to be found all in one place. They are the best counterweight to true believers of all stripes. Ultimately, intellectual due process is no less integral to democracy than is due process of law.

Within a democracy, the social world remains a deceptive place for the sophisticated and the innocent alike. The tendency of leaders and large numbers of citizens to underestimate this fact is a source of enormous human misery.

> What is the relationship between critical thinking and a democratic society?

Here is an example. In his book a few years ago and in the 2003 Oscar-winning documentary by Errol Morris, *The Fog of War*, former defense secretary Robert S. McNamara (1995) identifies the mistakes made by him and others that led to calamity in Vietnam. His account describes confident, mostly decent men who did what they thought was best, but who fell prey to a chilling list of errors that could serve as chapters in a textbook on critical thinking: dualistic thinking, wishful thinking, absence of intellectual humility, underestimating complexity, group-think, childlike credulity, rigid adherence to orthodoxy. These were intelligent, educated men whose logical reasoning skills were far above average. Yet McNamara finds it "incredible" that "[w]e failed to analyze our assumptions critically."

Perhaps the architects of the Vietnam war went wrong because they indulged in what Thomas Sowell (2002) calls "shibboleths" as substitutes for critical thinking. A shibboleth is a belief that serves the purpose of identifying the believer as one of the good guys, prominently planted on the side of the angels.

Shibboleths "transform questions about facts, causation, and evidence into questions about personal identity and moral worth":

> Mere facts cannot compete with shibboleths when it comes to making people feel good. Moreover, shibboleths keep off the agenda the painful question of how dangerous it is to have policies which impact millions of human beings without a thorough knowledge of the hard facts needed to understand just what that impact has actually been. . . .
>
> Shibboleths are dangerous, not only because they mobilize political support for policies that most of the supporters have not thought through, but also because these badges of identity make it harder to reverse those policies when they turn out to be disastrous.

What are shibboleths?
How are they related to critical thinking?
Why do they threaten society?

Like many other forms of uncritical thinking, shibboleths derive their power from the fact that humans are designed to be social animals more than truth-seeking ones. For all the societal benefits of critical thinking, at the individual level, uncritical thinking offers social and psychological rewards of its own.

References

Gould, Stephen Jay. 1997. The Positive Power of Skepticism. In Michael Shermer, *Why People Believe Weird Things: Pseudoscience, Superstition, and Other Confusions of Our Time*, ix–xii. New York: W.H. Freeman.

Hand, Learned. 1952 (1944). The Spirit of Liberty. In Irving Dillard, ed., *The Spirit of Liberty: Papers and Addresses of Learned Hand*. New York: Alfred A. Knopf.

Kuhn, Robert. 2003. Science as democratizer. *American Scientist* 91(5):388–390.

McNamara, Robert. 1995. *In Retrospect: The Tragedy and Lessons of Vietnam*. New York: Random House.

Sowell, Thomas. 2002. The high cost of shibboleths. Townhall.com. February 15. (Accessed December 1, 2006.)

My Definition of Critical Thinking

We know that good critical thinkers accurately define their terms before moving forward, so use the information in the preceding articles to define the primary focus of this text: critical thinking.

Move thoughtfully and carefully through the following questions to arrive at your personal definition.

1. List three basic components of critical thinking.
2. Explain what is not critical thinking.
3. What can you compare it to?
4. Why is it important?

Write out your definition as clearly and precisely as you can. Include in your definition the significance of critical thinking in the life of a college student.

With a good, clear understanding of critical thinking, you are now ready to move on to the relationship of critical thinking to reading and writing. Your approach to critical thinking will determine your potential as a reader and a writer. Review your notes in this chapter as necessary as you progress through the text. Continuing to adjust and refine your definition of critical thinking is important to your progress and success as a student.

What Do I Need to Know About Reading and Writing Critically?

Reading and writing are companion activities that engage people in the creation of thought and meaning, either as readers interpreting one or as writers constructing one. Clear thinking is the pivotal point that joins these two efforts. Now that you understand the range and power of critical thinking, you can use it on some sample reading and writing material. If you learn to read critically, you will naturally be able to write critically. You must process your thoughts on a higher level as you read in order to produce essays of your own at this level. In other words, you must "import" your critical reading in order to "export" critical writing. This next section explains the relationship of critical thinking to reading and writing and gives annotated examples of the reading and writing processes at work.

Reading Critically

Reading critically begins with developing a natural curiosity about an essay and nurturing that curiosity throughout the reading process. To learn as much as you can from an essay, you should first study any preliminary material you can find, then read the essay to get a general overview of its main ideas, and finally read the selection again to achieve a deeper understanding of its content. The three phases of the reading process explained below—preparing to read, reading, and rereading—will help you develop this "natural curiosity" so that you can approach any reading assignment with an active, inquiring mind.

Preparing to Read

Learning as much as you can about an essay and its context (the circumstances surrounding its development) before you begin reading can help you move through the essay with an energetic, active mind and then reach some degree of analysis before writing on the assigned topics. In particular, knowing where an essay was first published, studying the writer's background, and doing some preliminary thinking on the subject of a reading selection will help you understand the writer's ideas and form some valid opinions of your own.

As you approach any essay, you should concentrate on four specific areas to give you an overview of the material you are about to read. We use an essay by Lewis Thomas to demonstrate these techniques.

1. *Title.* A close look at the title will usually provide important clues about the author's attitude toward the topic, the author's stand on an issue, or the mood of an essay. It can also furnish you with a sense of audience and purpose.

To Err Is Human

From this title, for example, we might infer that the author will discuss errors, human nature, and the extent to which mistakes influence human behaviour. The title is half of a well-known proverbial quotation (Alexander Pope's "To err is human, to forgive, divine"), so we might speculate further that the author has written an essay intended for a well-read audience interested in the relationship between errors and humanity. After reading only four words of the essay—its title—we already have a good deal of information about the subject, its audience, and the author's attitude toward both.

2. *Synopsis.* The Rhetorical Contents in this text contains a synopsis of each essay, very much like the following, so that you can find out more specific details about its contents before you begin reading.

Physician Lewis Thomas explains how we can profit from our mistakes—especially if we trust human nature. Perhaps someday, he says, we can apply this same principle to the computer and magnify the advantages of these errors.

From this synopsis, we learn that Thomas's essay will be an analysis of human errors and of the way we can benefit from those errors. The synopsis also tells us that the computer has the potential to magnify the value of our own errors.

3. *Biography.* Learning as much as you can about the author of an essay will generally stimulate your interest in the material and help you achieve a deeper understanding of the issues to be discussed. From the biographies in this book, you can learn, for example, whether a writer is young or old, conservative or liberal, open- or closed-minded. You might also discover when in the author's career the essay was written or what gives the author credibility in addressing the topic. Such information will invariably provide a deeper, more thorough understanding of a selection's ideas, audience, and logical structure.

LEWIS THOMAS

Lewis Thomas was a physician who, until his death in 1998, was president emeritus of the Sloan-Kettering Cancer Center and scholar-in-residence at the Cornell University Medical Center in New York City. A graduate of Princeton University and Harvard Medical School, he was formerly head of pathology and dean of the New York University–Bellevue Medical Center and dean of the Yale Medical School. In addition to having written over 200 scientific papers on virology and immunology, he authored many popular scientific essays, some of which have been collected in *Lives of a Cell* (1974), *The Medusa and the Snail* (1979), *Late Night Thoughts on Listening to Mahler's Ninth Symphony* (1983), *Etcetera, Etcetera* (1990), and *The Fragile Species* (1992). The memoirs of his distinguished career have been published in *The Youngest Science: Notes of a Medicine Watcher* (1983). Thomas liked to refer to his essays as "experiments in thought": Although Thomas generally starts off with a clear intention of what he wants to write, he claims that unexpected ideas in the act of composition often lead him to new discoveries. For Thomas, the writing process is like being in a lab.

As this information indicates, Thomas was a prominent physician who published widely on scientific topics. We know that he considered his essays "experiments in thought," which makes us expect a relaxed, spontaneous treatment of his subjects. From this biography, we can also infer that he was a leader in the medical world and that, because of the positions he held, he was well respected in his professional life. Last, we can speculate that he had a clear sense of his audience because he was able to present difficult concepts in clear, everyday language.

4. *Prereading Questions.* The Preparing to Read sections following the biographies are intended to focus your attention and stimulate your curiosity before you begin each essay. They will also get you ready to form your own opinions of the essay and its topic. You may want to write your responses to these questions in a journal to have a record of your thoughts on the various topics.

Learning where, why, and how an essay was first written will provide you with a context for the material: Why did the author write this essay? Where was it first published? Who was the author's original audience? This type of information enables you to understand the circumstances surrounding the development of the selection and to identify any topical or historical references the author makes. All the selections in this textbook were published elsewhere first—in another book, a journal, a website, or a magazine. Some are excerpts from longer works. The author's original audience, therefore, consisted of the readers of that particular publication.

Preparing to Read

The following essay, which originally appeared in the *New England Journal of Medicine* (January 1976), illustrates the clarity and ease with which Thomas explains complex scientific topics. As you prepare to read this essay, take a few moments to think about the role mistakes play in our lives: What are some memorable mistakes you have made in your life? Did you learn anything important from any of these errors? Do you make more or fewer mistakes than other people you know? Do you see any advantages to making mistakes? Any disadvantages?

From the sample Preparing to Read material, we learn that Thomas's essay "To Err Is Human" was originally published in the *New England Journal of Medicine*, a prestigious periodical read principally by members of the scientific community. Written early in 1976, the article plays upon its audience's growing fascination with computers and with the limits of artificial intelligence—subjects just as timely today as they were in the mid-1970s.

The questions here prompt you to consider your own ideas, opinions, or experiences on the topic of errors in our lives. These questions are, ideally, the last step in preparing yourself for the active role you should play as a reader.

Reading

People read essays in books, newspapers, magazines, journals, and on websites for a great variety of reasons. One reader may want to be stimulated intellectually, whereas another seeks relaxation; one person reads to keep up with the latest developments in his or her profession, whereas the next wants to learn why a certain event happened or how something can be done; some people read in order to be challenged by new ideas, whereas others find comfort principally in printed material that supports their own moral, social, or political opinions. The selections in this textbook variously fulfill all these expectations. They have been chosen, however, not only for these reasons, but for an additional, broader purpose: Reading them can help make you a better writer.

Every time you read an essay in this book, you will also be preparing to write your own essay, concentrating on the same rhetorical pattern. For this reason, as you read each selection you should pay careful attention to both the content (subject matter) and the form (language, sentence structure, organization, and development of ideas) of each essay. You will also see how effectively experienced writers use particular rhetorical modes (or patterns of thought) to organize and communicate their ideas.

Each essay in this collection features one dominant pattern that is generally supported by several others. In fact, the more aware you are of each author's writing techniques, the more rapidly your own writing process will mature and improve.

The questions before and after each essay teach you a way of reading that can help you discover the relationship of a writer's ideas to one another as well as to your own ideas. These questions can also help clarify the connection between the writer's topic, his or her style or manner of expression, and your own composing process. The questions are designed to help you understand and generate ideas, discover various choices the writers make in composing their essays, and finally realize the freedom you have to make related choices in your own writing. Such an approach takes some of the mystery out of reading and writing and makes them manageable tasks at which anyone can become proficient.

Within each essay, at the bottom of the pages, are questions designed specifically to raise your level of thinking as you read. They provide a "bridge" between the personal prereading questions and the broader academic questions and assignments that follow each essay. As you move further into the text, these questions help you understand each essay on a deeper level by filtering the context through your own experience. They invite you to engage fully with your reading and bring it into your life so you understand it both instinctively and intellectually. If you take the time to produce a written response to these questions, you will quite naturally form your own opinions and arguments in preparation for the assignments that follow each essay.

To understand your reading material on the critical level, you should be prepared to read each essay at least three times. The first reading is an overview, during which you want to get a general sense of the essay in relation to its title, purpose, audience, and publication information. You should annotate the essay with your personal reactions and make sure you understand all of the author's vocabulary.

To illustrate this process, on the following pages is the Thomas essay with a student's comments in the margins, showing how she reacted to the essay while reading it for the first time. The student also circled words she didn't know and put the definitions in the margins.

LEWIS THOMAS

To Err Is Human

This is definitely true!

Everyone must have had at least one personal experience with a computer error by this time. Bank balances are suddenly reported to have jumped from $379 into the millions, appeals for charitable contributions are mailed over and over to people with crazy sounding names at your address, department stores send the wrong bills, utility companies write that they're turning everything off, that sort of thing. If you manage to get in touch with someone and complain, you then get instantaneously typed, guilty letters from the same computer, saying, "Our computer was in error, and an adjustment is being made in your account." 1

Last spring this happened to me.

Exactly

How can this be?

These are supposed to be the sheerest, blindest accidents. Mistakes are not believed to be part of the normal behavior of a good machine. If things go wrong, it must be a personal, human error, the result of fingering, tampering, a button getting stuck, someone hitting the wrong key. The computer, at its normal best, is infallible. 2

perfect

I wonder whether this can be true. After all, the whole point of computers is that they represent an extension of the human brain, vastly improved upon but nonetheless human, superhuman❶ maybe. A good computer can think clearly and quickly enough to beat you at chess, and some of them have even been programmed to write obscure verse. They can do anything we can do, and more besides. 3

In what way?

Can this be proven?

I expected this essay to be so much more stuffy than it is. I can even understand it.

It is not yet known whether a computer has its own consciousness, and it would be hard to find out about this. When you walk into one of those great halls now built for the huge machines, and stand listening, it is easy to imagine that the faint, distant noises are the sound of thinking, and the turning of the spools gives them the look of wild creatures rolling their eyes in the effort to concentrate, choking with information. But real thinking, and dreaming, are other matters. 4

In what way?

Good, clear comparison for the general reader

On the other hand, the evidences of something like an unconscious, equivalent to ours, are all around, in every mail. As extensions of the human brain, they have been constructed with the same property of error, spontaneous, uncontrolled, and rich in possibilities.❷ 5

So true—great image!

Mistakes are at the very base of human thought, embedded there, feeding the structure like root nodules. If we were not provided with 6

Reading Critically

❶ To what extent do you feel computers "extend" the human brain? Can humans do anything that computers can't do? If so, what?

❷ How could computer errors be "rich in possibilities"?

the knack of being wrong, we could never get anything useful done. We think our way along by choosing between right and wrong alternatives, and the wrong choices have to be made as frequently as the right ones. We get along in life this way. We are built to make mistakes, coded for error.❸

7 We learn, as we say, by "trial and error." Why do we always say that? Why not "trial and rightness" or "trial and triumph"? The old phrase puts it that way because that is, in real life, the way it is done.

8 A good laboratory, like a good bank or a corporation or government, has to run like a computer. Almost everything is done flawlessly, by the book, and all the numbers add up to the predicted sums. The days go by. And then, if it is a lucky day, and a lucky laboratory, somebody makes a mistake: the wrong buffer, something in one of the blanks, a decimal misplaced in reading counts, the warm room off by a degree and a half, a mouse out of his box, or just a misreading of the day's protocol. Whatever, when the results come in, something is obviously screwed up, and then the action can begin.

9 The misreading is not the important error; it opens the way. The next step is the crucial one. If the investigator can bring himself to say, "But even so, look at that!" then the new finding, whatever it is, is ready for snatching. What is needed, for progress to be made, is the move based on error.

10 Whenever new kinds of thinking are about to be accomplished, or new varieties of music, there has to be an argument beforehand. With two sides debating in the same mind, haranguing, there is an amiable understanding that one is right and the other wrong. Sooner or later the thing is settled, but there can be no action at all if there are not the two sides, and the argument. The hope is in the faculty of wrongness, the tendency toward error. The capacity to leap across mountains of information to land lightly on the wrong side represents the highest of human endowments.

11 It may be that this is a uniquely human gift, perhaps even stipulated in our genetic instructions.❹ Other creatures do not seem to have DNA sequences for making mistakes as a routine part of daily living, certainly not for programmed error as a guide for action.

12 We are at our human finest, dancing with our minds, when there are more choices than two. Sometimes there are ten, even twenty different ways to go, all but one bound to be wrong, and the richness of selection in such situations can lift us onto totally new ground. This process is called exploration and is based on human fallibility. If we had only a single center in our brains, capable of responding only when a correct decision was to be made, instead of the jumble of different, credulous, easily conned clusters of neurones that provide for being flung off into blind alleys, up trees, down dead ends, out into blue sky, along wrong turnings, around bends, we could only stay the way we are today, stuck fast.

Reading Critically

❸ Have you ever made an error that turned out to be beneficial? What happened?

❹ Do you agree with Thomas that we are genetically programmed to make mistakes in our lives? Explain your answer.

I love the phrase "splendid freedom"

Look up "maladroit"

I like this idea

13 The lower animals do not have this splendid freedom. They are limited, most of them, to absolute infallibility. Cats, for all their good side, never make mistakes. I have never seen a maladroit, clumsy, or blundering cat. Dogs are sometimes fallible, occasionally able to make charming minor mistakes, but they get this way by trying to mimic their masters. Fish are flawless in everything they do. Individual cells in a tissue are mindless machines, perfect in their performance, as absolutely inhuman as bees.

See ¶ 11

perfection

awkward

I never thought of mistakes this way

Thomas makes our technology sound really exciting

We need to program computers to make deliberate mistakes so they can help our natural human tendency to learn thru error

Not a contradition after all

14 We should have this in mind as we become dependent on more complex computers for the arrangement of our affairs. Give the computers their heads, I say; let them go their way. If we can learn to do this, turning our heads to one side and wincing while the work proceeds, the possibilities for the future of mankind, and computerkind, are limitless. Your average good computer can make calculations in an instant which would take a lifetime of slide rules for any of us. Think of what we could gain from the near infinity of precise, machine-made miscomputation which is now so easily within our grasp. We would begin the solving of some of our hardest problems. How, for instance, should we go about organizing ourselves for social living on a planetary scale, now that we have become, as a plain fact of life, a single community? We can assume, as a working hypothesis, that all the right ways of doing this are unworkable. What we need, then, for moving ahead, is a set of wrong alternatives much longer and more interesting than the short list of mistaken courses that any of us can think up right now. We need, in fact, an infinite list, and when it is printed out we need the computer to turn on itself and select, at random, the next way to go. If it is a big enough mistake, we could find ourselves on a new level, stunned, out in the clear, ready to move again.❺

Yes

So true

error or mistake

So mistakes have value!

After you have read the reading for the first time, summarize its main ideas in some fashion.The form of this task might be anything, from a drawing of the main ideas as they relate to one another, to a succinct written summary. You could draw a graph or map of the topics in the essay (in much the same way that a person would draw a map of an area for someone unfamiliar with a particular route); outline the ideas to get an overview of the piece; or summarize the ideas to check your understanding of the main points of the selection. Any of these tasks can be completed from your original notes and underlining. Each will give you a slightly more thorough understanding of what you have read.

Reading Critically

❺ What do the author's final words mean to you: "stunned, out in the clear, ready to move again"?

Next, read the questions and assignments following the selection to help focus your thinking for the second reading. Don't answer the questions at this time; just read them to make sure you are picking up the main ideas from the selection and thinking about relevant connections among those ideas.

Rereading

Following your initial reading, read the piece again, concentrating this time on how the author achieved his or her purpose. The temptation to skip this stage of the reading process is often powerful, but the second and third readings are crucial to your development as a critical reader in all of your courses. Rereading could be compared to seeing a good movie for the second or third time. The first viewing would provide you with a general understanding of the plot, the characters, the setting, and the overall artistic accomplishment of the director; during the second viewing, however, you would undoubtedly notice many more details and see their specific contributions to the artistic whole. Similarly, the second and third readings of an essay allow a much deeper understanding of the work under consideration and prepare you to analyze the writer's ideas.

During your second reading, you should answer the questions at the bottom of the pages of the essay (the Reading Critically questions). These questions are marked throughout the text both in the essay and at the bottom of the pages by numbers within circles. Then you might ask some additional questions of your own. You will get the most out of this process if you respond in writing. Here are some sample student responses to the bridge questions accompanying the Thomas essay.

1. Sample response: Computers usually supply us with more memory than we could ever have. Perhaps we even rely on them too much for this service. On the other hand, I think we can reason on more complex levels than the computer can.
2. Sample response: Errors on the computer, like errors in humans, might lead to new discoveries or new insights into old theories and observations.
3. Sample response: I have made several mistakes that turned out to be beneficial: I dated a guy who turned out to be a negative

force in my life, which helped me understand what it means to be happy; I followed a lead on the Internet that taught me an important lesson; and I learned a lot about myself when I discovered a mistake I made on a math test.

4. Sample response: Compared to cats and dogs, we are definitely programmed to make mistakes. We are not meant to do everything perfectly, and we learn from our mistakes—in both positive and negative ways.
5. Sample response: My guess is that Thomas means we will be stunned by our new discoveries and ready to break into the clear—like a football player running with the ball.

During your third reading, you should also be prepared to do some detective work and look closely at the assumptions the reading is based on: For example, how does the writer move from idea to idea in the essay? What hidden assertions lie behind these ideas? Do you agree or disagree with these assertions? Your assessment of these unspoken assumptions will often play a major role in your critical response to a piece of writing. In the case of Thomas's essay, do you accept the unspoken connection he makes between the workings of the human brain and the computer? What parts of the essay hinge upon your acceptance of this connection? What other assumptions are fundamental to Thomas's reasoning? If you accept his thinking along the way, you are more likely to agree with the general flow of Thomas's essay. If you discover a flaw in his premises or assumptions, your acceptance of his argument will start to break down.

Next, answer the questions that follow the essay. The Understanding Details questions will help you understand and remember what you have read on both the literal and the interpretive levels. Some of the questions ask you to restate various important points the author makes (literal); others help you see relationships between the different ideas presented (interpretive).

Understanding Details

Literal	1. According to Thomas, in what ways are computers and humans similar? In what ways are they different?

Literal/ Interpretive	2. In what ways do we learn by "trial and error"? Why is this a useful way to learn?
Interpretive	3. What does Thomas mean by the statement, "If we were not provided with the knack of being wrong, we could never get anything useful done" (paragraph 6)?
Interpretive	4. According to Thomas, in what important way do humans and "lower" animals differ? What does this comparison have to do with Thomas's main line of reasoning?

The Analyzing Meaning questions require you to analyze and evaluate some of the writer's ideas in order to form valid opinions of your own. These questions demand a higher level of thought than the previous set and help you prepare more specifically for the discussion/writing assignments that follow.

	Analyzing Meaning
Analytical	1. What is Thomas's main point in this essay? How do the references to computers help him make this point?
Analytical	2. Why does Thomas perceive human error as such a positive quality? What does "exploration" have to do with this quality (paragraph 12)?
Analytical	3. What could we gain from "the near infinity of precise, machine-made miscomputation" (paragraph 14)? In what ways would our civilization advance?

The Discovering Rhetorical Strategies questions ask you to look closely at what strategies the writer uses to develop his or her thesis, and how those strategies work. The questions address aspects of the composition process, such as word choice, use of detail, transitions, statement of purpose, organization of ideas, sentence structure, and paragraph development. By becoming aware of these factors, you can use them in creating your own essays. If you understand what choices a writer makes to create certain effects in his or her prose, you are more likely to discover the range of choices available to you as you write, and you will also become more aware of your ability to control your readers' thoughts and feelings.

Discovering Rhetorical Strategies

1. Thomas begins his essay with a list of experiences most of us have had at one time or another. Do you find this an effective beginning? Why or why not?
2. Which main points in his essay does Thomas develop in most detail? Why do you think he chooses to develop these points so thoroughly?
3. Explain the simile Thomas uses in paragraph 6: "Mistakes are at the very base of human thought, embedded there, feeding the structure like root nodules." Is the comparison between mistakes and root nodules useful in this context? Why or why not? Find another simile or metaphor in this essay, and explain how it works.

A final set of questions, Making Connections, asks you to consider the essay you have just read in reference to other essays in the book. Your instructor will assign these questions according to the selections you have read. The questions may have you compare the writers' treatment of an idea, the authors' style of writing, the difference in their opinions, or the similarities between their views of the world. Such questions will help you see connections in your own life—not only in your reading and your immediate environment, but also in the larger world around you. These questions, in particular, encourage you to move from specific references in the selections to a broader range of issues and circumstances that affect your daily life.

Making Connections

1. Jenn Lamothe ("Giving Up the Fight") refers to learning from her mistakes. Would Thomas agree with her approach to this topic? In what ways do these authors think alike about the benefits of making errors? In what ways do they differ on the topic? Explain your answer.
2. Lewis Thomas and Peter Nicholson ("Information-Rich and Attention-Poor") both discuss the usefulness of computers. In what ways do their ideas complement each other? In what ways do they differ?
3. Thomas says, "The lower animals . . . are limited, most of them, to absolute infallibility" (paragraph 13). Compare this perspective with that of Stanley Coren in "Dogs and Monsters." Do you think Coren would agree that "other creatures do not seem to have DNA sequences for making mistakes as a routine part of daily living, certainly not for programmed error as a guide for action" (paragraph 11)? Explain why or why not.

Writing Critically

The last stage of responding to the reading selections in this text offers you various Ideas for Discussion/Writing that will allow you to demonstrate the different skills you have learned in each chapter. You will be most successful if you envision each writing experience as an organic process that follows a natural cycle of prewriting, writing, and rewriting.

Preparing to Write

The prewriting phase involves exploring a subject, generating ideas, selecting and narrowing a topic, analyzing an audience, and developing a purpose. Preceding the writing assignments are Preparing to Write questions you should respond to before trying to structure your thoughts into a coherent essay. These questions will assist you in generating new thoughts on the topics and may even stimulate new approaches to old ideas. Keeping a journal to respond to these questions is an excellent technique, because you will then have a record of your opinions on topics related to the writing assignments that follow. No matter what format you use to answer these questions, the activity of prewriting generally continues in various forms throughout the writing process.

Preparing to Write

Write freely about an important mistake you have made: How did the mistake make you feel? What (if anything) did you learn from this mistake? What did you fail to learn that you should have learned? Did this mistake have any positive impact on your life? What were its negative consequences? How crucial are mistakes in our lives?

Responses to these questions can be prompted by a number of different "invention" techniques and carried out individually, with another student, in small groups, or as a class project. Invention strategies can also help you discover related ideas through the various stages of writing your papers. Because you will undoubtedly vary your approach depending on the assignment, you should be familiar with the following choices available to you:

Brainstorming. The basis of brainstorming is free association. Ideally, you should get a group of people together and bounce ideas, words, and thoughts off one another until they begin to cluster around related topics. In brainstorming with others, the exchange of thoughts usually starts orally, but should transfer to paper when your ideas begin to fall into related categories. When you brainstorm by yourself, however, you should write down everything that comes to mind. The act of recording your ideas in this case becomes a catalyst for other thoughts; you are essentially setting up a dialogue with yourself on paper. Then, keep writing down words and phrases that occur to you until they begin to fall into logical subdivisions, or until you stop generating new ideas.

Freewriting. Freewriting means writing to discover what you want to say. Set a time limit of about 10 minutes, and just write by free association. Write about what you are seeing, feeling, touching, thinking; write about having nothing to say; recopy the sentence you just wrote—anything. Just keep writing on paper, on a typewriter, or on a computer. After you have generated some material, locate an idea that is central to your writing assignment, put it at the top of another page, and start freewriting again, letting your thoughts take shape around this central idea. This second type of preparation is called *focused freewriting* and is especially valuable when you already have a specific topic.

Journal Entries. Journal entries are much like freewriting, except you have some sense of an audience—probably either your instructor or yourself. In a journal, anything goes. You can respond to the Preparing to Write questions, jot down thoughts, paste up articles that spark your interest, write sections of dialogue, draft letters (the kind you never send), record dreams, or make lists. The possibilities are unlimited. An excellent way of practising writing, the process of keeping a journal is also a wonderful means of dealing with new ideas—a way of fixing them in your mind and making them yours.

Direct Questions. This technique involves asking a series of questions useful in any writing situation to generate ideas, arrange thoughts, or revise prose. One example of this strategy is to use the inquiries journalists rely on to check the coverage in their articles:

Who:	*Who played the game?*
	Who won the game?
What:	*What kind of game was it?*
	What happened in the game?
Why:	*Why was the game played?*
Where:	*Where was the game played?*
When:	*When was the game played?*
How:	*How was the game played?*

If you ask yourself extended questions of this sort on a specific topic, you will begin to produce thoughts and details that will undoubtedly be useful to you in the writing assignments that follow.

Clustering. Clustering is a method of drawing or mapping your ideas as fast as they come into your mind. Put a word, phrase, or sentence in a circle in the centre of a blank page.

Then, put every new idea that comes to you in another circle and show its relationship to a previous thought by drawing a line to the circle containing the previous idea. You will probably reach a natural stopping point for this exercise in two to three minutes.

Although you can generate ideas in a number of different ways, the main principle behind the Preparing to Write questions in this text is to encourage you to do what is called *expressive writing* before you tackle any writing assignment. This is writing based on your feelings, thoughts, experiences, observations, and opinions. The process of answering questions about your own ideas and experiences makes you "think on paper," enabling you to surround yourself with your own thoughts and opinions. From this reservoir, you can then choose the ideas you want to develop into an essay and begin writing about them one at a time.

As you use various prewriting techniques to generate responses to the Preparing to Write questions, you should know that these responses can be expressed using lists, outlines, random notes, sentences and paragraphs, charts, graphs, or pictures—whatever keeps the thoughts flowing smoothly and productively. One of our students used a combination of brainstorming and clustering to generate the following thoughts in response to the prewriting exercise following the Thomas essay:

Brainstorming

Mistakes:

- *happen when I'm in a hurry*
- *make me feel stupid*
- *love*
- *Bob*
- *learned a lot about people*
- *people aren't what they seem*
- *getting back on track*
- *parents*
- *corrections*
- *relationships*
- *trip back East*
- *pride*
- *going in circles*
- *learning from mistakes*
- *I am a better person*
- *make my values clear*
- *mistakes help us change*
- *painful*
- *helpful*
- *valuable*

Clustering

From the free-flowing thoughts you generate, you next need to decide what to write about and how to limit your subject to a manageable length. Our student writer chose topic 2 from the Choosing a Topic list after the essay (see page 35). Her initial responses to the prewriting questions helped her decide to write on "A Time I Got Lost." She then generated more focused ideas and opinions in the form of a journal entry. It is printed here just as she wrote it, errors and all.

Journal Entry

The craziest mistake I think I ever made was on a trip I took recently—I was heading to the east coast from British Columbia and reached Fredericton. I was so excited because I was going to get to see the Atlantic Ocean for the first time in my life and Fredericton was one of my last towns before I reached the sea. In Fredericton I was going to have to change from a northeast direction to due east.

When I got there the highway was under construction. I took the detour, but got all skrewed up till I realized that I had gone the wrong direction. By this time I was lost somewhere in downtown Fredericton and didn't know which way was east. I stoped and asked a guy at a gas station and he explained how to get back on the east-bound highway. The way was through the middle of town. By the time I got to where I was supposed to turn right I could only turn left. So I started left and then realized I couldn't turn back the other way! I made a couple of other stops after that, and one jerk told me I "just couldn't get there from here." Eventually I found a truck driver heading toward the same eastbound highway, and he told me to follow him. An hour and forty minutes after reaching Fredericton's city limits I finally managed to leave going east. I felt as if I had spent an entire month there!

The thing I learned from this was just how egocentric I am. I would not have made this error if I had not been so damn cocky about my sense of direction. My mistake was made worse because I got flustered and didn't listen to the directions clearly. I find that the reason I most often make a mistake is because I don't listen carefully to instructions. This has been a problem all my life.

After I got over feeling really stoopid I decided this kind of thing was not going to happen again. It was too much a waste of time and gas, so I was going to be more careful of road signs and directions.

This all turned out to be a positive experience though. I learned that there are lots of friendly, helpful people. It was kind of reassuring to know that other folks would help you if you just asked.

I feel this and other mistakes are crucial not only to my life but to personal growth in general. It is the making of mistakes that helps people learn where they are misdirecting their energies. I think mistakes can help all of us learn to be more careful about some part of our lives. This is why mistakes are crucial. Otherwise, we would continue in the same old rut and never improve.

This entry served as the foundation upon which the student built her essay. Her next step was to consider *audience* and *purpose* (which are usually specified in the writing assignments in this text). The first of these features identifies the person or group of people you will address in your essay. The second is a declaration of your principal reason for writing the essay, which usually takes the form of a thesis statement (the statement of purpose or the controlling idea of an essay). Together these pieces of information consciously or subconsciously help you make most of the decisions you are faced with as you write: what words to choose, what sentence structures to use, what order to present ideas in, which topics to develop, and which to summarize. The more you know about your audience (age, educational background, likes, dislikes, biases, political persuasion, and social status) and your purpose (to inform, persuade, and/or entertain), the easier the writing task will be. In the rough draft and final draft of the essay in the section that follows, the student knew she was writing to a senior English class at her old high school in order to convince them that mistakes can be positive factors in their lives. This clear sense of audience and purpose helped her realize she should use fairly advanced vocabulary, call upon a variety of sentence structures, and organize her ideas chronologically to make her point most effectively to her intended audience.

At this stage of the writing process, some people benefit from assembling their ideas in the form of an outline. Others use an outline as a check on their logic and organization after the first draft has been written. Whether your outlines are informal (a simple list) or highly structured, they can help you visualize the logical relationship of your ideas to each other. We recommend using your outline throughout the prewriting and writing stages to ensure that your work will be carefully and tightly organized. Your outline, however, should be adjusted to your draft as it develops.

Writing

The writing stage asks you to draft an essay based upon the prewriting material you have assembled. Because you have already made the important preliminary decisions regarding your topic, your audience, and your purpose, the task of actually writing the essay should follow naturally. (Notice we did not say this task should necessarily be easy—just natural.) At this stage, you should look upon your essay as a way of solving a problem or answering a question: The problem/question is posed in your writing assignment, and the solution/answer is your essay. The three Choosing a Topic assignments that follow the prewriting questions in the text require you to consider issues related to the essay you just read. Although they typically ask you to focus on one rhetorical pattern, they draw on many rhetorical strategies (as do all writing assignments in the text) and require you to support your statements with concrete examples. The following assignments refer to the Lewis Thomas essay and emphasize the use of example, his dominant rhetorical strategy.

Choosing a Topic

1. You have decided to write an editorial for your local newspaper concerning the impact of computers on our lives. Cite specific experiences you have had with computers to help make your main point.
2. You have been invited back to your high school to make a speech to a senior English class about how people can learn from their mistakes. Write your speech in the form of an essay explaining what you learned from a crucial mistake you have made. Use examples to show these students that mistakes can be positive factors in their lives.
3. In an essay for your writing class, explain one specific human quality. Use Thomas's essay as a model. Cite examples to support your explanation.

The following essay is our student's first-draft response to topic 2. After writing her journal entry, the student drafted a tentative thesis statement: "I know there are positive attitudes that can come from making a mistake because I recently had an opportunity to learn some valuable lessons from one of my errors." This statement helped the student further develop and organize her ideas as she focused finally on one well-chosen example to illustrate her thesis. At this point, the thesis is simply the controlling idea around which the other topics take shape; it is often revised several times before the final draft.

First Draft: A Time I Got Lost

Parents and teachers frequently pressure us to avoid committing errors. Meanwhile, our friends laugh at us when we make mistakes. With all these different messages, it is hard for us to think of mistakes as positive events. But if any of you take the time to think about what you have learned from mistakes, I bet you will realize all the good things that have come from these events. I know there are positive attitudes that can come from making a mistake because I recently had an opportunity to learn some valuable lessons in this way.

While travelling back east this last summer, I made the mistake of turning west on an interprovincial detour in order to reach the Atlantic Ocean. The adventure took me into the heart of Fredericton, where I got totally lost. I had to get directions several times until two hours later I was going in the right direction. As I was driving out of town, I realized that although I had made a stupid mistake, I had learned a great deal. Overall, the detour was actually a positive experience.

The first thing I remember thinking after I had gotten my wits together was that I had definitely learned something from making the mistake. I had the opportunity to see a new city, filled with new people—3000 kilometres from my own hometown, but very much like it. I also became aware that the beach is not always toward the west, as it is in British Columbia. The entire experience was like getting a geography lesson firsthand.

As this pleasant feeling began to grow, I came to another realization. I was aware of how important other people can be in making a mistake into a positive experience. My first reaction was "Oh no, someone is going to know I made a mistake!" But the amazing part about this mistake was how supportive everyone was. The townspeople were entirely willing to help someone they did not know. This mistake helped me to learn that people tend to be nicer than I had imagined.

The final lesson I learned from getting lost in Fredericton was how to be more cautious about my actions, so as not to repeat the same mistake. It was this internalization of all the information I gleaned from making the mistake that I see as the most positive part of the experience. I realized that in order to avoid such situations in the future I would have to be less egocentric in my decisions and more willing to listen to directions from other people. I needed to learn that my set way of doing things was not always the best way. If I had not made the mistake, I would not have been aware of my other options.

By making this mistake I learned that there is a more comprehensive manner of looking at the world. In the future, if we could all stop after making a mistake and ask ourselves, "What can I learn from this?" we would be less critical of ourselves and have a great many more positive experiences. If I were not able to make mistakes, I would probably not be able to expand my knowledge of my environment, my sense of others, and my understanding of myself.

Rewriting

The rewriting stage includes revising, editing, and proofreading. The first of these activities, *revising*, actually takes place during the entire writing process as you change words, recast sentences, and move whole paragraphs from one place to another. Making these linguistic and organizational choices means you will also be constantly adjusting your content to your purpose (what you want to accomplish) and your audience (the readers) in much the same way you alter your speech to communicate more effectively in response to the gestures, eye movements, or facial expressions of your listener. Revising is literally the act of "reseeing" your essay, looking at it through your readers' eyes to determine whether or not it achieves its purpose. As you revise, you should consider matters of both content and form. In *content*, do you have an interesting, thought-provoking title for your essay? Do you think your thesis statement will be clear to your audience? Does your introduction capture the readers' attention? Is your treatment of your topic consistent throughout the essay? Do you support your assertions with specific examples? Does your conclusion sum up your main points? In *form*, is your essay organized effectively? Do you use a variety of rhetorical strategies? Are your sentence structures and vocabulary varied and interesting?

Editing entails correcting mistakes in your writing so that your final draft conforms to the conventions of standard written English. Correct punctuation, spelling, and mechanics will help you make your points and will encourage your readers to move smoothly through your essay from topic to topic. At this stage, you should be concerned about such matters as whether your sentences are complete, whether your punctuation is correct and effective, whether you have followed conventional rules for using mechanics, and whether the words in your essay are spelled correctly.

Proofreading involves reading over your entire essay, slowly and carefully, to make certain you have not allowed any errors to slip into your draft. (Most writing instructors don't look upon errors as kindly as Thomas does.) In general, good writers try to let some time elapse between writing the final draft and proofreading it (at least a few hours, perhaps a day or so). Otherwise, they find themselves proofreading their thoughts rather than their words. Some writers even profit from proofreading their papers backwards—a technique that allows them to focus on individual words and phrases rather than on entire sentences.

Following is the student's revised draft of her essay on making mistakes in life. The final draft of this typical student's essay represents the entire writing process at work. We have made notes in the margin to highlight various effective elements in her essay, and we have underlined substantial changes in words and phrases from earlier drafts.

Mistakes and Maturity

Catchy title; good change from first draft

Rapport with audience and point of view established

Parents and teachers frequently harp on us to correct our errors. Meanwhile, our friends laugh at us when we make mistakes. With all these negative messages, most of us have a hard time believing that problems can be positive experiences. But if we take the time to think about what we have learned from various blunders, we will realize all the good that has come from these events. I know making mistakes can have positive results because I recently learned several valuable lessons from one unforgettable experience.

Clear, stimulating introduction for high school seniors

Good brief summary of complex experience (see notes from Preparing to Write)

Background information

While I was travelling to the East Coast last summer, I made the mistake of turning west on an interprovincial detour in an attempt to reach the Atlantic Ocean. This adventure took me into the centre of Fredericton, where I became totally lost, bewildered, and angry at myself. I had to ask for directions several times until two hours later, when I finally found the correct highway toward the ocean. As I was driving out of town, I realized that although I had made a "dumb" mistake, I had actually learned a great deal. Overall, my adventure had been quite positive.

Good details

First topic (Topics are in chronological order)

The first insight I remember having after my wits returned was that I had definitely learned more about Canadian geography from making this mistake. I had become intimately acquainted with a town 4827 kilometres from home that greatly resembled my own city, and I had become aware that the beach is not always toward the west, as it is in British Columbia. I had also met some pleasant strangers. Looking at my confusion as a learning experience encouraged me to have positive feelings about the mistake.

Adequate number of examples

Nice close to this paragraph

As I relaxed and let this happy feeling grow, I came to another realization. I became aware of how important other people can be in turning a mistake into a positive event. Although my first reaction had been "Oh, no! Someone is going to know I'm lost," I was amazed by how supportive other people were during my panic and embarrassment. From an old man swinging on his front porch to an elementary school boy crossing the street with his bright blue backpack, I found that the townspeople of Fredericton were entirely willing to help someone they did not even know. I realized that people in general are nicer than I had previously thought.

Second topic

Clear explanation with details

Good summary statement

The final lesson I learned from making this mistake was how to be more cautious about my future decisions. This insight was, in fact, the most positive part of the entire experience. What I realized I must do to prevent similar errors in the future was to relax, not be so bullheaded in my decisions, and be more willing to listen to directions from other people. I might never have had these positive realizations if I had not made this mistake.

Third topic

Specific details

Thus, by driving in circles for two hours, I developed a more comprehensive way of looking at the world. If I were unable to make mistakes, I probably would not have had this chance to learn about my environment, improve my impressions of strangers, and reconsider the egocentric way in which I act in certain situations. Perhaps there's a lesson here for all of us. Instead of criticizing ourselves unduly, if each one of us could pause after making an error and ask, "How can I profit from this?" we would realize that mistakes can often be turned into positive events that will help us become more confident and mature.

Clear transition statement

Good summary of three topics without being repetitive

Concluding statement applicable to all readers

Nicely focused concluding remark

As these various drafts of the student paper indicate, the essay assignments in this book encourage you to transfer to your own writing your understanding of how form and content work together. If you use the short-answer questions after each reading selection as a guide, the writing assignments will help you learn how to give shape to your own ideas and to gain control of your readers' thoughts and feelings. In essence, they will help you recognize the power you have through language over your life and your environment.

Conclusion

As you approach the essays in this text, remember that both reading and writing function most efficiently as processes of discovery. Through them, you educate and expand your own mind and the minds of your readers. They can provide a powerful means of discovering new information or clarifying what you already know. Reading and writing lead to understanding. And just as you can discover how to read through writing, so too can you become more aware of the details of the writing process through reading. We hope your time spent with this book is both pleasant and profitable as you refine your ability to discover and express effectively the good ideas within yourself.

Reading and Writing Inventories

Because checklists can be a helpful method of review, we offer here a series of questions that represent the three stages of reading and writing just discussed. These guidelines can be generalized into a checklist for academic assignments in many disciplines.

READING INVENTORY

Preparing to Read

Title

✓ What can I infer from the title of the essay?
✓ Who do I think is the author's audience? What is the principal purpose of the essay?

Synopsis

✓ What is the general subject of the essay?
✓ What is the author's approach to the subject?

Biography

✓ What do I know about the author's age, political stance, and general beliefs?
✓ How qualified is the author to write on this subject?
✓ When did the author write the essay? Under what conditions? In what context?

Content

✓ Where was the essay first published?
✓ What would I like to learn about this topic?
✓ What are some of my opinions on this subject?

Reading

✓ What are the essay's main ideas?
✓ What words do I need to look up in a dictionary?
✓ What are my initial reactions to the ideas in this essay?

Rereading

✓ How does the author achieve his or her purpose in this essay?
✓ What assumptions underlie the author's reasoning?
✓ Do I have a solid interpretive understanding of this essay? Do I understand the relationship among ideas? What conclusions can I draw from this essay?
✓ Do I have an accurate analytical understanding of this essay? Which ideas can I take apart, examine, and put back together again? What is my evaluation of this material?
✓ Do I understand the rhetorical strategies the writer uses and the way they work? Can I explain the effects of these strategies?

WRITING INVENTORY

Preparing to Write

- ✓ Do I understand my topic or assignment?
- ✓ Have I narrowed my topic adequately?
- ✓ Do I have a specific audience for my essay? Do I know their likes and dislikes? Their educational level? Their knowledge of the topic?
- ✓ What is my purpose?

Writing

- ✓ Can I express my topic as a problem or question?
- ✓ Is my essay a solution or an answer to that problem or question?

Rewriting

Revising the Content

- ✓ Does my essay have a clear, interesting title?
- ✓ Will my statement of purpose (or thesis) be clear to my audience?
- ✓ Will the introduction make my audience want to read the rest of my essay?
- ✓ Have I included enough details to prove my main points?
- ✓ Does my conclusion sum up my central points?
- ✓ Will I accomplish my purpose with this audience?

Revising the Form

- ✓ Have I organized my ideas as effectively as possible for this audience?
- ✓ Do I use appropriate rhetorical strategies to support my main point?
- ✓ Is my sentence structure varied and interesting?
- ✓ Is my vocabulary appropriate for my topic, my purpose, and my audience?

Editing and Proofreading

- ✓ Have I written complete sentences throughout my essay?
- ✓ Have I used punctuation correctly and effectively? (Check especially the use of commas, apostrophes, colons, and semicolons.)
- ✓ Have I followed conventional rules for mechanics (capitalization, underlining or italics, abbreviations, and numbers)?
- ✓ Are all the words in my essay spelled correctly? (Use a dictionary or a spell-checker when in doubt.)

CHAPTER 1

DESCRIPTION

Exploring Through the Senses

All of us use description in our daily lives. We might, for example, try to convey the horrors of a recent storm to our relatives, or help a friend visualize someone we met on vacation, or describe the cars in an accident for a police report. Whatever our specific purpose, description is fundamental to the act of communication: We give and receive descriptions constantly, and our lives are continually affected by this simple yet important rhetorical technique.

Defining *Description*

Description may be defined as "the act of capturing people, places, events, objects, and feelings in words so that a reader (or listener) can visualize and respond to them." Unlike narration, which traditionally presents events in a clear time sequence, description essentially suspends its objects in time, making them exempt from the limits of chronology. Narration tells a story, while pure description contains no action or time. Description is one of our primary forms of self-expression; it paints a verbal picture that helps the reader understand or share a sensory experience through the process of *showing* rather than *telling*. *Telling* your friends, for example, that "the campgrounds were filled with friendly, happy activities" is not as engaging as *showing* them by saying, "The campgrounds were alive with the smell of spicy curry, the sound of high-pitched laughter, and the sight of happy families sharing the warmth of a fire." Showing your readers helps them understand your experience through as many senses as possible.

Descriptions fall somewhere between two extremes: (1) totally objective reports (with no trace of opinions or feelings), such as we might find in a dictionary or an encyclopedia, and (2) very subjective accounts, which focus almost exclusively on personal impressions. The same horse, for instance, might be described by one writer as "a large, solid-hoofed herbivorous mammal having a long mane and a tail" (objective) and by another as "a magnificent and spirited beast flaring its nostrils in search of adventure" (subjective). Most descriptive writing, however, falls somewhere between these two extremes: "a large, four-legged beast in search of adventure."

Objective description is principally characterized by its impartial, precise, and emotionless tone. Found most prominently in technical and scientific writing, such accounts might include a description of equipment to be used in a chemistry experiment, the results of a market survey for a particular consumer product, or a medical appraisal of a heart patient's physical symptoms. In situations like these, accurate, unbiased, and easily understandable accounts are of the utmost importance.

Subjective description, in contrast, is intentionally created to produce a particular response in the reader or listener. Focusing on feelings rather than on raw data, subjective description tries to activate as many senses as possible, thereby leading the audience to a specific conclusion or state of mind. Examples of subjective descriptions are a parent's disapproving comments about one of your friends, a professor's glowing analysis of your most recent "A" paper, or a basketball coach's critique of the team's losing effort in last night's big game.

In most situations, the degree of subjectivity or objectivity in a descriptive passage depends to a large extent upon the writer's purpose and intended audience. In the case of the heart patient mentioned above, the patient's physician might present the case in a formal, scientific way to a group of medical colleagues; in a personal, sympathetic way to the patient's spouse; and in financial terms to a number of potential contributors in order to solicit funds for heart disease research.

The following paragraph describes one student's fond memories of visiting "the farm." As you read it, notice the writer's use of subjective description to communicate to her readers the multitude of contradictory feelings she connects with this rural retreat.

> The shrill scream of the alarm shatters a dream. This is the last day of my visit to the place I call "the farm," an old ramshackle

house in the country owned by one of my aunts. I want to go out once more in the peace of the early morning, walk in the crisp and chilly hour, and breathe the sweet air. My body feels jarred as my feet hit the hard-packed clay dirt. I tune out my stiff muscles and cold arms and legs and instead focus on two herons playing hop-scotch on the canal bank: Every few yards I walk toward them, they fly one over the other an almost equal distance away from me. A killdeer with its piercing crystalline cry dips its body as it flies low over the water, the tip of its wing leaving a ring to reverberate outward. The damp earth has a strong, rich, musky scent. To the east, dust rises, and for the first time I hear the clanking and straining of a tractor as it harrows smooth the soil before planting. A crop duster rises close by just as it cuts off its release of spray, the acrid taste of chemical filtering down through the air. As the birds chatter and peck at the fields, I reluctantly return to my life in the city.

Thinking Critically Through Description

Each rhetorical mode in this book gives us new insight into the process of thinking by providing different options for arranging our thoughts and our experiences. The more we know about these options, the more conscious we become of how our minds operate and the better chance we have to improve and refine our thinking skills. (For a more thorough definition of the term *rhetorical mode*, see the glossary on the website **www.pearsoncanada.ca/flachmann**.)

As you examine description as a way of thinking, consider it in isolation for a moment, apart from the other rhetorical modes. Think of it as a muscle you can isolate and strengthen on its own in a weight-training program before you ask it to perform together with other muscles. By isolating description, you will learn more readily what it entails and how it functions as a critical thinking tool. In the process, you will also strengthen your knowledge of how to recognize and use description more effectively in your reading, in your writing, and in your daily life.

Just as you exercise to strengthen muscles, you will also benefit from doing exercises to improve your skill in using descriptive techniques. As you have learned, description depends to a great extent on the keenness of your senses. As you prepare to read and write descriptive essays, do the following tasks so that you can first learn what the process of description feels like in your own head. Really use your imagination to play with these exercises on as many different levels as possible. Also, write when you are asked to do so. The combination of thinking and writing is often especially useful when you practise your thinking skills.

1. Make a list of five descriptive words you would use to trigger each of the senses: taste, sight, hearing, touch, and smell.
2. Choose an unusual object and brainstorm about its physical characteristics. Then, brainstorm about the emotions this object evokes. Why is this object so unusual or special? Compare your two brainstorming results and draw some conclusions about their differences.

Reading and Writing Descriptive Essays

All good descriptions share four fundamental qualities: (1) an accurate sense of audience (who the readers are) and purpose (why the essay was written), (2) a clear vision of the object being described, (3) a careful selection of details that help communicate the author's vision, and (4) a consistent point of view or perspective from which a writer composes. The dominant impression or main effect the writer wishes to leave with a specific audience dictates virtually all of the verbal choices in a descriptive essay. Although description is featured in this chapter, you should also pay close attention to how other rhetorical strategies (such as example, division/classification, and cause/effect) can best support the dominant impression.

Reading Descriptive Essays

- What is the essay's dominant impression?
- Is the essay mainly objective or subjective?
- What senses does the author engage?

Preparing to Read. As you approach the reading selections in this chapter, you should focus first on the author's title and try to make some initial assumptions about the essay that follows: Does Edith Iglauer reveal her attitude toward her subject in the title "Red Smile"? Can you guess what the general mood of "What a Certain Visionary Once Said" will be? Then, scan the essay to discover its audience and purpose: What do you think Lisa Moore's purpose is in "Between the North Bridge and the King George IV Bridge"? Who is Joe Fiorito addressing in "Night Shift on the

Main"? You should also read the synopsis of each essay in the Rhetorical Contents (on pages v–xvii); these brief summaries will provide you with helpful information at this point in the reading process.

Next, learn as much as you can about the author and the conditions under which the essay was composed, information that is provided in the biographical statement before each essay. For a descriptive essay, the conditions under which the author wrote the essay, coupled with his or her purpose, can be very revealing: When and under what conditions did Jean Yoon write "Halmonee"? What do Edith Iglauer's interests tell you about her motivations for writing "Red Smile"? What concerns might have led Joe Fiorito to write "Night Shift on the Main"? What does Tomson Highway's background suggest about his perspective in "What a Certain Visionary Once Said"? Learning where the essay was first published will also give you valuable information about its audience.

Last, before you begin to read, try to do some brainstorming on the essay's title. In this chapter, respond to the Preparing to Read questions before each essay, which ask you to begin thinking and writing about the topic under consideration. Then, pose your own questions: What image do you have of "the North" (Highway)? What might you want to learn about the night life of a corner of Montreal (Fiorito)? What might give someone a red smile (Iglauer)?

Reading. As you read each essay for the first time, jot down your initial reactions to it. Try to make connections and see relationships among the author's biography; the essay's title, purpose, and audience; and the synopsis. In this way, you will create a context or framework for your reading. See if you can figure out, for example, what Highway might be saying about people's attitudes toward the land in his essay "What a Certain Visionary Once Said" or why Joe Fiorito wrote an essay about Montreal's The Main. Try to discover what the relationship is between purpose, audience, and publication information in Lisa Moore's essay.

Also determine at this point if the author's treatment of his or her subject is predominantly objective (generally free of emotion) or subjective (heavily charged with emotion).

In addition, make sure you have a general sense of the dominant impression each author is trying to convey. Such an initial approach to reading these descriptive selections will give you a foundation upon which to analyze the material during your second, more in-depth reading.

Finally, after your first reading of each essay, take a look at the questions that follow it and make certain you can answer them. This material will guide your rereading.

Rereading. As you reread these descriptive essays, you should be discovering exactly what each essay's dominant impression is and how the author created it. Notice each author's careful selection of details and the way in which these details come together to leave you with this impression. Also try to determine how certain details add to and detract from that dominant impression and how the writer's point of view affects it: How does Tomson Highway create a sense of respect for the environment in "What a Certain Visionary Once Said"? How does Jean Yoon help us to understand her grandmother?

Try to find during this reading other rhetorical modes that support the description. Although the essays in this chapter describe various persons, places, or objects, all of the authors call upon other rhetorical strategies (especially example and comparison/contrast) to communicate their descriptions. How do these various rhetorical strategies work together in each essay to create a coherent whole?

Finally, answering the questions after each essay will check your understanding of the author's main points and help you think critically about the essay in preparing for the discussion/writing assignments that follow.

For an inventory of the reading process, you may want to review the checklist on page 41 of the Introduction.

Writing Descriptive Essays

- Choose a dominant impression as your thesis.
- Find details that support your thesis.
- Engage all five senses.
- Choose a point of view.
- *Show* rather than *tell*.

Preparing to Write. Before you choose a writing assignment, use the prewriting questions that follow each essay to help you discover your own ideas and opinions about the general topic of the essay. Next, choose an assignment or read the one assigned to you. Then, just as you do when you read an essay, you should determine the audience and purpose for your essay (if these are not specified for you in the assignment). For whom are you writing? And why? Will an impartial, objective report be appropriate, or should you present a more emotional, subjective account to accomplish your task? In assessing your audience, you need to determine what they do and do not know about your topic. This information will help you make decisions about what you are going to say and how you will say it. Your purpose will be defined by what you intend your readers to know, think, or believe after they have read your descriptive essay. For example, do you want them to make up their own minds about the urban landscape you are describing, based on an objective presentation of data, or do you hope to sway their opinions through a more subjective display of information? Or perhaps you will decide to blend the two techniques, combining facts and opinions in order to achieve the impression of personal certainty based on objective evidence. What dominant impression do you want to leave with your audience? As you might suspect, decisions regarding audience and purpose are as important to writing descriptions as they are to reading descriptions, and such decisions will shape your descriptive essay from start to finish.

The clarity with which you present the object of your analysis is another fundamental quality of good description. Whenever possible, you should thoroughly investigate the person, place, moment, or feeling you wish to describe, paying particular attention to its effect upon each of your five senses. What can you see, smell, hear, taste, and touch as you examine your subject? If you want to describe your house, for example, begin by asking yourself a series of pertinent questions: How big is the house? What colour is it? How many exterior doors does the house have? How many interior doors? Are any of the rooms wallpapered? If so, what are the colours and texture of that wallpaper? How many different shades of paint cover the walls? Which rooms have constant noises (from clocks and other mechanical devices)? Are the kitchen appliances hot or cold to the touch? What is the quietest room in the house? The noisiest? What smells do you notice in the laundry? In the kitchen? In the basement? Most important, do any of these sensory questions trigger particular memories? Although you will probably not use all of these details in your descriptive essay, the process of generating and answering such detailed questions will help reacquaint you with the object of your description as it also assists you in designing and focusing your paper. To help you generate some of these ideas, you may want to review the prewriting techniques introduced on pages 28–34.

Writing. As you write, you must select the details of your description with great care and precision so that you leave your reader with a specific impression. If, for instance, you want your audience to feel the warmth and comfort of your home, you might concentrate on describing the plush carpets, the big upholstered chairs, the inviting scent of hot apple cider, and the crackling fire. If, on the other hand, you want to gain your audience's sympathy, you might prefer to focus on the sparse austerity of your home environment: the bare walls, the quietness, the lack of colour and decoration, the dim lighting, and the frigid temperature. You also want to make sure you omit unrelated ideas, like a conversation between your parents that you accidentally overheard. Your careful choice of details will help control your audience's reaction.

The next important quality of an effective descriptive essay is point of view, your physical perspective on your subject. Because the organization of your essay depends on your point of view, you need to choose a specific angle from which to consistently approach your description. If you verbally jump around your home, referring first to a picture on the wall in your bedroom, next to the microwave in the kitchen, and then to the quilt on your bed, no reasonable reader will be able to follow your description. Nor will he or she want to. If, however, you move from room to room in some logical, sequential way, always focusing on the details you want your audience to know, you will be helping readers form a clear, memorable impression of your home. Your vision will become their vision. In other words, your point of view plays a part in determining the organization of your description. Working spatially, you could move from side to side (from one wall to another in the rooms we have discussed), from top to bottom (from ceiling to floor), or from far to near (from the farthest to the closest point in a room), or you might progress from large to small objects, from uninteresting to interesting, or from funny to serious. Whatever plan you choose should help you accomplish your purpose with your particular audience.

To make your impression even more vivid, you might use figurative language to fill out your descriptions. Using words "figuratively" means using them imaginatively rather than literally. The two most popular forms of figurative language are *simile* and *metaphor*. A *simile* is a comparison between two dissimilar objects or ideas introduced by *like* or *as*: Fiorito describes "coleslaw, glistening like cut hay in the rain." A *metaphor* is an implied comparison between two dissimilar objects or ideas that is not introduced by *like* or *as*: Lisa Moore refers to the three women from the cruise as "Macbeth's three witches." Besides enlivening your writing, figurative language helps your readers understand objects, feelings, and ideas that are complex or obscure by comparing them to things that are more familiar.

Rewriting. As you reread each of your descriptive essays, play the role of your audience and try to determine what dominant impression you receive by the end of your reading.

- Do I communicate the dominant impression I want to convey?
- Do my details support this dominant impression?
- Do I have a clear point of view toward my subject?
- Which senses do I stimulate?
- Do I use similes or metaphors when appropriate?
- Am I *showing* rather than *telling* in my description?

For additional suggestions on the writing process, you may want to consult the checklist on page 42 of the Introduction.

Student Essay: Description at Work

In the following essay, a student relives some of her childhood memories through a subjective description of her grandmother's house. As you read it, pay particular attention to the different types of sensual details the student writer chooses in order to communicate to readers her dominant impression of her grandmother's home. Notice also her use of carefully chosen details to *show* rather than *tell* us about her childhood reminiscences, especially her comparisons, which make the memory as vivid for the reader as it is for the writer.

Grandma's House

Writer's point of view or perspective

My most vivid childhood memories are set in my Grandma Goodlink's house, a curious blend of familiar and mysterious

Dominant impression

treasures. Grandma lived at the end of a dead-end street, in the same house she had lived in since the first day of her marriage. That was half a century and 13 children ago. A set of crumbly steps made of concrete mixed with gravel led up to her front door. I remember a big gap between the house and the steps, as if someone had not pushed them up close enough to the house. Anyone who looked into the gap could see old toys and books that had fallen into the crack behind the steps and had remained there, forever irretrievable.

Comparison (simile) — Sight

Only a hook-type lock on the front door protected Grandma's many beautiful antiques. Her living room was set up like a church or schoolroom, with an old purple velvet couch against the far wall and two chairs immediately in front of the couch facing the same direction. One-half of the couch was always buried in old clothes, magazines, and newspapers, and a lone shoe sat atop the pile, a finishing touch to some bizarre modern sculpture. To one side was an aged and tuneless upright piano with yellowed keys. The ivory overlay was missing so that the wood underneath showed through, and many of the keys made only a muffled and frustrating thump, no matter how hard I pressed them. On the wall facing the piano was the room's only window, draped with yellowed lace curtains. Grandma always left that window open. I remember sitting near it, smelling the rain while the curtains tickled my face.

Comparison (simile) — Sight — Comparison (simile) — Sight — Sound — Sight — Sight — Sound — Sight — Smell — Touch

For no apparent reason, an old curtain hung in the door between the kitchen and the living room. In the kitchen, a large Formica-topped table always held at least a half-dozen varieties of homemade jelly, as well as a loaf of bread, gooseberry pies, or cherry pies with the pits left in, boxes of cereal, and anything else not requiring refrigeration, as if the table served as a small, portable pantry. Grandma's kitchen always smelled of toast, and I often wondered—and still do—if she lived entirely on toast. A hole had eaten through the kitchen floor, not just the warped yellow linoleum, but all the way through the floor itself. My sisters and I never wanted to take a bath at Grandma's house because we discovered that anyone who lay on the floor on his stomach and put one eye to the hole could see the bathtub, which was kept in the musty basement because the upstairs bathroom was too small.

Sight — Taste — Comparison (simile) — Smell — Sight — Sight — Smell

The back bedroom was near the kitchen and adjacent to the basement stairs. I once heard one of my aunts call that room a firetrap, and indeed it was. The room was wallpapered with the old newspapers Grandma liked to collect, and the bed was stacked high with my mother's and aunts' old clothes. There was no space between the furniture in that room, only a narrow path against

Sight — Sight

one wall leading to the bed. A sideboard was shoved against the opposite wall; a sewing table was pushed up against the sideboard; a short chest of drawers lay against the sewing table; and so on. But no one could identify these pieces of forgotten furniture without digging through the sewing patterns, half-made dresses, dishes, and books. Any outsider would just think this was a part of the room where the floor had been raised to about waist-level, so thoroughly was the mass of furniture hidden. Sight

Stepping off Grandma's sloping back porch was like stepping into an enchanted forest. Comparison (simile) The grass and weeds were hip-level, with a tiny dirt path leading to nowhere, as if it had lost its way in the jungle. Comparison (simile) A Sight fancy white fence, courtesy of the neighbours, bordered the yard in back and vainly attempted to hold in the Sight gooseberries, raspberries, and blackberries that grew wildly along the side of Grandma's yard. Huge crabapple, cherry, and walnut trees Sight shaded the house and hid the sky. I used to stand under them and look up, pretending to be deep in a magic forest. The ground was Touch cool and damp under my bare feet, even in the middle of the day, and my head would fill with the sweet fragrance of mixed spring flowers Smell and the throaty cooing of doves Sound I could never find but could always hear. But, before long, the wind would shift, and the musty aroma of petroleum Smell from a nearby refinery would jerk me back to reality.

Grandma's house is indeed a place for memories. Just as her decaying concrete steps store the treasures of many lost childhoods, her house still stands, guarding the memories of generations of children and grandchildren. Dominant impression rephrased

Some Final Thoughts on Description

Because description is one of the most basic forms of verbal communication, you will find descriptive passages in most of the reading selections throughout this textbook. Description provides us with the means to capture our audience's attention and clarify certain points in all of our writing. The examples chosen for the following section, however, are predominantly descriptive—the main purpose in each being to involve the readers' senses as vividly as possible. As you read through each of these essays, try to determine its intended audience and purpose, the object of the description, the extent to which details are included or excluded, and the author's point of view. Equipped with these four areas of reference, you can become an increasingly sophisticated reader and writer of descriptive prose.

DESCRIPTION IN REVIEW

Reading Descriptive Essays

Preparing to Read

✓ What assumptions can I make from the essay's title?
✓ What do I think the general mood of the essay will be?
✓ What are the essay's purpose and audience?
✓ What does the synopsis tell me about the essay?
✓ What can I learn from the author's biography?
✓ Can I predict the author's point of view toward the subject?

Reading

✓ Is the essay predominantly objective or subjective?
✓ What is the essay's dominant impression?
✓ What senses does the author engage?

Rereading

✓ What details support the essay's dominant impression?
✓ What other rhetorical modes does the author use?

Writing Descriptive Essays

Preparing to Write

✓ What is my purpose?
✓ Will I be primarily objective or subjective?
✓ Who is my audience?
✓ What is the dominant impression I want to convey?

Writing

✓ Do I have a dominant impression for my thesis?
✓ Did I select details that support my dominant impression?
✓ Did I engage all five senses?
✓ What is my point of view toward my subject (objective or subjective)?
✓ Do I show rather than tell my narrative?

Rewriting

✓ Do I create the dominant impression I want to convey?
✓ Do my details support this dominant impression?
✓ Which senses do I stimulate?
✓ Do I have a clear, consistent point of view toward my subject?
✓ Do I use similes or metaphors when appropriate?
✓ Am I showing rather than telling in my description?

TOMSON HIGHWAY

What a Certain Visionary Once Said (1992)

In the following essay, Tomson Highway (1951–) presents a loving and vibrant description of the region of Canada where he comes from. The 11th of 12 children, Highway was born and raised on the Brochet Reserve in northern Manitoba, where his first language was Cree. Highway didn't begin learning English until he was six years old, when he was sent away to a Catholic boarding school. He graduated from the University of Western Ontario with a B.A. in music and English, and he began writing at about age 30. Now a resident of Toronto, Highway is the founder and was the first director of the Native Earth Performing Arts Theatre and has received wide acclaim for the plays that he has written and produced, including the Dora Mavor Moore Award, the Toronto Arts Award (1990), and the Chalmers Canadian Play Award in 1986 for "The Rez Sisters" and again in 1990 for "Dry Lips Oughta Move to Kapuskasing."

Highway was made a Member of the Order of Canada in 1994 and was chosen by *Maclean's* magazine as one of the 100 most important Canadians in history.

In 1997, Highway published his first novel, *Kiss of the Fur Queen*, a largely autobiographical story about two Cree brothers. "Rose," a full-length musical sequel to "The Rez Sisters" and "Dry Lips," was first produced in 2000. These works were followed by a series of illustrated books for children and "Ernestine Shuswap Gets Her Trout," a play about British Columbia's Native peoples losing their rights, their land, and their language. Most recently, Highway has written the libretto for "The Journey or Pimooteewin," a musical adaptation of a classic First Nations myth, which is billed as the first opera in Cree. He currently divides his time between northern Ontario and the south of France and is working on his second novel.

This essay first appeared as an insert in *The Bank of Montreal Annual Report* (1992).

Preparing to Read

The following essay is a vivid description of a part of the country Tomson Highway respects and admires. Before reading, think about the Canadian North. In your mind, travel north from the 49th parallel. How does the weather change as you progress? What do you notice about the landscape and the terrain? What happens to the population? What observations do you make about the vegetation? What about the wildlife? Are there any assumptions that you make about the seasons? Does your mode of transportation change as you travel north? What colours stand out to you?

Are there any distinctive smells? What sounds do you hear? What sounds do you not hear?

As you travel north from Winnipeg, the flatness of the prairie begins to give way. And the northern forests begin to take over, forests of spruce and pine and poplar and birch. The northern rivers and northern rapids, the waterfalls, the eskers,❶ the northern lakes—thousands of them—with their innumerable islands encircled by golden-sand beaches and flat limestone surfaces that slide gracefully into water. As you travel farther north, the trees themselves begin to diminish in height and size. And get smaller, until, finally, you reach the barren lands. It is from these reaches that herds of caribou in the thousands come thundering down each winter. It is here that you find trout and pickerel and pike and whitefish in profusion. If you're here in August, your eyes will be glutted with a sudden explosion of colour seldom seen in any southern Canadian landscape: fields of wild raspberries, cloudberries,❷ blueberries, cranberries, stands of wild flowers you never believed such remote northern terrain was capable of nurturing. And the water is still so clean you can dip your hand over the side of your canoe and you can drink it. In winter, you can eat the snow, without fear. In both winter and summer, you can breathe, this is your land, your home. 1

Here, you can begin to remember that you are a human being.❸ And if you take the time to listen—really listen—you can begin to hear the earth breathe. And whisper things simple men, who never suspected they were mad, can hear. Madmen who speak Cree, for one, can in fact understand the language this land speaks, in certain circles. Which would make madmen who speak Cree a privileged lot. 2

Then you seat yourself down on a carpet of reindeer moss and you watch the movements of the sky, filled with stars and galaxies of stars by night, streaked by endlessly shifting cloud formations by day. You watch the movements of the lake which, within one hour, can change from a surface of glass to one of waves so massive in their fury they can—and have—killed many a man. And you begin to understand that men and women can, within maybe not one hour but one day, change from a mood 3

Reading Critically

❶ What are eskers?

❷ Have you ever seen or tasted a cloudberry? If so, describe it.

❸ What do you think Highway is suggesting in this sentence?

of reflective serenity and self-control to one of depression and despair so deep they can—and have—killed many a man.[4]

You begin to understand that this earth we live on—once thought insensate, inanimate, dead by scientists, theologians and such—has an emotional, psychological and spiritual life every bit as complex as that of the most complex, sensitive and intelligent of individuals. 4

And it's ours. Or is it? 5

A certain ancient aboriginal visionary of this country once said: "We have not inherited this land, we have merely borrowed it from our children."[5] 6

If that's the case, what a loan! 7

Eh? 8

UNDERSTANDING DETAILS

1. For Highway, what is the essential appeal of the North?
2. In contrast to the view of traditional scientists and theologians, how does Highway characterize the earth? In your own words, characterize Highway's attitude toward the earth.
3. How many senses does Highway invoke in this description? Give one example of each from this essay.

ANALYZING MEANING

1. What is Highway's purpose in writing this description? Whom is he writing it for?
2. In paragraph 2, Highway refers to "madmen." Who are these madmen, and why does Highway label them this way? Does he really believe that they are mad?
3. Explain Highway's conclusion. Why does he end on a questioning note?

DISCOVERING RHETORICAL STRATEGIES

1. Is this description objective or subjective? Explain. How might a land surveyor's description of this area differ from Highway's?
2. How many times does the writer use the words *north* or *northern* in this essay? What effect does this have on the reader? How would more specific place names change the impression?

Reading Critically

[4] Why does the author repeat this phrase?

[5] What do you think this quotation means? Do you agree or disagree? Explain your answer.

3. Does "What a Certain Visionary Once Said" contain the four fundamental qualities of descriptive essays that are outlined at the beginning of this chapter? Support your answer with specific details.

MAKING CONNECTIONS

1. Anita Rau Badami ("My Canada") describes travelling through the untamed parts of Canada, first in her search for orcas and then in exploring her adopted country. Does the land have the same effect on Badami that it has on Highway? Explain why or why not.
2. In "Pretty Like a White Boy: The Adventures of a Blue-Eyed Ojibway," Drew Hayden Taylor writes about the attitude of white people toward Native Canadians. How does this attitude compare with Highway's comments about perceptions of people who can "understand the language this land speaks"?

IDEAS FOR DISCUSSION/WRITING

Preparing to Write

Write freely about weather. How would you describe the climate of Canada generally? How would you describe the region where you live? What accommodations have you made in your life for the weather you experience? What kind of weather do you most enjoy? How does the weather influence your mood? Why is the weather such a common topic of conversation?

Choosing a Topic

1. In an essay for newcomers to your region of the country, describe your favourite season. Focus on the natural physical aspects of that season as well as the effects those aspects have on you and your community.
2. Think of a television program or movie that is set in the north (e.g., *North of 60, Atanarjuat, Northern Exposure*), and write an essay in which you discuss how its depiction of a northern community has either confirmed or changed your impressions.
3. Highway obviously feels very strongly about the place he describes. Write a short essay in which you describe a place that you very strongly dislike. Provide enough detail that your audience will be sure to avoid this spot.

JEAN YOON

Halmonee (2007)

Jean Yoon (1962–) is a writer, actor, and theatre artist born in Illinois and raised in Toronto. As an actor, Jean Yoon has appeared in productions by Tarragon Theatre, Cahoots Theatre Projects, and the Lorraine Kimsa Theatre for Young People; she also works regularly in film and television, and earned a Gemini nomination for her performance in the CBC mini-series *Dragon Boys*. A pioneer in the Asian Canadian theatre community, she is best known as the writer/creator of "The Yoko Ono Project." Other plays by Jean Yoon include "Sliding for Home & Borders," "Spite," and "Hongbu & Nolbu: The Tale of the Magic Pumpkins," a comic adaptation of a Korean folktale. Jean Yoon's poems, fiction, and essays have been published in a number of magazines and anthologies, including *Fireweed, what magazine, Canadian Theatre Review, Premonitions: The Kaya Anthology of New Asian North American Poetry*, and *Han Kŭt: Critical Art and Writing by Korean Canadian Women*, from which the piece here is taken.

Preparing to Read

"Halmonee" is a description of Yoon's grandmother, of both her life and her death. How would you describe your own grandparents? Does your image of them come from knowing them directly or from what you have learned from others? What image comes to mind when you hear the word *grandmother*? What iconic grandmothers can you think of from television, movies, or works of literature, such as fairy tales?

Halmonee is lying in bed, half-smoked cigarettes planted like spokes in a wide seashell that she uses as an ashtray. She is resting on her elbow, thick glasses sliding down her nose. Her hair is perfectly white and thinning on the very top, just where she can't see it herself with a mirror. She used to make my mother brush her hair carefully each night and pluck out the white ones until finally my mother refused because there were more white hairs than black. She is used to it now but every now and then she still begs my mother to help her dye her hair. My mother always refuses. Now her hair is short and so soft that when you run your fingers through it, it feels like spring grass. It is hard to believe she is so old.❶ 1

Reading Critically

❶ Why does Yoon find it hard to believe her grandmother is so old? Is she referring to Halmonee's appearance or to something else? Explain.

There is a book in her hand with very large print. The pages are thin and elegant so you can see, like veins in the skin, the words on the opposite page. I think it is the bible she is reading, but maybe it's a book of hymns. She doesn't sing herself but she enjoys calling the preacher and telling him that she is dying, soon, oh how her body aches, please speak up, there are bees in the air, oh please come soon, she had to phone herself because her terrible daughter doesn't believe her pain. . . .❷ And when the preacher comes, he brings his wife, a neat lady with shoes that match her pale peach dress. They hold her hand and sing energetic hymns. Halmonee reads all these hymns over and over so when the preacher and his wife do come, she knows exactly which ones she wants them to sing. 2

Her skin is without spots, like those I see on the faces of some other old people, and it is deliciously soft. Under her bed, she has a great brown purse with a gold clasp that is shaped like a daisy. Here and there the gold has rubbed off, leaving a dull grey finish. In her purse she has skin cream, powder, and a long rectangular tortoise shell comb. I like this the best. The teeth of the comb do not bend like the plastic comb I carry in my knapsack. They are stiff like wood and when you hold the comb to the light, it is like looking through a venetian blind, half-opened, made of earth marble. 3

There are other things hidden in her bag. Some candies, a case for her dentures, a tarnished silver spoon wrapped in a piece of Korean newspaper, some elastics and a package of long black hairpins. Sometimes she stows her jewelry in her purse, too. Her most treasured piece is a wide gold ring, notched in a familiar pattern of stars. About once a year she hands this ring over to my mother saying that since she's about to die soon, her only daughter should have it. My mother takes the ring with solemnity and cynicism. A few days later, when my grandmother is feeling better, my mother returns the ring and whatever else my grandmother has bestowed upon her.❸ 4

She was so pretty when she was young, my mother tells me. She was so pretty and spoiled. All her sisters pampered her and she was so strong-willed and stubborn that she could never learn 5

Reading Critically

❷ What insight does this description give into Halmonee's personality?

❸ Why do you think Yoon's mother returns these things?

anything from anyone. There is resentment in my mother's voice. She looks at me and holds her stare for a moment. You are a lot like her, she means to say. You are a lot like her.

6 I remember once imitating my grandmother. My father was sitting on the sofa, his belly taut like a drum from over-eating. He hadn't yet learned how to fend off my mother's appeals that he eat this and try that, just a bit more, honey, or it will have to be thrown away. His eyes were sleepy. He rubbed the stubble on his chin with one hand and held his stomach with the other. *"Aigoo, noh-moo mah-ni mogoh-soh-yoh."*

7 My mother was in the kitchen, walking quickly but ineffectively❹ from one end of the kitchen where the sink was to the other end where the stove and all the dirty pans were. My grandmother was leaning one elbow on the table, smoking a cigarette, talking in her cranky and insistent tone. Mom had obviously done something wrong. I watched as my mother grew increasingly agitated and my grandmother finally stopped talking, opened her purse, pulled out some pills and popped them in her mouth. She held the pills under her tongue, her cheeks puffed with air so that the bitter white taste wouldn't spread through her mouth. She walked slowly to the sink, her hands level with her elbows, sawing gently back and forth as she took each delicate step. She stepped up on the two inch platform that Dad put in front of the sink so we could all wash dishes without discomfort. (The sinks in every house we have ever lived in were just slightly too high.) She tossed back a glass of water and screwed up her face as she swallowed. You could see the tension exaggerated in her neck, the almost mimed gulp. She saw me watching her and quickly glanced away.

8 I knew then that she needed an audience. Every actor needs an audience. I could understand that.

9 She was sitting again, but now my mother was locked up tight. She refused to answer. I guess that's when I decided it was time for action.

10 "Look at this, Mom!" I said.

11 I sat opposite my grandmother, mirrored her smoking, her posture, the light groans as she shifted in her seat to relieve the pressure in her hip that was putting her foot to sleep. I stood

---

Reading Critically

❹ How would you define "walking quickly but ineffectively"?

slowly, pushing against the table for support, adding an extra moan for effect. I hobbled to the sink, popping pills as I went. I was extra slow turning the tap. It was so hard to do with an eighty-two year old wrist. Cheeks puffed, face squinching just so. Swallow. Finally a sigh that shudders through old old bones. *"Aigoo, mom-mee ulma-nah ahpoh-soh, chook-kae-soh-yoh!"*

12 I looked through the corner of my eye to see my mother frozen, like an animal that is seeing double and doesn't know which way to run.[5] I saw my father standing at the doorway now, suppressing a laugh, panic in his eyes. I saw my grandmother, her mouth open just about to cackle.

13 *"Aigoo, aigoo, aigoo, aigoo, aigoo . . . ,"* I sighed. Hurt tumbling downhill in a breeze. That's how she used to show she was tired. That's how my mother sounds now. That's probably how I'll sound at the end of a day, when and if I ever get as old as she did.

14 One thing I liked about my grandmother was that she could take a joke. She had lousy taste when it came to playing jokes on other people. She often told stories, marvelous dangerous stories about her deeply felt sufferings, the less truth the more convincing. She created constant havoc. She didn't seem to know when she was going too far, but she had a laugh that was healthy and selfish.[6]

15 "Godammy" she used to say. "Godammy you!" Later I taught her "son of a bitch," which through her lips came out something like, "son oba beach." A wicked smile used to flicker across her face when she swore in English. I loved that look. "Puck-ah! Puck-ah godammy son-oba-beach!"

16 When my grandmother finally died, it was a relief for everyone. She had been sick for a long time, but no one knew she was as sick as she was that summer of '83. She had been threatening death for almost twenty years. No one believed her anymore. I was working as an actor that summer and for some reason I just knew it was that day. All morning it had been raining, the sky was neurotically[7] sunny and thunderous. By three o'clock it was clearing up but the ground was still wet and in the park where we were playing, the ground would be muddy and dangerously slippery.

Reading Critically

[5] Why do you think Yoon's mother reacts this way?

[6] Explain the phrase, "she had a laugh that was healthy and selfish."

[7] What does this word mean? Do you know anyone who could be described as neurotic?

By five o'clock I was ready to hit the subway and get to work but I stalled, waited by the phone and at five-thirty I called the theatre. The show was cancelled. I rushed to Doctors' Hospital, still carrying my bag with all my warm-up clothes, some make-up that I needed for the show, a book to read on the train. I was worried because if the stage manager noticed I wasn't there when he made the cancellation official to the cast, I might get into a lot of trouble. But somehow I knew something was happening.

17 Halmonee had been in the hospital for two weeks, growing weaker each day. Her weight had dropped to almost eighty pounds. The doctors didn't know what it was but they were making us wear masks when we went to see her. Tuberculosis was whispered in my parents' bedroom. Tuberculosis, not of the lungs, but of some other internal organs. A tuberculosis which could not be detected by x-ray.

18 Doctors' Hospital is on Brunswick, just north of College. The hospital is small and made of yellow brick, the kind that was in style in the fifties. It has that flimsy ugliness of buildings put up in haste and optimism. My grandmother was on the eighth floor. There were two elevators. There were about five people waiting. Behind the silver triangular button was a red glow. Good, I thought, it can't be long.

19 I waited eight minutes. I could have walked up in that time.[8] For the first few minutes I was anxious. I drummed my fingers on my shoulder bag. I walked back and forth. The floor was grey tile marked off in square yards. I pressed my toes into the intersection of the tiles. Pirouette. The elevator still hadn't arrived. Several more minutes would pass before the door would open but I knew then that she had died.[9]

20 My mother was crying and holding my grandmother's hand. My father was not there. He was talking to the doctors and would be back soon. "You just missed her," my mother sobbed in Korean. I nodded. "I know."

21 Later my mother stepped out for a minute and I was left alone with my grandmother. She was still warm. Or at least, her face was. But she was so thin now it was awful to look at her. Her lips

---

Reading Critically

[8] Why do you think Yoon waited so long for the elevator instead of walking up the stairs?

[9] How did Yoon know that Halmonee had died?

were dry, as dry as the skin on your feet after you've been walking barefoot. There were deep cracks at the corners, a thin layer of red underneath. I pulled aside the sheet, gently, and looked at her feet. They were purple and swollen. Her flesh was filled with water wherever circulation was limited: her hands, her feet, the side of her hip. Her hands, her beautiful hands, were curled so tight, close to her face, and yet inside her thumb, across her palm, her flesh was black. She had such beautiful hands. She used to cream them gently and her nails were always perfect and unadorned.

There was a white plastic tube that had been inserted in her nose and I had seen it feeding her air; it was lying now on her pillow, no longer necessary. The intravenous tube was still in her left arm, the tape not covering the huge expanse of skin bruised and broken from so many needles. 22

She shouldn't have died like that. She was always setting the stage for a grand exit. Hymns, friends around her, the wailing of daughter and son, their vocal remorse, too late. She should have died at home, with a descending *aigoo, aigoo, aigoo . . .*, a softening whistle through her lips, her eyes open and knowing. 23

My three cousins, my brothers and I carried the coffin. We hadn't seen each other in several years. We traded sober compliments on how we'd all changed. My uncle stood by in a stiff new suit. My mother wept uncontrollably. I remember her hands trembling as she struggled to replace my grandmother's thick gold ring on the finger where she had worn it for so many years. My father protested that it was foolish to bury an heirloom, but my mother insisted. I think she was afraid my grandmother might return from the dead and ask for it back. 24

I still own some of Halmonee's old clothes, a grey coat of quilted silk to be worn on weddings and grand occasions. It is made of heavy cloth embroidered with silver. There are carefully hidden pockets inside the folds of dark purple lining. The coat still has the stale smell of baby powder, the acid tinge that hung lightly on her skin towards the end, a faint cigarette burn on the right cuff. And inside a pocket I had never noticed before I found a square wooden comb that I remember she said she couldn't find.⑩ Fine white hairs and dust as pale as breath. 25

Reading Critically

⑩ Why do you think Yoon tells us about finding the comb?

UNDERSTANDING DETAILS

1. Yoon describes herself imitating her grandmother (paragraph 11). Why does she do this? How does her grandmother react?
2. What activities does Halmonee enjoy?
3. Why does Yoon teach her grandmother to swear in English?

ANALYZING MEANING

1. Describe the relationship between the writer and Halmonee. What details help to make this relationship clear?
2. Why does Halmonee spend years telling everyone that she is dying? Does she really believe that she is about to die? Explain why or why not.
3. In paragraph 23, Yoon says, "She shouldn't have died like that." Explain what she means by this. Why does Yoon believe that her grandmother should have died at home?

DISCOVERING RHETORICAL STRATEGIES

1. Yoon's writing includes details that appeal to each of the five senses. Find at least one example of each and then decide which example you find most effective.
2. At several points in her essay, Yoon incorporates Korean words (paragraphs 6, 11, 13, 23). What is the effect of this choice?
3. Yoon uses many metaphors and similes in her writing. Find at least five examples of metaphors and/or similes. Explain the effect of this figurative language on Yoon's description of Halmonee.

MAKING CONNECTIONS

1. Yoon and Matt Cohen ("Zada's Hanukkah Legacy") both write about their grandparents. How are their relationships with their grandparents similar? How do they differ?
2. Yoon, Lisa Moore ("Between the North Bridge and the King George IV Bridge"), and Joe Fiorito ("Night Shift on the Main") all focus on people in their descriptions. What common aspects of their subjects do they include in their descriptions?

IDEAS FOR DISCUSSION/WRITING

Preparing to Write

Write freely about your impressions of one or more older people in your life: Who are they? What characteristics do they share? How are they different from each other? Different from you? Similar to you?

Choosing a Topic

1. Write an essay in which you describe someone to whom you are related. Incorporate details that will help the reader to understand your relationship with the person you are describing.
2. Think of a public figure in Canada who you believe deserves to be appointed to the Order of Canada, an honour that recognizes "a lifetime of outstanding achievement, dedication to the community and service to the nation." Write a descriptive essay as part of your nomination of this candidate for this designation.
3. Write a profile of yourself for an online dating or social networking site. Include specific details that give a clear sense of what you look like and who you are.

EDITH IGLAUER

Red Smile (2010)

Edith Iglauer's sense of humour and natural curiosity are reflected through her life and her writing. Iglauer was born in Cleveland, Ohio, in 1917 and was educated at Wellesley College (B.A.) and the Columbia University School of Journalism (M.S.)

Iglauer began her career working at *McCall's* magazine and worked in the radio newsroom in the Office of Strategic Services/Office of War Information at the beginning of WWII. She married in 1942 and she later went to work for *The Cleveland News* as a war correspondent in Italy and Yugoslavia. At the end of the war, she moved to New York where, from the mid-1940s to 1960, she published numerous articles for periodicals including *Harper's Magazine, The Christian Science Monitor, The New York Herald Tribune*, the *Atlantic Monthly*, and *Maclean's.*

In 1960, Iglauer became a staff writer and frequent contributor to *The New Yorker* magazine, writing influential articles about far-ranging topics including the building of the World Trade Center, air pollution, Canadian Prime Minister Pierre Trudeau, architect Arthur Erickson, New York's fair housing law, the opening of an ice road in the Canadian North, and Inuit cooperatives.

In 1974 Iglauer moved to Canada, where she continued writing articles as well as nonfiction books. Her first book, *The New People* (1966), later updated and reprinted as *Inuit Journey* (1979, 2000) documented the development of Inuit cooperatives in the Eastern Arctic in Canada. This was followed by *Denison's Ice Road* (1974); *Seven Stones: A Portrait of Arthur Erickson, Architect* (1981); *Fishing with John* (1988), a memoir—nominated for a Governor General's award—about the lives of Iglauer and her second husband aboard a commercial fishing boat; and *The Strangers Next Door* (1991).

Iglauer currently lives in Vancouver, and her more recent work has appeared in the *Vancouver Sun, Americas,* and *Geist,* the source of the essay here. Now in her mid-nineties, Iglauer is working on a new book.

Preparing to Read

In this essay, originally published in *Geist*, Iglauer relates the story of an introductory visit to a psychiatrist and the rituals that she performs before visiting any doctor. Before reading, think about rituals that you perform in situations such as visiting the doctor or going to a job interview. What do you do? Where did you learn these rituals? Why do you perform them? What would happen if you changed your routine?

When I was living in New York in the 1960s, almost everyone I knew was walking or running to the office of some psychiatrist. A hilarious drawing by the cartoonist Whitney Darrow, in *The New Yorker*,❶ depicting two parents and their children lying side by side on an office floor in session with a psychiatrist, was said to have been drawn from his own life—or so Whitney claimed. I might have travelled the psychiatry route, which my doctor urged me to do after a painful divorce, except for a ludicrous mistake that saved me. 1

My doctor referred me to a psychiatrist whose office was right around the corner from me, two blocks uptown and two streets across. On the morning of my appointment, I woke up early in a nervous fit.❷ I fiddled around, trying to decide what to wear; and then, what would I say when I got there? But time was running out, and a voice in my head said, Hey! You better hurry up, or you'll be late. 2

Before I could dress, I had to have a bath. I was going to a doctor, wasn't I? For as long as I can remember, I have never gone to a doctor or dentist or therapist appointment without performing three sacred rituals: a bath, then the toilet; and finally, brushing my teeth. 3

I rushed through my bath, put on my best suit, a red one imported from Switzerland with brass buttons and green trim, ran back into the bathroom to the toilet and then to the sink, grabbed my toothbrush and toothpaste and scrubbed my teeth. Then I reached for the mouthwash, a small bottle of red Lavoris, opened my mouth and sprayed inside. 4

A quick glance sideways in the mirror, a flash of red. Great heavens—my teeth were bright red! I shut my eyes and opened them again. I was not having a bad dream. My teeth actually were bright red. By mistake, I had picked up the small bottle beside the Lavoris, whose contents were also red, and sprayed my teeth with the red antiseptic Merthiolate. 5

I looked at my watch. Right now I should be on the street, halfway to my appointment. I shakily squeezed more toothpaste on my brush and scrubbed my teeth, hard. They were still bright red. The colour was not washing away. 6

Reading Critically

❶ Why did Iglauer's doctor refer her to a psychiatrist? Why do you think she went?

❷ Why do you think Iglauer is nervous about her appointment?

What a time for this to happen! And with a psychiatrist, of all people. One look and he would decide I was just plain nuts. I opened my mouth and bared my teeth in front of the mirror, and tried to imagine that I was the psychiatrist seeing me, the patient, for the first time. I definitely looked crazy. I hoped that eventually the red would wear off. In the meantime, after this appointment—which it was too late to cancel—I would have to go into hiding. 7

I ran to the elevator, which crept slowly down eight floors, fled out the front door of my building and sprinted up the street. I stopped only once, to grin at myself in the glass of a store window. I could only pray: please, Doctor, whoever you are, have a sense of humour. 8

I arrived at the psychiatrist's office, panting, with only one minute to spare. A small bald man in a white coat and gold-rimmed glasses opened the door. He introduced himself and led the way into his office, which was furnished with the usual desk and chair and another chair opposite, as well as a black leather couch off to one side. He sat down behind his desk and pointed to the chair facing him. I sank into it while he silently stared at me. I took a deep breath. Then I smiled my red smile. I thought, if he doesn't smile back, I'm lost. 9

"You may wonder why I have red teeth," I began hesitantly, continuing to smile. 10

He looked at me and waited. What could he possibly be thinking? 11

I stumbled through an explanation of how I had prepared for my appointment with him by taking a bath, putting on my clothes and brushing my teeth, then spraying them with Merthiolate. "A mistake," I said with a nervous laugh. "I . . . I . . . thought I was spraying my mouth with Lavoris, which I always do before I go to a doctor. You know, brush my teeth, take a bath . . . and . . . so on . . . My mother always . . ." My voice trailed off. Oh, those cold eyes! That stony face! As we used to say, not a laugh in a carload.❸ 12

After an awful silence, he said, "What do you do?" 13

"I'm a writer," I said. I brightened up. "As a matter of fact, I have a piece in *The New Yorker* magazine this week." 14

"What's it about?" he said. 15

I smiled again, producing another impressive view of my scarlet teeth. "Eskimo food," I said. 16

Reading Critically

❸ Explain the expression "not a laugh in a carload."

His eyebrows went up. Again he waited, silently. I stumbled through another explanation, this time of how I had just returned from a trip to Arctic Canada, where I had been observing attempts by Canadian government officials to introduce canned varieties of traditional Inuit❹ foods, seal and whale meat and whale blubber, into Native communities. During weather so bad that the Inuit could not go out to hunt, or when their main food, caribou, mysteriously disappeared, they were threatened with and sometimes died from starvation. 17

The challenge, I went on, was to convince the Inuit that foods they had always consumed fresh could safely be eaten from a can during periods of food scarcity. We had brought with us canned samples of whale meat, seal flippers and especially the blubber they loved to chew, for them to try. 18

The psychiatrist was not at all interested in an experiment that I thought was fascinating. He fiddled with the pencils on his desk, made a few notes and abruptly changed the subject. He spent the rest of our allotted time in a thinly disguised attempt to find out whether I would be able to pay for future sessions.❺ We made an appointment for the following week, and I departed. What an ordeal. 19

The day before I was to return for a further exploration of my psyche, I called up and cancelled. 20

There was a pause at his end of the phone. "I will of course expect you to pay for the cancelled session," he said. "You can give the payment to me when you come again the following week." 21

"Oh, Doctor, I won't be coming back," I said. "And since I am giving you plenty of notice, I will not be paying you for the cancelled session." 22

It was a long time before I sought help again. Then it was with a Danish therapist who read to me from Hans Christian Andersen, and helped me plan the menu for the first dinner party I was going to give in my whole life all by myself. I was going to have a pot roast because it was so easy, and I was agonizing over whether to serve rice or potatoes with it. 23

"Potatoes," he said. 24

Reading Critically

❹ Who are the Inuit?

❺ Why does the psychiatrist spend the appointment time trying to discern whether Iglauer will be able to pay? What might make him think that she will not be able to?

UNDERSTANDING DETAILS

1. Why does Iglauer initially go to the psychiatrist?
2. In what ways does Iglauer prepare for her initial meeting with the psychiatrist? Why?
3. How does Iglauer feel about the Danish therapist she eventually sees? How do you know this?

ANALYZING MEANING

1. Why does the psychiatrist respond to Iglauer as he does? Does he have a sense of humour? How do you know?
2. Why does Iglauer give the psychiatrist so much detail about her article in *The New Yorker*?
3. Describe Iglauer's attitude toward her subject. How is that attitude conveyed? Is the tone of this essay predominantly objective or subjective?

DISCOVERING RHETORICAL STRATEGIES

1. In telling the story, Iglauer uses the brand names of the mouthwash and the antiseptic. Why does she make this choice?
2. What senses does Iglauer appeal to in her description?
3. Describe Iglauer's tone in this essay. Use specific examples to show how her style (use of language) creates this tone.

MAKING CONNECTIONS

1. In relating this story, Iglauer has the ability to laugh at herself. Compare her approach to that of Jeannie Guy ("Newfoundland Cooking") and Barbara Kingsolver ("Life Without Go-Go Boots").
2. Iglauer's essay was originally published in *Geist* magazine. In what ways is the style similar to that of other essays from *Geist*, such as Stephen Osborne's "The Lost Art of Waving" or Faith Moosang's "Nancy Drew Knows It's Hard"?

IDEAS FOR DISCUSSION/WRITING

Preparing to Write

Write freely about an embarrassing experience you have had. Where did it happen? How long ago did it happen? Why was it embarrassing? How did others react to you in this situation? Would you still find it embarrassing if it happened to you today?

Choosing a Topic

1. Write an essay in which you relate the story of meeting a person with whom you didn't get along. Through the details you incorporate, show the reader the differences between you and the other person rather than telling about them explicitly.
2. Write a descriptive essay in which you depict a familiar routine. Use details that appeal to a range of senses and make sure that your attitude toward this routine is clearly conveyed in your essay.
3. Using both memory and imagination, take a journey back to a particular moment or event in your past. Write an essay in which you describe in the clearest and strongest possible detail what you felt, saw, smelled, tasted, and touched at that time. What exactly were you doing? How did you feel? Who was with you? What is the strongest thing about this event that you are trying to convey?

JOE FIORITO

Night Shift on the Main (1996)

Originally from Thunder Bay, Ontario, Joe Fiorito (1948–) began his writing career in Montreal, Quebec, where he worked as a columnist for the Montreal *Gazette* and *Hour* magazine. Fiorito has since contributed to a variety of publications, including the *National Post*, the *Globe and Mail*, and *enRoute*. He now lives in Toronto and contributes regular columns to the *Toronto Star*. Fiorito has worked for CBC Radio, and he is also a published poet. His book *Comfort Me with Apples* (1994) is a collection of essays that originally were published as a weekly column in *Hour* magazine. Although Fiorito has no formal journalism training, he won a National Newspaper Award in 1996 for his *Gazette* columns. A collection of these profiles, or "people pieces," was published in a book entitled *Tango on the Main* (1996); it is from this collection that the selection here is taken. More recently, Fiorito has written a memoir about his family, *The Closer We Are to Dying* (1999), and a novel entitled *The Song Beneath the Ice* (2002). His latest collection of essays, *Union Station: Love, Madness, Sex and Survival on the Streets of the New Toronto*, was published in 2006.

Preparing to Read

In this essay from *Tango on the Main*, Joe Fiorito spends an evening observing and experiencing the night shift at The Main, a restaurant on Montreal's Blvd. St-Laurent. Before reading it, think about night shifts. What kinds of businesses have night shifts? Have you ever worked a night shift? What associations do you have with working a night shift? What specific challenges is one likely to face in working a night shift?

Soft rain is falling on fresh snow. On the corner of the street, a young woman in a yellow slicker wades through a black puddle. Down the block, a pack of university kids chuck snowballs back and forth in the dark. 1

All the lights are on in all the restos on the street, and all the waiters are waiting at their stations, nervous as greyhounds before a race. The night shift is about to begin. 2

In the upstairs kitchen on the second floor of a smoked meat palace called The Main, a Salvadoran named Merino splashes 3 water in a double sink. He is a happy man. During the day, he works as a presser at a coat factory. At night he works here, washing pots.

Merino's day is seventeen hours long. He is twenty-two years old. Why is he smiling? His wife has just given birth to their second child. 4

Peter Varvaro isn't as young as Merino, but he works nearly as many hours. He owns The Main. He'll be cutting steaks until midnight, and he'll be back at work at ten tomorrow morning. He looks a little tired now. 5

What's the strangest thing that's ever happened on the night shift? Peter considers the question as he pushes a rib steak past the blade of the band saw. He's seen his share of louts and goofs, so many that they have become one lout, one goof. There have been robberies, two of them. 6

Then he remembers: A woman came into the restaurant one evening in the old days, years ago. She ordered a big meal, finished it, wiped her lips and then she walked out into the middle of the street and took off all her clothes.❶ 7

The cops took her away. 8

At nine, Barbara joins the two men in the upstairs kitchen. Barbara is the chef. She has a glass of coffee in one hand, a forbidden cigarette in the other. Her gaze is steady and unblinking. 9

Barbara is slim, in her thirties. She's dressed in a white sweater, a short apron and blue slacks. She learned to cook in Poland. 10

She takes six briskets out of the cooler and rubs them with salt and pepper. She layers the meat in roasting pans, and bathes them with oil. She chops onions, celery and carrots on top of the briskets. Into the oven they go. 11

She wipes the stainless steel counter, then sets a pot of water on the stove. She takes a bucket of liver and two dozen eggs from the cooler. She starts to fry a pot of onions. She boils the eggs. The liver—dark, thick and slippery—slides into the heat of a second oven. 12

Now she fills another pot with water. You could bathe in this pot, it is so big. With Merino's help, she sets it on the stove. She 13

Reading Critically

❶ Have you ever been in a restaurant late at night? What is the strangest thing that you have ever experienced in a restaurant?

tosses in dozens of beef ribs, adds a splash of salt, a handful of garlic, and turns on the gas burner.

She gives the onions a stir. The air begins to smell salty-sweet. Does she cook like this at home? "Yes, my husband is a very lucky man." 14

Last night, Barbara made a million latkes, matzoh balls and kishkas. She boiled more tongues than spoke at the tower of Babel. She made enough rice pudding and blintzes to satisfy the hunger of a thousand of those tongues. 15

Tonight she'll make a million varenekes, pronounced veronicas. You know them as perogies. No matter. Barbara takes a sip of coffee, shells her hardboiled eggs, and turns the liver in the oven. She doesn't stop. 16

Now she cores, quarters and slices seven heads of cabbage, some onions and some carrots. She mixes two gallons of dressing and voila!—coleslaw, glistening like cut hay in the rain. Peter and Merino go home. Barbara is just getting started. 17

Downstairs in one of the booths, a big woman talks to herself as she eats a pair of smoked meat sandwiches. The Main is practically empty. She should talk to the grill man. He's bored stiff. It's only midnight. It's still early. 18

Barbara wipes her forehead with the back of her hand. She sighs in one of the five languages she speaks, and assembles what she needs for the chopped liver. She passes the hardboiled eggs through the grinder. They fall into a basin, yellow and pale as daisies in a field. 19

Now the booths downstairs are suddenly full, and they will stay full until 4:00 a.m. The grill man is slathering mustard, he's slicing steamy sandwiches for dozens of sleepless old men, for kids with illegal smiles,❷ for punks and drunks and yuppies. They are a democracy of empty stomachs in a parliament of smoked meat. Some honourable members are starved. 20

I spy a well-dressed couple. The man has good hair and manners, the woman is shy. She spears a french fry with a silver fork. Her lips are swollen, scarlet. The tip of the fry is painted red with ketchup. She takes a dainty bite. The eros❸ of that gesture. 21

Reading Critically

❷ What does Fiorito mean by "kids with illegal smiles"?

❸ What does *eros* mean?

Back upstairs, Barbara is rolling a sheet of dough and cutting circles for the varenekes. She fills one circle with a mixture of potatoes, onions and cheese. She folds it over and pinches it stylishly shut. She will do this fifteen dozen times.❹ 22

It's early morning now. The chopped liver has been packed in tubs, the ribs and roasts are chilled, the buckets of coleslaw and the trays of varenekes put away. 23

A solitary couple slides into a booth downstairs. He has the bright eyes of a sled dog. She is pale, nearly albino, and she holds a blood-red rose in her hand. The effect is vaguely disturbing, as if the rose had leached the complexion from her cheeks. They order breakfast. 24

Barbara wipes her last counter. She comes downstairs and says goodnight to the waiters. She picks up a loaf of bread from the bakery down the street and heads for home. The man with the sled-dog eyes lights up another smoke. The white-blonde woman asks for more coffee. 25

The night shift comes to an end. 26

UNDERSTANDING DETAILS

1. What is The Main? Who works there? Who are the customers?
2. Make a list of all the foods named in Fiorito's essay. How many are there? What is the effect of his including lists of ingredients?
3. When is The Main open? When is it busiest?

ANALYZING MEANING

1. What is Fiorito's attitude toward The Main? How does he convey his attitude toward his subject in his essay?
2. Explain the comment, "He's seen his share of louts and goofs, so many that they have become one lout, one goof" (in paragraph 6).
3. Describe the overall feeling of The Main. To what senses does Fiorito appeal in creating his mental picture of The Main? Give an example of each.

Reading Critically

❹ How many times is "fifteen dozen"? Do you think this is an accurate number or an exaggeration?

DISCOVERING RHETORICAL STRATEGIES

1. One of the rhetorical strategies Fiorito employs is figurative language. Identify at least three examples of metaphors or similes in "Night Shift on the Main." Also identify at least three instances where Fiorito has used the stylistic devices of alliteration, rhyme, or repetition.
2. How does Fiorito link the beginning and the end of his essay? Does he have an effective introduction and conclusion?
3. Fiorito tends to write in short sentences and divide his writing into short paragraphs. What is the effect of this style of writing? Do you find it effective? Why or why not?

MAKING CONNECTIONS

1. Imagine that Judy Rebick is reading Fiorito's essay. Based on her comments in "The Culture of Overwork," how do you think Rebick would react to the lives of those working at The Main? Explain your answer."
2. Fiorito's writing is distinguished by a conversational tone and an informal writing style. Compare his style with that of Laura Robinson ("Sports Breeds Real-Life Violence") or Janice Gross Stein ("Whisper, Echo and Voice"). Whose style do you find most effective? Why?
3. In "Co-opting Dissent," Naomi Klein discusses the corporate trend toward branding. Does The Main have a corporate brand? If so, what slogan or tag line would you use to capture this brand identity? How do you think the owner would react to the idea of branding?

IDEAS FOR DISCUSSION/WRITING

Preparing to Write

Write freely about your favourite restaurant. Where is this restaurant? Is it a fancy place where you go on special occasions or a casual place where you go more regularly? Who goes to this restaurant with you? What kind of food is served there? How would you describe the staff? Do you have particular memories associated with this restaurant? What about it makes it your favourite?

Choosing a Topic

1. Think of a place where you have worked and write a short descriptive essay that makes the place come alive for readers

who have never experienced it directly. Incorporate specific details that appeal to a range of senses.

2. Think of a particular meal or dish that you love. In a short descriptive essay, write about that meal or dish for someone who may never have had it. Choose details and language that convey your attitude toward your subject without telling your audience explicitly how you feel about it.
3. From the information in Fiorito's essay, create a menu for The Main that includes a short description with the name of each item. Think about your purpose and your audience, and remember that the description should be both appealing and accurate.

LISA MOORE

Between the North Bridge and the King George IV Bridge (2010)

Lisa Moore (1964–) grew up near St. John's, Newfoundland, and knew from a young age that she was going to be a writer. She graduated from the Nova Scotia College of Art & Design with a Bachelor of Arts degree and studied at Memorial University, where she was a member of The Burning Rock Collective, a group of St. John's writers. Her first book, a collection of short stories titled *Degrees of Nakedness*, was published in 1995 and was followed by *Open* in 2002. She has also published two novels: *Alligator* (2005) and *February* (2010.) Moore's work has appeared in various anthologies, and she has written for television, radio, newspapers, and magazines.

Preparing to Read

In this essay, Lisa Moore describes a snapshot of the experience of the Edinburgh Fringe Festival in the literary magazine *Eighteen Bridges*. Before reading, think about street performers or buskers. Where have you seen street performers? What type of performances do they give? Why do they choose this type of venue rather than a more traditional stage? How do street performers attract an audience? How are they paid?

A bronze statue on a plinth[1] comes to life. It bops a passerby on the head with its sword. The man executes a double-take, fists clenched. He's wearing a kilt and black knee socks with red tassels. Even his silver buzz cut looks fierce, gilded by a shaft of setting sun. 1

But the statue is frozen again, blasé, nonplussed, the sword resting casually against its shoulder. 2

I watch a magician blow up a tube balloon so it's the length of his forearm. He promises to swallow the whole thing. He tilts 3

Reading Critically

[1] What is a plinth?

his head and opens his mouth wide and holds the balloon over it, but pauses to remark: Ladies, I sympathize.

There's a boy who calls himself Super Scott, further down the street. He cajoles and mocks the crowd that grows thick and presses closer. He takes volunteers—a beautiful girl who writhes with self-consciousness and two good-natured, smirking men. Super Scott gets the crowd to clap for them; he makes the men do goofy dances.❷ 4

Then he prepares to juggle batons of fire. 5

The two male volunteers grip each other's wrists to make a seat. The boy climbs. He makes a show of clasping the volunteers by the cheek or nose,❸ pulling himself up to a wobbly standing position. Once he's up, he flaps his kilt at half the audience and there's a burst of applause. And then he tells the girl volunteer to throw him the batons at her feet, one by one. He calls for a lighter. 6

I'm eighteen years old, he says. He produces a hat and drops it at his feet. 7

Please. Give enough to keep this kid on the streets where he belongs, he shouts. 8

The boy has lit all the batons. He is crouched, leaning forward. Super Scott is very handsome and young looking, wiry and wry—but all of that has emptied out. 9

The boy is staring forward with an intensity that makes him seem absent, a husk. It's as if he is possessed, caught. 10

Much later in the evening, I will eavesdrop on three women who are part of a cruise. They have finished their meal and the bones are sitting on the plates. One woman leans forward. 11

It would have been better, she says, if he had married Camilla in the beginning. She's the one he loved.❹ 12

The other women lean in too, Macbeth's three witches,❺ and discuss it with whispered urgency. 13

Super Scott has lit the torches and drops the lighter to the street below. He tosses the batons and they begin to cartwheel 14

Reading Critically

❷ Why do you think Super Scott makes the volunteers do goofy dances? Why would the men volunteer for this?

❸ Why does Super Scott make a show of having difficulty coming to stand on the arms of the volunteers?

❹ To whom are the women referring here? Why does Moore not explain this?

❺ To what is Moore alluding with her characterization of the women as "Macbeth's three witches?"

around him. Each baton tips end over end and touches down, slapping the boy's outstretched hands. The flames are tattered and clinging until they are circling him in a solid chain. They are circling faster and faster, licking and snapping, an orange wheel of ragged light.

The air around the boy goes liquid, a wavering film of heat. 15
His blue eyes stare straight ahead, big and wide, into the dusk beyond the glassy melting street.

UNDERSTANDING DETAILS

1. What is the Edinburgh Fringe Festival?
2. How can a bronze statue come to life? Why does it hit a passerby on the head with its sword?
3. What is the appeal of Super Scott?

ANALYZING MEANING

1. What is Moore's purpose in writing this description? Who is she writing it for?
2. Who are the three women from the cruise talking about? Why does Moore refer to them as "Macbeth's three witches"?
3. How does Moore feel about her subject? How do you know?

DISCOVERING RHETORICAL STRATEGIES

1. In this essay, Moore uses figurative language to strengthen her description. Identify at least one example of each of the following: alliteration, metaphor, simile.
2. In describing Super Scott, Moore uses a variety of verbs to describe his actions. List eight words she uses in this context and comment on the effect of these language choices.
3. What is Moore's point of view? Is it consistent through this essay?

MAKING CONNECTIONS

1. Writer Richard Ford has said of Moore that she has "a magnetizing gift for revealing how the earth feels, looks, tastes, smells" **(www.houseofanansi.com/February-P1028.aspx)**. Compare Moore's ability in this regard with that of Tomson Highway ("What a Certain Visionary Once Said").
2. Like Faith Moosang ("Nancy Drew Knows It's Hard"), Moore is a visual artist as well as a writer. How is their visual artistry reflected in the writing of these two authors?

IDEAS FOR DISCUSSION/WRITING

Preparing to Write

Write freely about a performer who has captured your attention. Who is the performer? What type of performance does he or she do? How did you first learn about this performer? Where have you seen this person perform? What is it about this performer that attracts you?

Choosing a Topic

1. Write a description of a performance that you have seen. Include details that appeal to the full range of senses so that your reader can share your experience of this performance most effectively.
2. Think of an event that you have attended. It could be a festival, a meeting, a demonstration or rally, or some other experience. Write a description of this event, making your attitude clear without stating it directly. Use specific details appealing to a range of senses to help the reader share your experience of the event you are describing.
3. Find a painting that particularly appeals to you and write a short descriptive essay that allows your readers to visualize it. Don't limit yourself to details that appeal solely to the sense of sight.

CHAPTER 2

NARRATION

Telling a Story

A good story is a powerful method of getting someone's attention. The excitement that accompanies a suspenseful ghost story, a lively anecdote, or a vivid joke easily attests to this effect. In fact, narration is one of the earliest verbal skills we all learn as children, providing us with a convenient, logical, and easily understood means of sharing our thoughts with other people. Storytelling is powerful because it offers us a way of dramatizing our ideas so that others can identify with them.

Defining *Narration*

Narration involves telling a story that is often based on personal experience. Stories can be oral or written, real or imaginary, short or long. A good story, however, always has a point or purpose. It can be the dominant mode (as in a novel or short story), supported by other rhetorical strategies, or it can serve the purpose of another rhetorical mode (as in a persuasive essay, a historical survey, or a scientific report).

In its subordinate role, narration can provide examples or explain ideas. If asked why you are attending college or university, for instance, you might turn to narration to make your answer clear, beginning with a story about your family's difficulties in the past. The purpose of telling such a story would be to show your listeners how important higher education is to you by encouraging them to understand and identify with your family history.

Unlike description, which generally portrays people, places, and objects in *space*, narration asks the reader to follow a series of actions through a particular *time* sequence. Description often complements the movement of narration, though. People must be depicted, for instance, along with their relationships to one another, before their actions can have any real meaning for us; similarly, places must be described so that we can picture the setting and understand the activities in a specific scene. The organization of the action and the time spent on each episode in a story should be based principally on a writer's analysis of the interests and needs of the audience.

To be most effective, narration should prolong the exciting parts of a story and shorten the routine facts that simply move the reader from one episode to another. If you were robbed on your way to work, for example, a good narrative describing the incident would concentrate on the traumatic event itself rather than on such mundane and boring details as what you had for breakfast and what clothes you had put on prior to the attack. Finally, just like description, narration *shows* rather than *tells* its purpose to the audience. The factual statement "I was robbed this morning" could be made much more vivid and dramatic through the addition of some simple narration: "As I was walking to work at 7:30 a.m., a huge and angry-looking man ran up to me, thrust a gun into the middle of my stomach, and took my money, my new phone, all my credit cards, and my pants—leaving me penniless and embarrassed."

The following paragraph written by a student recounts a recent skydiving experience. As you read this narrative, notice the writer's use of vivid detail to *show* rather than *tell* her message to the readers.

> I have always needed occasional "fixes" of excitement in my life, so when I realized one spring day that I was more than ordinarily bored, I made up my mind to take more than ordinary steps to relieve that boredom. I decided to go skydiving. The next thing I knew, I was stuffed into a claustrophobically small plane with five other terrified people, rolling down a bumpy, rural runway, droning my way to 3500 feet and an exhilarating experience. Once over the jump area, I waited my turn, stepped onto the strut, held my breath, and then kicked off into the cold, rushing air as my heart pounded heavily. All I could think was, "I hope this damn parachute opens!" The sensation of falling backward through space was unfamiliar and

> disconcerting till my chute opened with a loud pop, momentarily pulling me upward toward the distant sky. After several minutes of floating downward, I landed rudely on the hard ground. Life, I remembered happily, could be awfully exciting. And a month later, when my tailbone had stopped throbbing, I still felt that way.

Thinking Critically Through Narration

Rhetorical modes offer us different ways of perceiving reality. Narration is an especially useful tool for sequencing or putting details and information into some kind of logical order, usually chronological. Working with narration helps us see clear sequences separate from all other mental functions.

Practising exercises in narrative techniques can help you see clear patterns in topics you are writing about. Although narration is usually used in conjunction with other rhetorical modes, we are going to isolate it here so that you can appreciate its specific mechanics separately from other mental activities. If you feel the process of narration in your head, you are more likely to understand exactly what it entails and thus use it more effectively in reading other essays and in organizing and writing your own.

We will single out narration for some warm-up exercises to make your sequencing perceptions as accurate and successful as possible. In this way, you will actually learn to feel how your mind works in this particular mode and then be more aware of the thinking strategies available to you in your own reading and writing. As you become more conscious of the mechanics of the individual rhetorical modes, you will naturally become more adept at combining them to accomplish the specific purpose and the related effect you want to create.

The following exercises, which require a combination of thinking and writing skills, will help you practise this particular strategy in isolation. Just as in a physical workout, we will warm up your mental capabilities one by one as if they were muscles that can be developed individually before being used together in harmony.

1. Make a chronological list of the different activities you did yesterday, from waking in the morning to sleeping at night. Randomly pick two events to treat as the highlights of your day. Now, write freely for five minutes, explaining the story of your day and emphasizing the importance of these two highlights.

2. Recall an important event that happened to you between the ages of five and ten. Brainstorm about how this event made you feel at the time it happened. Then, brainstorm about how this event makes you feel now. What changes have you discovered in your view of this event?
3. Find a picture that appeals to you and write the story that goes with the picture. The story may be real or invented.

Reading and Writing Narrative Essays

In the narrative mode, making meaning in reading and writing is a fairly straightforward process. To read a narrative essay most effectively, you should spend your time concentrating on the writer's main story line and use of details. To create an effective story, you have some important decisions to make before you write and certain variables to control as you actually draft your narrative.

During the prewriting stage, you need to generate ideas and choose a point of view through which your story will be presented. Then, as you write, the preliminary decisions you have made regarding the selection and arrangement of your details (especially important in a narrative) will allow your story to flow more easily. Carefully controlled organization, along with appropriate timing and pacing, can influence your audience's reactions in very powerful ways.

Reading Narrative Essays

- What is the story's context?
- What is the essay's story line?
- What is the author's purpose?

Preparing to Read. As you prepare to read the narratives in this chapter, try to guess what each title tells you about that essay's topic and about the author's attitude toward that topic. Can you tell, for example, what Matt Cohen's attitude toward his subject is from his title, "Zada's Hanukkah Legacy," or how Steven Heighton feels about the Vimy Ridge memorial in "Elegy in Stone"? Can you anticipate what kind of fight Jenn Lamothe is writing about in "Giving Up the Fight"? Also, scan the essay and read its synopsis in the Rhetorical Contents to help you anticipate as much as you can about the author's purpose and audience.

The more you learn from the biography of the author and the circumstances surrounding the composition of a particular essay, the better prepared you will be to read the essay. For a narrative essay, the writer's point of view or perspective on the story and its characters is especially significant. From the biographies, can you determine something about Anik See's view of crossing borders in "Borderland" or K'naan's reason for writing his essay, "Between the Highs and the Lows, Life Happens"? What do you learn about Steven Heighton's views on war in "Elegy in Stone"?

Last, before you begin to read, answer the Preparing to Read questions and then try to generate some of your own inquiries on the general subject of the essay: What do you want to know about the celebration of Hanukkah (Cohen)? What is the Six String Nation (Taylor)? What do you think about the policy of fingerprinting and photographing anyone who is denied entry to the United States (See)?

Reading. As you read a narrative essay for the first time, simply follow the story line and try to get a general sense of the narrative and of the author's general purpose. Is See's purpose to make us feel sympathetic to her situation or angered by it? Is Steven Heighton trying to encourage us to visit the monument at Vimy Ridge, or is he simply trying to show us more about the nature of Canada? Record your initial reactions to each essay as they occur to you.

Based on the biographical information preceding the essay and the essay's tone, purpose, and audience, try to create a context for the narrative as you read. How do such details help you understand your reading material more thoroughly? A first reading of this sort, along with a survey of the questions that follow the essay, will help prepare you for a critical understanding of the material when you read it for the second time.

Rereading. As you reread these narrative essays, notice the author's selection and arrangement of details. Why does K'naan organize his essay one way and Heighton another? What effect does their organization create? Also pay attention to the timing and the pacing of the story line. What do the quotations add to Lamothe's narrative? What does the measured pace of See's "Borderland" communicate?

In addition, consider at this point what other rhetorical strategies the authors use to support their narratives. Which writers use examples to supplement their stories? Which use definitions? Which use comparisons? Why do they use these strategies?

Finally, when you answer the questions after each essay, you can check your understanding of the material on different levels before you tackle the discussion/writing topics that follow. For a general checklist of reading guidelines, see page 41 of the Introduction.

Writing Narrative Essays

- Decide on your thesis.
- Choose details to support your thesis.
- Arrange your details for a specific effect.
- Follow a time sequence.
- Show rather than tell.

Preparing to Write. First, you should answer the prewriting questions to help you generate thoughts on the subject at hand. Next, as in all writing, you should explore your subject matter and discover as many specific details as possible. (See pages 28–34 of the Introduction for a discussion of prewriting techniques.) Some writers rely on the familiar journalistic checklist of Who, What, When, Where, Why, and How to make sure they cover all aspects of their narrative. If you were using the story of a basketball game at your college or university to demonstrate the team spirit of your school, for example, you might want to consider telling your readers *who* played in the game and/or *who* attended; *what* happened before, during, and after the game; *when* and *where* it took place; *why* it was being played (or *why* these particular teams were playing each other or *why* the game was especially important); and *how* the winning basket was shot. Freewriting, or a combination of freewriting and the journalistic questions, is another effective way of getting ideas and story details on paper for use in a first draft.

Once you have generated these ideas, you should always let your purpose and audience ultimately guide your selection of details, but the process of gathering such journalistic information gives you some material from which to choose. You will also need to decide whether to include dialogue in your narrative. Again, the difference here is between showing and telling: Will your audience benefit from reading what was actually said, word for word, during a discussion, or will a brief description of the conversation be sufficiently effective? In fact, all the choices you make at this stage of the composing process will give you material with which to create emphasis, suspense, conflict, and interest in your subject.

Next, you must decide upon the point of view that will most readily help you achieve your purpose with your specific audience. Point of view includes the (1) person, (2) vantage point, and (3) attitude of your narrator. *Person* refers to who will tell the story: an uninvolved observer, a character in the narrative, or an omniscient (all-knowing) narrator. This initial decision will guide your thoughts on *vantage point*, which is the frame of reference of the narrator: close to the action, far from the action, looking back on the past, or reporting on the present. Finally, your narrator will naturally have an *attitude*, or *personal feeling*, about the subject: accepting, hostile, sarcastic, indifferent, angry, pleased, or any of a number of similar emotions. Once you adopt a certain perspective in a story, you must follow it for the duration of the narrative. This consistency will bring focus and coherence to the story.

Writing. After you have explored your topic and adopted a particular point of view, you need to write a thesis statement and to select and arrange the details of your story coherently so that the narrative has a clear beginning, middle, and end. The most natural way to organize the events of a narrative, of course, is chronologically. In your story about the school basketball game, you would probably narrate the relevant details in the order in which they occurred (i.e., sequentially, from the beginning of the game to its conclusion). More experienced writers may elect to use flashbacks: An athlete might recall a significant event that happened during the game, or a coach might recollect the contest's turning point. Your most important consideration is that the elements of a story follow some sort of time sequence, aided by the use of clear and logical transitions (e.g., *then, next, at this point, suddenly*) that help the reader move smoothly from one event to the next.

In addition to organization, the development of your essay with enough details is important. In this way, the details that you choose should *show* rather than *tell* your story. This approach will help your essay become interesting and believable to your readers. Furthermore, the point of view of your narrator should remain consistent throughout your essay; this will give it a high degree of credibility.

Rewriting. As you reread the narrative you have written, pretend you are a reader and make sure you have told the story from the most effective point of view, considering both your purpose and your audience:

- Is my purpose (or thesis) clearly stated?
- Does my narrator help me achieve my purpose?

Further, as you reread, make certain you can follow the events of the story as they are related:

- Does one event lead naturally to the next?
- Are all the details relevant to my purpose?
- Do I show rather than tell my message?

For more advice on writing and editing, see pages 34–39 of the Introduction.

Student Essay: Narration at Work

The following essay characterizes the writer's mother by telling a story about an unusual family vacation. As you read it, notice that the student writer states her purpose clearly and succinctly in the first paragraph. She then becomes an integral part of her story as she carefully selects examples and details that help convey her thesis.

A Vacation with My Mother

First-person narrator

General subject

I had an interesting childhood—not because of where I grew up and not because I ever did anything particularly adventuresome or thrilling. In fact, I don't think my life seemed especially interesting to me at the time. But now, telling friends about my supposedly ordinary childhood, I notice an array of responses ranging from astonishment to hilarity. The source of their surprise and amusement is my mother—gracious, charming, sweet, and totally out of synchronization with the rest of the world. One strange family trip we took when I was 11 captures the essence of her zaniness.

Specific subject

Thesis statement

My two sets of grandparents lived in Calgary and Regina, respectively, and my parents decided we would spend a few weeks driving to those cities and seeing all the sights along the relaxed and rambling way. My eight-year-old brother, David, and I had some serious reservations. If Dad had ever had Mom drive him to school, we reasoned, he'd never even consider letting her help drive

Narrator's attitude

us anywhere out of town, let alone out of Vancouver. If we weren't paying attention, we were as likely to end up at her office or the golf course as we were to arrive at school. Sometimes she'd drop us off at a friend's house to play and then forget where she'd left us. The notion of going on a long trip with her was really unnerving. Examples

Transition How can I explain my mother to a stranger? Have you ever watched reruns of the old *I Love Lucy* with Lucille Ball? I did as a child, and I thought Lucy Ricardo was normal. I lived with somebody a lot like her. Now, Mom wasn't a redhead (not usually, anyway), and Dad wasn't a Cuban nightclub owner, but at home we had the same situation of a loving but bemused husband trying to deal with the off-the-wall logic and enthusiasm of a frequently exasperating wife. We all adored her, but we had to admit it: Mom was a flaky, absent-minded, genuine eccentric. Narrator's vantage point

Transition As the first day of our trip approached, David and I reluctantly said goodbye to all of our friends. Who knew if we'd ever see any of them again? Finally, the moment of our departure arrived, and we loaded suitcases, books, games, some camping gear, and a tent into the car and bravely drove off. We bravely drove off again two hours later after we'd returned home to get the purse and traveller's cheques that Mom had forgotten. Careful selection of details

David and I were always a little nervous when using gas station bathrooms if Mom was driving while Dad napped: "You stand outside the door and play lookout while I go, and I'll stand outside the door and play lookout while you go." I had terrible visions: "Honey, where are the kids?" "What?! Oh, gosh . . . I thought they were being awfully quiet. Uh . . . Lethbridge?" We were never actually abandoned in a strange city, but we weren't about to take any chances. Use of dialogue Examples

Transition On the fourth or fifth night of the trip, we had trouble finding a motel with a vacancy. After driving futilely for an hour, Mom suddenly had a great idea: Why didn't we find a house with a likely looking backyard and ask if we could pitch our tent there? To her, the scheme was eminently reasonable. Vowing quietly to each other to hide in the back seat if she did it, David and I groaned in anticipated mortification. To our profound relief, Dad vetoed the idea. Mom never could understand our objections. If a strange family showed up on her front doorstep, Mom would have been delighted. She thinks everyone in the world is as nice as she is. We finally found a vacancy in the next town. David and I were thrilled—the place featured bungalows in the shape of teepees. Passage of time Example

Transition The Native motif must have reminded my parents that we had not yet used the brand-new tent, Coleman stove, portable mattress, and other camping gear we had brought. We headed to a national park the next day and found a campsite by a lake. It took hours to figure out how to get the tent up. It was one of those deluxe models with mosquito-net windows, canvas floors, and enough room for three large families to sleep in. It was after dark before we finally got it erected, and the night had turned quite cold. We fixed a hurried campfire dinner (chicken burned on the outside and raw in the middle) and prepared to go to sleep. That was when we realized that Mom had forgotten to bring along some important pieces of equipment—our sleeping bags. The four of us huddled together on our thin mattresses under the carpet from the station-wagon floor. That ended our camping days. Give me a stucco teepee any time.

Chrono-logical order

Careful selection of details

We drove through three provinces and saw lots of interesting sights along the way: a working mine, a logging camp, caves, mountains, waterfalls, even a haunted house. David and I were excited and amazed at all the wonders we found, and Mom was just as enthralled as we were. Her constant pleasure and sense of the world as a beautiful, magical place was infectious. I never realized until I grew up how really childlike—in the best sense of the word—my mother actually is. She is innocent, optimistic, and always ready to be entertained.

Examples (spatial order)

Transition

Looking back on that long-past family vacation, I now realize that my childhood was more special because I grew up with a mother who wasn't afraid to try anything and who taught me to look at the world as a series of marvellous opportunities to be explored. What did it matter that she thought England was bordered by Germany? We were never going to try to drive there. So what if she was always leaving her car keys in the refrigerator or some other equally inexplicable place? In the end, we always got where we were going—and we generally had a grand time along the way.

Narrator's attitude

Examples

Concluding remark

Some Final Thoughts on Narration

Just as with other modes of writing, all decisions regarding narration should be made with a specific purpose and an intended audience constantly in mind. As you will see, each narrative in this section is directed at a clearly defined audience. Notice, as you read, how each writer manipulates the various features of narration so that the readers are simultaneously caught up in the plot and deeply moved to feel, act, think, and believe the writer's personal opinions.

NARRATION IN REVIEW

Reading Narrative Essays

Preparing to Read

✓ What assumptions can I make from the essay's title?
✓ What do I think the general mood of the essay will be?
✓ What are the essay's purpose and audience?
✓ What does the synopsis tell me about the essay?
✓ What can I learn from the author's biography?
✓ Can I predict the author's point of view toward the subject?

Reading

✓ What is the essay's context?
✓ What is the essay's story line or plot?
✓ What is the author's purpose?

Rereading

✓ What details did the author choose, and how are they arranged?
✓ How does the author control the pace of the story?
✓ What other rhetorical modes does the author use?

Writing Narrative Essays

Preparing to Write

✓ What is my purpose?
✓ Who is my audience?
✓ What is my narrator's point of view—including person, vantage point, and attitude toward the subject?

Writing

✓ What is my thesis?
✓ What details will best support this thesis?
✓ How can I arrange these details to create a certain effect?
✓ Does my narrative essay follow a well-paced time sequence?
✓ Do I show rather than tell my story?

Rewriting

✓ Is my purpose (or thesis) clearly stated?
✓ Does my narrator help me achieve my purpose?
✓ Does one event lead naturally to the next?
✓ Are all the details relevant to my purpose?
✓ Do I show rather than tell my message?

STEVEN HEIGHTON

Elegy in Stone (1997)

This essay comes from Heighton's collection of essays, *The Admen Move on Lhasa: Writing and Culture in a Virtual World* (1997), which followed the publication of three collections of poetry: *Stalin's Carnival* (1989), *Foreign Ghosts* (1989), and *The Ecstasy of Skeptics* (1994); and two books of fiction: *Flight Paths of the Emperor* (1992) and *On Earth as It Is* (1995). Steven Heighton has consistently been recognized for his writing with awards, including the Canadian Authors Association Air Canada Award for most promising young writer in 1989, the Gerald Lampert Memorial Award in 1990, and a National Magazine Awards gold medal for fiction in 1992. In addition, Heighton's *Flight Paths of the Emperor* was a Trillium Book Award finalist in 1993, and *On Earth as It Is* was nominated for the Governor General's Award for poetry in 1995. More recently, Heighton has published three novels including *The Shadow Boxer* (2000) and *Afterlands* (2005).

Steven Heighton was born in Toronto in 1961 and grew up there and in Red Lake in Northern Ontario. After graduating from Queen's University with a B.A. and an M.A. in English, he spent time teaching in Japan and then returned to Kingston, Ontario, where he became editor of *Quarry* magazine. He has also lived in Alberta and British Columbia, and now lives with his family in Kingston, where he works as a writer. Heighton's latest collection of poetry is *Patient Frame* (2010) and his most recent novel, *Every Lost Country*, was published in 2010.

Preparing to Read

"Elegy in Stone" is taken from a collection of essays entitled *The Admen Move on Lhasa* (1997). In this essay, Steven Heighton relates his visit to the national park and monument at Vimy Ridge in France. Before reading Heighton's essay, think about war and the attitudes toward war. What images are evoked by the terms *honour*, *valour*, and *bravery*? How have attitudes toward war changed with new technologies that change the way wars are fought? How has increased understanding about the psychological effects of war on survivors (e.g., post-traumatic stress disorder) changed our attitudes toward war?

Vimy Ridge, April 1992

The park's entrance—a border crossing, really—was modest enough: a small sign you could easily miss if you were driving past. But we were on foot. And though it turned out to be a much longer walk than we'd expected, it was a good place to walk, the fields along the road billowing with mustard, wheat, and poppies, the oaks and maples fragrant with new growth. We could be in Canada, I thought—then remembered that, for official purposes, we were. 1

The wind as we neared the ridge grew chilly, the sky grey.❶ 2

Before long the road passed through a forest of natural growth and entered an old plantation of white pines, thick and towering, a spacious colonnade receding in the gloom. Fences appeared along the road, then signs warning us not to walk among the trees where sheep foraged above grassed-in trenches, shell holes, unexploded mines. In the blue-green, stained-glass light of the forest, the near-silence was eerie, solemn, as in the cathedral at Arras. 3

Finally we heard voices, saw a file of parked cars ahead through the trees and came out at the main exhibit site of the park, some distance below the monument that crowns Vimy Ridge. Here, in 1917, from a line of trenches now preserved in concrete and filled daily with French tourists, the Canadian troops had launched their attack. Preserved likewise is the first obstacle they had met: the front-line German trench, barely a grenade's throw away. This whites-of-their-eyes proximity surprised us and made stories of verbal fraternization between the lines—of back and forth banter in broken English and German—all the more plausible, and poignant.❷ 4

A few years after the end of the First World War the government of France gave Canada a sizeable chunk of the cratered, barren terrain around Vimy Ridge, where 20,000 Canadians fell before the ridge was finally taken on 12 April 1917. Today many Canadian visitors to France pass the memorial park en route to Arras or Lille without realizing the site is officially a small piece of Canada. Though "plot" might be a better word, for although the trenches where Canadian and Allied soldiers lived and died 5

Reading Critically

❶ What is the purpose of this sentence? Why does it stand alone?

❷ Why would the enemy soldiers talk to each other? Why might this be "poignant"?

during their siege have healed over, the fields are scarred with cemeteries and the woodlots filled with unmarked graves.

We'd arrived the night before in nearby Arras, finding a hotel and visiting the town's medieval cathedral. The hotel manager had elaborately regretted that we hadn't come two weeks earlier, on Easter Monday, when French President François Mitterrand and Prime Minister Brian Mulroney and a handful of Vimy veterans had arrived for the seventy-fifth anniversary of the ridge's fall. I told the manager that I'd read about the ceremony back home, but felt the park was probably best experienced without the crowds and fanfare of an official visit. I could have said more but didn't trust my French enough to try explaining how disturbed I'd been by photographs of those heads of state and their aides beaming glibly among the hunched veterans, whose nation-building sacrifice was clearly far from the politicians' minds.❸ 6

Nation-building sacrifice sounds far too much like the kind of pious, pushy rhetoric I've learned to mistrust and fear, yet for years the bloody achievement of the Canadians on Vimy Ridge did stand, like the ridge itself, as a landmark, a high point around which the idea of a distinct Canadian identity could form. 7

"*C'est magnifique*," the manager told us when we explained we wanted to go. "*Magnifique.*" 8

At the park's main exhibit site we went into a small, undistinguished brick building to see about a tour of the tunnel system under the trenches. The young guides, in Parks Canada uniforms, explained that we'd just missed the tour and unfortunately would have to wait for the next. But as we turned and went outside to confer, they must have noticed the small Canadian flag sewn onto my backpack, because one of them came out after us and beckoned us toward the tunnels. "You should have told us you're Canadian," he said with a soft Manitoba-French accent. "We don't get all that many."❹ 9

The low-ceilinged, labyrinthine "subways"—where men ate and slept before the attack and couriers ran with their messages and sappers set charges under the German lines—have been carefully restored, but more or less unembellished. The impression, as above in the trenches, was sobering. I was relieved that 10

Reading Critically

❸ Why did Heighton find these photographs disturbing?

❹ What reasons could there be for so few Canadians visiting the exhibit site?

this sad, clammy underworld had not been brightened up into some gaudy monument to Our Glorious Past; I was relieved that it still looked, and felt, like a tomb. It reminded me of the tunnels of the besieged Huguenots❺ under the cathedral in Arras.

11 It was good to get back up into the daylight. We agreed to meet Mario and the other guides for a beer that night in town.

12 We followed the road up the last part of the ridge to the monument, wind blowing over the bare fields in a steady barrage. Seventy-five years before, the Canadians had advanced at dawn through driving sleet and snow, and now, nearing the exposed crown of the ridge, we could see how weather of that intensity must be quite common. The monument stands atop Hill 145, the Canadians' final objective and the highest point for miles around—but on the morning of the attack it must have been invisible through the snow and the timed barrage behind which the men were advancing.

13 Before the hilltop and the monument came in sight I'd felt uneasy, recalling the many monuments I had seen that stylized or made over the true face of war so as to safeguard an ideology, to comply with aesthetic conventions, or to make life easier for the recruiters of future wars. But as we neared the monument—two enormous white limestone pillars that meet at the base to form a kind of elongated U—I was impressed. And, as before, relieved. I'd first become anxious when the hotel keeper had told us to expect something "*magnifique*," but now I saw that in a sense he was right, for here was something magnificent in its simplicity, its solemnity, its understatement. And brilliant in its implication, because the pillars did not quite form a triumphant V, as you might expect, but a shape uncannily resembling the sights mounted on machine guns of the First World War—the kind that claimed tens of thousands of Canadian lives in the war and several thousand on the morning of the attack.❻

14 I don't believe such resemblances can be assigned to chance. An artist's hand is always guided in large part by the subconscious. I don't know whether the architect of the Vimy monument was ever asked about his intentions, conscious or subconscious,

---

Reading Critically

❺ Who were the Huguenots?

❻ Why is the shape of the monument significant? Do you agree with Heighton's feelings about it? Why or why not?

but in a sense they're no longer the point; unlike so many other old monuments, Walter Seymour Allward's is strikingly modern because of the way it surpasses, or second-guesses, all conventional intent.

15 We drew closer. Our feeling that this monolith was more a cenotaph,[7] a vast elegy in stone instead of petrified hot air, grew stronger. And with it a feeling of pride. But a kind of pride very different, I think, from the tribal, intolerant swagger so many monuments have been built to inspire. A shy pride in our country's awkwardness at blowing its own horn—because sooner or later every country that does blow its own horn, with flamboyance, starts looking for somebody else to outblow. A pride in our reluctance—our seeming inability—to canonize brave, scared, betrayed adolescents as bearded heroes of mythic dimension, larger than life. Unreal.

16 And the monument is a cenotaph: we find its base inscribed with the names of the 11,285 Canadians whose final resting place is unknown. Blown to pieces. Lost in the mud, or buried anonymously in the graveyards below the ridge. The parade of names marches on and on, a kind of elegy whose heartbreaking syllables are English- and French-Canadian, Ojibway, Ukrainian, Dutch, German, Italian, Japanese . . .

17 Many are the names of our own distant relations.

18 The figures carved on and around the monument, though dated in style, are not blowing trumpets or beating breasts or drums. They seem instead to grieve. We round the monument and the Douai Plain fans out below us: another figure, much larger, cloaked, stands apart at the edge of the monument overlooking the plain. Behind her a sparely worded inscription, in English and French, tells of the ridge's fall.

19 The figure, we will learn later that night, is Canada, "mourning her lost sons."

20 Tonight in Arras we'll learn other things as well from the Canadian guides we meet for a beer. That the whole park is planted with shrubs and trees from Canada. That 11,285 pines were planted after the war for every lost man whose name appears on the monument. That the prime minister's Easter visit was indeed a grand and lavish affair—everything the monument

---

Reading Critically

[7] What is a cenotaph?

itself is not—but that the old soldiers on display carried themselves with dignity and a quiet, inconspicuous pride. And it's that feeling we end up coming back to towards the end of the night when the drinks have made us a bit more open and, I suppose, sentimental. Because we learn that these young expatriates have all felt just as we have about the austerity of the Vimy monument—and, by implication, the Canadian tendency to downplay the "heroism" of our achievements, to refuse to idealize, poeticize, and thus censor an obscene, man-made reality.❽

21 Or am I wrong to offer Canada these drunken toasts on a virtue that's largely a matter of historical and political necessity? Perhaps what I'm trying to say is that Canadians are lucky to have been spared, so far, that sense of collective power combined with intense tribal identity that makes every imperial nation so arrogant, competitive, and brutal. And as our friends guide us back to our hotel, I wonder if Canadians will ever stop berating themselves for not believing—as too many other nations have believed, and keep on believing—that they're better than others, that they're the chosen, the elect, the Greatest Nation on Earth, with God on their side.❾

22 "Make sure to let people back home know about the memorial," Mario calls out as we enter our hotel. And I reflect that a visit to the monument and the many battlefields around it might help convince some Canadians that there are worse things than uncertainty and understatement.

23 And if the monument doesn't convince them, or the battlefields, then surely the graveyards will. In the park or within walking distance lie thirty cemeteries where the remains of over 7,000 Canadians are buried. They are peaceful places, conscientiously tended. Flowers bloom over every grave. Many are poppies. The paint on the crosses is fresh, a dazzling white in the April sun. Here, no doubt, many of the boys whose names appear on the monument are actually buried, beneath long files of anonymous crosses, or stones ranked like chairs in a vast, deserted cathedral. Another endless parade, this time of the nameless—though here and there we do find stones inscribed with a name, an age. David Mahon, 1901–1917. IN MEMORY OF OUR DEAR AND ONLY CHILD.

Reading Critically

❽ What is the "obscene, man-made reality"?

❾ Which nations do you think the author is referring to?

We recite the words aloud, but this time the feeling they inspire has little to do with pride.[10] The huge limestone gunsight looms above us on the ridge as we enter yet another aisle, and read, yet again: 24

A SOLDIER OF THE GREAT WAR

A Canadian Regiment

Known Unto God

UNDERSTANDING DETAILS

1. What is the significance of Vimy Ridge? Explain why there is a park situated here.
2. What does the monument Heighton finds in the park look like? Draw a picture of the monument, incorporating as many details as possible. When was it built? By whom?
3. What is the role of Mario in Heighton's essay?

ANALYZING MEANING

1. According to Heighton, what aspects of Canada do the monument and park at Vimy Ridge reflect? Does Heighton see these aspects as positive or negative?
2. Why is Heighton glad he missed the prime minister's visit?
3. Describe Heighton's reaction to all that he finds at Vimy Ridge. Why is he "relieved that this sad, clammy underworld had not been brightened up into some gaudy monument to Our Glorious Past [and] . . . relieved that it still looked, and felt, like a tomb" (paragraph 10)?

DISCOVERING RHETORICAL STRATEGIES

1. What is the dominant tone of Heighton's essay? How does this tone suit the purpose of the essay?
2. Heighton incorporates many figures of speech into this essay. Find examples of alliteration, metaphor, simile, and personification. What is the effect of each of these on Heighton's essay?
3. While narration is the primary rhetorical strategy used in Heighton's essay, he also writes very descriptively. Find

---

Reading Critically

[10] What feeling do you think these words inspired in the author? Do they have the same effect on you? Why or why not?

examples in "Elegy in Stone" of particularly vivid descriptive images or passages. How do these enhance Heighton's narration?

MAKING CONNECTIONS

1. Heighton's essay is largely about war and the ways that citizens of different countries view war. Barbara Ehrenreich ("The Ecstasy of War") summarizes different theories about the way wars are waged. What do you think Heighton's "theory of war" would be?
2. Both Heighton and Anita Rau Badami ("My Canada") are writing about the national character of Canada and Canadians. Whose view do you agree with more strongly? Why?

IDEAS FOR DISCUSSION/WRITING

Preparing to Write

Write freely about monuments constructed to remember people or events. What purpose do monuments serve? Who builds them? Who maintains them? What kinds of monuments are public? Which are personal? What monuments are you familiar with? What kinds of emotions do they evoke?

Choosing a Topic

1. Write an essay in which you describe a place that is a good representation of Canada's identity or reflection of values. Link the aspects of the place clearly with the qualities you believe they represent.
2. Write a narrative essay about a visit you have made to some site of historical significance. Why did you go there? What was your predominant impression of this place?
3. Monuments are sometimes built in recognition of people who have been killed in some tragic way. Choose a situation such as a specific natural disaster and then outline, in a descriptive essay, what kind of monument you would design to recognize and remember this person or people.

K'NAAN

Between the Highs and the Lows, Life Happens (2010)

Singer-songwriter K'naan was born Keinan Abdi Warsame in Somalia in 1978 and grew up in Mogadishu. His interest in music and hip hop began early; his aunt, Magool, was one of Somalia's most famous singers, his grandfather was a poet, and his father, who was working in New York City, sent his son American rap albums, which K'naan learned to copy phonetically, even though he didn't yet know the language.

When civil war broke out in Somalia in 1991, K'naan and his family fled Mogadishu, living briefly in New York before settling in the Rexdale neighbourhood of Toronto. K'naan was soon writing poetry in English and posting it on Somali websites; he also dropped out of high school and was arrested numerous times. He kept writing, though, and eventually began to travel extensively; in 1999, when invited to address the United Nations High Commission for Refugees, he performed a spoken-word piece criticizing the UN's response to the crisis in Somalia and was given a standing ovation. This led to his introduction to Youssou N'Dour, a Senegalese musician, who invited K'naan to record with him. K'naan's first full-length album, *The Dusty Foot Philosopher*, won the 2006 Juno Award for Rap Recording of the Year. His next album, *Troubadour*, released in 2009, garnered three Juno nominations and was shortlisted for the 2009 Polaris Music Prize. His song "Wavin' Flag" was a worldwide hit; it was remixed as the promotional anthem for the FIFA World Cup in 2010 and rerecorded by Canadian artists to raise money for earthquake victims in Haiti. K'naan won the Juno for Artist of the Year in 2010 and continues to record and tour internationally.

Preparing to Read

In this essay that originally appeared in *The Globe and Mail*, K'naan explains how he became an artist and where the inspiration for his music comes from. Before reading, think about what you know of K'naan's music. How would you characterize the genre and the general tone of his songs? Where have you heard his songs? How well known is he as an artist? What has made his music popular?

It was not my dream to be an artist. 1

How could it have been? I thought artist, much like a leader, 2 was something you either were or weren't. Never something you set out to be. And as a boy in Mogadishu Somalia,❶ although art plainly encapsulated the world as I knew it, what I really wanted to be was an optometrist.

But there weren't any doctors in my family. My father, they 3 explained, was a civil servant of sorts, who then moved to New York for reasons all the poets in my life would fail to articulate. My mother was, by nature, a poet, but above all the distraction of talent, she was a mother. Her father was loved by all, a poet whose nickname was Ahyaa Wadani, meaning something like "The Passion of the Country" or, "the Soul of the Country" or, "The jewel ..." (Translating the Somali language into English is like squeezing an oversized person into a fitted shirt—always needs some stretching to make it work.)

One day when I was about seven, my mother took me along 4 for my grandmother's appointment with an eye doctor. Her eyesight, much like the prospects of the country, had been slowly dimming.❷

I remember clearly the glory of his entrance to the waiting 5 room where we sat. A white overcoat, a pen hugged by the cartilage of his ear, poking through what used to be a proud army of hair, now retreating. Everything about him suggested some incorruptible dignity. I've always wondered if he looked as impressive to my mother as he did to me. I wanted to be him.

He searched for fugitives with the light thing into grandma's 6 prisoner eyes for a while, like tolerable interrogation. Then with a great big sigh meant to prove his empathetic efforts, the sound of finality from someone who'd seen it all, he said, "I'm sorry, but there's nothing I can do, it's just old age."

I remember how overcome I was with disbelief. I thought, 7 if I was he, a doctor entrusted with that overcoat, I would fix grandma's eyes. Suddenly I went from wanting to be him, to *having* to be him.

Reading Critically

❶ Where is Mogadishu, Somalia?

❷ What does K'naan mean when he says that the prospects of the country were dimming?

I realize now that music in my life came in a similar fashion: much more of a need than a want—an antidote to a poison rather than a recreational drug. 8

I was a teenager in Toronto when it first hit me. The intolerable fear of insanity. You see, as Somalis, the fine art of psychoanalysis is not something we've learned to appreciate. You're either a crazy person or you're not. And since I didn't really know any Canadians, there was no one to explain to me the sudden flood of anxiety attacks, depression and insomnia. 9

It's fitting, I thought. I've escaped a war with minor injuries, adopted a new country where even laziness could be transformed into an opportunity for success, and I thought I would get away clean? Of course there had to be some tragic balance to this overbearing fortune. God, I thought, did I really have to choose between peace and sanity. I remember having these thoughts alone in a living room, pacing up and down, opening and closing windows in a frenzy, but one mid-afternoon when I ended up in a bathtub still half dressed,[3] I decided that I should tell someone. 10

Mom said that the answer was in the Koran.[4] My answer to her was, didn't the Koran say to seek help from professionals? And so we did. Doctor after doctor, blood test after blood test, and they would all conclude that I was fine, almost blushing about how perfectly healthy I was. It went on this way for a while, but the unsummoned tears continued, the voices in my head were getting more opinionated than my own voice. So I made excuses to hide from it. It was all beginning to be too painful to live with. 11

At this point I was already fancying myself as someone with some musical talent. I could often find a little poetry in me if I needed to. Kids in the neighbourhood thought I could rap and if, on a good day, I went to the mall with friends, I would spend all my time inside Radio Shack playing their little keyboards until they kicked me out for not buying. 12

My first songs were written in this condition. One song, called *Voices In My Head,* I remember writing during a particularly 13

Reading Critically

[3] What causes K'naan to end up "in a bathtub still half dressed"?

[4] What is the Koran? Why does K'naan's mother say that the answer is in the Koran?

torturous anxiety attack. I had gotten the news of a Somali boy who was a friend in Toronto, leaping to his death from the 20-something floor of an old high-rise we once lived in.

14 Another song, a kind of a happy one actually, *In The Beginning*, was written and recorded on my way to check into the emergency room. A minor stop to a major event, I thought. In reality, all my life was in the minor key, but it was out of defiance that I wrote it all on major.⑤

15 And where am I now? I suppose they're right to say that I'm flying high. I was recently honoured with two Juno awards for these songs of desperation.⑥

16 And at the moment, I'm writing this on a plane from China where I had just performed at the World Expo. But once again, it seems that the great balancing act is in motion. Somalia is worse now than it was when I left at age 13. And while my career has some mentionable highs, my romantic life is adorned with the quiet lows. So I suppose this all means more songs.

17 I didn't turn out to be an optometrist. But I do hope that in some way, my music opens an eye or two, to a great continent of both immeasurable beauty and struggle. And to my own life, written as a country disguised as a person.

UNDERSTANDING DETAILS

1. What did K'naan want to be? Why?
2. Why did K'naan end up becoming an artist?
3. According to K'naan, in what ways does the perception of mental health issues differ between Canada and Somalia?

ANALYZING MEANING

1. What is K'naan's thesis? Has he successfully supported his thesis through his essay? Explain why or why not.
2. Overall, how satisfied is K'naan with his life? Does he come across as an optimist or as a pessimist?
3. What is the source of K'naan's musical creativity? Why does he refer to "songs of desperation" (paragraph 15)?

Reading Critically

⑤ What is the difference between a major and a minor key? What emotions are typically associated with each?

⑥ What are Juno awards? For what did K'naan win these awards?

DISCOVERING RHETORICAL STRATEGIES

1. How has K'naan linked his introduction and conclusion to effectively bookend his essay?
2. How would you characterize the tone of this essay? How does K'naan achieve this tone? Is it effective for his subject matter and his audience?
3. What other rhetorical strategies has K'naan used in this essay to make his narrative effective and interesting?

MAKING CONNECTIONS

1. K'naan and Evelyn Lau ("More and More") both write about their responses to anxiety. In what ways are their experiences similar? In what ways do they differ?
2. K'naan says, "I realize now that music in my life came in a similar fashion: much more of a need than a want—an antidote to a poison rather than a recreational drug" (paragraph 8). How do you think that Jowi Taylor ("Beginning" from *Six String Nation*) would respond to this view of music?
3. Choose one of K'naan's songs and listen to it in the context of Daniel J. Levitin's essay ("The Music of My Mind.") Which of Levitin's strategies or methods for appealing to listeners can you identify in K'naan's song?

IDEAS FOR DISCUSSION/WRITING

Preparing to Write

Write freely about your childhood dreams for your life. When asked what you wanted to be when you grew up, what did you say? What made that choice appealing to you? Is that still your goal? What goals do you now have for your life?

Choosing a Topic

1. Write an essay in which you tell the story of how you came to be in your current educational situation.
2. Think of someone who inspired you or motivated you as a child. Choose a particular incident that stands out in your memory and tell that story, showing the effect that the incident had on you.
3. Think of an interesting story from your own family or cultural history that you have heard rather than read. Write this narrative, including specific descriptive details, to help others learn about your background and history.

ANIK SEE

Borderland (2004)

From the Sunshine Coast in British Columbia, but now living in Amsterdam and working as a writer and producer for Radio Netherlands Worldwide, Anik See is also a writer, book designer, and creator of handcrafted chapbooks and politically oriented broadsides. In addition, See is a traveller, as evidenced by the range of tales of food and travel collected in her book *A Fork in the Road* (2000). Most recently she has published *Saudade* (2008), a book of essays, and *postcard and other stories* (2009), a collection of short stories.

Preparing to Read

In this essay, Anik See writes about her experience of being denied entry to the United States when she attempts to visit some friends. Think about the ways in which our expectations about ease of travel have changed during your lifetime. What has made travel more accessible and easier? What has made travel more difficult or less appealing? How have security concerns changed the way that we travel since the beginning of this century? How do you react to the changes in security that people now typically experience when crossing borders? To what degree should a country be permitted to refuse entry to a person or detain a person whom it deems a potential risk or threat?

A couple of young guys behind me are talking about hockey. They're upset that Roman Turek, the Flames' regular goalie, is back—they hope Sutter trades him soon; they think that Sutter hopes so too. 1

The wind outside is picking up. It's going a good clip now, much stronger than it was an hour ago. It's almost a tumbleweed a-tumblin' kind of wind, and if it weren't for all the cornfields around, this would be a tumbleweed a-tumblin' kind of place. The kind of bright sunlight that you only see in southern Alberta, the kind that washes everything out. 2

I squint out the window and watch a Department of Homeland Security[1] officer drive my sister's car into a big shed, watch 3

Reading Critically

[1] What is the Department of Homeland Security?

as a corrugated metal door shuts behind it. One of the hockey guys asks me where I'm going. Minneapolis, to visit some friends, I say . . . and you? Salt Lake, they say, to visit some friends too, and, one of the guys leans forward with his eyes all lit up, maybe catch a game. He grins. I ask them how long it'll take. They don't know—they figure between eight and twelve hours, due south from here. No speed limit in Montana. Then Idaho, then sweet Utah. I-15 all the way.

The officer drives my sister's car out and parks it. Steps out of it and the wind nearly blows the car door back onto her. A big dust cloud tornadoes across the lot and she turns away, her hair standing on end. She comes inside, brushes herself off, crooks her finger at me once she's behind the counter. 4

Explain your passport to me, she says. I don't understand what you were doing in all these places. She flips back and forth through it. Like Cuba. 5

Just travelling, I say. In *Cuba*? she asks. Yes, I say, I went to a music festival. 6

And India? What's this India business? I was travelling, I say. 7

Why? 8

I'm naturally curious, I say. But she's halfway across the room before I finish, shaking her head. 9

Come over here, she says. She leads me into a room with a door that locks automatically behind me. Put your left index finger here, she says. Why? I ask. We're sending you back to Canada, she says. Why? I ask. We'll tell you that later. Now put your finger here. 10

I ask if I'm being charged or arrested for something. No, she says. It's policy. We fingerprint and photograph anyone who's denied entry. 11

I think about a friend of mine who had his address book photocopied by police once, in lieu of an unjustified arrest, and wonder which is worse.❷ I tell her I refuse to be fingerprinted on principle, since I've done nothing wrong, and never have, and since I'm being sent back to Canada anyway and it's not apparent why. She waves a man over and speaks to him in a low tone for about five minutes, points at the tourist visas in my passport. He nods, looks over at me. 12

Reading Critically

❷ Would you rather be arrested unjustly or have your address book photocopied by the police? Explain.

I understand you're being uncooperative in providing us with information, he says. No, I say, I've been honest and forthright. Biometric information, he says, pointing to the small electronic pad. You cannot leave without being fingerprinted and photographed, he says, and no, you do not have the right to legal representation at the U.S. border. 13

The hockey kids are long gone. Heading south on I-15 with all their eagerness bubbling in front of them. 14

The officer presses my finger against the touchpad. She holds it gently, picks it up and places it down, rubs the skin gingerly when it doesn't take. I can tell she has a child. If I ask, she might pause and think to herself how quickly time passes, how she always sees her son as eight, but how he's thirteen now. She asks me if I've ever cut my fingers because they can't get a good scan on either index finger. I tell her that I used to work in kitchens, that the prints probably burned off long ago. She nods, looking at her computer screen. Hold still. Clicks her mouse. The image finally takes. 15

She tells me I'm being sent back because I lack ties to Canada. That they need to see a bank statement, more proof of material possession—a house, say, or at least my own car—and more than three changes of clothes for a one-week stay. I tell her that I've lived in Canada for thirty-five years and if that isn't a tie, I don't know what is. But that's OK, I say, I won't come back. I will not be a part of paranoid policy.[3] 16

On the Canadian side, I give the customs officer a sheet of paper with my name and file number on it. She looks at it, looks at me, a smile of empathy. Why didn't they let you in? I open my mouth, but anger comes up so quickly from my stomach that I'm seized with silence. It's OK, she says, you don't have to tell me. It just makes a long day longer. She tells me I can go. 17

I drive north, the windshield all sun and sky and brown cornfields, a long sword of horizon. It's half an hour before I can breathe, I mean really breathe, take a breath that reminds me of where I am. All that space and air around me and half an hour goes by before the fingers wrapped around my throat loosen—fingers with unscannable tips, just like the ones I have wrapped around the steering wheel of my sister's car. 18

Reading Critically

[3] What does See mean by a "paranoid policy"? Do you think this is an accurate description of U.S. customs?

UNDERSTANDING DETAILS

1. Explain why See is not permitted to enter the United States. Are the "hockey kids" allowed to enter?
2. Why does See not tell the Canadian customs officer why she was denied entry to the United States?
3. Describe the attitude of the officers See encounters from the Department of Homeland Security. Is the attitude consistent between the two officers?

ANALYZING MEANING

1. Why is See fingerprinted and photographed by the U.S. Department of Homeland Security? Why does she initially resist this procedure? Why does she ultimately allow herself to be fingerprinted and photographed?
2. Explain See's comment that she can tell the officer has a child. How can she tell this? Why does she include this observation in her story?
3. Why is See made so angry by this experience at the border? What are the metaphorical "fingers wrapped around . . . [her] throat" (paragraph 18)?

DISCOVERING RHETORICAL STRATEGIES

1. What is See's purpose in telling this story? Does she successfully achieve her purpose? Explain why or why not.
2. What examples of figurative language can you find in See's essay? What is the effect of these language choices on the reader?
3. What is the tone of See's essay? How has See conveyed this tone throughout this piece of writing?

MAKING CONNECTIONS

1. In "Borderland," See relates a story about a situation in which she felt inappropriately treated. Compare this experience to the situation described in the essay by Edith Iglauer ("Red Smile").
2. June Callwood ("Forgiveness") characterizes the beginning of the 21st century as "the age of anger, the polar opposite of forgiveness." How do you think Callwood would explain See's reaction to being photographed and fingerprinted by the U.S. Department of Homeland Security as well as denied entry to the U.S.?

IDEAS FOR DISCUSSION/WRITING

Preparing to Write

Write freely about a time when you crossed a border. What places were you travelling between? What was the reason for your travel? Was the border one that was monitored or controlled? What questions did the border officials ask you? What was their attitude toward you? Were you permitted to cross the border? How did you feel throughout the process of crossing the border?

Choosing a Topic

1. If you have ever been denied entry to a place (e.g., a country, a building) in a way that you felt was unjust, write an essay in which you relate the story of this experience. Make sure that you include a clear thesis in your essay.
2. Write a narrative essay about an experience that made you very angry. Your anger should be clear to your reader but shouldn't affect the logical organization of your essay. Use specific details to help your reader appreciate why you reacted the way you did to the situation.
3. Choose an incident or event from your life that has given you particular insight into human nature. Relate the event in a narrative essay with a clear thesis.

MATT COHEN

Zada's Hanukkah Legacy (1995)

Acknowledgment of Matt Cohen's contribution to the literary world of Canada has taken many forms. Friends, family, colleagues, and readers recognize his talents as a writer of over 40 books, including novels, short stories, poetry, and books for children (under the pseudonym Teddy Jam), and he earned great respect for his work as an advocate for writers. At the corner of Bloor Street and Spadina Avenue in Toronto there is a park named in honour of Matt Cohen, featuring plaques with a biography of Cohen, along with excerpts from a selection of his novels. The 2002 publication *Uncommon Ground*, a collection of original essays, archival photographs, and author interviews, is another vehicle for celebrating Matt Cohen's life and legacy as a writer.

Born in Kingston, Ontario, in 1942, and raised in Ottawa, Cohen earned his bachelor's and master's degrees from the University of Toronto and began his career teaching political philosophy at McMaster University. Cohen went on to become a full-time writer whose work was recognized with the Toronto Arts Award (1998), two National Magazine Awards for short fiction, the John Glassco Translation Prize (1990), and the Governor General's Award for fiction (1999) for *Elizabeth and After*.

One of the founding members of the Writers' Union of Canada, Matt Cohen also served as writer-in-residence at several Canadian universities and was visiting professor at the University of Bologna in Italy in 1985. Matt Cohen died of cancer in December of 1999.

Preparing to Read

In "Zada's Hanukkah Legacy," first published in *Canadian Geographic* magazine in 1995, Matt Cohen reflects on his childhood celebration of Hanukkah with his family. Before reading the essay, think about Hanukkah. Do you celebrate Hanukkah? If so, in what way? If not, what traditions do you associate with Hanukkah? What is the general tone of the holiday of Hanukkah? Why is Hanukkah celebrated?

One winter, when I was a child, we travelled from Ottawa to Toronto to be with my father's parents for Hanukkah. As we drove slowly through the wintry twilight, the snow crunched and squeaked beneath the tires of our old snout-nosed Dodge. When we arrived, it was almost dark. 1

My grandmother opened the door before we could knock. As always, she was wearing a black dress that made her look even thinner than she was, and square-heeled shoes that emphasized the fragility of her legs and ankles. Although my grandmother lived into her 90s, she had been on the verge of death since she was 35. We children went in first, apparently out of politeness but in fact because my parents were even more terrified of my grandparents than we were. 2

The table was set. The silver gleamed and the ritual candelabra—the *menorah*—was in place along with the patterned white dinner service—big plates with wide soup bowls on top. From the kitchen came the familiar smells of chicken soup, *kasha* (buckwheat), and roast beef that had probably been in the oven since the Pleistocene Epoch.❶ 3

We had been delayed on the road and sunset, which marked the beginning of the holiday, was upon us. As soon as our coats were off, *Zada* (grandfather) led me to the menorah and asked me if I knew the blessing for the Hanukkah candles. He lowered his head so his face was almost level with mine. He wore his invariable dark suit pants, black belt, black shoes, white shirt with expansion bracelets on the arms, suspenders, a tie held in place by a golden tiepin, and of course his *yarmulkah* (skull cap). He had lost his hair following a bout of scarlet fever, but his moustache and beard, trimmed to a squarish spade a few inches below his chin, gave him—to my eyes—a wild and hairy look that was emphasized by the contrasting pinkness of his lips and tongue. Bearded, candid, utterly foreign, his face was an outburst from a past I couldn't begin to imagine. A devout believer, his passionate Jewishness made it completely natural to talk about biblical figures as though they were neighbours we had just met on the street. 4

Soon I was holding the match and reciting, in Hebrew, the blessing I'd learned in the car.❷ My grandfather, knowing full well this was a surface acquisition, nodded and hummed along. 5

Zada Cohen was a short and stocky man, renowned for feats of strength we grandchildren never saw but were told about—the most amazing being that during a fire he had carried two pigs, one under each arm, from a neighbour's barn. This was notable not only because carrying two pigs would be so difficult, 6

Reading Critically

❶ What and when was the Pleistocene Epoch?

❷ Why did Cohen learn the blessing in the car?

but because my grandfather had demonstrated an unsuspected ecumenical[3] streak. When the fire happened, I have no doubt he was wearing his usual costume, down to the tiepin, the suspenders and the yarmulkah.

7 The first time I remember meeting him was when I was six years old. He took me by the hand and walked me to an empty synagogue. We stood in the middle of what was—to me—a cavernous dusty room filled with the smell of old books and rotting cloth. My grandfather pointed out the ark where the Torah was kept, the gallery reserved for women, and the Bimah where the rabbi delivered his sermon and the cantor sang the sacred texts. Then he crouched down so his eyes were directly opposite mine.

8 "*You* will be a rabbi," my grandfather announced to me. Fortunately, even at the time, we both knew this was extremely unlikely.[4]

9 Over the years, he maintained this special way of fixing his eyes on mine. At such moments I knew that as the eldest (although religiously unworthy) grandson, I was being singled out to receive, absorb, and somehow shoulder the responsibility for some piece of Jewish lore he felt it essential for me to know.

10 "Mordecai," he always called me by my Hebrew name, "do you know—"

11 Of course, I never did.

12 Hanukkah, the Feast of Lights, is celebrated each year for eight days beginning on the 25th day of the Hebrew month Kislev. Since the Jewish calendar is based on the lunar month, Hanukkah's date in the modern calendar varies from late November to late December. For Jews, the year's most important holidays are Yom Kippur and Rosh Hashanah. Although these holidays often allow Jewish children to miss school during the World Series, they feature fasting, repentance and promises to be good.

13 Hanukkah, a relatively minor holiday in the Jewish religious pantheon, has not only presents, but a terrific story. "Do you know," Zada would ask me, "that we celebrate Hanukkah because a certain man with a name like yours, a Mattathias, had the courage to say no?" Or: "Do you know that to join his army, a young man had to be strong enough to rip a tree from the ground with his bare hands while galloping past on horseback?

Reading Critically

[3] What does *ecumenical* mean?

[4] Why do you think they both knew this?

At full speed?" At first I viewed the story merely as about wild battles won by out-numbered Jewish soldiers. But the real story of Hanukkah is broader, because it is also the story of the Jewish rejection—after a period of great temptation—of the Greek Empire and Greek culture.

In the 5th century BC, the Jewish people, after a brief exile in Babylon, returned to Judea and restored the Temple in Jerusalem. Then began a period of consolidation in which the scribes and the written word gained a predominant influence. Meanwhile, in the Greek city of Athens, another intellectual revolution was taking place. This was the era of Socrates, Plato and Aristotle. 14

In 334 BC, Alexander of Macedon began his conquests, which included Palestine. The Greeks allowed the Jews a prominent role in the founding of Alexandria, and it was in conjunction with the Greek Empire that the Jews began to establish themselves as a mercantile force in the Mediterranean basin. The Jews found themselves tremendously attracted to—and seduced by—Hellenic culture, customs and language. The translation of the Hebrew scriptures into Greek became a major event in Jewish intellectual life. During this period, the Jews, although Hellenized❺ in many respects, were still free to follow their own religious practices. 15

But in 175 BC, Antiochus, an Athens-born Greek warrior, ascended the throne. He soon established domination over Judea and in the process, Jerusalem was converted into a Greek city. A proclamation was issued that forced all citizens to follow the Greek religion. Even the Temple in Jerusalem would be used for pagan religious rituals, including the slaughter of pigs on its altar. 16

At this time, through the influence of the scribes, Judaism favoured piety and tolerance over fighting. As a result, thousands of religious Jews martyred themselves.❻ Even the less devout refused to fight on the Sabbath, and opposing armies soon learned that was the day on which the Jews were most easily attacked. 17

In 168 BC, in the marketplace of a small town called Modein to the northwest of Jerusalem, the Syrian soldiers erected an altar. The men of Modein were assembled there and the soldiers' captain ordered Mattathias, a Jewish priest and elder, to sacrifice a 18

Reading Critically

❺ What is the meaning of *Hellenized*?

❻ What does "martyred themselves" mean?

pig to Jupiter in honour of Antiochus. Mattathias did not budge. Another stepped forward, offering to perform the sacrifice. The plan was that those Jews who refused to eat the meat of the pig would be executed. Suddenly, the aged Mattathias snatched the sword from the captain, killed the traitor who had offered to perform the sacrifice, then killed the captain. Mattathias's sons then surrounded him, and they and their followers fled to the hills.

19 So began the Maccabee uprising. The rebels—not the first Jewish guerilla group in history—had made the singular decision to temporarily suspend the ordinance against fighting on the Sabbath, giving them a tremendous military advantage over their unsuspecting enemies. In a matter of four years, the Maccabees' victories brought them to Jerusalem itself, where their first task was to clean and reconsecrate the Temple. Removing the stones that had been used for pagan sacrifices, they built a new altar.

20 On the 25th day of Kislev, 165 BC, they lit the sacred lamp—only to discover there was enough oil for just one day. Horsemen were sent in every direction to find more oil. Eight days later, someone finally returned—but remarkably, the lamp had continued to burn. Hanukkah commemorates the reconsecration of the temple and the miracle of the lasting oil.

21 Because my wife is not Jewish, Hanukkah in our family doesn't compete with Christmas or replace it. It has its own special status and everyone enjoys it for what we have made it. Hanukkah is also familiar to my children from their classrooms and day-care. For them, this holiday is a normal part of their public and private lives.

22 The situation was entirely different in the late 1940s when I grew up. Then, Jews were still trying to come to terms with the enormity of their losses during World War II. If the word "holocaust" existed then, I never heard it. There was no single word to describe what had happened. Nor was Hanukkah celebrated and discussed in school on an equal footing with Christmas. Such a possibility was unthinkable because Judaism and Hanukkah had no public place.

23 On the contrary, being Jewish was something best kept to oneself: when I was in Grade 5, my refusal to say the Lord's Prayer led to my spending each morning in the corridor while the teacher, a Sunday School organist in his spare time, led the rest of the class through their religious exercises. For me, Jewish holidays were not only religious events, but also another way of being singled out, set aside, sent to the corridor until secular life resumed and I was returned to the main room.

Hanukkah's gift-giving aspects are constantly growing, but when I was a child it seemed a weak and almost pitiful counterpoint to the public splendour that made Christmas the emotional and commercial centrepiece of winter. For this extravaganza, people put up trees in their houses and store windows, chains of lights festooned downtown and residential areas, Santa Claus and his reindeer dashed through skies and shopping centres. On the day itself, I knew, Christian children would receive armloads of presents, then, after a huge lunch, settle down to watching television specials that celebrated the triumph of their virtues and their happiness. 24

For whatever reasons, the Jews of Ottawa did not compete by putting electric Stars of David on their roofs or erecting Hanukkah bushes in their living rooms. It's true that Jewish children got presents, but they weren't the sort of thing you'd brag about at school if you wanted to survive recess.❼ Nonetheless, though it took a long time, I came to value Hanukkah for its own virtues and—mostly because of my grandfather—to realize how complex and full of contemporary resonance its story was. 25

Now that I am an adult and a parent, I look forward to Hanukkah as a warm family celebration that over the years has become a mid-winter opportunity to explore with my children a little of the meaning and history of Judaism. It is also an occasion for gift-giving and family visiting which—aside from the potato pancakes and the candles—are the main attraction for the children. 26

When potato pancakes—*latkas*—were served at that long-ago Hanukkah at my grandparents' house, Zada explained the traditional holiday food had originated during the battles of the Maccabees: passing through a village one time, the Jewish guerillas were served the pancakes because that was the only food there was time to make. 27

After tea, presents were distributed. As they did every single Hanukkah for decades, my grandparents gave my brother and me white shirts. These were always "Eatonia" shirts, with starched collars and holes for cufflinks, and they were for wearing to synagogue—a place we didn't go very often. Then my grandfather recounted the battle when the Jews defeated the 28

Reading Critically

❼ What sort of presents did Jewish children get? What sort of presents did they need to survive recess?

Syrians, who rode powerful elephants instead of horses. He asked us if we thought we would be strong enough to tear trees out of the ground. Of course we would.

When the evening was finished—not before we'd all had several desserts and numerous helpings of chocolates and cookies—we went out to the car. Despite the cold, my grandparents stood in the open door, framed by the yellow light, and watched us drive off. They were, I suddenly realized, like survivors on some magical ark that had arrived from thousands of years ago. To them, Hanukkah had nothing to do with Christmas or being sent to the hallway or television specials—it was a magic ritual mysteriously connected to their mysterious past. One I could participate in and grow into until I, too, appeared to my children or grandchildren as a friendly but bizarre relic out of a past they will never otherwise touch. 29

UNDERSTANDING DETAILS

1. Explain why Cohen's family travelled to Toronto each winter. Who is the "Zada" of the title?
2. Summarize the historical events that led to the Maccabee uprising.
3. How is Hanukkah celebrated? How does Hanukkah compare with Christmas?

ANALYZING MEANING

1. As an adult, how does Cohen view Hanukkah? How does this compare with his childhood experience of this Jewish holiday?
2. What is the purpose of Cohen's essay? Has he successfully achieved this purpose? Explain why or why not.
3. Explain the title of Cohen's essay.

DISCOVERING RHETORICAL STRATEGIES

1. In addition to narration, Cohen has employed several other rhetorical modes in this essay. Identify at least two other rhetorical modes, and discuss their contribution to the essay.
2. What is Cohen's thesis? Where in the essay is it located?
3. In addition to his personal narrative, Cohen gives a chronological account of historical events. Explain how he has combined these two elements in a single essay. Is this an effective organizational strategy? Why or why not?

MAKING CONNECTIONS

1. In this essay Cohen contrasts his childhood view of Hanukkah with his adult view. Compare and contrast this dual perspective with those of Barbara Kingsolver ("Life Without Go-Go Boots") and Monte Hummel ("A Passion for the Environment: Two Accounts"). Describe the tone of each of the adult perspectives as the authors reflect on their childhood experiences.
2. Cohen and Steven Heighton ("Elegy in Stone") have both incorporated descriptions of historical events into their essays. Discuss the effectiveness of their portrayals of history.

IDEAS FOR DISCUSSION/WRITING

Preparing to Write

Write freely about religious traditions. Do you observe any religious holidays? Why or why not? If so, which ones? How are they observed? Have your practices changed over time? What religious traditions do other people in your community practise? What is your reaction to these observances? Do you understand their practices?

Choosing a Topic

1. Write a narrative essay in which you relate the story of a childhood celebration of a particular holiday (religious or not).
2. Write an essay in which you compare and contrast the observances of holidays from two different cultures or religions. For example, you might compare Tet (Vietnamese) with Rosh Hashanah (Jewish) or Nowrooz (Zoroastrian), or Ramadan (Muslim) with Lent (Christian).
3. Think of a grandparent (or other adult in your life) who made a particularly strong impression on you. Choose a story that highlights the key characteristics of your subject, and write a narrative essay in which you convey the impact of this person on your life.

JOWI TAYLOR

"Beginning" from *Six String Nation* (2009)

Broadcaster, producer, writer, and founder of the Six String Nation Project, Jowi Taylor (1962–) is from Toronto, Ontario, where he studied linguistics at the University of Toronto. During his years at university, Taylor worked as a volunteer radio host at CKLN-FM (at Ryerson Polytechnic) and, during a year of travel, hosted a show in Bangkok, Thailand. After working as a production coordinator at Harbourfront Centre for 10 years, Taylor went to CBC Radio, where he hosted *Global Village* for over a decade, hosted and co-produced a Peabody Award–winning series called *The Wire: The Impact of Electricity on Music* as well as the follow-up series *The Nerve: Music and the Human Experience*, wrote the Radio 2 blog, and now hosts and produces *Nightstream.*

Taylor has published articles in a variety of magazines including *Shift* and *Montage*, and he has also served as a board member for the Images Festival, ImagineNATIVE and the Ontario Council of Folk Festivals. His current focus is the Six String Nation guitar project, conceived and initiated in 1995 and completed 11 years later. The selection here is an excerpt from Taylor's book, *Six String Nation* (2009). It chronicles, in words and pictures, the story of Voyageur, a guitar built from 64 pieces representing diverse stories of Canada.

Preparing to Read

Before reading this selection that opens Jowi Taylor's book about his Six String Nation project, think about how you would define Canada. What makes Canada unique? What stories from Canadian history particularly characterize us as a nation? How is Canada different from other countries with which you are familiar?

Music has been the centre of my life since I first figured out how to drop a needle on a record. Before I started amassing a record collection at the age of nine, I had explored every groove in my parents' record cabinet. I think my parents were a little bit dismayed at the sheer volume of attention I paid to music—not to mention the sheer volume at which I liked to listen to it. 1

As music was to me, so politics was to them. While my parents hosted riding association meetings, I was in my teen-den in the basement with the headphones turned up loud. For me, music contained the spark of all kinds of power—physical, spiritual, emotional, social, cultural *and* political. The political power, for me, grew not just from lyrics (as it did in so much of my parents' collection) but in a song's very structure. The music of a Ghanaian drum ensemble or mid-period Talking Heads was more politically suggestive, I felt, than most protest songs.❶ Once you got lyrics involved, you got someone's point of view—possibly misinformed, possibly earnest, possibly missing the point entirely. 2

That's how I felt in 1995, as the province of Quebec steered hard in the direction of sovereignty with the October referendum.❷ As the decision loomed, the drama played out in the cool calculus of politics and the heated passions of culture, with warm (sometimes itchy) sentiment softening up the middle ground. I sympathized with Quebec nationalism as an expression of cultural confidence. Then again, I also understood those people who chartered buses simply so they could stand on the streets of Montreal to declare their undying—and normally unarticulated—love for Quebec as an essential part of Canada. 3

But as I listened to debates and then on referendum night watched those blue and red graph-bars battle for real estate on my TV screen, I felt we were missing something really important. This wasn't just about Quebec versus the rest of Canada, it wasn't about French versus English, or politicians and intellectuals grappling for control of our constitutional history. Canada is filled with stories from communities large and small, stories that flesh out the character of who we are. Sad tales, grand tales, tiny acts of revolution or invention that resonate with some small part of us, whether we're from First Nations or founding nations or the United Nations we have become. During the referendum, none of those stories passed the lips of pundits or politicians of any stripe.❸ 4

A few months before the referendum, I happened to meet a guitar-maker named George Rizsanyi. A Hungarian immigrant 5

Reading Critically

❶ Why does Taylor consider songs without lyrics "more politically suggestive" than those with words?

❷ What issue or question was the focus of the October 1995 Quebec referendum?

❸ What important thing does Taylor believe was missing in the referendum debates?

and former auto worker, George had made a name for himself building guitars from Canadian woods rather than the exotics favoured by most in the trade.[4] As he saw it, people paid huge sums, destroyed rainforests and skewed local economies just to get at materials for which there were equivalent or superior homegrown substitutes. George even made guitars using wood from his property in Greenbank, Ontario. This quietly patriotic act seemed counter to how Canadians tend to think—that if something is from here, it must be second-rate. Perhaps the reason for this referendum was that Quebecers were prepared *not* to think that way about themselves. And perhaps Canadians in every part of the country longed to express themselves as boldly as Quebecers did. If our local stories weren't constrained by self-doubt, perhaps we could all experience that boldness together.

6 I asked George if he could build a guitar using material from every part of the country—one piece from each province and territory. George agreed to give it a try. We thought we might have it done in time for the referendum. We couldn't have been more wrong.

7 I'm often asked how long it took to make the guitar. I have two answers. Aside from preparation time, George spent just six weeks between April and June of 2006 building Voyageur, with Sara Nasr parachuted into the workshop for one week to work on the fretboard inlays. But the other answer is that, with all the research, consultation, futile attempts to get funding, the meetings and letters and phone calls and e-mails and endorsements and false hopes, it took eleven years from that magic moment of conception until we heard the first sound from this guitar.

8 While I spun my wheels, other projects emerged that seemed to tap into the same zeitgeist[5]—a collective notion of nation. Author Charlotte Gray's *The Museum Called Canada* looked at the country through twenty-five virtual rooms filled with the objects of our memory, meaning and culture. Tyler Aspin, an artist from Pinette, PEI, built a sculpture called *The Canada Tree* made from items contributed by people from across the country. In tribute to Tyler, the rosette of the guitar includes pieces of the mallet used to build the tree. Tyler died of a lightning strike in 2001, before we had a chance to meet and become friends.

Reading Critically

4. What are the "exotics favoured by most in the trade?" Why do you think they are favoured?
5. What does *zeitgeist* mean? What zeitgeist is Taylor referring to here?

My guitar remained a frustrated dream even after an article on the front page of the November 26, 2005, *Globe and Mail* attracted all kinds of kudos but no funding. But when Mark Kristmanson, director of events for the National Capital Commission❻ in Ottawa, called to ask if the guitar would be ready in time to be featured in programming for Canada Day 2006, I took what funding promises I had, multiplied them in my head and simply said yes. Even though the main funding promise would ultimately fall through, I knew this was the best opportunity to debut the guitar the way I'd dreamed. Even if I was flat broke,❼ how could I say no? 9

UNDERSTANDING DETAILS

1. What motivated Jowi Taylor to begin the Six String Nation project?
2. What did Taylor choose to be the centrepiece of his project? Why?
3. Who is George Rizsanyi? What about him appealed to Taylor?

ANALYZING MEANING

1. Taylor says that Canadians tend to think that "if something is from here, it must be second-rate" (paragraph 5). Why does he see this as problematic? Do you agree with Taylor? Why or why not?
2. Explain Taylor's comment that, "other projects seemed to tap into the same zeitgeist—a collective notion of nation" (paragraph 8).
3. According to Taylor, what was the 1995 referendum really about? Do you agree with him? Why or why not?

DISCOVERING RHETORICAL STRATEGIES

1. Narrative is made effective through the careful selection of detail. What details in Taylor's essay were particularly effective for you as a reader? Why?
2. What is the dominant tone of Taylor's essay? How does this tone support the purpose of his essay?
3. What other rhetorical strategies has Taylor used in this essay to make his narrative effective and interesting?

Reading Critically

❻ What is the National Capital Commission?

❼ Why was Taylor flat broke? What costs do you think would be associated with this project?

MAKING CONNECTIONS

1. Seven rules for writing are outlined in Natalie Goldberg's essay ("The Rules of Writing Practice"). Which of these rules has Taylor followed? Are there any that he appears to have ignored or violated?
2. Taylor's Six String Nation project is about Canadian identity. How do you think Anita Rau Badami ("My Canada") would respond to Taylor's notion of Canada? What about Janice Gross Stein ("Whisper, Echo and Voice")?
3. Taylor posits that "perhaps Canadians in every part of the country longed to express themselves as boldly as Quebecers did. If our local stories weren't constrained by self-doubt, perhaps we could all experience that boldness together" (paragraph 5). How do you think K'naan ("Between the Highs and the Lows, Life Happens") would react to that statement?

IDEAS FOR DISCUSSION/WRITING

Preparing to Write

Write freely about the place of music in your life. What types of music do you particularly enjoy? What types of music do you not like? When do you typically listen to music? Are there times when you don't want to hear any music? Where do you find new music? What is your first memory of music? What would your life be like without music?

Choosing a Topic

1. Taylor wanted the pieces of the Six String Nation guitar to reflect the various stories of Canada. Imagine that you are embarking on a similar project; what is one Canadian story that you would want to include and what might you choose to represent that story?
2. Taylor set out to make a guitar that would contain one piece of material from each province and territory. If you were creating this guitar, describe what 13 materials you would choose to represent each of our provinces and territories.
3. Write a narrative about an experience you have had that felt uniquely Canadian. When and where was this experience? Make it clear how you felt about this experience.

JENN LAMOTHE

Giving Up the Fight (2007)

Jenn Lamothe (1980–) is a freelance writer living in Sudbury. Her writing has been published in *The Sudbury Star*, and the essay here was originally broadcast on CBC Radio's *This I Believe* series.

Preparing to Read

Before reading Lamothe's narrative about her response to her epilepsy, think about a condition such as epilepsy that causes seizures. What triggers epileptic seizures? Can seizures be controlled? Is there any cure for epilepsy? What is the appropriate action to take if you see someone having a seizure?

I believe that sometimes it's better to give up the fight. 1

Through most of my struggle with epilepsy, I followed the philosophy of Dylan Thomas and decided to "rage, rage against the dying of the light". I fought my doctors, my family, anyone who told me that there was nothing left to be done, that I would be a slave to the seizures for the rest of my life. I would not believe it, hearing over and over the stories of those who had found a cure after years of illness. Their doctors were wrong. They kept fighting and saw victory in the end. I decided that I too would fight until my dying breath.❶ 2

I fought with everything I had, and I never won. 3

The seizures always overwhelmed me, and always left me hopeless. Every time I suffered a seizure, I felt like a failure.❷ I told myself, "I'm not fighting hard enough, I'm not strong enough". With nothing to do but sit and wait for the seizures to come, I would punish myself, thinking of only the wrong in my 4

Reading Critically

❶ Can you think of examples of other illnesses that require the sufferer to fight?

❷ Why do you think the seizures made Lamothe feel like a failure?

life. Getting up in the morning became more difficult than anything I could imagine. I could never find a reason to rise.

5 It was a stormy winter day when it hit me. I sat on my worn out spot on the couch and the answer came to me as if I had known it all along. I am not only losing the battle, I am wasting my life. All the times I spent fighting, or what I thought was fighting, I was actually hiding myself away.[3] It was like I went to sleep for four years hoping that when I woke up it would all be over. But it never was. And I was tired of sleeping.

6 What happens if I stop fighting? What happens if I accept the seizures, accept the limitations, and work within them? The answers came so easily I knew they were right.

7 I remembered that I am a woman, not just an epileptic. I forgot Dylan Thomas' battle cry and replaced it with Lennon and McCartney's refrain: "for tomorrow may rain, so I'll follow the sun". I began to do what I could now, because later was so uncertain. I tried new things, as the opportunity may never come again. Even if it did, I may not be up for it. Not only did I get back on my feet, I began to treasure every moment. Every time I laughed it was louder. When I listened it was with a new focus, and I regained the sparkle in my eye.

8 I began leaving the house, wanting to go all the places I had feared before.[4] I saw that I was not an inconvenience, but I was truly loved by those who surrounded me. The essence of who I am overrules any first aid that might be required.

9 I will never again let go of my hopes or my dreams. I believe that my greatest freedoms come from knowing and respecting my boundaries. Giving up the fight has given me back my life.

UNDERSTANDING DETAILS

1. What condition does Lamothe have that made her feel she had to fight? Who and what was she fighting?
2. Why does Lamothe choose to stop fighting?
3. Explain the effect on Lamothe of giving up her fight. In giving up her fight has Lamothe given up? Why or why not?

Reading Critically

[3] What is Lamothe's revelation telling her?

[4] Why did Lamothe fear going out?

ANALYZING MEANING

1. Why does Lamothe believe that she has to fight? Why does she spend so much time and energy fighting?
2. In paragraph 6, Lamothe poses a series of questions to herself and then says that the answers came very easily. Articulate the answers that you think Lamothe came up with in response to each of these questions.
3. Why do you think that Lamothe has chosen to share her experience with such a broad audience by writing this personal essay? What is her purpose in sharing her belief that "sometimes it's better to give up the fight" (paragraph 1)?

DISCOVERING RHETORICAL STRATEGIES

1. Lamothe chooses quotations or lyrics from Dylan Thomas and Lennon and McCartney to characterize her two approaches to life. Why has she chosen to use others' words rather than simply describing her two different attitudes? What is the effect of incorporating these references?
2. How would you describe the pacing of Lamothe's narrative? How has she achieved this effect? How is it particularly well suited to the original form of this piece as an essay for radio broadcast?
3. How many of Lamothe's sentences begin with *I*? What is the effect of this choice in telling this story?

MAKING CONNECTIONS

1. Lamothe and Cynara Geissler ("Fat Acceptance: A Basic Primer") have both written personal essays about self-acceptance. Comment on the similarities as well as the differences in their style and approach to this task.
2. Like Lamothe, Anik See ("Borderland") and Barbara Kingsolver ("Life Without Go-Go Boots") use first-person narratives in their essays. Explain the effectiveness of this approach in achieving their purposes.

IDEAS FOR DISCUSSION/WRITING

Preparing to Write

Write freely about persistence and not giving up. Generally, how do we regard people who keep fighting? How do we describe people who give up the fight? How have we learned the value of sticking with something? How is this attitude reinforced?

Choosing a Topic

1. Write an essay describing a situation in which you achieved something significant because you did not give up. Make sure that you select and organize your details effectively to serve your purpose clearly.
2. Recall a time when you felt like a failure. Write a narrative essay in which you recreate the events and your feelings about them for your audience. Be sure to show your audience the events and feelings rather than telling about them.
3. This essay comes from a series of pieces on CBC Radio called *This I Believe*. Think of a deeply held belief and write a short personal essay (350–500 words) explaining this aspect of your personal philosophy. Begin your essay with "I believe . . ." and avoid sermonizing or editorializing.

CHAPTER 3

EXAMPLE

Illustrating Ideas

Citing an example to help make a point is one of the most instinctive techniques we use in communication. If, for instance, you state that being an internationally ranked tennis player requires constant practice, a friend might challenge that assertion and ask what you mean by "constant practice." When you respond "about three hours a day," your friend might ask for more specific proof. At this stage in the discussion, you could offer the following illustrations to support your statement: When not on tour, Venus Williams practises four hours per day; Roger Federer, five hours; and Maria Sharapova, six hours. Your friend's doubt will have been answered through your use of examples.

Defining *Example*

Well-chosen examples and illustrations are an essay's building blocks. They are drawn from your experience, your observations, and your reading. They help you show rather than tell what you mean, usually by supplying concrete details (references to what we can see, smell, taste, hear, or touch) to support abstract ideas (such as faith, hope, understanding, and love); by providing specifics ("I like chocolate") to explain generalizations ("I like sweets"); and by giving definite references ("Turn left at the second stoplight") to clarify vague statements ("Turn in a few blocks"). Though illustrations take many forms, writers often find themselves indebted to description or narration (or some combination of the two) in order to supply enough relevant examples to achieve their rhetorical intent.

As you might suspect, examples are important ingredients in producing exciting, vivid prose. Just as crucial is the fact that carefully chosen examples often encourage your readers to feel one way or another about an issue being discussed. If you tell your parents, for instance, that living in a college residence is not conducive to academic success, they may doubt your word, perhaps thinking that you are simply attempting to coerce them into giving you money for an apartment. You can help dispel this notion, however, by giving them specific examples of the chaotic nature of residence life: the party down the hall that ended at 2:00 a.m. when you had a chemistry exam that same morning at 8:00; the sound system next door that seems to be stuck on its highest decibel level at all hours of the day and night; and the new "friend" you recently acquired who thinks you are the best listener in the world—especially when everyone else has the good sense to be asleep. After such a detailed and well-documented explanation, your parents could hardly deny the strain of this difficult environment on your studies. Examples can be very persuasive.

The following paragraphs, written by a student, use examples to explain how he reacts to boredom in his life. As you read this excerpt, notice how the writer shows rather than tells the readers how he copes with boredom by providing exciting details that are concrete, specific, and definite:

> We all deal with boredom in our own ways. Unfortunately, most of us have to deal with it far too often. Some people actually seek boredom. Being bored means that they are not required to do anything; being boring means that no one wants anything from them. In short, these people equate boredom with peace and relaxation. But for the rest of us, boredom is not peaceful. It produces anxiety.
>
> Most people deal with boredom by trying to distract themselves from boring circumstances. Myself, I'm a reader. At the breakfast table over a boring bowl of cereal, I read the cereal box, the milk carton, the wrapper on the bread. (Have you ever noticed how many of those ingredients are unpronounceable?) Waiting in a doctor's office, I will gladly read weekly news magazines of three years ago, a book for five-year-olds, advertisements for drugs, and even the physician's odd-looking diplomas on the walls. Have you ever been so bored you were reduced to reading through all the business cards in your wallet? Searching for names similar to yours in the phone book? Browsing through the *National Enquirer* while waiting in the grocery line? At any rate, that's my recipe for beating boredom. What's yours?

Thinking Critically Through Examples

Working with examples gives you yet another powerful way of processing your immediate environment and the larger world around you. It involves a manner of thinking that is completely different from description and narration. Using examples to think critically means seeing a definite order in a series of specific, concrete illustrations that are related in some way that may or may not be immediately obvious to your readers.

Isolating this rhetorical mode involves playing with related details in such a way that they create various patterns that relay different messages to the reader. Often, the simple act of arranging examples helps both the reader and the writer make sense of an experience or idea. In fact, ordering examples and illustrations in a certain way may give one distinct impression, while ordering them in another way may send a completely different message. Each pattern creates a different meaning and, as a result, an entirely new effect.

With examples, more than with description and narration, patterns need to be discovered in the context of the topic, the writer's purpose, and the writer's ultimate message. Writers and readers of example essays must make a shift from chronological to logical thinking. A writer discussing variations in faces, for example, would be working with assorted memories of people, incidents, and age differences. All of these details will eventually take shape in some sort of statement about faces, but these observations would probably not follow a strictly chronological sequence.

The exercises here will help you experience the mental differences among these rhetorical modes and will also prepare you to make sense of details and examples through careful arrangement and rearrangement of them in your essay. These exercises will continue to give you more information about your mind's abilities and range.

Reading and Writing Example Essays

A common criticism of college- and university-level writers is that they often base their essays on unsupported generalizations, such as "All sports cars are unreliable." The guidelines discussed in this introduction will help you avoid this problem and use examples effectively to support your ideas.

As you read the essays in this chapter, take time to notice the degree of specificity the writers use to make various points. To a certain extent, the more examples you use in your essays, the clearer your ideas will be and the more your readers will understand and be interested in what you are saying.

Notice also that these writers know when to stop—when "more" becomes too much and boredom sets in for the reader. Most students err by using too few examples, however, so we suggest that when in doubt about whether or not to include another illustration, you should go ahead and add one.

Reading Example Essays

- What is the essay's context?
- What is the writer's main message?
- How do examples communicate this message?

Preparing to Read. Before you begin reading the essays in this chapter, take some time to think about each author's title: What can you infer about Anita Rau Badami's attitude toward her subject from her title, "My Canada"? Based on the title of Katrina Onstad's essay, "John Lennon, Michael Jackson: Do Celebrities Die Anymore?" how do you think the author views celebrity worship? In addition, try to discover the writer's audience and purpose at this point in the reading process. Scanning the essay and surveying its synopsis in the Rhetorical Contents will provide you with useful information for this task.

Also important as you prepare to read is information about the author and about how a particular essay was written. Most of this material is furnished for you in the biography preceding each essay. From it, you might learn, for example, why Barbara Kingsolver is qualified to write about fashion or why Naomi Klein wrote "Co-opting Dissent."

Finally, before you begin to read, take time to answer the Preparing to Read questions and to make some associations with the general subject of the essay: What are your opinions on celebrities (Onstad)? How familiar are you with branding (Klein)?

Reading. As you first read these essays, record any thoughts that come to mind. Make associations freely with the content of each essay, its purpose, its audience, and the facts about its publication. For example, try to determine why Stephen Osborne found waving a worthy subject or why Naomi Klein titles her essay "Co-opting Dissent." At this point, you will probably be able to make some pretty accurate guesses about the audience each author is addressing. Creating a context for your reading—including the writer's qualifications; the essay's tone, purpose, and audience; and the publication information—is an important first step toward being able to analyze your reading material in any mode.

Finally, after you have read an essay in this section once, preview the questions after the selection before you read it again. Let these questions focus your attention for your second reading.

Rereading. As you read the essays in this chapter for a second time, focus on the examples each writer uses to make his or her point: How relevant are these examples to the thesis and purpose of each essay? How many examples do the writers use? Do they vary the length of these examples to achieve different goals? Do the authors use examples their readers can easily identify with and understand? How are these examples organized in each case? Does this arrangement support each writer's purpose? For example, how relevant to her central idea are Anita Rau Badami's examples of people she met in Canada? How many examples does Barbara Kingsolver use to make each point? Does Ryan McNutt provide enough examples to support his assessment of Joanna Newsom? How does Naomi Klein organize her examples? Does this arrangement help her accomplish her purpose? In what way? Does Katrina Onstad use examples that a variety of readers can identify with? How effective are her examples? How effective are Osborne's examples?

As you read, consider also how other rhetorical modes help each writer accomplish his or her purpose. What are these modes? How do they work along with examples to help create a coherent essay?

Last, answering the questions after each essay will help you check your grasp of its main points and will lead you from the literal to the analytical level in preparation for the discussion/ writing assignments that follow.

For a thorough summary of reading tasks, you might want to consult the checklist on page 41 of the Introduction.

Writing Example Essays

- Draft a thesis statement.
- Choose relevant examples to support your thesis.
- Arrange your examples to prove your main point.

Preparing to Write. Before you can use examples in an essay, you must first think of some. One good way to generate ideas is to use some of the prewriting techniques explained in the Introduction (pages 28–34) as you respond to the Preparing to Write questions that appear before the writing assignments for each essay. You should then consider these thoughts in conjunction with the purpose and the audience specified in your chosen writing assignments. Out of these questions should come a number of good examples for your essay.

Writing. In an example essay, a thesis statement or controlling idea will help you begin to organize your paper. (See pages 34–35 of the Introduction for more information on thesis statements.) Examples become the primary method of organizing an essay when they guide the reader from point to point in reference to the writer's thesis statement. The examples you use should always be relevant to the thesis and purpose of your essay. If, for instance, the person talking about tennis players cited the practice schedules of only unknown players, her friend certainly would not be convinced of the truth of her statement about how hard internationally ranked athletes work at their game. To develop a topic principally with examples, you can use one extended example or several shorter examples, depending on the nature and purpose of your assertion. If you are attempting to prove that Canadians are more health conscious now than they were 20 years ago, citing a few examples from your own neighbourhood will not provide enough evidence to be convincing. If, however, you are simply commenting on a neighbourhood health trend, you can legitimately refer to these local cases. Furthermore, always try to find examples with which your readers can identify so that they can follow your line of reasoning. If you want your parents to help finance an apartment, citing instances from the lives of current famous musicians or movie actors will probably not prove your point because your parents may not sympathize with these particular role models.

The examples you choose must also be arranged as effectively as possible to encourage audience interest and identification. If you are using examples to explain the imaginative quality of Canada's Wonderland, for instance, the most logical approach would probably be to organize your essay by degrees (i.e., from least to most imaginative or most to least original). But if your essay uses examples to help readers visualize your bedroom, a spatial arrangement of the details (moving from one item to the next) might be easiest for your readers to follow. If the subject is a series of important events, like graduation weekend, the illustrations might most effectively be organized chronologically. As you will learn from reading the selections that follow, the careful organization of examples leads quite easily to unity and coherence in your essays. *Unity* is a sense of wholeness and interrelatedness that writers achieve by making sure all their sentences are related to the essay's main idea; *coherence* refers to logical development in an essay, with special attention to how well ideas grow out of one another as the essay develops. Unity and coherence produce good writing—and that, of course, helps foster confidence and accomplishment in school and in your professional life.

Rewriting. As you reread your example essays, look closely at the choice and arrangement of details in relation to your purpose and audience:

- Have I included enough examples to develop each of my topics adequately?
- Are the examples I have chosen relevant to my thesis?
- Have I selected examples that my readers can easily understand?
- Have I arranged these examples in a logical manner that my audience can follow?

For more detailed information on writing, see the checklist on page 42 of the Introduction.

Student Essay: Examples at Work

In the following essay, a student uses examples to explain and analyze her parents' behaviour as they prepare for and enjoy their grandchildren during the Christmas holidays. As you read it, study the various examples the student writer uses to convince us that her parents truly undergo a transformation each winter.

Mom and Dad's Holiday Disappearing Act

General topic

Details to capture holiday spirit

Often during the winter holidays, people find surprises: Children discover the secret contents of brightly wrapped packages that have teased them for weeks; cooks are astonished by the wealth of

Background information

smells and memories their busy kitchens can bring about; workaholics stumble upon the true joy of a few days' rest. My surprise over the past few winters has been the personality transformation my parents go through around mid-December as they change from Dad and Mom into Poppa and Granny. Yes, they become grandparents and are completely different from the people I know the other 11 and a half months of the year.

Thesis statement

First point

The first sign of my parents' metamorphosis is the delight they take in visiting toy and children's clothing stores. These two people, who usually despise anything having to do with shopping malls, become crazed consumers. While they tell me to budget my money and shop wisely, they are buying every doll, dump truck, and velvet outfit in sight. And this is only the beginning of the holidays!

Examples relevant to thesis

Transition

When my brother's children arrive, Poppa and Granny come into full form. First they throw out all ideas about a balanced diet for the grandkids. While we were raised in a house where everyone had to take two bites of broccoli, beets, or liver (foods that appeared quite often on our table despite constant groaning), the grandchildren never have to eat anything that does not appeal to them. Granny carries marshmallows in her pockets to bribe the littlest ones into following her around the house, while Poppa offers "surprises" of candy and cake to them all day long. Boxes of chocolate-covered cherries disappear while the bran muffins get hard and stale. The kids love all the sweets, and when the sugar revs up their energy levels, Granny and Poppa can always decide to leave and do a bit more shopping or go to bed while my brother and sister-in-law try to deal with their supercharged, hyperactive kids.

Second point

Humorous examples (organized from most to least healthy)

Transition

Once the grandchildren have arrived, Granny and Poppa also seem to forget all of the responsibility lectures I so often hear in my daily life. If little Tommy throws a fit at a friend's house, he is "overwhelmed by the number of adults"; if Mickey screams at his sister during dinner, he is "developing his own personality"; if Nancy breaks Granny's vanity mirror (after being told twice to put it down), she is "just a curious child." But, if I track mud into the house while helping to unload groceries, I become "careless"; if I scold one of the grandkids for tearing pages out of my calculus book, I am "impatient." If a grandchild talks back to her mother, Granny and Poppa chuckle at her spirit. If I mumble one word about all of this doting, Mom and Dad reappear to have a talk with me about petty jealousies.

Third point

Examples in the form of comparisons

When my nieces and nephews first started appearing at our home for the holidays a few years ago, I probably was jealous, and I complained a lot. But now I spend more time simply sitting back and watching Mom and Dad change into what we call the "Incredible Huggers." They enjoy their time with these grandchildren so much that I easily forgive them their Granny and Poppa faults.

Transition to conclusion

Writer's attitude

I believe their personality change is due to the lack of responsibility they feel for the grandkids: In their role as grandparents, they don't have to worry about sugar causing cavities or temporary failures of self-discipline turning into lifetime faults. Those problems are up to my brother and sister-in-law. All Granny and Poppa have to do is enjoy and love their grandchildren. They have all the fun of being parents without any of the attendant obligations. And you know what? I think they've earned the right to make this transformation—at least once a year.

Writer's analysis of situation

Specific reference to introduction

Concluding remark

Some Final Thoughts on Examples

Although examples are often used to supplement and support other methods of development—such as cause/effect, comparison/contrast, and process analysis—the essays in this section are focused principally on examples. A main idea is expressed in the introduction of each, and the rest of the essay provides examples to bolster that contention. As you read these essays, pay close attention to each author's choice and arrangement of examples; then, try to determine which organizational techniques are most persuasive for each specific audience.

EXAMPLE IN REVIEW

Reading Example Essays

Preparing to Read

✓ What assumptions can I make from the essay's title?
✓ What do I think the general mood of the essay will be?
✓ What are the essay's purpose and audience?
✓ What does the synopsis tell me about the essay?
✓ What can I learn from the author's biography?
✓ Can I predict the author's point of view toward the subject?

Reading

✓ What general message is the author trying to convey?
✓ What is the essay's context?
✓ How do examples communicate this message?

Rereading

✓ What examples help the author communicate the essay's message?
✓ How are these examples organized?
✓ What other rhetorical modes does the author use?

Writing Example Essays

Preparing to Write

✓ What is my purpose?
✓ Who is my audience?
✓ What is the message I want to convey?

Writing

✓ What is my thesis or controlling idea?
✓ Do the examples I am choosing support this thesis?
✓ Are these examples arranged as effectively as possible?

Rewriting

✓ Have I included enough examples to develop each of my topics adequately?
✓ Are the examples I have chosen relevant to my thesis?
✓ Have I arranged these examples logically so that my audience can follow them?

ANITA RAU BADAMI

My Canada (2000)

Born in eastern India, Anita Rau Badami (1961–) was raised and educated in India, where she began her writing career as a journalist. After coming to Canada with her husband and son in 1991, Badami registered for a creative writing course at the University of Calgary and, subsequently, a master's degree in English literature. From this start, Badami has become a successful fiction writer in Canada with the publication of several novels, including *Tamarind Mem* (1996); *The Hero's Walk* (2000), which won the 2001 Regional Commonwealth Best Book Prize; and *Can You Hear the Nightbird Call?* (2006). Her most recent novel, *Tell It to the Trees*, was published in 2011. Badami is now a resident of Montreal. You can read her blog, see her artwork, and find out more about her at **www.anitaraubadami.ca**.

Preparing to Read

In this essay, originally published in the *Imperial Oil Review*, Badami reflects on her attempts to define Canada and the process of coming to view Canada as her home. Think about the idea of home. Where do you consider "home"? Has your home changed at any point in your life? Do you expect that the place that is home for you now will always be home? What distinguishes a place where one lives from a place that one calls home?

Early one morning in June last year, my family and I travelled from Vancouver to Tofino, a small town on the western coast of Vancouver Island. We had come in search of whales, particularly the magnificent orca. If we were lucky, we might even get to see a whole pod of them.❶ 1

When I was growing up in India, nothing had seemed more remote and exotic to me than these great mammals. I had seen pictures of them in geography texts and wildlife magazines, but the depictions were extremely unsatisfactory. The creatures were generally obscured by water or captured as a dim submarine shape 2

Reading Critically

❶ What is a pod of whales?

by an underwater camera—sometimes there was merely a spout of water shooting upwards from a brief arc of grey that might well have been the shoulder of a wave. By the time I left India for Canada, the orca had assumed mythical proportions, and a huge desire had ballooned in me to see this whale in its natural habitat.

The trip to Tofino had been inspired by an advertisement for whale-watching tours in a Vancouver paper. "Let's go this weekend," I had said to my husband and son. After several telephone calls to book a room in a hotel, we were on our way. 3

It was a grey morning when we left to catch the ferry to Victoria. But nothing could keep my hopes down; we were going to see those whales no matter what. The intensity of my longing, I was convinced, would keep the rain away from Tofino. The crossing to Victoria was rough and cold, and by the time we had driven across the island and reached the small coastal town, we could barely see the way through the rain to our hotel. I had encountered rain like this only in India during the monsoons and had come to expect nothing more in this country than the gentle drizzle that was so characteristic of Vancouver. This wild downpour, accompanied by the roar of thunder and the crackle of lightning, was a glimpse of a Canada that I had never seen before—the country had been doing a slow dance for me over the nine years that I had lived here, showing me tantalizing little bits of itself every now and then.❷ 4

That first day, we were trapped inside our hotel room with nothing to do but gaze at the Pacific Ocean, which was hurling itself furiously at the beach. But the next morning, to our delight, was bright and sunny, and we rushed down to the jetty where the whale-watching tours began. "Too rough to go out in the open sea," said the tour operator regretfully. "I can take you on calmer waters between islands." A lone orca had been spotted grazing in those channels, and if we were lucky, we might catch a glimpse of it. We drifted in and out of dark green fingers of water whose otherwise still surface was now pocked by the rain that had started again. We saw a black bear at the edge of a stand of pines on a tiny island, an eagle gliding on currents of air against the grey sky, otters and stellar seals, but not a single whale. We started our journey home disappointed but determined to come back the next year. 5

Reading Critically

❷ Describe this image in your own words.

And then it happened. On the ferry from Victoria, a cry went up from the crowd of people strolling the decks. There, cleaving the steely, restless ocean, was a large pod of orca whales—bulls, cows, calves—rolling and diving, sending up plumes of water. I had hoped to see *one* of these creatures, and here I was being treated to a whole family when I least expected it. 6

Looking for the Canada that has gently seeped into my bloodstream is like looking for those whales. I find her at unexpected moments: in the sudden kindness of a stranger's smile; in the graceful flight of a hundred snow geese; or in the cascading, iridescent shimmer of the aurora borealis lighting up the midnight sky. Several years ago, a friend asked me what I thought of this land of vast, empty spaces, of mountains and trees and snow and water, where almost every person claims ancestry in another culture, another land, and where a hundred different histories mingle to create a new set of memories. I had said that Canada reminded me of a beautiful, enigmatic woman who looks down demurely most of the time, but then surprises the watcher with a sudden glance from a pair of mischievous eyes. A shy coquette, I said, pleased at having found the words to describe a country with which I was just beginning a relationship.❸ 7

In those early stages, I tried to define Canada in terms of other places, as a series of negatives: not as colourful and noisy as India, not as old as China, not as brash and individualistic as the United States.❹ I would read all the Canadian newspapers and magazines and watch all the Canadian television shows I could (including curling tournaments, even though I am not a sports enthusiast and couldn't see the point of a game that involved a teapotlike object and a broom). I travelled as much as possible into the mountains; breathed the moist air of ancient forests that held secrets of an unknowable past; wandered over the weird, moonlike surface of the Badlands at Drumheller, Alta., marvelling at the skeletal remains of dinosaurs that had roamed there aeons ago; tried skiing and ice-skating and rock climbing, ending up with little more than sore muscles. The more I looked, the less I seemed to see Canada.❺ Until that afternoon on the deck of the 8

Reading Critically

❸ What is the effect of Badami's personification of Canada?

❹ Do you use comparisons to define something or someone in your life?

❺ What does the author mean by, "The more I looked, the less I seemed to see Canada"? Why do you think the author had trouble "seeing" Canada?

ferry, when, as I watched the whales floating in the ocean, it came to me: there was no point in trying to find one fixed image of this land. It would always be an accumulation of events and experiences, smells, sights and sounds. I was, after all, seeing it through so many different lenses: a writer's, a woman's, an immigrant's, a lover's, a mother's. It was at that moment that I began to think of Canada without reference to any other country, to love it on its own terms for what it was, rather than what it wasn't.

9 We came to Canada from India a little more than nine years ago. My husband had woken up one morning and decided that he wanted to reinvent himself. He was tired of his engineering degree and his job in a vast, faceless corporation. Our relatives were alarmed by this sudden decision. They couldn't understand why we wanted to leave good jobs (I was a newspaper journalist) and comfortable lives for an uncertain future. And why Canada of all places, they wanted to know. Wasn't that somewhere near the North Pole? Horribly cold? With bears and wild animals that mauled people to death?

10 By September 1990, my husband had arrived in Canada and was taking a master's degree in environmental studies at the University of Calgary. By March of the next year, I had cleaned out our flat in the bustling metropolitan city of Bangalore, sold all our furniture and packed most of our other belongings in boxes and trunks to store in my parents-in-law's home. No point taking everything with us—we would be back in a few years,[6] I told myself and everybody else, resenting this move and quite certain that I would never want to live in a country that I knew basically as a vague band of land between the United States of America and the North Pole. At school we had learned a huge amount about Britain and Europe, and at university, American literature was one of the areas I had opted to study in addition to the standard menu of Shakespeare, the Renaissance poets, Victorian fiction and Indo-Anglian writing (works written in English by Indians). But I had studied almost nothing about Canada and had certainly never heard of Canlit.

11 I had once seen a picture in a geography book of a vast, flat prairie with a grain elevator rising from its heart. Another time, in an ancient issue of *Reader's Digest*, I had read about a forest fire

---

Reading Critically

[6] Why did Badami think she would be in Canada for only a few years?

in the Rockies. The article was accompanied by a lurid picture of dark stands of pines licked by flames against a red, yellow and orange sky. These, and the photographs of the aurora borealis and of a grizzly bear, were the sum of my experience of Canada, a country that had hitherto existed only in the outer edges of my imagination—until I found myself in the Calgary airport in March 1991, dressed in nothing warmer than a mohair sweater and a pair of canvas sneakers. My husband, who had already lived in the city for six months and had survived an extremely frigid winter, had buoyantly assured me that spring had come to Calgary. It was deliciously warm, there was joy in the air, all the trees were in bud, and I would love it. My four-year-old son and I emerged from the nearly empty airport to be hit by a blast of freezing air. I could see nothing for a few moments as my eyes and nose had started to water with the cold. My lungs had panicked and seized up. I was wheezing like an old pair of bellows. It was –15 Celsius, and we had just arrived from a city where the temperature had been hovering at 47 Celsius in the shade.❼ In the week that followed, the desire to go back from whence I'd come became ever stronger. I missed the noise, the bustle of people, the smells and the circuslike atmosphere of Indian streets. What was I doing in this barren city where the sky covered everything like blue glass, where I could hear my own footsteps echoing on an empty street, and where I was frequently the only passenger on a bus? I wanted to go home.❽

12 Two months later, the lilacs were in bloom, filling the air with their scent. There were daffodils thrusting up from the earth, followed by tulips and irises and hundreds of other flowers. The trees had burst into bloom, and I was looking at a different world. I had spent all my life in a country where the seasons merge into one another. This drama of death and regeneration was something I had never witnessed. I was instantly captivated. I would stay another year, I told myself, if for nothing other than to see the seasons change. Four years slipped by, and I was still in Canada. By now I had worked in a variety of places, including a china store, a book shop and a library. A few months after I'd arrived,

---

Reading Critically

❼ How would a drastic change like this affect you, both physically and emotionally?

❽ Have you ever felt homesick? Describe how it felt or how you think it would feel.

I had signed up for a creative writing course at the University of Calgary and then began a master's degree in English literature. I'd had several stories published, and I'd begun to love the crisp winter mornings, the sudden excitement of a chinook, which seems to melt the snow in minutes and peel veils of cloud away from the distant snowcapped mountains. Now, every time I stepped out of my house, I bumped into a friend or someone I knew. It was a wonderful feeling to know so many people in the city. All my fears about leaving my writing career in India, about forgetting how to write, seemed ridiculous. I had also found my métier❾ in fiction writing and had finished the first draft of a novel.

13 In 1995, my first novel was accepted for publication, and we moved to Vancouver. Once again I was filled with that wretched feeling of being torn from all that was familiar and beloved, of leaving home, except this time, home was Calgary, and what I yearned for was long silent streets and canola fields shimmering yellow under an endless blue sky.

14 In the years since I arrived here I have travelled the length and breadth of this land and collected many different images of it. Now if somebody asks me what I think or feel about Canada, I tell of all the people and places, sights and events that have woven a pattern in my heart.❿ I tell stories about Shinya and Mayo, who had come here from Japan and shared with us a passion for spicy eggplant curry and Charlie Chaplin. And Carole, who arrived like a Santa in the middle of our first spring with a bag full of toys for our son, just, she explained cheerfully, to make him feel at home. I talk about Serena and Mike, our neighbours, with whom we watched dozens of late-night movies after shared dinners and delicious fruit flans created by Mike. Or about Grant, who took us on a trip to Waterton Lakes National Park in southwestern Alberta, rowed us out to the middle of one of the many lakes and handed the paddles to my husband and me. "If you want to be Canadian," he declared, grinning, "you will have to learn to row a boat." And who, after watching us quarrel for 20 minutes, during which time we managed to describe tighter and tighter circles in the centre of the lake, decided that there were safer ways of becoming Canadian.⓫

Reading Critically

❾ Define *métier*. What does the author's diction tell you about her audience?

❿ What does the author mean by the phrase "woven a pattern in my heart"?

⓫ How proficient are Badami and her husband at rowing a boat? Explain how you know this.

There were all those evenings with Suni and Ravi and Mayura and Ratna, celebrating Indian festivals just as winter was beginning to take hold, nudging away those last warm fall days, and the many times that they took care of me while I tried to juggle work and school and home. 15

My Canada, I tell anyone who asks, is the driver who made sure that I was on the last bus out of Calgary's North Hill Centre when I was working the late shift there, even if it meant delaying the bus an extra 10 minutes. And the members of my creative writing group, who gave me their undiluted comments and prepared me for a career as a novelist. "When your first book is out there being trashed by the reviewers," they told me, "you'll thank us for your thick skin." My Canada includes all those people who made me feel like I belonged. 16

To my album of memories I will add an enchanted night spent lying on a sloping field in Calgary with a group of friends to watch a meteor shower streaking silver lines across the midnight sky. I will tell all who ask about the time I stood on Alberta's Athabasca Glacier surrounded by mountains eternally capped by snow, and drank crystalline water from a deep spring so ancient that time itself had no measure for it; of the moon full and golden, floating up over the mountains surrounding Lake Louise, and a lynx's eyes flaring green at us before the creature snarled and vanished into the darkness; of the flood of people on Main Street, Vancouver, celebrating the Sikh festival Baisakhi; of Chinatown, where a beautiful woman in a small, dark shop sold me exquisite paper and a stamp with a character that, she told me, meant "good luck"; of writers' festivals all over the country, where a medley of voices from many cultures was heard; and of a café in a remote Yukon town where I met a man who believed that he was the reincarnation of Elvis Presley. 17

I visited India recently, the second time that I had gone back since 1991. When it was time to leave, I realized with a small jolt that I felt none of the regret that I had experienced on the previous trip. The needle of my emotional compass had swung around and set itself in a different direction. While I still cherished the brilliant colours of India, I was also beginning to recognize and appreciate the subtle tints and textures of the Canadian fabric. And I knew that even though a part of me would always look with love towards the land of my birth, and deep inside I would for ever straddle two continents, two realities (the East and the West), my home was now here, in Canada. 18

UNDERSTANDING DETAILS

1. Where did Badami grow up? When and why did she come to Canada?
2. Why do Badami and her family travel to Tofino? Are their expectations met?
3. Where is Badami's home?

ANALYZING MEANING

1. Chart the shift in Badami's attitude toward Canada over time. What are the significant turning points in her perspective?
2. Badami tells the reader about her expectations in coming to Canada and then about the reality of what she found here. How does the reality compare with Badami's expectations?
3. What is the main point Badami is making in her essay? What examples serve to illustrate this thesis particularly effectively?

DISCOVERING RHETORICAL STRATEGIES

1. Although the author's dominant rhetorical method is the use of example, what other strategies has Badami used to organize her information? Give examples of these strategies.
2. Where in this essay do you find Badami's purpose most clearly stated? How does the organization of the major examples in this essay demonstrate the author's thesis statement?
3. Badami uses figurative language frequently in "My Canada." Identify at least three examples of her use of figurative language. What specific techniques has she used (e.g., metaphor, personification, simile), and what is the effect of these language choices on the reader?

MAKING CONNECTIONS

1. Both Badami and K'naan ("Between the Highs and the Lows, Life Happens") write about coming to Canada. How did their experiences before immigration differ? How did these experiences shape what happened after immigration?
2. Badami uses many personal examples to illustrate the points she makes in "My Canada." How does this compare with the use of examples by Katrina Onstad ("Michael Jackson, John Lennon: Do Celebrities Die Anymore?") and Barbara Kingsolver ("Life Without Go-Go Boots")?

IDEAS FOR DISCUSSION/WRITING

Preparing to Write

Write freely about Canada. How long have you lived in Canada? What are your dominant impressions of Canada? How would you describe Canada to someone in another country? What qualities or characteristics make Canada unique? Has Canada changed over the time that you have lived here? If so, in what ways? For better or for worse?

Choosing a Topic

1. Following Badami's lead, write an essay entitled "My Canada," in which you use specific examples to illustrate what Canada is to you. Make sure that your attitude toward your subject is clearly conveyed in your essay.
2. The reality of Canada that greeted Badami when she first arrived did not meet her expectations. Write an essay about a situation in which the reality you encountered was quite different from what you had expected. Use specific details to make your essay clear and effective.
3. Write about a place that you know well, using specific examples to create a clear, strong image of this place for your reader. Make sure that you define your place on its own terms rather than in comparison to another place.

RYAN McNUTT

The Music We Hate: Joanna Newsom (2010)

Ryan McNutt is a Halifax-based freelance writer. He has a B.A. in History and English from Acadia University and an advanced diploma in public relations from Nova Scotia Community College. In addition to working as part of the communications and marketing team at Dalhousie University, he writes about music and popular culture on his blog, *McNutt Against the Music*. His top three albums of the last decade were Arcade Fire's *Funeral*, Wilco's *Yankee Hotel Foxtrot*, and Radiohead's *Kid A*. The essay below was first published in *Maisonneuve*.

Preparing to Read

In this piece, Ryan McNutt discusses his objections to the music of Joanna Newsom, an American singer-songwriter whose compositions frequently feature the harp and piano. If you aren't familiar with Newsom's music, locate one of her songs on YouTube and form your own opinion before you read McNutt's article. If you already know her music, how do you feel about it?

When Joanna Newsom sings, it's as if the voices of a pre-pubescent girl and an elderly woman have been mashed together into a shrill, semi-consonant sound struggling to hold a tune as it quivers from note to note. Even if I couldn't come up with another reason for despising Newsom's brand of harp-based orchestral folk, I'd be content with just blaming her pipes. 1

Admittedly, Newsom and I didn't start on good terms. I'm not much for fussy, multi-part song constructions, so *Ys* probably wasn't an ideal introduction. Her simpler debut, *The Milk-Eyed Mender*, might have made a better first impression. But even then, other elements would have driven me bonkers: her preciousness, her insularity.[1] *Have One on Me*, released this year, is a turnoff in concept alone—the vanity of a triple album is hard to swallow. 2

Reading Critically

[1] What is "preciousness"? "Insularity"? If McNutt liked Newsom's music, what words might he use to describe these qualities in a positive way?

Am I being fair? Her voice—which the Village Voice mocked as having "a Monty Python quality"❷—may be off-putting, but there's no question it's unique, and it's hardly the first time a vocalist's distinctiveness has been a selling point (I spent my teenage years as a Billy Corgan apologist, after all). More troubling is that I enjoy the work of several male artists who play in the same genre sandbox, from Sufjan Stevens to Owen Pallett. 3

That said, I think my anti-Newsom stance is more a product of my pop sensibilities than any gender bias. Stevens and Pallett exhibit a passion almost wholly missing in Newsom's music. Their records sound ready to take on the world, whereas Newsom's albums—with their muted sense of rhythm and stubbornly-buried hooks❸—sound ready to win over an empty concert hall. 4

In a Pitchfork column titled "Why We Fight," Nitsuh Abebe argues that "Newsom's music feels private, a strange artifact waiting for you to come engage with it." I'd go further: Newsom's music doesn't care two figs what I think about it. It neither asks nor demands anything of its listener. It's simply there—quiet and complicated, but with no interest in reaching out and inspiring me to feel anything. If there's going to be a conversation about what role these songs could play in my life, the songs expect me to start it. 5

Is it wrong to want my music to fight for my attention? Should I not expect a record to make some argument—any argument—for why I should give a damn? I look for records that offer up something to react to: a kiss, a shove, anything in between. I want the tease of "Be My Baby," the rabid snarl of "Debaser," the fractured melody of "I Am Trying to Break Your Heart." Nothing about Newsom suggests the time and energy I could invest in her overlong madrigal muddles❹ would actually get me any closer to enjoying them. So I'm not interested. 6

On *Have One on Me,* there's one notable exception. At the record's end, following two exhausting hours of symphonic meanderings, the album concludes with a dissonant mess of piano, drums and strings, colliding into a wave of distortion. 7

Reading Critically

❷ What does a "Monty Python" quality suggest to you?

❸ Explain the idea of a musical "hook."

❹ What is a "madrigal"? How is "madrigal muddles" an apt description?

For the first time, Newsom seems conscious of the fact that someone is at the other end of the stereo, eager to make contact. And in a flash, it's over. If that's the extent of her come-hither, I say, No thanks.

UNDERSTANDING DETAILS

1. McNutt seems to have disliked Newsom's music from the beginning. What elements of Newsom's earlier work did he object to?
2. What problem does McNutt have with the album *Have One on Me* before even listening to it?
3. What potential advantage does McNutt say that a voice like Newsom's could have?

ANALYZING MEANING

1. Why does McNutt find it "more troubling" that he likes artists such as Sufjan Stevens and Owen Pallett? What is he worried about?
2. What is McNutt's main complaint about Newsom's music? How does her music differ from the kind of music he prefers?
3. What song on the album sparks McNutt's interest? What does he like about it? Why does he still say "no thanks"?

DISCOVERING RHETORICAL STRATEGIES

1. How does McNutt try to ensure that his criticism of Newsom is fair? Do you think he succeeds?
2. How does McNutt ensure that people unfamiliar with the music he is discussing can still follow his arguments?
3. McNutt uses a range of figurative language to describe Newsom's style. What descriptive phrases did you find most effective?

MAKING CONNECTIONS

1. Compare McNutt's review of Newsom's music to Jennie Punter's review of two movies in "Crime and Punishment in a Foreign Land." Which review did you find more persuasive? Why?
2. Both McNutt and Daniel J. Levitin ("The Music of My Mind") write about music. Compare their use of examples and their descriptions of specific songs. Which essay did you find more illuminating? Why?

IDEAS FOR DISCUSSION/WRITING

Preparing to Write

Make a list of your top 10 songs of all time. Looking at the list, what kind of music would you say you are most drawn to? Does most of the music fit into what McNutt calls a "genre sandbox"? If yes, why does this kind of music appeal to you? If not, what accounts for your eclectic taste in music? What kind of music do you dislike? What specifically do you dislike about it?

Choosing a Topic

1. Choose an album, an artist, or a genre, and write your own blog entry entitled "Music I Hate."
2. McNutt has a very strong reaction to Joanna Newsom's music and strives to find concrete reasons for his dislike. Other reviewers love her music, perhaps for the same reasons that McNutt dislikes it. Do you think that reviews of music can ever really transcend the subjectivity of taste? Write an essay on objectivity in music reviews.
3. Write a classification or definition essay for a particular "genre sandbox" for any art form (for example, hip hop music, horror films, mystery novels). Ensure that your examples are sufficiently detailed so that a reader not familiar with them can still follow your points.

KATRINA ONSTAD

John Lennon, Michael Jackson: Do Celebrities Die Anymore? (2011)

Katrina Onstad grew up in Vancouver and has degrees in English from McGill and the University of Toronto. A winner of a National Magazine Award, Onstad writes regularly for *The Globe and Mail* and *Toronto Life*, and has also been published in *The New York Times*, *The Guardian*, *Elle*, and *Salon*. Onstad was also the head film critic for CBC.ca, and has been featured on CBC radio and television and TVO's *Saturday Night at the Movies*. She is the author of two novels, *How Happy to Be* and *Everybody Has Everything*. Links to her writing can be found at **www.katrinaonstad.ca/**.

Preparing to Read

In this article, Onstad explores the business of dead celebrities: their presence in the media, their use in advertising campaigns, and the technology that allows old images or footage to be spliced into new photographs or film. What celebrities have been made more famous by their deaths than by their actions in life? Take a moment to make a mental list of deceased celebrities you have seen in ads. Do you find these ads effective? How do you think the advertisers get permission to use a dead celebrity's image?

It seems that George Lucas may be collecting dead people the way your grandma collects crystal fowl. In a recent Daily Mail interview, British director Mel Smith, who worked with Lucas years ago, said: "[Lucas has] been buying up the film rights to dead movie stars in the hope of using computer trickery to put them all together in a movie, so you'd have Orson Welles and Barbara Stanwyck appear alongside today's stars." 1

Although the Star Wars director hasn't confirmed this hobby, a penchant for splicing the dead and the living is very au courant. Michael Jackson, who died in 2009, was this year's top-earning dead celebrity, making $275-million, according to Forbes. His new 2 album features Dave Grohl and Lenny Kravitz, both rumoured to be alive.❶

3 Last year, the luxury chain of Dorchester Hotels released an ad campaign showing celebrities like Kristin Scott Thomas (living) dining with Albert Einstein, Grace Kelly and Orson Welles (dead, dead and dead). Let me put on John Lennon's new, remixed album—on the 30th anniversary of his assassination—and ponder the question: Doesn't anybody die anymore?

4 Technology has reshaped celebrity death. In 1997, Dirt Devil released an ad showing Fred Astaire dancing with a vacuum cleaner.

5 The press and public were appalled, and sales of the vacuum cleaner actually declined. Exhuming the dead for the purposes of shilling engendered a protective feeling in the audience. Astaire had no agency in this particular pas de deux❷ (not to mention poor, erased Ginger Rogers) and there was something chilling about the fact that the strings animating the corpse were held by a computer.❸

6 In 1981, Greil Marcus wrote with horror that Elvis Presley had become in the mere four years since his death "a T-shirt, a black velvet wall hanging, an emblem of working-class bad taste or upper-class camp." "A dead person is vulnerable in ways a living person is not," Marcus wrote. "A dead person can be summed up or dismissed."

7 Three decades later, dead celebrities aren't just reduced, but regurgitated, revived, remixed and reissued, making a silk-screened T-shirt seem like a folksy little problem. Today, anyone with a computer can put herself in a room with Elvis, add a Santa hat and send a Christmas card around the world. The Dorchester campaign didn't seem to generate any disgust at all. In the age of techno-mechanical reproduction, manipulation of the dead is a yawner.

8 And so, dead celebrities have become big business. In 2005, stock photo agency Corbis acquired a roster of "classic personalities," including Einstein and Mae West (psst—classic means dead).

Reading Critically

❶ Why does the author say these artists are "rumoured" to be alive?

❷ Explain this figure of speech.

❸ Do you agree with Onstad's assessment that there was something "chilling" in the computer re-animation of a dead celebrity?

The arm where they now reside at Corbis is called GreenLight, which reportedly earned $50-million in 2009 by renting dead stars for endorsements. "The nice thing about a dead celebrity is [that] scandal is behind them," a GreenLight VP told the Puget Sound Business Journal.

9 Living artists should be wary of these shenanigans, at least if they believe their work is what creates value. To split a dead performer from her context for fun or profit seems like some mad-scientist exercise in CGI onanism.❹ I don't think I want to see Barbara Stanwyck as Stella Dallas, her 73-year-old delivery divorced from its original meaning, spliced into a scene where she counsels Renée Zellweger on her dating issues.

10 Perhaps there's a filmmaker who could make a compelling film in this manner, but it probably isn't Lucas, who has always privileged technology above story❺ (the two most recent Star Wars movies seemed to be about intergalactic taxation). His grave-digging project tells today's actors what many of them must deeply fear (and know): You are really just a face and a body. You are a brand.

11 And the older the celebrity brand, the better. When Elvis died, rock critic Lester Bangs wrote: "I can guarantee you one thing, we will never again agree on anything as we agreed on Elvis." Guarantee fulfilled: Audiences today aren't in disagreement because they're rarely in conversation. We nest in our niches, listening to music recommended by our social networks and swooning over stars carefully cultivated for our own demographic.❻ Advertisers—and Lucas—know they have increasingly rare currency in Elvis or Marilyn Monroe (who appeared last month on the cover of Vanity Fair): a nostalgic, shared reference point, understood by everyone.

12 Freud wrote about the human death instinct, an inborn fascination with death that pushes and pulls against the lust for life—the kicking, thriving pleasure principle. Perhaps in a movie starring the living and the dead, we get both, and from the comfort of this side. It's a profitable endeavour—for the living, at least.

Reading Critically

❹ Explain this phrase.

❺ Do you agree with this assessment of Lucas's films?

❻ Can you give some examples of stars that are cultivated for certain demographics?

UNDERSTANDING DETAILS

1. What is George Lucas said to be collecting old film rights for?
2. What happened to Elvis after his death, according to Greil Marcus? Why does Marcus object to this?
3. What message does Lucas's project send to living celebrities? Why would they fear this message?

ANALYZING MEANING

1. Why did the public react badly to the use of Fred Astaire in a vacuum cleaner ad but not to the Dorchester campaign?
2. Why does Onstad object to splitting off a dead celebrity from his or her context?
3. Explain why advertisers consider celebrities such as Elvis and Marilyn Monroe to be "increasingly rare currency." From an advertiser's point of view, what advantages do dead celebrities have over living ones?

DISCOVERING RHETORICAL STRATEGIES

1. Onstad claims that dead celebrities are big business. Which examples were most effective in proving this?
2. How would you characterize Onstad's tone throughout the piece? Do you think this tone is appropriate for her argument?
3. Evaluate the effectiveness of Onstad's opening and closing paragraphs. Do you think Freud's "death instinct" is a good explanation for our fascination with dead celebrities? Can you think of an example of a movie starring "the living and the dead"?

MAKING CONNECTIONS

1. Imagine Onstad and Irshad Manji ("Status Anxiety? Consider Socrates and the Sewer Saviour") in conversation. What might Onstad say about status anxiety? What might Manji say about the practice of using dead celebrities in advertising?
2. What do you think Will Braun ("Seven Criteria for the Adoption of New Technology") might say about the technology that allows dead celebrities to animate current advertisements?

IDEAS FOR DISCUSSION/WRITING

Preparing to Write

Write about a celebrity death. How did you hear the news? How did the news of this death affect you? How did you feel about the public reaction to the death? Did the death of the person change how you felt about his or her work or public persona? Are there any living celebrities that you particularly admire? Do you think there is a difference between a "star" and a "celebrity"?

Choosing a Topic

1. In Shakespeare's *Macbeth,* a character remarks on how stoically the former Thane of Cawdor faced execution for treason, saying, "Nothing in his life became him like the leaving of it." Write an essay about a celebrity whose death seemed to redeem his or her life. What changed in the public's perception of the celebrity after his or her death?
2. Onstad suggests that our fascination with dead celebrities might be connected to what Freud called our "death instinct". Write an essay proposing your own theory for why we are so interested in celebrities who have died.
3. Do you think a company or individual should be allowed to purchase the rights to a dead person's image? How long should a person's image remain copyrighted after his or her death? Write an essay arguing for or against the sale of a dead person's image.

BARBARA KINGSOLVER

Life Without Go-Go Boots (2002)

In the FAQ section of her website (**www.kingsolver.com**), Barbara Kingsolver tells aspiring writers not to visualize themselves writing, but to simply write. Kingsolver has done much writing in the form of novels, short stories, essays, scientific articles, poems, and nonfiction books.

Kingsolver was born in Kentucky in 1955 and eventually left for Indiana to earn a degree in biology at DePauw University. Kingsolver pursued her studies further with a Master of Science degree at the University of Arizona and now makes her home with her family in Tucson, Arizona. While studying biology and ecology, Kingsolver worked at various points as an archaeologist, copy editor, X-ray technician, housecleaner, biology researcher, and translator of medical documents, but she eventually came to focus on a career as a writer. Her initial focus was on technical and scientific writing, after suffering from insomnia during her first pregnancy, she turned to writing fiction. Her first novel, *The Bean Trees*, was published in 1988. Her books include the novels *The Poisonwood Bible* (1998), *Prodigal Summer* (2000), and *The Lacuna* (2009); a collection of essays titled *Small Wonder* (2002); and *Animal, Vegetable, Miracle* (2007), her family's account of a year of eating locally.

Preparing to Read

"Life Without Go-Go Boots" was originally published in the catalogue of Lands' End, an American clothing company. Before reading the essay, think about the clothing that you wear. Where do you buy your clothes? How do you make your purchasing decisions? How would you describe the clothing sold by Lands' End? (If you are not familiar with Lands' End, see its website at **www.landsend.com**.) Why do you think a clothing company would include an essay in its catalogue?

Fashion nearly wrecked my life. I grew up beyond its pale,❶ convinced that this would stunt me in some irreparable way. I don't think it has, but for a long time it was touch and go. 1

Reading Critically

❶ What does Kingsolver mean by the phrase "I grew up beyond its pale"?

We lived in the country, in the middle of an alfalfa field; we had no immediate access to Bobbie Brooks sweaters. I went to school in the hand-me-downs of a cousin three years older. She had excellent fashion sense, but during the three-year lag her every sleek outfit turned to a pumpkin.❷ In fifth grade, when girls were wearing straight shifts with buttons down the front, I wore pastel shirtwaists with cap sleeves and a multitude of built-in petticoats. My black lace-up oxfords, which my parents perceived to have orthopedic value, carried their own weight in the spectacle. I suspected people noticed, and I knew it for sure on the day Billy Stamps announced to the lunch line: "Make way for the Bride of Frankenstein." 2

I suffered quietly, casting an ever-hopeful eye on my eighth-grade cousin whose button-front shifts someday would be mine. But by the time I was an eighth grader, everyone with an iota of social position wore polka-dot shirts and miniskirts. For Christmas, I begged for go-go boots. The rest of my life would be endurable if I had a pair of those white, calf-high confections with the little black heels. My mother, though always inscrutable near Christmas, seemed sympathetic; there was hope. Never mind that those little black heels are like skate blades in inclement weather. I would walk on air. 3

On Christmas morning I received white rubber boots with treads like a pair of Michelins. My mother loved me, but had missed the point. 4

In high school I took matters into my own hands. I learned to sew. I contrived to make an apple-green polyester jumpsuit that was supremely fashionable for about two months. Since it took me forty days and forty nights to make the thing, my moment of glory was brief. I learned what my mother had been trying to tell me all along: high fashion has the shelf life of potato salad. And when past its prime, it is similarly deadly. 5

Once I left home and went to college I was on my own, fashion-wise, having bypassed my cousin in stature and capped the arrangement off by moving to another state. But I found I still had to reckon with life's limited choices. After classes I worked variously as a house cleaner, typesetter, and artists' model. I could spend my wages on trendy apparel (which would be useless to 6

Reading Critically

❷ What does "turned to a pumpkin" remind you of?

me in any of my jobs, particularly the latter), or on the lesser gratifications of food and textbooks. It was a tough call, but I opted for education. This was Indiana and it was cold; when it wasn't cold, it was rainy. I bought an army surplus overcoat, with zip-out lining, that reached my ankles, and I found in my parents' attic a green pith helmet.[3] I became a known figure on campus. Fortunately, this was the era in which army boots were a fashion option for coeds. And besides, who knew? Maybe under all that all-weather olive drab was a Bobbie Brooks sweater. My social life picked right up.

7 As an adult, I made two hugely fortuitous choices in the women's-wear department: first, I moved out West, where the buffalo roam and hardly anyone is ever arrested for being unstylish. Second, I became a novelist. Artists (also mathematicians and geniuses) are greatly indulged by society when it comes to matters of grooming. If we happen to look like an unmade bed, it's presumed we're preoccupied with plot devices or unifying theories or things of that ilk.

8 Even so, when I was invited to attend an important author event on the East Coast, a friend took me in hand.

9 "Writers are *supposed* to be eccentric," I wailed.

10 My friend, one of the people who loves me best in the world, replied: "Barbara, you're not eccentric, you're an anachronism,"[4] and marched me down to an exclusive clothing shop.

11 It was a very small store; I nearly hyperventilated. "You could liquidate the stock here and feed an African nation for a year," I whispered. But under pressure I bought a suit, and wore it to the important author function. For three hours of my life I was precisely in vogue.

12 Since then it has reigned over my closet from its dry-cleaner bag, feeling unhappy and out of place, I am sure, a silk ambassador assigned to a flannel republic. Even if I go to a chichi restaurant, the suit stays home. I'm always afraid I'll spill something on it; I'd be too nervous to enjoy myself. It turns out I would rather converse than make a statement.

13 Now, there is fashion, and there is *style*. The latter, I've found, will serve, and costs less. Style is mostly a matter of acting as

---

Reading Critically

[3] What is a pith helmet?

[4] What is an anachronism?

if you know very well what you look like, thanks, and are just delighted about it. It also requires consistency.[5] A friend of mine wears buckskin moccasins every day of her life. She has daytime and evening moccasins. This works fine in Arizona, but when my friend fell in love with a Tasmanian geologist and prepared to move to a rain forest, I worried. Moccasins instantaneously decompose in wet weather. But I should have known, my friend has sense. She bought clear plastic galoshes to button over her moccasins, and writes me that she's happy.

I favor cowboy boots. I don't do high heels, because you never know when you might actually have to get somewhere, and most other entries in the ladies-shoes category look to me like Ol' Dixie and Ol' Dobbin trying to sneak into the Derby, trailing their plow. Cowboy boots aren't trying. They say, "I'm no pump, and furthermore, so what?" That characterizes my whole uniform, in fact: oversized flannel shirts, jeans or cotton leggings, and cowboy boots when weather permits. In summer I lean toward dresses that make contact with the body (if at all) only on the shiatsu acupressure points;[6] maybe also a Panama hat; and sneakers. I am happy. 14

I'm also a parent, which of course calls into question every decision one ever believes one has made for the last time. Can I raise my daughter as a raiment renegade? At present she couldn't care less. Maybe obsessions skip a generation. She was blessed with two older cousins whose sturdy hand-me-downs she has worn from birth, with relish. If she wasn't entirely a fashion plate, she also escaped being typecast. For her first two years she had no appreciable hair, to which parents can clamp those plastic barrettes that are gender dead giveaways. So when I took her to the park in cousin Ashley's dresses, strangers commented on her blue eyes and lovely complexion; when she wore Andrew's playsuits emblazoned with trucks and airplanes (why is it we only decorate our boys with modes of transportation?), people always commented on how strong and alert my child was—and what's his name? 15

This interests me. I also know it can't last. She's in school now, and I'm very quickly remembering what school is about: two parts ABCs to fifty parts Where Do I Stand in the Great Pecking 16

Reading Critically

5. Why does style require consistency?
6. What are "shiatsu acupressure points"? What does this tell you about Kingsolver's summer dresses?

Order of Humankind? She still rejects stereotypes, with extraordinary good humor. She has a dress-up collection to die for, gleaned from Goodwill and her grandparents' world travels, and likely as not will show up to dinner wearing harem pants, bunny ears, a glitter-bra over her T-shirt, wooden shoes, and a fez. But underneath it all, she's only human. I have a feeling the day might come when my daughter will beg to be a slave of conventional fashion.

17 I'm inclined to resist, if it happens. To press on her the larger truths I finally absorbed from my own wise parents: that she can find her own path. That she will be more valued for inward individuality than outward conformity. That a world plagued by poverty can ill afford the planned obsolescence of *haute couture.*[7]

18 But a small corner of my heart still harbors the Bride of Frankenstein, eleven years of age, haunting me in her brogues and petticoats. Always and forever, the ghosts of past anguish compel us to live through our children. If my daughter ever asks for the nineties equivalent of go-go boots, I'll cave in.

19 Maybe I'll also buy her some of those clear plastic galoshes to button over them on inclement days.

UNDERSTANDING DETAILS

1. As a child, why does Kingsolver want go-go boots? Do her parents oblige her in this desire? Why or why not?
2. Kingsolver's friend tells her she is "an anachronism" rather than eccentric (paragraph 10). What is the difference between the two? Do you agree with the friend?
3. As an adult, how does Kingsolver dress? Why?

ANALYZING MEANING

1. What is Kingsolver's thesis? How is it revealed in the examples that she relates in her essay?
2. Characterize Kingsolver's attitude toward fashion as a child. How does this compare with her attitude toward fashion as an adult?
3. What is the difference between fashion and style? How do you think the original audience for this essay would classify Kingsolver's appearance?

Reading Critically

[7] What does this sentence mean? What is "obsolescence"? What is "haute couture"?

DISCOVERING RHETORICAL STRATEGIES

1. Describe the tone of Kingsolver's essay. How is this tone achieved? Is it effective in making her point? Explain why or why not.
2. The use of examples to illustrate her point characterizes Kingsolver's essay. How many examples of fashion faux pas does Kingsolver include? Which example do you find the most effective?
3. Kingsolver's essay originally appeared in the catalogue of a clothing retailer. Describe the intended audience and purpose. Do you think Kingsolver has written an effective essay for this situation? Explain.

MAKING CONNECTIONS

1. Kingsolver's sense of humour is apparent in "Life Without Go-Go Boots," although she is making some serious points. Compare Kingsolver's use of humour with that of Drew Hayden Taylor ("Pretty Like a White Boy") or Katrina Onstad ("John Lennon, Michael Jackson: Do Celebrities Die Anymore?").
2. Kingsolver's essay focuses largely on the importance of acceptance by others. Compare her views with those of Irshad Manji ("Status Anxiety? Consider Socrates and the Sewer Saviour") and Cynara Geissler ("Fat Acceptance: A Basic Primer"). On what points do you think these women would agree? On which points might they disagree?
3. In "Life Without Go-Go Boots" Kingsolver reflects on her own childhood experiences and some of the reasons her parents might have made the choices they did. Compare the rationale for the choices made by Kingsolver's parents with the rationale for those made by Evelyn Lau's parents ("More and More").

IDEAS FOR DISCUSSION/WRITING

Preparing to Write

Write freely about fashion and the fashion industry. How would you describe your own sense of fashion? Is fashion important to you? Why or why not? Why is the fashion industry so big? How are fashion standards set? Why do people care about being "in fashion" when it comes to appearance?

Choosing a Topic

1. Kingsolver claims that artists (including writers), mathematicians, and geniuses are indulged by society in terms of their grooming. Are all writers a little eccentric? What makes anyone unique or special? Are we all a little odd? Are our odd qualities or apparent eccentricities sometimes assets? Using examples drawn from your own experience, write a character portrait of someone who seems eccentric to you.
2. Write an essay in which you use a series of specific examples to illustrate a particular lesson that you learned in growing up.
3. Kingsolver refers to the "planned obsolescence of *haute couture*." Write an essay in which you use specific examples to explain this phrase.

NAOMI KLEIN

Co-opting Dissent (2001)

Writer and activist Naomi Klein (1970–) is well known for her books *No Logo* (2000), *Fences and Windows* (2002), and *The Shock Doctrine* (2007); her magazine and newspaper columns and articles; and her public speaking engagements. Writing about current events and political/social issues, Klein is typically anti-globalization and critical of brand-oriented consumerism.

Born in Montreal to a politically and socially active family, Klein went to Toronto to attend the University of Toronto and there began writing for the student newspaper *The Varsity*. She has since gone on to write for a variety of publications, including *The Nation, The Globe and Mail, This Magazine, Harper's*, and *The Guardian.*

In 2004, Klein also became a documentary filmmaker as she, along with her husband, Avi Lewis, released *The Take*, a film profiling a group of Argentine factory workers who are laid off and eventually take back control of their plant and organize it into a co-operative. Her book *The Shock Doctrine*, which has been translated into over 25 languages, was also made into a full-length documentary by Michael Winterbottom in 2010. Descriptions of her work and links to her writing are available at **www.naomiklein.org**.

Preparing to Read

In this essay Klein writes about the change in the relationship between employer and employee and the trend toward hiring employees on a temporary or part-time rather than full-time basis. Think about employee status and the relationship between an employee and an employer. What obligations does an employee have to his or her employer? What obligations does an employer have to its employees? While the situation varies between organizations, do you think the current status is generally appropriate? If not, how should it change? Has the employer–employee relationship changed in Klein's lifetime? If so, what has caused the change?

When I was seventeen, I worked after school at an Esprit clothing store in Montreal. It was a pleasant job, mostly involving folding cotton garments into little squares so sharp that their corners could take your eye out.❶ But for some reason, 1

Reading Critically

❶ What is interesting about this image?

corporate headquarters didn't consider our T-shirt origami to be sufficiently profitable. One day, our calm world was turned upside down by a regional supervisor who swooped in to indoctrinate us in the culture of the Esprit brand—and increase our productivity in the process. "Esprit," she told us, "is like a good friend."

I was skeptical, and I let it be known. Skepticism, I quickly learned, is not considered an asset in the low-wage service sector. Two weeks later, the supervisor fired me for being in possession of that most loathed workplace character trait: "bad attitude." I guess that was one of my first lessons in why large multinational corporations are not "like a good friend," since good friends, while they may sometimes do horrible and hurtful things, rarely fire you. 2

So I was interested when, earlier this month, the TBWA/Chiat/Day advertising agency rolled out the new "brand identity" for Shoppers Drug Mart. (Rebranding launches are, in corporate terms, like being born again.) It turns out that the chain is no longer Everything You Want in a Drugstore—i.e., a place where you can buy things you need; it too is now a "caring friend," one that takes form as a chain of eight hundred drugstores with a $22 million ad budget burning a hole in its pocket. 3

Shoppers' new slogan is Take Care of Yourself,❷ selected, according to campaign creator Pat Pirisi, because it echoes "what a caring friend would say." Get ready for it to be said thousands of times a day by young cashiers as they hand you plastic bags filled with razors, dental floss and diet pills. "We believe this is a position Shoppers can own," Pirisi says. 4

Asking clerks to adopt this particular phrase as their mantra seems a bit heartless in this age of casual, insecure, underpaid McLabour. Service-sector workers are so often told to take care of themselves—since no one, least of all their mega-employers, is going to take care of them. 5

Yet it's one of the ironies of our branded age that as corporations become more remote by cutting lasting ties with us as their employees, they are increasingly sidling up to us as consumers, whispering sweet nothings in our ear about friendship and community. It's not just Shoppers: Wal-Mart ads tell stories 6

Reading Critically

❷ Which slogan do you prefer, and why?

about clerks who, in a pinch, lend customers their own wedding gowns, and Saturn ads are populated by car dealers who offer counselling when customers lose their jobs. You see, according to a new marketing book, *Values Added*, modern marketers have to "make your brand a cause and your cause a brand."❸

Maybe I still have a bad attitude, but this collective corporate hug feels about as empty today as it did when I was an about-to-be-unemployed sweater folder. Particularly when you stop to consider the cause of all this mass-produced warmth. 7

Explaining Shoppers' new brand identity to *The Financial Post*, Pirisi said, "In an age when people are becoming more and more distrustful of corporations—the World Trade Organization protests will attest to that—and at a time when the health care system isn't what it used to be, we realized we had to send consumers a message about partnership." 8

Ever since large corporations such as Nike, Shell and Monsanto began facing increased scrutiny from civil society—mostly for putting short-term profits far ahead of environmental responsibility and job security—an industry has ballooned to help these companies respond.❹ It seems clear, however, that many in the corporate world remain utterly convinced that all they have is a "messaging problem," one that can be neatly solved by settling on the right, socially minded brand identity. 9

It turns out that's the last thing they need. British Petroleum found this out the hard way when it was forced to distance itself from its own outrageous rebranding campaign, Beyond Petroleum. Understandably, many consumers interpreted the new slogan to mean the company was moving away from fossil fuels in response to climate change. Human rights and environmental activists, after seeing no evidence that BP was actually changing its policies, brought up embarrassing details at the company's annual meeting about BP's participation in a controversial new pipeline through sensitive areas of Tibet, as well as its decision to drill in the Alaska National Wildlife Refuge. With the new slogan being parodied on the Net as Beyond Preposterous, BP officials moved to abandon the Beyond Petroleum brand, though they have so far stuck with the new green flower logo. 10

Reading Critically

❸ What does the quote "make your brand a cause and your cause a brand" mean?

❹ What industry is Klein referring to?

As evidence of the state of corporate confusion, I frequently find myself asked to give presentations to individual corporations. Fearing that my words will end up in some gooey ad campaign, I always refuse. But I can offer this advice without reservation: nothing will change until corporations realize that they don't have a communications problem. They have a reality problem. 11

UNDERSTANDING DETAILS

1. Why was Klein fired from her job at the Esprit store?
2. Explain the term *McLabour* (paragraph 5).
3. What is corporate branding? Why do corporations "rebrand" themselves? Why was the BP rebranding not successful?

ANALYZING MEANING

1. Why does Klein object to the move by corporations such as Shoppers Drug Mart, Saturn, and Wal-Mart to brand themselves as "a caring friend"?
2. Why are people "becoming more and more distrustful of corporations" (paragraph 8)? How does Klein react to that increasing skepticism?
3. Klein ends with the following advice: "nothing will change until corporations realize that they don't have a communications problem. They have a reality problem." Explain what she means by this statement.

DISCOVERING RHETORICAL STRATEGIES

1. What is Klein's thesis? Where is it stated in her essay?
2. How many examples has Klein used to support her thesis? Are they effective examples? Explain why or why not.
3. What additional rhetorical strategies has Klein used in this essay?

MAKING CONNECTIONS

1. Like Arlene Perly Rae, Irshad Manji, and Anna Porter ("A Call to Arms"), Naomi Klein takes a strong position on a political topic. Compare and contrast the strategies these writers have used to make their points of view interesting to their readers.
2. How does Klein fit Irshad Manji's description of Socrates as a "gadfly" ("Status Anxiety? Consider Socrates and the Sewer Saviour")? How might Klein respond to the practice of using dead celebrities in advertising as described in Katrina

Onstad's essay ("John Lennon, Michael Jackson: Do Celebrities Die Anymore?")?

IDEAS FOR DISCUSSION/WRITING

Preparing to Write

Write freely about a large corporation with which you are familiar and the brand identity of that corporation. The corporation may be one where you are an employee or where you are a consumer (or possibly both). Describe the brand identity. How is that identity established? Has that brand identity changed over time? Has your own experience with this corporation reflected the brand identity that is promoted?

Choosing a Topic

1. Write a narrative essay in which you describe an experience with one of the corporations Klein mentions (or another similar company). In your narrative, use specific examples to illustrate how your experience was consistent or inconsistent with the brand identity that the corporation has adopted.
2. Write an essay in which you argue for or against the move toward globalization. Use specific examples to support your point of view.
3. Klein says she was fired for having a "bad attitude." Write a short essay for other students, explaining the three most beneficial employee characteristics and illustrating those with specific examples.

STEPHEN OSBORNE

The Lost Art of Waving (2010)

Stephen Osborne was born in Pangnirtung, Baffin Island, and has worked in publishing in Western Canada for most of his life. He is the publisher of *Geist*, a quarterly magazine focusing on Canadian arts, culture, and ideas, and the author of *Ice & Fire: Dispatches from the New World 1988–1998* (1998), a collection of narrative essays about travels and encounters across Canada. In 1971, he founded Pulp Press Book Publishers, now Arsenal Pulp Press (company motto: "Forty years of making trouble.") Osborne has won numerous awards, including the CBC Literary Award for Creative Non-fiction, the National Magazine Award for Outstanding Achievement, the Western Magazine Award for Lifetime Achievement, and the Vancouver Arts Award for Writing and Publishing. More of his writing can be found at **www.waysofpublishing.com**.

Preparing to Read

In this essay, Stephen Osborne looks at what a wave can mean, and why waving has become a lost art. Think about waving. When was the last time you waved at someone? Do you have different waves for different occasions? Aside from "good-bye," what can a wave mean? What other gestures can be used instead of a wave?

Some time ago, when she was four years old, or perhaps four and a half, which is a separate age at that time of life, my youngest protégé, whose name is Julia,[1] observed that not many people seemed to know how to wave properly. At the time she was demonstrating an improved method of holding hands, which required that I let my fingers hang straight down with no tilting, allowing her to grasp my fingers with hers at the right angle, and I could feel in a moment that there were no awkward forces pushing or pulling against us: we could walk together easily and she could skip along as she wished. She had been right about hand-holding so I hesitated to question her remark about people not 1

Reading Critically

[1] Who do you think Julia is? Why does the author call her his protégé?

knowing how to wave. Julia's own wave at the time resembled the wave of the Queen of England, a rather chilling twist of the hand. But later I noticed that she had injected a note of brio❷ into her waving, and now that she is five, or more precisely five and nearly three quarters, her wave has grown in stature and she often raises her hand rather grandly above her head, as she did the other day from the back seat of her mother's car as it pulled away from the curb. I could see that there was nothing uncertain in Julia's wave now and felt my own wave to be rather tentative, perhaps even hesitant; and as we who were left on the sidewalk waved back to her, I applied myself vigorously and kept waving until Julia was out of sight and then the car was out of sight. Only then did we stop waving, and we let our hands drift above our heads for a moment before finally lowering them. Is there an art of waving? Walter Benjamin seems to propose at least a typology of waving, in a few lines scribbled in a notebook circa 1930; his words may be all we have on the subject from great thinkers: "Waving from the mail coach, to the organic rhythm of the trotting horses. The senseless, desperate, cutting wave from the departing train. Waving has gone astray in the railroad station. On the other hand, the wave to strangers passing by on a moving train. This above all with children, who are waving to angels when they wave to the noiseless, unknown, never-returning people. (Of course, they are also saluting the passing train.)"

2 Who waves at trains today? Or at ships departing? Is waving at a cruise ship really waving, or are we merely enacting a role as seen in movies? (Are passengers leaving on a cruise ship not already on their way back?) At the airport no one waves; instead we embrace at the departure gate, forced to accept an unhappy substitute in the hug, a brief unprotracted moment, already a memory of parting. Once we watched and waved and watched more as our sight of the beloved diminished in the distance: eventually they were no more to be seen and so we turned back into the present and away from the past, where they had been earlier in the day: we were melancholy, even nostalgic. Let us note here the reduction in status of nostalgia, which for two hundred years, at least until the end of World War II and the onset of

---

Reading Critically

❷ Explain this phrase.

commercial air travel, had been an affliction common among students and military personnel; doctors treated nostalgia as they did influenza and other contagious diseases, with lots of bed rest and plenty of fluids. Who today is willing to be diagnosed as nostalgic? Who confesses to that once noble affliction, now reduced to a mere attribute of sentimentalism, a component of kitsch?❸

Certain species of waving will always be with us, of course: the pope waves, the queen waves, tyrants wave, clowns wave, mayors and prime ministers wave. Blondin waves to the Prince of Wales from his rope across Niagara.❹ Beauty queens wave and so do their maids in waiting and their runners-up. To what extent are we satisfied that their waving is true waving rather than a requirement in a job description? Let us define true waving as a continuum of mutual recognition, of contact soon but not quite yet to be broken or remade (the homecoming), and if broken, to be broken forever: this moment of breaking will never return; we continue to wave for another heartbeat or two with our hands in the air, beckoning, gesturing, making farewell yet always beckoning; then having lost not only eye contact but all visual residue of the departed, we hold our hands still in the air, in mute acknowledgement of a sundering now complete. 3

And then ships in passing, ferries, cruise ships, yachts: passengers wave to each other across the water. People living in the country wave to each other from their cars and their pickup trucks. Waving lends gravity and duration to the vanishing world, especially in glimpses of private farewells carried out in public spaces such as train stations and bus depots, but only weakly in airports, where the exchange of waves so meaningful in prior ages cannot be known or seen or even remembered by those too young to have known waving as some of us can still recall waving to each other on a darkened snowy evening, perhaps on the wooden platform at Sioux Lookout on a night of blizzard and cutting wind and nothing before us but the certainty of never seeing each other again, never being seen by each other again, although only to be separated for days or weeks at most but who could believe that, and the snow was hurting our faces 4

Reading Critically

❸ What is kitsch? Give some examples of things you feel qualify as kitsch.

❹ Who was Blondin? What does this example suggest about Osborne's intended audience?

and the big lamp was glaring and we had mittens on and scarves and the whistle was blowing. We embraced heavily in our awkward clothing; a clanging and the clash of iron and the screech of metal wheels: leaning out from the vestibule between cars, waving into the night and the blizzard for as long as we could, as the train pulled us apart, into the future, into the past. All was equally blank and without you, but was it an escape as well, a species of respite, even hope? The long and painful wailing of the whistle in the night, a lonely minor chord, D-sharp minor to be precise, on an air horn invented by Robert Swanson, the great whistle maker, at his whistle farm in a distant mountain valley. (Swanson was a composer of farewells: it was he who gave the minor chord to Canadian trains, the major chord to American trains.[5] Might there be a doctrine of farewells?) That was waving then, we want to say: those were the great days of waving, but how certain can we be? (Is this what Benjamin implies when he says that waving went astray in the railroad station?) Not long ago my protégé Julia began slipping into epileptic seizures, which went on for many weeks. During the seizures she would retreat for long moments to a distant place; we could see her leaving us and we would wave to her slowly, and she would wave back slowly, tracing a gesture in the air, and the wave would linger until the seizure had passed and we were together again. Who is it, we want to remember, who waves at angels, when they wave to the noiseless, unknown, never-returning people?[6]

UNDERSTANDING DETAILS

1. Why does the author not immediately dismiss four-year-old Julia's comment about people not knowing how to wave?
2. What "professions" require waves? How are these waves different from "true" waving? Explain Osborne's definition of "true" waving in your own words.
3. How was nostalgia once seen? How is it seen today? What is the link between nostalgia and waving?

Reading Critically

[5] Why does this detail prompt Osborne to ask if there is a "doctrine" of farewells?

[6] Whose question was this originally? Why does Osborne conclude his essay with it?

ANALYZING MEANING

1. Why would the widespread availability of air travel affect waving? Why does Osborne feel that a hug is an "unhappy" substitute for a wave? Why does he think waving lends more gravity to farewells in public places such as train stations but not airports?
2. Whom do you think Osborne is addressing in his description of waving from Sioux Lookout (paragraph 5) when he says, "All was equally blank and without you"? Why does he wonder if the departure was also "an escape [. . .], a species of respite, even hope"?
3. What meaning does waving take on for Osborne when Julia begins to have seizures?

DISCOVERING RHETORICAL STRATEGIES

1. Look at Osborne's use of long sentences. What effect do you think he is trying to create?
2. In addition to examples, identify two other rhetorical strategies that Osborne uses in this essay. How do they help build his argument about waving?
3. Osborne's examples of waving cover different time periods and social situations. Which examples of waving did you find most and least effective? Based on his examples, what can you surmise about Osborne's intended audience?

MAKING CONNECTIONS

1. Compare the types and range of Osborne's examples with those used by Barbara Kingsolver ("Life Without Go-Go Boots") and Naomi Klein ("Co-opting Dissent"). Which examples seem most effective to you? What accounts for their effectiveness?
2. How would you characterize the tone in this piece? Compare it to the tone of Evelyn Lau's "More and More" and Jean Yoon's "Halmonee." What similarities do you notice in the themes and writing styles of these three pieces?

IDEAS FOR DISCUSSION/WRITING

Preparing to Write

In addition to waving, make a list of possible ways to say goodbye. Include other gestures, physical actions (such as hugging), and phrases. Which do you use most frequently? Moments of departure can be awkward, intensely emotional, or suddenly liberating. Write about a memorable goodbye moment. Did you wave?

Choosing a Topic

1. Osborne feels that waving is a lost art. Write an essay about another gesture (such as bowing, standing up when an authority figure enters the room, a man opening a door for a woman, etc.) that has disappeared or is on its way out. Explain why the gesture might be disappearing and what is significant about this loss.
2. Osborne links the end of nostalgia with the arrival of commercial air travel. Others have connected the end of nostalgia to the Internet: because we can look up just about anything online, we never really have to long for what cannot be recovered. Write a descriptive essay on what you feel nostalgic for. What might you really be longing for when you feel this nostalgia?
3. Using Osborne's description of saying goodbye at Sioux Lookout as a model, write a narrative essay in the second person exploring a moment of departure.

CHAPTER 4

PROCESS ANALYSIS

Explaining Step by Step

Human nature is characterized by the perpetual desire to understand and analyze the process of living well. The bestseller list is always crowded with books on how to know yourself better, how to be assertive, how to become famous, how to avoid a natural disaster, or how to be rich and happy—all explained in three easy lessons. Open almost any popular magazine, and you will find numerous articles on how to lose weight, how elections are run in this country, how to dress for success, how political rallies evolved, how to gain power, or how to hit a successful topspin backhand. People naturally gravitate toward material that tells them how something is done, how something happened, or how something works, especially if they think the information will help them improve their lives in a significant way.

Defining *Process Analysis*

A *process* is a procedure that follows a series of steps or stages. *Analysis* involves taking a subject apart and explaining its components in order to better understand the whole. *Process analysis*, then, explains an action, a mechanism, or an event from beginning to end. It concentrates on either a mental or a physical operation: how to solve a chemistry problem, how to tune up your car, how the Canadian senate is formed, how the Internet works. In fact, the explanation of the writing process beginning on page 28 of this book is a good case in point: It divides writing into three interrelated verbal activities and explains how they work—separately and together.

A process analysis can take one of two main forms: (1) It can give directions, thereby explaining how to do something (directive), or (2) it can give information about how something happened (informative). The first type of analysis gives directions for a task the reader may wish to attempt in the future. Examples include how to make jelly, how to lose weight, how to drive to Saskatoon, how to assemble stereo equipment, how to make money, how to use a microscope, how to knit, how to resuscitate a dying relationship, how to win friends, how to discipline your child, and how to backpack.

The second type of analysis furnishes information about what actually occurred in specific situations or about how something works. Examples include how Hiroshima was bombed, how certain rock stars live, how the tax system works, how *Lord of the Rings* was filmed, how Mario Lemieux earned a place in the Hockey Hall of Fame, how gold was first discovered in Yukon, how computers work, how a kibbutz functions, and how the Canadian military became involved in Afghanistan. These analyses and others like them respond to a certain fascination we all have with mastering some processes and understanding the intricate details of others. This type of process analysis provides us with opportunities to raise our own standard of living, either by helping us directly apply certain processes to our own lives or by helping us understand how our complex world functions.

The following student paragraph analyzes the process of constructing a garden compost pit. Written primarily for people who might wish to make such a pit, this piece is directive rather than informative. Notice in particular the amount of detail the student calls upon to explain each stage of the process and the clear transitions she uses to guide us through her analysis.

> No garden is complete without a functioning compost pit. Here's a simple, inexpensive way to make your garbage work for you! To begin with, make a pen out of hog wire or chicken wire, four feet long by eight feet wide by four feet high, splitting it down the middle with another piece of wire so that you end up with a structure that looks like a capital *E* on its side. This is a compost duplex. In the first pen, place a layer of soda ash, just sprinkled on the surface of the dirt. Then, pile an inch or so of leaves, grass clippings, or sawdust on top of the soda ash. You're now ready

for the exciting part. Start throwing in all the organic refuse from your kitchen (no meat, bones, or grease, please). After the food is a foot or so deep, throw in a shovelful of steer manure and cover the entire mess with a thin layer of dirt. Then water it down. Continue this layering process until the pile is three to three-and-a-half feet high. Allow the pile to sit until it decomposes (from one month in warm weather to six months in colder weather). Next, take your pitchfork and start slinging the contents of pen one into pen two (which will land in reverse order, of course, with the top on the bottom and the bottom on the top). This ensures that everything will decompose evenly. Water this down and begin making a new pile in pen one. That's all there is to it! You now have a ready supply of fertilizer for your garden.

Thinking Critically Through Process Analysis

Process analysis embodies clear, careful, step-by-step thinking that takes one of three different forms: chronological, simultaneous, or cyclical. The first follows a time sequence from "first this" to "then that." The second forces you to deal with activities or events that happen or happened at the same time, such as people quietly studying or just going to work when the September 11th terrorist attacks hit New York and Washington. And the third requires you to process information that is continuous, such as the rising and setting of the sun. No other thinking pattern will force you to slow down as much as process analysis, because the process you are explaining probably won't make any sense if you leave out even the slightest detail.

Good process analysis can truly help your reader see an event in a totally new light. An observer looks at a product already assembled or at an event already completed and has no way of knowing without the help of a good process analysis how it got to this final stage. Such an analysis gives the writer or speaker as well as the observer a completely new way of "seeing" the subject in question. Separating process analysis from the other rhetorical modes lets you practise this method of thinking so that you will have a better understanding of the various mental procedures going on in your head. Exercising this possibility in isolation will help you feel its range and its intricacies so that you can become more adept at using it, fully developed, in combination with other modes of thought.

Reading and Writing Process Analysis Essays

Your approach to a process analysis essay should be fairly straightforward. As a reader, you should be sure you understand the author's statement of purpose and then try to visualize each step as you go along. As a writer, you need to adapt the mechanics of the way you normally write to the demands of a process analysis paper, beginning with an interesting topic and a number of clearly explained ideas or stages. As usual, the intended audience determines the choice of words and the degree of detail.

Reading Process Analysis Essays

- Is the essay *directive* or *informative*?
- What is the author's general message?

Preparing to Read. Preparing to read a process analysis essay is as uncomplicated as the essay itself. Titles such as Malcolm Gladwell's "Is the Belgian Coca-Cola Hysteria the Real Thing?" or Adam Goodheart's "How to Mummify a Pharaoh" tell us exactly what we're going to learn about. Scanning each selection to assess the author's audience will give you an even better idea of what to expect in these essays, while the synopsis of each in the Rhetorical Contents will help focus your attention on its subject.

Also important as you prepare to read these essays are the qualifications of each author to write on this subject: Has he or she performed the task, worked with the mechanism, or seen the event? Is the writer's experience first-hand? What makes Adam Goodheart a credible source on the ancient process of mummification? Has Maureen Littlejohn ("You Are a Contract Painkiller") actually experienced the effect of ASA on pain or fever? What is Stanley Coren's ("Dogs and Monsters") experience with dogs? How does he know about the genetic engineering of dogs? The biography preceding each essay will help you uncover this information and will give you other publication details that will encourage you to focus on the material you are about to read.

Finally, before you begin reading, answer the prereading questions, and then do some brainstorming on the subject of the essay: What do you want to know about mass hysteria (Gladwell)? How much do any of us really know about how ASA works, and why might we want to know more (Littlejohn)?

Reading. When you read the essays in this chapter for the first time, record your initial reactions to them. Consider the preliminary information you have been studying in order to create a context for each author's composition: Why did Littlejohn write "You Are a Contract Painkiller"? What circumstances prompted Coren's "Dogs and Monsters"? Who do you think is Nick Paumgarten's audience in "Master of Play"?

Also determine at this point whether the essay you are reading is *directive* (explaining how to do something) or *informative* (giving information about how something happened). This fundamental understanding of the author's intentions, along with a reading of the questions following the essay, will prepare you to approach the contents of each selection critically when you read it a second time.

Rereading. As you reread these process analysis essays, look for an overview of the process at the beginning of the essay so that you know where each writer is headed. The body of each essay is generally a discussion of the stages of the process.

This central portion of the essay is often organized *chronologically* (as in Bascaramurty's and Goodheart's essays), with clear transitions so that readers can easily follow the writer's train of thought. Other methods of organization are *cyclical* (such as the process of genetic engineering described by Coren), describing a process that has no clear beginning or end, and *simultaneous* (such as the effects of ASA outlined in Littlejohn's essay), in which many activities occur at the same time with a clear beginning and end. Most of these essays discuss the process as a whole at some point. During this second reading, you will also benefit from discovering what rhetorical modes each writer uses to support his or her process analysis and why these rhetorical modes work effectively. Do the historic examples that Maureen Littlejohn uses add to our understanding of the process she is explaining? How does Nick Paumgarten's use of description contribute to your understanding of video game development? How do all the rhetorical modes in each essay help create a coherent whole?

Also, as you reread, try to answer the Reading Critically questions. These questions will help in your critical analysis of each essay. After reading each essay for a second time, answer the questions that follow the selection to see if you understand your reading material on the literal, interpretive, and analytical levels before you take on the discussion/writing assignments.

For an overview of the entire reading process, consult the checklist on page 41 of the Introduction.

Writing Process Analysis Essays

- Provide an overview of the process.
- Draft a purpose statement or thesis.
- Make your essay directive or informative.
- Organize your essay chronologically, simultaneously, or cyclically.
- End with a description of the process as a whole.

Preparing to Write. As you begin a process analysis assignment, you first need to become as familiar as you can with the action, mechanism, or event you are going to describe. If possible, try to go through the process yourself at least once or twice. If you can't actually carry out the procedure, going through the process mentally and taking notes is a good alternative. Then, try to read something about the process. After all this preparation (and careful consideration of your audience and purpose), you should be ready to brainstorm, freewrite, cluster, or use your favourite prewriting technique (see pages 28–34 of the Introduction) in response to the prewriting questions before you start composing your paper.

Writing. The essay should begin with an overview of the process or event to be analyzed. This initial section should introduce the subject, divide it into a number of recognizable steps, and describe the result once the process is complete. Your thesis in a process essay is usually a purpose statement that clearly and briefly explains your approach to the procedure you will discuss: "Burning a CD can be divided into four basic steps" or "The American courts follow three stages in prosecuting a criminal case."

Next, the directive or informative essay should proceed logically through the various stages of the process, from beginning to end. The parts of a process usually fall nicely into chronological order, supported by such transitions as *at first, in the beginning, next, then, after that,* and *finally*. Some processes, however, are either simultaneous, forcing the writer to choose a more complex logical order for the essay (such as classification), or cyclical, requiring the writer to choose a starting point and then explain the cycle stage by stage. Playing the guitar, for example, involves two separate and simultaneous components that must work together: holding the strings against the frets with the fingers of one hand and strumming with the other hand. In analyzing this procedure, you would probably want to describe both parts of the process and then explain how the hands work together to produce music. An example of a cyclical process would be the changing of the seasons. To explain this concept to a reader, you would need to pick a starting point, such as spring, and describe the entire cycle, stage by stage, from that point onward.

In a process paper, you need to be especially sensitive to your intended audience, or readers will not be able to follow your explanation. The amount of information, the number of examples and illustrations, and the terms to be defined all depend on the prior knowledge and background of your readers. A writer explaining to a group of amateur cooks how to prepare a soufflé would take an entirely different approach to the subject than he or she would if the audience were a group of bona fide chefs hoping to land jobs in elegant French restaurants. The professional chefs would need more sophisticated and precise explanations than their recreational counterparts, who would probably find such an approach tedious and complicated because of the extraneous details.

The last section of a process analysis paper should consider the process as a whole. If, for example, the writer is giving directions on how to win an Xbox game, the essay might end with a good description or a screen capture illustrating the outcome. The informative essay on the American legal system might offer a summary of the stages of judging and sentencing a criminal. And the essay on cooking a soufflé might finish with a photograph of the mouth-watering dish.

Rewriting. In order to revise a process analysis essay, first make sure your main purpose is apparent throughout your paper:

- Is my purpose statement clear?

Next, you need to determine if your paper is aimed at the proper audience:

- Have I given my readers an overview of the process I am going to discuss?
- Do I go through the process step by step?
- At the end of the essay, do I help my readers see the process as a whole?

The checklist on page 42 will give you further guidelines for writing, revising, and proofreading.

Student Essay: Process Analysis at Work

The student essay that follows analyzes the process of using a "home permanent" kit. Notice that once the student gives an overview of the process, she discusses the steps one at a time, being careful to follow a logical order (in this case, chronological) and to use clear transitions. Then, see how the end of the essay shows the process as a whole.

Follow the Simple Directions

Although fickle hairstylists in Paris and Hollywood decide what is currently "in," many romanticists disregard fashion and yearn for a mane of delicate tendrils. Sharing this urge but resenting the cost, I opted for a "home perm" kit. Any literate person with normal dexterity could follow illustrated directions, I reasoned, and the eight easy steps would energize my limp locks in less than two hours. "Before" and "after" photos of flawless models showed the metamorphosis one might achieve. Confidently, I assembled towels, rollers, hair clips, waving lotion, neutralizer, end papers, and a plastic cap. While shampooing, I chortled about my ingenuity and economy.

Purpose statement for informative process analysis

Overview

First step (chronological order)

After towel-drying my hair, I applied the gooey, acidic waving lotion thoroughly. Then I wrapped an end paper around a parted section and rolled the first curl ("securely but not too tightly"). Despite the reassuring click of the fastened rollers, as I sectioned each new curl the previous one developed its own volition and slowly unrolled itself. Resolutely, I reapplied waving lotion and rewound—and rewound—each curl. Since my hair was already saturated, I regarded the next direction skeptically: "Apply waving lotion to each curl." Faithfully, however, I complied with the instructions. Ignoring the fragile state of the fastened rollers, I then feigned assurance and enclosed my entire head in a plastic cap. In forty minutes, chemical magic would occur.

Transition

Second step

Third step

Transition

Fourth step

Transition

Fifth step

Restless with anticipation, I puttered about the house; while absorbed in small chores, I felt the first few drops of lotion escape from the plastic tent. Stuffing wads of cotton around the cap's edges did not help, and the small drops soon became rivulets that left red streaks on my neck and face and splattered on the floor. (Had I overdone the waving lotion?) Ammonia fumes so permeated each room that I was soon asked to leave. Retreating to the bathroom, I opened the window and dreamed of frivolous new hairstyles.

Transition — Sixth step

Finally, the waving time had elapsed; neutralizing was next. I removed my plastic cap, carefully heeding the caution: "Do not disturb curlers as you rinse waving lotion from hair." With their usual impudence, however, all the curlers soon bobbed in the sink; undaunted, I continued. "This next step is critical," warned the instructions. Thinking half-hearted curls were better than no curls at all, I poured the entire bottle of neutralizer on my hair. After a drippy ten-minute wait, I read the next step: "Carefully remove rollers." As this advice was superfluous, I moved anxiously to the finale: "Rinse all solution from your hair, and enjoy your curls."

Transition — Seventh step
Transition — Eighth step

Final product

Lifting my head from the sink and expecting visions of Aphrodite, I saw instead Medusa's image in the mirror. Limp question-mark spirals fell over my eyes, and each "curl" ended in an explosion of steel-wool frizz. Reflecting on my ineptitude, I knew why the direction page was illustrated only with drawings. After washing a large load of ammonia-scented towels, I took two Aspirin and called my hairdresser. Some repair services are cheap at any price.

Concluding remark

Some Final Thoughts on Process Analysis

In this chapter, processes dictate the development and organization of each of the essays. Both directional and informational methods are represented here. Notice in particular the clear purpose statements that set the focus of some of the essays, as well as the other rhetorical modes (such as narration, comparison/contrast, and definition) that are used to help support the writers' explanations.

PROCESS ANALYSIS IN REVIEW

Reading Process Analysis Essays

Preparing to Read

✓ What assumptions can I make from the essay's title?
✓ What do I think the general mood of the essay will be?
✓ What are the essay's purpose and audience?
✓ What does the synopsis tell me about the essay?
✓ What can I learn from the author's biography?
✓ Can I predict the author's point of view toward the subject?

Reading

✓ Is the essay *directive* (explaining how to do something) or *informative* (giving information about how something happened)?
✓ What general message is the author trying to convey?

Rereading

✓ Does the author give an overview of the process?
✓ How is the essay organized—*chronologically*, *cyclically*, or *simultaneously*?
✓ What other rhetorical modes does the author use?

Writing Process Analysis Essays

Preparing to Write

✓ What is my purpose?
✓ Who is my audience?

Writing

✓ Do I provide an overview of the process at the beginning of the essay?
✓ Does my first paragraph introduce my subject, divide it into recognizable steps, describe the result once the process is complete, and include a purpose statement as my thesis?
✓ Is my process analysis essay either *directive* or *informative*?
✓ Do I proceed logically through the various steps of the process?
✓ Are the essay's details organized *chronologically*, *simultaneously*, or *cyclically*?
✓ Does my essay end with the process as a whole?

Rewriting

✓ Is my purpose statement clear?
✓ Have I given my readers an overview of the process I am going to discuss?
✓ Do I go through the process step by step?
✓ At the end of the essay, do I help my readers see the process as a whole?

MALCOLM GLADWELL

Is the Belgian Coca-Cola Hysteria the Real Thing? (1999)

Malcolm Gladwell (1963–) was born in England and lived there, as well as in the United States and Jamaica, before his family settled in Elmira, Ontario, in 1969. In 1984, he graduated from the University of Toronto with a history degree and got an internship at *The American Spectator* in Indiana. Less than a year later, he landed a job as a reporter at *The Washington Post* and, over time, moved from writing on topics with a business focus to those with a more general science bent. After complementing his work at *The Post* with freelance assignments for *The New Yorker*, Gladwell eventually won a contract as a staff writer with *The New Yorker* in 1996. Gladwell continues to write for *The New Yorker* and to do public speaking engagements based on his books: *The Tipping Point: How Little Things Can Make a Big Difference* (2000), in which he examines the idea of social epidemics; *Blink: The Power of Thinking Without Thinking* (2005), in which he explores rapid cognition; *Outliers: The Story of Success* (2008), about people whose abilities and accomplishments are far beyond the normal range; and *What the Dog Saw: And Other Adventures* (2009), a collection of essays. Links to many of his essays can be found on his website, **www.gladwell.com**.

Preparing to Read

In the summer of 1999, Malcolm Gladwell wrote the following essay, which appeared in *The New Yorker*. "Is the Belgian Coca-Cola Hysteria the Real Thing?" relates the story of an apparent food poisoning outbreak in Belgium and then speculates as to the real cause of the affliction that struck about 100 children. Before reading Gladwell's essay, think about food safety. What responsibility do food manufacturers have for food safety? How should a company respond to complaints that its products have caused illness? What role should government legislation play in upholding standards of food safety?

1 The wave of illness among Belgian children last month had the look and feel—in the beginning, at least—of an utterly typical food poisoning outbreak. First, forty-two children in the Belgian town of Bornem became mysteriously ill after drinking Coca-Cola

and had to be hospitalized. Two days later, eight more school children fell sick in Bruges, followed by thirteen in Harelbeke the next day and forty-two in Lochristi three days after that—and on and on in a widening spiral that, in the end, sent more than one hundred children to the hospital complaining of nausea, dizziness, and headaches, and forced Coca-Cola into the biggest product recall in its hundred-and-thirteen-year history. Upon investigation, an apparent culprit was found.❶ In the Coca-Cola plant in Antwerp, contaminated carbon dioxide had been used to carbonate a batch of the soda's famous syrup. With analysts predicting that the scare would make a dent in Coca-Cola's quarterly earnings, the soft-drink giant apologized to the Belgian people, and the world received a sobering reminder of the fragility of food safety.

2 The case isn't as simple as it seems, though. A scientific study ordered by Coca-Cola found that the contaminants in the carbon dioxide were sulfur compounds left over from the production process. In the tainted bottles of Coke, these residues were present at between five and seventeen parts per billion. These sulfides can cause illness, however, only at levels about a thousand times greater than that. At seventeen parts per billion, they simply leave a bad smell—like rotten eggs—which means that Belgium should have experienced nothing more than a minor epidemic of nose-wrinkling. More puzzling is the fact that, in four of the five schools where the bad Coke allegedly struck, half of the kids who got sick hadn't drunk any Coke that day. Whatever went on in Belgium, in other words, probably wasn't Coca-Cola poisoning. So what was it? Maybe nothing at all.

3 "You know, when this business started I bet two of my friends a bottle of champagne each that I knew the cause," Simon Wessely, a psychiatrist who teaches at the King's College School of Medicine in London, said.

4 "It's quite simple. It's just mass hysteria.❷ These things usually are."

5 Wessely has been collecting reports of this kind of hysteria for about ten years and now has hundreds of examples, dating back as far as 1787, when millworkers in Lancashire suddenly took ill after they became persuaded that they were being poisoned

---

Reading Critically

❶ How does Gladwell use syntax to make this sentence effective?

❷ What is your understanding of "mass hysteria"? Have you ever experienced this phenomenon?

by tainted cotton. According to Wessely, almost all cases fit a pattern. Someone sees a neighbor fall ill and becomes convinced that he is being contaminated by some unseen evil—in the past it was demons and spirits; nowadays it tends to be toxins and gases—and his fear makes him anxious. His anxiety makes him dizzy and nauseous. He begins to hyperventilate. He collapses. Other people hear the same allegation, see the "victim" faint, and they begin to get anxious themselves. They feel nauseous. They hyperventilate. They collapse, and before you know it everyone in the room is hyperventilating and collapsing.[3] These symptoms, Wessely stresses, are perfectly genuine. It's just that they are manifestations of a threat that is wholly imagined. "This kind of thing is extremely common," he says, "and it's almost normal. It doesn't mean that you are mentally ill or crazy."

6 Mass hysteria comes in several forms. Mass motor hysteria, for example, involves specific physical movements: shaking, tremors, and convulsions. According to the sociologist Robert Bartholomew, motor hysteria often occurs in environments of strict emotional repression; it was common in medieval nunneries and in nineteenth-century European schools, and it is seen today in some Islamic cultures. What happened in Belgium, he says, is a fairly typical example of a more standard form of contagious anxiety, possibly heightened by the recent Belgian scare over dioxin-contaminated animal feed. The students' alarm over the rotten-egg odor of their Cokes, for example, is straight out of the hysteria textbooks. "The vast majority of these events are triggered by some abnormal but benign smell," Wessely said. "Something strange, like a weird odor coming from the air conditioning."

7 The fact that the outbreaks occurred in schools is also typical of hysteria cases. "The classic ones always involve schoolchildren," Wessely continued. "There is a famous British case involving hundreds of schoolgirls who collapsed during a 1980 Nottinghamshire jazz festival. They blamed it on a local farmer spraying pesticides." Bartholomew has just published a paper on a hundred and fifteen documented hysteria cases in schools over the past three hundred years. As anyone who has ever been to

---

Reading Critically

[3] How does Gladwell's use of repetition affect the reader? What do you think his purpose is? Is it successful?

a rock concert knows, large numbers of adolescents in confined spaces seem to be particularly susceptible to mass hysteria. Those intent on pointing the finger at Coca-Cola in this sorry business ought to remember that. "We let the people of Belgium down," Douglas Ivester, the company's chairman, said in the midst of the crisis. Or perhaps it was the other way around.❹

UNDERSTANDING DETAILS

1. What were the symptoms experienced by the Belgian children in Gladwell's essay? What caused these symptoms?
2. List the steps in the setting in of mass hysteria.
3. What causes mass hysteria?

ANALYZING MEANING

1. How did Coca-Cola respond to the apparent poisoning of the people in Belgium? Was this response appropriate? Why or why not?
2. What is Gladwell's purpose in this essay? What is the main topic of Gladwell's essay?
3. Who is particularly susceptible to mass hysteria? Why?

DISCOVERING RHETORICAL STRATEGIES

1. A significant portion of Gladwell's essay is spent describing a series of events in Belgium. Explain why he spends so much time detailing these events.
2. Gladwell has quoted and cited other people in his essay. Why has he done this? What effect does this have?
3. What is Gladwell's purpose in this essay? Does he achieve this purpose?

MAKING CONNECTIONS

1. Gladwell is fascinated with the popularity of different social phenomena and the reasons people behave the way they do. Imagine a conversation between Gladwell and Judy Rebick ("The Culture of Overwork"). What do these two writers have in common? What topics of conversation do you imagine might engage them?

Reading Critically

❹ What is Gladwell suggesting? Is this an effective ending for the essay? Why or why not?

2. Barbara Kingsolver ("Life Without Go-Go Boots"), Judy Rebick ("The Culture of Overwork"), and Irshad Manji ("Status Anxiety? Consider Socrates and the Sewer Saviour") all cite examples of people's behaviour being modelled on the behaviour of those around them. Are these examples of the mass hysteria that Gladwell outlines? Why or why not?
3. Like Gladwell, Alison Gillmor ("Repress Yourself") is interested in factors that influence the behaviour of groups of people. Do you think that editing our emotions, as she suggests, would lead to more or fewer cases of mass hysteria?

IDEAS FOR DISCUSSION/WRITING

Preparing to Write

Write freely about contagious behaviour. What types of behaviour are "contagious"? What kinds of things do we do because we observe others around us doing them? Can yawning or blushing be caused by suggestion? If we observe others around us yawning, is it possible to keep ourselves from yawning as well?

Choosing a Topic

1. In a process essay directed to your classmates, explain how you believe a company should react in a case in which its product seems to be contaminated. Decide on your tone and purpose before you begin.
2. Write an essay for a local newspaper or magazine in which you outline the process for ensuring that the foods you consume at home are safe.
3. Gladwell explains how mass hysteria takes hold and what factors create it. Write a narrative essay in which you relate a story illustrating the power of the "mob mentality." How did the group dictate the actions of its individual members? Were the consequences of this behavioural influence positive or negative?

STANLEY COREN

Dogs and Monsters (2000)

You can see Stanley Coren as a guest on numerous television shows as well as in the role of host on his weekly television show, *Good Dog*. You can hear him on radio programs, such as *Dan Rather, Ideas, Quirks and Quarks*, and *The Osgood Report*. And you can read his work in articles published in *USA Today, The Globe and Mail, The New York Times, The Chicago Tribune, Time, People, Maclean's, Cosmopolitan*, and *Entertainment Weekly*. Coren has also published several books about dogs, including *How to Speak Dog: Mastering the Art of Dog–Human Communication* (2001), *Why We Love the Dogs We Do* (1998), *The Intelligence of Dogs* (1993, 2006), and *Sleep Thieves* (1996). He has published a multitude of academic and scientific writings related to his research into various areas of psychology and his current role as a professor and director of the Human Neuropsychology and Perception Laboratory at the University of British Columbia (UBC). If you wanted to meet Coren, you could take a course with the Vancouver Dog Obedience Training Club, or you could attend one of the many SPCA fundraising events that he participates in.

Coren was born in Philadelphia in 1942 and educated at the University of Pennsylvania (undergraduate) and Stanford University (doctorate). This prolific writer and researcher now lives in Vancouver with his wife, two dogs, and a cat. Links to many of his articles and excerpts from his books are available at **www.stanleycoren.com**.

Preparing to Read

A recent mobile phone ad campaign highlighted the similarities in appearance between people and the dogs they choose as pets. Do you have a dog? If so, what kind of dog do you have? What characteristics made you choose that type of dog? Generally, do you think dogs are good pets? Why or why not? How has the role of pets changed over the past century? In this essay, originally published in *Saturday Night* magazine in May 2000, Stanley Coren outlines the process of bioengineering dogs to adapt to the current technologies and needs of their human owners.

1 Today's headlines routinely raise fears about genetic engineering. The biggest concern is that "tampering with creation" to fashion new strains of plants and animals may result in the devastation of the world by upsetting the natural balance among

species. Even Prince Charles has joined the debate, claiming that genetic engineering "takes us into areas that should be left to God. We should not be meddling with the building blocks of life in this way." But the genetic manipulation of species is far from new. In fact, it began at least 14,000 years ago, when human beings created the first deliberately engineered organism—the dog.

2 The bioengineered canine was not created in a high-level biocontainment lab; rather, its beginnings were accidental. Wolves and jackals (the domestic dog's predecessors) were attracted to human camps because primitive humans left bones, bits of skin, and other scraps of leftover food scattered near their dwellings. The wolves and jackals learned that by loitering around the settlement they could grab an occasional bite to eat without the exertion involved in hunting. These primitive dogs were initially tolerated by humans because they functioned as de facto garbage-disposal units.❶

3 The dogs near the campsite provided another key benefit: security. They barked whenever wild beasts or strangers approached, removing the need for human guards to be posted at night, and thus affording the villagers more rest and increased safety. The bark was critical—the most effective guard dogs, obviously, were those with loud, persistent barks. And so a selective breeding program was begun: those dogs that barked loudly were kept and bred with other loud barkers, while those that did not bark were simply killed or chased off. In fact, one of the major distinctions between wild canines and domestic dogs today is that domestic dogs bark, while wild dogs seldom do. The persistent racket that irritates so many people is actually a human innovation.❷

4 It wasn't until the end of the fifteenth century, though, that the dog as a genetic creation became truly unique—almost more an invention than a species. At this point people began crossbreeding dogs, not just to cater to their changing needs, but to suit advancing technology. Typically, humans had tailored machines to suit organisms. With dogs, they began modifying an organism to fit a machine. The machine was the gun, and the organism was the gun dog.

Reading Critically

❶ What is Coren's purpose in comparing dogs to technology?

❷ Explain the irony of this statement.

The earliest gun dogs were the pointers, which appeared in Europe in the 1500s. The hunting weapon of choice at the time was the muzzle-loading musket, a primitive device that was notoriously laborious to use. On sighting his quarry, a hunter had to take out his powder horn, dump gunpowder down the barrel, followed by a lead ball wrapped with oiled paper or cloth, and tamp down the shot and powder with a tamping rod; then he had to fire the gun. The process took a minimum of thirty seconds, all in the service of a weapon with an effective range of twenty-five to fifty yards. To accommodate musket technology, the pointer was designed❸ to be slow, silent, and patient. The pointer's job was to find a bird, then to hold its position while pointing at the bird's location for the agonizingly long time it took the hunter to load and shoot his weapon. If a lucky shot actually killed a bird the pointer was expected to go out and bring the game back as well. But the retrieval was window-dressing; the pointer's genetic value lay in its ability to stretch time out, to live in a slow-motion world. 5

As weapons technology improved, guns became easier to load, with better range and accuracy. To match this new equipment, dog breeders in the late 1700s created a new kind of dog—the setter. Setters moved much more quickly than pointers, and indicated their proximity to the prey not by the stillness of their point but by the beat of their tails. The faster a setter wagged its tail, the closer it was to the game. 6

As more land was cultivated and cities and towns sprang up, hunters were forced to turn to wilderness areas, particularly wetlands, where they hid behind blinds and waited for their quarry to come to them. These circumstances placed a premium on a dog that was not simply quiet, as the pointer had been, but that possessed an almost preternatural obedience and patience. Thus, the retriever became the bioengineered star of the next century. Retrievers were bred to wait—to do nothing: not to point, not to flush, not to run, not to bark—and retrieve. They were bred to be less, not more, which, given the physiognomy❹ of the species, may have been the more remarkable biotechnological feat. 7

Reading Critically

❸ How does the word *designed* connect the concepts of selective breeding and bioengineering?

❹ What is the meaning of the word *physiognomy*? Why might this be an uncommon word?

Canada is responsible for the newest and most intriguing genetic invention in the retriever group: the Nova Scotia duck tolling retriever, a handsome, auburn-hued dog that stands about twenty inches high and weighs about forty-five pounds. The need for the toller arose when duck hunters found that they could better attract their quarry by having wooden "lures," or decoys, carved to look like ducks, floating in the nearby water. Ducks are also attracted to unusual movement and activities. This is where the toller comes in. Tolling simply means that the dog runs back and forth on the shore, spinning and making noise, or swims erratically near the shore to attract the birds. Curious ducks fly near to see what all the activity is about, and come within range of the hunter's gun. Tollers will do this for hours if needed. Of course, once the bird is shot the dog is then expected to swim out and bring it back to its lazy master.❺ 8

Like any piece of technology—the 78 rpm record player, or the pedal-driven sewing machine—a bioengineered dog can become outmoded and obsolete. One of the most common breeds of the eighteenth and nineteenth centuries, the Spanish pointer, was so popular in its day that it can be seen in scores of early paintings of hunts. These dogs were perfect for the era of the muzzle-loading musket—slow, quiet, and the most meticulous of the pointers. Today the breed is effectively extinct. Spanish pointers were simply too slow for impatient modern hunters, with their new, superior equipment—both guns and dogs. 9

Walk into homes today, and what you'll find are dogs engineered for a wholly different piece of technology: the TV remote control. Perhaps our faith in biogenetic engineering would be improved if we recognized that for those of us who don't hunt, some dogs have also been designed specifically to be our companions—to fit the couch-potato mentality of our current, leisure-addicted era. It is a wonder to me that starting with the DNA of a wolf, we have spent 14,000 years of biotechnology and genetic manipulation in the creation of the little white beast who is right now gently snoring with his head resting against my foot.❻ 10

Reading Critically

❺ Why do you think Coren uses the term *lazy master* to describe the hunter? What hint does this give us about his attitude toward hunting?

❻ What does this image say about the author's relationship with dogs?

UNDERSTANDING DETAILS

1. What is Coren's thesis? Where in the essay is it stated?
2. Outline the significant stages of development in the process of breeding dogs. What key characteristics identify each stage?
3. What has motivated humans to genetically engineer dogs over the past 14 000 years? What is the relationship between dogs and various forms of technology?

ANALYZING MEANING

1. Explain the title "Dogs and Monsters." Is it effective? Why or why not?
2. In the first paragraph of Coren's essay, he refers to the fears about genetic modification expressed in current headlines. How does Coren's discussion of the bioengineering of dogs relate to foods that are now the focus of the genetic modification controversy?
3. What is Coren's purpose in writing this essay? What gives him credibility in his discussion of genetic modification and bioengineering?

DISCOVERING RHETORICAL STRATEGIES

1. What strategies has Coren used to unify the introduction and conclusion of his essay?
2. In addition to chronologically outlining the history of the bioengineering of dogs, Coren uses other rhetorical strategies in his essay. What other methods of organization has he employed?
3. Which of the three forms of process analysis does Coren's essay follow? Explain your answer.

MAKING CONNECTIONS

1. Coren explains that dogs have been bred over time to adapt to the current technology available to people. Imagine that Coren is in conversation with Will Braun ("Seven Criteria for the Adoption of New Technology") about adaptation to new technology. In what ways have our skills and interests changed over time to adapt to the technology available? Do you think Coren and Braun would agree on the beneficial value of this type of adaptation?
2. Coren adds interest to his essay with the personal detail about his own dog in his conclusion. Compare this strategy with that

of Russell Smith ("Potty-Mouthed and Proud of It"), Sheema Khan ("Hijabs: Don't Kick Up a Fuss"), or Judy Rebick ("The Culture of Overwork").

IDEAS FOR WRITING/DISCUSSION

Preparing to Write

Coren opens his essay by pointing to recent fears about genetic modification. Write freely about genetic modification and the implications it has for our society. In what areas of our life are you aware of genetic modification happening? Do you see it as a good thing or a bad thing? Why does genetic modification frighten people? What are the benefits of genetic modification? Should the government prohibit the production of genetically modified organisms?

Choosing a Topic

1. Write an essay in which you argue for or against companies being allowed to bioengineer foods. Make sure you support your position with specific examples.
2. Humans are constantly inventing new tools to help them adapt to a changing environment. Think of one particular technological advance of the past 20 years, and outline how and why that change happened.
3. Write an essay for the humane society newsletter in which you outline the process for adopting a pet. Be sure to explain clearly how people should select the pets they wish to adopt.

MAUREEN LITTLEJOHN

You Are a Contract Painkiller (1997)

Maureen Littlejohn is a journalist who has specialized in pop culture for over 20 years. She began her journalistic career working on *Campus Digest* (now *Campus Canada*) after graduating with an honours B.A. (general arts) from the University of Toronto and completing the magazine journalism program at Ryerson Polytechnic Institute. She has since worked as a reporter, feature writer, and TV music critic, interviewing numerous performing artists, including Madonna, Tom Hanks, Mel Gibson, and Joni Mitchell, and has been managing editor of several trade and consumer magazines. A travel writer, Littlejohn has visited Nunavut, the Indian Himalayas, and the Amazon Basin of Ecuador. She is currently based in Toronto.

Littlejohn's articles have appeared in a variety of publications, including the *Financial Post* magazine, *Flare* magazine, the Canadian Airlines in-flight magazine, *The Music Scene*, *CARAS News*, *Canadian Musician*, *Network*, and *Equinox*, where the piece included here was first published.

Preparing to Read

ASA, or Aspirin, is a medication that is readily available and familiar to most of us. In this essay, Maureen Littlejohn outlines the process by which ASA works to relieve our pain and the process through which ASA was developed. Before reading this essay, think about familiar medications. What do you typically keep stocked in your medicine cabinet at home? Do you ever use ASA? When? Why? What other nonprescription medications do you use? Do you favour medications available from pharmacies or more natural remedies? Why?

You are a contract painkiller, code name ASA, also known to your clients as aspirin.[1] Pain is your gain—Canadians swallow almost one billion of your agents each year. You have achieved renown by destroying headaches but you are equally effective in countering sprains, burns, or blows. You stop swelling and reduce fever and research suggests you may even help prevent heart attack and stroke. 1

Reading Critically

[1] How effective is the opening sentence at grabbing your attention? Explain.

2 On your latest mission, your client has just had a fight with her boss, and her head is pounding. Involuntary muscle contractions on her scalp and at the back of her neck, triggered by the argument, are now causing swelling and throbbing. In reaction, her body has produced an enzyme called prostaglandin, which is sensitizing the nerve endings in her scalp, especially around her temples and sending a message of pain to her brain.

3 Taken with a modest stream of water or ginger ale, your chalky, round self begins the mission by moving through the host's esophagus, into the stomach, then the upper small intestine, where you are dissolved and passed into the bloodstream. There, you slop into a molecular chain of events and disable the enzyme that converts the acid in cell membranes into prostaglandins. The nerve endings are now desensitized, that pain message to the brain is stopped, and your host is smiling again.

4 You reduce fever in a similar way. If your host were suffering from the flu, her white blood cells would be fighting the virus by producing prostaglandins that, in turn, cause the body's temperature to rise. You head off the prostaglandins and bring the fever down.

5 You are not the only pain-relieving agent at work. Ibuprofen and other aspirinlike drugs known as nonsteroidal anti-inflammatory drugs (NSAIDs) do much the same thing. You all share possible side effects—in 2 to 6 percent of your clients, you cause stomach irritation and possibly bleeding and, in extreme cases, kidney failure. Prostaglandins help maintain the integrity of the stomach lining, and in their absence, the acidic NSAIDs give the host a queasy feeling.

6 As a tonic for hire,❷ you have been around for a century, but your family tree goes back much further. In ancient Greece, Hippocrates noted that chewing on willow leaves reduced fever. In the 1800s, two Italian chemists confirmed that willow bark contains one of your main ingredients, the antipyretic (fever-reducing) salicin. A Swiss pharmacist then found that meadowsweet, a shrub in the spirea family, has even more of the magic substance than willow bark. And while experimenting with salicin, a German chemist created salicylic acid (the SA of ASA). He called it *Spirsäure* after spirea, hence the "spirin" part of your name. The "a" was added for "acetyl," the substances—including a salt—that made the SA easier on the stomach. In 1893, Felix Hoffmann at the Bayer AG Chemical Works in Germany purified and stabilized you, and that's when

---

Reading Critically

❷ To what is Littlejohn comparing ASA here?

you first claimed celebrity status as one of the world's most popular, inexpensive pain relievers. Today you are synthesized from coal tar or petroleum instead of plants.❸

7 Beyond garden-variety aches and pains, you are prescribed as a remedy for arthritis because of your genius for blocking prostaglandins that trigger the pain and swelling of joints. Your most recent prostaglandin-fighting potential is to prevent heart attack and stroke. There is even talk that you may help ward off cancer and senility. Mission impossible? We'll see.

UNDERSTANDING DETAILS

1. What is ASA made from? What does *ASA* stand for?
2. When was ASA invented? By whom?
3. Explain how ASA works to relieve pain and reduce fever.

ANALYZING MEANING

1. Why has ASA become so popular over time? What do you anticipate its status will be in the future?
2. Describe Littlejohn's attitude toward her subject. What specific examples contribute to this impression?
3. Why might ASA be synthesized from coal tar or petroleum? Why have we moved beyond simply ingesting willow leaves and meadowsweet?

DISCOVERING RHETORICAL STRATEGIES

1. Littlejohn uses the second person to detail the history and the effect of ASA. What is the effect of casting the reader in the role of an ASA tablet? Why has she chosen this strategy? How effective is her choice to address the inanimate subject of her essay directly?
2. In this essay, Littlejohn uses an extended metaphor. To what does she compare ASA? List five examples of this comparison.
3. Is this essay a directive or a descriptive process analysis? Why is this an appropriate strategy for this topic?

MAKING CONNECTIONS

1. Littlejohn's use of an extended metaphor makes her subject more interesting and easier to understand. Explain how her use of figurative language compares with that of Joe Fiorito

---

Reading Critically

❸ Does this fact make ASA more or less appealing to you? Explain.

("Night Shift on the Main") or Ryan McNutt ("The Music We Hate: Joanna Newsom").

2. "You Are a Contract Painkiller" addresses the reader directly as "you" and, in fact, casts the reader as the subject of the essay. How is this approach similar to that of Joe Fiorito's "Night Shift on the Main"? How is the role of the reader different in these two essays?
3. Littlejohn is presenting scientific information in this essay and incorporating terminology that may initially be unfamiliar to her readers. What strategies has she used to make this subject accessible and interesting to her audience? How does her approach compare with that of Stanley Coren ("Dogs and Monsters"), Daniel J. Levitin ("The Music of My Mind") or Adam Goodheart ("How to Mummify a Pharaoh")?

IDEAS FOR DISCUSSION/WRITING

Preparing to Write

Write freely about common pain medications with which you are familiar. What do you do if you burn yourself with an iron? How do you remedy a headache? What do you do for bee stings? What is the best way to relieve sunburn pain? How do you treat a sprain? How did you learn about these treatments? How do you gauge their effectiveness?

Choosing a Topic

1. Think of a practice that was once commonly accepted for treating some ailment. It might be the use of mustard plasters or cod liver oil to cure or prevent colds, electric shock therapy to treat psychological problems, amputation to prevent the spread of infection, or lobotomies to cure psychological disorders. In a short essay, explain how and why this practice fell out of favour.
2. There are many things that we may find disagreeable but that we do because we recognize the benefits that they offer. This might include getting our teeth cleaned at the dentist's, exercising, or cleaning the bathroom. Describe one such process, focusing on its positive aspects.
3. Taking medication is one response to relieving pain, but many people are resistant to taking medications such as ASA. Write an essay in which you present some alternative responses to treating a headache or other "garden-variety aches and pains."

DAKSHANA BASCARAMURTY

My Parents Killed Santa (and Nobody Cared) (2011)

Dakshana Bascaramurty grew up in Winnipeg and now lives in Toronto. Her articles have appeared in the *National Post* and the *Ottawa Citizen*, and she has written radio content for CBC Ottawa. Since 2009, she has written for the Life section of *The Globe and Mail*. In 2011, she appeared at the Winnipeg Comedy Festival, and speculates that this appearance might be traced back to the first comic sketch she wrote and performed at age 10. Humour remains an element in her writing; an early essay for *The Globe and Mail* focused on her ability to nap while on the toilet.

Preparing to Read

"My Parents Killed Santa (and Nobody Cared)" originally appeared in the Facts & Arguments section of *The Globe and Mail*. In this essay, Bascaramurty, the daughter of Hindu parents, describes her desire for a traditional Christmas and her efforts to make her family conform to her longing. Before you read, think about important holidays in your community. In which holidays do you feel like an active participant? An intrigued outsider? Merely bored? Are there family holidays that you wish you didn't have to celebrate? Why?

As far as immigrant Hindu parents go, mine were pretty good at pretending they gave a damn about Christmas. 1

We did the tree, we did the Polaroids with Santa, we even did the stockings (though instead of stuffing them with dollar-store toys and clementines,[1] my mom hung them limp and empty on the tree). 2

"I think we're supposed to eat turkey," I told her after *Mickey's Christmas Carol* tipped me off. 3

"I hate turkey. It's so dry and bland," she said. So we'd eat chicken curry instead. 4

Reading Critically

[1] How do you think the young Bascaramurty knew the stockings were supposed to contain toys and clementines?

I'd write letters to the North Pole, detailing the year's requests, complete with cutouts from the Consumers Distributing catalogue. Most of the time, Santa delivered (though there was the one year I asked for a Cabbage Patch Kid and got a Chinatown knockoff instead). 5

Holiday commercials from cookie manufacturers taught me and my brother to leave out a glass of milk and Oreos on a plate on Christmas Eve. In the morning the cookies and milk were gone. Once, there was even a note from Santa expressing his gratitude for the midnight snack. He left a few carrots for us, explaining that they were leftovers from feeding the reindeer. 6

My brother sneered. "From the reindeer? Gross, I'm not eating those." 7

My mom peeled them and I giddily scarfed down those magical root vegetables. From the North Pole! How *exotic*! And then, when I was 8, we moved from Toronto to Winnipeg. We brought the tree, but left all the ornaments and holiday decor behind. When December hit, I started to get nervous. 8

"So, um, about that tree. Are we putting it up?" I asked. 9

"You're going to put up a tree with nothing on it?" my dad asked. "Not worth it. Not this year." 10

It sat in the basement untouched. 11

Would Santa skip over our house? I wondered. I was already a pretty neurotic kid, but this sent my anxiety into overdrive as the weeks wore on. We made decoupage ornaments in art class, but I had nothing on which to hang them. 12

We spent Christmas Eve at a family friend's house – it was their son's birthday. My eyes were on the clock as the men refilled their scotch glasses. "We should leave," I whispered to my mom, assuming that if we weren't home Santa would definitely skip our house. 13

We walked in the door at midnight. No presents in sight. I checked the kitchen (maybe he left them on the counter?), the dining room (under the table?), the living room (in that corner by the potted plants?). Maybe he was just running behind. *Yeah. That's what it is.* 14

My mother, looking exhausted, told my brother and me to wait downstairs while she trudged up to her bedroom. She came down toting two bags from The Bay (contents boxed, but not wrapped) and presented one to each of us halfheartedly. Mine contained a pair of green corduroy pants and a turtleneck with a micro floral pattern. 15

What was this? 16

"I guess you've figured out by now that Santa isn't real," my 17 mom said with a yawn and went up to bed.

The world slowed down. I looked to my brother to see if he 18 was as horrified as I was. He was unfazed.

Wait, was this true? The balloon I'd filled up with my beliefs 19 over the years was zooming around the room as the air hissed out of it.

My parents seemed relieved that the jig was up.❷ They'd 20 done their part – taken it way further than most non-Christians would have. Still, I felt cheated. I wanted to be one of those poorly adjusted kids who believed in Santa well into the double digits.

When my parents gave up on the Santa ruse, they gave up on 21 everything else, too. By the time my brother was away at university, I was the only one interested in seasonal pageantry.

I put up the tree for the last time when I was 17. I lugged 22 the box upstairs from the basement, assembled it and trimmed it with decorations bought on clearance at Zellers the year before. I watched *The Family Man* (yes, that Nicolas Cage masterpiece❸) for company while my parents were out grocery shopping. A friend called and asked what I was doing. "Putting up the Christmas tree."

"Oh, you're busy with your family! I'll let you go," he said. 23

"Nope. Just doing it on my own. That's Nic Cage you hear in 24 the background."

I suddenly felt empty, like I was doing all this for an eight-year- 25 old who didn't actually exist. I decided that day that I'd save it until I had a *real* eight-year-old to fuss over.

And I'm going to let that kid believe until she's in her double 26 digits.

UNDERSTANDING DETAILS

1. Where does Bascaramurty get her ideas about how to celebrate Christmas? How do her parents accommodate her wishes?
2. Why do her parents not put up the tree when they move to Winnipeg? Why is she so anxious about the lack of a tree? How does Bascaramurty find out there is no Santa Claus?

Reading Critically

❷ Explain this figure of speech.

❸ What is Bascaramurty's tone here?

3. What happens to Christmas in the Bascaramurty household after Santa is revealed to be a "ruse"?

ANALYZING MEANING

1. Why do you think Bascaramurty's parents go along with Christmas, even though they are Hindus? Aside from the title, what signs indicate that their hearts were not fully into the celebration?
2. Why does Bascaramurty feel cheated when she discovers the truth about Santa? Do you think there's another reason? What might Santa mean to her?
3. What does Bascaramurty realize when putting up the tree for the last time at age 17?

DISCOVERING RHETORICAL STRATEGIES

1. What process is being described in this piece? Which of the three forms of process analysis is used? What other rhetorical strategies does Bascaramurty use in this essay?
2. What image or persona does the author create for herself? How does her use of humour contribute to this persona?
3. How effective is the title? Why might Bascaramurty have chosen this as her title?

MAKING CONNECTIONS

1. Both Bascaramurty and Anita Rau Badami ("My Canada") write about a desire to adapt and belong. How are their experiences different?
2. Like Bascaramurty, K'naan ("Between the Highs and the Lows, Life Happens") also writes about his childhood experiences from an adult perspective. Compare the use of narrative in each of the essays. How are they similar? In what ways do they differ?

IDEAS FOR DISCUSSION/WRITING

Preparing to Write

Write freely about a holiday you loved as a child. Describe your anticipation, the lead-up to the day or days of celebration, the rituals, and the day immediately after. Do you still love this holiday as much as you did when you were a child? Why or why not? How has your celebration of the holiday changed?

Choosing a Topic

1. Write a process essay in which you describe your own discovery of something as a child. It could be a disappointing discovery, like Bascaramurty's, or a happier revelation.
2. Chose any holiday and write an informative or prescriptive process essay explaining how to celebrate it in the traditional style.
3. Research a holiday that is no longer celebrated (such as Saturnalia) or make up a new holiday. Write a persuasive essay arguing for the reinstatement or adoption of this celebration, showing how your community would benefit.

NICK PAUMGARTEN

Master of Play (2010)

Nick Paumgarten has been a staff writer at *The New Yorker* since 2005. His features have covered a wide range of topics, from video games to backcountry skiing, from Wall Street to online dating. He has appeared frequently on National Public Radio and the Public Broadcasting System to discuss the topics of his research. Before writing for *The New Yorker*, he was a reporter and senior editor at *The New York Observer*. He lives in Manhattan.

Preparing to Read

This essay below is an excerpt from a profile of Nintendo game designer and artist Shigeru Miyamoto, published in *The New Yorker* in 2010. The author first saw Miyamoto at an annual convention of video game makers, called E3 Expo, where Miyamoto was demonstrating the 14th installment of the Zelda game. Eventually, Paumgarten went to Japan to meet Miyamoto. As part of his research for this essay, Paumgarten borrowed a Wii and played some of the games he was writing about.

Nintendo has been in the business of play since 1889. Its founder, Fusajiro Yamauchi, made playing cards, or *karuta*. Well into the next century, the company's main product was *hanafuda*—cards made from crushed mulberry bark and lavishly illustrated with symbols such as animals and flowers—which replaced the painted seashells that the Japanese had traditionally used and which became widespread in Japan for gambling. As it happens, fortune and luck are intrinsic to the company's name. Made up of the three kanji characters *nin*, *ten*, and *do*, the name has been said to mean "Leave luck to heaven," or "Work hard, but in the end it is in heaven's hands," as the journalist David Sheff rendered it, in his 1993 portrait of the company, "Game Over: How Nintendo Zapped an American Industry, Captured Your Dollars, and Enslaved Your Children." (Sheff decided to write the book, which in spite of the title is generally admiring, after watching his young son Nic get hooked on Super Mario; Nic's addiction, years later, to methamphetamine became fodder for another book.) 1

In 1949, Yamauchi's headstrong and debonair great-grandson Hiroshi Yamauchi, aged twenty-two, took over Nintendo and began restlessly casting about for ways to extend its reach. He secured a licensing agreement with the Walt Disney Company and scored a big hit with American-style playing cards adorned with the image of Mickey Mouse. Other entrepreneurial gambits—instant rice, a taxi fleet—fared poorly. In the mid-nineteen-sixties, Yamauchi hired an engineer named Gunpei Yokoi and a crew of young tinkerers to think about making toys and games, and their experiments helped foster a culture of whimsy and risk❶ amid Nintendo's rigid corporate structure. As one of them told Sheff, years later, "Here were these very serious men thinking about the content of play." 2

The very serious men turned out a succession of silly gizmos. There was the Ultra Hand, a device with a gripping hand at the end of it; the Love Tester, a primitive electronic contrivance that purported to measure the level of ardor between a boy and a girl; the Beam Gun, which used a ray of light to hit simulated targets. (Nintendo converted abandoned bowling alleys into "shooting ranges," where you could fire at simulations of clay pigeons.) Across the ocean, a company called Atari, based in California, had created Pong, the first hit video game. Pong, originally an arcade game, was turned into a home version in 1975. Inspired by Atari, and by the craze for a new arcade game called Space Invaders,❷ Yamauchi, who told Sheff that he had never played a video game, led Nintendo into the arcade business, and also pushed for the development of a home console like Atari's, an apparatus that would come to be called the Family Computer, or Famicom. 3

In 1976, [Shigeru] Miyamoto, then age twenty-four, was a recent art-college graduate, with a degree in industrial design and an enduring fascination with the Japanese comic strips called manga. He liked to draw and paint, make toys, and play bluegrass on the banjo and the guitar, and wasn't sure how any of this was going to translate into earning a living. He had a vague idea that he'd create some kind of mass-market object. His father got him an interview with Yamauchi, through a mutual friend. Miyamoto showed the company some toys he'd made, two wooden clothes 4

Reading Critically

❶ How would a culture of whimsy and risk help a gaming company?

❷ Have you ever played Pong or Space Invaders? Aside from the obvious difference in graphics, how do these games differ from the games available now?

hangers for kids in the shape of crows and elephants. Yamauchi hired him to be an apprentice in the planning department.

5 What Miyamoto became, however, was Nintendo's first artist. He started out by designing the console for a car-racing game, and then by conceiving the look of the attackers for a knockoff of Space Invaders called Space Fever. His breakthrough came after an arcade game called Radar Scope, which Nintendo had hoped would be a hit in America, failed, leaving the company with an inventory in the United States of two thousand unsold Radar Scope cabinets. Yamauchi tapped Miyamoto to design a new game to replace Radar Scope in those cabinets.

6 The game he came up with was Donkey Kong. He had in mind a scenario based on Popeye, but Nintendo was unable to secure the rights, so he invented a new set of characters. The hero, the player's avatar, was a carpenter named Jumpman. (Miyamoto had initially called him Mr. Video, with the intention of using him in every game, much in the way that, he said, Hitchcock appears in many of his own films.) Jumpman's pet gorilla had kidnapped his girlfriend, Pauline, and escaped with her to the top of a construction site. The object of the game was to climb up through the girders while dodging the gorilla's projectiles, and then vanquish the gorilla and rescue the girl. The goal, in other words, was to get to the end of the game, not just to pile up points. ("Donkey" was the word Miyamoto found in a Japanese-English dictionary for "stubborn" or "goofy." "Kong" was a word for gorilla.) Prior to Donkey Kong, games had been developed by engineers and programmers with little or no regard for narrative or graphical playfulness. Donkey Kong, which débuted in 1981, had a story, a sense of humor, funny music (which Miyamoto helped write), and an ingenious game logic. It had four distinct screens, like a manga[3] panel. This was also a new and soon-to-be-ubiquitous genre: what Miyamoto has called a running/jumping/climbing game, otherwise known as a platform game.[4] At first, the Nintendo executives in America thought that Donkey Kong, as both a name and a game, was doomed. Looking for a better name for Jumpman, they settled on Mario, because of his resemblance to their landlord. To their surprise, the game was a huge hit.

Reading Critically

[3] What is a manga panel?

[4] Can you name any other games within this genre?

Mario, of course, went on to bigger things. When Nintendo released the Famicom in the United States, in 1985 (it was rechristened the Nintendo Entertainment System, or N.E.S.), Super Mario Bros. was the game that sold the machine and in turn laid claim to the eyes, and the thumbs, of the world. The market for home games had crashed, and several companies went under or got out. Super Mario represented a re-start. Again, the object was the rescue of a maiden, who has been kidnapped by Bowser, or King Koopa, an evil turtle. Mario, now a plumber, and joined by a lanky brother named Luigi, bounced through the Mushroom Kingdom, dodging or bopping enemies in the form of turtles, beetles, and squid, while seeking out magic mushrooms, coins, and hidden stars. When you set down these elements in ink, they sound ridiculous, but there is something in this scenario that is utterly and peerlessly captivating. There were eight worlds, with four levels each, which meant that you had to pass through thirty-two stages to get to the princess. You travelled through these worlds left to right, on what's called a side-scrolling screen. It wasn't the first side-scroll game, but it was the most charming and complex. What's more, the complexity was subtle. Yokoi, Miyamoto's mentor, and the inventor of the Game Boy device, had urged him to simplify his approach. The game had just fifteen or twenty dynamics in it—how the mushrooms work, how the blocks react when you hit them—yet they combined in such a way to produce a seemingly limitless array of experiences and moves, and to provide opportunities for an alternative, idiosyncratic style of play, which brings to mind nothing so much as chess. Will Wright [creator of the video games Sims and Spore] cited the theory of emergence—the idea that complex systems arise out of the interaction of several simple things. "The hardware wasn't much better than Atari's," he said. "The polish and the depth of the games were. Super Mario was so approachable, so simple, so addictive, and yet so deep."[5] The game's musical score, an entrancing suite by the Nintendo composer Koji Kondo, may be to one generation what "In-A-Gadda-Da-Vida" was to another.[6] 7

Reading Critically

[5] If you have played Super Mario Brothers, do you agree with this assessment?

[6] Look up the original "In-A-Gadda-Da-Vida" song. What generation or era does it belong to?

Jamin Brophy-Warren, who publishes a video-game arts and culture magazine called *Kill Screen*, told me that there is something in the amplitude and dynamic of Mario's jumps—just enough supernatural lift yet also just enough gravitational resistance—that makes the act of performing that jump, over and over, deeply satisfying. He also cited the archetypal quality of Mario's task, that vague feeling of longing and disappointment which undergirds his desperate and recurring quest for the girl. "It's a story of desire," Brophy-Warren said. 8

There are generally two approaches to thinking about games: narratology and ludology. The first emphasizes story, the second play. The next time I played Super Mario, on the Wii (you can order all the vintage games), I found myself in a narratological mode. Mario reminded me of K. and his pursuit of the barmaid Frieda, in Kafka's "The Castle," and of the kind of lost-loved-one dreams that "The Castle" both mimics and instigates. But then a Koopa Troopa got me, and I had the distinct thrill of starting over with the press of a button—quarters hoarded now only for parking meters.❼ If the game was anything, it was unpretentious, and it was better to approach it that way. As Wright had said, "When you play his games, you feel like you're a kid and you're out in the back yard playing in the dirt." 9

UNDERSTANDING DETAILS

1. What did Nintendo make before it made video games? When did the corporate culture of Nintendo begin to change? How did Nintendo end up in the arcade game business?
2. Where did the name Donkey Kong come from? How was Donkey Kong different from earlier video games developed by engineers and programmers?
3. In what way does Super Mario Brothers remind the author of chess?

ANALYZING MEANING

1. Explain what makes Mario's jumps so satisfying. What is an archetype? Explain the "archetypal quality" of Mario's task (paragraph 8).

Reading Critically

❼ What quarters is the author referring to here?

2. What did the game Super Mario Brothers do for Nintendo? What makes the game so captivating?
3. Explain the difference between narratology and ludology. How does the author experience both when he plays Super Mario on the Wii?

DISCOVERING RHETORICAL STRATEGIES

1. What role did the artist Shigeru Miyamoto play in the development of the individual games mentioned in this excerpt and the overall development of Nintendo?
2. Paumgarten uses a number of technical terms associated with gaming, as well as Japanese words, and the names of games and companies with which general readers might have little or no familiarity. How does he accommodate general readers in an essay about a technical subject?
3. Consider the author's use of description in this essay. How do his descriptions contribute to his process analysis? How do you think he feels about the games he is describing?

MAKING CONNECTIONS

1. Compare Paumgarten's use of process analysis with that of Stanley Coren ("Dogs and Monsters"). What differences do you see in their purpose and approach?
2. Paumgarten incorporates a great deal of information into his profile of Shigeru Miyamoto—a brief history of video games, descriptions of specific games, as well as references to literature, psychology, philosophy, and music. Compare how he handles this information with the way Stephen Osborne ("The Lost Art of Waving") and Russell Smith ("Potty-Mouthed and Proud of It") handle explanations, references, and allusions in their essays. What demands does this writing style make on the reader? What are the rewards for the reader?

IDEAS FOR DISCUSSION/WRITING

Preparing to Write

What games do you remember playing as a child? Did you play board games? Card games? Video games? Activity-based games like hide-and-seek? Games of make-believe? What was your favourite game? Why? Have you felt nostalgia for any of these games or any of the games described in this essay? Do you play video games on a regular basis now? Aside from video games, what activities do adults engage in that preserve the qualities of childhood "play"? What qualities of childhood play are missing in these adult activities?

Choosing a Topic

1. Write an essay that explains the object and basic rules of any game, along with its appeal. Include the historical development of the game, if relevant.
2. Choose a character, theme, or genre in popular culture and write a process essay explaining its development over time. For example, you might choose to explore the development of a particular kind of monster such as Godzilla, a genre such as the vampire movie, or a character such as the gangster anti-hero.
3. Write a classification essay outlining the ways that adults "play."

ADAM GOODHEART

How to Mummify a Pharaoh (1995)

Adam Goodheart is an American historian and well-known essayist with a special interest in linking the past and present in his writing. He studied American history and literature at Harvard University, and, since graduating in 1992, has written on a wide range of cultural, political, and historical topics. His work has appeared in *The New York Times*, *National Geographic*, *Smithsonian*, and *The Atlantic*, as well as in various anthologies. He has also appeared on National Public Radio, C-Span, and CNN. He was a founding editor of *Civilization*, the award-winning magazine of the U.S. Library of Congress, and has served as an editorial board member and contributing editor to several American magazines. Goodheart has won numerous awards for his writing, including the Henry Lawson Award for Travel Writing in 2005. In 2006, he was appointed director of Washington College's C.V. Starr Center for the Study of American Experience.

Preparing to Read

This essay about the steps in the mummification process originally appeared in *Civilization* magazine (May/June 1995) in a column entitled "Lost Arts." Other "lost arts" featured in Goodheart's column included "How to Host a Roman Orgy" and "How to Hunt a Woolly Mammoth." Before you begin reading, think about what you know about Ancient Egypt and how you know it. Did you study the pharaohs and pyramids in history class? Have you seen an Egyptian exhibit at a museum? Or do many of your associations come from films like *The Mummy*? As you read Goodheart's essay, pay attention to his tone.

Old Pharaohs never died—they just took really long vacations. Ancient Egyptians believed that at death, a person's spirit, or ka, was forcibly separated from the body. But it returned now and then for a visit, to snack on the food that had been left in the tomb. It was crucial that the body stay as lifelike as possible for eternity—that way the ka (whose life was hard enough already) would avoid reanimating the wrong corpse. So mummification became a fine art, especially where royalty was concerned. These days dead pharaohs are admittedly a bit hard to come by. So if you decide to practice on a friend or close relative, please make [sure] the loved one is fully deceased before you begin. 1

The early stages of the process can be a bit malodorous, so it's recommended you move to a well-ventilated tent. (You'll have trouble breathing anyway since tradition also prescribes you wear the jackal-head mask in honour of Anubis, god of the dead.) After cleansing the body, break the pharaoh's nose by pushing a long iron hook up the nostrils. Left or right, you choose. Then use the hook to remove the contents of the skull. The brain can be discarded since the Egyptians attached no special significance to it. 2

Next, take a flint knife and make a long incision down the left side of the abdomen—actually, it's best to have a friend do this, since the person who cuts open the body must then be pelted with stones to atone for the profanation. After you've stoned your friend, use a bronze knife to remove the pharaoh's internal organs through the incision. Wash them in palm wine as a disinfectant and set them aside to inter later in separate alabaster jars. Leave the heart in place. Egyptians believed it was the seat of consciousness. 3

Once the abdominal cavity is empty, fill it with natron, a natural salt found in the delta of the west bank of the Nile. Heap more natron on until he is completely covered. According to ancient papyrus, he should be left for 42 days after which he will [be] almost completely desiccated.❶ Having removed the natron, anoint the head with frankincense and the body with Sacred oil. Pack the skull and abdomen with myrrh and other spices, and cover the incision with a sheet of gold. 4

For extra life-like effect, you can stuff the corpse's skin with a compound of sawdust, butter and mud. Don't overdo it though. Queen Henettowey, wife of Pinedjem I, was so overstuffed that when archaeologists found her, her face had split open like an old sofa. 5

If you thought mummies wrapped in bedsheets were stuff of B-movies, think again: Even pharaohs were usually wound in strips cut from household linens. Pour molten pine resin over the body; in the course of centuries this will turn the flesh black, glassy and rock hard. While the resin's still tacky, bandage each of the extremities separately; including fingers and toes. Then brush another coat and repeat. (Go easy on the second coat of resin—Tutankhamen stuck to his coffin and had to be chipped out piece by piece.) Amulets can be placed between the layers of 6

Reading Critically

❶ What is meaning of the word *desiccated*?

bandages; a scarab over the heart is the minimum.❷ The last layers should secure the arms and legs to the body. Your mummy is now ready to be entombed in grand style.

A note on sarcophagi: careful name-tagging will prevent embarrassing mix-ups later on. A mummy long thought to be a 21st dynasty princess was recently x-rayed and found to be . . . a pet baboon.❸ 7

Hide your mummy well—you've got more than just tomb-robbers to worry about. In renaissance Europe, powdered mummy was eaten as a remedy for everything from ulcers to epilepsy (though 17th century writers did complain of a "stink in the mouth.") Later, English manufacturers ground up mummies to use as fertilizer, and one entrepreneur from Maine made wrapping paper from mummy bandages. 8

UNDERSTANDING DETAILS

1. How many general steps does Goodheart describe in the mummification process? Make a list of all the required materials and tools. What function did natron serve? What effect does the resin have over time?
2. Why does Goodheart recommend getting a friend to make the incision in the abdomen? Why did the ancient Egyptians discard the brain? Where did they think consciousness resided?
3. How were mummy remains used later in history?

ANALYZING MEANING

1. What was the purpose of mummification, according to Goodheart?
2. Goodheart explains why it is important to label the mummy properly and hide it well. What do his reasons tell us about the attitudes of later civilizations toward Ancient Egyptian culture?
3. How does Goodheart treat his topic? What other kinds of writing were you reminded of when you read this piece? How did Goodheart's tone affect your own attitude toward the topic?

DISCOVERING RHETORICAL STRATEGIES

1. What do you think Goodheart's purpose was in writing this essay? Who do you think he was writing it for?

Reading Critically

❷ What is a scarab? What do you think it represents? Why is this the "minimum"?

❸ What is the author's purpose in using an ellipsis here?

2. Consider the contrast between Goodheart's subject matter and his tone. How does his use of syntax and diction contribute to this contrast?
3. Goodheart chose to address the reader directly in this essay. How would the essay change if he shifted the entire piece from second person to third person point of view? What other changes would he have to make if he wrote the essay in third person?

MAKING CONNECTIONS

1. Compare the tone of Maureen Littlejohn's "You Are a Contract Painkiller" to Goodheart's "How to Mummify a Pharaoh." In what ways are their tones similar? How do they differ?
2. Goodheart and Stephen King ("Why We Crave Horror Movies") both deal with gruesome topics. In what ways are their strategies and writing styles similar? In what ways do they differ?

IDEAS FOR DISCUSSION/WRITING

Preparing to Write

Goodheart frequently writes about history. Write about your interest in history. What did you like or not like about history class in elementary and high school? What eras or cultures were you most interested in? Have you studied history at the post-secondary level? Do you visit museums, and if yes, what exhibits are you particularly drawn to? Do you watch historical films or television programs about history? Do you think that dramatizing historical events or persons on screen allows for a better understanding of history? What disadvantages might there be in learning about history from TV and film?

Choosing a Topic

1. Goodheart has written several essays on the "lost arts" of past civilizations. Write an essay about an "art" you feel you have lost in your own life (such as the lost art of playing outside, or the lost art of summer vacation), or a "lost art" you think our society should revive.
2. Mummies have long been a staple of Hollywood films, along with vampires, werewolves, ghosts, and various prehistoric and futuristic monsters. Write a process essay describing how to defeat or deal with one of these creatures.
3. It has often been noted that the rituals surrounding death are more important for the living than the dead. Write an essay describing the rites and rituals associated with death in your culture and exploring what functions they serve for family and friends of the deceased.

CHAPTER 5

DIVISION/ CLASSIFICATION

Finding Categories

Both division and classification play important roles in our everyday lives: bureau drawers separate one type of clothing from another; kitchen cabinets organize food, dishes, and utensils into proper groups; grocery stores shelve similar items together so shoppers can easily locate what they want to buy; school notebooks with tabs help students divide up their academic lives; newspapers classify local and national events in order to organize a great deal of daily information for the general public; and our own personal classification systems assist us in separating what we like from what we don't so that we can have access to our favourite foods, our favourite cars, our favourite entertainment, our favourite people. The two processes of division and classification are so natural to us, in fact, that we sometimes aren't even aware we are using them.

Defining *Division/Classification*

Division and classification are actually mirror images of each other. Division is the basic feature of process analysis, which we studied in the last chapter: It moves from a general concept to subdivisions of that concept or from a single category to multiple subcategories. Classification works in the opposite direction, moving from specifics to a group with common traits, or from multiple subgroups to a single, larger, and more inclusive category. These techniques work together in many ways. A college, for example, is *divided* into departments (single to multiple), whereas courses are *classified* by department (multiple to single); the medical field is *divided* into specialties, whereas doctors are *classified* by a single specialty; a cookbook is *divided* into chapters, whereas recipes are *classified* according to type; and athletics is *divided* into specific sports, whereas athletes are *classified* by the sport in which they participate. Division is the separation of an idea or an item into its basic parts, such as a home into rooms, a course into assignments, or a job into various duties or responsibilities; classification is the organization of items with similar features into a group or groups, such as identifying all green-eyed people in a large group, cutting out all carbohydrates from your diet, or watching only the aquatic events during the Olympics.

Classification is an organizational system for presenting a large amount of material to a reader or listener. This process helps us make sense of the complex world we live in by letting us work with smaller, more understandable units of that world. Classification must be governed by some clear, logical purpose (such as focusing on all lower-level course requirements), which will then dictate the system of categories to be used. The plan of organization that results should be as flexible as possible, and it should illustrate the specific relationship to each of the other items in a group and of the groups themselves to one another.

As you already know, many different ways of classifying the same elements are possible. If you consider the examples at the outset of this chapter, you will realize that bureau drawers vary from house to house and even from person to person; that no one's kitchen is set up exactly the same way as someone else's; and that grocery stores have similar but not identical systems of food classification. (Think, for instance, of the many different schemes for organizing dairy products, meats, organic foods, etc.) In addition, your friends probably use a method different from yours to organize their school notes; different newspapers vary their presentation of the news; and two professors will probably teach the same course material in divergent ways. We all have distinct and uniquely logical methods of classifying the elements in our own lives.

The following student paragraph about friends illustrates both division and classification. As you read it, notice how the student writer moves back and forth smoothly from general to specific and from multiple to single:

The word *friend* can refer to many different types of relationships. Close friends are "friends" at their very best: people for whom we feel respect, esteem, and, quite possibly, even love. We regard these people and their well-being with kindness, interest, and goodwill; we trust them and will go out of our way to help them. Needless to say, we could all use at least one close friend. Next come "casual friends," people with whom we share a particular interest or activity. The investment of a great amount of time and energy in developing this type of friendship is usually not required, though casual friends often become close friends with the passage of time. The last division of "friend" is most general and is composed of all those individuals whose acquaintance we have made and who feel no hostility toward us. When one is counting friends, this group should certainly be included, since such friendships often develop into "casual" or "close" relationships. Knowing people in all three groups is necessary, however, because all types of friends undoubtedly help us live healthier, happier lives.

Thinking Critically Through Division/Classification

As mentioned, the thinking strategies of division and classification are the flip sides of each other: Your textbook is *divided* into chapters (one item divided into many), but chapters are *classified* (grouped) into sections or units. Your brain performs these mental acrobatics constantly, but to be as proficient at this method of thinking as possible, you need to be aware of the cognitive activities you go through. Focusing on these two companion patterns of thought will develop your skill in dealing with these complex schemes as doing so simultaneously increases your overall mental capabilities.

You might think of division/classification as a driving pattern that goes forward and then doubles back on itself in reverse. Division is a movement from a single concept to multiple categories, while classification involves gathering multiple concepts into a single group. Dividing and/or classifying helps us make sense of our subject by using categories to highlight similarities and differences. In the case of division, you are trying to find what differences break the items into separate groups, while, with classification, you let the similarities among the items help you put the material into meaningful categories. Processing your material in this way helps your readers see your particular subject in a new way and often brings renewed insights to both reader and writer.

Experimenting with division and classification is important to your growth as a critical thinker. It will help you process complex information so that you can understand more fully your options for dealing with material in all subject areas. Practising division and classification separately from other rhetorical modes makes you concentrate on improving this particular pattern of thinking before adding it to your expanding arsenal of critical thinking skills.

1. Describe the people in your class. How could they be divided and classified into groups? What do you learn by looking at the group in this way?
2. Study the table of contents of a magazine that interests you. Into what sections is the magazine divided? What distinguishing features does each section have? Now study the various advertisements in the same magazine. What different categories would you use to classify these ads? List the ads in each category.
3. Make a chart classifying the places where you do your shopping. Explain your classification system to the class.

Reading and Writing Division/ Classification Essays

Writers of division/classification essays must first decide if they are going to break down a topic into many separate parts or group together similar items into one coherent category; a writer's purpose will, of course, guide him or her in this decision. Readers must likewise recognize and understand which of these two parallel operations an author is using to structure an essay. Another important identifying feature of division/classification essays is an explanation (explicit or implicit) of the significance of a particular system of organization.

Reading Division/Classification Essays

- What is the essay's context?
- Does the essay divide and/or classify?

Preparing to Read. As you approach the selections in this chapter, you should study all the material that precedes each essay so you can prepare yourself for your reading. First of all, what hints does the title give you about what you are going to read? To what extent does Alex Boyd reveal in his title his attitude toward graffiti? Who is Will Braun's intended audience in "Seven Criteria for the Adoption of New Technology"? Then, see what you can learn from scanning each essay and reading its synopsis in the Rhetorical Contents.

Also important as you prepare to read the essays in this chapter is your knowledge of each author and the conditions under which each essay was written: What does the biographical material tell you about Daniel J. Levitin's "The Music of My Mind" or Faith Moosang's "Nancy Drew Knows It's Hard"? Knowing where these essays were first published will give you even more information about each author's purpose and audience.

Finally, before you begin to read, answer the Preparing to Read questions, and then think freely for a few minutes about the general topic: How do you make decisions about adopting new technology? Who might need Will Braun's "Seven Criteria for the Adoption of New Technology"? What are some of your own stories about graffiti (Boyd)?

Reading. As you read each essay for the first time, write down your initial reactions to the topic itself, to the preliminary material, to the mood the writer sets, or to a specific incident in the essay. Make associations between the essay and your own experiences.

In addition, create a context for each essay by drawing on the preliminary material you have just read about the essay: What is Alison Gillmor's attitude to emotional excess? What is Alex Boyd saying about the role of graffiti in our society? According to Daniel J. Levitin, what is it about music that makes it pleasing to us?

Also, in this first reading, notice whether the writers divided (split up) or classified (gathered together) their material to make their point. Finally, read the questions after each essay, and let them guide your second reading of the selection.

Rereading. When you read these division/classification essays a second time, notice how the authors carefully match their dominant rhetorical approach (in this case, division or classification) to their purpose in a clear thesis. What, for example, is Gillmor's dominant rhetorical approach to her subject? How does this approach further her purpose? What other rhetorical strategies support her thesis? Then, see how these writers logically present their division or classification systems to their readers, defining new categories as their essays progress. Finally, notice how each writer either implicitly or explicitly explains the significance or value of his or her division/classification system. How does Braun explain his system of organization? How does Levitin help us to anticipate his categories through skimming and scanning his essay? Now, answer the questions after each essay to check your understanding and to help you analyze your reading in preparation for the discussion/writing topics that follow.

For a more complete survey of reading guidelines, you may want to consult the checklist on page 41 of the Introduction.

Writing Division/Classification Essays

- Decide on a purpose/thesis.
- Divide the subject into categories.
- Arrange the categories logically.
- Define each category.
- Explain the significance of your approach.

Preparing to Write. You should approach a division/classification essay in the same way you have begun all your other writing assignments—with some kind of prewriting activity that will help you generate ideas, such as the Preparing to Write questions featured in this chapter. The prewriting techniques outlined in the Introduction on pages 28–34 can help you approach these questions imaginatively. Before you even consider the selection and arrangement of details, you need to explore your subject, choose a topic, and decide on a specific purpose and audience. The best way to explore your subject is to think about it, read about it, and then write about it. Look at it from all possible angles and see what patterns and relationships emerge. To choose a specific topic, you might begin by listing any groups, patterns, or combinations you discover within your subject matter. Your purpose should take shape as you form your thesis, and your audience is probably dictated by the assignment. Making these decisions before you write will make the rest of your task much easier.

Writing. As you begin to write, certain guidelines will help you structure your ideas for a division/classification essay:

1. Declare an overall purpose for your classification.
2. Divide the item or concept you are dealing with into categories.
3. Arrange these categories into a logical sequence.
4. Define each category, explaining the difference between one category and another and showing that difference through specific examples.
5. Explain the significance of your classification system. (Why is it worth reading? What will your audience learn from it?)

All discussion in such an essay should reinforce the purpose stated at the beginning of the theme. Other rhetorical modes—such as narration, example, and comparison/contrast—will naturally be used to supplement your classification.

To make your classification as workable as possible, take special care that your categories do not overlap and that all topics fall into their proper places. If, for example, you were classifying all the jobs performed by students in your writing class, the categories of (1) indoor work and (2) outdoor work would probably be inadequate. Most delivery jobs, for example, fall into both categories. At a pizza restaurant, a florist, or a gift shop, a delivery person's time would be split between indoor and outdoor work. So you would need to design a different classification system to avoid this problem. The categories of (1) indoor work, (2) outdoor work, and (3) a combination of indoor and outdoor work would be much more useful for this task. Making sure your categories don't overlap will help make your classification essays more readable and more accurate.

Rewriting. As you rewrite your division/classification essays, consider carefully the probable reactions of your readers to the form and content of your paper:

- Does my thesis communicate my purpose clearly?
- Have I divided my topic into separate and understandable categories?
- Are these categories arranged logically?
- Are the distinctions between my categories as clear as possible?
- Do I explain the significance of my particular classification system?

More guidelines for writing and rewriting are available on page 42 of the Introduction.

Student Essay: Division/Classification at Work

The following student essay divides skiers into interesting categories based on their physical abilities. As you read it, notice how the student writer weaves the significance of his study into his opening statement of purpose. Also, pay particular attention to his logical method of organization and clear explanation of categories as he moves with ease from multiple to single and back to multiple again throughout the essay.

People on the Slopes

Subject

When I first learned to ski, I was amazed by the shapes who whizzed by me and slipped down trails marked only by a black diamond signifying "most difficult," while others careened awkwardly down the "bunny slopes." These skiers, I discovered, could be divided into distinct categories—for my own entertainment and for the purpose of finding appropriate skiing partners.

Thesis statement

Overall purpose

First category

Definition

First are the poetic skiers. They glide down the mountainside silently with what seems like no effort at all. They float from side to side on the intermediate slopes, their knees bent perfectly above parallel skis, while their sharp skills allow them to bypass slower skiers with safely executed turns at remarkable speeds.

Supporting details

Second category

Definition

The crazy skiers also get down the mountain quickly, but with a lot more noise attending their descent. At every hill, they yell a loud "Yahoo!" and slam their skis into the snow. These go-for-broke athletes always whiz by faster than everyone else, and they especially seem to love the crowded runs where they can slide over the backs of other people's skis. I often find crazy skiers in mangled messes at the bottoms of steep hills, where they are yelling loudly, but not the famous "Yahoo!"

Supporting details (with humour)

Transition

Third category

Definition

After being overwhelmed by the crazy skiers, I am always glad to find other skiers like myself: the average ones. We are polite on the slopes, concentrate on improving our technique with every run, and ski the beginner slopes only at the beginning of the day to warm up. We go over the moguls (small hills) much more cautiously than the crazy or poetic skiers, but we still seek adventure

Supporting detail (comparative)

with a slight jump or two each day. We remain a silent majority on the mountain.

Transition

Fourth category

Below us in talent, but much more evident on the mountainside, are what I call the eternal beginners. These skiers stick to the same beginner slope almost every run of every day during their vacation. Should they venture onto an intermediate slope, they quickly assume the snowplough position (a pigeon-toed stance) and never leave it. Eternal beginners weave from one side of the run to the other and hardly ever fall, because they proceed so slowly; however, they do yell quite a bit at the crazies who like to run over the backs of their skis.

Definition

Supporting details

Transition

Having always enjoyed people-watching, I have fun each time I am on the slopes observing the myriad of skiers around me. I use these observations to pick out possible ski partners for myself and others. Since my mother is an eternal beginner, she has more fun skiing with someone who shares her interests than with my dad, who is a poetic skier with solitude on his mind. After taking care of Mom, I am free to find a partner I'll enjoy. My sister, the crazy skier of the family, just heads for the rowdiest group she can find! As the years go by and my talents grow, I am trusting my perceptions of skier types to help me find the right partner for life on and off the slopes. No doubt watching my fellow skiers will always remain an enjoyable pastime.

Significance of classification system

Concluding remarks

Some Final Thoughts on Division/Classification

The essays collected in this chapter use division and/or classification as their primary organizing principle. All of these essays show both techniques at work to varying degrees. As you read, you might also want to be aware of the other rhetorical modes that support these division/classification essays, such as description and definition. Finally, pay particular attention to how these authors bring significance to their systems of classification and, as a result, to the essays themselves.

DIVISION/CLASSIFICATION IN REVIEW

Reading Division/Classification Essays

Preparing to Read

✓ What assumptions can I make from the essay's title?
✓ What do I think the general mood of the essay will be?
✓ What are the essay's purpose and audience?
✓ What does the synopsis tell me about the essay?
✓ What can I learn from the author's biography?
✓ Can I predict the author's point of view toward the subject?

Reading

✓ What is the context of the essay?
✓ Did the author divide or classify?

Rereading

✓ How does division or classification help the author accomplish his or her purpose?
✓ What other rhetorical strategies does the author use?
✓ How does the writer explain the significance of his or her division/classification system?

Writing Division/Classification Essays

Preparing to Write

✓ What is my purpose?
✓ Who is my audience?

Writing

✓ Do I declare an overall purpose for my essay?
✓ Do I divide my subject into distinct categories?
✓ Do I arrange these categories into a logical sequence?
✓ Do I clearly define each category?
✓ Do I explain the significance of my approach?

Rewriting

✓ Does my thesis communicate my purpose clearly?
✓ Have I divided my topic into clear, separate categories?
✓ Are these categories arranged logically?
✓ Do I explain the significance of my classification system?

ALISON GILLMOR

Repress Yourself (2006)

Alison Gillmor studied at the University of Winnipeg and at York University, where she obtained an M.A. in art history. She has taught art history at the University of Winnipeg, and her articles and reviews have appeared in *The Walrus*, *The Globe and Mail*, *enRoute*, and *Azure*, and on **www.CBC.ca**. She is currently the film critic for the *Winnipeg Free Press*.

Preparing to Read

In this essay, Alison Gillmor discusses emotionally cool and inhibited characters from *CSI* and *Desperate Housewives*. If you watch these shows, think about your favourite characters. Why do you prefer these characters over the others? What characters from other TV shows do you like? Do you agree with commentators like Gillmor who believe we have lost the values of modesty and decorum? What are the negative consequences of living in a society that values modesty and propriety over freedom of expression?

Dr. Goldfine: *Bree, how does this reconciliation have a chance if the two of you can't be honest about the innermost parts of your lives?* 1

Bree: *We're, um, wasps, Dr. Goldfine. Not acknowledging the elephant in the room is what we do best.* 2

Bree Van De Kamp is the most quietly desperate of the *Desperate Housewives*. As played by the exquisitely uptight Marcia Cross, Bree spent the first season silently navigating marital problems with husband Rex. She has since survived Rex's sudden death—after which her only public sign of grief was a series of stunning black outfits—and accepted a dubious marriage proposal because she felt it would have been rude to decline. ("Obviously there is a downside to having good manners," as she later explains to Dr. Goldfine.) The buttoned-up Bree may not be as conventionally sexy as her barely dressed neighbour Gabrielle, but she exudes a certain steely eroticism. Check out any fan forum and you'll find fired-up admirers waiting for that preternaturally neat red hair to be mussed. 3

Meanwhile, over at the Las Vegas crime lab, Gil Grissom is hot. Despite being middle-aged and a bit pudgy, despite geeky hobbies such as entomology,❶ despite a set of emotional inhibitions that would bring an ox to its knees, the head of the *CSI* graveyard shift (as played by William Petersen) is way, way hot. At csi-forensics.com, one of the many websites that encourage fans to post their fictional expansions of the show's characters, Gil is at least as big a draw as hipster Greg, and much bigger than all-American frat-boy Nick, or tall, cool Warrick. Of particular interest to the fan-fic crowd is the unexpressed relationship between Gil and Sara Sidle, which has been confined mostly to significant glances over blood-spatter patterns and—on one memorably romantic occasion—some deeply submerged flirting while the two tracked the insect infestation of a dead pig. 4

So why are these characters, who at one time might have been dismissed as charmless, turning out to be this season's sex symbols? Could prime-time TV—of all things—be helping to re-brand reticence?❷ 5

The values of privacy, modesty, discretion, and restraint have taken a hit in the last forty years. This distrust of emotional reserve is partly a hold-over from the 1960s, when failure to voice even stray feelings and thoughts was considered hypocritical and phony. An ideological divide hardened into rigid stereotypes about who is expected to wear their hearts on their sleeves and who is expected to tuck them tidily into breast pockets. Conservatives supposedly support a collective stiff upper lip, while liberals believe in free-to-be-you-and-me emotionalism. Men are evidently from Mars, a planet where communication consists of Gary Cooperesque "yups" and "nopes," while women are caring and sharing Venusians. Wasps are expected to stare mutely into their drinks, while the sons and daughters of the Mediterranean engage in the loud, wildly gestural fights so beloved by the Italian neo-realists. All rich people are stuffy and stiff, while all poor people are given to exuberant, spontaneous outbursts of dancing, like the steerage passengers on James Cameron's *Titanic*. Young people routinely embark on romantic affairs by saying, "Let's promise to always tell each other everything," while their 6

Reading Critically

❶ What is entomology?

❷ What does Gillmor mean by "re-brand reticence"?

more cautious elders have retreated to the fallback "don't ask, don't tell" position.

7 These either/or categories put progressive repressives like me in a bind. If we admit that over-emotionalism leaves us feeling faint and exhausted, we risk being aligned with a whole set of values that we might not actually embrace (if we were given to embracing at all, which, generally speaking, we are not). Fortunately, recent blips on the pop-culture radar seem to be offering a way to rehabilitate reserve without coming off as completely pompous. Where the control of passion was once viewed as hopelessly square, it can now be seen as sexy, smart, and self-aware. Done right, emotional repression could be the new cool.❸

8 Emotional coolness has a history. The Stoics❹ believed that while we cannot control external events, we can control our emotional responses to them through the exercise of reason. (Stoicism saw a brief millennial revival with the release of Tom Wolfe's *A Man in Full*, in which the writings of Epictetus inspire a stoic televangelistic crusade, and *Gladiator*, in which the aging Marcus Aurelius praises the virtues of forbearance and fortitude while a stripped-to-the-waist Russell Crowe acts on them. In the end, though, contemporary North American culture had a hard time sustaining a philosophy that declares that "wealth is the greatest of human sorrows." In his discourses on the virtues of the Renaissance courtier, Baldassare Castiglione advocated modesty, gentleness, grace, good sense, and discretion (along with the abilities to run, jump, swim, ride, throw darts, cast stones, vault, wrestle, play tennis, speak the classical languages, and compose poetry). In keeping with his belief that extreme positions contain their opposites, Castiglione argued for both emotion and reason, which he felt could be reconciled through the virtue of temperance.❺

9 Later, the Victorians became the image of emotional propriety; their very name is now synonymous with prudery and primness, though the layered realities of Victorian life actually illustrate how complex the balance between emotion and expression can be. While middle-class Victorians believed that some feelings should not enter into polite conversation, they could

---

Reading Critically

❸ How do you think emotional repression can be "done right"?

❹ Who were the Stoics? What era were they from?

❺ How would you explain this sentence in your own words?

also—in modern terms—turn into sentimental mush balls, weeping publicly over the death of Dickens' Little Nell or writing letters replete with flowery declarations of friendship. Queen Victoria herself took her protracted private mourning for Prince Albert to almost necrophiliac[6] extremes.

10 Over the centuries, artists and thinkers have characterized this tension in various ways: reason vs. passion, mind vs. body, super-ego vs. id. The current skirmish involves neuroscientists who are searching for the hard-wired emotions that enable the human species to survive vs. those postmodernists who view emotions as social constructions. Apparently, in whatever way the human heart has been mapped out, the control of feeling has never been as neat or complete as the Stoics would have wished.

11 Emotional expression, meanwhile, has not always been as tiresome as it has become in our full-disclosure culture. When the Romantics proclaimed that "Feeling is all!" it meant something, and their exploration of the individual psyche and its most powerful emotions—sorrow, awe, ecstasy, longing—was fired by great-souled ambition. This revolutionary fervour seems to have dwindled. Rather than expanding the self to meet the world, latter-day romantics have been shrinking the world to fit the self. Leftover Romanticism has been topped up with misreadings of Freud, who has been brought in to champion emotional anarchy in ways the good bourgeois Viennese gentleman could never have anticipated.[7] André Breton and the Surrealists hoped that Freud's theory of dreams and the unconscious would waken humankind to complete social, sexual, and emotional liberation, something Freud found vaguely embarrassing. He himself was content with the rather more modest project of converting "neurotic misery into ordinary unhappiness."

12 "Ordinary unhappiness" would never cut it in the American self-help movement, of course. Postwar pop psychology's tendency to zero in on instant personal fulfillment reinforced the idea that any thwarting of emotion could be instantly converted into unhealthy neurosis or even physical disease. Amid this emotional free-for-all, our culture began to jettison the idea of decorum, the notion that displays of feeling should occasionally be

---

Reading Critically

[6] What is a necrophiliac?

[7] Explain what Gillmor is saying in this sentence.

circumscribed by time, place, or audience—that not everything needs to be expressed, for instance, "in front of the children," on a cell phone in a crowded elevator, at the wedding of one's former lover, or during a teary appearance on daytime TV. We increasingly used self-expression as a justification for all sorts of bad behaviour on the grounds that to do anything other than what our natural feeling dictates is hypocritical.

But, really, what's wrong with a little hypocrisy, wonders Judith Martin, a.k.a. Miss Manners, North America's best-known arbiter of etiquette. Though occasionally expected to pronounce on matters of fish-knife placement, Martin spends much more time dealing with the moral foundations of civilized society. Within this framework, she finds social hypocrisy vastly preferable to expressions of unkindness, no matter how existentially authentic they may be.[8] As she writes in the modestly titled *Miss Manners Rescues Civilization*: "People seem to have an inordinate amount of interest nowadays in their own feelings. This does not strike Miss Manners as quite decent. First they put an enormous effort into examining themselves, in the hope of discovering what their feelings actually are. . . . Then they act on those feelings. This requires no thought at all. 13

"All of this puzzles Miss Manners, who always knows exactly how she feels, and considers the question of how and when to express or to act upon one's feelings to be a highly complex subject—namely, etiquette.["] Martin wishes to remind her "gentle readers" of the difference between feelings, to which we are all entitled, and the notion that all feelings must be yanked, half-formed and gasping, into the open air.[9] 14

We should make clear that those of us who find reticence sexy—let's call ourselves the New Repressives—are not advocating cold-fishiness of any sort. We seek not to extinguish emotions but to focus them by using reflection, self-knowledge, and the judicious ability to occasionally shut the hell up. We're for feeling passionately but expressing selectively, because it's in this gap that interesting things happen. 15

Reading Critically

[8] What is meant by the phrase "no matter how existentially authentic they may be"?

[9] What kind of image does the phrase "the notion that all feelings must be yanked, half-formed and gasping, into the open air" invoke?

The last decade has established the tedium of hyperemotionalism with a queasy display of over-sharing celebrities and tell-all autobiographies, chair-throwing talk shows and invasive reality TV, and the cyber-exhibitionism of blogging. We may have reached a tipping point, though, if the recent fascination with buttoned-up TV characters is any indication. It's doubtful that this development marks a pop-culture paradigm shift. It's probably not even a trend. Emotional subtlety and stringent self-analysis will likely remain the territory of Booker Prize winners and Joan Didion memoirs. But the mass media's puppy-like attention span has seized on the prickly pleasures of uptightness—at least for a moment. 16

Consider the contrasting celebrity trajectories of Tom Cruise and Madonna. Though he's known for his portrayals of callow, cocky operators, Cruise once maintained a sense of mysterious depth through the ruthless gatekeeping of his public image. And then suddenly there he was, getting all schmoopy with Katie Holmes and scaring Oprah by going down on his knees, pounding the floor, leaping on the furniture, and screaming his love on national television. (According to urbandictionary.com, the phrase "jumping the couch" is now used to describe "a defining moment when you know someone has gone off the deep end.") Meanwhile, we have Madonna, the "Express Yourself" girl once known for nude hitch-hiking. With her cool eye for zeitgeist zig-zags, she sensed that total exposure had temporarily exhausted itself and embarked on a calculated dalliance with British propriety and reserve. In last August's *Vogue* the reinvented Madge was pictured on the English estate she shares with husband Guy Ritchie, feeding the chickens in a ladylike dress and cardie.[10] 17

Public reaction to these PR reversals suggests a new mood. Cruise nearly scuttled the *War of the Worlds* publicity push when his fans discovered that, um, actually, they didn't want to see "the real Tom" and his icky, inappropriate public displays of affection after all. The newly demure Mrs. R., on the other hand, piqued our interest—even if it was only to marvel at her unabashed media manipulation. 18

Madonna's passing passion for primness—she's already reworked herself as a disco diva—may have been a shrewd 19

Reading Critically

[10] What is a cardie?

show of self-marketing. And *CSI* producer Jerry Bruckheimer, known for loud, bombastic movies such as *Armageddon* and *Pearl Harbor*, is probably backing his uncommunicative investigators for strategic reasons. As shrewd pop-culture prognosticators,[11] they have both seized on emotional repression as a novelty, a cool contrast to the emotionally overheated effects of most mass media, including the web.

20 Cyber-theorist Rebecca Blood's early optimism that the blogosphere could be a community dedicated to self-awareness, self-reliance, and critical thinking was a wonderful leap of Rousseauian idealism, and the blogs that live up to that standard are models of democratic social engagement, with writing fresh enough to merit Blood's definition of blogging as "a coffeehouse conversation in text." Unfortunately, most of blog-world material doesn't warrant this kind of optimism. Instead, it offers sullen and adolescent evidence that personal expression does not necessarily lead to a greater understanding of the self and others. Blood believes that "each of us [bloggers] speaks in an individual voice of an individual vision," but just try googling the phrase "I hate my mom" or "Nobody understands me" or "My love life sucks" and see how many hits you get—and how drearily alike the entries are. Many bloggers seem to be caught in circular thinking and world-obliterating self-absorption.[12] They can't be doing anything for their audience, and it's not even clear what they're doing for themselves.

21 It's hardly surprising that it is British researchers who have discovered that venting may not necessarily be good for you. According to a 2004 study of 153 Staffordshire University students, people who write in journals—the online diary's low-tech cousin—are more likely to suffer from insomnia, head-aches, social dysfunction, anxiety, indigestion, and generally feeling crappy. The most morose are those who go back and reread old entries. Psychologist Elaine Duncan of Glasgow Caledonian University speculates that rather than providing a cathartic experience, diary-keeping traps many of its practitioners in a "ruminative, repetitive cycle."[13]

Reading Critically

[11] What do prognosticators do?

[12] Do you agree that bloggers "seem to be caught in circular thinking and world-obliterating self-absorption"? Why or why not?

[13] Have you ever kept a journal? If so, would you agree or disagree with this speculation?

22 Emotion usually benefits from editing. Unmediated feeling has a certain raw power, but once it's out there it has only one place to go. Its limitations remind us of George Lucas's legendary piece of advice for the actors in the original *Star Wars* movie: "Faster, more intense." Reality television is a good example of a genre that has gotten about as fast and intense as fast and intense can be, without getting any better.⓮ Turning the camera on friends and family as they indulge in psychological slapfests of resentment, envy, self-pity, petulance, spite, and self-entitlement, these shows routinely remind us that many feelings are unhelpful or just plain unseemly. *The Jerry Springer Show* ("I Slept With My Sister's Fiancé," "Wives vs. Mistresses!") is an instant, ice-water antidote to the warm, fuzzy idea that any emotion is valid simply because one happens to feel it.

23 It may seem counterintuitive, but emotional expression is often one-dimensional, while sublimation has a thousand fascinating faces—irony, enigma, understatement, indirection, Cole Porter-style insouciance,⓯ and blessed quiet. One of the advantages of scripted dramas, which have recently made a hard-fought comeback against reality TV, is that characters can finally be ordered to stop talking. Prime time is now awash in meaningful silences. Along with the familiar stoics of *Law & Order* reruns (the sardonic Lennie Briscoe; the stiff, upright Benjamin Stone; Adam Schiff, the weariest man on television), we have the down-to-business gang at *Without a Trace*, led by the literally and figuratively tight-lipped Jack Malone (Anthony LaPaglia), and the oh-so-complicated Jack Bauer (Kiefer Sutherland) of *24*.

24 The model of Gil Grissom's remote paterfamilias leading his crime-lab family has proven so effective that the expanding *CSI* franchise has continued to replicate this dynamic, first with Horatio Caine (David Caruso) in Miami and later with Mac Taylor (Gary Sinise) in New York. Each *CSI* episode presents viewers with a puzzle about how some poor stiff came to die, but the larger, underlying mystery involves the living characters—their feelings, their pasts, and their tortuously tamped-down relationships. Eschewing the common TV practice of lunkheaded exposition, the writers tease out backstories gradually, often over many episodes or even

---

Reading Critically

⓮ Do you enjoy reality TV? Explain why you like or dislike it.

⓯ What is insouciance?

years. (Sara has daddy issues; Warrick was a compulsive gambler.) Everyone gets one case a season to take personally—because of parallels with some hidden desire or past trauma—but the rest of the time the staffers are expected to behave with terse professionalism.

CSI treats its characters with a certain tact, allowing them private lives that remain private, and the show's consistently high ratings over five seasons suggest that audiences are intrigued rather than frustrated by this emotional circumspection. Tired of having every subplot handed to them, people want to make discoveries for themselves. 25

In his landmark 1960 work, *Art and Illusion*, art historian E.H. Gombrich argued for the importance of "the beholder's share," suggesting that ambiguity allows viewers to actively engage with a work, to indulge in the pleasure of projection, to exercise their imaginations, and—on a slightly less elevated plane—to be flattered by the feeling of being "in the know." *CSI*'s fervent fan-fiction following is a cyber-age confirmation of Gombrich's ideas. These viewers are driven to fill the show's suggestive gaps with their own stories, and it's no coincidence they like the emotionally cagey characters the best. (Fan-fiction has a significant history with emotional repression: in the 1930s, a group calling itself the Baker Street Irregulars began writing stories about that desiccated calculating machine, Sherlock Holmes. *Spockanalia,* an early fanzine first published in 1967, was devoted to *Star Trek*'s resident rationalist, Mr. Spock.) 26

The ambiguity of *Desperate Housewives* lies in its odd tone. Is it wacky comedy or dark mystery, a satirical take on middle-class hypocrisy or an affectionate homage to the women who hold suburban life together? *Desperate Housewives* exposes Wisteria Lane's dark secrets (the murderer in the minivan, the country-club prostitute, the noises in the basement), but it also celebrates such retro notions as "the polite fiction" and "the social obligation." TV audiences seem to be fascinated by the mix of hidden sin and surface decorum—a tone that soap operas invented of course—and this uneven show works best when it's almost impossible to tease them apart. Take a scene in which Bree politely plays out her hostile relationship with son Andrew by blackmailing him into attending a dinner party. He's stunned, but she acts as if she's merely being punctilious.[16] "You don't know the lengths I'd 27

Reading Critically

[16] How is Bree acting?

go to for even seating," Bree tells him, and, you know, we really don't know.

28 Freud believed that the requirements of civilization hunker down on our instincts "like a garrison in a conquered town." If it's true that we're condemned to this internal division, then the gap between emotion and expression is more than just a way to heat up TV ratings: it's a place where we can learn something essential about what it means to be human. Within this view, emotion and expression aren't in stark opposition; they're in a tricky, tantalizing, revealing relationship. Words left unspoken, feelings kept constrained take on a different kind of eloquence. If we have to live with the forces of repression and denial, then why not find a way to explore, even enjoy them?

29 "You'd settle for that?" Dr. Goldfine asks Bree. "A life filled with repression and denial?"

30 "And dinner parties," she replies. "Don't forget the dinner parties."

UNDERSTANDING DETAILS

1. What stereotypes arose out of the sixties? Who falls on the side of emotional expression? Who falls on the side of repression?
2. Gillmor gives us a history of emotional coolness, from the Stoics to modern times. What does each era have in common? Who are the New Repressives? What do they stand for?
3. What do the career trajectories of Tom Cruise and Madonna suggest to the author? How does the popularity of *CSI* support her theory?

ANALYZING MEANING

1. How does the original Romantic emotionalism differ from the expression of emotion today? Why was decorum jettisoned by postwar pop psychology?
2. Why does Gillmor say that emotion benefits from editing? Why is sublimation more interesting to her than full expression?
3. Explain E.H. Gombrich's theory of "the beholder's share" (paragraph 26). How do "emotionally cagey" characters fit in to this theory?

DISCOVERING RHETORICAL STRATEGIES

1. What kinds of research does Gillmor use to develop her classification? Does she make a distinction between "high" art and popular culture?

2. Where does Gillmor use formal diction? Where does she use informal diction? How is her use of diction appropriate for this essay?
3. Gillmor explores a wide range of examples and ideas in this essay. Analyze the transitions Gillmor uses to link these examples and ideas. Where are these transitions most often located?

MAKING CONNECTIONS

1. Compare the attitudes of Gillmor's "New Repressives" with the attitude of the people described in Cynara Geissler's "Fat Acceptance"? How is the behaviour Geissler describes different from the behaviour Gillmor is advocating?
2. How do you think Gillmor would react to Evelyn Lau's essay "More and More"? How might she react to Russell Smith's defence of profanity ("Potty-Mouthed and Proud of It"?)

IDEAS FOR DISCUSSION/WRITING

Preparing to Write

Write freely about your favourite television character. What do you like best about this character? Is this character emotionally expressive or restrained? Would you identify yourself as one of Gillmor's "New Repressives" or one of the "Leftover Romantics"? Do you write in a journal? Why or why not? How do you feel when others express strong feelings in public?

Choosing a Topic

1. Do you agree with Miss Manners, who finds social hypocrisy vastly preferable to expressions of unkindness? Write an essay illustrating your argument with a range of examples.
2. Gillmor analyzes several TV programs to demonstrate changing attitudes toward emotional expression. Choose one or two other popular TV programs that support a trend you have noticed in society. Write an essay that explains the trend, using details of the TV programs to support your analysis.
3. Gillmor explores the tension between expression and restraint. In an essay, classify different genres of something (such as television programs, movies, or music) in order to illustrate the tension between two other opposing ideas (such as authenticity vs. "selling out," "real" vs. scripted, liberal vs. conservative, etc.).

WILL BRAUN

Seven Criteria for the Adoption of New Technology (2010)

Will Braun grew up in a Mennonite farm family in Manitoba, where he says that he was taught to care about the world around him. That care has manifested itself in his life in a number of ways, including his decision in 2002 to stop flying. Braun uses his bicycle as a primary mode of transportation and when invited to a festival in Kitchener, Ontario, chose to ride his bike over 1300 kilometres to get there rather than fly from his home in Winnipeg.

A writer, editor, and organic vegetable farmer, Braun and Aiden Enns launched *Geez Magazine* in 2005, an ad-free magazine for "the over-churched, out-churched, un-churched and maybe even the un-churchable" (**www.geezmagazine.org/about**) and the source of the essay here. Braun now works as the staff person for the Interfaith Task Force on Northern Hydro Development.

Preparing to Read

In this essay, Will Braun, who was key in spearheading the *Geez Magazine* "De-Motorize Your Soul" campaign, contemplates whether he and his wife should get a car. Before reading, think about owning a car. Do you own a car? If so, why? What do you use your car for? What would your life be like without your car? How did you choose the car you have? If you do not own a car, why not? Have you owned a car in the past or do you aspire to own one in the future? Do you participate in a car-sharing program?

Technology stresses me right out. Not so much the high-tech stuff, but the very notion of stuff itself; this phenomenon of technology that churns out better freezer bags, nicer church pulpits and an endless (literally) array of other stuff. Technology is all about evermore stuff. I'm stressed by this seemingly unstoppable momentum. And by my inability to resist.❶ 1

Reading Critically

❶ What is Braun unable to resist? Why do you think he can't resist?

As the world rushes toward an overcrowded but new and improved grave full of "articulated task lamps" with "industrial style charm," wines with "velvety" appeal, and cordless window shades that are "safe® for children and pets" (that's just one section of today's paper), I find my supposedly simple-living self caught on the same slow slide toward more. The bike I ride now is better than the one I had a year ago. Before long I'll need a new computer, and it will be better than the one I have now. The force of inevitability takes over. 2

What is one to do? How exactly, and realistically, can a person resist, or cope, or somehow do something other than just get swept along? My impulse is to rant. 3

But invective❷ doesn't help much with the practical decisions we all face regularly. More helpful I propose, would be a systematic means to assess the pros and cons of particular technologies. This is precisely what is missing from our culture of more. Our belief in progress is unquestioning, dogmatic. To question is to be "backward" (a term that could as easily be a compliment if we were at peace with the past). But question we must, so I set out to establish criteria for the acquisition of new technology. 4

I gave my search a practical context. My wife and I need to decide whether to get a car. Neither of us has ever owned one (though we've done some intensive borrowing). We live in the middle of a small city, and thus can manage well without. But we feel called and compelled to move to the rurals,❸ where carlessness is much trickier. I dread the decision. 5

I decided to consult three sources: Wendell Berry, who is a Kentucky farmer and thinker; Donald Kraybill, who is a Pennsylvania sociologist with 30 years experience studying the Amish; and David Kline, an Ohio farmer, writer and Amish bishop.❹ 6

The plain folk

I chose Kline because I wanted to better understand how Amish groups decide which technologies to adopt. Contrary to the stigma, the Amish are not stuck in time, but are ever adapting to the broader society. 7

Reading Critically

❷ What does *invective* mean?

❸ What are "the rurals"?

❹ Do these seem like good, credible sources to consult? Explain why or why not.

Often, observers of the Amish ridicule the seeming inconsistencies in their approach to technology. For instance, Kline spoke with me from a phone "shanty," or homemade booth, located about 300 metres from his house and shared with neighbours. These shanties are permitted, but phones in homes are not. Similarly incongruous, you can't own a car but you can ride in your non-Amish neighbour's car in certain circumstances. Restrictions on technology vary widely among the 40 Amish sub-groups, but they all draw lines that some observers consider duplicitous. 8

To me, these lines do not demonstrate hypocrisy but an intentional process of selecting technology based on certain criteria. "These people are not Luddites,"❺ says Kraybill, "they are selectively making decisions and adapting." To dismiss this adaptation system is to imply that the mainstream approach of embracing every new gadget without reservation somehow exhibits superior ethical integrity. 9

Journey backward

I have long admired the Amish, usually from a distance, for their seemingly unmatched ability to control the forces of progress. So I was eager to speak with Kline. 10

He talks freely about the varying and evolving restrictions on electricity, cars, tractors and cell phones among different Amish groups. He tells me of his own "journey backward," from a more lenient group to a more conservative one. And he tells me about two young men in his area who recently gave up their cars when they were baptized into the church. Kline, it turns out, did the same thing 45 years ago. 11

Young people are given freedom to experiment with worldly ways, and about 85 to 90 percent return to Amish life.❻ "I have no yearning for it," Kline says now of car ownership. His tone is light, gracious and convincing. He explains the advantages horses have over cars. They limit the size of farms, in contrast to the unlimited expansion of the agribusiness model. They limit the distances people can travel, thus contributing to cohesion of family and community. 12

Reading Critically

❺ Explain what Luddites are.

❻ Why do you think so many return to Amish life?

"The car would pull the local community apart," Kraybill explains in his book *The Riddle of Amish Culture.* "The car was perfect for a complicated, individuated and mobile society," but the Amish are a "stable, simple, local people." 13

The Amish, he writes, "intuitively grasp [technology's] long-term social impact," and impacts on family and community are of particular concern. "If it's bad for the family, you don't have it," Kline says. He gives the example of phones in homes, which he says would interrupt and deteriorate family life. I can't argue — when the phone rings while I'm reading to my 3-year-old son, he intuitively grasps the social impact of technology. 14

But still, I tolerate the interruptions rather than submit to the sort of limitations the Amish accept. Submission and limitation are particularly unpopular notions in our culture, but when Kline speaks positively about them, I find it a refreshing alternative to the limitlessness and individuality of my society. And when he says of his low-tech, limited life: "I don't feel deprived at all, I feel free," the sparkle in his voice leaves little doubt.❼ 15

With this, I begin drafting criteria about family, living in smaller circles and limitation. 16

A good technology

I glean further criteria from the writings of Wendell Berry (who Kline credits with keeping him on the Amish path when, as a young man, modern agriculture tempted him). In Berry's essay, "A Good Scythe," he compares a well-designed, well-crafted Marugg hand scythe to a gas-powered weed eater he had purchased. He compares, among other factors, weight, cost, safety, ease of use, and noise. The hand scythe wins in most categories. 17

But what interests me most is the notion of systematic assessment itself, as well as the pleasure, satisfaction and affection that Berry expresses in writing about the good scythe. He wants his tools to be a joy to use. This appeals to me, so I add it to my criteria.❽ 18

I also re-read Berry's 1987 essay, "Why I am not Going to Buy a Computer." Or at least I try. A few paragraphs in, I become bogged down in feelings of inadequacy. The guy uses a pencil 19

Reading Critically

❼ In what ways might submission and limitation be freeing?

❽ Do you agree that tools should be a joy to use?

and prefers to write during the day, when electric light is not needed, because, he says: "I would hate to think that my work as a writer could not be done without a direct dependence on strip-mined coal." That's an intimidating degree of integrity. My laptop and my energy provider are not ethically justifiable, but I remain addicted.

20 Feeling the stress of the decisions and compromises forced upon us by technological progress, I skip to the end of the essay where he lists "standards for technological innovation." I add the one about the quality of work done by an item to my own list and decide it's time to try applying my criteria to my family's pending car decision.

A good car?

1. How would the technology affect dynamics of family and community? Having a car in the country would allow us to connect with friends and non-immediate family who live beyond biking range. It would decrease the likelihood of connecting with people geographically nearest to us, including one another. It would contribute to a more scattered existence (I don't deal well with scatteredness). It would require money, and thus we would spend more time working and less with family. 21
2. Would it help me live in smaller, more stable circles? This one is easier: No. 22
3. Is there a way to limit it, or would it push us down the slippery slope to even more? Sharing a vehicle with another household would be one limit—we couldn't just grab the keys and go. Using veggie oil for fuel would be another limiting (read: inconveniencing) factor. On the other hand, it would require further purchases: fuel, tools, tires, repairs, possibly fuzzy dice (depending on local culture[9]), lubricants, insurance and surely more. Yikes. 23
4. Drawing on Berry: would it do "work that is clearly and demonstrably better" than the thing it replaces? That's tricky. There's a reason Kline says the car is "probably the most loved thing in the world" – it has some huge advantages over human- or animal-powered transportation. Does that make the work it 24

Reading Critically

[9] What local culture might require the purchase of fuzzy dice?

does "better"? Is it a qualitatively better way to move over the earth? Measuring betterness is more complicated here than in Berry's scythe example.[10]

5. Who would want us to get it, and who would not? (I come up with this criterion myself.) My parents would probably be glad for visits from the grandkids, as would the grandkids. Friends in the city would enjoy seeing us. People to whom we would potentially sell and deliver garden produce would appreciate us having a car (or van or truck). Rex W. Tillerson would be in favour. He's the CEO of Exxon. The local mechanic, tire shop and car wash would also benefit. Those not in favour, theoretically, would include people negatively affected by oil extraction, people concerned with climate change and possibly our children, at least down the road, when climate change visits consequences upon them. 25

6. Would it bring joy and satisfaction to life? Would we like it? I would surely enjoy benefits of an automobile, but I find no pleasure in driving per se. It brings me none of the good energy I get from biking or walking. A car would cause me guilt, concern about theft, worries about breakdowns and stress about ongoing costs.[11] 26

7. Does it represent what I believe in? No. 27

Oh shit. The car clearly fails the test, but I just don't know if we can do the rural thing without wheels. I should have married into the Amish.[12] 28

Roadkill

The criteria help me see consequences and values more clearly. But I also fear the force of technological inevitability will run those values over, like roadkill on hot asphalt. Car culture is a hard force to overcome, especially on your own. "You would probably need an automobile," Kline tells me, "because you don't have the community we have." Surrounded by resourceful Amish neighbours and businesses, he can get almost everything he needs, including socialization, within a horse-friendly radius. 29

Reading Critically

[10] Why is measuring betterness more complicated here?

[11] How do you feel about driving? Do you share Braun's sentiments?

[12] Why does Braun say that he should have married into the Amish?

That's one of the lessons of the Amish, Kraybill tells me, "you can't do it alone."

30 So our family's options are not great: 1) Remain carless urbanites and just sit on our rural calling. 2) Attempt a carless rural life of relative isolation, considerable inconvenience, economic fragility, but transportational integrity. 3) Become morally compromised, but conveniently motorized ruralites. I don't know what we will do.

Horse-drawn

31 I knew from the beginning that criteria alone are of little use unless I can find it in myself to die to my worldly desires,[13] as the Amish would say, when an item fails the test. I think of it in terms of being drawn by values more compelling than convenience, mobility and efficiency. A critical reaction to technology is not enough; one must be drawn to something that truly seems better than what progress offers. The Amish genius – by which I do not mean to imply perfection – is not a sophisticated critique of technology but an adherence to long-lived convictions about separation from the influences of the world, finding meaning in family and community, humility, simplicity, loving others and reliance on God. Kline's voice does not become animated when talking about the dangers of technology, which he does gently and briefly, but when he talks about the humility of his neighbours from the most conservative Amish sub-group, or the young guys opting for something better than car ownership.

32 What's at play here, according to *The Amish Way: Patient Faith in a Perilous World*, are different "assumptions about contentment and the meaning of life." In this new book, Kraybill and his co-authors write about how the Amish define "the good life" differently.[14] I like what I see of their idea of a "good life" but I feel trapped in a different world. This I find stressful.

33 Kline doesn't share my tech-induced anxiety. Though he lives at acute odds with the high-tech society right around him, he says the prospect of technological encroachment does not cause him worry. The Amish, it seems, are best viewed not as a people holed up in a cultural bunker desperately fending off the

---

Reading Critically

[13] Explain the phrase "to die to my worldly desires."

[14] How do you define "the good life"?

beast of progress, but as a rich community deliberately navigating tricky times from a point of identity and strength.

34 None of this provides me with a quick fix to my car dilemma. Perhaps that's part of the point – the Amish don't believe in quick fixes.[15] Kraybill and his co-authors write about the "uncommon patience" of the Amish. "When they are faced with problems, their first instinct is to wait and pray rather than seek a quick fix."

35 I add another possibility to my list of options regarding car ownership: get a car, move to the country (but close to basic services), experiment with other tech limits, soothe my conscience with grace and open sky, try to live into deeper values, pray for neo-Amish-like neighbours, and devise a 10-year plan for de-motorization. Who knows, maybe by year five I would be ready to pull out those criteria and see how horse and buggy ownership measures up.

UNDERSTANDING DETAILS

1. What is it about technology that stresses Braun out?
2. In considering whether to get a car, what three sources does Braun decide to consult? Why does he choose these sources?
3. List the criteria that Braun identifies to make the decision about whether to get a car.

ANALYZING MEANING

1. How effective are Braun's criteria in his decision making? Explain why.
2. Explain the view of the Amish people conveyed in Braun's essays. How does Braun feel about the Amish?
3. This essay comes from *Geez Magazine,* described on its website as follows: "a quarterly, ad-free magazine for the over-churched, out-churched, un-churched and maybe even the un-churchable. We hope to untangle the narrative of faith from the fundamentalists, pious self-helpers and religio-profiteers. We explore the point at which word, action and image intersect, and then ignite." (**www.geezmagazine.org/magazine**) How does this essay help *Geez* to accomplish its purpose?

Reading Critically

[15] Why don't the Amish believe in quick fixes? What is the alternative?

DISCOVERING RHETORICAL STRATEGIES

1. In his essay, Braun incorporates quotations from a variety of other writers. Why does he include these quotations? How do they help him to achieve his purpose?
2. In addition to classification and division, what rhetorical strategies does Braun use in this essay?
3. Describe the tone of Braun's essay. How does he achieve this tone?

MAKING CONNECTIONS

1. Irshad Manji ("Status Anxiety? Consider Socrates and the Sewer Saviour") writes about stresses connected with the social networking site Facebook. How do you think Braun would feel about Facebook?
2. Peter Nicholson ("Information-Rich and Attention-Poor") writes about the effects of technology on our attention spans. What do you think Braun would say about the current situation that Nicholson describes. Do you think he would share Nicholson's perspective or disagree? Explain.

IDEAS FOR DISCUSSION/WRITING

Preparing to Write

Write freely about a time when you had to make a major purchasing decision. What criteria did you use to help you to make your decision? Where all criteria weighted equally? Were the criteria helpful in making your decision?

Choosing a Topic

1. Think of a major decision that you are likely to need to make in the next three years. Write an essay in which you identify a set of criteria that you could use to help you make that decision. Focus on identifying your criteria and your rationale for them rather than on your answers or applying those criteria to your situation.
2. Will Braun says that technology stresses him out. How do you feel about technology? Write an essay in which you categorize the effects technology has on you.
3. Write about a difficult decision that you had to make. Who influenced your decision either directly or indirectly? Write an essay that explains your decision-making process.

FAITH MOOSANG

Nancy Drew Knows It's Hard (2009)

Faith Moosang is a Vancouver-based photographic artist. She received a B.F.A. from Emily Carr University of Art + Design and an M.F.A. from the School for the Contemporary Arts at Simon Fraser University.

Moosang's photography and video and film installations have been shown in solo and group exhibitions in North America and Europe. She has also published *First Son: Portraits by C.D. Hoy*, a collection of photograps by Chinese immigrant Chow Dong Hoy, curated by Moosang and accompanied by her text.

Preparing to Read

In this essay, which first appeared in *Geist*, Faith Moosang writes about "a world terrorized by crime." Think about terrorism. What is terrorism? When did you first become aware of the concept of terrorism? What examples of terrorist activities are you familiar with? Do you think that terrorism is increasing or decreasing globally?

Nancy Drew knows it's hard to live in a terrorized world.❶ Of course, certain events occurring in late 2008 in the country to the south of Canada have all but wiped the scourge of terror from the face of the earth, never to be seen again. But Nancy knows that we still live in a world terrorized by crime—to be specific, a world terrorized by perps—and she wants to help. 1

Nancy has been 18 years old for 79 years. In that time she has solved 56 mysteries, bringing down 15 conglomerates, 11 syndicates, 10 gangs, one nature cult and a panoply of unaffiliated creeps.❷ These are *perps*—bad to the bone—and you can defeat them. Some tips, inspired by Nancy Drew: 2

Reading Critically

❶ Why is the world "terrorized"? What is the source of the terror?

❷ Explain the phrase "panoply of unaffiliated creeps."

Recognizing perps. The higher up a perp is in the echelons of organized crime, the darker the clothes. Hats are always pulled low, coats dark, suits ill-fitting. If your perp runs with the crowd that likes to wear disguises, watch out for added facial hair and the overwhelming propensity to dress in the costume[3] of other cultures. 3

Appearance of perps. Watch out for people who have broken nails or whiny voices, who are crafty, dour, glum, shifty-eyed, strident, smirking, quarrelsome, clumsy, nervous, leering, haggard, scarred, balding or are in their fifties. 4

Behaviour of perps. You can easily identify perps simply by watching them. It is commonly and mistakenly assumed that their activities are surreptitious, guarded, well concealed. Nothing is further from the truth. Beware the man running with a sack, or throwing bombs. 5

Perp-catching tools. A purse that is co-ordinated with her knit separates is de rigueur for Nancy. However, the purse not only pulls together the whole outfit, it also carries the essentials of good sleuthing. In it, you will find ID, change for important phone calls, a flashlight, quizzing glass,[4] matches, a handkerchief which you can breathe through if, for example, a ceiling falls on you), a vial of perfume for sterilizing things or reviving unconscious people, and a burlap bag. As well, you will find a wig and glasses, for hastily changing your appearance, and lipstick for writing help messages. 6

Fighting form. But the strong core of your perp-fighting arsenal has to be your own being. You need to be in excellent shape and know the value of a hearty lunch; for example, and I quote: "heaping amounts of lobster, puffed shrimp, tomatoes, coleslaw, potatoes, hot biscuits, lemonade and apple pie."[5] Where she puts it, I don't know. Your skills should also include the ability to swim carrying an unconscious person in a stormy lake, fly a plane, play championship tennis and golf, arrange flowers, throw your voice,[6] throw a rock like a boy and do ballet well enough to take the leading dancer's place at a moment's notice. 7

Reading Critically

- [3] Why does Moosang use the word *costume* here rather than *outfit* or *attire*?
- [4] What is a quizzing glass?
- [5] Why does Moosang incorporate a quotation with all the details of the lunch here?
- [6] What does it mean to "throw your voice"?

UNDERSTANDING DETAILS

1. What are perps?
2. Who is Nancy Drew and why has she "been 18 years old for 79 years" (paragraph 2)?
3. According to Moosang's essay, how difficult is it to identify criminals? How can they be identified?

ANALYZING MEANING

1. Why does Moosang look to Nancy Drew for inspiration?
2. What are the "events occurring in late 2008" to which Moosang refers (paragraph 1)? Does Moosang believe that "the scourge of terror" has really been "wiped . . . from the face of the earth"?
3. What is Moosang's purpose in this essay? Has she successfully achieved this purpose? Explain.

DISCOVERING RHETORICAL STRATEGIES

1. How many categories of tips from Nancy Drew does Moosang identify? What organizing principle does she use for these categories?
2. What is the tone of Moosang's essay? How does she achieve this tone?
3. What other rhetorical strategies has Moosang used in her essay to make it effective and interesting?

MAKING CONNECTIONS

1. Moosang's essay was originally published in *Geist* magazine, which is also the source of Stephen Osborne's "The Lost Art of Waving." What commonalities in these essays reflect the common original intended audience?
2. Like Drew Hayden Taylor ("Pretty Like a White Boy"), Moosang has chosen to present her ideas with humour. Compare the use of humour in the writing of these two authors.

IDEAS FOR DISCUSSION/WRITING

Preparing to Write

Write freely about a fictional character with whom you are familiar. This might be someone from a book or series of books you read as a child, a character from a book you have read more recently, or a character from a movie or television show (avoid choosing anyone from a reality television show.) Why does this character stand out in your mind? What do you like about this character? What is this character best known for?

Choosing a Topic

1. Write an essay in which you explain what genre of books, movies, or music you particularly enjoy. Use the characteristics that define this category or genre to help explain its appeal to you.
2. Write an essay in which you present tips from a memorable fictional character on how to deal with some aspect of current life.
3. Write your own classification or division essay on the distinctive behaviours of a specific group of people you know well.

DANIEL J. LEVITIN

The Music of My Mind: A Neuroscientist Examines the Recipe for Listening Ecstasy (2006)

Daniel J. Levitin received his first tape recorder when he was three and has been involved with music and recording ever since. He left Stanford University (because—according to his website—he was told he couldn't major in the saxophone) to pursue a career in music, and for 10 years worked as a musician, songwriter, record producer, sound engineer, music consultant for feature films, and custom modifier of guitar amplifiers. Levitin eventually returned to university and now has degrees in cognitive psychology, cognitive science, and psychology. An associate professor of psychology at McGill University, he has been very vocal in the debates over intellectual property and the downloading of music. He is the best-selling author of *This Is Your Brain on Music: The Science of a Human Obsession* (2006) and *The World in Six Songs: How the Musical Brain Created Human Nature* (2008). He writes for music magazines, such as *Grammy*, *Billboard*, and *Audio*, as well as for academic journals, and has appeared as a commentator on CBC and National Public Radio. Levitin has won awards for his teaching, popular writing, academic writing, recordings, and soundtracks for films.

Preparing to Read

This essay comes from *Paste*, an independently published American entertainment magazine. There is a general assumption that everyone likes music of some sort, although their specific tastes may vary. Before you begin reading, think about what music you particularly enjoy. What musicians or songs stand out as your favourites? What is it about that music that you like? What songs or pieces of music have stood the test of time and still appeal to you after repeated listening?

I have to admit a bias—I like brains, almost as much as I like blistering guitar solos or throat-shredding vocals. Most people don't realize that music wouldn't exist without this three-pound mass of cells and water. I'm not just talking about the brains required to compose a song, or to control the precision finger movements of a virtuoso guitarist—I'm talking about *listeners'* brains. 1

Musicians exploit facts about the way our ears, and then brains, perceive music in order to create some of the most surprising, rewarding and pleasurable effects of listening to music. They do this in a variety of ways, often intuitively, without even knowing the mental principles involved. Here's a list of some actions that lead to convergences between music and neuropsychology:❶ 2

1) Violate Expectations: Pitch We're used to melodies being composed of different notes. But in "Something" by The Beatles, the melody plays the same note—the tonic—for the song's first six notes. When Harrison finally comes off the tonic, he hits the least likely note in the scale, the leading tone. He has masterfully violated our expectations that melodies need to move from one note to another and, further, that they need to move from a leading tone to a tonic. McCartney holds a single pitch for the first seven notes of "You Never Give Me Your Money" and the first six notes of "For No One." Antonio Carlos Jobim's "One Note Samba" takes this to an extreme. 3

2) Violate Expectations: Rhythm A lifetime of musical experience has taught us that music contains steady beats, and that when the beat stops, the music's over. 4

Musicians work hard to establish a song's groove and, when they stop, it becomes sort of a neuromusical joke, the equivalent of tripping someone as they walk down the street. Near the end of The Doobie Brothers' "Long Train Runnin'," the band stops at the end of a chorus and lead vocalist Patrick Simmons seems to be ending the song with "Where would you be now?" After a second of silence, the guitar riff❷ comes back and your brain realizes it's been had—the band members were keeping time all along in their brains, waiting for the right moment to surprise the listener. We hear this in many songs, including "Good Lovin'" by The Rascals. 5

3) Variations on a Theme Our brains have evolved to love variety—in food, sex and music. A classic trick is when musicians restate a musical idea on a different instrument. The guitar 6

Reading Critically

❶ What is neuropsychology?

❷ What is a guitar riff?

solo in "And I Love Her" by The Beatles—which plays the same melody as the vocal—does just this, as does the solo in Coldplay's "Don't Panic."

4) Paradox[3] and Contradiction Another form of variation involves contradiction. Musicians often surprise us by playing songs we wouldn't expect them to, or in a style we wouldn't expect. When Van Halen was the newest, hippest group around it surprised fans by launching into a hard-rock version of an older not-quite-hip-at-the-time song by The Kinks, "You Really Got Me." Unapologetically unsentimental rockers The Rolling Stones had done the opposite a few years earlier by using violins on "Lady Jane." Tori Amos recorded a soft-ballad version of Nirvana's abrasive classic "Smells Like Teen Spirit." The inherent juxtaposition of styles is musically (and neurally) rewarding.[4] 7

5) Juxtapose Expectations: Rhythms and Genre The Police made a career out of violating rhythmic expectations. Rock's standard rhythmic convention is to have a guitar or piano play downbeats (ones and threes) while a snare drum plays backbeats on the two and the four. Reggae turns this around, putting guitar on two and four with the backbeat. The Police combined reggae with rock to create a new sound that simultaneously fulfilled some—and violated other—rhythmic expectations. Sting often played bass parts that were entirely novel, avoiding the rock clichés of playing on the downbeat or of playing synchronously with the bass drum. "Spirits in the Material World" from *Ghost in the Machine* takes this rhythmic play to such an extreme that it can be hard to tell where the downbeat even is. 8

6) Violate Structural Expectations In "Yesterday," the main melodic phrase is seven measures long; The Beatles surprise us by violating one of the most basic assumptions of popular music: the four—or eight—measure phrase (nearly all rock/pop songs have musical ideas organized into phrases of those lengths). We've heard thousands of songs thousands of times 9

Reading Critically

[3] What is a paradox?

[4] Explain what this sentence means.

and, even without being able to explicitly describe it, we've incorporated this tendency as a "rule" about music we know. So when "Yesterday's" seven-measure phrase comes along, it's a surprise.[5] Even though we've heard the song 1,000 or even 10,000 times, it still interests us because it violates schematic expectations that are even more firmly entrenched than our memory of this particular song.

7) Don't Do the Same Thing Twice Master musicians add subtle shadings of nuance and difference to their parts; each time they play a part, they change it a bit. In Stevie Wonder's "Superstition," for example, the beat on the hi-hat is never played exactly the same way twice. The genius of Wonder's playing is that he keeps us on our mental toes by changing the pattern's aspects every time, making just enough of it the same to keep us grounded and oriented. 10

8) Unfold Chords One Note at a Time Instead of playing the guitar chords all at once, composers will often spoon-feed them to us one note at a time. This builds tension and exercises our brains by forcing them to assemble the notes into a coherent harmonic object. We become participants in the music's creation by creating in our heads the chords the guitarist implies. This is one of the oldest tricks there is, found in Beethoven's sonatas, The Beatles' "Because" (based on Beethoven's "Pathétique" sonata), The Cure's "Kyoto Song," Death Cab For Cutie's "Technicolor Girls" and countless others. 11

UNDERSTANDING DETAILS

1. What aspect of music's appeal is Levitin explaining in this essay? Why?
2. How many different musical examples does Levitin include in his essay? How many are classical and how many belong to more contemporary genres?
3. In paragraph 11, Levitin describes composers as "spoon-feed[ing]" chords to us "one note at a time." Explain what he means by this.

Reading Critically

[5] Can you think of any other examples of songs that use a five- or seven-measure phrase in this way?

ANALYZING MEANING

1. Levitin gives examples of each of the strategies used to make music rewarding to listeners. Identify at least one additional example to illustrate each of the eight categories that Levitin outlines.
2. Many of Levitin's categories have to do with violation of our expectations. Explain how and where we learned the "rules" or expectations of music that are being violated.
3. This essay was published in a magazine in 2006, but most of the examples Levitin uses to illustrate his categories are from decades earlier. Explain why Levitin has chosen the examples he has rather than more current songs and newer artists.

DISCOVERING RHETORICAL STRATEGIES

1. Explain Levitin's introduction. Why does he admit his bias for this audience?
2. While Levitin divides his explanation of the effect of music on the brain into eight categories, he links these categories. Identify the transitions he uses to make these links and thereby give his essay coherence and cohesiveness.
3. While Levitin is dividing his points into multiple categories as a primary organizational technique, he also uses other rhetorical strategies. Identify and explain at least one additional rhetorical strategy used in this essay.

MAKING CONNECTIONS

1. Levitin is a neuroscientist writing to explain aspects of brain function to a general audience. Compare his strategies and style to those of Carmen Everest Wahl in "Gluten Intolerance."
2. Levitin, K'naan ("Between the Highs and Lows, Life Happens," and Jowi Taylor ("Beginning" from *Six String Nation*) all write about the appeal of music. How are their perspectives similar? In what ways do they differ?

IDEAS FOR DISCUSSION/WRITING

Preparing to Write

Think about a musician or musical group that you particularly like. When did you first hear this musician/group? What is it about that music that appeals to you? What aspects of the music stand out in your mind? Is this a long-standing favourite or a recent discovery?

Choosing a Topic

1. Write an essay for *Paste* magazine introducing your favourite musician (or group), and explain the appeal of this subject. Use specific examples to illustrate your points.
2. On Levitin's website (**www.psych.mcgill.ca/levitin**), he includes lists of what is on his iPod and what he is currently listening to. Choose one of the songs Levitin has listed, and write an explanation of its appeal based on the categories Levitin has described. Be sure to cover all the ways in which this song appeals to listeners' brains.
3. Music is typically categorized according to genre for marketing promotion and sales. For people new to the music business, write an explanation of at least eight musical genres (e.g., R&B, hip hop, rock, pop, roots, opera) to help them classify new songs and musicians they are promoting. Use specific examples to help make your classification system clear.

ALEX BOYD

In Defense of Graffiti (2003)

According to Alex Boyd (1969–) in an interview in *The Danforth Review,* "If good writing can do anything, it can try and observe and capture something unique. It can fight against cliché, it can remind us that there is more to life than obsessing with our sex lives, watching TV and buying things" (**http://epe.lac-bac.gc.ca/100/202/300/danforth/2009/no27/features/interviews/alex_boyd.htm**).

Boyd is a writer whose fiction, poems, essays, reviews, and articles have been published in newspapers and periodicals, including *The Globe and Mail, Books in Canada, Taddle Creek,* and *Quill & Quire.* He currently coordinates the IV Lounge Reading Series in Toronto, where he lives, and co-edits the online journal *Northern Poetry Review.* In 2008 he won the Gerald Lampert Memorial Award for his book of poetry, *Making Bones Walk.* In 2008 he also established Digital Popcorn, a site for personal film reviews, and in 2009 helped establish the Best Canadian Essays series.

Preparing to Read

The title of this essay clearly identifies Boyd's subject and his position on that subject. Before reading, think about graffiti. What is your reaction to graffiti that you see? Do you believe graffiti is a form of vandalism or do you see it as a form of artistic expression? Is your reaction always the same? Why do people create graffiti? Have you ever created any graffiti in a public place? If so, what motivated you?

There are two types of graffiti: one rambling, obscure, and sometimes offensive, the other more tangible, more political and accessible. Whatever negative associations people sometimes have of graffiti and whatever steps are taken against it are usually the result of a perception based on the first kind of graffiti. But I believe there are often enough examples of the second kind to demonstrate that graffiti deserves more consideration. If, after all, there is any value to it at all, then it deserves something more than automatic dismissal despite our comfortable and cherished notions of privacy and property. 1

In walking the streets of Toronto, I find it's simple enough to collect examples of fairly useless, or even damaging graffiti: stupid 2 racist remarks, empty slogans, illegible signatures or comments like "Nick and Gloria sparkle." How excellent for Nick and Gloria. But the more overtly political and useful examples of graffiti are everywhere too. Here are some examples from the Toronto area:

Greed = Death
Just because YOU said so?
Fur is Dead
Creative survival
The most common way people lose power is by thinking they don't have any
Happiness can be yours forever! Order now!
*Peace, no religion*❶

In yet another category of Toronto graffiti are the cryptic yet interesting examples, like "Fix Signs," and in the category of trite but somehow warming comes "I Love You," placed at least a dozen times all over the downtown core this summer, as unconditional as they are blunt. 3

Anywhere attempts are made to smother freedom of speech, graffiti becomes an affordable, accessible method of communication. In El Salvador, graffiti takes the form of important and passionate social commentary: 4

We demand Freedom
Today it's the turn of the victim
The People first
Respect for the rights of others is peace

While living in Scotland, I noticed that a public debate had taken place entirely through graffiti. The first remark had been a confused, general statement about gay men (as opposed to pedophiles) sexually abusing children. Someone crossed out the remark and commented on the ignorance of the first person, and then the first person had returned to not only cross out the second person's comments but include a threatening remark as well.❷ All the remarks were still legible, though, resulting in a permanent posted conversation that fairly obviously demonstrated 5

Reading Critically

❶ Do you think these are good examples of useful graffiti? Explain.

❷ Have you ever seen this kind of debating graffiti? Can you think of places where this type would likely be found?

that the first person was completely inflexible in his beliefs and would allow no dissent.

6 At Maeshowe, a Stone Age tomb in Scotland, there are examples of historical graffiti. In the twelfth century several groups of Norsemen broke into the tomb and left markings, some as simple as "Ingigerth is the most beautiful of all women," with the image of a slavering dog carved next to it. Another man stood on some shoulders or got a boost in order to write, "Tholfir Kolbeinsson carved these runes high up." Other runes explain the Viking's purpose, but the most startling thing is that the majority of examples, like the ones that I've provided, demonstrate how amazingly similar it is to modern graffiti. The simple fact that they've survived almost a thousand years gives them historical value and, therefore, legal protection, yet present attempts to make permanent statements are the acts of "vandals."❸

7 Some simply assume that everyone hates graffiti, and websites advertise cleaning services that fight those "vandals and their weapons of destruction—cans of spray paint and colored markers." The use of the words "vandals," and "weapons" particularly struck me. My dictionary defines a vandal as someone who willfully damages or destroys things, especially beautiful or valuable ones (doesn't strike me as fair when applied to graffiti, which has the potential to be esthetically pleasing, and may cover a neutral or unused surface). The Vandals were a member of the Germanic peoples living south of the Baltic who plundered Gaul, Spain, and North Africa and even sacked Rome in AD 455, destroying many books and works of art. Again, not a very good fit with messages between citizens tucked away in alleys or emblazoned on corners.

8 As a culture we make little or no official effort to preserve or at least photograph what these "vandals" have done with their "weapons" before whitewashing it.❹ The obvious lessons being that something must survive in order to be called history, but also that we choose what survives, and are in the habit of being extremely shortsighted about it, or leaving it to luck, as demonstrated by Maeshowe.

Reading Critically

❸ Is there a difference between Norsemen runes and modern-day graffiti? How would people in that era have felt about the Norsemen breaking into a tomb and carving runes?

❹ Do you think that today's graffiti should be preserved or photographed? If so, who should decide what is worthy of preservation?

Today graffiti isn't legal,[5] so it becomes difficult to trace the whereabouts and details of all those who do it, but I suspect most graffiti is done by young people, whether they call themselves artists or not. I say this not just because it's rebellious but also because young people don't yet have the same kind of investment in society, and have a different perspective, a slightly distanced position. Not only are they still defining an identity and searching for a role, they may be more capable on some level of recognizing a basic unfairness: that a message with money behind it is called advertising while a public one is mere graffiti. 9

The message of most graffiti may not be about struggle, but its existence does involve an ongoing struggle between those who have and those who don't. It is not the wealthiest people who leave graffiti. It's more likely to be someone young, someone poor, or someone who is poor because they are young. Those of us who are most opposed to it are likely those of us who can afford to own at least a home if not other buildings, and take offense to anyone who would stain it with their own personal message.[6] Yes, it can be an unwelcome intrusion on private property, but it's possibly the voice of someone who may never own his or her own house, business or anything else, which only leaves them the option of needling, in some small way, those who have money and power. This is perhaps the best reason for someone to call cans of spray paint weapons—they create the potential for a permanent, articulate voice for the disadvantaged. If it allows those who have less to be articulate, and critical of those who have more, naturally anyone in the better position will see it as a "weapon." 10

I don't believe I would want to live in a world where every inch of space cries out for my attention, (regardless of whether they were ads or private thoughts). But I also encourage everyone to be open to reading graffiti and to think of it as something that, like poetry, puts a finger on the real and honest pulse of the world. There is little financial profit in something like poetry, but there is even less in graffiti (in fact there is the risk of arrest, and it's fair to assume a belief in the importance of the statement to 11

Reading Critically

5. Should graffiti be legal? Why or why not?
6. Do you agree with Boyd's theory of who is more likely to leave graffiti and who is most likely to oppose it? Explain.

take such a risk. I've noticed that the more meaningful messages are concise, to conserve time in writing it, and the more useless ones are to be found all over alleys and in more hidden locations). This kind of logical assumption in the basic sincerity of graffiti has led corporations to try and co-opt it in advertising campaigns giving the impression, as long as you don't think about it too hard, that the word on the street favours whatever corporation uses it. But ultimately, this has to be rejected. Graffiti is not a contrived or manufactured thing designed to make money. And for that reason alone, we should be willing to watch and read.

UNDERSTANDING DETAILS

1. Explain Boyd's view of the value of graffiti. Does he see all graffiti as equal? Explain.
2. In what ways does Boyd see graffiti as similar to poetry?
3. Outline the categories into which Boyd groups different examples of grafitti. Are his categories all clear-cut?

ANALYZING MEANING

1. What is Boyd's purpose in writing this essay? Does he achieve his purpose? Explain.
2. What, according to Boyd, is the reason that people create graffiti? Do you agree with him that this is the typical motivation? What examples have you seen that would support or refute this position?
3. Why does graffiti create such conflict? Why does Boyd feel the need to defend it?

DISCOVERING RHETORICAL STRATEGIES

1. How does Boyd organize the classification system that he uses to present his argument about graffiti?
2. How many examples does Boyd include to illustrate each of the types of graffiti he identifies? Are his examples sufficient? Explain why or why not.
3. What is Boyd's thesis? Where in his essay is it stated? Does he provide adequate support for his thesis to make his essay effective?

MAKING CONNECTIONS

1. Boyd, like Steven Heighton ("Elegy in Stone"), Evelyn Lau ("More and More"), and Barbara Kingsolver ("Life Without Go-Go Boots"), writes poetry as well as prose. What aspects of these authors' essays reflect their poetic interests?
2. Imagine Naomi Klein ("Co-opting Dissent") in conversation with Alex Boyd about the role of graffiti in our culture. How do you expect that Klein would react to Boyd's position?

IDEAS FOR DISCUSSION/WRITING

Preparing to Write

What constitutes artistic expression? Write freely about art and what fits—or doesn't fit—within the broad classification of art. What value does art have within our society? Does its value change according to the assessment of experts, or is art "in the eye of the beholder"?

Choosing a Topic

1. Boyd presents graffiti as an accessible medium for young people to share their ideas and publicly voice their opinions and concerns. Write an essay in which you outline other media that young people use for these purposes. Draw on specific examples to illustrate your points.
2. Do you see graffiti as a crime or as art? Write an article for your local paper explaining your perspective and persuading others to adopt your view.
3. Compare and contrast graffiti with other art forms that audiences might have dismissed at some point in history.

CHAPTER 6

COMPARISON/ CONTRAST

Discovering Similarities and Differences

Making comparisons is such a natural and necessary part of our everyday lives that we often do so without conscious effort. When we were children, we compared our toys with those of our friends, we contrasted our height and physical development with other children's, and we constantly evaluated our happiness in comparison with that evidenced by our parents and childhood companions. As we grew older, we habitually compared our dates, teachers, parents, friends, possessions, and physical attributes. Now, in college or university, we learn about anthropology by writing essays on the similarities and differences between two African tribes, about political science by contrasting the Liberal and Conservative platforms, about business by comparing annual production rates, and about literature by comparing Atwood with Ondaatje or Shakespeare with Marlowe. Comparing and contrasting various elements in our lives helps us make decisions, such as which course to take or which house to buy, and it justifies preferences that we already hold, such as liking one city more than another or loving one person more than the next. In these ways and in many others, the skilful use of comparison and contrast is clearly essential to our social and professional lives.

Defining *Comparison/Contrast*

Comparison and *contrast* allow us to understand one subject by putting it next to another. Comparing involves discovering likenesses or similarities, whereas contrasting is based on finding differences. Like division and classification, comparison and contrast are generally considered part of the same process because we usually have no reason for comparing unless some contrast is also involved. Each implies the existence of the other. For this reason, the word *compare* is often used to mean both techniques.

Comparison and contrast are most profitably applied to two items that have something in common, such as cats and dogs, or cars and motorcycles. A discussion of cats and motorcycles, for example, would probably not be very rewarding or stimulating because they do not have much in common. If more than two items are compared in an essay, they are still most profitably discussed in pairs: for instance, motorcycles and cars, cars and bicycles, or bicycles and motorcycles.

An *analogy* is an extended, sustained comparison. Often used to explain unfamiliar, abstract, or complicated thoughts, this rhetorical technique adds energy and vividness to a wide variety of college-level writing. The process of analogy differs slightly from comparison/contrast in three important ways: Comparison/contrast begins with subjects from the same class and places equal weight on both of them. In addition, it addresses both the similarities and the differences of these subjects. Analogy, conversely, seldom explores subjects from the same class, and it focuses principally on one familiar subject in an attempt to explain another, more complex one. Furthermore, analogy deals only with similarities, not with contrasts. A comparison/contrast essay, for example, might study two veterans' ways of coping with the trauma of the Gulf War by pointing out the differences in their methods as well as the similarities. An analogy essay might use the familiar notion of a fireworks display to reveal the chilling horror of the lonely hours after dark during this war: "Nights in the Persian Gulf were similar to a loud, unending fireworks display. We had no idea when the next blast was coming, how loud it would be, or how close. We cringed in terror after dark, hoping the next surprise would not be our own death." In this example, rather than simply hearing about an event, we participate in it through this highly refined form of comparison.

The following student paragraph compares and contrasts married and single life. As you read it, notice how the author compares similar social states and, in the process, justifies her current lifestyle:

Recently I saw a bumper sticker that read, "It used to be wine, women, and song, and now it's beer, the old lady, and TV." Much truth may be found in this comparison of single and married lifestyles. When my husband and I used to date, for example, we'd go out for dinner and drinks and then maybe see a play or concert. Our discussions were intelligent, often ranging over global politics, science, literature, and other lofty topics. He would open doors for me, buy me flowers, and make sure I was comfortable and happy. Now, three years later, after marriage and a child, the baby bottle has replaced the wine bottle, the smell of diapers wipes out the scent of roses, and our nights on the town are infrequent, cherished events. But that's OK. A little bit of the excitement and mystery may be gone, but these intangible qualities have given way to a sturdy, dependable trust in each other and a quiet confidence about our future together.

Thinking Critically Through Comparison/Contrast

Comparison and contrast are basic to a number of different thought processes. We compare and contrast quite naturally on a daily basis, but all of us would benefit greatly from being more aware of these companion strategies in our own writing. They help us not only in perceiving our environment but also in understanding and organizing large amounts of information.

The basic skill of finding similarities and differences will enhance your ability to create accurate descriptions, to cite appropriate examples, to present a full process analysis, and, of course, to classify and label subjects. It is a pattern of thought that is essential to more complex thinking strategies, so perfecting the ability to use it is an important step in your efforts to improve your critical thinking.

Reading and Writing Comparison/Contrast Essays

Many established guidelines regulate the development of a comparison/contrast essay and should be taken into account from both the reading and the writing perspectives. All good comparative studies serve a specific purpose. They attempt either to examine their subjects separately or to demonstrate the superiority of one over the other. In evaluating two different types of cars, for example, a writer might point out the amazing gas mileage of one model and the smooth handling qualities of the other, or the superiority of one car's gas consumption over that of the other. Whatever the intent, comparison/contrast essays need to be clear and logical and have a precise purpose.

Reading Comparison/Contrast Essays

- What is the writer comparing?
- What is the essay's thesis?
- How is the essay organized?

Preparing to Read. As you begin reading this chapter, pull together as much preliminary material as possible for each essay so that you can focus your attention and have the benefit of prior knowledge before you start to read. In particular, you are trying to discover what is being compared or contrasted and why. What does Irshad Manji's's title ("Status Anxiety? Consider Socrates and the Sewer Saviour") suggest to you? From the title of his essay, can you tell what Michael McKinley is comparing in "Opera Night in Canada"? From glancing at the essay itself and reading the synopsis in the Rhetorical Contents, do you know what Jennie Punter's essay ("Crime and Punishment in a Foreign Land") is trying to accomplish?

Also, before you begin to read these essays, try to discover information about the author and the conditions under which each essay was written. Why is Michael McKinley qualified to write about hockey and opera? What was Monte Hummel's job? To what extent do you expect this to colour his comparison of a natural environment at two different times?

Finally, just before you begin to read, answer the Preparing to Read questions, and then make some free associations with the general topic of each essay. For example, what are some of the similarities and differences between hockey and opera (Michael McKinley)? Have you ever given much thought to clotheslines (Christopher DeWolf)?

Reading. As you read each comparison/contrast essay for the first time, be sure to record your own feelings and opinions. Some of the issues presented in this chapter are highly controversial. You will often have strong reactions to them, which you should try to write down as soon as possible.

In addition, you may want to comment on the relationship between the preliminary essay material, the author's stance in the essay, and the content of the essay itself. For example, what motivated Jennie Punter to write "Crime and Punishment in a Foreign Land"? Who was her primary intended audience? What prompted Irshad Manji to write "Status Anxiety? Consider Socrates and the Sewer Saviour"? Answering these questions will provide you with a context for your first reading and will prepare you to analyze the essays in more depth on your second reading.

You should make certain you understand each author's thesis and then take a close look at his or her principal method of organization: Is the essay arranged (1) point by point, (2) subject by subject, (3) as a combination of these two, or (4) as separate discussions of similarities and differences between two subjects? (See the chart on page 269 for an illustration of these options.) Last, preview the questions that follow the essay before you read it again.

Rereading. When you read these essays a second time, you should look at the comparison or contrast much more closely. First, look in detail at the writer's method of organization (see the chart on page 269). How effective is it in advancing the writer's thesis?

Next, you should consider whether each essay is fully developed and balanced: Does McKinley compare similar items? Is Manji's treatment of her subjects well balanced? Do all the writers in this chapter use well-chosen transitions so that you can move smoothly from one point to the next? Also, what other rhetorical modes support each comparison/contrast essay in this chapter? Finally, answering the questions after each selection will let you evaluate your understanding of the essay and help you analyze its contents in preparation for the discussion/writing topics that follow.

For a more thorough inventory of the reading process, turn to page 41 in the Introduction.

Writing Comparison/Contrast Essays

- Draft a thesis.
- Choose items in the same category.
- Introduce your subjects and your reason for comparing them.

- Include the limits of your discussion.
- Organize your essay.
- Balance the treatment of your subjects.

Preparing to Write. As you consider various topics for a comparison/contrast essay, you should answer the Preparing to Write questions that precede the assignments and then use the prewriting techniques explained in the Introduction to generate even more ideas on these topics.

As you focus your attention on a particular topic, keep the following suggestions in mind:

- Generally, compare/contrast items in the same category (e.g., compare two professors, but not a professor and a swimming pool).
- Have a specific purpose or reason for writing your essay.
- Discuss the same qualities of each subject (i.e., if you evaluate the teaching techniques of one professor, do so for the other professor as well).
- Use as many pertinent details as possible to expand your comparison/contrast and to accomplish your stated purpose.
- Deal with all aspects of the comparison that are relevant to the purpose.
- Balance the treatment of the different subjects of your comparison (i.e., don't spend more time on one than on another).
- Determine your audience's background and knowledge so that you will know how much of your comparison should be explained in detail and how much can be skimmed over.

Next, in preparation for a comparison/contrast project, you might list all the elements of both subjects that you want to compare. This list can then help you give your essay structure as well as substance. At this stage in the writing process, the task may seem similar to pure description, but a discussion of two subjects in relation to each other rapidly changes the assignment from description to comparison.

Writing. The introduction of your comparison/contrast essay should (1) clearly identify your subjects, (2) explain the basis of your comparison/contrast, and (3) state your purpose and the overall limits of your particular study. Identifying your subject is, of course, a necessary and important task in any essay. Similarly, justifying the elements you will be comparing and contrasting creates reader interest and gives your audience some specifics to look for in the essay. Finally, your statement of purpose or thesis (for example, to prove that one professor is superior to another) should include the boundaries of your discussion. You cannot cover all the reasons for your preference in one short essay, so you must limit your consideration to three or four basic categories (perhaps teaching techniques, the clarity of the assignments given, classroom attitude, and grading standards). The introduction is the place to make all these limits known.

You can organize the body of your paper in one of four ways: (1) a point-by-point, or alternating, comparison; (2) a subject-by-subject, or divided, comparison; (3) a combination of these two methods; or (4) a division between the similarities and differences. (See the chart on page 269.)

The point-by-point comparison evaluates both subjects in terms of each category. If the issue, for example, is which of two cars to buy, you might discuss both models' gasoline consumption first; then, their horsepower; next, their ease in handling; and, finally, their standard equipment. Following the second method of organization, subject by subject, you would discuss the gasoline consumption, horsepower, ease in handling, and standard equipment of car A first and then follow the same format for car B. The third option would allow you to introduce, say, the interior design of each car point by point (or car by car) and then explain the mechanical features of the automobiles (kilometres per litre, horsepower, gear ratio, and braking system) subject by subject. To use the last method of organization, you might discuss the similarities between the two models first and the differences second (or vice versa). If the cars you are comparing have similar kilometres-per-litre (km/L) ratings but completely different horsepower, steering systems, and optional equipment, you could discuss the gasoline consumption first and then emphasize the differences by mentioning them later in the essay. If, instead, you are trying to emphasize the fact that the km/L ratings of these models remain consistent despite their differences, then reverse the order of your essay.

Methods of Organization

Point by Point
km/L, car A
km/L, car B
horsepower, car A
horsepower, car B
handling, car A
handling, car B
equipment, car A
equipment, car B

Subject by Subject
km/L, car A
horsepower, car A
handling, car A
equipment, car A
km/L, car B
horsepower, car B
handling, car B
equipment, car B

Combination
interior, car A
interior, car B
----
km/L, car A
horsepower, car A
km/L, car B
horsepower, car B

Similarities/Differences
similarities:
  km/L, cars A and B
differences:
  horsepower, cars A and B
  handling, cars A and B
  equipment, cars A and B

When confronted with the task of choosing a method of organization for a comparison/contrast essay, you need to find the pattern that best suits your purpose. If you want single items to stand out in a discussion, for instance, the best choice will be the point-by-point system; it is especially appropriate for long essays, but has a tendency to turn into an exercise in making lists if you don't pay careful attention to your transitions. If, however, the subjects themselves (rather than the itemized points) are the most interesting feature of your essay, you should use the subject-by-subject comparison; this system is particularly good for short essays in which the readers can retain what was said about one subject while they read about a second subject. Through this second system of organization, each subject becomes a unified whole; this approach to an essay is generally effective unless the theme becomes awkwardly divided into two separate parts. You must also remember, if you choose this second method of organization, that the second (or last) subject is in the most emphatic position because that is what your readers will have seen most recently. The final two options for organizing a comparison/contrast essay give you some built-in flexibility so that you can create emphasis and attempt to manipulate reader opinion simply by the structure of your essay.

Using logical transitions in your comparison/contrast essays will establish clear relationships between the items in your comparisons and will also move your readers smoothly from one topic to the next. If you wish to indicate comparisons, use such words as *like, as, also, in like manner, similarly,* and *in addition;* to signal contrasts, try *but, in contrast to, unlike, whereas,* and *on the one hand/on the other hand.*

The conclusion of a comparison/contrast essay summarizes the main points and states the deductions drawn from those points. As you choose your method of organization, remember not to get locked into a formulaic approach to your subjects, which will adversely affect the readability of your essay. To avoid making your reader feel like a spectator at a verbal table tennis match, be straightforward, honest, and patient as you discover and recount the details of your comparison.

Rewriting. When you review the draft of your comparison/contrast essay, you need once again to make sure that you communicate your purpose as effectively as possible to your intended audience. Two guidelines previously mentioned should help you accomplish this goal:

- Do I identify my subjects clearly?
- Does my thesis clearly state the purpose and overall limits of my particular subject?

You will also need to pay close attention to the development of your essay:

- Are my compare/contrast items from the same general category?
- Do I discuss the same qualities of each subject?
- Do I balance the treatment of my subjects?
- Do I organize my topic as effectively as possible?
- Does my conclusion summarize and analyze my main points?

For further information on writing and revising your comparison/contrast essays, consult the checklist on page 42 of the Introduction.

Student Essay: Comparison/Contrast at Work

The following student essay compares the advantages and disadvantages of macaroni and cheese versus tacos in the life of a harried first-year college or university student. As you read it, notice that the writer states his intention in the first paragraph and then expands his discussion with appropriate details to produce a balanced essay. Also, try to determine what effect he creates by using two methods of organization: first subject by subject, then point by point.

Student Chef

Topics

Basis of comparison

To this day, I will not eat either macaroni and cheese or tacos. No, it's not because of any allergy; it's because during my first year at college, I prepared one or the other of these scrumptious dishes more times than I care to remember. However, my choice of which culinary delight to cook on any given night was not as simple a decision as one might imagine.

Thesis statement: Purpose and limits of comparison

Paragraph on subject A: Macaroni and cheese

Point 1 (price)

Point 2 (preparation)

Point 3 (odour)

Macaroni and cheese has numerous advantages for the student chef. First of all, it is inexpensive. No matter how poor one may be, there's probably enough change under the couch cushion to buy a box at the market. All that starch for only 89¢. What a bargain! Second, it can be prepared in just one pan. This is especially important given the meagre resources of the average student's kitchen. Third, and perhaps most important, macaroni and cheese is odourless. By odourless, I mean that no one else can smell it. It is a well-known fact that students hate to cook and that they love nothing better than to wander dejectedly around the kitchen with big, sad eyes after someone else has been cooking. But with macaroni and cheese, no enticing aromas are going to find their way into the nose of any would-be mooch.

Paragraph on subject B: Tacos

Transition

Point 1 (price)

Point 2 (preparation)

Point 3 (odour)

Tacos, on the other hand, are a different matter altogether. For the student cook, the most significant difference is obviously the price. To enjoy tacos for dinner, the adventurous student gourmet must purchase no fewer than five ingredients from the market: corn tortillas, beef, lettuce, tomatoes, and cheese. Needless to say, this is a major expenditure. Second, the chef must adroitly shuffle these ingredients back and forth among his very limited supply of pans and bowls. And finally, tacos smell great. That wouldn't be a problem if the tacos didn't also smell great to about 20 of the cook's newest—if not closest—friends, who appear with those same pathetic, starving eyes mentioned earlier. When this happens, the cook will be lucky to get more than two of his own creations.

Subject B Paragraph on point 4: Taste

Tacos, then, wouldn't stand much of a chance if they didn't outdo macaroni and cheese in one area: taste. Taste is almost—but not quite—an optional requirement in the opinion of a frugal student hash-slinger. Taste is just important enough so that tacos are occasionally prepared, despite their disadvantages. Transition

Transition Paragraph on point 5: Colour

But tacos have other advantages besides their taste. With their enticing, colourful ingredients, they even look good. The only thing that can be said about the colour of macaroni and cheese is that it's a colour not found in nature. Subject B Subject A

Transition Paragraph on point 6: Time

On the other hand, macaroni and cheese is quick. It can be prepared in about ten minutes, while tacos take more than twice as long. And there are occasions—such as final exam week—when time is a scarce and precious resource. Subject A Subject B

Transition Analysis

As you can see, quite a bit of thinking went into my choice of food in my younger years. These two dishes essentially got me through my first year and indirectly taught me how to make important decisions (like what to eat). But I still feel a certain revulsion when I hear their names today. Summary Concluding statement

Some Final Thoughts on Comparison/ Contrast

The essays in this section demonstrate various methods of organization as well as a number of distinct stylistic approaches to writing a comparison/contrast essay. As you read these selections, pay particular attention to the clear, well-focused introductions; the different logical methods of organization; and the smooth transitions between sentences and paragraphs.

COMPARISON/CONTRAST IN REVIEW

Reading Comparison/Contrast Essays

Preparing to Read

✓ What assumptions can I make from the essay's title?
✓ What do I think the general mood of the essay will be?
✓ What are the essay's purpose and audience?
✓ What does the synopsis tell me about the essay?
✓ What can I learn from the author's biography?
✓ Can I predict the author's point of view toward the subject?

Reading

✓ What is the writer comparing?
✓ What is the essay's thesis?
✓ How is the essay organized?

Rereading

✓ Is the writer's method of organization effective?
✓ Is the essay fully developed?
✓ What other rhetorical strategies does the author use?

Writing Comparison/Contrast Essays

Preparing to Write

✓ What is my purpose?
✓ Who is my audience?

Writing

✓ Did I draft a thesis?
✓ Am I comparing/contrasting items in the same general category?
✓ Does my introduction (1) clearly identify my subjects, (2) explain the basis of my comparison/contrast, and (3) state my purpose and the overall limits of my particular study?
✓ Does my thesis include the boundaries of my discussion?
✓ Is my paper organized effectively: point by point, subject by subject, as a combination of the two, or as separate discussions of similarities and differences between two subjects?
✓ Do I balance the treatment of my subjects?

Rewriting

✓ Does my thesis clearly state the purpose and overall limits of my particular study?
✓ Do I compare/contrast items from the same general category?
✓ Do I discuss the same qualities of each subject?
✓ Do I balance the treatment of my subjects?
✓ Have I organized my topic as effectively as possible?
✓ Does my conclusion summarize and analyze my main points?

MONTE HUMMEL

A Passion for the Environment: Two Accounts (2000)

The Order of Canada recognizes outstanding achievement in a variety of fields of human endeavour. Monte Hummel's appointment as an Officer of the Order of Canada in 2000 reflects the difference he has made to Canada in the realm of the environment.

Born in Toronto in 1947, Monte Hummel spent his childhood in White Dog Falls in Northern Ontario. He earned a B.A., an M.A., and an M.Sc. in forestry at the University of Toronto, and has spent his career in various environmental advocacy roles, ranging from executive director and chairman of Pollution Probe (which he co-founded) to president of World Wildlife Fund Canada (a position he held for almost 20 years).

In addition, Hummel has written several books, including *Arctic Wildlife* (1985); *Wild Hunters: Predators in Peril* (1992), co-authored with his wife, Sherry Pettigrew; *Protecting Canada's Endangered Spaces* (2000); and *Wintergreen: Reflections from Loon Lake* (2002). His most recent book is *Caribou and the North: A Shared Future* (2008).

Now a resident of Beeton, Ontario, Hummel continues to win recognition for his environmental work, including Canadian Geographic's Lifetime Achievement Award (2004) and the Douglas H. Pimlott Award from the Canadian Nature Federation (2005).

"A Passion for the Environment" first appeared in the *Queen's Quarterly*.

Preparing to Read

Before reading Hummel's essay, think about changes to the natural environment. What changes have you observed in your lifetime? Are those changes positive or negative? What has caused those changes? What future changes do you anticipate? What value do you attach to preservation of the natural environment? Where should this fit in governmental, societal, and commercial priorities?

On a sunny day in August 1959, my honey-coloured spaniel Roxy and I went fishing. At the time, my family lived in a hydro camp at White Dog Falls, north of Kenora in northwestern Ontario. Roxy and I scrambled over familiar rocks along the river 1 bank, caught frogs for bait, shared a sandwich for lunch, landed a couple of medium-sized pike out of dark swirling pools below the rapids, and rested looking up through pines at osprey who were also fishing these northern waters. Two men noticed us, and asked if I would show them where I caught the fish, which I was pleased to do if they would let me fillet anything they caught at 25 cents each. It was truly a Huck Finn kind of upbringing, and deeply formative of "a passion for the environment."

2 On a sunny day in August 1969, I returned to visit my home river of those halcyon❶ boyhood days, with the ink barely dry on a university degree. Memories welled up as I picked my way down to the shore to see what a small sign said, posted right by the water. "Fish for Fun Only." This message was screened against the background of a skull and crossbones, by authority of the Government of Ontario.❷ The English-Wabigoon river system had become tragically contaminated by mercury from an upstream chlor-alkali plant associated with the pulp and paper industry. The fish were no longer fit to eat. The Ojibway kids I went to school with had lost their commercial white-fish fishery and jobs guiding sport anglers, so the economic base of their reserve was in tatters. So was my Huck Finn upbringing. On that day, "a passion for the environment" came crisply into focus.

UNDERSTANDING DETAILS

1. What is Hummel comparing and contrasting?
2. What served as the economic base of the Ojibway reserve in 1959?
3. What changes to his childhood home does Hummel find when he returns from university? What was responsible for these changes?

ANALYZING MEANING

1. Explain Hummel's purpose in this essay. What is his thesis?
2. Hummel refers to his "Huck Finn kind of upbringing" (paragraph 1). Explain this reference.

Reading Critically

❶ What is the meaning of the word *halcyon*?

❷ What other signs bearing warnings might we see as a result of environmental changes?

3. Writing in his fifties, Hummel chose to relate incidents from several decades earlier. Why did this experience have such a strong impact on Hummel? Given his range of experience related to the environment, why didn't Hummel focus on a more current example?

DISCOVERING RHETORICAL STRATEGIES

1. Find three examples of repetition of phrases in Hummel's essay. What is the effect of this repetition?
2. Has Hummel organized his comparison/contrast to focus on one side at a time or point by point? Is this an effective choice? Why or why not?
3. Hummel uses several specific examples in his essay. Explain the effect of the incorporation of these examples.

MAKING CONNECTIONS

1. The title of Hummel's essay clearly indicates his attitude toward the environment. How does his stance toward the environment compare with that of Tomson Highway ("What a Certain Visionary Once Said")?
2. Hummel's essay appeared in the *Queen's Quarterly* as part of a series about people's passions. How does Hummel's portrayal of his passion compare with that of Marguerite Andersen ("Passion for Language")?

IDEAS FOR DISCUSSION/WRITING

Preparing to Write

What do you feel passionate about? What has created that passion in you? What continues to fuel that passion? How is that passion expressed? How do others respond to your passion? Have your passions changed over time or remained consistent?

Choosing a Topic

1. Write about your passion. What has created your passion, and how is your passion expressed?
2. Imagine you are a representative for the chlor-alkali plant that has caused the changes to the English-Wabigoon river system. Write an essay in which you justify the actions taken by your company, and explain the benefits that have resulted from your company's industry in this area.

3. Think of a particular interest that you pursued at one point in your life that has significantly diminished or heightened in importance to you. This might be a sport, a hobby, a community issue, or a social/political cause. Write a comparison/contrast essay in which you compare your engagement in this interest at different stages of your life, and account for the change over time.

MICHAEL McKINLEY

Opera Night in Canada (2000)

Michael McKinley (1961–) is a screenwriter, journalist, and author of several books about hockey, including *Hockey Hall of Fame Legends: The Official Book* (1993), *Etched in Ice: A Tribute to Hockey's Defining Moments* (1998), *Putting a Roof on Winter: Hockey's Rise from Sport to Spectacle* (2000), *The Magnificent One: The Mario Lemieux Story* (2002), and *Hockey: A People's History* (2006). His most recent book, *The Penalty Killing* (2010), is a mystery novel set in the world of hockey. In addition, McKinley, who graduated from the University of British Columbia and Oxford University, wrote and produced *Sacred Ballot*, a documentary on papal elections, for CBC's *Witness* and produced several CNN documentaries, including one on historical evidence related to the life of Jesus Christ. He has also written an episode of *South Park*. In his role as a journalist, McKinley has written for many publications, including the *Chicago Sun-Times*, the *Daily Mail* (London), *The Guardian* (London), the *Los Angeles Times*, *The New York Observer*, *Food and Wine*, and *Sports Illustrated*. You can read more about him, his work, and his love for hockey at **http://michaelmckinley.net**.

Preparing to Read

"Opera Night in Canada" first appeared in *Saturday Night* magazine with the subtitle "hockey and opera are more similar than you think, which is bad news for hockey." In this essay Michael McKinley shows the commonalities between these two apparently disparate forms of entertainment. What are your thoughts about hockey? Do you play hockey? Do you like to watch hockey? Do you attend hockey games? Do you like opera? Have you ever attended an opera? To what types of people do these forms of entertainment typically appeal? Why do you think McKinley sees the similarities between hockey and opera as bad news for hockey?

In late August, a new opera by composer Leslie Uyeda and librettist Tom Cone debuted at Festival Vancouver, an international showcase for music. Of course, the premiere of an opera at a music festival is hardly newsworthy, but the subject matter of this opera was: *Game Misconduct* is an opera about hockey. 1

The ninety-minute opera takes place in the seventh game of a playoff series between a Canadian team and their American rivals, and follows eight characters over three periods, plus overtime, as they watch the action from the bleachers. Each character represents a theme: there's Larry, a hot-dog and popcorn vendor, who will lose his job of twenty years when the arena is torn down; Rita, a fan whom Larry loves; Rene, the father of the Canadian team's goalie; Blossom, who loves hockey for the fighting; Snake and Sylvia, for whom hockey fills the gaps in their relationship; Hugo, an obnoxious fan from Anaheim; and Trish, a hockey virgin at her first game.❶ 2

For those of us who love both hockey and opera, the idea of these two art forms being united after all this time is as shocking as Pinkerton returning to marry Madame Butterfly or the Leafs being united with the Stanley Cup. Hockey and opera would seem to exist on opposite ends of the cultural spectrum; a closer look, however, reveals that they have a lot in common. Hockey has three periods; most operas have three acts. Hockey has six positions—a centre, two wingers, two defencemen, and the goalie—while opera has six major "positions"—soprano, mezzo, contralto, tenor, baritone, and bass. Opera's favourite themes are love and death, and hockey echoes these themes, giving us something to love (the game) in the season of death (winter).❷ 3

Perhaps the most interesting parallel, though, is that both opera and hockey were, in the early stages of their development, hugely popular, and populist, forms of entertainment. Venice saw the world's first public opera house open in 1637, and by 1670, the city had twenty of them. Opera houses had also sprouted up in Rome, Florence, Genoa, Bologna, and Modena. In fact, all across Europe, "real people" were piling in to see tragedy and comedy set to a few good tunes, even if they couldn't understand the Italian, an oversight that Mozart addressed in 1791 when he wrote *The Magic Flute* in his native language of German—a move that brought even more common folk into the stalls. 4

Reading Critically

❶ Do you think this production would appeal more to hockey fans, opera fans, or both? Explain.

❷ Which of these three similarities do you find the most convincing? Which one is the least convincing? Explain.

A century later, opera enjoyed a similar flowering on this side of the Atlantic. Places as far-flung as Dawson City built ice rinks in the service of hockey—but an opera house was just as important to a Canadian small town. Indeed, the country's towns and cities did not consider themselves civilized until they had an opera house to call their own, and both urban Brahmin and rugged frontiersmen would think nothing of going to the opera one night and a hockey game the next. When the Kenora Thistles won the Stanley Cup in 1907, the team from the smallest town ever to win the trophy (population 10,000) could only hold their civic reception in a place as hallowed as the ice rink: the Kenora Opera House. The champion Thistles sat in the opera boxes, their faces reflecting the "barricade of silverware"—including the Cup—that lined the stage as the ecstatic townspeople serenaded their heroes with speeches and song. The occasion itself was operatic. 5

Nearly a quarter of a century later, Conn Smythe was inventing the Maple Leafs as "Canada's Team" (or English Canada's Team) and looking to raise them a temple at Carlton and Church Streets. He wanted to build a place that could not only house the Stanley Cup champions to come, but where people could also dress as though they were going to the opera. On November 12, 1931, 13,000 people—many of them in evening dress, as if at *Siegfried* (or later, under Harold Ballard, at *I Pagliacci*)—turned out for the Gardens opening. As speeches droned on at centre ice, impatient shouts of "Play hockey!" roared down from the rafters, where sat many of the men who had built the place, eager to see if the one-dollar MLG common shares they had taken were going to be worth anything. 6

The image of proles❸ in the cheap seats shouting "Get on with it" recalls the vocal passion of early opera audiences, but it also highlights the downward trajectory of opera in the twentieth century. Movies, radio, and eventually television rendered a night at the opera a largely upper-class pursuit; the importance of opera to the common folk was confined to that parodic phrase beloved of sports announcers: "It ain't over until the fat lady sings." Opera drifted from its populist roots, becoming rarefied, 7

Reading Critically

❸ Who are the proles? Where did this term come from?

culturally adrift, and, arguably, irrelevant, at least to the public at large.

8 Opera's current cultural relevance—or lack of same—is one of the reasons that *Game Misconduct*'s composer chose to tackle hockey as a theme. "'Contemporary' has become a frightening word to a lot of people," Uyeda says. "I don't understand why people don't want to see themselves reflected [in opera]. And that is exactly the reason that I went for this theme of hockey, because it has something to do with me, and with this great country."

9 Ironically, just as people no longer see themselves reflected in opera, it may not be long before they no longer see themselves reflected in hockey. Just as opera has its corporate-sponsorship drives, the NHL now fights for the corporate patron with its mega-arenas bearing corporate logos and perks like wine cellars and humidors and, at the Staples Center in Los Angeles, fireplaces in the corporate boxes. In fact, top tickets for a Maple Leafs game cost a whopping $325 each, or almost three times what you'd pay to sit in the front row at a Canadian Opera Company performance.❹

10 When the swank Air Canada Centre opened in Toronto, Leafs coach Pat Quinn saw the future of hockey—and it was not good. Asked if he feared losing the blue-collar fan, Quinn said, "We've already lost the blue-collar fan. I'm worried about the white-collar fan." It's something that *Game Misconduct* worries about too. Opera, once central, lost touch with the common fan. In the ultimate irony of the hockey-opera relationship, the fat lady may be singing for the national game as well.

UNDERSTANDING DETAILS

1. The differences between opera and hockey are obvious; McKinley focuses on similarities. List the similarities he identifies.
2. Why did Uyeda choose to create an opera about hockey?
3. Why has the popularity of opera diminished over time? What effects have these forces had on hockey?

Reading Critically

❹ Would you pay $325 for hockey tickets? Would you pay a third of this for opera tickets?

ANALYZING MEANING

1. Why has McKinley chosen to compare opera and hockey? What is his purpose in this essay?
2. Explain the "parodic phrase beloved of sports announcers: 'It ain't over until the fat lady sings'" (paragraph 7). What does McKinley mean by his reference to this phrase in the final sentence of his essay?
3. Is McKinley's outlook for the future of hockey optimistic or pessimistic? Explain.

DISCOVERING RHETORICAL STRATEGIES

1. Which of the four main methods of organizing a comparison/contrast essay has McKinley used? Why do you think he has made this choice?
2. In addition to comparison and contrast, what rhetorical strategies has McKinley employed in his essay? Where do you see evidence of these strategies?
3. How does McKinley give his essay cohesiveness? What details link the conclusion back to the beginning of the essay?

MAKING CONNECTIONS

1. McKinley and Aaron Wherry ("Violently Happy") both write about hockey. If they were to attend a hockey game together, on what aspects of the experience do you think they would agree? Where might their views differ?
2. Imagine McKinley in conversation with Alison Gillmor ("Repress Yourself"). What might Gillmor say about the vocal passion of both opera and hockey fans?

IDEAS FOR DISCUSSION/WRITING

Preparing to Write

McKinley writes about the popular and populist beginnings of both opera and hockey, but he suggests that both have become "rarefied" or inaccessible to the public at large. Write freely about entertainment events and their appeal. What types of events have the broadest public appeal? Where do they take place? What types of events do you like to attend? To what do you attribute their appeal? What type of audience do those events tend to attract? Is there a cost associated with those events? Are there types of entertainment events that you avoid? If so, why? How do you learn about events that are happening in your community? Are there types of events you have attended in the past but that have now become inaccessible?

Choosing a Topic

1. Write an essay for a group of your classmates in which you propose attending an event or participating in an activity that won't have immediate appeal. To convince them to participate, show the similarities between this type of event or activity and another that you know they enjoy.
2. Write an essay in which you compare and contrast two events that you have attended. Make sure you point out both similarities and differences, and clarify for your audience which one you preferred.
3. Hockey is often considered the national sport of Canada (although that title is officially shared with lacrosse). Compare and contrast the role of hockey in Canada with the role of baseball in the United States, football in Brazil or Italy, cricket in the West Indies, tae kwon do in Korea, or sumo wrestling in Japan. Have the roles of these sports changed over time? If so, in what way?

IRSHAD MANJI

Status Anxiety? Consider Socrates and the Sewer Saviour (2010)

Author and activist Irshad Manji left Uganda at age four with her family when Idi Amin expelled all Asians from the country. She grew up near Vancouver and attended the University of British Columbia, where she studied the history of ideas. Manji has written for a wide range of newspapers, including *The Globe and Mail* and *The Huffington Post*, has hosted several political and cultural TV shows, including *QueerTelevision*, and has spearheaded numerous projects promoting freedom of thought and conscience, such as the Moral Courage Project, at New York University School of Public Service, which encourages young people to challenge censorship and intellectual conformity. Her first book, *The Trouble with Islam Today: A Muslim's Call for Reform in Her Faith* (2005), was published in 30 countries (but was banned in several others). *Allah, Liberty and Love: The Courage to Reconcile Faith and Freedom* was published in 2011. Named by the World Economic Forum as a Young Global Leader, and awarded *O Magazine's* first Chutzpah Award for "audacity, nerve, boldness and conviction," Manji sees her mission as guiding people about Muslim reform and moral courage. Her website is **www.irshadmanji.com**.

Preparing to Read

In the following essay, first published in *The Globe and Mail*, Manji writes about the concern we feel for how others perceive us. Connecting the movie *The Social Network* (about the founding of Facebook), the philosopher Socrates, and the animated film *Ratatouille*, Manji explores the pressure to conform and the idea of liberation. Before you read, take a moment to think about her three subjects of comparison. Can you see any immediate similarities among them? What connections do you expect Manji to draw?

There's an assumption that, if you haven't yet seen *The Social Network*, Aaron Sorkin's hit movie about the launching of Facebook, you're a bit of a loser. 1

To which the proper response might be, "So I'm a loser. Big whoop. At least I know that a rat can cook."❶ 2

Reading Critically

❶ How is this an effective introduction?

Allow me to explain. 3

According to the philosopher Alain de Botton, humans are steeped in "status anxiety." Most people agonize over how others judge us. Being social creatures, we'll always care about the way we're perceived. The question is: Can we care less? 4

In The Social Network, Harvard student-turned-Facebook founder Mark Zuckerberg strives not to care. He fails–spectacularly. 5

His best friend is on the verge of getting into an exclusive fraternity, while the Zuckerberg character, courted by no swanky club, self-inflicts further humiliation by driving his girlfriend nuts. She dumps him. For solace and revenge, our boy wonder adopts an explosive alchemy❷ of ambition and algorithms. Hence the birth of a multibillion-dollar venture. 6

But it's not just one entrepreneur's dream. Facebook helps incubate the reputation of every user, tapping into base emotions: our aspiration for approval and our tormenting fear of being deemed pathetic. To the end, the Zuckerberg character struggles to regain respect for himself, if he had any at all. 7

However fictionalized this particular drama, a real burden confronts our vulnerable humanity. We instinctively know what it means to survive. What, though, does it mean to succeed? 8

I walked out of the theatre thinking about Socrates. The Greek philosopher relished people's nasty opinions about him. To guard against society's becoming mentally lazy and morally arrogant, he interrogated his fellow Athenians. Not exactly a way to win friends. 9

Socrates attended the debut of a play and realized that the tale revolved around mocking him. Legend has it he stood up mid-performance, not to storm out but to stand out. He wanted to make himself an even easier target. 10

Which enraged his detractors more. They ridiculed him as a gadfly, an insect that flits around, crawls under the skin and irritates to the point of inviting a swatter. Socrates embraced the label. Gadflies, after all, annoy packs of mules. 11

He believed that's what too many citizens had become. Mr. de Botton tells us that Socrates was asked by an onlooker in the marketplace, "Don't you worry about being called names?" Socrates reportedly shot back, "Why? Do you think I should resent it if an ass had kicked me?" 12

Reading Critically

❷ What does *alchemy* mean? Why is this an appropriate word here?

Ultimately, his haters sentenced Socrates to death. The charge: corrupting youth by replacing the traditional gods of worship with a new god – one's conscience. He drank the hemlock that killed his body but not his legacy. 13

Here's the paradox: Socrates achieved iconic status by being free of status anxiety.❸ He never buckled to the envy of others. This is how he acquired self-knowledge. This is what illuminated his uniqueness. And this is why we know his name today. 14

I realize that Socrates can make for pretty tough reading. You might prefer going to the movies. In that case, skip *The Social Network*. Instead, rent *Ratatouille*, the gorgeously animated saga of Remy, a young French rat who accepts himself for everything he is, including one heck of a chef. 15

The odds of success couldn't be lower. His father disapproves, pressing Remy to accept the rodent's supposed fate of scrounging. The inept dishwasher whom he befriends goes hot and cold on Remy, often transferring his own esteem crises to the saviour from the sewer. The restaurant's proprietor, caving to fast-food culture, spurns any effort at culinary excellence and schemes to squash Remy. And the ghost of the restaurant's founder pushes and prods Remy to stay true to his purpose. But what's the recipe for self-awareness? 16

Above all, the most famous food critic in France, a harsh crank who lives to demolish dreams (for he's lost sight of his own), is coming to dinner. The restaurant's future rides on his every terrifying word. Or so he'd have Paris believe. 17

Throughout the adventure, status anxiety gets turned on its head. Like Socrates the gadfly, Remy the rat teaches us that purpose is attained – and sustained – by liberating yourself from the politics of others. 18

The timeless bottom line? "Friend" yourself before you can love your social network. 19

UNDERSTANDING DETAILS

1. What is status anxiety? How does Manji see this anxiety reflected in Facebook?

Reading Critically

❸ Can you think of contemporary figures who have achieved iconic status for this reason?

2. According to Manji's summary of *The Social Network,* what motivates Mark Zuckerberg in the movie to start his multibillion-dollar adventure?
3. How did Socrates react when others insulted him? How did he achieve his current status as an icon, according to Manji?

ANALYZING MEANING

1. What does Manji mean when she says "Facebook helps incubate the reputation of every user" (paragraph 7)? Why does she consider the desire for approval a "base emotion"? Do you agree?
2. Explain Socrates's role as a "gadfly" (paragraph 11). Why did he embrace this role? List some contemporary "gadflies."
3. What does Manji mean when she refers to "the politics of others" (paragraph 18)? Why would she use the term "politics"?

DISCOVERING RHETORICAL STRATEGIES

1. How effectively does Manji link Socrates to the movies *The Social Network* and *Ratatouille*? Of her three subjects, which most effectively supports her thesis about liberating ourselves from status anxiety? Why?
2. Look at the transitions Manji uses to connect her three very different topics throughout the essay. How does she tie all three together in the conclusion?
3. Consider Manji's diction in this article. What kind of persona does she create through her use of informal diction?

MAKING CONNECTIONS

1. Both Michael McKinley ("Opera Night in Canada") and Manji compare topics not commonly linked. To what extent did the unusual nature of these comparisons contribute to your interest in the essays?
2. Both Manji and Cynara Geissler ("Fat Acceptance: A Basic Primer") write about the importance of self-acceptance. How do these essays differ in tone?

IDEAS FOR DISCUSSION/WRITING

Preparing to Write

Whether or not you are a regular user of a social networking site such as Facebook, write freely about the idea of online networking and online friendships. If you use a social networking site, in what ways do you think it enriches your life? What are some of the disadvantages of using the site? If you do not use a social networking site, write about why you have not set up an account. Do you feel that you are missing out on something valuable? Did you see the movie *The Social Network*? Did it change the way you see Facebook and other social networking sites?

Choosing a Topic

1. If you are a Facebook user, take a minute to think about what you love and what you dislike about the site. Write an email addressed to the company with a list of suggested improvements. Explain how your suggestions will improve the Facebook experience.
2. Write an essay comparing or contrasting two social networking sites, or a process essay explaining how to successfully use Facebook or any other social networking site.
3. Manji connects three disparate characters to discuss the phenomenon of status anxiety. Find two other dissimilar characters to discuss another social or psychological phenomenon such as *schadenfreude* (the pleasure we take in the misfortune of others), cyberbullying, binge drinking, or snobbery.

CHRISTOPHER DeWOLF

Montrealers, Cherish Your Clotheslines (2007)

Born and raised in Calgary, Christopher DeWolf now lives and works in Hong Kong. A writer and photographer, DeWolf founded **urbanphoto .net** in 1999, a blog that publishes photographs and articles about people and places all over the world. DeWolf has a degree in Canadian studies and history from McGill University, and his writing has appeared in the Montreal *Gazette* and the *Mirror*, the *National Post*, and *Time*. From 2004 until 2009, he wrote about urban affairs for *Maisonneuve*, and now contributes to the *South China Morning Post* and CNNGo. He also serves as an editor-at-large for *Surface Asia*, a magazine dedicated to design and architecture. He claims that his interest in cityscapes and urban issues began with his early experiences building Lego cities with his father.

Preparing to Read

In the essay below, Christopher DeWolf compares attitudes toward clotheslines in several Canadian cities. Before you begin to read, take a moment to think about your laundry. Do you always use a dryer? When, if ever, do you hang clothes outside? Are there clotheslines outside in your neighbourhood? If not, would it bother you if people suddenly started hanging their clothes outside? Why or why not? What do clotheslines make you think of? What are the advantages of using a clothesline?

Nobody hangs their laundry out to dry in Calgary. In fact, there are hardly any clotheslines. My grandmother's house had one, but I don't think she ever used it. She, like everyone I knew while growing up there, had a washer and dryer set tucked neatly in a musty corner of her basement, across from a half-century-old furnace. 1

It was an eye-opening experience to travel to Newfoundland as a teenager, where I discovered that St. John's was precisely the opposite of Calgary: everyone had clotheslines. Clothes hung over alleyways and backyards, billowing in the salty Atlantic breeze like flags of chores vanquished.❶ There was something 2

Reading Critically

❶ What does this simile make you think of?

inexplicably romantic, something timeless, about clothes drying on lines, whether in the city or in a stark outport on the Avalon Peninsula.

3 Montreal is similar to St. John's, at least in that regard. Here, the clothesline tradition never really died. Although they're less prevalent today than in the past, you'll still see an abundance of them if you wander down the laneways of just about any neighbourhood. Immigrant neighbourhoods in particular have a ton of clotheslines, probably because they're home to so many people who come from countries where drying your clothes outside is still the norm. I remember, earlier this fall, driving east through St. Michel on the elevated Metropolitan Expressway, staring at long rows of triplexes tied together by strands of billowing clothes.

4 I wouldn't be surprised if that kind of scene became even more common in the future. That's because clotheslines are no longer just quaint—they're fashionable. The growing marketability of anything "green" has led to a resurgence of interest in drying clothes outside. It's cheaper than clothes dryers, which can consume as much as 900 kilowatt hours of energy per year, and better for your clothes. According to *La Presse*, which extolled the benefits of clotheslines last summer, the sun eliminates odours and removes stains, and is easier on natural fibres than clothes dryers.

5 But, as much as I like to know that the sun can whiten my whites, it's the clothesline aesthetic that really appeals to me. I'm still charmed by the sight of them, which is good because they're ubiquitous❷ in my back alley from March until November. More than that, though, clotheslines domesticate the street. We've spent so much effort over [the] past half-century trying to sterilize our cities, to turn them into machines, that we need these kinds of reminders that they are, first and foremost, places where people live, messy as that may be.

6 Still, prejudices linger. Many new subdivisions include provisions in house purchase agreements that ban residents from drying their clothes outside. It's a class thing more than anything else, since clotheslines are still associated by many with poverty.❸

Reading Critically

❷ What does the word *ubiquitous* mean?

❸ Why do you think clotheslines are associated with poverty?

There has been a clear shift in attitude, however. Earlier this month, Ontario's environment minister announced that he wants to override those clothesline bans.

7 I'm not alone in enjoying the look of clotheslines, either. There are plenty of Flickr groups dedicated to clotheslines, including one called Les cordes à linge de Montréal.

UNDERSTANDING DETAILS

1. Why is the author surprised by the clotheslines in St. John's? Why do they appeal to him?
2. How is Montreal like St. John's in terms of clotheslines? Why are clotheslines more prevalent in immigrant neighbourhoods?
3. What are the practical advantages of drying clothes outside? Are these advantages the main reason the author likes clotheslines?

ANALYZING MEANING

1. Why are clotheslines becoming fashionable?
2. What does DeWolf mean when he says that "clotheslines domesticate the street" (paragraph 5)?
3. Why do prejudices linger against clotheslines, according to DeWolf?

DISCOVERING RHETORICAL STRATEGIES

1. What is the author's thesis? Where is this thesis most clearly expressed?
2. Which method of organization does the author use to discuss clotheslines in different cities?
3. What other rhetorical strategies does DeWolf use?

MAKING CONNECTIONS

1. Both DeWolf and Stephen Osborne ("The Lost Art of Waving") write about something that is disappearing from contemporary urban areas. Compare the tone of both essays. Which one appeals to you more? Why?
2. Some cities have bans on clotheslines. Compare this negative view of clotheslines to the negative view people have of graffiti (Alex Boyd, "In Defense of Graffiti"). What do you think these views have in common?

IDEAS FOR DISCUSSION/WRITING

Preparing to Write

Write freely about things that appeal to you in an urban landscape. What details do you find most appealing? Least appealing? Do you prefer an urban landscape in summer or winter? Spring or fall? What areas of your city or town do you find most beautiful? What areas do you find ugly? Which kind of landscape do you find more romantic—densely urban or completely rural or something in between?

Choosing a Topic

1. Do you think clotheslines should be banned in your city or town? Write an essay fully justifying your response.
2. What else, other than clotheslines, do you think should be banned in your city? Write an article for your local newspaper explaining what city council should ban, and why.
3. DeWolf writes about his first "eye-opening" trip to the city of St. John's (paragraph 2). Write a descriptive essay on an "eye-opening" visit you have taken to another city.

JENNIE PUNTER

Crime and Punishment in a Foreign Land (2010)

Writer and film critic Jennie Punter has written widely on arts and entertainment. Her articles and reviews have appeared in *The Globe and Mail* and the *Toronto Star*. She contributes regularly to *Variety*, a magazine about the film industry. Punter has also worked in documentary film production. She tweets at **http://twitter.com/#!/JenniePunter**.

Preparing to Read

The essay below appeared in *Queen's Quarterly*, a journal of essays, reviews, articles, fiction, and poetry published by Queen's University. In this piece, Punter compares two foreign crime movies, *The Secret in their Eyes* (Argentina) and *The Girl with the Dragon Tattoo* (Sweden). Have you seen either film? Have you read the "Millennium Trilogy"? As a rule, are you drawn to films about crime? Why or why not?

On the eve of leaving for the cottage earlier this summer I finished, in late-night page-turning frenzy, *The Girl Who Kicked the Hornet's Nest*, the final book of the late Swedish author Stieg Larsson's "Millennium Trilogy" of crime novels, which have sold 40 million copies worldwide. I couldn't save it for the beach. Such is the grip of these bestsellers; high literature they ain't, but they are highly addictive. Before the wave of popularity that began in Scandinavia washed over North America, news hit that the trilogy is set for a Hollywood film franchise treatment produced by Sony Pictures. "Millennium" fans clamour every time a showbiz reporter uploads a rumour. What rugged 40-something actor will play muckraking investigative journalist Mikael Blomkvist? And, more important, what gutsy ingénue could possibly inhabit the diminutive, flatchested, chain-smoking, tattoo-adorned, anti-social, bisexual, genius computer hacker Lisbeth Salander, one of the most compelling characters in recent popular fiction? (Daniel Craig, best known as the latest James Bond, and newcomer Rooney Mara, it turns out.) 1

The adaptation of the first book, *The Girl with the Dragon Tattoo* (the original, more provocative, title in Swedish is *Män som hatar kvinnor* or "Men Who Hate Women," a running theme in the trilogy), will be directed by David Fincher, known for the creepy noirish thrillers *Se7en*, *Fight Club*, and *Zodiac*. Screenwriter Steven Zaillian, Oscar-winner for *Schindler's List*, is currently penning the script; he too knows his way around a thriller, with credits on straightforward fare like *Clear and Present Danger*, *The Interpreter*, and *American Gangster*. It could be a good film. But it's easy to speculate a Hollywood treatment of *Dragon Tattoo* would tone down the sexual violence essential to the story (to get that PG rating) and juice up the action. The reality since the 1980s is that most Hollywood crime movies target the young male demographic. With the odd exception, we get formulaic, male-centred narratives—heist, gangster, or buddy cop flicks.❶ At best, they entertain by fulfilling expectations. At worst, they have you kicking yourself because you didn't stay home and get your crime fix by renting a season of HBO's *The Sopranos* or *The Wire*. 2

The contemporary investigative procedural narrative—the whodunit—tends to rely heavily on the "magic" of science and technology.❷ Characters await DNA lab results. Footage from security cameras, cell phone signals, and other gadgetry is used to identify and track. What is left for a modern protagonist but to throw himself into the hyperactivity that too often passes for action these days? (Even the recent *Sherlock Holmes*, starring Robert Downey Jr, "rebooted" the famous sleuth into this formula with lacklustre results.) But two high-profile foreign films, released this spring here, prove good, old-fashioned pondering of clues and run-of-the-mill legwork can still be immensely rewarding and even magical to watch in a crime drama. The mesmerizing Argentinean film *The Secret In Their Eyes* won an Academy Award earlier this year for best foreign language film. The Swedish-language *The Girl With The Dragon Tattoo* is the first of three Millennium trilogy features produced by Yellow Bird (a company cofounded by celebrated Swedish crime novelist Henning Mankell no less). Both *Secret* and *Dragon Tattoo* were box 3

Reading Critically

❶ Can you give an example for each of these genres?

❷ What does Punter mean by the "magic" of science and technology?

office hits at home and are as slick and eye-catching a cinematic experience as anything Hollywood turns out. But they are made for grown-ups (young cinephiles included). That means, for starters, they give us complex, appealing characters that linger long after mysteries are solved. I saw the films within a few weeks of each other. Although the films differ in many respects, I was struck by their similarities. They make a revelatory double bill, in that they are a kind of crime movie that rarely gets made anymore—masterfully plotted, lavishly detailed, engaged with the past and present, unsettling but never melodramatic, full of surprises but not tricks, bubbling with real chemistry between the two leads.

4 *The Secret in Their Eyes*, the more accomplished of the two, opens with the meeting in a Buenos Aires courthouse of retired criminal investigator Benjamin (Ricardo Darin), who lives alone, and Irene (Soledad Villamil), a judge who is married with children. They have not seen each other for years. He tells her he has been struggling to write about a case they were involved with 25 years earlier, soon after she became Benjamin's much younger boss. The case has haunted him all these years. We don't know exactly why, yet. But we do know this will be a film about unfinished business—of the case's loose ends and of the unspoken emotion between Benjamin and Irene (their eyes are actually not very secretive).

5 The film shuffles smoothly back and forth in time in a beautifully orchestrated way that gradually answers questions and builds suspense. As events surrounding the 1974 case—the brutal rape and murder of a young wife—unfold, we slide to present day (2000) as Benjamin toils on his book, regularly visiting Irene, ostensibly to get feedback. She says she has no interest in reading his drafts, no interest in revisiting the past. But the case drew them together years ago, and once again they are swept up. "Start with what you remember most," Irene advises him. That is, as it turns out, the moment Irene walked into the cluttered office, wearing a red beret and flashing a beautiful smile and a sharp wit that left Benjamin tongue-tied.

6 Darin's superb performance gives us a likeable man too smart for his own good, always irreverent but doggedly responsible. Somehow he was beaten down by the murder case and has been living with a feeling of, if not failure, then deep regret. At first we believe it's because the murder was unsolved, but the reasons are more complex. The murder story is set just before the

military dictatorship,[3] when democracy was still rule of law but corruption was taking hold. For writer-director Juan José Campanella (a veteran director of such TV shows as *Law & Order*, who returns to Argentina to makes films) politics is a backdrop. "I always compare it to World War II in *Casablanca*," he explained in an interview. "It's happening and it emerges in personal ways, in attitudes. But you would not describe *Casablanca* as a war movie."

7 Benjamin has barely returned from the crime scene when a career climbing rival investigator announces an arrest that turns out to be bogus. Benjamin discovers two immigrant workmen confessed after a beating. Outraged, he launches proceedings that get his rival sent to the boonies. This righteous act comes back to bite him when his rival gains power as a regional bureaucrat in league with thugs.

8 During the reopened investigation Benjamin is inspired by conversations with the murdered woman's stoic husband Morales (Pablo Rago), whose expressions of undying love for his wife often describe things Benjamin wishes he could say about Irene. "I still don't know where I got the courage to talk to such a beautiful girl," Morales babbles as Benjamin flips through a photo album. His eye catches the image of Gomez, who appears in several photos looking sidelong at Morales' wife; Benjamin knows that look and is convinced he should track him down. The hunch proves promising when Gomez proves a slippery fellow. Benjamin and fellow investigator Sandoval (Guillermo Francella)—a notorious barfly played as a nimble, melancholy clown—engage in some funny fumbling amateur sleuthing (Campanella is a fan of 1960s Italian comedies). In the film's thrilling tour de force centrepiece, the camera soars high over a roaring soccer stadium then plunges, without cutting, into the dense crowd where the investigators hopelessly search for Gomez in the stands. Against all odds they spot him. After an exciting foot chase (with Keystone Kops grace notes[4]) Gomez lands in the courthouse. Irene dangerously takes the lead in the interrogation, playing the role of a disdainful woman, enraging Gomez to the point that he brandishes his penis and confesses.

Reading Critically

❸ What military dictatorship is referred to here?

❹ Look up the Keystone Kops. What are grace notes? What does this tell you about Punter's intended audience?

But this twisted criminal does not remain long behind bars. 9 Benjamin's former rival, the corrupt bureaucrat, gleefully springs Gomez ("a model prisoner" who spied on guerrillas in jail) and sets him up as an armed agent hunting down so-called terrorists. In one scene Gomez steps into an elevator and slowly, wordlessly cocks his gun with his back turned to Benjamin and Irene—it's utterly sinister, bordering on darkly humorous, as the pair stand there trapped, terrified, and completely helpless as the elevator does its thing; one feels here a subtle comment on the shift in the political scene. Indeed, Benjamin makes a veiled suggestion to Morales that he should simply take matters into his own hands. "Life in prison would have been fair," Morales counters—why should Gomez die, and thus be released from punishment, while he continues to suffer? The system is broken, and so is Benjamin. Just when he realizes Irene's heart is open to his love, he runs out of time. His own life is in danger, and he leaves the city quickly and for a very long time.

Here the film enters the present day, and Irene and Benjamin— 10 the actors beautifully playing more confident but jaded versions of their younger selves—face each other and the case again. Benjamin cannot leave his story dangling in the past; he seeks its conclusion, and ultimately emotional closure, by trying to locate Gomez and Morales. Campanella writes crisp, witty dialogue punctuated by inspired monologues. The best, a plot-advancing rant on the predictable nature of "a guy's passion" by the booze-wise Sandoval, resonates 25 years later as Benjamin confronts the truth in a quietly chilling finale.

The Girl with the Dragon Tattoo also revolves around the unfin- 11 ished business of an ancient investigation that ignites the obsessive nature of the film's male protagonist and puts him in mortal danger. The film is a more straightforward action-mystery, albeit with Swedish Gothic kick, but also features a backdrop of political pessimism, the stench of corruption wafting (and fully fragrant in the sequels).

Middle-aged journalist Blomkvist (Michael Nyqvist), pub- 12 lisher of the magazine *Millennium,* has just lost a libel case against a Swedish tycoon. It's clear he's been set up, but he must serve a short prison term in six months. Out of the blue he is hired by elderly industrialist Henrik Vanger (Sven-Bertil Taube), who will pay him handsomely to investigate a cold case—the disappearance, in a "closed-room" scenario, of his beloved 16-year-old niece Harriet 40 years earlier on the remote island that has served as the Vanger family compound for decades.

Henrik believes Harriet was murdered by a family member when the entire dysfunctional clan was gathered for a corporate meeting on the island—where some family members, including an old Nazi, still live. Holed up in a cabin on the island, Blomkvist discovers he is being remotely "helped" by Salander (described in the first paragraph of this article). She had been hired to investigate his background but has been keeping tabs ever since for personal reasons. Soon she is on site, a more than efficient partner whose unusual gifts include a photographic memory, a knack with surveillance gear, and defensive fighting skills. 13

Danish director Niels Arden Oplev radically streamlines the sprawling novel, cutting or diminishing characters, tossing out tasty background and bits of business, integrating Blomkvist and Salander's storylines and investigative moves in a more direct way. Fans may disagree, but I think the film is an improvement on Larsson's messy, if enjoyable, book. One great example is how the film handles photography. Like Benjamin, Blomkvist pores over photos (though a much larger archive) and eventually gets a hunch. In prose this process involves lengthy descriptions, but in the film we flip realtime through images, via a Mac program, becoming one with Blomkvist's evolving thought process—the scenes are reminiscent of *Blow Up* as the protagonist intuitively knows he's stumbled on something significant but strains to figure out what. 14

The film's standout improvement is Salander, a more fierce and proactive version than we find in the book and played to perfection by Noomi Rapace. In *Secret*, one woman is a victim, the other an investigator with power; in *Dragon Tattoo*, Salander is both. The film does not eschew the novel's harrowing scenes of sexual violence. The incorruptible Salander is brutally raped by her new legal guardian, who mistakes her sullenness for mental incompetence and expects she will keep mute; later she exacts what she believes is fitting punishment. This experience, one of Salander's many secrets, fuels her desire to speed up Blomkvist's investigation—Salander knows something far darker is at play on the island than the 40-year-old mystery. 15

Some view Salander as a feminist icon;[5] others see an emotionally damaged vigilante, but one thing is for sure—with the 16

Reading Critically

[5] Why might Salander be seen as a feminist icon? Name other feminist icons.

release of the two Swedish sequels this year and a Hollywood franchise around the corner, this singular and complex character will leave a permanent mark on the crime film map.

UNDERSTANDING DETAILS

1. What is Punter's main complaint against most crime movies since the 1980s? Who is the audience for these crime movies?
2. Why was the recent *Sherlock Holmes* "reboot" lacklustre, according to Punter? How are the two foreign crime movies different?
3. In what ways is the film version of *The Girl with the Dragon Tattoo* an improvement over the novel?

ANALYZING MEANING

1. How does Punter think the Hollywood version of *The Girl with the Dragon Tattoo* will differ from the Swedish original? Why will it be changed?
2. What does Punter mean when she says the two foreign crime movies were made for "grown-ups" (paragraph 3)? What themes do the two movies have in common?
3. What role does politics play in both movies?

DISCOVERING RHETORICAL STRATEGIES

1. What method of organization does Punter use to make her comparison? Why would she choose this method?
2. What is Punter's main purpose in writing this essay? Were you persuaded by her argument? Why or why not?
3. Punter describes both films in great detail and yet manages to avoid giving away key plot spoilers. Make a list of things she hints at but does not reveal. Do you feel she has still revealed too much?

MAKING CONNECTIONS

1. Both Punter and Irshad Manji ("Status Anxiety? Consider Socrates and the Sewer Saviour") compare films in their essays. How do their audiences differ? How do you know?
2. Both Punter and Ryan McNutt ("The Music We Hate: Joanne Newsom") are faced with the challenge of translating essentially sensory art forms into words. How effective were these writers in conveying film and music on the page?

IDEAS FOR DISCUSSION/WRITING

Preparing to Write

Write freely about a movie you have seen that was adapted from a book. If you read the book before you saw the film, how did you feel about the adaptation? If you saw the film first, were you inspired to read the book after? Why or why not? In terms of telling a story, which medium, film or print, do you feel has the greatest advantage? Is there anything a novel can do that film cannot?

Choosing a Topic

1 Write a comparison of a Hollywood film and a foreign film within the same genre, or a comparison of an original film and a remake (or "reboot," as Punter calls it.) What differences in style or approach do you see, and what do you think explains these differences?
2. Punter writes about crime films. Write an argumentative essay explaining what you think accounts for the popularity of crime films and "investigative procedural" television shows.
3. Choose a book that you think would make an excellent film and write a persuasive essay outlining why this book would work as a movie, who it would appeal to, and why. Suggest actors and actresses for the main roles, and note any changes that the film would have to make to the book's structure.

CHAPTER 7

DEFINITION

Limiting the Frame of Reference

Definitions help us function smoothly in a complex world. All effective communication, in fact, is dependent on our unique human ability to understand and employ accurate definitions of a wide range of words, phrases, and abstract ideas. If we did not work from a set of shared definitions, we would not be able to carry on coherent conversations, write comprehensible letters, or respond to even the simplest radio and television programs. Definitions help us understand concrete terms (such as *electrons, isometric exercises*, and *gross national product*), discuss various events in our lives (such as snowboarding, legal proceedings, and a New Year's celebration), and grasp difficult abstract ideas (such as the concepts of democracy, ambition, and resentment). The ability to comprehend definitions and use them effectively helps us keep our oral and written level of communication accurate and accessible to a wide variety of people.

Defining *Definition*

Definition is the process of explaining a word, object, or idea in such a way that the reader (or listener) knows as precisely as possible what we mean. A good definition sets up intellectual boundaries by focusing on the special qualities of a word or phrase that set it apart from other similar words or phrases. Clear definitions always give the writer and the reader a mutual starting point on the sometimes bumpy road to successful communication.

Definitions vary from short, dictionary-length summaries to longer, extended accounts that determine the form of an entire essay. Words or ideas that require expanded definitions are usually abstract, complex, or unavoidably controversial; they generally bear many related meanings or many shades of meaning. Definitions can be *objective* (technically precise and generally dry) or *subjective* (coloured with personal opinion). They can be used to instruct or entertain, or to accomplish a combination of these two fundamental rhetorical goals.

In the following excerpt, a student defines *childhood* by putting it into perspective with other important stages of life. Though mostly entertaining, the paragraph is also instructive as the student objectively captures the essence of this phase of human development:

> Childhood is a stage of growth somewhere between infancy and adolescence. Just as each developmental period in our lives brings new changes and concerns, childhood serves as the threshold to puberty—the time we learn to discriminate between good and bad, right and wrong, love and lust. Childhood is neither a time of irresponsible infancy nor responsible adulthood. Rather, it is marked by duties that we don't really want, challenges that excite us, feelings that puzzle and frighten us, and limitless opportunities that help us explore the world around us. Childhood is a time when we solidify our personalities in spite of pressures to be someone else.

Thinking Critically Through Definition

Definitions are building blocks in communication that help us make certain we are functioning from the same understanding of terms and ideas. They give us a foundation to work from in both reading and writing. Definitions force us to think about meanings and word associations that make other thinking strategies stronger and easier to work with.

The process of thinking through our definitions forces us to come to some understanding about a particular term or concept we are mentally wrestling with. Articulating that definition helps us move to other modes of thought and higher levels of understanding. Practising definitions in isolation to get a feel for them is much like separating the skill of pedalling from the process of riding a bike. The better you get at pedalling, the more natural the rest of the cycling process becomes. The following exercises ask you to practise definitions in a number of different ways. Being more conscious of what definition entails will make it more useful to you in both your reading and your writing.

1. Define one of the concrete words and one of the abstract words listed here in one or two sentences.

   Concrete: *cattle, book, truck, water, gum*

   Abstract: *freedom, progress, equality, fairness, boredom*

   What were some of the differences between the processes you went through to explain the concrete word and the abstract word? What can you conclude from this brief exercise about the differences in defining abstract and concrete words?
2. In what ways can you "define" yourself? What qualities or characteristics are crucial to an understanding of you as a person?

Reading and Writing Definition Essays

Extended definitions, which usually range from two or three paragraphs to an entire essay, seldom follow a set pattern of development or organization. Instead, as you will see from the examples in this chapter, they draw on a number of different techniques to help explain a word, object, term, concept, or phenomenon.

Reading Definition Essays

- What is the essay's context?
- How is the definition introduced?
- Is the essay *objective* or *subjective*?
- What other rhetorical modes support the definition?

Preparing to Read. As you begin to read each of the definition essays in this chapter, take some time to consider the author's title and the synopsis of the essay in the Rhetorical Contents: What is June Callwood's attitude toward her topic in "Forgiveness"? What do you sense is the general mood of Lawrence Hill's "Don't Call Me That Word"? How much can you learn about Cynara Geissler's topic from her title "Fat Acceptance: A Basic Primer"?

Equally important as you prepare to read is scanning an essay and finding information from its preliminary material about the author and the circumstances surrounding the composition of the essay. What do you think Douglas Glover will be describing in "On Winning and Responsibility"? And what can you learn about Drew Hayden Taylor and his qualifications for writing "Pretty Like a White Boy: The Adventures of a Blue-Eyed Ojibway"?

Last, as you prepare to read these essays, answer the prereading questions before each essay, and then spend a few minutes thinking freely about the general subject of the essay at hand: What is your experience of being judged based on your body shape or size (Geissler)? What is your own definition of *terrorism* (Black)? What is your reaction to the word *nigger* (Hill)?

Reading. As you read a definition essay, as with all essays, be sure to record your initial reactions to your reading material. What are some of your thoughts or associations in relation to each essay?

As you get more involved in the essay, reconsider the preliminary material so that you can create a context within which to analyze what the writer is saying: Who do you think Taylor's primary audience is? Do you think his essay will effectively reach that group of people? For whom is Lawrence Hill writing? How would he have to change his essay to appeal to another audience? In what ways is Cynara Geissler qualified to write about fat acceptance?

Also, determine at this point whether the author's treatment of his or her subject is predominantly objective or subjective. Then, make sure you understand the main points of the essay on the literal, interpretive, and analytical levels by reading the questions that follow.

Rereading. When you read these definition essays for a second time, check to see how each writer actually sets forth his or her definition: Does the writer put each item in a specific category with clear boundaries? Do you understand how the item being defined is different from other items in the same category? Did the author name the various components of the item, explain its etymology (linguistic origin and history), discuss what it is not, or perform a combination of these tasks?

To evaluate the effectiveness of a definition essay, you need to reconsider the essay's primary purpose and audience. If Taylor is trying to get the general reader to understand the experience of not "looking the part," how effective is he in doing so?

Similarly, how effective is Geissler in persuading you to respect and value all body sizes and shapes? Especially applicable is the question of what other rhetorical strategies help the author communicate this purpose. What other modes do Simon Black and June Callwood use to enhance your understanding of terrorism and forgiveness?

For an inventory of the reading process, you can review the guidelines on page 41 of the Introduction.

Writing Definition Essays

- Compose a thesis statement.
- Approach the definition creatively.
- Define the word or concept.
- Use other rhetorical strategies to support your definition.

Preparing to Write. As with other essays, you should begin the task of writing a definition essay by answering the prewriting questions featured in this text and then by exploring your subject and generating other ideas. (See the explanation of various prewriting techniques on pages 28–34 of the Introduction.) Be sure you know what you are going to define and how you will approach your definition. You should then focus on a specific audience and purpose as you approach the writing assignment.

Writing. The next step toward developing a definition essay is usually to describe the general category to which the word belongs and then to contrast the word with all other words in that group. To define *exposition*, for example, you might say that it is a type of writing. Then, to differentiate it from other types of writing, you could go on to say that its main purpose is to "expose," or present information, as opposed to rhetorical modes such as description and narration, which describe and tell stories. In addition, you might want to cite some expository methods, such as example, process analysis, division/classification, and comparison/contrast.

Yet another way to begin a definition essay is to provide a term's etymology. Tracing a word's origin often illuminates its current meaning and usage as well. *Exposition*, for example, comes from the Latin *exponere*, meaning "to put forth, set forth, display, declare, or publish" (*ex* = out; *ponere* = to put or place). This information can generally be found in any good dictionary or encyclopedia.

Another approach to defining a term is to explain what it does *not* mean. For example, *exposition* is not creative writing. By limiting the readers' frame of reference in these various ways, you are helping to establish a working definition for the term under consideration.

Finally, the rhetorical methods that we have already studied (description, narration, example, process analysis, division/classification, and comparison/contrast) are particularly useful to writers in expanding their definitions. To clarify the term *exposition*, you might describe the details of an expository theme, **narrate** a story about the wide use of the term in today's classroom, or **give examples** of assignments that would produce good expository writing. In other situations, you could **analyze** various writing assignments and discuss the **process** of producing an expository essay, **classify** exposition apart from creative writing and then **divide** it into categories similar to the headings of this book, or **compare** and **contrast** it with creative writing. Writers also quite often use definition to support other rhetorical modes.

Rewriting. Reviewing and revising a definition essay is a relatively straightforward task:

- Have I chosen an effective beginning for my paper?
- Did I create a reasonable context for my definition?
- Have I used appropriate rhetorical strategies to develop my ideas?
- Have I achieved my overall purpose as effectively as possible?

Other guidelines to direct your writing and revising appear on page 42 of the Introduction.

Student Essay: Definition at Work

In the following essay, a student defines "the perfect yuppie." Notice how the writer puts this term in a category and then explains the limits of that category and the uniqueness of this term within the category. To further inform her audience of the features of "yuppiness," the student calls on the word's etymology, its dictionary definition, an itemization of the term's basic characteristics, a number of examples that explain those characteristics, and, finally, a general discussion of causes and effects that regulate a yuppie's behaviour.

The Perfect Yuppie

Etymology/ dictionary definition — General category of word being defined

Many people already know that the letters *YUP* stand for "young urban professional." *Young* in this context is understood to mean thirtyish; *urban* often means suburban; and *professional* means most definitely college-educated. Double the *P* and add an *I* and an *E* at the end, and you get yuppie—that 1980s bourgeois, the marketers' darling, and the 1960s' inheritance. But let's not generalize. Not every 30-year-old suburban college graduate qualifies as a yuppie. Nor is every yuppie in his or her thirties. True yuppiness involves much more than the words that make up the acronym. Being the little sister of a couple of yups, I am in an especially good position to define the perfect yuppie. I watched two develop.

Subject

Limitations set — Why the dictionary is inadequate

Writer's credibility

The essence of yuppiness is generally new money. In the yuppie's defence, I will admit that most yuppies have worked hard for their money and social status. Moreover, the baby boom of which they are a part has caused a glut of job seekers in their age bracket, forcing them to be competitive if they want all the nice things retailers have designed for them. But with new money comes an interesting combination of wealth, naïveté, and pretentiousness.

General characteristic

Cause/effect

General characteristic — Cause/effect

For example, most yuppies worthy of the title have long ago traded in their fringed suede jackets for fancy fur coats. Although they were animal rights activists in the 1960s, they will not notice the irony of this change. In fact, they may be shameless enough to parade in their fur coats—fashion-show style—for friends and family. Because of their "innocence," yuppies generally will not see the vulgarity of their actions.

Specific example

Specific example

Because they are often quite wealthy, yuppies tend to have a lot of "things." They are simply overwhelmed by the responsibility of spending all that money. For example, one yup I know has 14 pairs of sunglasses and 7 watches. She, her husband, and their three children own at least 20 collections of everything from comic books to Civil War memorabilia. Most yuppies have so much money that I often wonder why the word *yuppie* does not have a dollar sign in it somewhere.

General characteristic

Specific example

Specific example

Perhaps in an effort to rid themselves of this financial burden, all good yuppies go to Europe as soon as possible. Not Germany or France or Portugal, mind you, but Europe. They do not know what they are doing there and thus generally spend much more money than they need to—but, after all, no yuppie ever claimed to be frugal. Most important, they bring home slides of Europe

Cause/effect

General characteristic

Cause/effect

General characteristic

and show them to everyone they know. A really good yuppie will forget and show you his or her slides more than once. Incidentally, when everyone has seen the slides of Europe twice, the yuppie's next stop is Australia.

General characteristic

A favourite pastime of yuppies is having wine-tasting parties for their yuppie friends. At these parties, they must make a great to-do about tasting the wine, cupping their faces over the glass with their palms (as if they were having a facial), and even sniffing the cork, for goodness sake. I once knew a yuppie who did not understand that a bottle of wine could not be rejected simply because he found he "did not like that kind." Another enjoyed making a show of having his wife choose and taste the wine occasionally, which they both thought was adorable.

Specific example

Specific example

Specific example

What it is not

Some yuppie wanna-bes drive red or black BMWs, but don't let them fool you. A genuine, hard-core yuppie will usually own a gold or silver Volvo station wagon. In this yuppie-mobile, the yuppie wife will chauffeur her young yupettes to and from their modelling classes, track meets, ballet, the manicurist, and Boy Scouts, for the young yuppie is generally as competitive and socially active as his or her parents. On the same topic, one particularly annoying trait of yuppie parents is bragging about their yupettes. You will know yuppies by the fact that they have the smartest, most talented children in the world. They will show you their kids' report cards, making sure you notice any improvements from last term.

General characteristic

Specific example

Cause/effect

General characteristic

Specific example

Perhaps I have been harsh in my portrayal of the perfect yuppie, and, certainly, I will be accused by some of stereotyping. But consider this: I never classify people as yuppies who do not so classify themselves. The ultimate criterion for being yuppies is that they will always proudly label themselves as such.

Division/classification

General characteristic and concluding statement

Some Final Thoughts on Definition

The following selections feature extended definitions whose main purpose is to explain a specific term or idea to their readers. Each essay in its own way helps the audience identify with various parts of its definitions, and each successfully communicates the unique qualities of the term or idea in question. Notice which approaches to definition each writer takes and how these approaches limit the readers' frame of reference in the process of effective communication.

DEFINITION IN REVIEW

Reading Definition Essays

Preparing to Read

✓ What assumptions can I make from the essay's title?
✓ What do I think the general mood of the essay will be?
✓ What are the essay's purpose and audience?
✓ What does the synopsis tell me about the essay?
✓ What can I learn from the author's biography?
✓ Can I predict the author's point of view toward the subject?

Reading

✓ What is the essay's context?
✓ How is the definition introduced?
✓ Is the essay predominantly subjective or objective?
✓ What other rhetorical strategies support the thesis?

Rereading

✓ How does the author lay out the definition?
✓ What are the essay's main purpose and audience?
✓ What other rhetorical strategies does the author use?

Writing Definition Essays

Preparing to Write

✓ Do I know what I am going to define and how I will approach my topic?
✓ Who is my audience?

Writing

✓ Did I compose a thesis statement?
✓ Does the beginning of the essay suit my purpose?
✓ Do I use effective strategies to define my word or concept?
✓ What rhetorical strategies do I use to expand my definition essay?

Rewriting

✓ Have I chosen an effective beginning for my essay?
✓ Did I create a reasonable context for my definition?
✓ Have I used appropriate rhetorical strategies to develop my ideas?
✓ Have I achieved my overall purpose as effectively as possible?

DREW HAYDEN TAYLOR

Pretty Like a White Boy: The Adventures of a Blue-Eyed Ojibway (1991)

Living in Toronto but originally from the Curve Lake Reserve near Peterborough, Ontario, Drew Hayden Taylor (1962–) has claimed to hate the technical part of writing, yet he had achieved enviable success by his early thirties—as a writer.

Since graduating from the broadcasting program at Seneca College, Taylor has worked as a radio reporter, a sound recordist for a film company, a promoter at the Canadian Native Arts Foundation, and a freelance writer. In addition to articles and stories that have appeared in *Maclean's*, *The Globe and Mail*, *This Magazine*, *Anishinabek News*, *Cinema Canada*, and *Windspeaker*, Taylor has written episodes for *The Beachcombers* and *Street Legal*. He is also an award-winning playwright who has served as the writer-in-residence for the Native Earth Performing Arts Theatre.

Taylor is the author of over 20 books, including several plays ("Only Drunks and Children Tell the Truth," "The Baby Blues," "The Boy in the Treehouse/Girl Who Loved Her Horses," and "alterNatives"), several collections of essays, and a book of short stories, *Fearless Warriors* (1998). Taylor brings a strong sense of humour to his work, which centres primarily on Native issues. He wrote and directed *Redskins, Tricksters and Puppy Stew*, a documentary on Native humour for the National Film Board of Canada. He has also edited two anthologies, *Me Funny*, a book about Native humour (2006), and its follow-up, *Me Sexy* (2008). Most recently, Taylor has published a novel entitled *Motorcycles & Sweetgrass* (2010), which was nominated for the Governor General's Award, and *NEWS: Postcards from the Four Directions*, a collection of articles and essays.

Taylor hopes that others will have a more accurate picture of the diversity of Native Peoples if they read more stories written by Native writers. The essay "Pretty Like a White Boy: The Adventures of a Blue-Eyed Ojibway" conveys Taylor's frustrating experiences of not "looking the part."

Preparing to Read

In this essay, Drew Hayden Taylor presents examples from his own life that illustrate the problems that occur as we categorize and define people by their heritage and appearance. Taylor's definition of a new term that accurately defines who he is provides a concluding summary to his discussion of stereotypes and the difficulties of not fitting neatly into the already existing categories. As you prepare to read, consider the terms *Indians*, *Native people*, and *white man*. What associations do you have with each of these? Are they positive labels or negative ones? How do you distinguish people from these groups from people from other groups? What does an Indian look like? In what way does a white person differ in appearance from a Native person? What does the title of this essay tell you about the author's attitude toward his topic?

In this big, huge world, with all its billions and billions of people, it's safe to say that everybody will eventually come across personalities and individuals that will touch them in some peculiar yet poignant way. Individuals that in some way represent and help define who you are. I'm no different, mine was Kermit the Frog. Not just because Natives have a long tradition of savouring Frogs' legs, but because of his music. If you all may remember, Kermit is quite famous for his rendition of "It's Not Easy Being Green." I can relate. If I could sing, my song would be "It's Not Easy Having Blue Eyes in a Brown Eyed Village." 1

Yes, I'm afraid it's true. The author happens to be a card-carrying Indian.❶ Once you get past the aforementioned eyes, the fair skin, the light brown hair, and noticeable lack of cheekbones, there lies the heart and spirit of an Ojibway storyteller. Honest Injun, or as the more politically correct term may be, honest aboriginal. 2

You see, I'm the product of a white father I never knew, and an Ojibway woman who evidently couldn't run fast enough.❷ As a kid I knew I looked a bit different. But, then again, all kids are paranoid when it comes to their peers. I had a fairly happy childhood, frolicking through the bulrushes. But there were certain things that, even then, made me notice my unusual appearance. Whenever we played cowboys and Indians, guess who had to be the bad guy, the cowboy. 3

It wasn't until I left the Reserve for the big bad city, that I became more aware of the role people expected me to play, and the fact that physically I didn't fit in. Everybody seemed to have this preconceived idea of how every Indian looked and acted. One guy, on my first day of college, asked me what kind of horse I preferred. I didn't have the heart to tell him "hobby."❸ 4

Reading Critically

❶ What is "a card-carrying Indian"?

❷ What does this sentence imply?

❸ What is a "hobby horse"? Why do you think Taylor jokes about this?

I've often tried to be philosophical about the whole thing. 5 I have both white and red blood in me, I guess that makes me pink. I am a "Pink" man. Try to imagine this, I'm walking around on any typical Reserve in Canada, my head held high, proudly announcing to everyone "I am a Pink Man." It's a good thing I ran track in school.❹

My pinkness is constantly being pointed out to me over 6 and over and over again. "You don't look Indian?" "You're not Indian, are you?" "Really?!?" I got questions like that from both white and Native people, for a while I debated having my status card tattooed on my forehead.

And like most insecure people and specially a blue-eyed 7 Native writer, I went through a particularly severe identity crisis at one point. In fact, I admit it, one depressing spring evening, I dyed my hair black. Pitch black.

The reason for such a dramatic act, you may ask? Show 8 Business. You see, for the last eight years or so, I've worked in various capacities in the performing arts, and as a result I'd always get calls to be an extra or even try out for an important role in some Native oriented movie. This anonymous voice would phone, having been given my number, and ask if I would be interested in trying out for a movie. Being a naturally ambitious, curious, and greedy young man, I would always readily agree, stardom flashing in my eyes and hunger pains from my wallet.

A few days later I would show up for the audition, and 9 that was always an experience. What kind of experience you may ask? Picture this, the picture calls for the casting of seventeenth-century Mohawk warriors living in a traditional longhouse.❺ The casting director calls the name "Drew Hayden Taylor" and I enter.

The casting director, the producer, and the film's director 10 look up from the table and see my face, blue eyes flashing in anticipation. I once was described as a slightly chubby beachboy. But even beachboys have tans. Anyway, there would be a quick flush of confusion, a recheck of the papers, and a hesitant "Mr. Taylor?" Then they would ask if I was at the right audition. It

---

Reading Critically

❹ Why does Taylor consider calling himself a "Pink Man"?

❺ What is a longhouse? Can you think of any other types of dwellings that 17th-century Indians lived in?

was always the same. By the way, I never got any of the parts I tried for, except for a few anonymous crowd shots. Politics tells me it's because of the way I look, reality tells me it's probably because I can't act. I'm not sure which is better.

11 It's not just film people either. Recently I've become quite involved in Theatre, Native theatre to be exact. And one cold October day I was happily attending the Toronto leg of a province-wide tour of my first play, *Toronto at Dreamer's Rock.* The place was sold out, the audience very receptive and the performance was wonderful. Ironically one of the actors was also half white.❻

12 The director later told me he had been talking with the actor's father, an older non-Native type chap. Evidently he had asked a few questions about me, and how I did my research. This made the director curious and he asked about his interest. He replied "He's got an amazing grasp of the Native situation for a white person."

13 Not all these incidents are work related either. One time a friend and I were coming out of a rather upscale bar (we were out Yuppie watching) and managed to catch a cab. We thanked the cab driver for being so comfortably close on such a cold night, he shrugged and nonchalantly talked about knowing what bars to drive around. "If you're not careful, all you'll get is drunk Indians." I hiccupped.

14 Another time this cab driver droned on and on about the government. He started out by criticizing Mulroney, and eventually his handling of the Oka crisis. This perked up my ears, until he said "If it were me, I'd have tear-gassed the place by the second day. No more problem." He got a dime tip. A few incidents like this and I'm convinced I'd make a great undercover agent for one of the Native political organizations.

15 But then again, even Native people have been known to look at me with a fair amount of suspicion. Many years ago when I was a young man, I was working on a documentary on Native culture up in the wilds of Northern Ontario. We were at an isolated cabin filming a trapper woman and her kids. This one particular nine-year-old girl seemed to take a shine to me. She followed me around for two days both annoying me and endearing herself to me.

Reading Critically

❻ Why does Taylor find this ironic?

But she absolutely refused to believe that I was Indian. The whole film crew tried to tell her but to no avail. She was certain I was white.

16 Then one day as I was loading up the car with film equipment, she asked me if I wanted some tea. Being in a hurry I declined the tea. She immediately smiled with victory crying out "See, you're not Indian, all Indians drink tea!"

17 Frustrated and a little hurt I whipped out my Status card and thrust it at her. Now there I was, standing in a Northern Ontario winter, showing my Status card to a nine-year-old non-status Indian girl who had no idea what one was. Looking back, this may not have been one of my brighter moves.❼

18 But I must admit, it was a Native woman that boiled everything down in one simple sentence. You may know that woman, Marianne Jones from "The Beachcombers" television series. We were working on a film together out west and we got to gossiping. Eventually we got around to talking about our respective villages. Hers on the Queen Charlotte Islands, or Haida Gwaii as the Haida call them, and mine in central Ontario.

19 Eventually childhood on the Reserve was being discussed and I made a comment about the way I look. She studied me for a moment, smiled, and said "Do you know what the old women in my village would call you?" Hesitant but curious, I shook my head. "They'd say you were pretty like a white boy." To this day I'm still not sure if I like that.

20 Now some may argue that I am simply a Métis with a Status card. I disagree, I failed French in grade 11. And the Métis as everyone knows have their own separate and honourable culture, particularly in western Canada. And of course I am well aware that I am not the only person with my physical characteristics.

21 I remember once looking at a video tape of a drum group, shot on a Reserve up near Manitoulin Island. I noticed one of the drummers seemed quite fairhaired, almost blond. I mentioned this to my girlfriend of the time and she shrugged saying "Well, that's to be expected. The highway runs right through the Reserve."❽

Reading Critically

❼ Why does Taylor feel this way about his actions?

❽ How does this statement reflect Taylor's own origins?

Perhaps I'm being too critical. There's a lot to be said for both cultures. For example, on the left hand, you have the Native respect for Elders. They understand the concept of wisdom and insight coming with age. 22

On the white hand, there's Italian food. I mean I really love my mother and family but seriously, does anything really beat good Veal Scaloppine? Most of my aboriginal friends share my fondness for this particular brand of food. Wasn't there a warrior at Oka named Lasagna? I found it ironic, though curiously logical, that Columbus was Italian. A connection I wonder? 23

Also Native people have this wonderful respect and love for the land. They believe they are part of it, a mere link in the cycle of existence. Now as many of you know, this conflicts with the accepted Judeo-Christian i.e. western view of land management. I even believe somewhere in the first chapters of the Bible it says something about God giving man dominion over Nature. Check it out, Genesis 4:?, "Thou shalt clear cut." So I grew up understanding that everything around me is important and alive. My Native heritage gave me that. 24

And again, on the white hand, there's breast implants. Darn clever them white people. That's something Indians would never have invented, seriously. We're not ambitious enough. We just take what the Creator decides to give us, but no, not the white man. Just imagine it, some serious looking white man, and let's face it people, we know it was a man who invented them, don't we? So just imagine some serious looking white doctor sitting around in his laboratory muttering to himself, "Big tits, big tits, hmmm, how do I make big tits?" If it was an Indian, it would be "Big tits, big tits, white women sure got big tits" and leave it at that. 25

So where does that leave me on the big philosophical scoreboard? What exactly are my choices again? Indians—respect for Elders, love of the land. White people—food and big tits. In order to live in both cultures I guess I'd have to find an Indian woman with big tits who lives with her grandmother in a cabin out in the woods and can make Fettuccini Alfredo on a wood stove.[9] 26

Reading Critically

[9] What is our reaction to this statement? Explain.

Now let me make this clear, I'm not writing this for sympathy, or out of anger, or even some need for self-glorification. I am just setting the facts straight. For as you read this, a new Nation is born. This is a declaration of independence, my declaration of independence. 27

I've spent too many years explaining who and what I am repeatedly, so as of this moment, I officially secede from both races. I plan to start my own separate nation. Because I am half Ojibway and half Caucasian, we will be called the Occasions. And I of course, since I'm founding the new nation, will be a Special Occasion. 28

UNDERSTANDING DETAILS

1. Does Taylor affiliate himself more closely with Native or white culture? Give specific examples to support your answer.
2. What advantages does Taylor associate with being Native? What advantages does he link with being White?
3. According to Taylor, why would he make a great undercover agent for a Native political organization?

ANALYZING MEANING

1. What is the author's purpose in this essay? Does he take an objective or a subjective approach in defining his subject?
2. Explain why Taylor does not consider himself to be Métis.
3. Why do you think Taylor did not get the parts in the films for which he auditioned?

DISCOVERING RHETORICAL STRATEGIES

1. What tone is established in this essay? How does Taylor create this tone? Is it effective?
2. What rhetorical strategies is Taylor employing in this essay in addition to definition? Give specific examples to support your answer.
3. Why does Taylor settle on the term "Special Occasion" rather than "Pink Man" as a way to define himself? What definition strategy has resulted in his final title?

MAKING CONNECTIONS

1. Taylor credits Tomson Highway ("What a Certain Visionary Once Said") with "helping him to get his feet wet" in Native theatre. What similarities are there between Taylor's essay and Highway's?

2. Imagine Edith Iglauer ("Red Smile") and Taylor having a conversation about being judged based on appearances. In what respects are their experiences similar? How do they differ? Do the two respond to these judgments in the same way? Give specific examples to support your answer.
3. Taylor has chosen humour as a vehicle for making a difficult subject more palatable to his readers. Compare this strategy to that of Simon Black ("The Search for Mandela's Gun") and Lawrence Hill ("Don't Call Me That Word"). Explain which you think is the more effective approach.

IDEAS FOR DISCUSSION/WRITING

Preparing to Write

Write freely about your ethnic background, race, or heritage. How would you define yourself? Do existing categories work for you, or do you feel the need to create a new category to capture who you are? What physical characteristics define you as part of the group you have identified? What personality characteristics affiliate you with this group? How would you categorize children of mixed heritage?

Choosing a Topic

1. Think of a term to define yourself in a way that reflects various aspects of your heritage/background. Others may belong to this group, but focus on the aspects that make you unique compared with other already existing categories. Write an essay for a general interest magazine in which you define your term using examples from your own life to make your definition clear.
2. Write an essay for college or university students in which you define a particular job or profession based on your knowledge of someone in that position.
3. In paragraph 1, Taylor refers to "[i]ndividuals that in some way represent and help define who you are." Describe one such individual in your life and explain how he or she has contributed to making you who you are.

JUNE CALLWOOD

Forgiveness (2002)

For her life-long activism and support of social justice, June Callwood has sometimes been called "Canada's conscience." Born in Chatham, Ontario, in 1924, Callwood grew up in poverty, quitting high school at age 16 to help support her family. She moved to Toronto two years later and talked her way into a job at *The Globe and Mail*. When she married, a year after being hired, she kept her original name because the newspaper did not employ married women at the time. The author of over 10 books, Callwood founded numerous organizations devoted to social justice and freedom of expression. Some of these enduring organizations include the Writers' Union of Canada; PEN Canada; the Canadian Civil Liberties Association; Casey House, the first hospice in the world to provide palliative care to people with AIDS; Digger House, a shelter for homeless youth; and Nellie's, one of Canada's first shelters for women in crisis. Among her many awards are the Order of Canada, the Order of Ontario, and 17 honorary degrees. On her 80th birthday, the University of Toronto created the June Callwood Professorship in Social Justice. In a speech to inaugurate the professorship, Callwood declared, "I am missing a formal religion, but I am not without a theology, and my theology is that kindness is a divinity in motion" (**http://www.caseyhouse.com/en/june_callwood/biography/**). She died of cancer in 2007.

Preparing to Read

The word *forgive* is from the Old English *forgiefan*, *for* meaning "completely" and *giefan* meaning "to give." What is "given completely" in forgiveness? What is given up? Do you think some actions are unforgivable? Have you ever been unable to forgive someone? What do you think of the saying "To know all is to forgive all"? Who benefits most when one person forgives another—the forgiver or the transgressor?

A small boy in an industrial city in Ontario was beaten severely many times by his father, to the extent that the boy not infrequently required a doctor to stitch up the wounds. His father, a policeman, sincerely believed that if he beat his son with chains, belts, sticks, and his fists, the boy would not grow up to be gay. That boy, now in his thirties and indelibly a gay man, says he will never forgive his father. 1

"What he did is not forgivable," the man says with composure. "How can it ever be all right to abuse a child? But I have let it go." 2

And a woman, raised on the Prairies in a Finnish home, married a black man and had a son. She showed the infant proudly to her mother, whose reaction was a look of naked disgust. Her mother and that son, now a charming and successful adult, have since developed an affectionate relationship, but the daughter has not forgotten or forgiven the expression on her mother's face. "The best I can do," she says, "is that I have stopped hating her." 3

The ability to forgive is a central tenet of every major religion in the world—Christian, Judaic, Hindu, Buddhist, and Islamic. Those faiths urge followers to forgive their enemies and, indeed, even to find a way to love those who wrong them. As the twenty-first century dawns, however, the world is making a spectacular mess of such pious admonitions. Instead of goodwill, this is the age of anger, the polar opposite of forgiveness.❶ Merciless ethnic, tribal, and religious conflicts dominate every corner of the planet, and in North America individuals live with high levels of wrath that explode as domestic brutality, road rage, vile epithets, and acts of random slaughter. 4

Many people, like the gay man or the woman in a biracial marriage, find forgiveness an unreasonable dictate. Some assaults on the body or soul are unconscionable,❷ they feel, and forgiveness is simply out of the question. It satisfies the requirements of their humanity that they gradually ease away from the primitive thoughts of revenge that once obsessed them. 5

When Simon Wiesenthal, the famed Nazi hunter, was in a German concentration camp, he found himself in a strange situation. He was taken to the bedside of a dying SS officer, a youth who had killed many Jews, and the young man asked him, a Jew, for forgiveness. Wiesenthal was silent and left the room, but was haunted ever after. Thirty years later, he contacted some of the world's great thinkers and asked, what should I have done? Theologians such as Bishop Desmond Tutu and the Dalai Lama gently hinted that he should have been forgiving, for his own 6

Reading Critically

❶ Callwood makes it sound as if this age of anger were new. Do you think she is right? Why or why not?

❷ What does *unconscionable* mean?

sake, but others, notably philosopher Herbert Marcuse, said that great evil should never be forgiven.❸ In *The Sunflower*, a collection of fifty-three responses to Wiesenthal's question, Marcuse wrote sternly that forgiveness condones the crime.❹

7 The moral vacuum left by the pervasive disuse and misuse of religious tenets has allowed a secular forgiveness industry to spring into being. People who yearn desperately to rid themselves of an obsession for vengeance will seek help in curious places. Since 1985, the University of Wisconsin–Madison has offered forgiveness studies, and an International Forgiveness Institute was founded there. Four years ago, the world's first international conference on forgiveness drew hundreds of delegates to Madison. Stanford University has a forgiveness research project and people in California, a state on the cutting edge of self-absorption, are taking part in studies on the art and science of forgiveness. Self-help shelves in bookstores abound in titles such as *Forgive Your Parents: Heal Yourself.*

8 An odious US daytime television show, *Forgive or Forget*, features guests who say they owe someone an apology. They describe their offence, and then, *ta-dah*, the injured party appears on the appropriately tacky set and either grants or withholds forgiveness. Will the former foes embrace one another? The titillated audience can't wait.

9 Apologies are iffy because often they are contrived or coerced. Apologies extracted by judges, mediators, and parents are thin gruel for the wronged person. One familiar genre of apology, the one which commences, "I am sorry you are feeling badly," is particularly counterproductive because there is no admission of any responsibility; it is the other person's problem for being thin-skinned. A sincere and remorseful acceptance of blame, however, can close a wound.❺

10 Psychologists are engrossed by the topic and so are theologians, philosophers, psychiatrists, and—surprise—cardiologists. Unforgiving people, some studies show, are three times more

---

Reading Critically

❸ What do you think Wiesenthal should have done and why?

❹ What is meant by the phrase "forgiveness condones the crime"? Do you agree? Why or why not?

❺ Do you think this is true? Whose wound does this close? Which do you think has more power, a sincere apology or forgiveness? Which is harder to give?

likely to have heart disease as people who don't carry grudges. These findings raise the suspicion that the researchers may have the cart before the horse. Heart attacks occur more often in blowtop people who have unfortified egos, the very ones most apt to be relentlessly unforgiving. On the other hand, people who hold tolerant views of human nature and don't seem to nurse grievances unduly tend to have blood pressures in the normal range.

11 Clergy, counsellors, and people who lecture and write books about forgiveness all preach reductionism as a strategy for overcoming hot resentment of someone's nasty behaviour. They say that people who have been harmed should see the hurtful as deeply flawed human beings working out nameless aggressions. Pitiable and inferior, they are examples of failure to thrive. Adults still distressed by abuse, neglect, or rejection in childhood are urged to consider what happened in their parents' childhoods—often, bad parenting comes from being badly parented. The theory is that understanding the reasons for their parents' limitations will enable the offspring to acquire a measure of compassion.

12 Maybe it works. Hillary Clinton apparently forgave her sleazy husband because she knows he had an unhappy childhood.[6]

13 This technique can be applied to almost any injustice and falls within the rapists-were-beaten-as-children, *poor them* school of thought, which for some skeptics veers perilously close to non-accountability. The law and commonsense hold that adults are responsible for what they do. While empathy may help people appreciate why others behave badly, the exercise is somewhat patronizing. The offender is reduced to a contemptible hive of neuroses and ungovernable aberrations, which accordingly elevates the injured party to a morally superior person.

14 Demonizing the enemy[7] is a common coping mechanism in times of adversity. In military terms, it captures the high ground. Catastrophes such as divorce, job loss, rape, robbery, infidelity, and slander are all assaults on personal dignity and self-respect. A sense of being intact—*safe*—has been violated, and people are

---

Reading Critically

[6] Do you think this is a good example? Why or why not?

[7] What is meant by the phrase "demonizing the enemy"? How is this accomplished?

dismayed to find themselves for some time emotionally crippled by anger and grief. Betrayal and loss take big chunks out of people's confidence and leave them feeling excruciatingly vulnerable to random harm.

15 The starting place, some therapists say, is to accept that something appalling has happened, and it hurts. Denial, a recourse more favoured by men than by women, won't help.[8] The next step they say, is to develop an off switch. When fury threatens to make the brain reel, people should grasp for distractions. Brooding about revenge only serves to unhinge reason. If people don't rid themselves of wrath, personal growth stops cold. The hard part comes at the end of the process. The choices are to enter a state of forgiveness, which is a triumph of generosity, or just to put the matter in a box, cover it with a lid, place a brick on the lid, and move on. In healthy people, a perverse state of mind eventually wears itself out.

16 In yoga, they say that it takes six years of regularly practising meditation to gain spiritual insight. Forgiveness of a great wrong may take longer. The process can't even begin until the injured person stops crying.

17 Some people are marvellously unbroken by great injustices. Nelson Mandela smiled gently at his adversaries after twenty-seven years of brutal imprisonment. A worldwide figure of wonder, he even invited his white jailer to his inauguration as South Africa's president. In Cambodia, a pastor whose family had been wiped out by the Khmer Rouge baptized and forgave a notorious Khmer Rouge leader known as Duch. A university professor in Virginia had an urge to kill the intruder who beat his mother to death, but stopped himself with the thought, "Whose heart is darker?" And the father of a young girl casually murdered in a street encounter with a teenager she didn't know attended the trial and sat quietly throughout the appalling testimony. He said he would visit the youth in prison. "I do not think I can forgive him," he explained, "but perhaps if I know him I will not hate him."

18 Forgiveness is hard work. A woman, a devout Roman Catholic who forgave the man who tortured and killed her seven-year-old daughter, said, "Anyone who says forgiveness is for wimps hasn't tried it." The reward for giving up scalding thoughts of reprisal is peace of mind. It is worth the candle.

Reading Critically

[8] Do you agree that men are more likely to be in denial than women? Explain.

UNDERSTANDING DETAILS

1. What comprises the "secular forgiveness industry" (paragraph 7)? How did it come about? Why do people turn to this "industry"?
2. Some people find forgiveness "an unreasonable dictate" (paragraph 5). How do these people satisfy "the requirements of their humanity"? How is this different from forgiveness?
3. What are the steps in the forgiveness process? Why might the process take so long?

ANALYZING MEANING

1. What is the author's objection to the TV program *Forgive or Forget*?
2. Why are apologies "iffy" (paragraph 9)? What kinds of apologies does the author discuss?
3. What is reductionism? How does it help people to forgive? Why do some skeptics have a problem with it?

DISCOVERING RHETORICAL STRATEGIES

1. What kinds of examples does the author use to illustrate the complexities of forgiveness? How are the examples at the beginning different from the ones at the end? If these examples were reversed, how would that affect your reading of the article?
2. What reasons does Callwood give for why people should forgive one another? Which of these reasons did you find most compelling?
3. Look up the origin of the phrase "not worth the candle." How is this a fitting last line to the article?

MAKING CONNECTIONS

1. Compare Callwood's definition of forgiveness with Alison Gillmor's analysis of repression ("Repress Yourself"). What views or attitudes do the authors share?
2. Both Callwood and Evelyn Lau ("More and More") write about painful emotional issues. Compare their approaches. Which did you find more effective and why?

IDEAS FOR DISCUSSION/WRITING

Preparing to Write

Write freely about a time you wanted revenge. How did you feel? What thoughts went through your mind? Did you take revenge?

How did you feel after? If you didn't go through with your plans, what stopped you? Similarly, think about a time you have hurt another person. How did you feel after? Were you forgiven for your actions? In general, do you find it easy to apologize? Do you see yourself as a forgiving person? Is the decision to forgive within a person's conscious control? Aside from deciding to forgive someone, what factors might bring about forgiveness?

Choosing a Topic

1. Should some things not be forgiven? Write an essay giving your own answer to Simon Wiesenthal's question in paragraph 6.
2. Think about an incident in your life when you have wronged or been wronged by another person. In a narrative essay, write the story in three parts. First, tell your side of the story. Then describe the story from the other person's point of view. Finally, write the story from a third party's point of view. Try to adapt the narrative voice to match each speaker.
3. Callwood writes about the "secular forgiveness industry" (paragraph 7). Write a definition essay about another trend in pop psychology (such as the confessional TV talk show or a principle of the New Age movement).

DOUGLAS GLOVER

On Winning and Responsibility (2010)

Douglas Glover was born in 1948 and grew up on a family farm in southwestern Ontario. He has a Bachelor of Arts degree in philosophy from York University, a Master of Letters in philosophy from the University of Edinburgh, and a Master of Fine Arts (M.F.A) from the Iowa Writers' Workshop at the University of Iowa.

Glover worked on a series of daily newspapers in New Brunswick, Ontario, Quebec, and Saskatchewan early in his career before publishing *Precious* in 1984. Glover is the author of four novels, five collections of short stories, a compilation of essays, and a book about Don Quixote and novel form. Glover's work has also been included in many anthologies. Glover has won many accolades for his writing, including the 2003 Governor General's Award for fiction. He was a finalist for the 2005 International IMPAC Dublin Literary Award for his novel *Elle* and won the 2006 Writers' Trust of Canada Timothy Findley Award.

In addition to his writing, over the past two decades he has taught at a variety of upstate New York colleges and served as writer-in-residence at four universities in Canada and the U.S. Glover is currently on the faculty of the Vermont College of Fine Arts M.F.A in Writing program.

Preparing to Read

In this essay, first published in *Global Brief*, Douglas Glover explores the notion of winning. Before reading, think about your sense of winning and what it means to win. In what realms of life do we talk about winning? Is winning always positive? What does it take to be a "winner"?

The idea of winning smacks of the absolute and archaic. The pulse of history, liberal guilt and the end-of-history, millenarian dream of global homogeneity are against it. We all go to the worms. Civilizations rise and fall. What remains of countless 'wins' are a few stone remnants[1] and a museum display of corroded armour. 1

Reading Critically

[1] What are the "few stone remnants" to which Glover refers?

Language, as always, is dire with prognostication. One can win the battle but not the war. And even if one wins, it might be a Pyrrhic victory.❷ In the modern parlance, quagmire is a metaphor turned into a technical term for a victory that won't stick. Paradoxically, it seems, both sides have to agree on who won – otherwise [one] does not get victory; one gets a festering sore or a quagmire. We see an early model in the Book of Judges: after wandering in the Wilderness, fording the River Jordan, and conquering city after city, the Israelites find total victory slipping from their grasp (quagmire) due to an inability to compass Jehovah's original programme of ethnic cleansing. 2

Winning is elitist and anti-democratic.❸ Only a few can win; the masses are losers. Think of the difference between performing an action in order to do it well (from aesthetic or utilitarian motives) and performing the same act in order to win (to defeat an opponent). Competition drives excellence,❹ we think, in imitation of the ancient Greeks; although nowadays it also drives the invention of credit default swaps, offshore manufacturing, and the bankrupting of middle-class homeowners. Winning outcomes are always asymmetrical, or they are shadowed by their opposites – failure, resentment and loss. The legendary priest-kings of the Grove of Nemi won their crowns by slaughtering previous kings in combat, only to be slaughtered in turn by new champions. 3

As often as not, winning is a matter of who tells the story, and where the story ends. George W. Bush had his 'Mission Accomplished' moment,❺ only to watch the story of Iraq unfold new chapters of anarchy. If history teaches a lesson, it is that winning is temporary, relative, and open to question. Human beings are a wayward and squabbling lot; as far as winning is concerned, someone is always moving the goalposts or changing the rules. And sometimes one wishes that politicians and their enablers, the media, would scale back the dramatic hyperbole. We should perhaps forget winning and think: temporary advantage in the chaos of life. 4

Reading Critically

❷ What is a "Pyrrhic victory"? Why would this type of victory not be satisfying?

❸ Do you agree with this statement? Why or why not?

❹ What is one example of a situation in which competition drives excellence?

❺ What was Bush's "Mission Accomplished" moment?

In the culture of sports (not to mention politics and the arts, treated as a sport as they often are in the media) where the ancient dramas of *agon* – struggle, defeat and victory – are played out in a glamourous and gossipy arena, winning has become a fantasy of inhuman ability (thank goodness for steroids), fabulous wealth and hysterical spectator identification, a fact not lost on marketing shills – hence the taint of commercial tawdriness attached to winners these days. Above all, winning is entertainment.[6] Disguised as an index of achievement, the cult of winning packages experience as a dramatic action: desire, conflict, suspense, climax and catharsis. 5

People who forget other people speak easily of winning and turn life into a game. And perhaps there is nothing more human than wanting to transform the most awful circumstances – say, war, or the ruthless competition for scarce resources – into a tennis match, all gallantry, rules and referees. But this is pure escapism, denial and tragedy. As the planet grows smaller (and the cosmos beyond grows more mysteriously expansive), it becomes indispensable to compose a larger theory of winning that includes the entire human race and Nature herself within a broad and unconventional accommodation to Fate and Law. 6

At its very best, the ideal of globalization is about winning on a planetary scale – not about the politics of conflict and advantage at the level of tribes, villages, regions or states – but about negotiation, planning and compromise at the level of the species. The radically conservative ideology of eco-politics posits not a programme of competition, conquest and consumption, but of renewal and sustainability. The great, nearly half-century of war from 1914 to 1945 ended not with the punitive hubris of the Treaty of Versailles, but with the Marshall Plan that turned Germany into a winner of a different sort, and irrevocably altered Europe's moral trajectory.[7] 7

There is a definition of the word 'winning' that has little to do with conquest or chicanery, with struggle, defeated opponents and humiliation. We speak of a winning smile or disposition, winning as charming and agreeable, winning that is persuasive, seductive, 8

Reading Critically

[6] What realms can you think of in which winning is primarily entertainment?

[7] What was the Marshall Plan? What effect did it have on Europe? In what way did it make Germany a sort of winner?

and ultimately results in possession. Winning in this regard is not a matter of violence and triumph, but of attraction by force of personality, nobility, generosity and beauty – winning as an expression of play and rhetoric, under the sign of the winged god Eros.

UNDERSTANDING DETAILS

1. How does Glover characterize winning in sports?
2. What does Glover mean when he says, "Language, as always, is dire with prognostication" (paragraph 2)?
3. How is the word *winning*, used "under the sign of the winged god Eros" (paragraph 8), different from the other uses of *winning*?

ANALYZING MEANING

1. How many definitions of winning does Glover present? How many does he portray as positive and how many as negative?
2. Glover says, "We should perhaps forget winning and think: temporary advantage in the chaos of life" (paragraph 4). Explain what he means by this.
3. Glover's essay is entitled "On Winning and Responsibility." What responsibility does he see as coming with winning?

DISCOVERING RHETORICAL STRATEGIES

1. What do you think Glover's purpose is in this essay? Has he successfully achieved that purpose?
2. Is "On Winning and Responsibility" an effective title? Why or why not?
3. Glover makes several literary, historical, and political references in his essay. Identify at least four of these references and then discuss their function in the essay.

MAKING CONNECTIONS

1. What is Glover's thesis in this essay? Where is it expressed? Why has Glover made this choice?
2. According to Glover's essay, "Competition drives excellence, we think" (paragraph 3). How do you think John Moore ("Sporting Life") would respond to that statement?

IDEAS FOR DISCUSSION/WRITING

Preparing to Write

Write freely about competition. In what realms of your life do you experience competition? Do you enjoy competition? Why or why not? What are the positive outcomes of competition? What are the negative outcomes? When is competition explicit and when is it implicit? Do you consider yourself to be a competitive person?

Choosing a Topic

1. Write about a time when you won something. It might have been a sports competition, an academic award, a game, a contest, or something else. Make it clear how it felt to be a winner.
2. Glover says, "Only a few can win; the masses are losers" (paragraph 3). Write a short essay in which you define the term *loser*. Take into account the various definitions of the word and incorporate examples to help illustrate your definition.
3. According to Glover, "Above all, winning is entertainment." (paragraph 5). Think of one of the popular competition reality TV shows. Illustrate Glover's thesis by writing about how that show is structured.

CYNARA GEISSLER

Fat Acceptance: A Basic Primer (2010)

Vancouver-based writer, cultural critic, poet, and podcaster Cynara Geissler has a B.A., Honours from the University of Winnipeg and is a Master of Publishing candidate at Simon Fraser University. Her poetry, fiction, and essays have appeared in various print and online magazines, including *Juice Magazine*, *milo*, *Fatshionista*, *Shameless*, and *Geez Magazine*, where this essay first appeared. In addition, Geissler is marketing manager at Arsenal Pulp Press and does public speaking engagements.

Prior to moving to B.C., Geissler was programming coordinator for the Manitoba Writers' Collective and in that role helped organize Speaking Crow, Winnipeg's longest-running open-mic poetry series.

Preparing to Read

In this essay, first published in *Geez Magazine*, Cynara Geissler champions the fat acceptance movement and her own transformation as she accepted her body. Before reading, think about our cultural expectations regarding body size and shape. What is seen as desirable? What is the prevailing attitude toward people who are considered fat? What is considered beautiful? Unattractive? What industries support our cultural attitudes toward body size and weight?

Fat acceptance – also known as size acceptance, body positivity, weight neutrality and not-waxing-rhapsodic-about-dieting – is a social and corporeal justice principle, founded on the revolutionary idea that it is not productive to spend every waking moment of every day actively hating your body. We live in a fat-fearing and food-moralizing culture where magazines, movies (often involving the hackneyed application of fat suits)❶ and a multi-million dollar "health" and diet industry all pump out the message "thinner is better" – not unlike an unrelenting, cacophonous and extremely distracting trumpet. 1

Reading Critically

❶ Why are fat suits used in magazines and movies?

A lot of time, effort and capital has been invested in making us believe that fat is a dirty word, a state indicative of moral decrepitude, visual shorthand for lazy, undisciplined, incapable and out of control.[2] To stand pointedly and unapologetically outside a narrow beauty politic constitutes a radical act. It takes a lot of stones to tell well-meaning but misinformed friends, relatives and health care professionals who've become accustomed to the brass quartet of lazy-science-and-blanket-judgment that you're not sorry for your size, you're pretty down with your bad self and actually, while we're on the subject, what you do with and put in your body is your own business thankyouverymuch.[3] 2

The fat acceptance movement – which counts activists, academics, doctors and rock stars among its diverse ranks – catches a lot of fire because if there's one thing that makes people uncomfortable it's questioning the efficacy of shame as a motivational tool. Pervasive rhetoric – capitalist, religious, economic – tells us that suffering and self-sacrifice both pave the way to success, and allow us to explain away injustice, to believe that swallowing a daily dose of shit is acceptable, part of the game. So of course people bristle when told that not only do diets – which represent a bodily act of contrition[4] – not work, but that you can opt out, and that once you do, there are other much better places to play. And while it's a big relief to have someone point out, as feminist critic Dorothy Allison has, "that suffering does not ennoble; it destroys," it can start out feeling like a slap in the face especially if you, as I did, devoted much of your conscious life to the pursuit of thinness. 3

When you open up to the possibility that you can live your life *right now* instead of waiting for an arbitrary number on the scale, or on the tag in your pants, it blows your world apart. When you adopt a stance of body autonomy and accept the notion that not only is health not intrinsically connected to height and weight, but is relative, personal, highly variable and not a moral debt to be paid, life becomes enjoyable and navigable in ways you never thought possible. This concept – that your body is your business and that you should feed it, move it, and adorn it for no grander purpose than that it is pleasurable and *feels good*, 4

Reading Critically

[2] Why has our society invested so much in creating this response to fat?

[3] Why has Geissler run these words together into one?

[4] Explain how diets are an act of contrition.

no matter what your weight yesterday, today, or tomorrow – is the basis of Health at Every Size.

And one of the disarming ironies of fat acceptance is that, once you step outside the panopticon of self-loathing and cease obsessing about your body and the ways it deviates from an impossible ideal, you become much more aware of the mechanics of what makes you feel satisfied, invigorated, and inspired and your choices – about food, physical activity, and personal presentation – reflect *your* needs and your identity. More than that, in accepting your body as it is, you help to create a culture that respects and values the diversity of all bodies,[5] a culture that, to return to Allison, "refuses lying myths and easy moralities," that sees people as "human, flawed and extraordinary." Back when I was punishing my body with four-hour workouts and styrofoam food that filled me with little else than despair, I never felt any sort of triumph or control over myself or my life, or deep engagement with the world around me. All my time and energy was spent buying into a loser's game with a moving set of goal posts because – surprise! – capitalist diet culture is in the business of manufacturing failure, a self-sustaining economy of never-ending problems with impermanent purchasable solutions in the form of magic herbs, vibrating hot pants and "fixing" creams. It was only when I shut out the racket of diet discourse and refused to subject myself to an unforgiving beauty politic[6] – reclaiming my body as *my own* – that I felt I had any agency, and valued it in others. 5

UNDERSTANDING DETAILS

1. What is the fat acceptance movement?
2. According to Geissler, how does our society generally view people who are fat?
3. What is the effect on Geissler of accepting her body size?

ANALYZING MEANING

1. How does Geissler feel about other people telling her what to do with her body and what to put in it? Explain her position.

Reading Critically

[5] Do you agree with Geissler's statement? Explain why or why not.

[6] Describe the message that Geissler was getting from the "unforgiving beauty politic."

2. What is the "impossible ideal" to which Geissler refers (paragraph 5)? Do you agree that it is impossible? Explain why or why not.
3. Explain Geissler's conclusion. Evaluate its effectiveness.

DISCOVERING RHETORICAL STRATEGIES

1. How would you describe Geissler's tone in this essay? Give three examples of particular words or phrases that contribute to this tone.
2. What other rhetorical modes has Geissler used in this essay? How do these strategies enhance her definition of fat acceptance?
3. Is Geissler's definition primarily objective or subjective? Explain.

MAKING CONNECTIONS

1. Evelyn Lau ("More and More") and Geissler both write about family and societal expectations around eating and body weight. In what ways are their experiences similar? In what ways do they differ?
2. How do you think Douglas Glover ("On Winning and Responsibility") would respond to Geissler claim that "Pervasive rhetoric – capitalist, religious, economic – tells us that suffering and self-sacrifice both pave the way to success" (paragraph 3)?
3. Seven rules for writing are outlined in Natalie Goldberg's essay ("The Rules of Writing Practice"). Which of these rules has Geissler followed? Are there any that she appears to have ignored or violated?

IDEAS FOR DISCUSSION/WRITING

Preparing to Write

Write freely about your most central beliefs. Where do these beliefs come from? Which of your family members share these beliefs? How different are your core beliefs from those of your parents? What about your grandparents? What beliefs do you think you might have in common with your great-grandparents? Try to imagine what your own great-grandchildren might be like. What would they know about you? How might their beliefs differ from yours?

Choosing a Topic

1. Geissler says, "Pervasive rhetoric – capitalist, religious, economic – tells us that suffering and self-sacrifice both pave the way to success" (paragraph 3). Write about one way in which you have experienced or witnessed this message being conveyed other than in terms of body weight.
2. According to Geissler, "what you do with and put in your body is your own business" (paragraph 2). Do you agree or disagree? Write a short essay in which you support or refute this statement.
3. Write an essay in which you define *beauty* as the term applies to people. Include specific examples in your essay to make your definition clear and strong.

SIMON BLACK

The Search for Mandela's Gun (2006)

A freelance writer, Simon Black has written extensively on social and political issues in his "Politics as Usual" column for *Pound*, a Canadian urban music magazine. His interest in urban music and politics is also evident in the university course he is developing, which will use hip hop culture as a lens through which to examine contemporary social and political issues. His column on sports from a radical's perspective appears in *Canadian Dimension*, and his writing has also appeared in the *Toronto Star, The Independent, Relay, New Labor Forum,* and ZNet, and on **http://rabble.ca**. Black has degrees in sociology and labour studies and is working on a Ph.D. in political science at York University. He has studied at the New School for Social Research in New York City and, in 2008–2009, was a visiting Fulbright student-fellow at the City University of New York's Graduate Center. He has lectured in Toronto high schools on philosophy and social justice; the essay below arose out of a conversation with high school students.

Preparing to Read

In his essay, Black explores the definition of *terrorism*. What is your definition of a terrorist? What factors have contributed to your definition? Who, by your definition, would count as a terrorist? What do you know about Nelson Mandela? Which groups would have considered him a terrorist? Do you think that violence for a political cause is ever justified? How is this form of political violence the same as or different from terrorism?

Recently I was speaking to high school students about the role of social movements in the political system. One movement I spoke of was the Black freedom struggle in South Africa. The kids knew little about apartheid[1] but they all recognized the name of Nelson Mandela. Sensing their interest, I embarked on a slight digression, telling them the story of Nelson Mandela's handgun. The gun was a gift given to him by an Ethiopian army 1

Reading Critically

[1] What is apartheid? Where and for how long did it exist?

officer while he undertook military training in Addis Ababa. Prior to his arrest and subsequent 27-year imprisonment, Mandela buried the gun behind his farmhouse hideout situated just north of Johannesburg. This year, historians and activists from the ruling African National Congress party—of which Mandela was leader—went on a mission to dig up the long lost gun and put it in a museum. Upon hearing the story, the class was astonished: "Mandela had a gun?" "Why did he have a gun?" "Not *the* Nelson Mandela, right?" I told them that Mandela had been active in forming the Umkhonto we Sizwe (or MK for short), an armed resistance group which sabotaged (i.e. bombed) key sites of white South African rule.❷ The students couldn't believe that the Mandela they knew—the grandfatherly elder statesman, the Nobel Peace Prize winner, the friend of Bill Clinton—had organized "terrorism."

2 I understood their confusion. In these times of omnipresent "terrorist" threats, it seems natural for us to understand terrorism as a cut and dry issue, a matter of good versus evil—as George Bush would have us believe. We're told that the cliché of "one man's terrorist is another man's freedom fighter" is horribly out of date in our post 9/11 world. Yet the discussion around what constitutes the legitimate use of violence for political ends is as relevant as ever. Who would dare compare Al-Qaeda's nihilistic❸ program to the sabotage campaign carried out by Mandela's MK? The British Empire arrogantly supposed that anyone who didn't like living under the thumb of colonial rule was a "terrorist," from the Mau Mau's in Kenya to the Indian resistance.❹ The U.S. government labeled the Black Panther Party "terrorists," when much of the terror of American politics was being carried out by the CIA at home and the U.S. military abroad (Vietnam, Cambodia, Chile, Nicaragua etc.). It goes on: The Israeli government denounces Palestinian "terrorism" whether it is speaking of suicide bombings in busy town centers or the gunning down of Israeli soldiers who are illegally occupying the Palestinian territories of the West Bank and Gaza Strip.

Reading Critically

❷ Why does the author put the word *bombed* in parentheses?

❸ What is the meaning of *nihilistic*? Do you think Al-Qaeda's actions of 9/11 were nihilistic? Explain why or why not.

❹ Who were the Mau Mau? Who made up the Indian resistance? What is the difference between them?

Even within so-called terrorist movements, political violence eschews black or white distinctions. The Irish Republican Army's (IRA) bombing of British shoppers in Manchester was not only heinous, but a horrible strategic mistake for those concerned with the civil rights struggle of Northern Irish Catholics. Yet that same IRA's defense of Catholic communities under British army bombardment in Belfast must be seen in a different light. This nuanced approach to political violence should be applied to all social struggles that opt for the bullet when the ballot is not available (to paraphrase Malcolm X).❺ When people are denied political participation, violence becomes a justifiable means to assert their rights and the line that separates "terrorism" from "resistance" becomes blurred. 3

The term terrorism has become all things to all people, so amorphous❻ that it does little to explain complex conflicts which desperately require solutions and not heated political rhetoric. More often than not, it is the people with power who define what "terrorism" is and who the "terrorists" are. For those of us who forget the murky ethical dilemmas that surround the use of political violence, a history lesson is in order. Maybe the search for Mandela's gun can teach us something about the nature of political violence in this age of the "global war on terror." 4

UNDERSTANDING DETAILS

1. Why were Black's students shocked to find out that Nelson Mandela had a gun?
2. What was MK? What was Mandela's role in it?
3. According to Black, when does violence become a justifiable means for a people to assert their rights?

ANALYZING MEANING

1. Why do some people consider the cliché "one man's terrorist is another man's freedom fighter" (paragraph 2) to be out of date after 9/11? Why is it not out of date to the author?
2. Why is political violence hard to categorize even within so-called terrorist movements?
3. Who gets to define *terrorism*, according to the author? Why is this problematic?

Reading Critically

❺ Give an example of what the author means by "opt[ing] for the bullet when the ballot is not available."

❻ What does the word *amorphous* mean?

DISCOVERING RHETORICAL STRATEGIES

1. Look at the author's use of examples in the second paragraph. Can you discern any pattern in the way the examples are listed? What is the overall effect of these examples?
2. Why does the author put quotation marks around *terrorism, terrorist,* and *global war on terror*? How does this strategy contribute to his definition of terrorism?
3. In the end, how is Black defining *terrorism*? What can the search for Mandela's gun teach us?

MAKING CONNECTIONS

1. Imagine June Callwood ("Forgiveness") and Black in a discussion of forgiveness and the repercussions of political violence. Where might they agree? Where might they disagree?
2. Black and Adam Gopnik ("Shootings") write about different types of violence, but both use examples to support their arguments. Compare their use of examples. Which essay did you find more persuasive?

IDEAS FOR DISCUSSION/WRITING

Preparing to Write

Most people have vivid memories of September 11, 2001. They remember where they were and what they were doing at the exact moment they first heard about the attacks. Write freely about your memories of that day. How did your life change in the days and weeks following 9/11? Which of those changes were temporary? Which were permanent? Do you feel you are living in one of the most dangerous or one of the most peaceful times in human history?

Choosing a Topic

1. Nelson Mandela was awarded the Nobel Peace Prize in 1993. Read about the history of the Nobel Peace Prize at **www.nobelprize.org**. Then write an argumentative essay nominating someone who you believe deserves the award.
2. What constitutes the legitimate use of violence for political ends? Write an argumentative essay, supporting your thesis with concrete examples.
3. Choose another contentious word, such as *terrorist*, and write your own expanded definition.

LAWRENCE HILL

Don't Call Me That Word (2002)

Racial identity is a recurring theme in the work of Lawrence Hill. Born in 1957, Hill grew up in a suburb of Toronto, grappling with his identity as the child of a Black father and a White mother. This experience informs much of the writing, teaching, and speaking that he does today.

With a B.A. in economics and an M.A. in writing, Hill is a writer of both fiction and nonfiction. His nonfiction book *Black Berry, Sweet Juice: On Being Black and White in Canada* (2001) examines what it is like to grow up as a mixed-race person. *The Deserter's Tale: The Story of an Ordinary Soldier Who Walked Away from the War in Iraq*, written with Joshua Key, was released in 2007. Hill's novels include *Some Great Thing* (1992), *Any Known Blood* (1997), and *The Book of Negroes* (2007). *The Book of Negroes* won the 2008 Commonwealth Writers' Prize for Best Book and the 2007 Rogers Writers' Trust Fiction Prize. Hill won a National Magazine Award in 2006 for the essay "Is Africa's Pain Black America's Burden?" and the American Wilbur Award in 2005 for best national television documentary for *Seeking Salvation: A History of the Black Church in Canada*. He has also published two books about Black history.

Hill, who speaks French and Spanish in addition to English, has led cultural exchanges in Niger, Cameroon, and Mali as a volunteer with Canadian Crossroads International, and he volunteers with a variety of other Canadian Black history and writers' groups.

Hill has also taught writing through Ryerson University, Johns Hopkins University, and the Writers in Electronic Residence program of the Writers' Trust of Canada. He lives in Burlington, Ontario, with his wife and five children.

Preparing to Read

Hill's essay comes from *Maclean's* magazine. Before you begin reading, think about name-calling. What is the effect of being called a name that has negative connotations? Have you ever been called names as a child or as an adult? If so, what were those names? How did those names make you feel? Have you ever called other people names with negative overtones? If so, why did you use those names? What was the intended effect on your audience? What negative names specifically relate to race or ethnicity?

Growing up in the 1960s in the affluent, almost all-white Don Mills, Ont., I was told by my black father that education and professional achievement were the only viable options for black people in North America. He laid down three rules as if they had been received from the mouth of God: 1) I was to study like the dickens; 2) anything less than complete success in school or at work was to be regarded as failure; 3) if anybody called me "nigger," I was to beat the hell out of him. 1

This is the legacy of being black in Canada. You overcompensate for the fluke of your ancestry, and stand on guard against those who would knock you down.❶ Over 400 years of black history here, we have had to overcome numerous challenges: the chains of slave vessels, the wrath of slave owners, the rules of segregation, the killing ways of police bullets, our own murderous infighting, and all the modern vicissitudes of polite Canadian oppression.❷ 2

Blacks in Canada, like our metaphorical brothers and sisters all over the world, have a vivid collective memory. We know what our ancestors have been through, and we know what our children still face. Most of us cringe when we hear the word "nigger." No other word in the English language distills hatred so effectively, and evokes such a long and bloody history. 3

These days, more people than ever are talking about the word "nigger," as a result of the publication this year of the book *Nigger: The Strange Career of a Troublesome Word*, by Randall Kennedy, a black American law professor at Harvard University. It's a fascinating read, but it raises a troublesome argument that I ultimately reject: Kennedy praises "African American innovators" (by which he means comedians and hip hop stylists)❸ for "taming, civilizing, and transmuting 'the filthiest, dirtiest, nastiest word in the English language.'" 4

Some misguided white people have bought into this same way of thinking. We have hit the pinnacle of absurdity when white teenagers sling their arms around black friends and ask, "Whassup my nigger?" And some white people seem to want 5

Reading Critically

❶ What is being echoed here?

❷ What does Hill mean by "the modern vicissitudes of polite Canadian oppression"?

❸ Who might Kennedy be referring to?

a piece of that word, and feel the need to apply it to their own difficult experiences. The Irish have been referred to as "the niggers of Europe." In the 1970s, Québécois writer Pierre Vallieres titled one of his books *White Niggers of America*. And just the other night, when I visited a drop-in centre catering mostly to black junior high and high school students in Toronto's Kensington Market area, a white teenager decked out in baggy pants and parroting what he imagined to be blackspeak complained that some kids accused him of being a "wigger"—an insulting term for whites who are trying to act black. Whatever that means.❹

6 As Randall Kennedy rightly asserts, the word abounds in contemporary black urban culture. True, when it crops up in hip hop lyrics, it's not intended to carry the hate of the racist. It signals an in-group, brotherly, friendly trash talk. This is well known in American culture but it has penetrated black Canadian culture, too. Choclair, a leading black Canadian hip hop artist, uses the word "nigga"—a derivation of "nigger"—frequently in his lyrics.

7 Some people might say that the N-word is making a comeback. That the old-style, racist use of the word has faded into history and that it's now kosher to use the word in ordinary conversation. This argument fails on two counts. First, racists and racism haven't disappeared from the Canadian landscape. The comeback argument also fails because it suggests that reappropriating the word reflects a new linguistic trend.❺ This is naive. As a way of playing with the English language's most hateful word, black people—mostly young black males—have called themselves "nigger" for generations. The difference now is that these same young blacks have broadcast the word, via music and TV, to the whole world. In the middle-class black cultures I've encountered in Canada and the United States, such a young man usually gets slapped or tongue-lashed by his mother, at just about that point, and he learns that the only time it's safe to use that word is when he's chilling on the street with his buddies. Black people use the word "nigger" precisely because it hurts so much that we

---

Reading Critically

❹ How does Hill effectively use syntax here?

❺ What does *reappropriating* mean? Can you think of examples of other words that have been reappropriated?

need to dance with our own pain, in the same way that blues music dives straight into bad luck and heartbreak. This is very much part of the black North American experience: we don't run from our pain, we roll it into our art.❻

8 But does that take the sting out of the word? No. And what's the proof of that? We don't use the word around our mothers, our teachers, the people we fall in love with, or our children. "Nigger" is a word that young black men use on each other. But the word still pains most black Canadians. Let me share an image of just how much the word hurts. A friend of mine—a black woman, community activist and graduate student—was dying to read Kennedy's book. She bought it last week, but couldn't bring herself to start devouring it on the subway to work until she had ripped off the cover: she wouldn't allow herself to be seen on the subway with the word "nigger" splashed on the cover of a book, so close to her face.

UNDERSTANDING DETAILS

1. What is the word to which Hill refers in his title? How, physically, is it set apart in the text of the essay?
2. Describe Randall Kennedy's view of the word *nigger*.
3. Hill points out that "[s]ome people might say that the N-word is making a comeback. That the old-style, racist use of the word has faded into history and that it's now kosher to use the word in ordinary conversation" (paragraph 7). Does Hill agree with this position? Why or why not?

ANALYZING MEANING

1. Explain the difference between the word *nigger* being used by young Black men among themselves and by anyone else.
2. Why do some people believe that "the N-word is making a comeback" (paragraph 7)? Do you agree with them? Explain.
3. Why does Hill call the word *nigger* "the English language's most hateful word" (paragraph 7)? What other words have a similar impact?

Reading Critically

❻ What does Hill mean by the statement "we don't run from our pain, we roll it into our art"?

DISCOVERING RHETORICAL STRATEGIES

1. How effective is the title of Hill's essay? What is the effect of using *That Word* rather than *Nigger*?
2. What is Hill's purpose in writing this essay? Has he successfully achieved his purpose?
3. Is Hill's definition primarily an objective or a subjective one? Explain your conclusion.

MAKING CONNECTIONS

1. Drew Hayden Taylor ("Pretty Like a White Boy") and Hill both talk about terms that label people based on their race or ethnicity. In what ways do labels affect perception?
2. Both Russell Smith ("Potty-Mouthed and Proud of It") and Hill write about taboo words. Do you think they would agree with each other's point of view?

IDEAS FOR DISCUSSION/WRITING

Preparing to Write

Hill says of the Black North American experience that "we don't run from our pain, we roll it into our art" (paragraph 7). Write freely about rolling pain into art. What does it mean to roll your pain into your art? What types of pain take form in art? What forms of art reflect people's pain?

Choosing a Topic

1. Write an essay in which you explore the meaning of a name given to people of a community to which you belong. This community might be distinguished by race, ethnicity, socioeconomic status, residence, religion, age, sexual orientation, or political stance. Be clear about your attitude toward the term you are defining.
2. Many musicians cause controversy by using language that is commonly considered offensive. Write an essay about the inclusion of such language in the work of contemporary musicians. Use specific examples of musicians to give your essay clarity and credibility.
3. What is the attraction of art (e.g., music, visual art, dance) that reflects pain? Write an essay defining the appeal of such work.

CHAPTER 8

CAUSE/EFFECT

Tracing Reasons and Results

Wanting to know why things happen is one of our earliest, most basic instincts: Why can't I go out, Mommy? Why are you laughing? Why won't the dog stop barking? Why can't I swim faster than my big brother? These questions, and many more like them, reflect our innately inquisitive nature. Closely related to this desire to understand *why* is our interest in *what* will happen in the future as a result of some particular action: What will I feel like tomorrow if I stay up late tonight? How will I perform in the marathon if I train with a team? What will be the result if I mix together these two potent chemicals? What will happen if I turn in my next English assignment two days early?

A daily awareness of this intimate relationship between causes and effects allows us to begin to understand the complex and interrelated series of events that make up our lives and the lives of others. For example, trying to understand the various causes of the conflict in the Middle East teaches us about international relations; knowing our biological reactions to certain foods helps us make decisions about what to eat; understanding the interrelated reasons for the outbreak of World War II offers us insight into historical trends and human nature; knowing the effects of sunshine on various parts of our bodies helps us make decisions about how much ultraviolet exposure we can tolerate and what sunscreen lotion to use; and understanding the causes of Canada's most recent recession will help us respond appropriately to the next economic crisis we encounter. More than anything else, tracing causes and effects teaches us how to think clearly and react intelligently to our multifaceted environment.

In college or university, you will often be asked to use this natural interest in causes and effects to analyze particular situations and to discern general principles. For example, you might be asked some of the following questions on essay exams in different courses:

Anthropology: Why did the Mayan culture disintegrate?

Psychology: Why do humans respond to fear in different ways?

Biology: How do lab rats react to caffeine?

History: What were the positive effects of building the Trans-Canada Highway?

Business: Why did so many dot.com businesses go bankrupt in the late 1990s? What effect did this dot.com bust have on the economy?

Your ability to answer such questions will depend in large part on your skill at understanding cause and effect relationships.

Defining *Cause/Effect*

Cause/effect analysis requires the ability to look for connections between different elements and to analyze the reasons for those connections. As the name implies, this rhetorical mode has two separate components: *cause* and *effect*. A particular essay might concentrate on cause (Why do you live on campus?), on effect (What are the resulting advantages and disadvantages of living on campus?), or on some combination of the two. In working with causes, we are searching for any circumstances from the past that may have caused a single event; in looking for effects, we seek occurrences that took place after a particular event and resulted from that event. Like process analysis, cause/effect makes use of our intellectual ability to analyze. Process analysis addresses *how* something happens, whereas causal analysis discusses *why* it happened and *what* the result was. A process analysis paper, for example, might explain how to advertise more effectively to increase sales, whereas a cause/effect study would discover that three specific elements contributed to an increase in sales: effective advertising, personal service, and selective discounts. The study of causes and effects, therefore, provides many different and helpful ways for humans to make sense of and clarify their views of the world.

Looking for causes and effects requires an advanced form of thinking. It is more complex than most rhetorical strategies we have studied because it can exist on a number of different and progressively more difficult levels. The most accurate and effective causal analysis develops from digging for the real or ultimate causes or effects, as opposed to those that are merely superficial or immediate. The crime scene investigators would have been out of work on the TV show *CSI*, for example, if they had stopped their investigation at the immediate cause of death (accidental drug overdose) rather than searching diligently for the real cause (victim was asphyxiated by assailants after being incapacitated by a mixture of Xanax and heroin). Similarly, voters would be easy to manipulate if they considered only the immediate effects of a tax increase (a slightly higher tax bill) rather than the ultimate benefits that would result (the many years of improved health care that our population would receive because of the ability to train and hire health-care professionals). Only the discovery of the actual reasons for an event or an idea will lead to the logical and accurate analysis of causes and effects important to a basic understanding of various aspects of our lives.

Faulty reasoning assigns causes to a sequence of actions without adequate justification. One such logical fallacy is called *post hoc, ergo propter hoc* ("after this, therefore because of this"): The fact that someone lost a job after walking under a ladder does not mean that the two events are causally related; by the same token, if we get up every morning at 5:30 a.m., just before the sun rises, we cannot therefore conclude that the sun rises *because* we get up (no matter how self-centred we are!). Faulty reasoning also occurs when we oversimplify a particular situation. Most events are connected to a multitude of causes and effects. Sometimes one effect has many causes: A student may fail a history exam because she's been working two part-time jobs, she was sick, she didn't study hard enough, and she found the instructor very boring. One cause may also have many effects. If a house burns down, the people who lived in it will be out of a home. If we look at such a tragic scene more closely, however, we may also note that the fire traumatized a child who lived there, helped the family learn what good friends they had, encouraged the family to double their future fire insurance, and provided the stimulus that they needed to make a long-dreamed-of move to another city. One event has thus resulted in many interrelated effects. Building an argument on insecure foundations or oversimplifying the causes or effects connected with an event will seriously hinder the construction of a rational essay. No matter what the nature of the cause/effect analysis, it must always be based on clear observation, accurate facts, and rigorous logic.

In the following paragraph, a student writer analyzes some of the causes and effects connected with the controversial issue of euthanasia. Notice how he makes connections and then analyzes those connections as he consistently explores the immediate and ultimate effects of being able to stretch life beyond its normal limits through new medical technology:

> Along with the many recent startling advances in medical technology have come a number of complex moral, ethical, and spiritual questions that beg to be answered. We now have the ability to prolong the life of the human body for a very long time. But what rights do patients and their families have to curtail cruel and unusual medical treatment that stretches life beyond its normal limits? This dilemma has produced a ripple effect in society. Is the extension of life an unquestionable goal in itself, regardless of the quality of that life? Modern scientific technology has forced doctors to re-evaluate the exact meaning and purpose of their profession. For example, many medical schools and undergraduate university programs now routinely offer classes on medical ethics—an esoteric and infrequently taught subject only a few years ago. Doctors and scholars alike are realizing that medical personnel alone cannot be expected to decide on the exact parameters of life. In like manner, the judicial process must now evaluate the legal complexities of mercy killings and the rights of patients to die with dignity and without unnecessary medical intervention. The insurance business, too, wrestles with the catastrophic effects of new technology on the costs of today's hospital care. In short, medical progress entails more than microscopes, chemicals, and high-tech instruments. If we are to develop as a thoughtful, just, and merciful society, we must consider not only the physical well-being of our nation's patients, but their emotional, spiritual, and financial status as well.

Thinking Critically Through Cause/Effect

Thinking about causes and effects is one of the most advanced mental activities that we perform. It involves complex operations that we must consider carefully, making sure all connections are reasonable and accurate. Unlike other rhetorical patterns, cause/effect thinking requires us to see specific relationships between two or more items. To practise this strategy, we need to look for items or events that are causally related—that is, one has caused the other. Then, we can focus either on the causes (the initial stimulus), the effects (the results), or a combination of the two.

Searching out causes and effects requires a lot of digging that is not necessary for most of the other modes. Cause/effect necessitates the ultimate in investigative work. The mental exertion associated with this thinking strategy is sometimes exhausting, but it is always worth going through when you discover relationships that you never saw before or you uncover links in your reasoning that were previously unknown or obscure to you.

If you've ever had the secret desire to be a private eye or an investigator of any sort, practising cause/effect reasoning can be lots of fun. It forces you to see relationships among multiple items and then to make sense of those connections. Completing the following exercises in this skill will help you perfect the logistics of cause/effect thinking before you mix and match it with other thinking strategies.

1. Choose a major problem you see in our society. On one side of a piece of paper, list what you think are the main causes of this problem; on the other side, list the effects. Compare the two lists to see how they differ. Then, compare and contrast your lists with those written by other students.
2. List the effects of one of the following: getting a speeding ticket, winning an Olympic medal, graduating from college or university, or watching TV until early in the morning.

Reading and Writing Cause/Effect Essays

Causal analysis is usually employed for one of three main purposes: (1) to prove a specific point (such as the necessity of tighter airport security), in which case the writer generally deals totally with facts and with conclusions drawn from those facts; (2) to argue against a widely accepted belief (for example, the assertion that cocaine is addictive), in which case the writer relies principally on facts, with perhaps some pertinent opinions; or (3) to speculate on a theory (for instance, why the crime rate is higher in most major cities than it is in rural areas), in which case the writer probably presents hypotheses and opinions along with facts. This section will explore these purposes in cause/effect essays from the standpoint of both reading and writing.

Reading Cause/Effect Essays

- What is the essay's thesis?
- What are the real causes and effects?
- What are the author's assertions?

Preparing to Read. As you set out to read the essays in this chapter, begin by focusing your attention on the title and the synopsis of the essay you are about to read and by scanning the essay itself: What do you think Peter Nicholson will discuss in "Information-Rich and Attention-Poor"? In Evelyn Lau's essay "More and More," what could *more* refer to?

Also, at this stage in the reading process, you should try to learn as much as you can about the author of the essay and the reasons he or she wrote it. Ask yourself questions such as the following: What is Evelyn Lau's intention in "More and More"? Who is Jeannie Guy's intended audience in "Newfoundland Cooking"? And what is Stephen King's point of view in "Why We Crave Horror Movies"?

Finally, before you begin to read, answer the prereading questions for each essay and then consider the proposed essay topic from a variety of perspectives: For example, do you have any dietary restrictions (Wahl)? Do you enjoy watching Olympic sports (Moore)? What do you want to know about eating disorders (Lau)?

Reading. As you read each essay in this chapter for the first time, record your spontaneous reactions to it, drawing as often as possible on the preliminary material you already know: What do you think of horror movies (King)? Why did Lau choose the title she did? Have you ever tried any adventure sports (Moore)?

Whenever you can, try to create a context for your reading: What is the tone of Moore's comments about Xtreme sports? How does this tone help him communicate with his audience? What do you think the purpose is in Guy's essay about the food of her childhood in Newfoundland? How clearly does she get this purpose across to you?

Also, during this reading, note the essay's thesis and check to see if the writer thoroughly explores all possibilities before settling on the primary causes and/or effects of a particular situation; in addition, determine whether the writer clearly states the assertions that naturally evolve from a discussion of the topic.

Finally, read the questions following each essay to get a sense of the main issues and strategies in the selection.

Rereading. When you reread these essays, you should focus mainly on the writer's craft. Notice how the authors narrow and focus their material, how they make clear and logical connections between ideas in their essays, how they support their conclusions with concrete examples, how they use other rhetorical modes to accomplish their cause/effect analysis, and how they employ logical transitions to move us smoothly from one point to another. Most important, however, ask yourself if the writer actually discusses the real causes and/or effects of a particular circumstance: What does King say are the primary reasons people crave horror movies? What causes does Wahl propose for the increase in gluten intolerance? What are the primary causes and effects of eating disorders? In your critical analysis of each essay, don't forget to consider the Reading Critically questions as well.

For a thorough outline of the reading process, consult the checklist on page 41 of the Introduction.

Writing Cause/Effect Essays

- State your purpose in your thesis.
- Explore all causes and effects.
- Use concrete evidence.
- Summarize and draw conclusions.

Preparing to Write. Beginning a cause/effect essay—and any other essay—requires exploring and limiting your subject, specifying a purpose, and identifying an audience. The Preparing to Write questions before the essay assignments, coupled with the prewriting techniques outlined in the Introduction, encourage you to consider specific issues related to your reading. The assignments themselves will then help you limit your topic and determine a particular purpose and audience for your message. For cause/effect essays, determining a purpose is even more important than usual because your readers can get hopelessly lost unless your analysis is clearly focused.

Writing. For all its conceptual complexity, a cause/effect essay can be organized quite simply. The introduction generally presents the subject(s) and states the purpose of the analysis in a clear thesis. The body of the paper then explores all relevant causes and/or effects, typically progressing either from least to most influential or from most to least influential. Finally, the concluding section summarizes the various cause-and-effect relationships established in the body of the paper and clearly states the conclusions that can be drawn from those relationships.

The following additional guidelines should assist you in producing an effective cause/effect essay in all academic disciplines:

- Narrow and focus your material as much as possible.
- Consider all possibilities before assigning real or ultimate causes or effects.
- Show connections between ideas by using transitions and key words such as *because, reasons, results, effects,* and *consequences* to guide your readers smoothly through your essay.
- Support all inferences with concrete evidence.
- Be as objective as possible in your analysis so that you don't distort logic with personal biases.
- Understand your audience's opinions and convictions so that you know what to emphasize in your essay.
- Qualify your assertions to avoid overstatement and oversimplification.

These suggestions apply to both cause/effect essay assignments and exam questions.

Rewriting. As you revise your cause/effect essays, ask yourself the following important questions:

- Is my thesis stated clearly at the outset of my paper?
- Does it include my subject and my purpose?
- Do I accomplish my purpose as effectively as possible for my particular audience?
- Do I use logical reasoning throughout the essay?
- Do I carefully explore all relevant causes and/or effects?
- Do I clearly state the conclusions that can be drawn from my analysis?

More specific guidelines for writing and revising your essays appear on page 42 of the Introduction.

Student Essay: Cause/Effect at Work

In the following essay, the student writer analyzes the effects of contemporary TV soap operas on young people. Notice that she states her subject and purpose at the beginning of the essay and then presents a combination of facts and opinions in her exploration of the topic. Notice also that, in her analysis, the writer is careful to draw clear connections between her perceptions of the issue and various objective details in an attempt to trace the effects of this medium in our society today. At the end of her essay, look at her summary of the logical relationships she establishes in the body of the essay and her statements about the conclusions she draws from these relationships.

Distortions of Reality

Background

Television's contributions to society, positive and negative, have been debated continually since this piece of technology invaded the average Canadian household in the 1950s. Television has brought an unlimited influx of new information, ideas, and cultures into our homes. However, based on my observations of my 13-year-old cousin, Katie, and her friends, I think we need to take a closer look at the effects of soap operas on adolescents today. The distortions of reality portrayed on these programs are frighteningly misleading and, in my opinion, can be very confusing to young people.

Thesis statement

Transition

During the early 1990s, the lifestyle of the typical soap opera "family" has been radically transformed from comfortable pretentiousness to blatant and unrealistic decadence. The characters neither live nor dress like the majority of their viewers, who are generally middle-class Canadians. These television families live in large, majestic homes that are flawlessly decorated. The actors are often adorned in beautiful designer clothing, fur coats, and expensive jewellery, and this opulent lifestyle is sustained by people with no visible means of income. Very few of the characters seem to "work" for a living. When they do, upward mobility—without the benefit of proper education or suitable training—and a well-planned marriage come quickly.

First distortion of reality

Concrete examples

Transition

From this constant barrage of conspicuous consumption, my cousin and her friends seem to have a distorted view of everyday economic realities. I see Katie and her group becoming obsessed with the appearance of their clothes and possessions. I frequently

First effect

Concrete examples

hear them berate their parents' jobs and modest homes. With noticeable arrogance, these young adolescents seem to view their parents' lives as "failures" when compared to the effortless, luxurious lifestyles portrayed in the soaps.

Transition

One of the most alluring features of this genre is its masterful use of deception. Conflicts between characters in soap operas are based on secrecy and misinformation. Failure to tell the truth and to perform honourable deeds further complicates the entangled lives and love affairs of the participants. But when the truth finally comes out and all mistakes and misdeeds become public, the culprits and offenders hardly ever suffer for their actions. In fact, they appear to leave the scene of the crime guilt-free.

Concrete examples

Second distortion of reality

Transition

Regrettably, Katie and her friends consistently express alarming indifference to this lack of moral integrity. In their daily viewing, they shrug off underhanded scenes of scheming and conniving, and they marvel at how the characters manipulate each other into positions of powerlessness or grapple in distasteful love scenes. I can only conclude that continued exposure to this amoral behaviour is eroding the fundamental values of truth and fidelity in these kids.

Concrete examples

Second effect

Transition

Also in the soaps, the powers-that-be conveniently disregard any sense of responsibility for wrongdoing. Characters serve jail terms quickly and in relative comfort. Drug or alcohol abuse does not mar anyone's physical appearance or behaviour, and poverty is virtually nonexistent. Usually, the wrongdoer's position, wealth, and prestige are quickly restored—with little pain and suffering.

Third distortion of reality

Concrete examples

Adolescents are clearly learning that people can act without regard for the harmful effects of their actions on themselves and others when they see this type of behaviour go unpunished. Again, I notice the result of this delusion in my cousin. Recently, when a businessman in our community was convicted of embezzling large sums of money from his clients, Katie was outraged because he was sentenced to five years in prison, unlike her daytime TV "heartthrob," who had been given a suspended sentence for a similar crime. With righteous indignation, Katie claimed that the victims, many of whom had lost their entire savings, should have realized that any business investment involves risk and the threat of loss. Logic and common sense evaded Katie's reasoning as she insisted on comparing television justice with real-life scruples.

Third effect

Concrete examples

The writers and producers of soap operas argue that the shows are designed to entertain viewers and are not meant to be reflections of reality. Theoretically, this may be true, but I can actually see how these soap operas are affecting my cousin and her crowd. Although my personal observations are limited, I cannot believe they are unique or unusual. Too many young people think that they can amass wealth and material possessions without an education, hard work, or careful financial planning; that material goods are the sole measure of a person's success in life; and that honesty and integrity are not necessarily admirable qualities. Ultimate effect

Proposed solution Soap operas should demonstrate a realistic lifestyle and a responsible sense of behaviour. The many hours adolescents spend in front of the television can obviously influence their view of the world. As a society, we cannot afford the consequences resulting from the distortions of reality portrayed every day in these shows.

Some Final Thoughts on Cause/Effect

The essays in this chapter deal with both causes and effects in a variety of ways. As you read each essay, try to discover its primary purpose and the ultimate causes and/or effects of the issue under discussion. Note also the clear causal relationships that each author sets forth on solid foundations supported by logical reasoning. Although the subjects of these essays vary dramatically, each essay exhibits the basic elements of effective causal analysis.

CAUSE/EFFECT IN REVIEW

Reading Cause/Effect Essays

Preparing to Read

✓ What assumptions can I make from the essay's title?
✓ What do I think the general mood of the essay will be?
✓ What are the essay's purpose and audience?
✓ What does the synopsis tell me about the essay?
✓ What can I learn from the author's biography?
✓ Can I predict the author's point of view toward the subject?

Reading

✓ What is the essay's thesis?
✓ What are the real causes and/or effects?
✓ What are the author's assertions?

Rereading

✓ How does the writer narrow and focus the essay?
✓ Does the writer make clear and logical connections between the ideas?
✓ What concrete examples support the author's conclusions?
✓ Does the writer discuss the real causes and effects?

Writing Cause/Effect Essays

Preparing to Write

✓ What is my purpose?
✓ Who is my audience?

Writing

✓ Do I state my purpose in my thesis?
✓ Do I explore all possible causes or effects?
✓ Do I show connections between ideas by using transitions and key words?
✓ Do I use concrete evidence?
✓ Do I summarize and draw conclusions?

Rewriting

✓ Is my thesis stated clearly at the outset of my essay?
✓ Does it include my subject and my purpose?
✓ Do I carefully explore all relevant causes and/or effects?
✓ Do I accomplish my purpose as effectively as possible?
✓ Do I use logical reasoning throughout the essay?
✓ Do I state clearly the conclusions that can be drawn from my essay?

STEPHEN KING

Why We Crave Horror Movies (1982)

Stephen King (1947–) has observed that people seem to have an unending appetite for horror. This insight may help justify his phenomenal success as a writer of horror fiction since the mid-1970s. His books have sold over one hundred million copies, and the movies made from them have generated more income than the gross domestic product of several small countries.

After early jobs as a janitor, a laundry worker, and a high-school English teacher in Portland, Maine, King turned to writing full-time following the spectacular sales of his first novel, *Carrie* (1974), which focuses on a shy, socially ostracized young girl who takes revenge on her cruel classmates through newly developed telekinetic powers. King's subsequent books have included *The Shining* (1977), *Firestarter* (1980), *Cujo* (1981), *Pet Sematary* (1983), *Misery* (1987), *The Stand* (1990), *Dolores Claiborne* (1993), *Rose Madder* (1995), *Desperation* (1996), *Bag of Bones* (1998), *Dreamcatcher* (2001), and seven novels in the Dark Tower series.

Asked to explain why readers and moviegoers are so attracted to his tales of horror, King recently explained that most people's lives are characterized by fear, but those fears are not supposed to be acknowledged. In the absence of other channels to deal with these emotions, the horror writer can give people a place to put their fears. In the context of a horror story it is okay to be afraid because it is not real.

A cheerful though somewhat superstitious person, King, who now lives in Bangor, Maine, admits to doing most of his best writing during the morning hours.

Preparing to Read

As you prepare to read this article, consider your thoughts on our society's emotional condition: How emotionally healthy are Canadians? Were they more emotionally healthy 20 years ago? A century ago? What makes a society emotionally healthy? Emotionally unhealthy? How can a society maintain good health? What is the relationship between emotional health and a civilized society?

I think that we're all mentally ill; those of us outside the asylums only hide it a little better—and maybe not all that much better, after all. We've all known people who talk to themselves, people who sometimes squinch❶ their faces into horrible grimaces when they believe no one is watching, people who have some hysterical fear—of snakes, the dark, the tight place, the long drop . . . and, of course, those final worms and grubs that are waiting so patiently underground. 1

When we pay our four or five bucks and seat ourselves at tenth-row center in a theater showing a horror movie, we are daring the nightmare.❷ 2

Why? Some of the reasons are simple and obvious. To show that we can, that we are not afraid, that we can ride this roller coaster. Which is not to say that a really good horror movie may not surprise a scream out of us at some point, the way we may scream when the roller coaster twists through a complete 360 or plows through a lake at the bottom of the drop. And horror movies, like roller coasters, have always been the special province of the young; by the time one turns 40 or 50, one's appetite for double twists or 360-degree loops may be considerably depleted. 3

We also go to reestablish our feelings of essential normality; the horror movie is innately conservative, even reactionary. Freda Jackson as the horrible melting woman in *Die, Monster, Die!* confirms for us that no matter how far we may be removed from the beauty of a Robert Redford or a Diana Ross, we are still light-years from true ugliness. 4

And we go to have fun. 5

Ah, but this is where the ground starts to slope away, isn't it? Because this is a very peculiar sort of fun, indeed. The fun comes from seeing others menaced—sometimes killed.❸ One critic has suggested that if pro football has become the voyeur's version of combat, then the horror film has become the modern version of the public lynching. 6

It is true that the mythic, "fairy-tale" horror film intends to take away the shades of gray. . . . It urges us to put away our 7

Reading Critically

❶ Have you ever encountered the word *squinch*? Do you think this is a real word or did King invent it?

❷ What does King mean by the phrase "we are daring the nightmare"?

❸ Do you think it is "fun" to see the characters in horror films menaced or killed? Why or why not?

more civilized and adult penchant for analysis and to become children again, seeing things in pure blacks and whites.❹ It may be that horror movies provide psychic relief on this level because this invitation to lapse into simplicity, irrationality, and even outright madness is extended so rarely. We are told we may allow our emotions a free rein . . . or no rein at all.

8 If we are all insane, then sanity becomes a matter of degree. If your insanity leads you to carve up women, like Jack the Ripper or the Cleveland Torso Murderer, we clap you away in the funny farm (but neither of those two amateur-night surgeons was ever caught, heh-heh-heh); if, on the other hand, your insanity leads you only to talk to yourself when you're under stress or to pick your nose on your morning bus, then you are left alone to go about your business . . . though it is doubtful that you will ever be invited to the best parties.

9 The potential lyncher is in almost all of us (excluding saints, past and present; but then, most saints❺ have been crazy in their own ways), and every now and then, he has to be let loose to scream and roll around in the grass. Our emotions and our fears form their own body, and we recognize that it demands its own exercise to maintain proper muscle tone. Certain of these emotional muscles are accepted—even exalted—in civilized society; they are, of course, the emotions that tend to maintain the status quo of civilization itself. Love, friendship, loyalty, kindness—these are all the emotions that we applaud, emotions that have been immortalized in the couplets of Hallmark cards and in the verses (I don't dare call it poetry) of Leonard Nimoy.

10 When we exhibit these emotions, society showers us with positive reinforcement; we learn this even before we get out of diapers. When, as children, we hug our rotten little puke of a sister and give her a kiss, all the aunts and uncles smile and twit and cry, "Isn't he the sweetest little thing?" Such coveted treats as chocolate-covered graham crackers often follow. But if we deliberately slam the rotten little puke of a sister's fingers in the door, sanctions follow—angry remonstrance from parents, aunts and uncles; instead of a chocolate-covered graham cracker, a spanking.

11 But anticivilization emotions don't go away, and they demand periodic exercise. We have such "sick" jokes as, "What's

---

Reading Critically

❹ What does King mean by "mythic" horror films? Can you think of any examples of horror films that do require analysis?

❺ Who do you think King is referring to and why?

the difference between a truckload of bowling balls and a truckload of dead babies?"❻ (You can't unload a truckload of bowling balls with a pitchfork . . . a joke, by the way, that I heard originally from a ten-year-old.) Such a joke may surprise a laugh or a grin out of us even as we recoil, a possibility that confirms the thesis: If we share a brotherhood of man, then we also share an insanity of man. None of which is intended as a defense of either the sick joke or insanity but merely as an explanation of why the best horror films, like the best fairy tales, manage to be reactionary, anarchistic, and revolutionary all at the same time.

The mythic horror movie, like the sick joke, has a dirty job to do. It deliberately appeals to all that is worst in us. It is morbidity unchained, our most base instincts let free, our nastiest fantasies realized . . . and it all happens, fittingly enough, in the dark. For those reasons, good liberals often shy away from horror films. For myself, I like to see the most aggressive of them—*Dawn of the Dead*, for instance—as lifting a trap door in the civilized forebrain and throwing a basket of raw meat to the hungry alligators swimming around in that subterranean river beneath.❼ 12

Why bother? Because it keeps them from getting out, man. It keeps them down there and me up here. It was Lennon and McCartney who said that all you need is love, and I would agree with that. 13

As long as you keep the gators fed. 14

UNDERSTANDING DETAILS

1. Why, in King's opinion, do civilized people enjoy horror movies?
2. According to King, in what ways are horror films like roller coasters?
3. According to King, how are horror films like public lynchings?
4. What is the difference between "emotions that tend to maintain the status quo of civilization" (paragraph 9) and "anticivilization emotions" (paragraph 11)?

Reading Critically

❻ What is the connection between horror films and "sick" jokes?

❼ Explain this figure of speech. What are the "hungry alligators"? What is the "subterranean river"?

ANALYZING MEANING

1. How can horror movies "reestablish our feelings of essential normality" (paragraph 4)?
2. What is "reactionary, anarchistic, and revolutionary" (paragraph 11) about fairy tales? About horror films?
3. Why does the author think we need to exercise our anticivilization emotions? What are some other ways we might confront these emotions?
4. Explain the last line of King's essay: "As long as you keep the gators fed" (paragraph 14).

DISCOVERING RHETORICAL STRATEGIES

1. What is the cause/effect relationship King notes in society between horror movies and sanity?
2. Why does King begin his essay with such a dramatic statement as "I think that we're all mentally ill" (paragraph 1)?
3. Who do you think is the author's intended audience for this essay? Describe it in detail. How did you come to this conclusion?
4. What different rhetorical strategies does King use to support his cause/effect analysis? Give examples of each.

MAKING CONNECTIONS

1. In "Repress Yourself," Alison Gillmor considers the appeal of various television shows. What do you think she might say about the appeal of horror movies?
2. The effect of a horror movie can be contagious, like the hysterical behaviour described by Malcolm Gladwell ("Is the Belgian Coca-Cola Hysteria the Real Thing?"). In what way might a horror movie trigger mass hysteria?
3. Imagine a panel discussion with Aaron Wherry ("Violently Happy"), Laura Robinson ("Sports Breeds Real-Life Violence"), and King on the topic of violence in sports and entertainment. Whose point of view would you be most likely to agree with?

IDEAS FOR DISCUSSION/WRITING

Preparing to Write

Write freely about how most people maintain a healthy emotional attitude: How would you define *emotional well-being*? When are people most emotionally healthy? Most emotionally unhealthy?

What do your friends and relatives do to maintain a healthy emotional life? What do you do to maintain emotional health? What is the connection between our individual emotional health and the extent to which our society is civilized?

Choosing a Topic

1. Think of a release other than horror films for our most violent emotions. Is it an acceptable release? Write an essay for the general public explaining the relationship between this particular release and our "civilized" society.
2. If you accept King's analysis of horror movies, what role in society do you think other types of movies play (e.g., love stories, science fiction, comedies)? Choose one type, and explain its role to your class.
3. Your psychology instructor has asked you to explain your opinions on the degree of sanity or insanity in Canada at present. In what ways are we sane? In what ways are we insane? Write an essay for your psychology instructor explaining in detail your observations along these lines.

PETER NICHOLSON

Information-Rich and Attention-Poor (2009)

A native of Nova Scotia, Peter Nicholson has bachelor's and master's degrees in physics from Dalhousie University and a Ph.D. in operations research from Stanford University, along with honorary doctorates from three Canadian universities. Dr. Nicholson is a member of the Order of Canada and has held various positions in government, business, science, and higher education.

He began his career in the academic sector, teaching computer science at the University of Minnesota. Since then, Nicholson has served as Deputy Chief of Staff, Policy, in the Office of the Prime Minister of Canada; member of the Nova Scotia Legislature; Clifford Clark Visiting Economist in the Department of Finance Canada; Special Advisor to the Secretary-General of the Organisation for Economic Co-operation and Development (OECD) in Paris; as well as Senior Vice-President at Scotiabank and Chief Strategy Officer at BCE Inc.

He has also served as a volunteer on several organizations promoting science and technology in Canada. He was a member of the Prime Minister's National Advisory Board on Science and Technology, Chair of the Board of the Fields Institute for Research in Mathematical Sciences, and Chair of both the Canada Foundation for Innovation and the Millennium Scholarship Foundation.

In 2006, Peter Nicholson became the inaugural president of the Council of Canadian Academies, a post he held until 2010. Currently he holds the following positions: Chair of the External Advisory Council at Wealth Creation, Preservation and Donation (WCPD); Member at the Alberta Research and Innovation Authority; Chair at the Standing Selection Committee, Networks of Centres of Excellence; and Chair of the External Advisory Committee at Halifax Marine Research Institute.

Preparing to Read

This essay, which originally appeared in *The Globe and Mail* in 2009, explores the effects of the wealth of information available to us. Peter Nicholson says that the amount of information available as a result of advances in technology has led to a diminished attention spans. Before reading, think about your own attention span. How would you characterize your ability to pay attention to things? What holds your attention? Do you think that your attention span has changed over time? Do you see shorter attention spans as a problem or an effective strategy for functioning in today's world?

Twenty-eight years ago, psychologist and computer scientist Herbert Simon observed that the most fundamental consequence of the superabundance of information created by the digital revolution was a corresponding scarcity of attention. In becoming information-rich, we have become attention-poor. 1

The three technologies that have powered the information revolution – computation, data transmission and data storage[1] – have each increased in capability (and declined in cost per unit of capability) by about 10 million times since the early 1960s. It is as if a house that cost half a million dollars in 1964 could be bought today for a nickel, or if life expectancy had been reduced from 75 years to four minutes.[2] 2

This has unleashed a torrential abundance of data and information. But economics teaches that the counterpart of every new abundance is a new scarcity – in this case, the scarcity of human time and attention. The cost of one's time (approximated, for example, by the average wage) relative to the cost of data manipulation, transmission and storage has increased roughly 10-million-fold in just over two generations – a change in relative "prices" utterly without precedent. This, above all, is what is driving the evolution of online behaviour and culture, with profound implications for the production and consumption of knowledge. The primary consequence is the growing emphasis on speed at the expense of depth. 3

Behaviour inevitably adapts to conserve the scarce resource – in this case, attention and time – and to "waste" the abundant resource. Thus, for example, much of the new technology's capability has been spent on simplifying interfaces[3] and reducing communications latencies essentially to zero; both of these conserve precious time for users. The same motive has also spawned a plethora of indexing and searching schemes, of which Google is the chief example. These are all seeking to be attention-optimizers. 4

Today's information technology is nowhere near its theoretical physical limits, though many engineering and cost hurdles may slow development after 2015. Nanotechnologies 5

Reading Critically

[1] Distinguish among these three technologies. How are they linked?

[2] Why do you think Nicholson has included these analogies? What is their effect on you as a reader?

[3] What is one technology with which you are familiar where the interface has been simplified?

and quantum phenomena nevertheless promise to support a new growth path for decades to come. For example, a recently announced storage technology using carbon nanotubes may allow digital information to be held without degradation for a billion years or more[4] – an innovation that would eliminate the major shortcoming of the digital archive.

6 We may think metaphorically of the production of knowledge as a function of "information" and "attention," with attention understood as the set of activities by which information is ultimately transformed into various forms of knowledge. By virtue of its unprecedented impact on the relative prices of information and human attention, information technology is driving a correspondingly profound transformation of knowledge production, the main feature of which is a shift of emphasis from "depth" to "speed." This is simply because depth and nuance require time and attention to absorb. So as attention has become the dominant scarcity, depth has become less "affordable." Moreover, with information so abundant, strategies are needed to process it more quickly, lest something of vital interest or importance is missed.[5]

THE 24-HOUR KNOWLEDGE CYCLE

7 Knowledge is evolving from a "stock" to a "flow." Stock and flow – for example, wealth and income – are concepts familiar to accountants and economists. A stock of knowledge may be thought of as a quasi-permanent repository – such as a book or an entire library – whereas the flow is the process of developing the knowledge. The old Encyclopedia Britannica was quintessentially a stock; Wikipedia is the paradigmatic example of flow. Obviously, a stock of knowledge is rarely permanent; it depreciates like any other form of capital. But electronic information technology is profoundly changing the rate of depreciation. By analogy with the 24-hour news cycle (which was an early consequence of the growing abundance of video bandwidth as cable television replaced scarce over-the-air frequencies), there is now the equivalent of a 24-hour knowledge cycle – "late-breaking knowledge," as it were. Knowledge is becoming more like a river than a lake, more and more dominated by the flow than by the stock. What is driving this?

Reading Critically

[4] Why is this longevity of information storage important? How does this compare to current digital archives?

[5] Do you see this shift as essentially positive or negative? Explain.

Most obvious is the fact that the media by which electronic information is presented and manipulated permit it to be changed continuously and almost at no cost. Information products are therefore constantly evolving, for the simple reason that, faced with the option, who would not choose an updated over an outdated version? By the time information products eventually come to rest, they are very likely to be considered obsolete. In the cutthroat competition for attention, they are no longer "news." 8

Consequently, there is little time to think and reflect as the flow moves on. This has a subtle and pernicious❻ implication for the production of knowledge. When the effective shelf-life of a document (or any information product) shrinks, fewer resources will be invested in its creation. This is because the period during which the product is likely to be read or referred to is too short to repay a large allocation of scarce time and skill in its production. As a result, the "market" for depth is narrowing. 9

There is also under way a shift of intellectual authority from producers of depth – the traditional "expert" – to the broader public. This is nowhere more tellingly illustrated than by Wikipedia, which has roughly 300,000 volunteer contributors every month. The upshot is that thousands of heads working in parallel are, in an environment of information superabundance, presumably better than one, even if that one is an expert.❼ 10

What makes the mobilization of "crowd wisdom" intellectually powerful is that the technology of the Web makes it so easy for even amateurs to access a growing fraction of the corpus of human knowledge. But while hundreds of thousands of Web-empowered volunteers are able to very efficiently dedicate small slices of their discretionary time, the traditional experts– professors, journalists, authors and filmmakers – need to be compensated for their effort, since expertise is what they have to sell.❽ Unfortunately for them, this has become a much harder sell because the ethic of "free" rules the economics of so much Web content. Moreover, the value of traditional expert authority is itself being diluted by the new incentive structure created by 11

Reading Critically

❻ What does *pernicious* mean in this context?

❼ What is your sense of Wikipedia as a reliable source of information? Do you believe that thousands of people working together create a better source of information that a single person?

❽ Do you value the ideas and views of the traditional experts enough to pay for them? Explain why or why not.

information technology that militates against what is deep and nuanced in favour of what is fast and stripped-down.

12 The result is the growing disintermediation of experts and gatekeepers of virtually all kinds. The irony is that experts have been the source of most of the nuggets of knowledge that the crowd now draws upon in rather parasitic fashion – for example, news and political bloggers depend heavily on a relatively small number of sources of professional journalism, just as many Wikipedia articles assimilate prior scholarship. The system works because it is able to mine intellectual capital. This suggests that today's "cult of the amateur" will ultimately be self-limiting[9] and will require continuous fresh infusions of more traditional forms of expert knowledge.

13 With almost all of the world's codified knowledge at your fingertips, why should you spend increasingly scarce attention loading up your own mind just in case you may some day need this particular fact or concept? Far better, one might argue, to access efficiently what you need, when you need it. This depends, of course, on building up a sufficient internalized structure of concepts to be able to link with the online store of knowledge. How to teach this is perhaps the greatest challenge and opportunity facing educators in the 21st century.

14 For now, the just-in-time approach seems to be narrowing peripheral intellectual vision and thus reducing the serendipity that has been the source of most radical innovation. What is apparently being eroded is the deep, integrative mode of knowledge generation that can come only from the "10,000 hours" of individual intellectual focus – a process that mysteriously gives rise to the insights that occur, often quite suddenly, to the well-prepared mind. We appear to be seeing fewer of the great synthetic innovations associated with names like Newton, Einstein or Watson and Crick.

THE AGE OF DIGITAL NATIVES

15 So we decry the increasing compartmentalization of knowledge – knowing more and more about less and less – while awaiting the great syntheses that some day may be achieved by millions of linked minds, all with fingertip access to the world's codified

---

Reading Critically

[9] Explain the term *cult of the amateur*. Do you agree that it will be self-limiting?

knowledge but with a globe-spanning spectrum of different perspectives. The hyperlinked and socially networked structure of the Internet may be making the metaphor of the Web as global "cyber-nervous system" into a reality – still primitive, but with potential for a far more integrated collective intelligence than we can imagine today.

16 Those of us who are still skeptical might recall that Plato, in the *Phaedrus*, suggested that writing would "create forgetfulness in the minds of those who learn to use it."[10] This is a striking example of a particular kind of generation gap in which masters of an established paradigm can only see the shortcomings, and not the potential, of the truly novel. Today, the electronic screen, with its lack of linear constraint, its ephemeral scintilla[11] and its hyperlinked multimedia content, portends a very different paradigm. How this may condition the habits of thought of the so-called "digital natives" – who, after all, are about to become both the custodians and creators of human knowledge – is one of the deepest and most significant questions facing our species. The challenge is to adapt, and then to evolve, in a world where there continues to be an exponential increase in the supply of information relative to the supply of human attention.

UNDERSTANDING DETAILS

1. What are the three technologies that have powered the information revolution? How much has their capability increased in the last 50 years?
2. In what ways has the new technology's capability been used to "conserve the scarce resource"? In what ways has the new technology adapted to "'waste' the abundant resource" (paragraph 4)?
3. What is the just-in-time approach? What is the effect of this approach?

ANALYZING MEANING

1. According to Nicholson, "economics teaches that the counterpart of every new abundance is a new scarcity" (paragraph 3).

Reading Critically

[10] Why does Nicholson include this quotation from Plato?

[11] What is "ephemeral scintilla"? Why does Nicholson use this term rather than more familiar language?

What is the scarcity that Nicholson identifies as the result of the abundance of information? What is the larger consequence of this new scarcity?
2. Explain what Nicholson sees as the greatest challenge and opportunity for 21st-century educators. Do you agree with him? Why or why not?
3. Explain why "depth has become less 'affordable'" (paragraph 6). What is the risk that Nicholson sees as a result of this?

DISCOVERING RHETORICAL STRATEGIES

1. Assess the effectiveness of Nicholson's introduction and his conclusion. How has he linked the beginning and end to frame his essay?
2. Does Nicholson focus primarily on causes or effects in this essay?
3. Describe Nicholson's tone in this essay. Use specific examples to show how his style (use of language) creates this tone.

MAKING CONNECTIONS

1. Nicholson refers to the philosopher Plato; in "Opera Night in Canada," Michael McKinley discusses three different operas; in "Sporting Life," John Moore cites the Bible, author and culture critic Witold Rybczynski, and writers Ernest Hemingway and Robert Ruark; in "Status Anxiety? Consider Socrates and the Sewer Saviour," Irshad Manji references philosophers Alain de Botton and Socrates. What function do these cultural references have in their respective essays?
2. Nicholson says that the consequence of the constant flow of knowledge is that "there is little time to think and reflect as the flow moves on" (paragraph 9). How do you think Judy Rebick ("The Culture of Overwork") would respond to this situation?

IDEAS FOR DISCUSSION/WRITING

Preparing to Write

Write freely about the effects of technology. What technological developments have made us more efficient? What expectations have changed as a result of changing technology? What positive effects do you see from things such as computers, mobile phones, and other personal electronic devices? What negative consequences have these pieces of equipment had on our lives?

Choosing a Topic

1. Do you consider yourself a "digital native"? If so, explain what makes you a digital native and how you use technology differently than those who are not part of this group. If you do not consider yourself a digital native, explain why not and how you use technology differently than those who are.
2. How has one specific form of technology (e.g., the BlackBerry, email, mobile phone, Android device, Facebook, Twitter) changed your life? Write an essay in which you outline the impact this technology has had on you. Be specific in the effects you identify and think carefully about the most effective way to organize your points.
3. Nicholson contrasts the perspective of the Internet as contributing to the diminishment of "the deep, integrative mode of knowledge generation" (paragraph 14) and traditional expertise with the view of the Internet as eventually enabling "great syntheses . . . [of] millions of linked minds" (paragraph 15). Which position do you agree with more readily? Explain why.

JOHN MOORE

Sporting Life (2006)

Born in Vancouver and now living in Squamish, B.C., John Moore (1950–) is a freelance writer and author of one book of poetry, *New Moon and Money* (1983); and three novels/novellas, *The Blue Parrot* (1999), *Three of a Kind* (2001), and *The Flea Market* (2003)

Moore's articles, including book reviews, wine reviews, general features, and news reports, have been published in a variety of magazines and newspapers, including *The Vancouver Sun*, *North Shore News*, and the *Vancouver Review*, where this essay first appeared.

Preparing to Read

This essay earned John Moore first place in the Travel and Leisure category of the Western Magazine Awards. In "Sporting Life," Moore writes about the popularity of adventure sports. Before reading, think about adventure sports. What are some examples of adventure sports? Who participates in them? What is the appeal of these sports? Have you ever participated in any adventure sports? If so, how would you describe the experience? If not, would you like to?

When we bought a house in Squamish back in the early 1990s, three people I worked with immediately hit on me about my garage, seeking storage for wind-surfboards, hang-gliders and kayaks. Plus the guy who asked if he could park a trailer with twin Ski-Doos in my side yard under a tarp. They all lived in apartments in downtown Vancouver. 1

"Why did you buy these goddamn toys if you have no place to keep them?" I felt like screaming, but I already knew the answer because back then I was scratching a living by writing outdoor adventure features for local periodicals. They bought them so that for one or two days of the week they could play at being someone who doesn't live in a 500-square-foot shoebox in the claustrophobic density of Vancouver's West End or Yaletown, while still being able to drive their Stupid Unnecessary Vehicles back from Whistler in 2 time to make the scene at some bistro in mud-spattered togs for a round of crantinis and pre-dinner bragging.❶

3 At that time, small companies had begun offering guided "wilderness experiences" that combined physical challenges with a supposedly non-intrusive, more spiritual experience of the natural world. Mostly run by people trying to make a living doing what they loved, they were usually happy to take a journalist along in exchange for the publicity value of an editorial feature—about 10 times more effective than a paid advertisement of equivalent size none of them could afford.❷ I bluffed my way into sea-kayaking, rock climbing, paragliding, rafting river rapids, mountain biking, avalanche survival and winter camping courses, the whole bag. Often I was treated to lunch and more beer than was good for me. Then I got paid to write about my experiences. For a writer, this is as good as it gets.

4 Time is a D-8 Cat❸ that scrapes away the vacant lot where you played baseball and flattens the woods where you built your tree fort. A scant dozen years later, even the wisdom of turning wilderness areas into adventure theme parks for weekend warriors and tourists to defray the cost of their "preservation" now seems problematic. We're more aware that *any* kind of development shrinks the planet, and the so-called "eco-tourism" and "adventure tourism" industries have turned out to be fraternal rather than identical twins, with very different agendas.

5 Eco-tourism purists object to snowmobiles and ATVs spewing gasoline fumes and wildlife-spooking noise into the pure wilderness they've promised clients. They deplore the harassment of cetacean mammals by powerboats over-laden with seasick whale voyeurs spewing vegan lunches into the pristine waters. The wider and more boisterous adventure tourism fraternity, which has spun off whole sub-genres of Xtreme sports, sees these criticisms as party-pooping and maintains that getting people out into the wilderness by any means is justified by the end of making them more sensitive to the plight of embattled Nature.

6 This Jacob and Esau cage-match will probably be a headliner for decades to come, but despite its internecine tensions, the outdoor recreation industry and its Xtreme sports spin-offs have

---

Reading Critically

❶ Describe Moore's tone. Why is he adopting this approach?

❷ Why is an editorial feature so much more valuable than paid advertising?

❸ What is a D-8 Cat?

already caused a fundamental paradigm shift in our culture. The postmodern *zeitgeist*[4] has caught up with sport. The modern age of the passive-ironic "disinterested spectator" in both the arts and popular culture is over; we have become a culture of *participants*.

* * *

"Just Do It"

—*NIKE slogan from the 1990s*

Nowhere is this shift more apparent than in the only "global" cultural event our species has managed to produce: the *modern* Olympic Games. I stress the word *modern* because when the Olympics were revived in late 19th-century Europe, we'd already become an industrialized urban culture of spectators. McGill University architecture professor and culture critic Witold Rybczynski notes in his history of leisure time, *Waiting for the Weekend* (Viking, 1991), that the shift to corporate-sponsored team sports played by professional athletes had occurred 100 years earlier, led by pub owners who noticed that they sold more ale and pies when the local farm boys got up a game of cricket on the nearby village green. In no time, players were on the payroll of the breweries, the green fenced on game days, and admission charged. Sport became something you *watched* while consuming large quantities of beer and junk food. *Plus ça change . . .*[5] 7

But watching the 2006 Winter Olympics on TV (lager and Cheezy-Poofs at hand), I couldn't help but suspect that the whole Olympic Idea might be on the verge of core-level marketing failure. Except for a few moments, like when the freestyler shot his bindings on a jump and nailed his landing without skis, or when the Netherlands bobsled pair took the bottom half of the run upside down, the Turin Olympics seemed, well, let's be honest, kind of *dull*.[6] 8

Seeing a bunch of people "race" on cross-country skis or on skates—not even allowed to thump or trip each other like *Rollergirls*—can't help but under-whelm TV viewers accustomed to watching people with double-digit IQs drive ATVs off sheer 9

Reading Critically

[4] What is the "postmodern *zeitgeist*"?

[5] Explain this comment. Why does Moore use a French expression rather than an English one?

[6] Do you agree that watching Olympic sports is somewhat dull? Explain your position.

cliffs or try to jump bikes to the top of apartment buildings from home-made plywood ramps on Real TV programs like the *Max X List*, never mind the sadistic stunts contrived by *Fear Factor*. Who wants to watch a pair of girls in modest maillots do synchronized swimming once you've seen a 42D-cup bimbo in a Malibu bikini (or some buff young stud in a Speedo) undo padlocks underwater in a clear plastic tank filled with giant pinching crabs for a $50,000 jackpot?

10 Yet the real problem with all Olympic events isn't their lack of appeal to cathode-lobotomized sofa lizards. Such people are no longer a dominant majority. For the first time in history since the classical age, many of the people who make up the audience for the Games are *themselves* weekend warriors—amateur athletes who regularly engage in Xtreme sports that that would give a pampered Olympian the yellow squirts. If you spend your weekends para-gliding, base-jumping, wind-surfing, ice-climbing or riding a bike down steep mountain trails at top speed, it's no wonder you're a bit blasé watching some coddled "star" flit down a pre-set engineered course to a "victory" measured in hundredths of a second.

* * *

11 As kids, we do things our parents warn us against to define ourselves as individuals—chicks that no longer cower in the nest waiting for Mom and Dad to hork up pre-digested social values. For my post-WW2 generation that came of age in the 1960s, this took the form of risky politics, risky drugs and risky sex. The acid test of any form of rebellion is whether or not it gives you what psycho-neurologists try to quantify as an endorphin/adrenaline high—the feeling you got when you climbed to the top of the forbidden cherry tree, rode your bike no-hands down the steepest hill in the neighbourhood, or played Knock On Ginger on the meanest old man on the block and he chased you with a flashlight and a nine-iron.❼

12 The sand pit was a place we were absolutely forbidden to play, a big semi-circular hole dug out of the side of a ridge not far from Cleveland Dam in North Vancouver. From up in the hot resinous shadows of the scrub firs, it was about five times higher than the roof of your house, as kids measure. The trick was seeing

---

Reading Critically

❼ What did you do as a child to achieve this "endorphin/adrenaline high" and define yourself as an individual?

that halfway down, big slopes of pure soft sand would break your fall, cushioning your slide to the bottom. You just needed the jam to take that first screaming step off the edge to slide down to glory and shake a bucket of grit out of your jeans.

13 Today's guided adventures and Xtreme sports depend on the courage to take that step: to launch yourself out the door of the plane at 10,000 feet, turn your kayak or canoe into whitewater, stretch for the hand-hold that gets you around the overhang, stay on your bike when the trail dives down a shale slope of plus-45 degrees. Make one split-second decision to hang in and the rest is reflex, will to survive, and the perversity to brag about seriously hurting yourself when you do.

14 The adrenaline rush of fear, then relief, is a high-colonic[8] for the brain. Portrayal of this kind of risk-taking as "a healthy active lifestyle" masks the discovery that adrenaline and endorphins appear to be the body's natural cocaine and heroin speedball—improving performance, blunting pain and producing delusions of invulnerability. Like all good things, this enzyme junk is addictive, even potentially lethal. It can also lead to reality-TV madness like the annual international Eco-Challenge race, in which teams of annoying over-achievers from around the world pay obscene amounts of money to whine about undergoing the kind of hardships that in wartime would result in atrocity trials.

15 Nostalgia for the euphoria of risk has become a billion-dollar industry. Every time baby boomers roll over in bed, some clever dick invents a new technologically enhanced mattress and makes a bundle to stick under it simply because there's so many of us with so much money that even a moderate market share of any product sector translates into mass sales.

16 When our parents hit their 40s, they accepted middle age gracefully, taking up low-impact social sports, like curling and golf, which involve a lot of innocent fibbing in plush cocktail lounges. They adopted cardigan sweaters and elastic-waist slacks and skirts that looked vaguely sporty while taking into account the natural state of the human body in its pre-senile phase.

17 Not us, man. Maybe we did transfer out of that Creative Ceramics major into an MBA program, or drop out and write the Securities & Exchange Commission exam to become a real estate agent or stockbroker. That doesn't mean we sold out.

Reading Critically

[8] What is a "high colonic for the brain"?

When some Jurassic rock radio station plays The Who's "My Generation," we crank up the sound system in the Volvo wagon and screech along, "Hope I die before I get old!"

So when we find ourselves still alive and looking five-oh in the mirror, we won't abide any polyester polo-necked golf shirts or Sansabelt slacks in our walk-in closets—bigger than family apartments in some parts of the world. We're jogging, running marathons, doing triathlons, mountain biking, rock-climbing, para-sailing, spelunking and deep-sea diving, white-water or sea kayaking, cross-country skiing—anything that will give us back the adrenaline rush of youth our generation assumes is an inalienable human right—and our closets and storage lockers are stuffed with over-priced gear to prove it.[9] 18

Most X-sports require physical courage, but no special moral or political commitment. They're just the natural organic version of the vicious sex, dangerous drugs and hedonistic head-banger music of the late 1970s and the money-and-gluttony worship of the odious Decade of Greed[10] that followed. We're fitter and we get more fresh air, but it's still just all about Us Having Fun. 19

* * *

Yet outdoor adventure tourism and Xtreme sports bridge what was called the generation gap in our wild youth. Not just a boomer fad, they're hugely popular with young people who still set the cultural tone and now even have their own X Games. X-sports are the participatory physical incarnation of postmodernism: they embody the now, the instant of being intensely alive in the moment, and through the postmodern aesthetic of playful radical juxtaposition they create new activities, taking a technique or piece of equipment originally designed for one purpose and adapting it to another. 20

Look at the reincarnation of the bicycle as an all-terrain vehicle. Invented in the late 19th century, it was a mechanical pony meant to reduce the vast daily tonnage of horse-shit fouling city streets at a time when automobiles were still hand-built toys of the rich. It was a contraption meant for paved or graded roads: a cheap, clean mode of urban transportation. When bikes began 21

Reading Critically

[9] Summarize the shift in responses to getting older. How did your grandparents respond to aging? Your parents? You?

[10] What was the "Decade of Greed"? What other terms have been used to characterize this decade?

reappearing in traffic as ecologically sound rides, I approved in principle, but as a hiker and dog person, I was appalled when they left pavement. Bikes may be eco-friendly in the city, but in the woods they rapidly degrade trails, creating mud-wallows in the low spots and eroding the edges.⓫

22 Mountain bikers also had serious attitude problems where safety and courtesy were concerned. In the late 1980s in lower Mosquito Creek where I walked my dog, I was nearly de-gendered by a spandexed biker hurtling out of the salmonberries. I caught his handlebars in time to stop him from giving me a free vasectomy and dumped him in the brambles accompanied by strong language. As I stalked off, ignoring his attempted apology, he recovered enough to shout, "By the way, I'm *not* an asshole." Chain leash wrapped around my fist, I offered to introduce him to the concept of obedience training. White-faced, he remounted and pedalled off, no doubt convinced he'd encountered one of the mentally ill our provincial government had recently expelled from supervised care facilities in order to save young urban stooges enough tax money to spend on $3,000 trail bikes.

23 Wind-surfboards gave the traditional Hawaiian sport, which went global as a subculture in the 1960s, new life by marrying it to quick-response sailing that is still a tradition in coastal Europe. The latest twist is kite-boarding, which combines a para-glider wing with a snowboard-length surfboard to maximize the aerial and aquatic thrill factors. As for a "sport" like street-luge—putting wheels on the one-man bobsled to run downhill races on pavement—the first time I saw this on TV I instantly recalled the kamikaze crates we used to rig from a single plank, two-by-four axles, wheels pried off a stolen shopping cart and a short rope for steering. Frills like soapbox coachwork and brakes were overlooked in our haste to launch down hills, praying posted lookouts were sharp-eyed and that none of the wheels would fall off. Just to survive with nothing more than bruises and the loss of a few yards of skin made you feel like an indestructible superhero.

24 Enhanced by contemporary materials like Kevlar,⓬ the ancient Inuit kayak is an ideal craft for up-close exploring and

---

Reading Critically

⓫ Explain Moore's apparently contradictory reaction to the increasing popularity of bicycles.

⓬ What is Kevlar? In addition to kayaks, where else are you aware of it being used?

low-impact adventuring in coastal waters. An Inuit hunter might approve of new sea kayaks on the basis of improved materials, but the idea of running *any* kayak down class-five river rapids would strike him as typically insane white-man behaviour. Rivers are full of rocks. Discovering them at high speed, upside down when you're busy drowning, may interfere with the appreciation of your newfound intimacy with the riparian environment.

True mother of all X-sports is the parachute, invented in World War I to give pilots and balloon observers a marginal chance of survival and later used to drop spies or troops behind enemy lines. Those pilots and paratroops would never have imagined that in the second half of the 20th century people would *pay* to jump out of planes and deliberately prolong free-fall to do mid-air stunts—including riding and flipping on snowboards, a sort of air-surfing that may be the ultimate Po-Mo[13] sport. 25

* * *

Even traditionally conservative recreational activities like mountaineering have been transformed by the postmodern *zeitgeist.* Originally practice activities for the final acts of peak ascension, rock-climbing and bouldering detached themselves and became a separate sport during the latter half of the 20th century in the North American southwest, where Dali-esque rock formations[14] and monotonously fine weather let climbers free the body from bulky clothing and packs to push the possibilities of climbing technique [to] the limit. 26

There's nothing especially postmodern about a specialist skill-set becoming a separate sport. What is supremely Po-Mo is the increasing number of climbers who learn their basic skills *indoors*, in climbing gyms that began to appear in North America in the early 1990s. Goofing on artificial walls, top-roped for safety with Pink Floyd's *Dark Side of The Moon* booming out of a dozen speakers may be a blast, but it doesn't prepare you for real rock that turns cold and slick when the weather changes, numbing your fingers after a few moves; or the brain-poaching effects of the sun if you start a pitch at the wrong time of day; or horseflies that chow down on your calves when an instinctive slap at them will cost you your hold and probably your life. 27

Reading Critically

[13] What does *Po-Mo* mean? Why does Moore use this abbreviation rather than the full term?

[14] What do "Dali-esque rock formations" look like?

When I took a rock-climbing course on the Smoke Bluffs in Squamish, the instructor turned up with a couple of ropes, slings and a handful of hardware he casually tossed on the ground. His modest gear cache did not impress a couple in their early 40s, clad from neck to ankle in matching superhero lycra. The guy in particular kept casting covetous glances at young rock-rats on neighbouring pitches whose chests were crossed with Rambo bandoliers dangling every nut, chock and widget in the catalogue. I made a point of asking, in front of everyone, "Does all that stuff really help?"⓯ 28

"It helps keep Mountain Equipment Co-op in business," the instructor answered with a smirk, provoking a scowl from the guy who'd been eyeing their racks. "Special gear is only useful if you already possess excellent basic climbing fundamentals. If you don't, having all that stuff is actually dangerous. It gives you too much to think about and it can make you think you're a better climber that you actually are. That's how you get hurt." 29

In the postmodern century, we no longer sell things on the basis that they make you look rich enough to *afford* them. We sell things, from cars to computers to sports gear, on the premise that they make you appear competent to *use* them. Replacing the image of wealth as the dominant status mode of our culture, the image of competence socially disenfranchises those who acquire wealth merely by the windfall of inheritance, luck, or even the kind of acquisitive drive worshipped during the 1980s. Thorstein Veblen, the early 20th-century economist who coined the term "conspicuous consumption" to explain the need of the rich to be seen to be so, would understand the necessity of buying $250 "trail shoes" to go for a walk in the woods. 30

This paradigm shift is one of the eccentric shortcuts by which something resembling "progress" in human culture occurs. Competence is harder to fake than wealth. Just buying top-of-the-line gear won't cut it; you have to learn how to use it or look like a horse's ass. And no matter how odious I personally find [them,] some X-sports [. . .] can have life-transforming effects for large numbers of people, regardless of income. This makes them much more inclusive than the passive supposed solidarity of a whole 31

Reading Critically

⓯ Why does Moore ask this question in front of everyone?

nation watching televised Olympic events restricted to an élite of athletic champions.[16]

* * *

32 Adventure tourism and X-sports have morphed into more than recreational activities. Like the hippie movement of the 1960s, they are a form of non-confrontational social revolution[17] for a culture so terminally disgusted with politics that "taking it to the streets" means grinding bikes and skateboards or doing free-form gymnastics off public structures, and "dropping out" entails an abrupt loss of real altitude.

33 In the 19th century, mountaineering was a subculture of eccentric amateurs, some inherently rich, others not so, who spent every free moment among the cliffs, crags and snows. Many people still climb in that spirit, taking low-paying jobs in the hospitality industry, which offers portable skills. They work as little as they need to, enabling them to travel from Squamish to Joshua Tree to the Dolomites[18]—wherever there's steep rock and fresh challenges. Like the so-called surf bums who follow the sun around the world or ski bums who follow the snow, they're actually more than a bunch of drop-outs marginalized by a passion for a particular physical activity.

34 Today's eco/adventure tourism and X-sport destinations are the moveable *gymnasia* of the Global Village, places where the young and quick meet kindred spirits, some old and wise, from all over the world, making social and philosophical connections, spawning sub-cultures with networks that may be possible models for future supra-national societies. We ought to be grateful for these signs of sanity in a younger generation, instead of whining because they're too smart to be loyal to corporate employers who treat them as members of an untouchable caste on principle.[19]

35 Our society, too, often evaluates cultural phenomena on a balance sheet, but even in those terms it's obvious that outdoor adventure recreation generates far greater long-term economic benefits than any number of Olympic blowouts. Proliferating

---

Reading Critically

[16] Explain why some extreme sports are more inclusive than a population watching the Olympic Games.

[17] Do you agree with Moore? Why or why not?

[18] Where are these three places? What do they have in common?

[19] Who is guilty of this whining that Moore describes? Who are they whining about?

variations of postmodern sports are all characterized by the investment of large amounts of money in lessons, specialized equipment, and branded clothing that identifies the user as blessed with the status of a high disposable income as well as that of a supposedly serious athlete and adventurer. Add on the entrepreneurial opportunities for niche-market services like instruction and guiding, the manufacture of clothing and gear, factor in the travel and tourism spin-offs, and you've got an industry. Not a closely held, hierarchical, traditional heavy industry, but possibly the new business model of a quiet social revolution these sub-cultures are engendering.

36 Some forward-looking nations (Belize, for instance) have staked their economic future on guided eco/adventure tours and X-sports, mainly because of their minimal environmental impact. Even the most egregious of these activities remain things post-millennial yuppies do on weekends—things that don't take you too far from an ATM and a good restaurant. Since those engaged in them don't penetrate wilderness areas permanently or to any significant depth, the worst damage they do is the equivalent of dog-earing the pages of a library book.

37 Cranky purists (don't look at me like that) may question the authenticity of the experiences offered by eco/adventure tourism. As a survivor of a wide random sampling, I have to admit that these experiences are no more authentic than the guided African safaris of the 1950s written up by Ernest Hemingway and Robert Ruark. But "authenticity" is often a reactionary concept that appeals to an idealized past, a supposed "golden age" that frequently proves to be more fabulous than fact.

38 When Hemingway and Ruark were affirming their manhood at the expense of big game on the veldt, they may not even have been aware that their Great White Hunter and native guides were discreetly covering them in accordance with Rule 1 of the adventure tourism industry; Don't Let the Client Get Killed. The Africa they described was a beautiful fiction of magnificent beasts and noble savages—a place that existed only in their writing, Hollywood films, and the animatronic Riverboat Ride attraction at Walt Disney's first theme park. The real Africa of their time was a continent-sized slave-labour camp perpetuated by febrile colonial administrations and global economic factors long before the term Third World had been coined.

39 *That* was the story a generation of writers completely missed, and it's a cautionary reminder that writing can be wonderful even

when it's unintentionally describing a creature by looking at the wrong end. When a friend read my breathless report of spending a couple of winter nights in an emergency shelter I'd built out of snow, he sent me a copy of Ernest Shackleton's excruciating saga of survival after the failure of his Antarctic expedition. Humbled, I took his point.[20] With appropriate postmodern irony, guided adventures and X-sports often trivialize the original activity that inspired them. White-water rafting and kayaking turn the death-defying river voyages of explorers like Simon Fraser and Alexander Mackenzie[21] into jolly day-trip outings to scenic water-park attractions.

40 But is it reasonable to value these experiences against a revisionist and possibly fictional notion of "authenticity"? Every human experience is unique to its time and place and thus authentic, in a sense. If somebody rides down the Thompson River rapids in a fat guided raft on some inane corporate team-building outing and has a life-changing experience, should we dismiss it because they weren't in [a] brigade canoe piloted by indentured, toqued, suicidal voyageurs? Surely it's the ultimate result that counts, the long-term effect on human beings and the way they see themselves in relation to their own culture.

41 The *gratuitous* aspect of X-treme sports, their postmodern, self-conscious novelty, makes them fun to watch, even fun to try, but don't expect many of them to become Olympic events.[22] The inclusion of snowboarding in the Olympics in the 1990s was a cynical marketing attempt to appeal to a younger generation who think the discus competition is just a really lame Frisbee event. But while the playful silliness of most X-sports may mark their cards as ephemeral fads, by the time the International Olympic Committee gets around to even considering them, whole subcultures of weekend warriors will be long gone, off to some global adventure play park or *doing* something else, instead of *watching* the tube.

Reading Critically

[20] What was Moore's friend's point?

[21] Who were Simon Fraser and Alexander MacKenzie? When and where did they live?

[22] Why are these sports unlikely to be included as Olympic events? Do you think that they should be? Why or why not?

UNDERSTANDING DETAILS

1. Summarize the two perspectives on adventure tourism.
2. What is the "fundamental paradigm shift in our culture" (paragraph 6) that Moore describes? How has this affected the Olympic Games?
3. What is the appeal of adventure or Xtreme sports? To whom do these activities appeal?

ANALYZING MEANING

1. What is Moore's thesis? Where in his essay is it stated?
2. What is Moore's attitude toward Xtreme sports? How is this revealed?
3. Explain why some people believe that adventure sports are not authentic. Do you agree? Why or why not?

DISCOVERING RHETORICAL STRATEGIES

1. Of the three common purposes of causal analysis essays (to prove a specific point, to argue against a widely accepted belief, or to speculate on a theory), which do you think is Moore's purpose in this essay? Has he successfully achieved that purpose?
2. What additional rhetorical strategies has Moore used in this essay? How have they helped him to achieve his purpose?
3. Moore's writing uses literary allusions, sophisticated language, and complex sentence structures. What is the effect of these choices on you as you read his essay?

MAKING CONNECTIONS

1. Moore discusses the differences between adventure tourism and eco-tourism. Explain which of these two Tomson Highway ("What a Certain Visionary Once Said") or Monte Hummel ("A Passion for the Environment") would likely support.
2. According to Moore, "adventure tourism and X-sports have morphed into more than recreational activities . . . they are a form of non-confrontational social revolution" (paragraph 32). What relationship do you think Alex Boyd would see between adventure tourism and X-sports and graffiti ("In Defense of Graffiti")?

IDEAS FOR DISCUSSION/WRITING

Preparing to Write

Write freely about sports. What sports do you like to watch? Do you typically watch live sports events or televised sports events? Which sports do you like to participate in? Have your preferences changed over time? If so, what has contributed to the change? Have you tried any of the Xtreme sports that Moore describes? If so, how did you find the experience? If not, do any of them appeal to you?

Choosing a Topic

1. Write about the sport that you like the best. What effect does watching or participating in this sport have on you?
2. Moore says that he found the 2006 Winter Olympics somewhat dull (paragraph 8.) Do you share this view of the modern Olympics? Explain why or why not.
3. According to Moore, "adventure tourism and X-sports have morphed into more than recreational activities . . . they are a form of non-confrontational social revolution." Write an essay in which you either promote the value of eco/adventure tours or persuade your audience that they are inauthentic and therefore participating in them is not worthwhile.

CARMEN EVEREST WAHL

Gluten Intolerance: Why Are More People Suffering Than Ever Before? (2010)

Carmen Everest Wahl is a local food writer from Waterloo with a background in environmental education and nutrition. She is enthusiastic about local food and writes regularly for *Edible Toronto,* one of the Edible Communities publications that strives to transform people's relationship to local food (**www.ediblecommunities.com/content/**).

Preparing to Read

In this essay, first published in *Edible Toronto and the Golden Horseshoe,* Wahl explores reasons for the growing prevalence of gluten intolerance and the responses of some food retailers to this change. Before reading, think about wheat and all the products that are made with wheat or wheat flour. How much of a staple are they in your diet? How significant is the production of wheat to Canada's economy? How would you react if you could no longer eat bread or other products containing wheat?

Hailed as the staff of life❶ because of its historical importance in the human diet, wheat has been a staple food in most civilizations throughout Europe, West Asia and North Africa for over ten thousand years. Statistics Canada❷ reported in 2008 that the average consumption of wheat flour per person in this country is almost 44 kilograms a year, the equivalent of nearly one cup of flour every day. The Food and Agriculture Organization (FAO) is forecasting the world's wheat production for 2010 to be 646 million tonnes, 21 million tonnes of which will be harvested from Canadian soil. Wheat is big business in our country and around the world, and has long been considered essential to a healthy and complete diet. But not for everyone. 1

Reading Critically

❶ Explain the phrase "staff of life."

❷ Is Statistics Canada a reliable source of information? How do you know?

Gluten intolerance, once thought to be fairly uncommon, is being identified in a growing number of people who exhibit an adverse reaction to gluten, the main protein in wheat. Just a decade ago, it was believed that gluten intolerance was experienced by one in 2,500 people worldwide. Within the past few years, it has generally been accepted that one in 133 people (or up to 270,000 Canadians) can now be classified into one of three distinct categories of gluten intolerance: celiac disease, non-celiac gluten sensitivity, or wheat allergy. 2

Hereditary celiac disease❸ occurs when the body's immune system mounts a defensive attack against normal tissue – including the intestinal lining – in response to eating gluten. As a result, celiac patients are at increased risk of malnutrition since the damaged intestine is incapable of absorbing nutrients. Celiac sufferers are also at higher risk of developing other auto-immune disorders such as thyroid, joint, and liver diseases, as well as diabetes mellitus. 3

The most common gluten-intolerance disorder is the non-celiac response to gluten, which manifests itself through abdominal pain and distension, flatulence, diarrhea, and a general feeling of lethargy. While relatively uncommon, the consumption of wheat can also lead to an allergic reaction, a histamine response similar to a peanut allergy, which manifests itself through skin rashes and swelling, wheezing, and abdominal pain. 4

While these three conditions have different symptoms and outcomes, they are all triggered by the consumption of wheat – the omnipresent and culturally significant food grain – and its protein components. 5

What exactly is this protein that has the potential to wreak such havoc in the human body? Gluten, which means glue in Latin, is formed when two other proteins found in wheat flour – gliadin and glutenin – are mixed with water. As this sticky mass is kneaded, the gluten strands become entangled, forming a strong, elastic web. During the process of making bread, the web catches the carbon dioxide formed from yeast growth, allowing the dough to rise into beautifully rounded loaves of bread. Other grains such as barley, rye, spelt and oats also contain trigger proteins similar to gluten. 6

Reading Critically

❸ What does it mean if a disease is hereditary?

Until recently it was believed that all cases of gluten intolerance were diagnosed and ultimately treated in childhood. Current research indicates, however, that onset among adults, especially between the ages of thirty and sixty, is occurring more frequently than previously thought. An epidemiological study recently published in the Annals of Medicine has provided evidence that celiac disease is increasing and that, as we age, the chances of being diagnosed increase. Why an individual is born with or develops gluten intolerance continues to baffle researchers but many hypotheses exist. 7

Historically, children afflicted with celiac disease would have died in infancy due to malabsorption of nutrients and complications such as anemia and diarrhea, and a likely diagnosis of Chronic Wasting Disease. Those children wouldn't have been able to pass along their genetic predisposition to gluten intolerance and the road to diagnosis would have ended there. Today, enhanced diagnostic tools have been developed that not only identify gluten intolerance in children but also point to wheat sensitivity in the aging population. 8

We do know that the wheat we eat today is dramatically different from the grains eaten by our ancestors. Active genetic selection has taken the wheat plant from a grass with few grains and little gluten to heavy seed heads loaded with that all-important bread-making protein. A Dutch study published in Theoretical and Applied Genetics supports the claim that older varieties of wheat produce less gluten than modern ones. Since the aim of wheat breeding was to create strains that served the bread industry's need for high yields and better baking qualities, high levels of gluten have obviously been seen as desirable. As the researchers note, however, the impact of high-gluten flours on the human digestive tract were never considered.❹ 9

Gluten is not only an important component in creating yeast-risen breads, but is increasingly found as an additive in processed foods. From soups and soya sauce to self-basting turkeys and bags of shredded cheese, gluten is used as a stabilizer, emulsifier, thickener, or flow agent in an effort to obtain a perfect final product. Gluten is even used in many nonfood items such as cosmetics, lickable stamps and envelopes, art supplies 10

Reading Critically

❹ Why do you think that the effect of high-gluten flours on the digestive tract was not considered?

and household cleaners. Gluten powder can be found inside latex and rubber gloves and as a coating on pills. It is also often used in the packaging of items like chewing gum. Needless to say, we are exposed to wheat and gluten in far more ways than just through the consumption of baked goods. While our bodies may have adapted to eating grain over the past several thousand years, the ways of modern life might have inundated us with a toxic component that at one time seemed quite harmless and indeed beneficial.❺

11 For the legions of people who have been given a diagnosis of gluten intolerance, celiac disease, or wheat allergy, the cure is the simple act of removing the offending food from their diets (no more wheat, barley, rye or oats) and a rigorous review of all food labels. (Since non-food-ingredient labels don't exist, several reputable websites have published lists of items containing hidden gluten.) "Simple," you say? Faced with this diagnosis, most people feel as if they have just been given a life sentence with no chance of parole in a World Without Bread, complete with a diet devoid of pastries, muffins, cookies, hot dogs and even birthday cake! How can one possibly live the good life given that kind of cure?

12 Bakeries are increasingly responding to the needs of this growing community. It is refreshing to find new products on the shelves that fulfill a niche in the food market, in contrast to the many over-processed, over-packaged, and often unhealthy new products that tempt our children and appeal to our sense of convenience. For Rhonda Barr, owner of Ya'd Never Know in Dundas, Ontario, the key to converting her conventional catering business into a dedicated gluten-free bakery last year was finding the right combinations of starches and bean flours that could replicate the texture and rising properties of wheat.❻

13 Today, forty-five fresh, gluten-free products that help to normalize the diet of gluten-intolerant consumers are baked and sold under the Ya'd Never Know label. Customers can walk right into the bakery and choose from a wide variety of breads, loaves, cookies, pasta dishes, quiches and gluten-free dressings. Craving an apple pie? No problem, Rhonda has created gluten-free pie shells that are ready to fill. Your son is having a birthday party and his best friend cannot eat wheat? A quick trip to the bakery will supply gluten-free

---

Reading Critically

❺ Can you think of any other products that fit this description?

❻ Why is it important for these bakers to replicate these properties of wheat?

hot dog buns, pizza, and even birthday cake that can be served to all of the party guests. And the surprise . . . ya'd never know by the taste that they were gluten-free. If it isn't convenient to drive to the Dundas bakery, many of these baked goods are also available at the Dundas and Ancaster farmers' markets, where Rhonda herself can often be seen searching for local fruits and vegetables to bake into her sweet and savoury products. For those further afield, online ordering with next-day delivery is also available.

14 Not content to merely rework tried and true recipes and offer fresh and wholesome foods to her customers, Rhonda is communicating the gluten-free lifestyle through her weekly cooking show on the local cable TV station, Channel 14. She is about to launch a consulting service that will assist people in transforming their kitchens into gluten-free zones. And, to put the icing on the cake, Rhonda has just published her first cookbook, *What's up with Gluten: A Chef's Perspective From My Kitchen to Yours*, a collection of recipes for gluten-free hors d'oeuvres, starters, mains and desserts. According to Rhonda, her mission is simply "to give people so deprived something normal again in their lives."

15 Roland Berchtold of Waterloo-based Grainharvest Breadhouse couldn't agree more. In 2004, he and his partner Hubert Wurm launched their Circle of Life Bakery division, which specializes in gluten-free, dairy-free, and sugar-free baked goods. Roland has observed parents and children coming into the bakery and leaving overjoyed at having found alternatives for lunches and snacks, even if they cost more. "Money doesn't seem to be an issue when you are trying to get kids to eat something," and with dozens of cookies, muffins, bars and biscotti, there are plenty of choices to satisfy both kids and adults alike.

16 Roland has noticed over the past few years that his clientele is shifting from mainly children to a greater percentage of adults, even those who have no issues with gluten. People have become aware that more and more processed foods contain wheat and they are searching for alternative grains in their everyday foods. The breads and other baked goods at Circle of Life are made from brown and white rice flours and, according to Roland, nobody seems to notice that they aren't made from wheat flour.❼

Reading Critically

❼ Do you believe these customers really do not notice that the products are not made with wheat flour?

17 Most of us couldn't conceive of a world without bread. Aside from being the perfect accompaniment to butter, cheese, meat and eggs, bread is satisfying for the way it feels in our mouths and fills our tummies. Talented bakers have realized that eating good gluten-free bread is just as important as eating any good bread, and today eating gluten-free need not be the life sentence it once was.

UNDERSTANDING DETAILS

1. List and briefly describe the three categories of gluten intolerance.
2. How common is gluten intolerance today? How does this compare to the past? What accounts for the change?
3. What is the solution for people with gluten intolerance?

ANALYZING MEANING

1. Explain why gluten is such a common ingredient in both food and non-food products.
2. What is Wahl's purpose in writing this essay? Has she successfully achieved it?
3. Discuss why some bakers have started focusing on gluten-free products. Do you think this is a passing trend or a fundamental shift? Explain.

DISCOVERING RHETORICAL STRATEGIES

1. Describe the tone of Wahl's essay. How does she achieve this tone? Is it an effective choice for her topic?
2. Does Wahl focus on causes, effects, or both? Explain.
3. In addition to cause/effect, what rhetorical strategies does Wahl use in this essay?

MAKING CONNECTIONS

1. In this essay, Wahl discusses those people whose diet is dictated, in part, by intolerance to a common food ingredient. Compare and contrast this approach to diet to that discussed by Cynara Geissler ("Fat Acceptance: A Basic Primer").
2. Wahl profiles a few food vendors who have shifted to gluten-free products to serve a growing population requiring such foods. Do you think that The Main that Joe Fiorito describes

in "Night Shift on the Main" would be a likely candidate for a similar reinvention? Why or why not?

3. Imagine that Wahl was going to write an essay for one of the Edible Communities publications about the local food of Newfoundland and Labrador. How might her essay be similar to Jeannie Guy's ("Newfoundland Cooking")? In what ways would it probably differ? (You might want to explore the Edible Communities website at **www.ediblecommunities.com/content/** for more information about the intended audience and purpose of these publications.)

IDEAS FOR DISCUSSION/WRITING

Preparing to Write

Write freely about a dietary restriction that you have experienced or that someone you know has experienced (e.g., gluten intolerance, an allergy, lactose intolerance, vegetarianism, veganism, keeping kosher, eating halal foods) What was the reason for the restriction (e.g., health, religion, ethics)? Was it a temporary restriction or long-term dietary modification? How easy or difficult was it to incorporate this dietary restriction into your life?

Choosing a Topic

1. Choose a food ingredient that you particularly enjoy and write an essay in which you imagine the effects on your life if you had to eliminate that ingredient from your diet.
2. Visit a local supermarket. Based on the information available on product labels, create a menu for a dinner party at which you know at least one of your guests is gluten intolerant.
3. Many restaurants and food producers are actively responding to the growing number of people with dietary restrictions. Write an essay in which you advocate for restaurants to provide clearly identified options for customers who are gluten intolerant or who have some other specific dietary restriction.

JEANNIE GUY

Newfoundland Cooking (2009)

Jeannie Guy attended Memorial University of Newfoundland and obtained a B.A. in English. While there, she then became distracted by collections of other people's writing and subsequently started her career in federal government libraries at the RCMP Crime Lab Library in Ottawa. After completing her master's degree in library science at Dalhousie University, she continued in library management (at the Office of the Auditor General, Canada Post Corporation, Fisheries and Oceans Canada, and the Privy Council Office, among others) where she found the work always sufficiently lucrative, interesting, and absorbing.

Preparing to Read

In this essay from *Newfoundland Quarterly*, Jeannie Guy talks about the meals of her childhood and the routines that dictated what her family typically ate each day. Before reading, think about your own meals growing up. Did you have regular dishes that reflected the other routines in your family life? Did you have favourite dishes? How much variety was there in your meals? Was your experience similar to that of your friends and neighbours? Who typically prepared the meals in your home?

Everyone was like me when I was young, or so I thought. Oh, not in the obvious things like the colour of their hair, or whether they were tall or little, or their religion or where they went to school. I learned pretty quickly that some people could run faster than me no matter how hard I tried, or that I was not even close to being the best at playing "alleys"❶ on my street, and that I was the youngest and smallest in the gang and there was no way to change that. But I thought that everyone went to school and church and everyone had a mom and dad and sisters or brothers, and ate the same food. It was all pretty much the same. At least it was like that for me until I went to university in the 1960s. 1

Reading Critically

❶ What is the game "alleys"?

That first year I took classes in general arts and sciences: maths, English and French, philosophy, anthropology and sociology. And that is where I found out that in Newfoundland and Labrador we had something called culture. We were different from everyone else. I remember it hit me like a thunderbolt in Sociology of the Family class. Our prof was probably from the Caribbean or South America and probably doing his PhD.❷ He had to teach us on Monday evening at 7:00. We were almost all students from the province and had not travelled much. Maybe to Halifax or to London, England or Montreal or Toronto. For most of us, St. John's was the big time. 2

He told us that he had never come across people before who ate the same dishes on a certain day of the week. He said in all his reading and studying people around the world, he had never encountered it. It was something foreign to him and he wanted to understand why we did it. I remember we students looked at each other shyly, strangely, out of the corner of our eyes when he said it. We did not know what he was talking about but we did not want to embarrass him or ourselves. What did he mean? 3

Well, you know. On Sunday at the noon meal—dinner—what did we have? Roast beef or roast chicken, of course, but at Christmas, turkey, we replied. Right after we came home from church. And we had mashed potatoes, with boiled carrots and turnip with gravy, right? And bread stuffing made with Mount Scio savory if it was chicken or turkey. And then cold-cuts for supper from the leftovers with salads and Jello with fruit cocktail and Nestle's thick cream. 4

Yes. Why was that? 5

We explained. 6

On Mondays when your Mom had clothes to wash and hang outside on the line (winter or not) and no time to be fooling around cooking fussy stuff, you had leftovers again. If she was starting to run out, you might have to load up on homemade bread and butter with sweet mustard pickles or homemade rhubarb pickles. In my house it was always served in Grandmother's little blue dish. Every Monday, right after school and Brownies or Guides you had leftovers. That's right. 7

Yes. And on Tuesdays, what about Tuesdays? 8

Reading Critically

❷ Why do you think Guy is vague about the origin of her professor and his reason for being at the university?

That was followed on Tuesdays, by "boiled dinner" for supper. Mom did the ironing on Tuesdays, and everything was all cotton in the early days: bedsheets, pillow cases, Dad's shirts, our school uniform blouses, aprons, her dresses . . . the works . . . all pure cotton. So ironing was a major chore, and she had little time for niceties.[3] Especially if it had been raining on Monday and she was still trying to get the clothes dry on the clothes line in the kitchen. Boiled dinner. Some people called it Jiggs' dinner or corned beef and cabbage. She just threw everything in one pot: corned beef, cabbage. Right. With pease pudding (just like in the nursery rhyme). Hot in a cotton cloth pudding bag. And boiled potatoes and here we go again: boiled carrots and turnip. When it got to the table, we kids would fight for the sweet mustard pickles. We did not know what ketchup was. 9

And what about the rest of the week? 10

So ironing day was followed by grocery day. Wednesdays Mom walked uptown for groceries: Lawlors' Meat Market, and Bowrings for the rest until the supermarkets came along. Then she could get everything there in one shop, and get it delivered. But she had to get home in time for them to deliver, so we had fish and brewis with scruncheons.[4] She must have put the hard tack in [to] soak the night before to have it soft enough to cook on Wednesday evenings. 11

On Thursdays she must have put clothes away, or did darning, and concentrated on cooking. That was perhaps an optional day when we could have anything: bottled moose with potatoes, or rabbit stew, or partridge, or in the spring seal flipper pie. Or sometimes in later years you got modern, foreign kind of food for supper like pork chops. 12

On Fridays we started getting ready for Sundays so she scrubbed the floors . . . on her knees . . . and waxed and polished them by hand. Wooden floors in the living room and dining room but canvas and later linoleum tile in the rest of the house. Until Dad got the polisher for her. Most of my friends had fish on Fridays. Which meant cod. Trout was popular too any time of year but usually not in the winter. Fish on Fridays.[5] That was not culture. That was religion. 13

Reading Critically

[3] What are the niceties that Guy is referring to?

[4] What are brewis and scruncheons?

[5] Explain why Guy uses so many sentence fragments rather than complete sentences.

Saturdays were big cleaning days and preparation for Sundays. Baking: cookies, squares and fresh bread were always on the go. You could not get near the kitchen . . . or dared not in case you ended up helping. And it meant pea soup for lunch with carrots diced into it with dumplings. I loved the dumplings: light and fluffy. My Grandmother Guy's recipe. My mother always complained that she could never make dumplings like Mrs. Guy. And the soup had bits of salt meat or riblets. Saturday evening was saltfish with potatoes and scruncheons. No question. 14

Sometimes Mom would make tea buns too with raisins but she was never happy with them, and Father used to tease her that they were heavy and hard enough that he could use them as sinkers . . . that's the lead weights you put on a fishing line to sink it.[6] Not like Gammy Guy's tea buns but wonderful all the same, hot with a bit of Good Luck margarine melting on them, not real butter. We used to tease the young kids when we were small if we did not want to play with them. "Go home! Your mother got buns!" That meant that their mothers had been baking and there was fresh bread or biscuits at home, so they had better go quickly or they would miss out. Everyone knew that. That was culture. Go into any house on my street, Forest Road, and it was pretty much the same. 15

Then on Sundays, Mom started from the top again and we had a so-called day of rest: no movies, no playing cards, no knitting. Nothing. Go to church and Sunday school and eat roast beef. Life was simple. It had structure and predictability. We had culture and we did not know it. We had *haute cuisine de terre neuve.* A professor at the university had told me. 16

UNDERSTANDING DETAILS

1. In what way did Guy believe that everybody was like her when she was young?
2. What is it about the people of Newfoundland that Guy's professor finds so interesting? Why?
3. In Guy's childhood, what primarily dictates what the families ate each night of the week? Make a chart that plots out the typical week of Guy's childhood in terms of meals and other family or household activities.

Reading Critically

[6] Why does Guy include the detail about her father's teasing about the tea buns?

ANALYZING MEANING

1. In the final paragraph, Guy says, "Life was simple. It had structure and predictability." How does she feel about this simplicity, structure, and predictability? Is she presenting this as a positive or a negative? Explain.
2. At university, Guy says, she learned that the place she came from had "culture." Explain what this culture is and why she didn't realize it earlier in her life.
3. Explain the importance of the university professor being the one to identify the "culture" of Guy's home province.

DISCOVERING RHETORICAL STRATEGIES

1. Throughout her essay, Guy incorporates details such as the names of the shops, the brand of margarine, and the materials from which the floors were made. Why does she incorporate this level of detail? What is the effect on the reader?
2. What is Guy's tone in this essay? How does she achieve this tone? Is it effective? Why or why not?
3. Explain Guy's conclusion. Evaluate its effectiveness. How is the conclusion linked back to the introduction?

MAKING CONNECTIONS

1. Guy says, "I found out that in Newfoundland and Labrador we had something called culture" (paragraph 2). Imagine that Jowi Taylor wanted to weave this culture into the Six String Nation guitar. How might he represent the Newfoundland and Labrador culture that Guy depicts?
2. Guy uses a first person narrative to depict this aspect of Newfoundland and Labrador culture. How does her approach and tone in this essay compare to that of Edith Iglauer ("Red Smile") and Barbara Kingsolver ("Life Without Go-Go Boots")?
3. Imagine that you were growing up with Guy in Newfoundland and Labrador with some form of gluten intolerance (Carmen Everest Wahl, "Gluten Intolerance"). How easy or difficult would this be?

IDEAS FOR DISCUSSION/WRITING

Preparing to Write

Write freely about the family routines of your childhood. What regular events dictated the flow of your life? How were your routines different from those of your friends and their families? In what ways were they the same? Were there particular days of the week to which you looked forward or days of the week that you did not like? Why?

Choosing a Topic

1. Think of some routine event from your childhood. Describe the event and discuss the effects that it had on your life.
2. Despite globalization, there are still some things that are unique to particular places. Write a narrative about something that is unique to the place where you grew up. This might be a certain food or drink or it might be another kind of experience, such as a particular festival, a type of transportation, or a local ritual. Include specific detail to show the link between the experience and the place, and be clear about why this experience is not one you can find elsewhere.
3. Guy discusses the experience of going to university and learning that the place she came from had "culture." Write an essay in which you discuss the effects on you of going to college or university. Consider both the tangible and intangible effects of your post-secondary experience.

EVELYN LAU

More and More (2001)

Evelyn Lau (1971–) has typically focused her artistry, her vision, and her poignant portrayals of characters and situations on the dark fringes of society.

The hard, gritty details of Lau's life first became familiar to many with the success of her book, *Runaway: Diary of a Street Kid*, published in 1989. This autobiographical work that was, five years later, made into a television movie, chronicles Lau's experiences as a 14-year-old runaway who became a prostitute and a junkie on the way to becoming a writer. She has also published five books of poetry, including *Oedipal Dreams* (1992)—which made her the youngest nominee ever for the Governor General's Award for poetry—two books of short stories, entitled *Fresh Girls and Other Stories* (1993) and *Choose Me* (1999), and a novel, *Other Women* (1995). Lau's most recent book is *Living Under Plastic* (2010).

Preparing to Read

In this selection, taken from a book entitled *Addicted: Notes from the Belly of the Beast*, a collection of essays about addiction, Evelyn Lau writes about her childhood addiction to sweets. Before you begin reading, think about the foods that you particularly enjoy. Are there foods for which you get cravings? What typically creates those cravings? How do you respond when you feel cravings for particular foods? Do you deny yourself foods you desire, or do you satisfy those desires? At what point does a craving become an addiction?

1 When did it begin? The sensation of a depthless hole opening up inside me, a cavernous feeling of need. The surrendering to compulsion, which was like getting on a treadmill and not being able to get off. The craving for perfection, so that if I slipped and had one of something "bad," then the day had fallen into disarray, and I had to keep having another and another until the darkness fell.

2 It began in childhood, innocently. My normal child's greed for candy magnified until it became all-consuming, until the thought of the next candy crowded out every other thought in my mind—though there was little pleasure in eating it beyond

the first sweet jolt on the tongue. After that moment it could have been soap or sawdust, but the urge to consume grew in me as steadily as an anxiety attack.❶ The craving was compounded by secrecy, fuelled by being forbidden; this was the most direct route I could see to escaping the control my mother exerted over me, to sabotaging her constant vigilance. Eating surreptitiously was a way of rebelling, of declaring my body my own.❷ I chewed smuggled sweets in bed, tossing the wrappers into the darkness behind the nearby sofa until one day, to my mortification, my father pulled the furniture away from the wall to vacuum and found the dusty, crumpled evidence. I disowned responsibility the way only a child could, claiming I didn't know how the wrappers could have gotten there, it had nothing to do with me.❸

3 Once, very early on, this desire for more must have had something to do with pleasure. Once I must have enjoyed a piece of cake or a scoop of ice cream and only wanted more of that enjoyment. But I can no longer remember such a time. I remember instead the growing panic, the desperate need that was a kind of clawing inside me. My quest for satiation blotted out everything in its path. When I was caught stealing a chocolate bar at a local drugstore, my mother screamed and hit at me wildly the moment I came home—was the food she cooked not good enough for me? Did I want people to think she was starving me? I had stolen two chocolate bars that day, but the store detective, emptying out my schoolbag, had found only one—the other had slipped between the pages of a textbook and lodged there. I hid the second bar in a drawer that afternoon, eager to get rid of it but unable to throw it away. The next day I shoved pieces of it into my mouth, fearful and ashamed, chewing miserably until it was gone. The chocolate was dark, it was bitter, it tasted like despair.❹

4 I hid sweets in my desk drawers, between the pages of books, even sometimes tucked inside my underwear when I came home from school, so that when my mother searched my pockets for contraband she would come up empty-handed. The food I

Reading Critically

❶ What is an anxiety attack? Have you ever experienced one? If so, describe how it felt.

❷ Why do you think Lau needs to feel in control of her own body? What illnesses is this a symptom of?

❸ Why does Lau lie about the candy wrappers?

❹ What do you think despair tastes like? Explain.

ate became one of the few things my parents could not always supervise. Whenever they left me alone in the house I hurried to the orange kitchen as soon as I heard the door close behind them. Heart racing, palms sweaty, I ransacked the cupboards, consuming bits of food—a biscuit, a handful of nuts, a mouthful of whisky—that I hoped would not be missed. My mother had begun keeping meticulous track of the food in the house and forcing me every week onto the bathroom scale, which had the opposite effect of what she wanted. I was twelve, thirteen, humiliated by her mocking comments as she peered at the dial on the scale; though I was never more than ten pounds overweight, I must have seemed impossibly fleshy next to her own ninety-pound frame. When she asked me to undress, when she slapped my thighs or pinched my waist or criticized my large breasts, I detached in my mind the same way I would years later when strangers ran their hands over my body. I dreaded these intrusions, and my compulsive behaviour grew in direct proportion to her increasingly frantic efforts to monitor every aspect of my life.[5]

5 Sometimes I would scurry down to the basement, where I would scoop up spoonfuls of sugar from the sacks in storage, gagging on the crystals lining my tongue. From my mother's purse I stole dimes and quarters that bought greasy paper bags of day-old cookies and doughnuts from the bakery on the way home from school. I still remember the taste of two dozen stale shortbread cookies consumed in a matter of blocks, the thick buttery dust of them in my throat, the nausea that pressed up inside me. I remember hiding behind a tree to finish the cookies before turning the corner onto the block where we lived, cramming them into my mouth; within moments I had reached a sugar and carbohydrate plateau where the clamour inside me dulled and my head felt thick, dazed. The storm of anxiety, of helpless rage, had passed for the time being. The frustration of never being good enough, of knowing I could never please my parents by winning a scholarship to medical school, of realizing that the life they wanted for me was not one I was capable of living. This happened day after day, bags of candies and pastries tearfully choked down along the corridor of streets between school and home. An hour later

Reading Critically

[5] How does her mother's behaviour contribute to Lau's problem? What does it tell you about her mother's personality?

I would have to eat dinner, feeling so full I could hardly breathe, and that night in bed I would vow never to binge again; the next day I would wake up and be perfect at last.[6]

But the next day I would wake in darkness, not perfect at all, and I knew I would do it again. I was driven by something larger than myself, some force I could hardly explain, let alone fight against. The tension that filled our household after my father lost his job, my mother's obsessive calibration of groceries and finances, my parents' expectations for my future . . . These things overpowered me and somehow manifested themselves in my need to keep eating until I was physically incapable of continuing. 6

It was as if I were trying to reach someplace that didn't exist, except in sleep or death. A perfect blankness, a white light. The search for this obliteration began with food, but later it wouldn't matter if it was food or alcohol or drugs or sleeping with men for money—the feeling was the same one I'd had as a child behind the shut door of my bedroom, gobbling up one candy, barely tasting it, so I could reach for the next, and the next. The urge was to keep going until the anxiety and rage stopped, until as a teenager I threw up or passed out or felt so blank that I no longer was myself. 7

One afternoon when I was sixteen or seventeen, years after I had run away from home, I sat sullenly in my psychiatrist's office with my parents. I wore a leather jacket and a miniskirt and was barely able to look at them across the room, my father's face lowered in pain and bewilderment, my mother twisting the strap of her purse between her thin fingers. My doctor was coaxing my father into telling me that he loved me. 8

"Chinese people don't talk about these things," my father tried to explain, haltingly. "It's not our tradition. But she knows. My wife—her mother—even when we couldn't afford any food, she would always have a cup of hot water waiting for her when she came home from school." 9

"She needs to hear you say it, Dad. Can you look at her and tell her?" 10

In a moment of what, even then, I knew was bravery worthy of a medal, my father lifted his face and looked straight at me. "Of course I love you," he said. 11

Reading Critically

[6] Are you a perfectionist? What are the advantages and/or disadvantages of trying to be perfect?

That was a moment I would remember from the session, 12
though at the time I stared back at him hard-eyed. Also his mention of the hot water, how I winced at the pathos of that, and how my mother clutched my arm as my parents left the doctor's office and tried to persuade me to come home with them for dinner. Was it so simple as food equalling love? Was it their love I was after, in all the years of my life when I threw one thing after another into that bottomless well, and all of those things—food, drugs, alcohol, men—simply fell in and disappeared?[7] What happened in the beginning that caused this? Something my mother did when I was an infant at her breast? Did she not come when I cried, did she hold me too tightly or turn her back when she should have stayed? Was there a chemical deficiency in my brain, a lack of serotonin, a predisposition toward these moods and impulses and compulsions? Was it a milder version of the mental illnesses that had stunted the lives of several of my mother's sisters, consigning them to a lifetime of antipsychotic medications and hospitals? Was it nature or nurture, creation or circumstance?

One substance replaced another, changing with the seasons. 13
I gave up food for drugs, cigarettes for alcohol, moved fluidly back and forth, tried various combinations. As a teenager it was marijuana, LSD, tranquilizers, painkillers and cocaine. I binged on these drugs, finding a more complete oblivion through chemicals, a more extensive loss of self, of memory and pain. Candy is dandy, but liquor is quicker. . . and nothing is so quick as a few lines of white glitter, a syringe dripping with a morphine derivative. Even when the acid gave me bad trips, even when the world morphed into a greater nightmare than it already seemed, being high was still better than staying inside myself. I sought through drugs to be somebody else—anybody else.

At nineteen, when I stopped smoking three packs of ciga- 14
rettes a day, I began my mornings instead with a drink in hand. That drink led to another and another, as the day devolved and the sun spiralled down in the sky. I no longer used street drugs, but started to mix alcohol with the prescription tranquilizers—Halcion, Ativan, Xanax—I obtained from various men, including the middle-aged married psychiatrist with whom I had a destructive yearlong affair. Twenty was a lost year, a calendar of

---

Reading Critically

7 In what way did all these things disappear?

blackout evenings, mornings where I could remember nothing of what I had said or done the night before, or how I had gotten home in the end. When I stopped taking pills, the bulimia that had come and gone in earlier times became one long unbroken stretch of binging and purging. I was throwing up seven or eight times a day and spending nearly as much on food as I had on drugs or alcohol.[8]

15 Once, in my early twenties, I went out for lunch with two of my aunts. I was hungover from the night before. I could barely touch the greasy dim sum, and I lost my temper when one of them kept insisting that I eat. When we were ready to leave, I said I'd wait for them outside while they used the washroom. A few minutes later I changed my mind and went to use the bathroom myself; as soon as I opened the door I could hear them talking about me behind the closed doors of their stalls.

16 "I know why she's the way she is," one aunt declared, in Chinese. "It's not her fault. Her mother stayed in bed too long when she was pregnant, she didn't move around enough. I think it did something to Evelyn's brain, that's why she's like this. She can't help it, she's disturbed . . ."

17 I turned on my heel and slammed the door on my way out, enraged. How dare she assume there was something wrong with me? I refused to believe it myself. Yet that was how my whole family had dealt with my running away and becoming involved in drugs and prostitution—I was "mentally ill," which, in an odd way, absolved me of blame and responsibility.[9] Once, to my psychiatrist's amusement, he received a phone call from this aunt, who insisted that I must be hearing voices; it was the only explanation for my behaviour. In her way, she believed I was pure, that none of it was my choice, that no one sane would choose such a life.

18 Was it a choice? Many people believe addicts are weak, that their suffering stems from a lack of willpower, that an addiction or a dependency can be overcome by strength of character alone. Intellectually I lean toward this belief as well, but emotionally it is a different story. I think of how many people would like to

---

Reading Critically

[8] Why do you think Lau doesn't have one specific addiction? Do you think most addicts can switch substances as easily as Lau? Why or why not?

[9] Does being "mentally ill" absolve a person of blame and responsibility? Why or why not?

have more than one cookie out of the bag they bring home from the supermarket. Some of them do have several cookies, savouring them, then place the rest of the bag in the cupboard. Others have a harder time doing that; they eat too many cookies, half the package perhaps, then feel repentant and disgusted with themselves. But imagine ratcheting that urge up further. Imagine that you are unable to sleep because of the cookies in your cupboard, that you can't work or read or leave the house knowing the uneaten cookies are there. That a feeling of anxiety begins to build in you, a desperation and a kind of anger, until you break down and cram the cookies into your mouth several at a time, devouring them until you throw up. If, after you throw up, there are still some cookies left in the bag, you have to keep eating them, even though by then you are sick of their taste and texture. If there are ten bags of cookies and no way that you can eat them all, you will have to bury the rest of them immediately at the bottom of the garbage pail—first crushing them and soaking them in water, say, to prevent your retrieving them later—in order to be rid of them.⑩

19 Is this behaviour something that can be changed by force of will? The feelings behind that scenario: what are they? Are they symptoms of some other hunger, some emotional lack or faulty wiring in the brain? I don't know, but I have lived with those feelings, those uncontrollable impulses, all my life.

20 I don't like the word "addiction." It conjures up dismal pictures of sober or lapsed strangers sitting together talking about their dependencies week after week, year after year, mired in the language of abstinence and recovery. I find myself impatient with people who identify themselves so closely with their affliction. There is something in me that scorns the weak-chinned, bleary-eyed, sad-sack faces of recovering addicts whose lives and vocabulary have been overtaken by their illness. And yet the emotions they cycle through, the force that dictates their behaviour, must not be so different from mine.⑪

21 Sometime toward my mid-twenties, the fog began to clear. Your body tires, your life changes, you climb out of the whirlpool and onto dry land. Certainly there were still days when I ate or

---

Reading Critically

⑩ What insight does this paragraph give you into an addict's cravings?

⑪ What is "the language of abstinence and recovery"? How do you think Lau feels about other addicts?

drank to the point of vomiting, there were unhealthy relationships to become obsessed with, but I didn't lose myself in the same way any more. With adulthood came the knowledge that emotions and experiences that seemed decimating at the time would pass, and sooner rather than later. I was no longer always facing the end of the world.

I became like everyone around me, with a mortgage and RRSPs and responsibilities, and if there were nights when I went out and drank too many martinis or glasses of wine, then stayed up all night throwing up in the bathroom—well, who didn't? 22

Now I'm almost thirty, the once unimaginable age. "Time to give up childish things," my psychiatrist chides. Once in a while I still binge and purge, but one lapse no longer triggers a six-month cycle as it used to. I often eat too much to quell some anxiety or emptiness, but now I can usually stop it from escalating into the sort of frenzy that leads to forced vomiting. Sometimes I drink vast quantities of alcohol and lose myself, but this is no different from the behaviour of many people I know.[12] It's never a problem for me to have only one glass of wine at dinner, or to keep alcohol around the apartment without consuming it, or to go for days without a drink. Illegal drugs haven't interested me for a decade, and pills—well, there are vials of tranquilizers in my drawer that have lain there untouched for eight years. But a little part of me is still glad when I get a headache. Even the small amount of codeine in several Tylenol 1's makes me feel more confident and slightly elevated. So, after all these years of almost never taking a sleeping pill or a painkiller, I must still be cautious.[13] The old desire for oblivion is not gone, only lying dormant, as are the temptation to slip into sleep rather than live through a difficult emotion and the longing to give in. And yet I know that if I give in, the next day will be harder as a result. That in the morning the previous day's anxiety, temporarily muffled by pills, will be back—tripled, quadrupled. That my hands will shake, my nerves will be frayed, and I will be less armoured than before. 23

The compulsions, the feelings of need and lack, are still there. They are always there. At one time, it was worth any price to get away from them—to feel bright and confident, to find the clearing 24

Reading Critically

[12] Do you agree that these behaviours are normal for many people?

[13] Why does Lau need to be cautious about taking over-the-counter medications?

in the forest where the sun streamed down and I was complete. I think now that these urges will stay with me for the rest of my life. The feelings will ebb and flow; maybe one day things will be a lot easier, and maybe they won't. At least I no longer wake up every morning expecting to be perfect, then destroying myself if I am not. Though I would never have believed it as a teenager, you do move beyond things, outgrow the person you were. Sometimes, just by staying alive, you find you have become someone who can live in the world after all.

UNDERSTANDING DETAILS

1. What are the immediate reasons that Evelyn Lau begins overeating as a child?
2. How does Lau's family respond to her eating behaviour?
3. Explain why Lau's father has difficulty telling his daughter that he loves her.

ANALYZING MEANING

1. Why does Lau overeat? How does it make her feel? What are the effects of her overeating?
2. In what way is Lau's overeating in childhood connected to her drinking, drug use, and promiscuity later in her life? What causes all these behaviours?
3. At her current age, is Lau an addict? Why or why not?

DISCOVERING RHETORICAL STRATEGIES

1. Lau uses many specific examples in her essay. Explain the effect of these examples on the overall effectiveness of "More and More."
2. Identify Lau's intended audience in this essay. What leads you to this conclusion?
3. Describe the tone of Lau's essay. Is this an appropriate tone for an essay on this topic? What language choices contribute to creating this tone?

MAKING CONNECTIONS

1. Lau, Steven Heighton ("Elegy in Stone"), and K'naan ("Between the Highs and Lows, Life Happens") are all poets as well as writers of prose. What aspects of their essays reflect their poetic interests?

2. Lau and Jean Yoon ("Halmonee") both write about intensely personal experiences. Which of these first-person essays appeals to you more? Why?

IDEAS FOR DISCUSSION/WRITING

Preparing to Write

Write freely about addiction. What is an addiction? What causes addiction? What types of things do people become addicted to? How is addiction generally viewed in our society? How can a person overcome an addiction?

Choosing a Topic

1. Write about a type of addiction you have experienced personally or that you've witnessed in someone else. Explain the causes of the addiction and the effects both on the addict and on others.
2. Lau says that she doesn't like the word *addiction.* From your own perspective, explain the effect of the word *addiction* or *addict.* Is there a another similar word that has less negative connotations?
3. Lau's addictive behaviour begins with food. Write an essay about the role of food in your family. How is food viewed? What emotions are attached to food? What associations or expectations accompany food in your family?

CHAPTER 9

ARGUMENT/ PERSUASION

Inciting People to Thought or Action

Almost everything we do or say is an attempt to persuade. Whether we dress up to impress a potential employer or argue openly with a friend about an upcoming election, we are trying to persuade various people to see the world our way. Some aspects of life are particularly dependent upon persuasion. Think, for example, of all the television, magazine, and online ads we see, urging us to buy certain products, or of the many impassioned appeals we read and hear on such controversial issues as the carbon tax, gun control, and same-sex marriage. Religious leaders devote their professional lives to persuading people to live a certain way and believe in certain religious truths, whereas scientists and mathematicians use rigorous logic and natural law to convince us of various hypotheses. Politicians make their living persuading voters to elect them and then support them throughout their terms of office. In fact, anyone who wants something from another person or agency, ranging from federal money for a research project to a new bicycle as a birthday present, must use some form of persuasion to get what he or she desires. The success or failure of this type of communication is easily determined: If the people being addressed change their actions or attitudes in favour of the writer or speaker, the attempt at persuasion has been successful.

Defining *Argument/Persuasion*

The terms *argument* and *persuasion* are often used interchangeably, but one is actually a subdivision of the other. Persuasion names a purpose for writing. To persuade your readers is to convince them to think, act, or feel a certain way. Much of the writing you have been doing in this book has persuasion as one of its goals. A description of an African tribe has a "dominant impression" you want your readers to accept; in an essay comparing various ways of celebrating the New Year, you are trying to convince your readers to believe that these similarities and differences actually exist; and in writing an essay exam on the causes of the strife in the Middle East, you are trying to convince your instructor that your reasoning is clear and your conclusions sound. In a sense, some degree of persuasion propels all writing.

More specifically, however, the process of persuasion involves appealing to one or more of the following: reason, emotion, or a sense of ethics. An argument is an appeal predominantly to your readers' reason and intellect. You are working in the realm of argument when you deal with complex issues that are debatable; opposing views (either explicit or implicit) are a basic requirement of argumentation. But argument and persuasion are taught together because good writers are constantly blending these three appeals and adjusting them to the purpose and audience of a particular writing task. Although reason and logic are the focus of this chapter, you need to learn to use all three methods of persuasion as skilfully as possible to write effective essays.

An appeal to reason relies upon logic and intellect and is usually most effective when you are expecting your readers to disagree with you. This type of appeal can help you change your readers' opinions or influence their future actions through the sheer strength of logical validity. If you wanted to argue, for example, that pregnant women should refrain from smoking cigarettes, you could cite abundant statistical evidence that babies born to mothers who smoke have lower birth weights, more respiratory problems, and a higher incidence of sudden infant death syndrome (SIDS) than the children of nonsmoking mothers. Because smoking clearly endangers the health of the unborn child, reason dictates that mothers who wish to give birth to the healthiest possible babies should avoid smoking during pregnancy.

Emotional appeals, however, attempt to arouse your readers' feelings, instincts, senses, and biases. Used most profitably when your readers already agree with you, this type of essay generally validates, reinforces, and/or incites in an effort to get your readers to share your feelings or ideas. In order to urge our lawmakers to impose stricter jail sentences for alcohol abuse, you might describe a recent tragic accident involving a local 12-year-old girl who was killed by a drunk driver as she rode her bicycle to school one morning. By focusing on such poignant visual details as the condition of her mangled bike, the bright blood stains on her white dress, and the anguish on the faces of parents and friends, you could build a powerfully persuasive essay that would be much more effective than a dull recitation of impersonal facts and nationwide statistics.

An appeal to ethics, the third technique writers often use to encourage readers to agree with them, involves cultivating a sincere, honest tone that will establish your reputation as a reliable, qualified, experienced, well-informed, and knowledgeable person whose opinions on the topic under discussion are believable because they are ethically sound. Such an approach is often used in conjunction with logical or emotional appeals to foster a verbal environment that will result in minimal resistance from its readers. Wayne Gretzky used the ethical, trustworthy persona he had created as a hockey player to persuade television viewers to drink Pepsi. In fact, the old gag question "Would you buy a used car from this man?" is our instinctive response to all forms of attempted persuasion, whether the salesperson is trying to sell us on Seagram's whisky or anti-smoking legislation, hair gel or organ donation. The more believable we are as human beings, the better chance we will have of convincing our audience.

The following student paragraph is directed primarily toward the audience's logical reasoning ability. Notice that the writer states her assertion and then gives reasons to convince her readers to change their ways. The student writer also brings both emotion and ethics into the argument by choosing her words and examples with great precision.

> Have you ever watched a pair of chunky thighs, a jiggling posterior, and an extra-large sweatshirt straining to cover a beer belly and thought, "Thank God I don't look like that! I'm in pretty good shape . . . for someone my age." Well, before you become too smug and self-righteous, consider what kind of shape you're really in. Just because you don't look like Shamu the Whale doesn't mean you're in good condition. What's missing, you ask? Exercise. You can diet

all day, wear the latest slim-cut designer jeans, and still be in worse shape than someone twice your age if you don't get a strong physical workout at least three times a week. Exercise is not only good for you, but it can also be fun—especially if you find a sport that makes you happy while you sweat. Your activity need not be expensive: Jogging, walking, basketball, tennis, and handball are not costly, unless you're seduced by the glossy sheen of the latest sporting fashions and accessories. Most of all, however, regular exercise is important for your health. You can just as easily drop dead from a sudden heart attack in the middle of a restaurant when you're slim and trim as when you're a slob. Your heart and lungs need regular workouts to stay healthy. So do yourself a favour and add some form of exercise to your schedule. You'll feel better and live longer, and your looks will improve, too!

Thinking Critically Through Argument/Persuasion

Argument and persuasion require you to present your views on an issue through logic, emotion, and good character in such a way that you convince an audience of your point of view. This rhetorical mode comes near the end of this book because it is an extremely complex and sophisticated method of reasoning. The more proficient you become in this strategy of thinking and presenting your views, the more you will get what you want out of life (and out of school). Being persuasive means getting the pay raises you need, the refund you deserve, and the grades you've worked so hard for.

In a successful argument, your logic must be flawless. Your conclusions should be based on clear evidence, and your evidence must be organized in such a way that it builds to an effective, convincing conclusion. You should constantly have your purpose and audience in mind as you build your case; at the same time, issues of emotion and good character should support the flow of your logic.

Exercising your best logical skills is extremely important to all phases of your daily survival—in and out of the classroom. Following a logical argument in your reading and presenting a logical response to your course work are the hallmarks of a good student. Right now, put your best logic forward and work on your reasoning and persuasive abilities in the series of exercises that follow. Isolate argument and persuasion from the other rhetorical strategies, so that you can practise them and strengthen your ability to argue before you combine them with other methods.

1. Choose a particular social issue that you believe is important and brainstorm the various views people might hold about this issue. Choose one of these views and identify the types of evidence you would need to support this view. Make a five- to ten-minute presentation arguing your point to your class or to a small group within your class.
2. Take to class two magazine ads—one ad that tries to sell a product and another that tries to convince the reader that a particular action or product is wrong or bad (unhealthy, misinterpreted, politically incorrect, etc.). How does each ad appeal to the reader's logic? How does the advertiser use emotion and character in his or her appeal?
3. Fill in the following blanks: The best way to ________ is to ________. (For example, "The best way to lose weight is to exercise.") Then, list ways you might persuade a reader to see your point of view in this statement.

Reading and Writing Persuasive Essays

Although persuasive writing can be approached in three different ways—logically, emotionally, and/or ethically—our stress in this chapter is on logic and reason, because they are at the heart of most post-secondary writing. As a reader, you will see how various forms of reasoning and different methods of organization affect your reaction to an essay. Your stand on a particular issue will control the way you process information in argument and persuasion essays. As you read the essays in this chapter, you will also learn to recognize emotional and ethical appeals and the different effects they create. In your role as writer, you need to be fully aware of the options available to you as you compose. Although the basis of your writing will be logical argument, you will see that you can learn to control your readers' responses to your essays by choosing your evidence carefully, organizing it wisely, and seasoning it with the right amount of emotion and ethics—depending on your purpose and audience.

Reading Persuasive Essays

- What is the author's main assertion or thesis?
- What ideas do you agree with?

- What ideas do you disagree with?
- What appeals does the author use?

Preparing to Read. As you prepare to read the essays in this chapter, spend a few minutes browsing through the preliminary material for each selection: What does Laura Robinson's title ("Sports Breeds Real-Life Violence") prepare you for? What can you learn from scanning Daniel Fricker and Lars Kushner's article ("Anti-Gay Bullying") and from reading its synopsis in the Rhetorical Contents?

Also, you should bring to your reading as much information as you can from the authors' biographies: Why do you think Arlene Perly Rae, Irshad Manji, and Anna Porter came together to write about fighting anti-Semitism in "A Call to Arms on Anti-Semitism"? Do they have the appropriate qualifications to write on this topic? What is the source of Fricker and Kushner's essay? For the essays in this chapter that present two sides of an argument, what biographical details prepare us for each writer's stand on the issue? Who were the original audiences for these pro and con arguments?

Last, before you read these essays, try to generate some ideas on each topic so that you can take the role of an active reader. In this text, the Preparing to Read questions will ready you for this task. Then, you should speculate further on the general subject of the essay: Do you believe 16 is too young to begin driving ("Raise the Driving Age")? What do you think Adam Gopnik will argue in "Shootings"?

Reading. Be sure to record your spontaneous reactions to the persuasive essays in this chapter as you read them for the first time: What are your opinions on each subject? Why do you hold these opinions? Be especially aware of your responses to the essays representing opposing viewpoints at the end of the chapter; know where you stand in relation to each side of the issues here.

Use the preliminary material before an essay to help you create a framework for your responses to it: Who was Russell Smith's primary audience when his essay on swearing was first published? In what ways is the tone of his essay appropriate for that audience? What motivated Sheema Khan to publish her arguments on the hijab ("Hijabs: Don't Kick Up a Fuss")? Why is Stein so interested in Canada's ability to speak up and make a difference ("Whisper, Echo and Voice")?

Your main job at this stage of reading is to determine each author's primary assertion or proposition (thesis statement) and to create an inquisitive environment for thinking critically about the essay's ideas. In addition, take a look at the questions after each selection to make sure you are picking up the major points of the essay.

Rereading. As you reread these persuasive essays, notice how the writers integrate their appeals to logic, to emotion, and to ethics. Also, pay attention to the emphasis the writers place on one or more appeals at certain strategic points in the essays: How do Perly Rae, Manji, and Porter integrate these three appeals in "A Call to Arms on Anti-Semitism"? Which of these appeals do they rely on to help bring their essay to a close? How persuasive is their final appeal? What combination of appeals does Gopnik use in "Shootings"? How does his tone contribute to his argument? How does he establish the tone?

Also, determine what other rhetorical strategies help these writers make their primary points. How do these strategies enable each writer to establish a unified essay with a beginning, a middle, and an end?

Then, answer the questions after each essay to make certain you understand it on the literal, interpretive, and analytical levels in preparation for the discussion/writing assignments that follow.

For a list of guidelines for the entire reading process, see the checklist on page 41 of the Introduction.

Writing Persuasive Essays

- Write a debatable thesis.
- Justify the significance of the issue.
- Choose evidence for your thesis.
- Organize your essay effectively.
- Use logical, ethical, and emotional appeals.
- Conclude with a summary and recommendations.

Preparing to Write. The first stage of writing an essay of this sort involves, as usual, exploring and then limiting your topic. As you prepare to write your persuasive paper, first try to generate as many ideas as possible—regardless of whether they appeal to logic, emotion, or ethics. To do this, review the prewriting techniques in the

Introduction and answer the Preparing to Write questions. Then, choose a topic. Next, focus on a purpose and a specific audience before you begin to write.

Writing. Most persuasive essays should begin with an assertion or a proposition stating what you believe about a certain issue. This thesis should generally be phrased as a debatable statement, such as, "If the national government instituted a guaranteed income supplement for seasonal workers, it would provide security for workers in the natural resource sectors of the economy and minimize the draw on the Employment Insurance Fund." At this point in your essay, you should also justify the significance of the issue you will be discussing: "Such a program would help to support workers in industries vital to Canada's economy, would help to maintain the EI Fund for people who become unexpectedly out of work, and would improve the image of seasonal workers among Canadians."

The essay should then support your thesis in a variety of ways. This support may take the form of facts, figures, examples, opinions by recognized authorities, case histories, narratives/anecdotes, comparisons, contrasts, or cause/effect studies. This evidence is most effectively organized from least to most important when you are confronted with a hostile audience (so that you can lead your readers through the reasoning, step by step) and from most to least important when you are facing a supportive audience (so that you can build on their loyalty and enthusiasm as you advance your thesis). In fact, you will be able to engineer your best support if you know your audience's opinions, feelings, and background before you write your essay, so that your intended "target" is as clear as possible. The body of your essay will undoubtedly consist of a combination of logical, emotional, and ethical appeals—all leading to some final summation or recommendation.

The concluding paragraph of a persuasive essay should restate your main assertion (in slightly different terms from those in your original statement) and should offer some constructive recommendations about the problem you have been discussing (if you haven't already done so). This section of your paper should clearly bring your argument to a close in one final attempt to move your audience to accept or act on the viewpoint you present. Let's look more closely now at each of the three types of appeals used in such essays: logical, emotional, and ethical.

To construct a *logical* argument, you have two principal patterns available to you: inductive reasoning or deductive reasoning. The first encourages an audience to make what is called an "inductive leap" from several particular examples to a single, useful generalization. In the case of a guaranteed income supplement, you might cite a number of examples, figures, facts, and case studies illustrating the effectiveness of a guaranteed income supplement plan, thereby leading to your firm belief that implementation of this program is essential to the survival of many of Canada's core industries. Used most often by detectives, scientists, and lawyers, the process of inductive reasoning addresses the audience's ability to think logically by moving it systematically from an assortment of selected evidence to a rational and ordered conclusion.

In contrast, deductive reasoning moves its audience from a broad, general statement to particular examples supporting that statement. In writing such an essay, you would present your thesis statement about a guaranteed income supplement first and then offer clear, orderly evidence to support that belief. Although the mental process we go through in creating a deductive argument is quite sophisticated, it is based on a three-step form of reasoning called the *syllogism*, which most logicians believe is the foundation of logical thinking. The traditional syllogism has the following:

- **A major premise:** e.g., Seasonal workers are essential to the Canadian economy.
- **A minor premise:** e.g., All workers must make enough money, through wages and/or supplements, to support themselves year round.
- **A conclusion:** e.g., Therefore, for the survival of the Canadian economy, seasonal workers need to receive enough money, through wages and/or supplements, to live adequately for the entire year.

As you might suspect, this type of reasoning is only as accurate as its original premises, so you need to be careful with the truth of the premises as well as with the logical validity of your argument.

In constructing a logical argument, you should take great care to avoid the two types of fallacies in reasoning found most frequently in college papers: giving too few examples to support an assertion and citing examples that do not represent the assertion fairly. If you build your argument on true statements and abundant, accurate evidence, your essay will be effective.

Persuading through *emotion* necessitates controlling your readers' instinctive reactions to what you are saying. You can accomplish this goal in two different ways: (1) by choosing your words with even greater care than usual and (2) by using figurative language whenever appropriate. In the first case, you must be especially conscious of using words that have the same general denotative (or dictionary) meaning but bear decidedly favourable or unfavourable connotative (or implicit) meanings. For example, notice the difference between *slender* and *scrawny*, *patriotic* and *chauvinistic*, or *compliment* and *flattery*. Your careful attention to the choice of such words can help readers form visual images with certain positive or negative associations that subtly encourage them to follow your argument and adopt your opinions. Second, the effective use of figurative language—especially similes and metaphors—makes your writing more vivid, thus triggering your readers' senses and encouraging them to accept your views. Both of these techniques will help you manipulate your readers into the position of agreeing with your ideas.

Ethical appeals, which establish you as a reliable, well-informed person, are accomplished through (1) the tone of your essay and (2) the number and type of examples you cite. Tone is created through deliberate word choice: Careful attention to the mood implied in the words you use can convince your readers that you are serious, friendly, authoritative, jovial, or methodical—depending on your intended purpose. Similarly, the examples you supply to support your assertions can encourage readers to see you as experienced, insightful, relaxed, or intense. In both of these cases, winning favour for yourself will usually also gain approval for your opinions.

Rewriting. To rework your persuasive essays, you should play the role of your readers and impartially evaluate the different appeals you have used to accomplish your purpose:

- Is my thesis statement clear?
- Is the main thrust of my essay argumentative (an appeal to reason)?
- Will the balance of these appeals effectively accomplish my purpose with my intended audience?

- Does my conclusion restate my argument, make a recommendation, and bring my essay to a close?

You should also look closely at the way your appeals work together in your essay:

- When I use logic, is that section of my paper arranged through either inductive or deductive reasoning?
- Is that the most effective order to achieve my purpose?
- In appealing to the emotions, have I chosen my words with proper attention to their denotative and connotative effects?
- Have I chosen examples carefully to support my thesis statement?
- Are these examples suitable for my purpose and audience?

Any additional guidance you may need as you write and revise your persuasive essays is provided on pages 34–39 of the Introduction.

Student Essay: Argument/Persuasion at Work

The following essay, written by an American student, uses all three appeals to make its point about the power of language in shaping our view of the world. First, the writer sets forth her character references (ethical appeal) in the first paragraph, after which she presents her thesis and its significance in paragraph 2. The support for her thesis is a combination of logical and emotional appeals, heavy on the logical, as the writer moves her paragraphs from general to particular in an effort to convince her readers to adopt her point of view and adjust their language use accordingly.

The Language of Equal Rights

Ethical appeal

Up front, I admit it. I've been a card-carrying feminist since junior high school. I want to see an Equal Rights Amendment to the U.S. Constitution, equal pay for equal—and comparable—work, and I go dutch on dates. Furthermore, I am quite prickly on the subject of language. I'm one of those women who bristles at terms like *lady doctor* (you know they don't mean a gynecologist), female policeman (a paradox), and *mankind* instead of *humanity* (are they really talking about me?).

Emotional appeal

Many people ask "How important are mere words, anyway? You know what we really mean." A question like this ignores the symbolic and psychological importance of language. What words "mean" can go beyond what a speaker or writer consciously intends, reflecting personal and cultural biases that run so deep that most of the time we aren't even aware they exist. "Mere words" are incredibly important: They are our framework for seeing and understanding the world.

Assertion or thesis statement

Significance of assertion

Logical appeal

Man, we are told, means "woman" as well as "man," just as *mankind* supposedly stands for all of humanity. In the introduction of a sociology textbook I recently read, the author was anxious to demonstrate his awareness of the controversy over sexist language and to assure his female readers that, despite his use of noninclusive terms, he was not forgetting the existence or importance of women in society. He was making a conscious decision to continue to use *man* and *mankind* instead of *people*, *humanity*, etc., for ease of expression and aesthetic reasons. "Man" simply sounds better, he explained. I flipped through the table of contents and found "Man and Society," "Man and Nature," "Man and Technology," and, near the end, "Man and Woman." At what point did *Man* quit meaning "people" and start meaning "men" again? The writer was obviously unaware of the answer to this question, because it is one he would never think to ask. Having consciously addressed the issue only to dismiss it, he reverted to form.

Examples organized deductively

Emotional appeal

Logical appeal

The very ambiguity of *man* as the generic word for our species ought to be enough to combat any arguments that we keep it because we all "know what it means" or because it is both traditional and sounds better. And does it really sound all that much better, or are we just more used to it, more comfortable? Our own national history proves that we can be comfortable with a host of words and attitudes that strike us as unjust and ugly today. A lot of white folks probably thought that Negroes were getting pretty stuffy and picky when they began to insist on being called Blacks. After all, weren't there more important things to worry about, like civil rights? But Black activists recognized the emotional and symbolic significance of having a name that was parallel to the name that the dominant race used for itself—a name equal in dignity, lacking that vaguely alien, anthropological sound. After all, whites were called *Caucasians* only in police reports, textbooks, and autopsies. *Negro* may have sounded better to people in the bad old days of blatant racial bigotry, but we adjusted to the word *Black* and have now moved on to African American, and more and

Examples organized deductively

Emotional appeal

more people of each race are adjusting to the wider implications and demands of practical as well as verbal labels.

Logical appeal

In a world where *man* and *human* are offered as synonymous terms, I don't think it is a coincidence that women are still vastly underrepresented in positions of money, power, and respect. Children grow up learning a language that makes maleness the norm for anything that isn't explicitly designated as female, giving little girls a very limited corner of the universe to picture themselves in. Indeed, the language that nonfeminists today claim to be inclusive was never intended to cover women in the first place. "One man, one vote" and "All men are created equal" meant just that. Women had to fight for decades to be included even as an afterthought; it took constitutional amendments to convince the government and the courts that women are human, too.

Examples organized deductively

Conclusion/ restatement

The message is clear. We have to start speaking about people, not men, if we are going to start thinking in terms of both women and men. A "female man" will never be the equal of her brother.

Some Final Thoughts on Argument/ Persuasion

As you can tell from the selections that follow, the three different types of persuasive appeals usually complement each other in practice. Most good persuasive essays use a combination of these methods to achieve their purposes. Good persuasive essays also rely on various rhetorical modes we have already studied—such as example, process analysis, division/classification, comparison/contrast, definition, and cause/effect—to advance their arguments. In the following essays, you will see a combination of appeals at work and a number of different rhetorical modes furthering the arguments.

ARGUMENT/PERSUASION IN REVIEW

Reading Persuasive Essays

Preparing to Read

✓ What assumptions can I make from the essay's title?
✓ What do I think the general mood of the essay will be?
✓ What are the essay's purpose and audience?
✓ What does the synopsis tell me about the essay?
✓ What can I learn from the author's biography?
✓ Can I predict the author's point of view toward the subject?

Reading

✓ What is the author's main assertion or thesis?
✓ What ideas do I agree with?
✓ What ideas do I disagree with?
✓ What appeals does the author use?

Rereading

✓ How does the writer integrate the appeals in the essay?
✓ What is the tone of the essay? How does the author establish this tone?
✓ What other rhetorical strategies does the author use?

Writing Persuasive Essays

Preparing to Write

✓ Do I narrow and focus my material as much as possible?
✓ What is my purpose?
✓ Who is my audience?

Writing

✓ Is my thesis a debatable question?
✓ Do I justify the significance of the issue?
✓ Is my essay organized effectively for what I am trying to accomplish?
✓ Did I choose evidence that supports my thesis?
✓ Do I conclude with a summary and recommendations?

Rewriting

✓ Is my thesis statement clear?
✓ Is the main thrust of my essay an appeal to reason?
✓ Will the balance of these appeals effectively accomplish my purpose with my intended audience?
✓ Have I chosen examples carefully to support my thesis statement?
✓ Is my tone suitable for my purpose and audience?
✓ Does my conclusion restate my argument, make a recommendation, and bring my essay to a close?

ARLENE PERLY RAE, IRSHAD MANJI, AND ANNA PORTER

A Call to Arms on Anti-Semitism (2004)

Arlene Perly Rae, Irshad Manji, and Anna Porter are all Toronto-based writers who have collaborated on the essay here, which originally appeared in the *Toronto Star*.

Arlene Perly Rae is best known for her columns, reviews, and books about children's literature. *Everybody's Favourites*, a guide to the best children's books, was published in 1997. Her work has appeared in the *Toronto Star* and *Maclean's*, and she has worked extensively for the national Campaign Against Child Poverty and the United Way of Greater Toronto.

An outspoken advocate for change in Islam, Irshad Manji is the author of the best-selling *The Trouble with Islam Today: A Muslim's Call for Reform in Her Faith* (2005) and *Allah, Liberty and Love: The Courage to Reconcile Faith and Freedom* (2011). Formerly the host of *Queer Television* on Toronto's Citytv, she is currently director of the Moral Courage Project at New York University, a program that teaches young people to stand up for the truth in their communities. (You can read a more detailed biography of Manji on page 284.)

Originally from Hungary, Anna Porter began her publishing career in England and now lives in Canada, where she founded Key Porter Books. She is the author of four novels, including *Kasztner's Train*, which won the 2007 Nereus Writers' Trust Non-Fiction Prize, and a memoir, *The Storyteller: A Memoir of Secrets, Magic and Lies* (2006). Her most recent book, *The Ghosts of Europe: Journeys through Central Europe's Troubled Past and Uncertain Future*, won the Shaughnessy Cohen Prize for Political Writing in 2011.

Preparing to Read

In this essay, three writers make a strong argument for Canada to take a leading role in fighting anti-Semitism. Before you begin reading, think about anti-Semitism. What is anti-Semitism? Have you ever experienced or witnessed anti-Semitism? What causes anti-Semitism? What other forms of discrimination are comparable to anti-Semitism?

The Jewish High Holidays are wrapping up. Ramadan, the Muslim month of fasting and atonement, is upon us. Before you know it, it will be Christmas. Is this the preamble to some bad interfaith joke? 1

Not this time. As a Christian, a Muslim and a Jew, we are collaborating to address something serious. It is the resurgence—in many places and in various forms—of anti-Semitism. We believe Canada can be a leader in the fight against it. 2

Worldwide, it is generally acknowledged that this ancient hatred is, once again, on the rise. 3

To be sure, other forms of prejudice are also raging, including fear of Muslims and persecution of Christians. Make no mistake; we unreservedly condemn Islamophobia and anti-Christian hostility wherever they occur. But a centuries-old racism directed against Jews has proven itself sustainable and promiscuous.❶ 4

The past few years have witnessed an increase in attacks on Jews, their synagogues, homes, cemeteries and other sites of gathering. 5

Incidents in Canada include vandalism, graffiti, and the desecration of gravestones. Most are the work of misfits, but the results cannot be easily dismissed. Last spring, a Jewish elementary school in Montreal was firebombed, its library destroyed. Clerics, politicians, media and ordinary citizens eloquently denounced this act. Prime Minister Paul Martin repudiated both the attack and its perpetrators, vowing that they have no place in our proudly pluralistic society.❷ 6

He also declared that our country can and should do more to combat anti-Semitism. 7

Canada now has that opportunity. 8

For the first time, a stand-alone resolution naming and condemning anti-Semitism may be put before the United Nations General Assembly. First it needs one or more sponsors—countries who speak to it at the committee level. 9

The sponsor should probably not be Israel, to avoid any confusion with the Middle East conflict as well as run the risk of rejection simply because many countries would—virtually automatically—vote against it.❸ 10

After the committee stage, the resolution comes before a full meeting of the general assembly. The greater the support in 11

Reading Critically

❶ How do you think this racism is "sustainable" and "promiscuous"?

❷ What effect does the authors' use of alliteration have in this sentence?

❸ Why would many countries automatically vote against the resolution if Israel were the sponsor?

committee, the better the chance the resolution has of being adopted by the larger body.

12 We feel that this resolution is both urgent and important. It should be given the best opportunity for adoption by the United Nations.

13 To help ensure that a strong international condemnation of anti-Semitism has a fighting chance—something that for decades after the Holocaust would have passed easily, but now may be more problematic—we are urging Canada to sponsor the resolution. In so doing, we would as a nation declare publicly this country's profound opposition to all forms of this insidious form of racism.

14 Such a move would testify to Canada's celebrated diversity, our embrace of universal human rights and our determination to combat racism of all kinds. It would also indicate our respect for the international community.❹ Canadians like a multilateral approach to contentious issues.

15 It is useful to consider what gave birth to this historic moment. At an April, 2004 Berlin meeting of the Organization for Security and Co-operation in Europe (OSCE), the 55 member states, Canada among them, unanimously endorsed a strong statement against anti-Semitism. It became known as the "Berlin Declaration."

16 Reaffirming the guarantees promoted in the Universal Declaration of Human Rights—such as freedom from discrimination based on religion or race—the Berlin Declaration went on to condemn all manifestations of anti-Semitism.

17 Moreover, it proclaimed unambiguously that political issues, including those in Israel and elsewhere in the Middle East, never justify anti-Semitism.

18 Two months later, U.N. Secretary-General Kofi Annan offered valuable support. He spoke approvingly of the Berlin Declaration in his opening remarks to a U.N. seminar on "unlearning intolerance."

19 Annan went on to say that the resurgence of hatred and violence directed toward Jews is a threat to people everywhere. "In fighting anti-Semitism we fight for all humanity." He went on to say: "We hope that people of all faiths, nationalities and political beliefs will stand up proudly and agree."

Reading Critically

❹ Do you agree that having Canada sponsor the resolution would have these effects? Why or why not?

None of this will solve the Israeli-Palestinian dispute, nor is it meant to. 20

But U.N. adoption of the Berlin Declaration, or a resolution with wording very close to it, will help distinguish between what is at issue and, equally importantly, what is not. 21

Again, in the words of Annan: "When we seek justice for the Palestinians—as we must—let us firmly disavow anyone who tries to use that cause to incite hatred against Jews in Israel or elsewhere." 22

This autumn there is a chance that the world will step up, acknowledge that virulent anti-Semitism hurts us all, and do what it can to put a stop to it. The secretary-general has expressed his hope that the U.N. family will adopt the principles of the Berlin Declaration. 23

As people who know what it means to take a leap of faith, we share that hope. As Canadians, we encourage our country to lead the way. 24

UNDERSTANDING DETAILS

1. What is the Berlin Declaration?
2. What specifically is it that the authors of this essay are advocating?
3. What gives these three writers credibility in writing on this topic?

ANALYZING MEANING

1. What is anti-Semitism? Why has there been a recent rise in anti-Semitism?
2. Explain the comment "Canadians like a multilateral approach to contentious issues" (paragraph 14). Do you agree with this view?
3. Why do you think these three writers have chosen to collaborate as co-authors rather than have one person write the essay and quote the others in it?

DISCOVERING RHETORICAL STRATEGIES

1. Have these writers used primarily logical or emotional appeals in "A Call to Arms on Anti-Semitism"? Is this an effective choice?
2. Three people have collaborated to write this essay. Is the voice of the essay unified and consistent, or do you have the sense of three different voices?

3. Canadian representatives at the United Nations are the people who have the ability to take the action that Perly Rae, Manji, and Porter are advocating in this essay, and yet the essay was published in a daily Toronto newspaper. Who is the intended audience for this essay? Does the essay effectively address that audience?

MAKING CONNECTIONS

1. The authors of this essay, like Naomi Klein ("Co-opting Dissent"), are advocates for social change. Compare and contrast the writing styles of these authors.
2. Perly Rae, Manji, and Porter are taking a strong position against a particular form of prejudice or discrimination. How does their approach to this topic compare with that of Daniel Fricker and Lars Kushner ("Anti-Gay Bullying") or Lawrence Hill ("Don't Call Me That Word") in their discussions of discrimination?

IDEAS FOR DISCUSSION/WRITING

Preparing to Write

There is a reference in this essay to Kofi Annan's talking about "unlearning intolerance" (paragraph 18). Write freely about the idea of "unlearning intolerance." What does this phrase mean? What does the phrase "unlearning intolerance" suggest about the nature and causes of intolerance? What perpetuates intolerance? How might someone "unlearn intolerance"? How easy or how difficult do you think this would be?

Choosing a Topic

1. These writers refer to "Canada's celebrated diversity, our embrace of universal human rights and our determination to combat racism of all kinds" (paragraph 14). Write an essay in which you compare the prevalence of racism in Canada with that in another country with which you are familiar.
2. In an essay for members of your school community, persuade your readers to take an active stand against a particular form of racism or discrimination. How can you convince your audience to be proactive in this situation?
3. In an essay for your local paper, advocate a position you would like your government representatives to take on a specific current issue. Make careful choices about the type of appeal you use, and be clear about the audience for whom you are writing.

JUDY REBICK

The Culture of Overwork (2001)

A noted feminist and political commentator, Judy Rebick (1945–) was the host of CBC Newsworld's *Straight from the Hip* and *Face Off*, a national debate show. She has appeared on a variety of other TV and radio news shows, and has written regular columns for *Elm Street*, the *Ottawa Citizen*, *The London Free Press*, and *CBC Online*. She is the author of four books: *Politically Speaking* (1996), *Imagine Democracy*, (2000), *Ten Thousand Roses: The Making of a Feminist Revolution* (2005), and *Transforming Power: From the Personal to the Political* (2009).

Rebick, who has a degree in psychology from McGill University, served as the president of Canada's largest women's organization, the National Action Committee on the Status of Women, from 1990 to 1993. Rebick held the Canadian Auto Workers' Sam Gindin Chair in Social Justice and Democracy at Ryerson University from 2002 until 2010, and was the founder of **http://rabble.ca**, an online community of rabble-rousers.

Preparing to Read

In "The Culture of Overwork," which first appeared in *Elm Street* magazine in 2001, Judy Rebick discusses the growing problem of overwork and its effects on individuals and society. Before you begin reading, think about overwork. How often do you respond "Busy" when people ask how you are? Do you feel overworked? Are the general expectations of your workplace (if you have one) realistic or excessive? How many hours do you think the ideal workweek should be? How would you spend your remaining time? Who should determine the appropriate number of hours in a standard workweek? What is a workaholic?

The other day I sat down at the computer in my home office and found that I just couldn't do any work. I was exhausted. At first I thought I was getting sick. Then I realized that I hadn't taken a day off in more than six weeks. I wound up sleeping and watching videos all weekend to recover. Still, I felt a little twinge of guilt that my work wasn't getting done even though years ago I had decided to break from the workaholic behaviour that was driving my life. 1

Overwork is becoming a cultural norm and it's bad for us. Non-standard jobs, self-employment, cutbacks, weakened labour 2 standards, technology that permits us to work everywhere from the car to the home, and the very male-defined norm that you have to work endless hours to be a success are all contributing.

3 A Statistics Canada report from November 1999 says that one-third of those aged 25 to 44 describe themselves as workaholics.❶ Studies show that long work hours are a major contributor to stress, depression, burnout and a variety of other illnesses. StatsCan data indicates that those who switched to a workweek longer than 40 hours increased cigarette and alcohol consumption and gained weight.

4 Irregular and long hours are stressful to families, too. A U.S. study shows that family breakup is three to eight times more likely in couples with children if one parent works nights or does shift work. In Quebec, one parent works nights or weekends in more than half of families.

5 But we don't just bring it on ourselves. In many of the fastest-growing sectors, such as dot-coms, entertainment and business services, small firms demand long hours and pay scant attention to labour standards.

6 Two years ago, Tara Cleveland, now 25, got a job as a Web page designer in a brand new dot-com business, so new that they were working out of the owner's living room for a while. "I worked 40 hours a week but they wanted more. They expected us to stay late every night and on weekends, too. They were never prepared to pay overtime." Cleveland, whose mother is a social activist, refused the overtime and still kept the job. But "most kids don't know what their rights are and they're just grateful to have an interesting job," notes Cleveland.❷

7 If working long hours makes us unhappy and unhealthy, why do we do it? Money is the obvious answer but, according to StatsCan, most of the one-fifth of Canadians who worked overtime during the first quarter of 1997 did so for free.

8 Chris Schenk, research director of the Ontario Federation of Labour, says downsizing in the recession of the early 1990s meant fewer people had to do more work. "It became an expectation to work long hours and take work home, even in the broader

---

Reading Critically

❶ Do you know any workaholics? What kind of behaviours do they exhibit? Are workaholics addicted to their work or just overworked?

❷ What are employees' rights when it comes to overtime? What could be the consequences of refusing to work extra hours?

public sector," he explains. Just ask nurses or teachers how their workload has increased.

9 Given these time stresses, you'd think that the length of a workweek would be a major issue in Canada, but it wasn't even mentioned in the recent federal election. Quebec—where the reality of women's lives seems to get more attention—has just reduced its legal workweek from 44 hours to 40 hours, joining four other provinces with a 40-hour week. But Ontario is going in the opposite direction with a proposal to extend the workweek to 60 hours if the employee and the employer agree.❸

10 In Europe, people want to live and work differently. France adopted a legal 35-hour workweek last February. Norway just added a fifth week of paid vacation, Denmark a sixth. Last spring, the Netherlands passed a law permitting people who want to work a shorter week to request it from their employer, with the onus on the employer to explain why it couldn't be implemented. The same law permits part-time workers to request longer hours.❹

11 So what can we do about the situation at home? I'm going to start booking time off in my agenda. We can challenge the culture of overwork by refusing overtime whenever possible and refusing to take work home. But individual action goes only so far. Women have to make overwork a major public policy issue. Let's look to Europe for the example and start demanding that the culture of work reflect the best interests of women and our families.

UNDERSTANDING DETAILS

1. What is "the culture of overwork"? According to Rebick, who and what is creating it?
2. What are the consequences of overwork?
3. How do the standards relating to working time in Europe compare with those in North America?

ANALYZING MEANING

1. How significant is the problem of overwork? Who does the culture of overwork affect the most?

Reading Critically

❸ What would be the advantages and disadvantages of a 60-hour work week? Would you want to work that many hours? Why or why not?

❹ How do you feel about Europe's attitudes toward work hours?

2. What is Rebick's thesis? What exactly is she advocating? Do you agree with this position? Why or why not?
3. Explain why people continue to work long hours despite the negative effects of this behaviour.

DISCOVERING RHETORICAL STRATEGIES

1. What is Rebick's purpose in writing this essay? Given the original source of this essay, who do you think is her intended audience?
2. In this essay, Rebick frequently uses statistics and quotations from authorities. Explain why she has incorporated these elements. How do they enhance her argument?
3. Is Rebick's essay an appeal primarily to logic, to emotion, or to ethics? Why do you think Rebick has made this choice?

MAKING CONNECTIONS

1. Compare Rebick's argument about overwork with observations made by Peter Nicholson ("Information-Rich and Attention-Poor") and Will Braun ("Seven Criteria for the Adoption of New Technology"). Where do their observations about excess overlap?
2. Discuss the relative balance of the logical, emotional, and ethical appeals in the essays by Rebick, Janice Gross Stein ("Whisper, Echo and Voice"), and Russell Smith ("Potty Mouthed and Proud of It"). Which author uses logic most? Who relies most heavily on emotion? Whose ethical appeal is the strongest? What does the dominance of the appeal have to do with the subject matter of each essay?

IDEAS FOR DISCUSSION/WRITING

Preparing to Write

Write freely about changing societal expectations. How do you go about shifting attitudes toward an issue such as overwork? What kind of action is appropriate to encourage a change in attitudes or public policy? What kind of action is effective? Can an individual make a difference? Why or why not?

Choosing a Topic

1. Write a letter to the premier of your province or the prime minister of Canada about the problem of overwork. Be clear about what actions you are responding to and what you expect from your reader.

2. Rebick argues that we need to reduce the average workweek, but she mentions a proposal in one province to extend the workweek to 60 hours. In a coherent essay, persuade your colleagues that overwork is not a serious social problem and that the workweek should be lengthened.
3. Rebick concludes her essay with a call to action: "Let's look to Europe for the example and start demanding that the culture of work reflect the best interests of women and our families." Write an essay in which you either advance this argument or justify the culture of overwork that Rebick identifies.

DANIEL FRICKER AND LARS KUSHNER

Anti-Gay Bullying (2010)

Daniel Fricker has a degree in film and media studies from Queen's University and has worked as a producer and journalist for CTV News and as a communications manager for Telus. His work has appeared in *Outlooks*, a magazine for Canada's lesbian, gay, bisexual and transgender community, and on the LGBT film website **www.hotpinkshorts.com**.

Lars Kushner studied at the ESADE business school and at the University of Western Ontario and is Associate Counsel at RGP Law Group in Vancouver.

Preparing to Read

All individuals in Canada have the right to protection from discrimination under Canada's *Charter of Rights and Freedoms*, including discrimination on the basis of sexual orientation (recognized as implicitly prohibited in the charter by the Supreme Court of Canada in 1995). After bullying led several gay teenagers to commit suicide in 2010, Fricker and Kushner wrote this essay, which originally appeared in *Outlooks*, calling for change. In it, the authors discuss solutions to the widespread bullying of young people that occurs because of their sexual orientation. Before you read, think about bullying you have witnessed or experienced. How often was sexual orientation a factor? Do you think this kind of bullying ends after grade school or high school?

When I was younger, the term "bullying" had kind of an after-school special feel to it; nobody took it very seriously. I think *Family Matters* did a few bully-themed episodes, and SBTB [*Saved by the Bell*] may have dabbled as well (Screech, presumably the victim of some jocks' name-calling/locker-cramming). It served as the title of low-budget grade school PSAs and filler news segments: Bullying: It Could Happen to You (I can picture the b+w, slow-mo❶ playground footage now). It was just a soft topic that everyone knew about, but nobody really gave too much focus. Sticks and stones, right? 1

Reading Critically

❶ What do the authors use this terminology instead of "black and white" and "slow motion"?

Well – wakeup call. It is, indeed, serious. This fall, people everywhere have taken notice of what some are even referring to as an "epidemic," a bullying crisis in schools across North America. International news outlets, celebrities, local not-for-profits, churches and school councils everywhere are all speaking out against bullying, specifically in support of LGBTQ youth. 2

Justin Aaberg was fifteen. Tyler Clementi was eighteen. Asher Brown and Seth Walsh were only thirteen years old. Over the past few months, these kids and others like them have all taken [. . .] their own lives in response to bullying. Hurt, made fun of, outed or physically assaulted for their perceived sexual orientation, these teens were forced towards a breaking point. Their stories are tragic and unnecessary. Our thoughts are with each of their families. 3

Adolescence is difficult. Grade school is no cake walk, and everyone is bound to go through their own stage of awkward/embarrassing (I once threw up from motion sickness at the back of the bus on a grade eight field trip . . . naturally, I was laughed at for weeks). They always say it, and it's true – kids can be cruel. For gay teens though, it's arguably much harder. While progress is made every day, there are still vast parts of our culture that willingly foster hate, intolerance and violence against gays. It's unfortunate, it's backwards and it needs to change – for our children, if for no one else. 4

Please bear with me❷ while I rattle off some stats (from a 2009 school climate survey conducted by the GLSEN): 5

- Nine out of ten LGBTQ students have experienced verbal/physical harassment at school;
- More than two two-thirds of students frequently hear slurs such "dyke" and "faggot";
- Gay teens are up to four times more likely to attempt suicide than their hetero peers; and
- Suicide is the third leading cause of death for young people under the age of 25.

This is a problem. 6

This is no after after-school special with Screech; this is an epidemic. 7

Things must change. 8

Reading Critically

❷ Why do the authors ask for our permission to provide statistics?

So what now? Bullying both warrants and demands a resolution. The first and most important step: awareness. While I refuse to find any silver lining in the wake of young lives lost, what remains is that people everywhere have finally taken notice. The attention of a nation has been captured, and there have been outcries of support, perhaps most notably the "It Gets Better Project." 9

The IGB Project was introduced as a vehicle for both outreach and optimism. Together, famous actors, writers, musicians and everyday people across the world have uploaded video monologues about the trials and tribulations of growing up gay. These are available online for everyone to see, produced in an effort to reach out to bullied teens and raise general awareness with the public. While each story and video is unique, they all proclaim the same unifying moral – aptly, it gets better. 10

The concept began with Seattle columnist Dan Savage, author of the widely acclaimed Savage Love column. Savage started the project as an immediate response to the suicide of Billy Lucas, a 15 year old from Indiana who had been the victim of anti-gay taunts and intimidation at school. In Savage's premiere video, he and his partner Terry discuss their family vacations, snowboarding together and their love of their adopted son – life as out, accepted and accomplished members of society. As role models for this generation's youth, their message is simple: while it may be tough now, it does get better. 11

In an era of tweeting, Facebooking, social networks and viral videos, the IGB Project has figured out a way to reach isolated kids in small towns/big cities everywhere. As of press time, the website (**itgetsbetterproject.com**) has almost one thousand uploaded vids. Along with Savage and his family, a host of celebrities, supporters, queer youth and allies have logged on to share their stories. There are clips from a handful of municipal politicians, a gay Jehovah's Witness, a video from the cast of Wicked and more. The diversity of the diarists across age, race, geography and sexual orientation truly demonstrates how bullying transcends society, affecting everyone in some shared capacity. 12

Neil Patrick Harris, one of this generation's most iconic out and proud leaders, recorded his own personal message with MTV News. In it, Harris calls out to the kids who are "just trying to fit in." With genuine empathy and poise, Neil asks teens to "stay strong" and to remain "individuals," inspiring words for those alienated and struggling with conformity. In the same way, Ellen DeGeneres devoted time on her daytime talk show 13 last month to encourage her viewers to take action (video a quick Google search away online). She takes a break from her daily antics/dancing to deliver a gripping message about bullying. Ellen bravely comments on the latent and blatant❸ homophobia in our culture today, and implores her viewers not to "let intolerance and ignorance take another life."

Although videos from the rich and famous (Dan, Neil and Ellen alike) have been widely-circulated, it is an IGB Project video from Ft. Worth, Texas that has truly had a viral impact. The video is of City Councilman Joel Burns speaking at a local town hall meeting. In the video, Burns poignantly shares his own personal story of bullying, in an attempt to reach out to teenagers both in Ft. Worth and across the continent. He speaks of his days as the skinny, awkward teenage son of a Methodist minister who was less-than-accepted❹ at school, having once been told to "go to hell where he belongs." Burns' message is intimate, direct and emotional, evident from the shaking in his voice and tears in his eyes. He, like many others recently, is determined to reach out to alienated youth. As of press time, the video has had over 1,500,000 YouTube hits. 14

Another moving story worth mentioning is that of Marco Melgoza, a seventh grader from Desmond Middle School in Madera, California. Marco decided to take his own stand against anti-gay bullying and protest on the front lawn of his school, the Advocate reported last month. In front of his classmates and teachers, he stood proudly waving a giant sign that read "Bullying is a Weapon." Marco has been a victim of slurs and violence himself, and is determined to make change in his school for himself and his peers. 15

People like Marco Melgoza, Joel Burns and Ellen DeGeneres are standing up. What youth need is simply understanding and support. Young people deserve the opportunity for a safe learning environment, one void of hate, harassment and intimidation – with more resources, positive spaces, GSAs [Gay Straight Alliances] and people simply to listen. There needs to be education on the impact and consequences of bullying, with ways to intervene. There needs to be change; things must change. 16

What every great social movement needs is a unifying cause, a rallying point that inspires a call for action. In a press conference shortly following the death of their son, Joe and Jane Clementi had 17

Reading Critically

❸ Give examples of latent and blatant discrimination. Which form do you think is more harmful? Why?

❹ What is the effect of this use of understatement?

these solemn words to share with the public: "Our hope is that our family's personal tragedy will serve as a call for compassion, empathy and human dignity." These recent suicides have been an alarming reminder that endless work still needs to be done to educate society about tolerance and mutual respect, to teach our children to embrace diversity and put an end to the hate and violence. Marco, Joel and Ellen are trying – now it's your turn.

For more information on how you can get involved here in Canada, visit Jer's Vision online (**jersvision.org**). JV is Canada's Youth Diversity Initiative, a national youth-led organization dedicated to addressing discrimination and promoting diversity by giving support to youth inspired to change. 18

Self-worth and acceptance should be the right of every youth . . . – even the Screeches of the world. 19

Make change happen today. 20

UNDERSTANDING DETAILS

1. Fricker and Kushner support their call for change with a number of general suggestions and concrete solutions. Make a list of both the general and specific things they suggest to help end bullying of LGBTQ kids.
2. How has the It Gets Better Project served to achieve the first and most important step toward a solution to the problem of bullying? What does the diversity of diarists show?
3. How is the video of Ft. Worth City Councilman Joel Burns different from the other popular videos on the It Gets Better site?

ANALYZING MEANING

1. What do the authors' descriptions of various television shows in the first paragraph suggest about how bullying was depicted in the past? Why is this approach to bullying no longer appropriate? Do you think it was ever effective?
2. Why do the authors say they "refuse to find any silver lining in the wake of young lives lost" (paragraph 9)?
3. What role does the idea of the "after-school special" play throughout this article?

DISCOVERING RHETORICAL STRATEGIES

1. Why might the authors have chosen to begin with their own memories of television programs on bullying? What tone do they establish in this opening paragraph? How does it compare to the tone of the next paragraph?

2. What audience do you think Fricker and Kushner had in mind for this essay? Who is the "you" the authors are addressing?
3. Fricker and Kushner use a combination of logical, emotional, and ethical appeals in this essay. Which appeal did you find most persuasive? Why?

MAKING CONNECTIONS

1. Fricker and Kushner show that self-worth and self-acceptance do not exist in a vacuum. Imagine Irshad Manji ("Status Anxiety? Consider Socrates and the Sewer Saviour") in conversation with Fricker and Kushner, discussing self-acceptance and the need for belonging. Where might they find common ground? Where might they disagree?
2. Cynara Geissler also writes about self-acceptance in "Fat Acceptance: A Basic Primer." Compare her strategies with those of Fricker and Kushner. Where do they differ? What accounts for the differences in their suggested solutions?

IDEAS FOR DISCUSSION/WRITING

Preparing to Write

Why do you think sexual orientation is such a focal point for bullies in grade school and high school? Many of the cases Fricker and Kushner describe occurred in the United States. Do you think LGBTQ youth suffer from similar levels of discrimination and bullying in Canada? What do you think accounts for homophobia and discrimination based on sexual orientation in Canadian society?

Choosing a Topic

1. Think of an area of your life in which things improved greatly when you reached a certain age. Write a script for your own video, addressed to your younger self. Explain to your younger self how things will get better.
2. Fricker and Kushner suggest that social movements often take off if they have a unifying cause or rallying cry. Write an essay analyzing a single event, image, or slogan that you think inspired social change. What made this event, image, or slogan so powerful?
3. Write a critique of an anti-bullying movie, television show, or educational program, exploring its approach to the problem of bullying. How effectively does it deal with bullying? How realistic are the solutions it presents?

JANICE GROSS STEIN

Whisper, Echo and Voice (2000)

Educated at McGill and Yale universities in the 1960s, Janice Gross Stein is the Harrowston Professor of Conflict Management in the Department of Political Science and the director of the Munk Centre for International Studies at the University of Toronto. An expert on conflict resolution and international relations, particularly related to the Middle East, Stein has written more than 80 books and articles, including (as co-author) *We All Lost the Cold War* (1994) and *Citizen Engagement in Conflict Resolution: Lessons for Canada in International Experience* (1997). Her 2001 Massey Lectures on "The Cult of Efficiency" are now available in print.

In addition, Stein appears frequently on television panels and comments on foreign policy on TVO's *Studio 2* and *Diplomatic Immunity*, as well as CBC's *The National*. She is currently a member of the International Security Committee of the American Academy of Arts and Sciences and the Committee on International Conflict Resolution of the National Academy of Sciences. She is a Member of the Order of Canada and the Order of Ontario, and a Fellow of the Royal Society of Canada.

Stein's essay here was originally printed as part of the Dominion Institute's ongoing Great Questions of Canada program (**www.greatquestions.com**), which invites high school, college, and university students to participate in an essay contest for a $1500 cash prize.

Preparing to Read

Janice Gross Stein's essay was originally written as part of a debate with Allan Gotlieb (Canada's former ambassador to the United States) on Canada and the world, and the steps that Canada might take to make sure it has a significant voice in international discussions. How would you characterize Canada's place in the international community? What roles does Canada play in relation to other nations, and in international organizations like the United Nations? How is Canada seen by other nations? Should Canada be more vocal on international issues?

In a global economy, sovereignty❶ is no longer what it was and states no longer have the same power to protect, or to abuse, their citizens. Canada is no exception: It is but a shadow of its 1

Reading Critically

❶ Explain the concept of sovereignty.

former self, with only a whisper for a voice. On this, Canadian champions and the critics of "globalization" agree.

2 But both are wrong. Each underestimates the capacity Canada retains to make a difference on global issues, even as the face of sovereignty changes.

3 We can only make a difference, however, if we build the domestic platform❷ needed to participate effectively in a knowledge-based global system; what we do at home shapes our choices abroad.

4 In the post–Cold War world, powerful enemies are largely absent and global market forces are ever present. In the global marketplace, Canada is not as significant a player as it was 50 years ago, and it is likely to become even less important as China, Brazil, Argentina and Indonesia mature. Canada also faces a special challenge: it lives next door to the mighty❸ United States.

5 The most serious threat to Canada's survival as a nation with a distinct identity is no longer military attack, but the pull and push of the U.S. economy and its entertainment industries. More and more innovative, risk-acceptant young Canadians are being drawn to the United States to work. More and more Canadians are watching programs produced in the United States, listening to music by American recording artists and reading books and magazines written and edited in the United States.

6 It is no surprise that managing the Canada–U.S. relationship is front and centre on our government's agenda. If there is to be a Canada at all—much less a Canada that speaks with authority on global issues—strategic choices must be made.

7 Ottawa, the provincial governments and the private sector must invest strategically in educating a scientifically and technically literate population and in promoting innovation. We have just begun, for example, to renovate our decaying scientific infrastructure through the Canadian Foundation for Innovation, but far more must be done.

8 Telecommunications and computer companies, software developers and biotechnology firms must partner with universities, colleges and governments to provide world-class opportunities for young Canadians. How Canada will fare in a global knowledge-based economy will depend largely on the skills of

---

Reading Critically

❷ What is a domestic platform?

❸ Why do you think Stein uses this adjective to describe the United States?

our citizens. Here we must do far better than in the past if Canada is to be a player in global markets.

9 But scientific and technical literacy alone will not provide a sufficient platform for authoritative participation in world politics. Canadians know alarmingly little about their own history, and they are unfamiliar with the cultures and practices of their diverse fellow citizens.❹ Our schools, post-secondary institutions and national public broadcaster must do significantly better in teaching Canadians about the richness of their past and the diversity of their present.

10 Participation in global politics is no longer restricted to a cadre of trained experts, as it was half a century ago. In the future, larger and larger numbers of Canadians will move abroad, come home and move out again. If we do not know our history, we will quickly forget who we are as we spend more time away from home. Canadian identity will blur and Canada's voice will gradually become mute.❺

11 We will also be unable to exploit one of our most important assets in global politics—our richly diverse population. Networks of immigrants now connect Canada around the globe. These networks are invaluable channels as Canada seeks to make its voice heard on international issues. We should lead in developing practices of multiple citizenship to strengthen these connections. Access to Canadian citizenship should be made easier rather than more difficult, and dual, even triple, citizenship should become possible. Canadians who move in and out of the country strengthen our international connections and help "brand" Canada❻ to those who might not know us otherwise.

12 But even if we invest strategically in engineering a better knowledge platform than we have in the past, living permanently in the shadow of the United States is still no easy task. It is even harder now, in this "unipolar" moment.❼

13 Canada must watch its economic back continuously. It does, and should, devote a great deal of attention to monitoring and lobbying Washington. Officials must also use the dense networks

---

Reading Critically

❹ Do you think this statement is true? How much do you know about Canada's history? How familiar are you with the different cultures of Canada's citizens?

❺ Do you agree with this prediction? Why or why not?

❻ What do you think Stein means by "branding" Canada?

❼ What does the author mean by a "unipolar" moment?

of political, social, and economic connections between Canadians and Americans to promote Canadian interests in Washington. We must also continue to promote multilateral regimes and rules of fair play. Logic dictates that Canada will generally do better on a regulated multilateral playing field than in one-to-one contests with Washington. When there is no choice but to deal with an issue bilaterally, there will inevitably be conflict and compromise; Canada will win some, but lose more.

14 Above all, Canada must have a responsible, independent voice in global politics. What Canada says and does globally helps us to define ourselves, and we have the power to speak strategically in several important ways. We can, for example, lead where the United States—particularly the executive branch—wishes it could go but sometimes cannot. We did so recently, for example, in Havana, and at the United Nations when sanctions against Iraq were once again on the agenda. In both cases, political constraints prevented the United States from exploring new openings. Despite rhetoric to the contrary in Congress, Canada's leadership was both helpful, and seen as helpful, in the American government.

15 Canada can also speak directly to some of the most difficult problems bedevilling[8] the global system. Ethnic and religious intolerance, governments unaccountable to their citizens, legal systems ungoverned by the rule of law, social inequity and the fracturing of communities in an age of global markets—all often spill over into violence. Canadian culture in its deepest sense—our habits of tolerance, our respect for human rights and our civility—provides the kind of expertise needed when the big powers or international institutions seek to prevent conflict or to reconstruct war-torn societies.

16 Canada has taken the lead on a basket of humanitarian issues—the ban on land mines, the creation of an International Criminal Court—and has built a coalition of 12 states, including Norway and South Africa, committed to enhancing the protection of citizens, even, if necessary, against their own governments. Seizing the moment when sovereignty is in retreat, Canada has made a difference globally. We can continue to do so if we use our human resources well and choose our issues carefully. But this capacity for significant engagement in global politics will be

---

Reading Critically

[8] What do you think this word means? Is it a real word?

impaired if we are reduced to echoing the United States. Unease with the weight of American economic, cultural, military and political power is not just a Canadian concern; Europe and Japan are worried as well, and they are not stilling their voices. On the right issues it is imperative that Canada have an independent voice, even if that voice occasionally irritates our neighbours.

17 The gravest threat, not only to our capacity to engage in the world but also to our survival, is the tendency to whisper or echo when we can indeed speak and make a difference.

UNDERSTANDING DETAILS

1. According to Stein, what do Canadian champions and critics of globalization agree on?
2. In what direction does Stein believe Canada should be moving? How does Stein propose this should be done? In what direction has Canada been moving over the past 50 years? Why?
3. In global politics, where can Canada lead that the United States cannot?

ANALYZING MEANING

1. Why does Stein believe Canada should have a louder voice in the global marketplace? How can Canada make a difference in global issues?
2. What reasons does Stein give for Canada's ability to lead in areas where the United States cannot?
3. This essay was written in 2000. Do you think Stein would view things differently now? Explain.

DISCOVERING RHETORICAL STRATEGIES

1. Who do you think is Stein's intended audience? Explain your conclusion.
2. Explain how Stein effectively frames her essay with the introduction and conclusion.
3. Is Stein's argument primarily an emotional, logical, or ethical one? Why has she chosen this approach?

MAKING CONNECTIONS

1. Anita Rau Badami ("My Canada") writes about Canada in comparison with the United States. How do you think she would respond to Stein's position that "The most serious threat to Canada's survival . . . is . . . the pull and push of the U.S. economy and its entertainment industries" (paragraph 5)?

2. Stein says, "Canadians know alarmingly little about their own history, and they are unfamiliar with the cultures and practices of their diverse fellow citizens" (paragraph 9). Imagine a conversation on this topic among Stein, Sheema Khan ("Hijabs: Don't Kick Up a Fuss"), Steven Heighton ("Elegy in Stone"), Dakshana Bascaramurty ("My Parents Killed Santa (and Nobody Cared)") and Anita Rau Badami ("My Canada"). On what points do you think these writers would agree? In what areas might they disagree?

IDEAS FOR DISCUSSION/WRITING

Preparing to Write

Stein contends that the U.S. economy and the American entertainment industries are the greatest threat to Canada's survival. Write freely about the influence of the United States on Canada. In what areas do you believe U.S. influence is the strongest? Is U.S. influence a problem? What should Canadians do about this influence? What should the Canadian government do about this influence?

Choosing a Topic

1. In paragraph 15, Stein lists many of the "most difficult problems bedevilling the global system." Choose one of the problems she mentions and write an essay in which you take a strong persuasive stance on the position Canada should take on this issue in the international arena.
2. How much do you know about Canadian history? Write an essay in which you support or refute Janice Gross Stein's position that "Canadians know alarmingly little about their own history" (paragraph 9).
3. In paragraphs 7 to 9, Stein identifies a number of steps that she believes need to be taken to ensure that, going forward, there is a Canada that speaks with authority on global issues. Select one of the propositions Stein makes and write a persuasive essay in which you encourage the appropriate party or parties to follow Stein's recommended course of action.

RUSSELL SMITH

Potty-Mouthed and Proud of It (2004)

Russell Smith is one of Canada's most well-known authors and cultural commentators. Born in South Africa in 1963, Smith was raised in Halifax, where his father, whom he mentions in the essay below, was professor of English and African Studies at Dalhousie University. Smith has an M.A. in French from Queen's University and has published several novels, including *How Insensitive* (1994), *Noise* (1998), *Diana: A Diary in the Second Person* (2003), *Muriella Pent* (2004), and *Girl Crazy* (2010); the short story collection *Young Men* (1999); and an illustrated fable, *The Princess and the Whiskheads* (2002). Smith is also the author of *Men's Style: The Thinking Man's Guide to Dress* (2005) and the editor of the online men's fashion magazine **www.dailyxy.com**. His column "Virtual Culture" in *The Globe and Mail* often explores the relationship between culture and language.

Smith has often provoked controversy with his writing, as when he invited readers of *The Globe and Mail* to submit their definitions of *pornography* after he wrote a column on whether porn should be available on cell phones.

Preparing to Read

In this essay, first published in *The Globe and Mail,* Russell Smith questions the censorship of taboo words on television. How do you feel about swearing on television, in movies, and in music? Do you agree with people who feel that taboo words are a threat to civility? Or do you side with Brabantio in *Othello,* who said, "Words are words. I never yet did hear / That the bruised heart was pierced through the ear"? Formerly taboo words such as *hell* and *damn* are now considered very mild. What does this say about the nature of profanity?

---

1 Why are taboo words taboo? What magical power do they have? And why, if they are inherently dangerous, do they change over the ages? Why is mention of the Communion goblet or the Eucharist-holder taboo in Quebec, while here merely evidence of academic interest? Why do we feel children are particularly sensitive to these magical powers?

None of these questions troubles the spate of warriors for linguistic chastity currently clamouring for censorship in the United States.❶ A couple of high-profile American lawmakers—Michael K. Powell, the chairman of the Federal Communications Commission, and Congressman Doug Ose—are calling for new regulations and even laws to stop the disgraceful use of taboo words on network television. Powell has called for a reversal of a recent FCC ruling on whether a rock star's televised use of the word "fucking" was obscene. The FCC had decided that it was not, because it was used as an adjective rather than a verb. No one has yet attempted to explain what difference this could possibly make, but then the whole debate is so irrational and nonsensical that trying to make sense of these arguments is like trying to make sense of a dream. A dream isn't about an argument, it's about a vague terror. 2

At any rate, Powell wants the word to be obscene, used adjectivally or not. He also wants the fines raised tenfold for television networks who permit these words to be spoken aloud. In a speech at a National Press Club luncheon, Powell said, "I personally believe that the growing coarseness and use of such profanity at a time when we are very likely to know that children are watching is abhorrent and irresponsible." 3

Shortly afterward, various representatives expressed their support for this idea. Congressman Fred Upton proposed a hearing on indecency. Senator John McCain pushed for stiffer fines for rude networks in a recent bill. Then Ose introduced his bill that listed which specific words should be banned from network television. They are, as Doug Saunders reported in this paper last week, basically the comedian George Carlin's famous list of "seven words you can't say on television," with "tit"—apparently no longer objectionable—replaced by "asshole." (Nothing indicates the arbitrary nature of the list better, I think, than this random substitution.❷ 4

And where is quim? Meat syringe? I can think of a whole lot of rude words that aren't on this list. Where, for God's sake, is arse?) Now lobby groups have joined the push, including the powerful Parents' Television Council, which has also issued statements stressing the vulnerability of children to such words. 5

Reading Critically

❶ Explain this sentence. What effect does Smith create by using alliteration? What does his choice of words tell us about his point of view?

❷ Why do you think the word *tit* was dropped from the list?

What the words will do to children is never stated. Is the argument that they will frighten children? (Probably not, since they are commonly heard in schoolyards and in pop music and—sadly for the FCC—on television.) 6

Is the argument that they will degrade the expressive capacity of children? This is a slightly more sophisticated thought, but still not a provable one. There is a fundamental contradiction in the idea that eliminating words improves one's vocabulary. (I myself grew up in a house in which no words were taboo. My father's colourful curses are some of my earliest memories. The words he used were so impressive and so gleefully awful they instilled in me a delight in language's chromatic, dramatic and sensual effects. Now I'm a professional writer. So bad language obviously didn't limit my vocabulary.) 7

Is the argument that the acts or objects that the bad words represent are too disgusting to contemplate? (This is implausible, since most of the words are not used to represent anything literal; they are all-purpose negatives.) 8

Or is it that the repetition of these words so weakens them that they actually become distanced from the thing or act they once represented, which dulls their power? (If so, surely we should encourage their use?) We'll never know what the argument is, because no argument is ever made. 9

A person with a basically mystical view of the word believes that words are not, as a linguist would say, merely constative. They are also performative—that is, they do not only describe, they also act. They cast spells merely by being uttered. Hence the taboo, in various cultures, on saying the name of the deity—the word is the property of the deity himself; to use it is to usurp a god's power. This is especially strong in Christianity and explains those ecclesiastical Québécois curses, and those gorgeous Elizabethan curses❸ derived from various parts of the Lord's anatomy: 'slid (from "God's eyelid"), zounds (from "God's wounds"), 'sblood (from "God's blood"). These words would have been considered indecent on Victorian television, had there been Victorian television,❹ and they are meaningless and powerless today. (Note to Mr. Powell: Magic words become less magic as society changes.) 10

Reading Critically

❸ Why does Smith describe Elizabethan curses as "gorgeous"?

❹ Why do you think these words would have been considered indecent in Victorian times?

Now it's using colloquial terms for sex acts and body parts that's the dangerous usurping of power: The spirit of the carnal is not for casual dabbling; it is not to be released into the society.

11 Every writer loves bad words. They don't diminish one's vocabulary; they expand it. They are harsh and colourful and often very funny. And their proliferation on television, more than almost any other development in the medium, has made television better in the past 10 years. The realism of the swearing was what I loved about *The Larry Sanders Show*, for example—and who can imagine *The Sopranos* without vulgarity? Foul language makes dialogue seem real, for the simple reason that most people in North America speak this way. Even the upstanding President of the United States [George W. Bush] has been caught saying "asshole" in an unguarded moment. He didn't get in any trouble from the right because he thought he was speaking in private, and we all know that there are two standards of behaviour when it comes to social conservatism—one private, one public. This goes for both sex and the language about it.

12 Of course, the censors will argue, we wouldn't want television to be about reality, we want it to be a role model, a guiding light, an instrument of change—an instrument that shows the world the way we want it to be. What could be more scary for a social conservative than reality?

UNDERSTANDING DETAILS

1. Why are the words for Communion goblet and Eucharist-holder considered taboo in Quebec?
2. What is the difference between a constative and a performative view of language (paragraph 10)? Why is it taboo to say the name of the deity in some cultures?
3. How, according to Smith, has swearing made television better in the past 10 years?

ANALYZING MEANING

1. What is the difference between Elizabethan curses and swearing today? What does this change in language imply about the differences in the two societies?
2. Why does Smith consider the list of seven taboo words arbitrary?
3. What does Smith mean when he says there are two standards of behaviour in social conservatism (paragraph 11)? How does this relate to his argument about language?

DISCOVERING RHETORICAL STRATEGIES

1. As he develops his argument, Smith asks many rhetorical questions, only some of which he answers explicitly. How are these questions an effective approach to his subject? Which of his answers did you find most persuasive?
2. Many of Smith's points can be found in parentheses. Why might he have chosen to do this?
3. How does Smith establish his credibility? How important is this credibility to his overall argument?

MAKING CONNECTIONS

1. Both Smith and Douglas Glover ("On Winning and Responsibility") challenge accepted notions that people may feel strongly about but rarely bother to question. Which essay did you find more persuasive? Why?
2. Smith and Alex Boyd ("In Defense of Graffiti") both defend things that are frequently dismissed as bad. Are they equally effective in their defence of profanity and graffiti?

IDEAS FOR DISCUSSION/WRITING

Preparing to Write

What swear words do you yourself use? In what contexts? Where did you learn these words? Write freely about your earliest memory of a taboo word. Who used the word? In what context? Think about the worst words you know in English and in any other languages you speak. What do these words have in common? Why are so many taboo words related to sex and bodily functions?

Choosing a Topic

1. Choose one of Smith's rhetorical questions and write an essay that answers it fully.
2. In Canada, the Canadian Radio-television and Telecommunications Commission (CRTC) is responsible for regulating what we see and hear on TV. Do you feel the CRTC should censor more of what is shown on television? Or do you believe viewers themselves are responsible for turning off what they don't want to see and hear? Write a persuasive essay on censorship in Canadian television.
3. Smith wonders if the repetition of a word dulls its power. Write an essay that explores how frequent usage has changed the power or impact of one word.

SHEEMA KHAN

Hijabs: Don't Kick Up a Fuss (2007)

Born in India, Sheema Khan came to Canada at the age of three, grew up in Montreal, and completed a Ph.D. in chemical physics at Harvard. She holds a number of pharmaceutical patents and is now a technical consultant in intellectual property law in Ottawa. In 2000, she founded the Canadian Council on American-Islamic Relations (CAIR-CAN), a grassroots advocacy group, and served as its chair until 2005. Khan writes a monthly column for *The Globe and Mail* on Islamic issues, and frequently speaks on issues of diversity and cultural integration. Her essays have been collected in a book, *Of Hockey and Hijab: Reflections of a Canadian Muslim Woman* (2009).

Preparing to Read

In this essay, Khan responds to an incident in Quebec in which an 11-year-old soccer player was ejected from a game because her hijab was considered a safety threat. When the case was taken before FIFA (Fédération Internationale de Football Association), the organization answered ambiguously, saying its rules were already clear. Since head scarves are not expressly forbidden—or even mentioned—under FIFA regulations, referees must continue to interpret the rules as they see fit. What are your thoughts on the subject? Do you think the hijab presents a safety risk for soccer players?

"Soccer moms 'R' us" is a good way to describe the recreational league I play in. We are women, over 30 years of age, who get together every week in friendly, competitive matches. I am the only hijabi in the league, but no one has ever raised the issue of my head scarf being a safety hazard (unless I secretly wear hoop earrings underneath). I can see the ball clearly, and the head scarf is not hanging loosely around my jersey. In fact, I don't think anyone notices it any more. I'm simply known as "No. 13." 1

The past few weeks have been good. We've had two shutouts, both solid team efforts, and I've managed to score in a number of games. I've also avoided pulling muscles or twisting my ankle—an added bonus at my age—and the hijab is no impediment. 2

I first played soccer in high school and loved it from the start. I coached a few girls' teams and played both competitively and recreationally (including a stint with a team called the "Dirty Sox"). I am also an accredited coach with the Canadian Soccer Association.❶ 3

Soccer's a great sport—it offers the challenge of controlling a ball, deking past a defender, passing to a teammate and timing a header (hopefully, into the net). It's great exercise and an inexpensive way of staying fit. It encourages teamwork and is the most popular sport on Earth—loved by more people than baseball, basketball and hockey (which I also play) combined. 4

That is why I shook my head in disbelief when I heard yesterday about Asmahan Mansour, 11, who was barred from playing in a Quebec tournament for wearing her hijab. Apparently, the referee ruled it a safety hazard. 5

Yet the refs in Asma's two other tournament games had no problems with her headgear. Neither has this ever been an issue in Ontario, where Asma plays regularly. Her team, along with five other Ontario teams, boycotted the remainder of the weekend tournament in support of Asma.❷ 6

Quebec soccer officials cited FIFA, the soccer world's governing body, as the source for their ban. According to Brigitte Frot, executive director of the Quebec Soccer Federation, FIFA rules don't allow for any jewellery or headgear. But on FIFA's website, laws governing player's equipment state that "equipment such as headgear, facemasks, knee and arm protectors made of soft, lightweight, padded material are not considered to be dangerous and are therefore permitted." There are pictures of soccer players wearing bandanas, glasses and headbands in action.❸ 7

The brouhaha in Laval, Que., seems to be a replay of what happened last May in Australia. A referee refused to allow Afifa Saad to play with her hijab. Both her team and the opposition supported her, and the match was called off. The Victorian Soccer Federation said 8

Reading Critically

❶ Why is this personal anecdote so important to Khan's argument? What does the tone of this opening tell you about her personality?

❷ Why is it significant that five other teams also boycotted the tournament? What does this suggest about the players' attitudes toward the hijab?

❸ Could any of these items be considered dangerous for players? Could any of them be more dangerous than wearing a hijab? Explain.

Ms. Saad, 21, one of the state's most promising strikers, deserved an apology. The federation also formally adopted a new rule allowing Muslim women to wear hijab in the field.

9 VSF chief executive Damien Brown said "the hijab has been deemed from the outset not to be dangerous and on that basis there is no issue whatsoever with people wearing it." Mr. Brown even proposed the hijab policy for possible adoption by FIFA, saying "we're trying to set an example that will be applied across the world."

10 Aside from his progressive stand on the rules, Mr. Brown captured the essential spirit of soccer, noting that "one of the real advantages of soccer over any other sport is, of course, its cultural diversity and its appeal across all boundaries." It is this spirit that has escaped Quebec soccer officials.

11 In the delightful comedy *Bend It Like Beckham*, plucky Jesminder Bhamra tries to satisfy her parents' traditions with her desire to play professional soccer. It's a metaphor of a dilemma faced by so many young people—how to maintain a multiplicity of identities while remaining true to oneself.

12 Too bad that Quebec soccer officials, with their unbendable rules, have stood in the way of a Muslim girl and her soccer dreams. However, Asma, along with her teammates, coaches and supporters, have been true to themselves by making sure that the principle of fair play speaks louder.

UNDERSTANDING DETAILS

1. How does her hijab affect Khan's ability to play soccer? Under what conditions does Khan say her hijab would be a safety hazard?
2. According to this article, what is FIFA's stand on headgear? Why might this stand be considered ambiguous?
3. How was a similar incident in Australia resolved?

ANALYZING MEANING

1. Why does Khan say, "I'm simply known as 'No. 13'" (paragraph 1)? How does she feel about being known as a number?
2. Why does the author say that the spirit of soccer has escaped Quebec soccer officials?
3. What is the movie *Bend It Like Beckham* a metaphor for? How is this metaphor related to Khan's argument? How does the author extend this metaphor?

DISCOVERING RHETORICAL STRATEGIES

1. How important is the appeal to ethics in this essay? How does Khan establish her credibility?
2. What other appeals does Khan use to make her argument?
3. Evaluate the effectiveness of the first and last paragraphs. What links them?

MAKING CONNECTIONS

1. Compare how Khan, Russell Smith ("Potty-Mouthed and Proud of It"), and Rafe Mair ("Raise the Driving Age") use the appeal to ethics in their arguments.
2. Khan praises soccer for encouraging teamwork. Imagine her in a discussion with Aaron Wherry ("Violently Happy") and Laura Robinson ("Sports Breeds Real-Life Violence") about the values developed or conveyed in sports. Would their views overlap on any points?

IDEAS FOR DISCUSSION/WRITING

Preparing to Write

Khan writes about a common dilemma: maintaining "a multiplicity of identities while remaining true to oneself" (paragraph 11). What "multiplicity of identities" do you maintain? What does it mean to you to be true to yourself? Cases like Asmahan Mansour's often raise questions about Canadian identity, assimilation, and integration. Is Canada a successful example of a country that contains a multiplicity of identities while remaining true to itself?

Choosing a Topic

1. How do you think FIFA should have responded to Asmahan Mansour's case? Write a persuasive essay defending your opinion.
2. Asmahan Mansour's case raised questions about diversity and multiculturalism in Canada. Write an essay critiquing or defending the Canadian Multiculturalism Act or another aspect of Canadian diversity.
3. Write an essay suggesting a solution to a controversy in another sport or physical activity. Use a range of rhetorical strategies to support your argument.

RAFE MAIR

Raise the Driving Age (2007)

A former lawyer and cabinet minister, Rafe Mair is a well-known West Coast broadcaster, commentator, and author who often stirs controversy with his outspoken style. He is a self-proclaimed contrarian who has made a habit of challenging authority since he was a child. In 2008, the Supreme Court of Canada cleared him of libel after he compared an opponent of gay rights to Hitler and the Ku Klux Klan. Referring to Mr. Mair's comparison, Mr. Justice Ian Binnie wrote in the decision that freedom of expression must cover outrageous as well as moderate opinions.

Mair has been a regular commentator on OMNI Television's current affairs program *The Standard*, and on CBC. He is the author of *Canada: Is Anyone Listening?* (1998); *Rants, Raves and Recollections* (2000); *Still Ranting: More Rants, Raves and Recollections* (2002); *Rafe: A Memoir* (2004); *Hard Talk* (2005); and *Over the Mountains: More Thoughts on Things That Matter* (2006). Mair has won awards for his journalism, including the Michener Media Award for public benefit and the Bruce Hutchinson Lifetime Achievement Award in B.C. journalism. He currently contributes a column to the online magazine *The Tyee* and blogs at **www.rafeonline.com**.

Preparing to Read

In this essay, which first appeared in the online magazine *The Tyee*, Rafe Mair argues that the driving age should be raised to 19. Before you read the essay, take a moment to think about your reaction to his proposal. How strongly do you support or oppose the idea? What are your reasons? If you were 15, how would you feel about the idea? Do you think that driving is a right or a privilege?

1 As a general rule I place the musings of insurance [companies] right up there with Pinocchio when his nose was longest.[1] Especially I have little if any regard for the musings of Allstate with whom I once worked as an adjustor and who later on were

---

Reading Critically

[1] Does this opening grab your attention? Why or why not? What is Mair suggesting about insurance companies?

occasional clients of my law firm. Allstate was dubbed "All heart" by those who had a claim only to have their insurance canceled or who were at the business end of a claim against the company. But here is what caught my eye in *The Economist* a few weeks ago,

"A 16-year-old can't see an NC-17 rated movie, drink alcohol or vote—but drive a 5,000 pound car at 60 mph? That's OK." 2

Allstate has a point—a very good point. The evidence of teenage recklessness almost seems to be a daily headline. Young kids racing—two people dead. Senior killed by hit and run young driver. On and bloody (literally) on it goes. 3

The police are driven to distraction by this epidemic❷ and spend far too much of their time on it. For example—every time there's a hit and run accident the police must investigate, taking them away from other duties meaning that teenage accidents compel a use of police time that would be much better spent on other matters.❸ 4

Courts seem loath to give out severe sentences and find that, like the police, a disproportionate amount of time is spent on cases that wouldn't happen if the age one can get a drivers' license were extended to 19. 5

The blows to the family, friends and communities are hard and the pain runs deep. 6

As a father who lost a 17-year-old daughter due to reckless driving (her own), I know about the pain and what it so tragically does to the security of the family affected. 7

No fear

I'm not one of those who looks back to my teenage days as unblemished by any stupid behaviour. Far from it. I got my license when I was 16 and was technically a good driver (the inspector said my reactions were in the top 90 per cent) but had little fear and almost no judgment. I was involved in several accidents and fortunately no one was hurt. We had drag races and often played "tag" with another car the object being to lose him. Up and down lanes and busy streets we went—what fun it was, especially when homeowners, pedestrians and other drivers shook their fists at us. 8

Reading Critically

❷ Why does Mair refer to teenage driving accidents as an "epidemic"?

❸ What other matters could the police be spending time on? Do you agree that the number of teenage driving accidents is taking the police away from other duties? Why or why not?

I had no business having a driver's license nor did 75 per cent of my friends. (That figure would be higher today because when I was a kid, girls were much safer than boys—a difference that no longer exists).❹ 9

We kids didn't hesitate for a moment to get behind the wheel because we had been drinking. In fact that was the situation most times we drove our parents' car full of our teenage friends. Other drugs weren't fashionable in those days but with the amount of booze we drank it didn't matter. On a Monday morning when, just before school went in, we were having a cigarette down the alley, you could depend upon one kid saying "I was so shit-faced Saturday night I drove home with one eye on the centre line and the other closed." That would usually be matched by an even more hair-raising story.❺ 10

Just wait a bit

It seems to me we must ask ourselves a question. Is a driver's license a right or a privilege? Actually that's easy—the courts have long held that it's a privilege. Now comes the harder question. Do we extend that privilege to people as soon as they are big enough to drive a car? The answer is no because there are lots of kids of 12 who are big enough. It must be, then, that we grant the license when a person is mature enough and we have arbitrarily decided that this happens on the 16th birthday. 11

We ought to have our collective heads read.❻ 12

Of course there are some very responsible drivers under the age of 19 and it would be unfair to take away their right—I mean privilege—to drive. But who ever said life would be "fair"? And is it really that unfair? We set all sorts of rules so we can have an orderly society. And, remember that here we're talking about a society extending a privilege—surely they're entitled to say, "We know that many young drivers are good and we also know that many older drivers are terrible but the issue is public safety and a hugely disproportionate number of injuries and deaths on the 13

Reading Critically

❹ What could account for this change in young female driving statistics?

❺ Why do you think that Mair and his friends were unaware of their dangerous driving habits? Do you think kids of that age today are more or less aware? Explain.

❻ What does this sentence imply? Why does Mair set it apart?

road are caused by drivers under 19." To argue that other drivers are bad too is a diversion, not an argument.

14 Move the time to 19 when other perks and responsibilities of adults are granted. This may require a special "when driving during employment" exception. So be it. Let everyone else wait until adulthood to exercise a very important privilege—driving a car and doing so carefully.❼

UNDERSTANDING DETAILS

1. Why does the author say he had no business driving at 16?
2. Why, according to the author, was the driving age set at 16?
3. Why does society have a right to change the age to 19, even though this may be unfair?

ANALYZING MEANING

1. Why might courts be loath to give out severe sentences to teenagers for reckless driving?
2. What does Mair mean when he says, "To argue that other drivers are bad too is a diversion, not an argument" (paragraph 13)? Do you agree with this statement?
3. What are Mair's main arguments for changing the driving age to 19?

DISCOVERING RHETORICAL STRATEGIES

1. How does Mair's appeal to ethics contribute to the persuasiveness of his argument?
2. Evaluate the comparisons in the following statement, and determine if the analogy makes a valid argument: "A 16-year-old can't see an NC-17 rated movie, drink alcohol or vote—but drive a 5,000 pound car at 60 mph? That's OK" (paragraph 2).
3. Mair states several times that young people are responsible for more accidents on the road than other drivers. Are you satisfied with the evidence he provides to support his claim?

MAKING CONNECTIONS

1. Daniel Fricker and Lars Kushner also advocate for change in their essay ("Anti-Gay Bullying"). Compare their tone and approach to Mair's. Which is more effective, in your opinion?

Reading Critically

❼ Do you agree with Mair's proposal? Why or why not?

2. Compare the appeals to logic, emotion, and ethics used by Mair, Sheema Khan ("Hijabs: Don't Kick Up a Fuss"), and Russell Smith ("Potty-Mouthed and Proud of It"). Which essay contains the strongest appeal to logic? Emotion? Ethics?

IDEAS FOR DISCUSSION/WRITING

Preparing to Write

Do you drive? How old were you when you got your licence? What do you remember about the process? Do you think you are a good driver? How do you know? If you don't drive, write freely about why not. Do you feel deprived, relieved, or indifferent that you don't have a licence or a car? Have you ever been in a vehicle with a really bad driver? Have you ever been in a car accident? In general, do you feel safe on the road? What makes you feel unsafe?

Choosing a Topic

1. At various times, people have argued that the legal age for something (driving, drinking, smoking, sex, marriage, retirement) should be raised or lowered. Pick an activity that is regulated by society either through licensing or age of consent, and write an essay arguing for or against the age requirements.
2. People have suggested that video racing games like "Need for Speed" are encouraging young people to drive recklessly in real life, causing serious accidents and, in some cases, death. Write an essay exploring the relationship between racing games and reckless driving.
3. Tailgating, driving while talking on a cell phone, speeding, driving too slowly . . . What bad driving habits do you find most irritating? Most dangerous? Write a classification essay that explores the behaviour of drivers on the road.

ADAM GOPNIK

Shootings (2007)

Adam Gopnik grew up in Montreal, the child of professors. He has a B.A. from McGill University and an M.A. from the Institute of Fine Arts in New York, and has written for *The New Yorker* since 1986. Gopnik is the author of *Paris to the Moon* (2000); *Through the Children's Gate: A Home in New York* (2006); *Angels and Ages: A Short Book about Darwin, Lincoln, and Modern Life* (2009); and *The Table Comes First: Family, France, and the Meaning of Food* (2011); and the editor of *Americans in Paris: A Literary Anthology* (2004). He has also written a children's book, *The King in the Window* (2005). Much of his writing consists of what he calls the "comic-sentimental essay," a form that uses personal experience for a purpose, whether to make an argument or derive a lesson. The essay, he has argued, is the only form that allows a writer to blend emotion and intellect seamlessly.

Preparing to Read

In this essay, Adam Gopnik discusses the cause of the 2007 Virginia Tech shootings, in which a single gunman killed 32 people before committing suicide. Before you begin reading, take a moment to think about mass shootings. Where do they most often take place? Who are the victims? What do you know about the shooters? What do you think is the root cause of these shootings? How can they be prevented?

The cell phones in the pockets of the dead students were still ringing when we were told that it was wrong to ask why.❶ As the police cleared the bodies from the Virginia Tech engineering building, the cell phones rang, in the eccentric varieties of ring tones, as parents kept trying to see if their children were O.K. To imagine the feelings of the police as they carried the bodies and heard the ringing is heartrending; to imagine the feelings of the parents who were calling—dread, desperate hope for a sudden answer and the bliss of reassurance, dawning grief—is unbearable.❷ But the parents, and the rest of us, were told 1

Reading Critically

❶ Why does the first sentence grab your attention?

❷ What picture does this opening paint?

that it was not the right moment to ask how the shooting had happened—specifically, why an obviously disturbed student, with a history of mental illness, was able to buy guns whose essential purpose is to kill people—and why it happens over and over again in America. At a press conference, Virginia's governor, Tim Kaine, said, "People who want to . . . make it their political hobby horse to ride, I've got nothing but loathing for them. . . . At this point, what it's about is comforting family members . . . and helping this community heal. And so to those who want to try to make this into some little crusade, I say take that elsewhere."

2 If the facts weren't so horrible, there might be something touching in the Governor's deeply American belief that "healing" can take place magically, without the intervening practice called "treating." The logic is unusual but striking: the aftermath of a terrorist attack is the wrong time to talk about security, the aftermath of a death from lung cancer is the wrong time to talk about smoking and the tobacco industry, and the aftermath of a car crash is the wrong time to talk about seat belts.[3] People talked about the shooting, of course, but much of the conversation was devoted to musings on the treatment of mental illness in universities, the problem of "narcissism," violence in the media and in popular culture, copycat killings, the alienation of immigrant students, and the question of Evil.

3 Some people, however—especially people outside America—were eager to talk about it in another way, and even to embark on a little crusade. The whole world saw that the United States has more gun violence than other countries because we have more guns and are willing to sell them to madmen who want to kill people. Every nation has violent loners, and they tend to have remarkably similar profiles from one country and culture to the next. And every country has known the horror of having a lunatic get his hands on a gun and kill innocent people. But on a recent list of the fourteen worst mass shootings in Western democracies since the nineteen-sixties the United States claimed seven, and, just as important, no other country on the list has had a repeat performance as severe as the first.

4 In Dunblane, Scotland, in 1996, a gunman killed sixteen children and a teacher at their school. Afterward, the British gun laws, already restrictive, were tightened—it's now against the

---

Reading Critically

[3] Do you agree with these statements? Why or why not?

law for any private citizen in the United Kingdom to own the kinds of guns that Cho Seung-Hui used at Virginia Tech—and nothing like Dunblane has occurred there since. In Quebec, after a school shooting took the lives of fourteen women in 1989, the survivors helped begin a gun-control movement that resulted in legislation bringing stronger, though far from sufficient, gun laws to Canada.❹ (There have been a couple of subsequent shooting sprees, but on a smaller scale, and with far fewer dead.) In the Paris suburb of Nanterre, in 2002, a man killed eight people at a municipal meeting. Gun control became a key issue in the Presidential election that year, and there has been no repeat incident.

So there is no American particularity about loners, disenfranchised immigrants, narcissism, alienated youth, complex moral agency, or Evil. There is an American particularity about guns. The arc is apparent. Forty years ago, a man killed fourteen people on a college campus in Austin, Texas; this year, a man killed thirty-two in Blacksburg, Virginia. Not enough was done between those two massacres to make weapons of mass killing harder to obtain.❺ In fact, while campus killings continued—Columbine being the most notorious, the shooting in the one-room Amish schoolhouse among the most recent—weapons have got more lethal, and, in states like Virginia, where the N.R.A. is powerful, no harder to buy. 5

Reducing the number of guns available to crazy people will neither relieve them of their insanity nor stop them from killing. Making it more difficult to buy guns that kill people is, however, a rational way to reduce the number of people killed by guns. Nations with tight gun laws have, on the whole, less gun violence; countries with somewhat restrictive gun laws have some gun violence; countries with essentially no gun laws have a lot of gun violence. (If you work hard, you can find a statistical exception hiding in a corner, but exceptions are just that. Some people who smoke their whole lives don't get lung cancer, while some people who never smoke do; still, the best way not to get lung cancer is not to smoke.) 6

It's true that in renewing the expired ban on assault weapons we can't guarantee that someone won't shoot people with a semi-automatic pistol, and that by controlling semi-automatic 7

Reading Critically

❹ How do you feel about the Canadian gun laws?

❺ Why has the American government failed to address this problem?

pistols we can't reduce the chances of someone killing people with a rifle. But the point of lawmaking is not to act as precisely as possible, in order to punish the latest crime; it is to act as comprehensively as possible, in order to prevent the next one. Semi-automatic Glocks and Walthers, Cho's weapons, are for killing people.❻ They are not made for hunting, and it's not easy to protect yourself with them. (If having a loaded semi-automatic on hand kept you safe, cops would not be shot as often as they are.)

8 Rural America is hunting country, and hunters need rifles and shotguns—with proper licensing, we'll live with the risk. There is no reason that any private citizen in a democracy should own a handgun. At some point, that simple truth will register. Until it does, phones will ring for dead children, and parents will be told not to ask why.❼

UNDERSTANDING DETAILS

1. What was the main difference between the way Americans talked about the shootings and the way people in other countries saw the tragedy?
2. What does Gopnik mean when he says, "there is no American particularity about loners, disenfranchised immigrants, narcissism, alienated youth, complex moral agency, or Evil" (paragraph 5)?
3. What is the point of lawmaking?

ANALYZING MEANING

1. Why were people told it was not the time to question the cause of the shooting? What was the cause, according to Gopnik?
2. Explain Gopnik's objection to Governor Kaine's plea for healing.
3. What is Gopnik's solution to the problem? Where does he state it most clearly?

DISCOVERING RHETORICAL STRATEGIES

1. Where does Gopnik address the opposition in this essay? How does this add to his argument?

Reading Critically

❻ Why do you think so many of these weapons are made?

❼ Explain what makes the last sentence so powerful.

2. Where does the author use an appeal to emotion? Where does he use an appeal to logic? Does he use each appeal equally?
3. Identify and evaluate the effectiveness of the analogies Gopnik uses in his argument.

MAKING CONNECTIONS

1. Like Gopnik, Laura Robinson ("Sports Breeds Real-Life Violence") and Aaron Wherry ("Violently Happy") deal with the problem of violence. Compare their views. Who makes the most persuasive argument?
2. Like June Callwood ("Forgiveness"), Gopnik writes about human actions that cause enormous pain and grief. How do you think he would respond to Callwood's discussion of forgiveness? Who do you think he would say needs to be forgiven?

IDEAS FOR DISCUSSION/WRITING

Preparing to Write

Mass shootings receive a great deal of media coverage and are sometimes followed by copycat shootings. Do you think the media sensationalizes these shootings? Do you find the subsequent panel discussions with experts illuminating? What do you think of the interviews with the distraught friends and families of the victims? Does media coverage of a mass shooting do more harm than good?

Choosing a Topic

1. "There is no reason that any private citizen in a democracy should own a handgun" (paragraph 8). Do you agree with Gopnik? Write an essay supporting your point of view.
2. Some people, including Stephen King ("Why We Crave Horror Movies"), believe that violent entertainment is a form of catharsis. Others believe that it desensitizes people to the horror of bloodshed, making it easier for them to act out violently. Write an essay explaining where you stand in the debate.
3. Gopnik proposes a solution to decrease gun violence in the United States. Write an essay proposing a solution to decrease violent crime in your city or province.

OPPOSING VIEWPOINTS

Hockey Violence

Aaron Wherry studied journalism at the University of Western Ontario, where he was editor-in-chief of the student newspaper, *The Gazette*. He has written extensively on music, film, and sports for the *National Post* and *Maclean's*. His blog for *Maclean's*, The Commons, presents a daily sketch from the House of Commons in Ottawa. His essays and articles have appeared in *Arts & Opinion*, *Maisonneuve*, and *NOW*. He tweets at **http://twitter.com/#!/aaronwherry**.

A former member of the Canadian cycling team and a national rowing champion, Laura Robinson is a coach, sports writer, and journalist. She has written two books for children: *Great Girls: Profiles of Awesome Canadian Athletes* (2004), co-written with her 14-year-old niece, Majia; and *Cyclist BikeList: The Book for Every Rider* (2010). Her books for adults include *She Shoots, She Scores: Canadian Perspectives on Women and Sport* (1997) and *Black Tights: Women, Sport, and Sexuality* (2002). Her book *Crossing the Line: Violence and Sexual Assault in Canada's National Sport* (1998) details abuse in the world of minor league hockey.

Preparing to Read

The following essays deal with the subject of violence in sports, particularly hockey. Both articles discuss Todd Bertuzzi, a player for the Vancouver Canucks, who attacked Colorado Avalanche player Steve Moore in 2004, fracturing three vertebrae in Moore's neck. Bertuzzi was given a year's suspension from the game. He was also charged with criminal assault, pleaded guilty, and was given a conditional discharge. Steve Moore has not played hockey since and has filed a civil lawsuit for damages against Bertuzzi, the Canucks, and their parent company. Before you read, think about popular professional sports in Canada and the United States. Which sports have the most and least body contact? Which sports are the most and least violent? Do you play any of these sports? Have you ever been injured because of another player's aggression? Do you think that professional leagues should do more to limit violence in sports?

AARON WHERRY

Violently Happy: Why the NHL Needs to Make Hockey Safe Again for Those Who Appreciate Bloodshed (2007)

The other night at a local drinking establishment, a co-worker and I got into an argument about Todd Bertuzzi. 1

I was, and still am, convinced that Bertuzzi's nearly paralyzing another player was worth a lifetime suspension from the NHL and not the one-year ban he received.❶ My co-worker believed I was a weak-kneed, liberal wuss. In hindsight, he might have been right about this last part. 2

But if we'd stopped bickering long enough to think about it, we likely would have realized there is one facet of this issue on which we can agree. Namely that hockey violence is awesome. At least as long as nobody gets hurt. 3

Violence in hockey is actually one of the least interesting subjects in sports—largely because, though weak-kneed, liberal wusses periodically make an issue of it, there is almost no real debate on the subject. Those who oppose it are just too vastly outnumbered. The people have spoken.❷ 4

For instance, if you search for "NHL" at YouTube (a league partner) and sort by view count, eleven of the first thirty videos involve some form of violence—from Buffalo's Brian Campbell dealing the unfortunate R.J. Umberger an impressive concussion during last year's playoffs to the infamous clip of goaltender Clint Malarchuk getting his throat slit by a skate and nearly bleeding to death. If you look up "NHL + fight," a total of 1,327 videos come up, including at least one compilation set to death metal. "Hockey + fight" yields 5,216 videos. 5

This is, essentially, where the NHL went wrong. 6

Reading Critically

❶ Which punishment do you believe Bertuzzi should have been given?

❷ What does Wherry mean by "The people have spoken"?

When, in the final years of the last century, those in charge of the league decided its future was in the wilds of Florida, Tennessee and North Carolina, it became accepted wisdom that the American sports fan would not tolerate barbaric violence. That the game would only succeed on its grace and beauty. That it must be, to quote Don Cherry, a "silver ballet." 7

This worked for about six years—from the summer of 1988, when Wayne Gretzky was traded to Los Angeles, to the spring of 1994, when *Sports Illustrated* proclaimed the NHL "hot" in light of a thrilling finale between the Rangers and Canucks. Everything since has been a disaster. Primarily because when the sport, as all sports do from time to time, suffered a competitive downswing, there wasn't nearly enough blood to keep people interested. 8

Now, after a brief post-lockout upswing, interest is bottoming out again in the United States. At this point, *The Mighty Ducks* movie starring Emilio Estevez probably appears more often on US basic cable than the hockey team it once inspired. 9

In the twelve years since 1994, coincidentally, stock car racing and football have come to dominate the professional sports scene in North America—both have succeeded in some of the southern US markets where the NHL has failed. Not coincidentally, these two sports share an inherent zest for bodily harm.❸ 10

No sport destroys the human body quite like football, while no other can claim a greater likelihood of flame-engulfed demise than NASCAR. In fact, neither sport would exist without the explicit possibility that something gruesome might happen at any given moment.❹ 11

But the answer to the NHL's current woes is not unbridled violence. Endorsing that would obviously contradict my stance that Bertuzzi should be tossed from the NHL and forced to work as a bouncer outside some sparsely attended Northern Ontario dive until he dies hopeless, penniless, cold and alone. And—make no mistake—I'm still 100 percent in support of that. 12

In fact, if Bertuzzi was a defensive end or race-car driver, and had done something roughly equivalent, he would have been banned for life. Unofficially run out of the sport at the very least. This is because 13

Reading Critically

❸ Do you think of hockey as being more or less violent than other sports? Explain.

❹ Do you think this could be the reason people watch football and stock car racing? Why or why not?

both the NFL and NASCAR understand that the appeal of violence disappears as soon as there are real-life ramifications. Essentially, it's all fun and games until someone breaks their neck.

You see, for all of the NFL's groin-pulling, ligament-shredding destruction, the league has gone to great lengths to limit the chaos. There are explicit restrictions on making contact with defenceless quarterbacks, receivers and kickers. Defenders are not allowed to trip, clothesline or grab an opponent's face mask. Protecting the star players is paramount. 14

Sure, if you're a 6-foot-5, 265-pound linebacker with low self-esteem, you're still more than welcome to try and deal your opponent a career-limiting brain injury. But the NFL has done everything it can to make sure you don't do this in any way that might get replayed endlessly on the evening news.❺ 15

NASCAR, meanwhile, has provided some of the most horrific scenes in sports history, but rarely do the most spectacular wrecks result in serious injury. Most often, the 25-year-old kid who just flipped his car end-over-end seventeen times and saw his chassis separated into 206 different parts is unlucky to walk away with a bloody nose. Deaths do occur, sure. But considering that the possibility of death looms over every lap of every race, the mortality rate is admirably low. 16

What NASCAR and the NFL have essentially achieved is the possibility of grievous injury without the reality of grievous injury. But the great minds behind the NHL have never quite figured this out. That some of us enjoy seeing another person get punched in the face, even if we'd never want to see anyone get hurt. 17

The line between these two ideas is not nearly as thin as you might believe. It's for the same reason that *America's Funniest Home Videos* is still on television. It also explains most video games, more than 87 percent of movies, approximately 74 percent of prime time television, the collected works of Wile E. Coyote and why more people supported the war in Iraq *before* it actually began. As a general rule, violence is acceptable as long as the effects are fictional, non-existent or at least within what society deems [to be] reasonable parameters.❻ 18

This also explains why Todd Bertuzzi should have been banned for life. An anecdotal study of sports history shows 19

Reading Critically

❺ Do you think this is hypocritical? Why or why not?

❻ Do you agree with this statement? Why or why not?

that violence only becomes abhorrent when either A) someone is attacked from behind, B) someone attacks an innocent fan, C) someone's career is ending prematurely, D) someone is crippled, E) someone is killed or F) a steel chair is involved. In Bertuzzi's case, he was responsible for A, C and nearly D.

20 But the NHL refused to make an example of him. While going out of their way over the last twenty years to cut down on fighting and rough play in the game, league officials couldn't bring themselves to deal out the ultimate punishment for arguably the worst case of reckless violence in league history. This is, obviously, rather hypocritical.

21 Worse, in doing so they ruined the game both for those who love violence and those who oppose it. First, for those who enjoy a good scrap, there is still less fighting. And any fighting that does occur is tainted by the prospect of another Bertuzzi-esque massacre. Without the explicit threat of banishment to Northern Ontario, there is little reason to believe something similar won't happen again. It's a vicious cycle, really.

22 Second, those who were uncomfortable with violence in hockey can still cite Bertuzzi as proof the league hasn't cleaned up its act. Anyone who wasn't watching hockey already because of its barbaric tendencies won't give it a chance in his lifetime after viewing the untimely end of Steve Moore's career.

23 The answer then is to both limit and promote the violence; legislate the fisticuffs to save the fisticuffs. Create an environment safe enough to promote the possibility of physical harm.[7] Ensure your stars are protected and egregious acts are severely deterred and then let the blood flow freely.

24 The NHL must get back to the days when a bench-clearing brawl seemed a constant possibility. When fine, upstanding young men like John Kordic had a place. When a 6–0 game was guaranteed to come apart in the final minutes. When attempting to re-align another person's facial structure with your fist was fine, but a crime if attempted with your stick.

25 A little blood never hurt anybody. And it does not seem too much to ask that we weak-kneed, liberal wusses be able to comfortably enjoy such stuff. Simply put: violence is the answer.

Reading Critically

7. Do you think it is possible to create this environment? Would it regenerate interest in hockey?

LAURA ROBINSON

Sports Breeds Real-Life Violence (2007)

The needless death last week of 15-year-old Manny Castillo, a Grade 10 junior rugby player at Lorne Park Secondary School in Mississauga, is just one more example of a long list of near fatal and fatal injuries boys and young men have sustained while acting out their part in the passion play that is aggressive male sport. Castillo was killed during the last seconds of the game by an opposing player who, police say, picked him up and, away from the playing area, drilled him into the ground. 1

This senseless act of violence is eerily reminiscent of Todd Bertuzzi's after-the-fact-attack on Steve Moore in 2005 that broke Moore's neck and has prevented him from playing or even having the kind of life a healthy man in his twenties, hockey player or not, should expect. 2

In Tuesday night's play-off game between Ottawa and Anaheim, the Ducks' Rob Niedermayer received a five minute major and a game misconduct for driving Tomas Holmstrom's face into the glass. Teammate Chris Pronger helped him. Holmstrom lay crumpled on the ice for several minutes and received 13 stitches. 3

Professional hockey and professional sport in general sell ideals of masculinity to a country that, for all its progressive rhetoric about women and gender, still worships a very traditional maleness.❶ The public broadcaster—the CBC—would not pay Don Cherry to be a commentator if this model of masculinity wasn't so desired, and wasn't played out by boys who are at a loss when searching for anyone remotely balanced and non-violent in the mediated culture boys tune into and from which they model their behaviour. 4

Media images of violent and aggressive male bodies abound.❷ If that male body represents something we deem as good, we allow it a sentimentality and margin of error seen in few other venues. 5

Reading Critically

❶ How do you think violence is associated with "traditional maleness"?

❷ Where do we see these "images of violent and aggressive male bodies" in the media?

Witness the placing of Bertuzzi on the 2006 Canadian Olympic hockey team, and the belief that violence on the ice or the playing field really isn't violence, but "part of the game." Also witness the almost saint-like status given by the sports media to professional male athletes who have killed or maimed members of their family, friends, strangers, teammates or themselves simply by being behind the steering-wheel in a car accident.❸ 6

This steady stream of sporting triumphs and maudlin tragedies is what keeps the wheels of the sports media spinning. Not surprisingly then, there was no national coverage earlier this month of Dr. Graham Pollett, medical officer and CEO for Middlesex-London in Ontario, and his report on the relationship between the eye-for-an-eye violence that occurs within NHL, CHL, and younger leagues, and male violence against women and children. Despite how big and strong adolescent athletes may look, it is crucial to remember that they are still children. 7

"Hockey violence negatively impacts the game at all levels. For these reasons alone, it should be expected that Hockey Canada would take whatever actions are necessary to minimize violence," states the report entitled Violence in Amateur Hockey. When violence is "coupled with hockey's role as a model for boys and men for dealing with emotionally charged situations, the need for change is that much more apparent" the report continues. 8

Canadians are terribly reticent about the frequency with which women and children face violence, but when doing so calls into question a tradition that is so deeply ingrained in our culture that hockey becomes our international calling card, Dr. Pollett runs the risk of being tarred as a traitor.❹ (Interestingly, in international tournaments fighting is disallowed and we still manage—as the world championships clearly showed—to play great hockey). 9

Dr. Pollett is adamant and wonders why officials did not make the correlation his report makes decades ago. With the death of Manny Castillo, Dr. Pollett's warning is made so very real: "This form of vigilante justice is accepted even by the referees who only intercede after one player has clearly beaten the other or both players fall to the ice" he writes. "A child who watches and/or plays hockey could be left with the perception that acts of violence are acceptable. This sends the wrong message to all children at this impressionable age." 10

Reading Critically

❸ Can you think of some examples of these car accidents?

❹ What does the phrase "being tarred as a traitor" mean?

Anyone who argues that Canadian boys don't learn, at least partly, how to be boys by watching hockey is in denial. Dr. Pollett is arguing that boys take those lessons from hockey and replay them in their everyday lives. 11

UNDERSTANDING DETAILS

1. What do Robinson and Wherry think about the consequences meted out to Todd Bertuzzi for his attack on Steve Moore?
2. What happens to hockey fans when violence in the game is restricted, according to Wherry? What is Robinson's view of hockey that is played without violence?
3. What does Wherry think the NHL should do about the problem of violence in hockey? What solution is given in Robinson's article?

ANALYZING MEANING

1. Why is Wherry accepting of violence in sports? Why is Robinson alarmed by it?
2. Both authors discuss the depiction of violence in the media. What causes do they attribute to the popularity of violent images?
3. To what extent do Robinson and Wherry agree on the negative consequences of real-life violence? Where do they disagree?

DISCOVERING RHETORICAL STRATEGIES

1. Compare the evidence each author presents. Which essay had the most persuasive evidence?
2. Compare the tone of each essay. How does the tone contribute to each author's argument?
3. Analyze the balance of appeals by each author. Who uses more of a logical appeal? Who uses more of an emotional appeal? Who relies most on the appeal to ethics?

MAKING CONNECTIONS

1. Compare the claims about violence put forward by Wherry, Robinson, and Barbara Ehrenreich ("The Ecstasy of War"). Do their ideas overlap anywhere?
2. Compare how hockey is depicted by Wherry, Robinson, and Michael McKinley ("Opera Night in Canada"). Which depiction do you feel is most accurate?

IDEAS FOR DISCUSSION/WRITING

Preparing to Write

Write freely about sports. Do you enjoy watching sports, such as hockey and football? Or do you prefer noncontact sports, like basketball and soccer? If you are a hockey fan, do you prefer European-style hockey, with its limited body contact, or NHL hockey? What role, if any, do you think your gender plays in these preferences?

Choosing a Topic

1. Do you agree with Wherry that "a little blood never hurt anybody" (paragraph 25) or with Robinson, who says that boys learn to be boys by watching hockey (paragraph 11) and other violent sports? Write an essay defending your opinion.
2. Robinson argues against the model of masculinity promoted by hockey and other sports. Write an essay defining another model of masculinity or femininity that is promoted by some aspect of popular culture.
3. The popularity of extreme sports has grown in recent years. What do you think accounts for the rise in popularity of high-risk activities?

CHAPTER 10

DOCUMENTED ESSAYS

Reading and Writing from Sources

We use sources every day in both informal and formal situations. We explain the source of a phone message, for example, or we refer to an instructor's comments in class. We use someone else's opinion in an essay, or we quote an expert to prove a point. We cite sources both in speaking and in writing through summary, paraphrase, and direct quotation. Most of your instructors will ask you to write papers using sources so that they can see how well you understand the course material. Using sources in academic papers requires you to understand what you have read and to integrate it with your own opinions and observations—a process that requires a high level of skill in thinking, reading, and writing.

Defining *Documented Essays*

Documented essays draw on the thinking, reading, and writing abilities you have built up over the course of your academic career, and they often require you to put all the rhetorical modes to work at their most analytical level. Documented essays demonstrate the process of analytical thinking at its best in different disciplines.

In the academic world, documented essays are also called *research papers*, *library papers*, and *term papers*. Documented essays are generally written for one of three reasons: (1) to **report**, (2) to **interpret**, or (3) to **analyze**.

The most uncomplicated type of documented essay **reports** information, as in a survey of problems that children have in preschool. The second type of documented essay both presents and **interprets** its findings. It examines a number of different views on a specific issue and weighs these views as it draws its own conclusions. A topic that falls into this category would be whether children who have attended preschool are more sociable than those who have not. After considering evidence on both sides, the writer would draw his or her own conclusions on this topic. A documented essay that **analyzes** a subject presents a hypothesis, tests the hypothesis, and analyzes or evaluates its conclusions. This type of essay calls for the most advanced form of critical thinking. It might look, for example, at the reasons preschool children are more or less socially adaptable than nonpreschool children. At its most proficient, this type of writing requires a sophisticated degree of evaluation that forces you to judge your reading, evaluate your sources, and ultimately scrutinize your own reasoning ability as the essay takes shape.

Each of these types of documented essays calls for a higher level of thinking, and each evolves from the previous category. In other words, interpreting requires some reporting, and analyzing draws on both reporting and interpreting.

In the following paragraph, a student reports, interprets, analyzes, and uses sources to document the problem of solid waste in the United States. Notice how the student writer draws her readers into the essay with a commonly used phrase about America and then questions the validity of its meaning. The student's opinions give shape to the paragraph, while her use of sources helps identify the problem and support her contentions.

> "America the Beautiful" is a phrase used to describe the many wonders of nature found throughout our country. America's natural beauty will fade, however, if solutions to our solid waste problems are not discovered soon. America is a rich nation socially, economically, and politically. But these very elements may be the cause of Americans' wastefulness. Americans now generate approximately 160 million tons of solid waste a year—3 1/2 pounds per person per day. We live in a consumer society where *convenience, ready-to-use,* and *throwaway* are words that spark the consumer's attention (Cook 60). However, many of the products associated with these words create a large part of our problem with solid waste (Grossman 39). We are running out of space for our garbage. The people of America are beginning to produce responses to this problem. Are we too late? A joint effort between individuals,

businesses, government industries, and local, state, and federal governments is necessary to establish policies and procedures to combat this waste war. The problem requires not one solution, but a combination of solutions involving technologies and people working together to provide a safe and healthy environment for themselves and future generations.

Documented Essay Reference Chart

A documented essay is really just an essay with supporting material that comes from outside sources. The following chart compares a standard essay and a research paper.

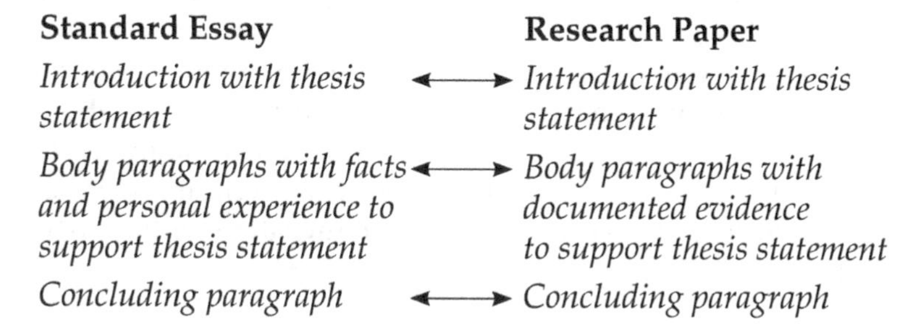

Standard Essay		**Research Paper**
Introduction with thesis statement	⟷	*Introduction with thesis statement*
Body paragraphs with facts and personal experience to support thesis statement	⟷	*Body paragraphs with documented evidence to support thesis statement*
Concluding paragraph	⟷	*Concluding paragraph*

Keep this outline in mind as you read how to construct a good documented essay. Laying out some clear guidelines is the best place to start.

Reading Documented Essays

You should read a documented essay in much the same way that you read any essay. In all cases, you should prepare to read and then reread several times—each time with a slightly different purpose. The main difference is that you are paying attention to not only what the writer concludes but also how the writer's sources support that conclusion

Preparing to Read. First, take a few minutes to look at the preliminary material for the selection: What can you learn from scanning Barbara Ehrenreich's essay ("The Ecstasy of War") or from reading the synopsis in the Rhetorical Contents? What questions do you have about facilitated communication before you read Lawrence Norton's essay ("Facilitated Communication & the Power of Belief")?

Also, you should learn as much as you can from the authors' biographies: What is Norton's interest in the use of facilitated communication with autistic children? What biographical details prepare us for his approach to this topic? Who was the original audience for Ehrenreich's essay?

Another important part of preparing to read a documented essay is surveying the sources cited. Turn to the end of the essay and look at the sources. What publications does Norton draw from? Are these books and magazines well respected? Do you recognize any of the authorities that Ehrenreich cites?

Last, before you read these essays, try to generate some ideas on the topics so that you can participate as fully as possible in your reading. The Preparing to Read questions will get you ready for this task. Then, try to speculate further on the topic of the essay: What is the connection for Ehrenreich between war and ecstasy? What does this relationship tell us about human nature in general? What do you want to know from Norton about the efficacy of facilitated communication? What are the effects of using facilitated communication with autistic children?

Reading. As you react to the material in this chapter, you should respond to both the research and the writing. Record your responses as you read the essay for the first time: What are your reactions to the information you are reading? Are the sources appropriate? How well do they support the author's main points? Use the preliminary material before each essay to help you create a framework for your responses to it: What motivated Norton to publish his review of the *Time* magazine article on facilitated communication? Do you find it convincing?

Questions at the bottom of the pages of each essay will guide you to higher-level forms of critical thinking in preparation for your writing assignments at the end of each selection. As in previous chapters, writing out your responses to these questions is the best strategy for shaping your own thoughts about these issues.

Your main job at this stage is to determine the author's primary assertion (thesis statement), note the sources the author cites to support this thesis, and begin to ask yourself questions about the essay so that you can respond critically to your reading. In addition, take a look at the questions after the selection to make certain you comprehend the major ideas of the essay.

Rereading. As you reread these documented essays, take some time to become aware of the difference between fact and opinion, to weigh and evaluate the evidence brought to bear on the arguments, to consider the sources the writer uses, to judge the interpretation of the facts cited, to determine what the writer has omitted, and to confirm your own views on the issues at hand. During this stage, you will also need to critique your sources to determine whether or not their information is credible. All these skills demand the use of critical-thinking strategies at their most sophisticated level.

You need to approach this type of argument with an inquiring mind, asking questions and looking for answers as you read the essay. Be especially conscious of the appeals (logical, emotional, and ethical) at work in the essay (see Chapter 9), and take note of other rhetorical strategies that support each author's main argument.

Also, be aware of your own thought processes as you sort fact from opinion. Know where you stand personally in relation to each side of the issues here.

Following is a list of guidelines that summarize the reading process for documented essays.

READING DOCUMENTED ESSAYS IN REVIEW

Reading Documented Essays

Preparing to Read

✓ What assumptions can I make from the essay's title?
✓ Can I guess what the general mood of the essay is?
✓ What are the essay's purpose and audience?
✓ What does the synopsis tell me about the essay?
✓ What can I learn from the author's biography?

Reading

✓ What is the author's main assertion or thesis?
✓ What are my personal associations with the essay?
✓ What sources does the author cite to support the thesis?
✓ What questions do I have about this topic?

Rereading

✓ How does the author use facts and opinions in the essay?
✓ Are the sources the writer cites valid and reliable?
✓ Does the author interpret facts accurately?
✓ What do I agree with in the essay?
✓ What do I disagree with in the essay?
✓ What are my own conclusions on this topic?

BARBARA EHRENREICH

The Ecstasy of War (1997)

Barbara Ehrenreich (1941–) is a respected author, lecturer, and social commentator on a wide range of topics. After earning a B.A. from Reed College in chemistry and physics and a Ph.D. from Rockefeller University in cell biology, she turned almost immediately to freelance writing, producing a succession of books and pamphlets on a dazzling array of subjects, including student uprisings, health care in America, poverty, welfare, economic justice for women, and the sexual politics of disease. Her books include *Blood Rites: Origins and History of the Passions of War* (1998), *Nickel and Dimed: On (Not) Getting By in America* (2001), *Bait and Switch: The (Futile) Pursuit of the American Dream* (2005), *Dancing in the Streets: A History of Collective Joy* (2007), and *This Land Is* Their *Land: Reports from a Divided Nation* (2009). Her most recent book, *Bright-Sided: How Positive Thinking Is Undermining America*, was published in 2009. Ehrenreich is also well known as a frequent guest on television and radio programs, including The *Today Show*, *Good Morning America*, and *Canada AM*. Her many articles, columns, and reviews have appeared in *The New York Times Magazine*, *Esquire*, *The Atlantic Monthly*, *The New Republic*, *Vogue*, *Harper's*, *The Wall Street Journal*, and *Time* magazine. Ehrenreich lives in Syosset, New York.

Preparing to Read

Taken from *Blood Rites: Origins and History of the Passions of War* (1998), the following essay analyzes the psychology of war. Its citations and bibliography illustrate proper MLA (Modern Language Association) documentation form. As you prepare to read this article, take a few minutes to think about aggression in society today: Do you think aggression plays a significant role in North American society? In other societies? What do you think is the origin of aggression? In your opinion, what role does aggression play in war? In everyday life? How do you react to aggressive behaviour? Do you make any connection between real war and war as a theme in entertainment? Search the Internet for descriptions of current video games with a war theme. You might visit websites for Electronic Arts, Activision, or Take-Two Interactive Software to peruse their current game lists. Consider the techniques and intents of these games while reading Ehrenreich's essay.

"*So elemental is the human need to endow the shedding of blood with some great and even sublime significance that it renders the intellect almost entirely helpless*" (Van Creveld 166). 1

Different wars have led to different theories of why men fight them. The Napoleonic Wars, which bore along with them the rationalist spirit of the French Revolution, inspired the Prussian officer Carl von Clausewitz to propose that war itself is an entirely rational undertaking, unsullied by human emotion. War, in his famous aphorism, is merely a "continuation of policy . . . by other means," with policy itself supposedly resulting from the same kind of clear-headed deliberation one might apply to a game of chess. Nation-states were the leading actors on the stage of history, and war was simply one of the many ways they advanced their interests against those of other nation-states. If you could accept the existence of this new superperson, the nation, a battle was no more disturbing and irrational than, say, a difficult trade negotiation—except perhaps to those who lay dying on the battlefield. 2

World War I, coming a century after Napoleon's sweep through Europe and northern Africa, led to an opposite assessment of the human impulse of war. World War I was hard to construe as in any way "rational," especially to that generation of European intellectuals, including Sigmund Freud, who survived to ponder the unprecedented harvest of dead bodies.❶ History textbooks tell us that the "Great War" grew out of the conflict between "competing imperialist states," but this Clausewitzian interpretation has little to do with the actual series of accidents, blunders, and miscommunications that impelled the nations of Europe to war in the summer of 1914.[A] At first swept up in the excitement of the war, unable for weeks to work or think of anything else, Freud was eventually led to conclude that there is some dark flaw in the human psyche, a perverse desire to destroy, countering Eros and the will to live (Stromberg 82).❷ 3

So these are, in crude summary, the theories of war which modern wars have left us with: That war is a means, however risky, by which men seek to advance their collective interests and improve their lives. Or, alternatively, that war stems from subrational drives not unlike those that lead individuals to commit violent crimes.❸ In our own time, most people seem to hold both views at once, avowing that war is a gainful enterprise, intended 4

Reading Critically

❶ How does the phrase "the unprecedented harvest of dead bodies" make you feel? Explain.

❷ What do you think of Freud's conclusion about the human psyche?

❸ What do you think of these "theories of war"?

to meet the material needs of the groups engaged in it, and, at the same time, that it fulfills deep and "irrational" psychological needs. There is no question about the first part of this proposition—that wars are designed, at least ostensibly, to secure necessaries like land or oil or "geopolitical advantage." The mystery lies in the peculiar psychological grip war exerts on us.

5 In the 1960s and '70s, the debate on the psychology of war centered on the notion of an "aggressive instinct," peculiar to all humans or only to human males. This is not the place to summarize that debate, with its endless examples of animal behavior and clashes over their applicability to human affairs. Here I would simply point out that, whether or not there is an aggressive instinct, there are reasons to reject it as the major wellspring of war.

6 Although it is true that aggressive impulses, up to and including murderous rage, can easily take over in the heat of actual battle, even this statement must be qualified to take account of different weaponry and modes of fighting. Hand-to-hand combat may indeed call forth and even require the emotions of rage and aggression, if only to mobilize the body for bursts of muscular activity. In the case of action-at-a-distance weapons, however, like guns and bows and arrows, emotionality of any sort can be a distinct disadvantage. Coolness, and the ability to keep aiming and firing steadfastly in the face of enemy fire, prevails. Hence, according to the distinguished American military historian Robert L. O'Connell, the change in the ideal warrior personality wrought by the advent of guns in the fifteenth and sixteenth centuries, from "ferocious aggressiveness" to "passive disdain" (119). So there is no personality type—"hot-tempered," "macho," or whatever—consistently and universally associated with warfare.❹

7 Furthermore, fighting itself is only one component of the enterprise we know as war. Wars are not barroom brawls writ large, or domestic violence that has been somehow extended to strangers. In war, fighting takes place within battles—along with much anxious waiting, of course—but wars do not begin with battles and are often not decided by them either. Most of war consists of preparation for battle—training, the organization of supplies, marching and other forms of transport—activities which are hard to account for by innate promptings of any kind.

Reading Critically

❹ Do you agree with Ehrenreich's conclusion concerning personality type? Why or why not?

There is no plausible instinct, for example, that impels a man to leave his home, cut his hair short, and drill for hours in tight formation. As anthropologists Clifton B. Kroeber and Bernard L. Fontana point out, "It is a large step from what may be biologically innate leanings toward individual aggression to ritualized, socially sanctioned, institutionalized group warfare" (166).

8 War, in other words, is too complex and collective an activity to be accounted for by a single warlike instinct lurking within the individual psyche. Instinct may, or may not, inspire a man to bayonet the first enemy he encounters in battle. But instinct does not mobilize supply lines, manufacture rifles, issue uniforms, or move an army of thousands from point A on the map to B. These are "complicated, orchestrated, highly organized" activities, as social theorist Robin Fox writes, undertaken not by individuals but by entities on the scale of nations and dynasties (15). "The hypothesis of a killer instinct," according to a commentator summarizing a recent conference on the anthropology of war, is "not so much wrong as irrelevant" (McCauley 2).

9 In fact, throughout history, individual men have gone to near-suicidal lengths to avoid participating in wars—a fact that proponents of a warlike instinct tend to slight. Men have fled their homelands, served lengthy prison terms, hacked off limbs, shot off feet or index fingers, feigned illness or insanity, or, if they could afford to, paid surrogates to fight in their stead.❺ "Some draw their teeth, some blind themselves, and others maim themselves, on their way to us" (Mitchell 42), the governor of Egypt complained of his peasant recruits in the early nineteenth century. So unreliable was the rank and file of the eighteenth-century Prussian army that military manuals forbade camping near a woods or forest: The troops would simply melt away into the trees (Delbrück 303).

10 Proponents of a warlike instinct must also reckon with the fact that even when men have been assembled, willingly or unwillingly, for the purpose of war, fighting is not something that seems to come "naturally" to them. In fact, surprisingly, even in the thick of battle, few men can bring themselves to shoot directly at individual enemies.[B] The difference between an ordinary man or boy and a reliable killer, as any drill sergeant could

---

Reading Critically

❺ How do you feel about fighting in a war? Would you consider any of these options to avoid it?

attest, is profound. A transformation is required: The man or boy leaves his former self behind and becomes something entirely different, perhaps even taking a new name. In small-scale, traditional societies, the change was usually accomplished through ritual drumming, dancing, fasting, and sexual abstinence—all of which serve to lift a man out of his mundane existence and into a new, warriorlike mode of being, denoted by special body paint, masks, and headdresses.

11 As if to emphasize the discontinuity between the warrior and the ordinary human being, many cultures require the would-be fighting man to leave his human-ness behind and assume a new form as an animal.[C] The young Scandinavian had to become a bear before he could become an elite warrior, going "berserk" (the word means, "dressed in a bear hide"), biting and chasing people. The Irish hero Cuchulain transformed himself into a monster in preparation for battle: "He became horrible, many-shaped, strange and unrecognizable," with one eye sucked into his skull and the other popping out of the side of the face (Davidson 84). Apparently this transformation was a familiar and meaningful one, because similarly distorted faces turn up frequently in Celtic art.

12 Often the transformation is helped along with drugs or social pressure of various kinds.[6] Tahitian warriors were browbeaten into fighting by functionaries called Rauti, or "exhorters," who ran around the battlefield urging their comrades to mimic "the devouring wild dog" (Keeley 146). The ancient Greek hoplites drank enough wine, apparently, to be quite tipsy when they went into battle (Hanson 126); Aztecs drank pulque;[7] Chinese troops at the time of Sun Tzu got into the mood by drinking wine and watching "gyrating sword dancers" perform (Griffith in Sun Tzu 37). Almost any drug or intoxicant has served, in one setting or another, to facilitate the transformation of man into warrior. Yanomamo Indians of the Amazon ingest a hallucinogen before battle; the ancient Scythians smoked hemp, while a neighboring tribe drank something called "hauma," which is believed to have induced a frenzy of aggression (Rolle 94–95). So if there is a destructive instinct that impels man to war, it is a weak one, and often requires a great deal of help.

Reading Critically

6. What could be the purpose of using drugs to help the transformation into a warrior?
7. What is "pulque"?

In seventeenth-century Europe, the transformation of man into soldier took on a new form, more concerted and disciplined, and far less pleasant, than wine. New recruits and even seasoned veterans were endlessly drilled, hour after hour, until each man began to feel himself part of a single, giant fighting machine. The drill was only partially inspired by the technology of firearms. It's easy enough to teach a man to shoot a gun; the problem is to make him willing to get into situations where guns are being shot and to remain there long enough to do some shooting of his own. So modern military training aims at a transformation parallel to that achieved by "primitives" with war drums and paint: In the fanatical routines of boot camp, a man leaves behind his former identity and is reborn as a creature of the military—an automaton[8] and also, ideally, a willing killer of other men. 13

This is not to suggest that killing is foreign to human nature or, more narrowly, to the male personality. Men (and women) have again and again proved themselves capable of killing impulsively and with gusto. But there is a huge difference between a war and an ordinary fight. War not only departs from the normal; it inverts all that is moral and right: In war one should kill, should steal, should burn cities and farms, should perhaps even rape matrons and little girls. Whether or not such activities are "natural" or at some level instinctual, most men undertake them only by entering what appears to be an "altered state"—induced by drugs or lengthy drilling, and denoted by face paint or khakis. 14

The point of such transformative rituals is not only to put men "in the mood." Returning warriors may go through equally challenging rituals before they can celebrate victory or reenter the community—covering their heads in apparent shame, for example; vomiting repeatedly; abstaining from sex (Keeley 144). Among the Maori, returning warriors could not participate in the victory celebration until they had gone through a whaka-hoa ritual, designed to make them "common" again: The hearts of slain enemies were roasted, after which offerings were made to the war god Tu, and the rest was eaten by priests, who shouted spells to remove "the blood curse" and enable warriors to re-enter their ordinary lives (Sagan 18). Among the Taulipang Indians 15

Reading Critically

[8] What is an "automaton"? Why does the military need its soldiers to be automatons?

of South America, victorious warriors "sat on ants, flogged one another with whips, and passed a cord covered with poisonous ants, through their mouth and nose" (Métraux 397). Such painful and shocking postwar rites impress on the warrior that war is much more than a "continuation of policy . . . by other means." In war men enter an alternative realm of human experience, as far removed from daily life as those things which we call "sacred."

Notes

A. See, for example, Stoessinger, *Why Nations Go to War*, 14–20.

B. See Grossman, *On Killing*.

C. In the mythologies of the Indo-European tradition, Dumézil relates, thanks "either to a gift of metamorphosis, or to a monstrous heredity, the eminent warrior possesses a veritable animal nature" (140).

Works Cited

Davidson, Hilda Ellis. *Myths and Symbols in Pagan Europe: Early Scandinavian and Celtic Religions*. Syracuse, NY: Syracuse UP, 1988.

Delbrück, Hans. *The Dawn of Modern Warfare*. Vol. 4 of History of the Art of War. Lincoln: U of Nebraska P, 1985.

Dumézil, Georges. *Destiny of the Warrior*. Chicago: U of Chicago P, 1969.

Fox, Robin. "Fatal Attraction: War and Human Nature." *The National Interest* (Winter 1992/93): 11–20.

Grossman, Lt. Col. Dave. *On Killing: The Psychological Cost of Learning to Kill in War and Society*. Boston: Little, Brown, 1995.

Hanson, Victor Davis. *The Western Way of War: Infantry Battle in Classical Greece*. New York: Knopf, 1989.

Keeley, Lawrence H. *War Before Civilization: The Myth of the Peaceful Savage*. New York: Oxford UP, 1996.

Kroeber, Clifton B., and Bernard L. Fontana. *Massacre on the Gila: An Account of the Last Major Battle Between American Indians, with Reflections on the Origin of War*. Tucson: U of Arizona P, 1986.

McCauley, Clark. "Conference Overview." *The Anthropology of War*. Ed. Jonathan Haas. Cambridge: Cambridge UP, 1990, 1–25.

Métraux, Alfred. "Warfare, Cannibalism, and Human Trophies." *Handbook of South American Indians*, vol. 5. Ed. Julian H. Steward. New York: Cooper Square Publishers, 1963, 383–409.

Mitchell, Timothy. *Colonizing Egypt*. Berkeley: U of California P, 1991.

O'Connell, Robert L. *Of Arms and Men: A History of War, Weapons, and Aggression*. New York: Oxford UP, 1989.

Rolle, Renate. *The World of the Scythians*. Berkeley: U of California P, 1989.

Sagan, Eli. *Cannibalism: Human Aggression and Cultural Form*. New York: Harper and Row, 1974.

Stoessinger, John G. *Why Nations Go to War*. New York: St. Martin's Press, 1993.

Stromberg, Roland. *Redemption by War: The Intellectuals and 1914*. Lawrence: U of Kansas P, 1982.

Sun Tzu. *The Art of War*. Trans. Samuel B. Griffith. London: Oxford UP, 1971.

Van Creveld, Martin. *The Transformation of War*. New York: Free Press, 1991.

UNDERSTANDING DETAILS

1. What do you think Ehrenreich's main purpose is in this essay?
2. What does Ehrenreich say are the various components of what we call "war"?
3. In what ways do some cultures ritualize the transformation from regular citizen to warrior? Give three examples.

ANALYZING MEANING

1. Do you believe war can ever be emotionless and rational, like "a difficult trade negotiation" (paragraph 2)?
2. What do Clifton B. Kroeber and Bernard L. Fontana mean when they say, "It is a large step from what may be biologically innate leanings toward individual aggression to ritualized, socially sanctioned, institutionalized group warfare" (paragraph 7)?
3. Are you convinced by this essay that "In war men enter an alternative realm of human experience, as far removed from daily life as those things which we call 'sacred'" (paragraph 15)?

DISCOVERING RHETORICAL STRATEGIES

1. Who do you think is Ehrenreich's main audience? How did you come to this conclusion?
2. The author begins her discussion of war with different "theories of why men fight" wars (paragraph 2). Is this an effective beginning for what Ehrenreich is trying to accomplish? Explain your answer.
3. What tone does the author establish by frequently citing statistics and referring to other sources in her essay?

MAKING CONNECTIONS

1. Compare and contrast Ehrenreich's insights on the psychology of war with Stephen King's theories on "Why We Crave Horror Movies." How do their ideas support one another? How do they contradict each other?

2. Compare Ehrenreich's use of examples with those of Lawrence Norton ("Facilitated Communication & the Power of Belief: How *Time* Magazine Got It Wrong")
3. In a conversation between Ehrenreich and Steven Heighton ("Elegy in Stone") about the glorification of war in American society, on what points would they agree and disagree? Give examples.

IDEAS FOR DISCUSSION/WRITING

Preparing to Write

Write freely about aggression in general: Why do people fight? Why do countries go to war? What are some ways in which people take out their aggression? Have you ever noticed people fighting just for the sake of fighting? When is aggression acceptable? When is it unacceptable?

Choosing a Topic

1. Ehrenreich claims that no personality type has a "single warlike instinct" (paragraph 8). How do her theories apply to video game users? Revisit the video game websites you found before reading Ehrenreich's essay. Then develop a documented essay in which you test Ehrenreich's theories by applying them to video game users. Be sure to use credible sources to support your claims.
2. Ehrenreich claims that "even when men have been assembled, willingly or unwillingly, for the purpose of war, fighting is not something that seems to come 'naturally' to them" (paragraph 10). Do you agree or disagree with this statement? Explain your reaction in a clearly reasoned argumentative essay. Cite Ehrenreich's selection whenever necessary.
3. In the last paragraph of her essay, Ehrenreich suggests that warriors often have to go through rituals to return to their civilizations. Use Ehrenreich's article as one of your sources; then read further on such transformations. Next, write a clear, well-documented argument expressing your opinion on a specific transformation. Organize your paper clearly and present your suggestions logically, using proper documentation (citations and bibliography) to support your position.

LAWRENCE NORTON

Facilitated Communication & the Power of Belief: How *Time* Magazine Got It Wrong (2006)

Dr. Lawrence Norton lives and works in Anchorage, Alaska, where he is a school neuropsychologist. In this role he provides school-related evaluations for children with cognitive and neurological issues, such as dyslexia, ADHD, and traumatic brain injury. Norton also serves as consultant to the regional Fetal Alcohol Spectrum Disorder Diagnostic Clinic and is an adjunct professor of psychology at the University of Alaska. This essay originally appeared in *eSkeptic*, the online newsletter of the Skeptics Society, in response to a 1996 article in *Time* magazine that described the dramatic effects realized by using facilitated communication with children with autism.

Preparing to Read

Before reading this article, think about credibility and proof. When do you believe the things you read or hear? When are you sceptical? How do you respond when you doubt what you read or hear? What sources do you generally consider reliable? What sources do you generally not trust? What gives a source credibility? How are things proven? When you are doing research, what steps do you take to prove your points or ideas?

The cover article of *Time* magazine dated May 15, 2006 was entitled, "New Insights Into the Hidden World of Autism." The article began with the story of a 13-year old profoundly autistic girl whose language was "limited to snatches of songs, echoed dialogue, and unintelligible utterances" and who was "most likely retarded."❶ However, a few days before her 13th birthday, Hannah was introduced to a communication technique known as 1

Reading Critically

❶ What do you know about autism? How common is it? Have you ever known anyone with autism?

facilitated communication.❷ This is a technique whereby a "facilitator" helps stabilize an autistic person's hand and arm so that they are able to type a message on a keyboard. On that day, the girl was asked by the facilitator, "Is there anything you'd like to say, Hannah?" Hannah, with the assistance of the facilitator, then typed out, "I love Mom." A year and a half later, Hannah is working her way through high school biology, algebra, and ancient history.[A]

2 If you are sceptical of this claim, you have good reason to be. Facilitated communication is a technique originally developed in Australia to assist individuals with physical limitations such as cerebral palsy to communicate via a keyboard. The technique was introduced in the United States in 1990 by Dr. Douglas Bicklen, a professor of special education at Syracuse University. While facilitated communication was never intended for use with autistic children, Bicklen believed it had the potential to provide a means of expressive communication for uncommunicative autistic individuals. Bicklen believed that while autistic children understood language, they were unable to express their thoughts due to a type of developmental apraxia that impaired their ability to control voluntary movement. It was their inability to express themselves, according to Biklen, which often masked the autistic individuals' true cognitive and linguistic abilities.[B]

3 Like 13-year old Hannah, parents of autistic children in the early 1990s found that when assisted by a facilitator their autistic children demonstrated extraordinary abilities. Five and six year old autistic children were writing complete sentences. Others wrote poems and short stories, while autistic adolescents successfully completed high school and college courses despite never having been taught to read or write or having demonstrated such abilities.[C]

4 Public schools around the country spent millions of dollars to hire and train facilitators. Parents made plans to have their child's facilitator accompany them to college. Parents, teachers and therapists did not question the validity of the facilitated communications. They believed facilitated communication was a breakthrough technique that completely redefined autism. The messages their autistic children typed, such as Hannah's "I love mom," was all the validation many parents would ever need.

Reading Critically

❷ Have you heard about this technique before?

However, some began to doubt the validity of the facilitated communications and began to ask difficult questions. Why would a child be able to successfully communicate with the assistance of a facilitator at school, but not at home with his or her own parents? How could a child demonstrate extraordinary literacy, writing grammatically correct sentences, when they had never been taught to read or write? How could a child type a message on a keyboard while they were staring at the ceiling? And most importantly, were the facilitated communications real? Were the autistic children authoring these writings, or were the facilitators?❸ 5

The question of whether the facilitated communications were real took on increased urgency when accusations of child sexual abuse began to surface around the country. As a result of these accusations, autistic children were removed from their homes by child welfare agencies while their parents were charged with child sexual abuse. 6

One of the first investigations of the efficacy of facilitated communication resulted from one of these sex abuse accusations. A profoundly autistic adolescent girl had accused her parents and grandparents of sexual abuse. The girl's facilitated communication skills were subsequently evaluated by Dr. Howard Shane, a speech pathologist and expert in augmentative communication. He first showed the adolescent girl and her facilitator a picture or object. The typed messages that followed correctly identified the picture or object both had seen. However, when the facilitator and child were shown a different picture or object, the message typed out on the keyboard was consistently what the facilitator had seen. It soon became apparent that it had not been the adolescent girl who had authored the accusations, but rather the facilitator.❹ 7

Individual case studies were followed by larger controlled studies that sought to determine the validity of facilitated communication. These studies typically included autistic as well as moderately and severely mentally retarded individuals—precisely those individuals whom Bicklen and facilitated communication advocates claimed needed facilitated communication in order to express their hidden thoughts. 8

Reading Critically

❸ Who do you think would have been the first to ask these questions—the parents, teachers, or therapists?

❹ What motive could a facilitator have for making these accusations? Why do you think this was a widespread phenomenon rather than a few isolated incidents?

In a well-controlled 1996 study, for example, the efficacy of facilitated communication was assessed in 12 individuals ranging in age from 7–36. Six of the participants had a diagnosis of autism, while six had severe to profound cognitive impairments. All subjects had demonstrated unexpected literacy once they began using facilitated communication. The facilitators in this study were those who had demonstrated the most success with each subject. Four of the facilitators were the subject's mothers, two were special education teachers, two were resident assistants, and one a teacher's aide. The amount of time each facilitator had been facilitating with each subject ranged from six months to two years. 9

The subjects were assessed in a familiar environment. The subjects or their facilitator were allowed to stop at any point if they felt uncomfortable. The subjects were presented with either an auditory or visual stimulus, and were then asked to identify that same stimulus. When the facilitators were unable to see or hear what the subjects saw or heard, the autistic subjects' unexpected literacy via facilitated communication was no longer evident.[D] 10

In a 1995 study, the subjects included 18 preschool through secondary students diagnosed with autism. All were nonverbal or had extremely limited verbal-expressive abilities. The student's teachers attended a two-day training session on facilitated communication taught by Douglas Bicklen. After a 15-week period during which the teachers used facilitated communication on a daily basis with the students, the students' ability to communicate using facilitated communication was evaluated. Several students demonstrated the ability to correctly respond to requests and questions when the facilitator knew the answer. When the facilitator did not know the correct answer, however, none of the students were able to respond correctly.[E] 11

In a 1993 study with 21 elementary and secondary autistic students, the researchers found no support for facilitated communication and concluded that "no client showed unexpected literacy or communicative abilities when tested via the facilitator screening procedure, even after 20 hours of training."[F] 12

A 1994 study examined the facilitated communications of 19 developmentally disabled adults ranging in age from 23–50. All the subjects in the study had been successfully using facilitated communication in their day treatment facility. The study required the individual via their facilitator to identify the color, shape, and the number of shapes they saw on a card. When the 13 facilitator did not see the same card shown to the subject, no subject was found to perform at levels that exceeded chance.[G]

In a 1996 study of 14 students with autism, none of the students were able to produce functional, typed communication following 10 weeks of instruction in the use of facilitated communication.[H] 14

These studies, along with many others, failed to validate the claims of facilitated communication advocates.[I] The empirical data was clear. It was not the autistic children who were authoring the typed messages, but their facilitators. The results of the scientific studies prompted the American Psychological Association in 1994 to adopt a resolution that stated, in part, that "facilitated communication is a controversial and unproved communication procedure with no scientifically demonstrated support for its efficacy." 15

Parents, their relatives and friends, teachers and therapists had all had wanted to believe that the facilitated communications were real. Any caring, empathetic person would want them to be real. Unfortunately, the scientific results were unequivocal.❺ 16

What were the costs of uncritically accepting these facilitated messages? False accusations of sexual abuse were made, parents were investigated for child sexual abuse (some were even jailed), children were placed in long term foster care, families were torn apart, millions of public school dollars were spent to hire and train facilitators, and years of schooling were wasted as autistic children sat in advanced classes rather than learning the life skills they would need. 17

This recent *Time* magazine article will undoubtedly be eagerly devoured by the parents, relatives, friends, therapists, and teachers of autistic children. Despite the overwhelming scientific evidence accumulated over a decade ago that clearly demonstrated that facilitated communication is an illusion, a minority of parents of autistic or severely mentally impaired children have continued to believe in the technique. Whether advocates of facilitated communication will one day succeed in bringing facilitated communication back into the mainstream is unclear, although this recent article is certainly troubling. The history of 18

Reading Critically

❺ What emotions do you think the parents felt once they learned the scientific results?

facilitated communication, however, should remind us of the significant costs that are often incurred when we, as a society, uncritically accept what we want to believe to be true based on emotion, rather than accepting what is based on fact.

References and Notes

A. Wallis, C. 2006. "Inside the Autistic Mind." *Time*, May 15, 42–51.

B. Bicklen, D. 1990. "Communication Unbound: Autism and Praxis." *Harvard Educational Review*, 60, 291–314; Bicklen, D., Morton, W.M., Gold, D., Berrigan, C., & Swaminathan, S. 1992. "Facilitated Communication: Implications for Individuals with Autism." *Topics in Language Disorders*, 12, 1–28.

C. Palfreman, J. 1993. *Prisoners of Silence*. Frontline, PBS.

D. Beck, A.R. & Pirovano, C.M. 1996. "Facilitated Communicators' Performance on a Task of Receptive Language." *Journal of Autism and Developmental Disorders*, 26 (5), 497–512.

E. Simpson, R.L., & Myles, B.S. 1995. "Effectiveness of Facilitated Communication with Children and Youth with Autism." *The Journal of Special Education*, 28 (4), 424–439.

F. Eberlin, M., McConnachie, G., Ibel, S., & Volpe, L. 1993. "Facilitated Communication: A Failure to Replicate the Phenomenon." *Journal of Autism and Developmental Disorders*, 23 (3), 507–530.

G. Regal, R.A., Rooney, J.R., & Wandas, T. 1994. "Facilitated Communication: An Experimental Approach." *Journal of Autism and Developmental Disorders*, 24 (3), 345–355.

H. Bomba, C., O'Donnell, L., Markowitz, C., & Holmes, D. 1996. "Evaluating the Impact of Facilitated Communicative Competence of Fourteen Students with Autism." *Journal of Autism and Developmental Disorders*, 26 (1), 43–57.

I. Green, G., & Shane, H.C. 1993. "Facilitated Communication: The Claims vs. the Evidence." *Harvard Mental Health Letter*, 10, 4–5; Montee, B.B., Miltenberger, R.G., & Wittrock, D. 1995. "An Experimental Analysis of Facilitated Communication." *Journal of Applied Behavior Analysis*, 28, 189–200; Moore, S., Donovan, B., Hudson, A., Dykstra, J., & Lawrence, J. 1993. "Evaluation of Facilitated Communication: Eight Case Studies." *Journal of Autism and Developmental Disorders*, 23, 531–539; Mostert, M.P. 1995. "Facilitated Communication Since 1995: A Review of Published Studies." *Journal of Autism and Developmental Disabilities*, 31 (3), 287–313; Szempruch, J., & Jacobson, J.W. 1993. "Evaluating the Facilitated Communications of People with Developmental Disabilities." *Research in Developmental Disabilities*, 14, 253–264.

UNDERSTANDING DETAILS

1. Explain the practice of facilitated communication. For whom was it originally developed? When, by whom, and why was

this communication method introduced for use with autistic children?
2. What is Norton's assessment of facilitated communication as a technique for use with autistic children?
3. What were the costs of accepting as real the facilitated messages from autistic children?

ANALYZING MEANING

1. Why is Norton so critical of the *Time* magazine article on facilitated communication and autism? Why do you think *Time* would have published the 1996 article in spite of the empirical evidence available on this subject?
2. According to Norton, "Parents, teachers and therapists did not question the validity of the facilitated communications" (paragraph 4). Why not? What do you think is Norton's opinion of those parents, teachers, and therapists?
3. What is Norton's purpose in writing this essay? Explain why you think he is, or is not, successful in achieving this purpose.

DISCOVERING RHETORICAL STRATEGIES

1. Describe Norton's tone in this article. How does he achieve this tone? Is it appropriate for his purpose?
2. In this article, is Norton reporting, interpreting, or analyzing? How do Norton's sources and statistics help advance his argument?
3. What main rhetorical modes does Norton use to make his case? Give examples of each.

MAKING CONNECTIONS

1. Imagine that Norton is having a conversation with Naomi Klein ("Co-opting Dissent") and Jenn Lamothe ("Giving Up the Fight") about the tendency of people to "uncritically accept what we want to believe to be true" rather than look at the factual evidence. What examples might Klein and Lamothe cite to support Norton's position? Where might their views differ?
2. Imagine that Norton has read the argument and persuasion essays by Adam Gopnik ("Shootings"); Russell Smith ("Potty-Mouthed and Proud of It"); and Arlene Perly Rae, Irshad Manji, and Anna Porter ("A Call to Arms on Anti-Semitism"). Which do you think he would assess as having the most convincing logical (rather than emotional) argument?

IDEAS FOR DISCUSSION/WRITING

Preparing to Write

Write freely about making decisions based on emotion rather than reason. Do you tend to focus more on emotion or reason when making decisions? What has been the result of that strategy? Have you ever believed something because you wanted it to be true even though the factual evidence pointed in the other direction? How did you deal with that contradiction?

Choosing a Topic

1. Write about a time when you made a faulty decision because emotion blinded you to reason. What decision did you make? What was the consequence of this decision?
2. Write an essay illustrating the saying "If it seems too good to be true, it probably is" and advocating a healthy dose of scepticism.
3. Research and report on (in a well-documented essay) the types of interventions that have shown some success with autistic children.

Preparing to Write Documented Essays

Choosing a Topic. Just as with any writing assignment, you should begin writing a documented essay by exploring and limiting your topic. You might be choosing a subject from infinite possibilities or working with an assigned topic, but as you consider your options, you should ask one very important question: Will you be able to find enough information to back up your thesis statement? To make sure you will have enough persuasive evidence, do preliminary research to see what information is available.

In your preliminary search, you should seek out both primary and secondary sources related to your topic. **Primary sources** are works of literature, historical documents, letters, diaries, speeches, eyewitness accounts, and your own experiments, observations, and conclusions; **secondary sources** explain and analyze information from other sources. Any librarian can help you search for both types. Make sure you take time to assess the relevance and credibility of the sources you find.

After you have found a few sources on your general topic, scan and evaluate what you have discovered, to limit your topic further. Depending on the required length of your essay, you want to find a topic broad enough to be researched, established enough so that you can find sources on it, and significant enough to demonstrate your abilities to grapple with ideas and draw conclusions. The Preparing to Write questions can help you generate and focus your ideas.

Once you have established these limitations, you might be tempted to write a thesis. At this point, however, asking a question and attempting to find an answer is probably more productive.

Our student writer decided to write on topic 1 (under Choosing a Topic on page 485) after reading and rereading Ehrenreich's essay. She narrowed her subject in the following way:

General Subject: Video games
More Specific: Video games and "warlike instincts"
More Specific: How video war-games can awaken "warlike instincts" in adolescents

This limited topic would be perfect for a documented essay, allowing our student writer to search for books and periodicals on the relationships among video games, violence, and war.

Writing a Good, Clear Thesis Statement. A thesis statement is the controlling idea that will guide the writing of your entire paper. Your assignments throughout college will usually be broad topics. To compose a good documented essay, you need to narrow a broad topic to an idea that you can prove within a limited number of pages. A working thesis statement will provide the direction for your essay, but you should keep in mind that your thesis is likely to be revised several times as the range of your knowledge changes and your paper takes different turns while you research and write.

Just as in a standard essay, the thesis statement in your documented essay is a contract between you and your readers. If you don't deliver what your thesis statement promises, your readers will be disappointed. The thesis statement is usually the last sentence in the introduction. It outlines your purpose and position on the essay's general topic and gives your readers an idea of the type of resources you will use to develop your essay.

Our student wrote the following thesis statement for her essay after reading several sources:

> In a community where violence is an integral part of entertainment, war-based video games normalize the "aggressive instinct" and create an illusion of war that becomes both desirable and natural.

Her entire essay responds to Ehrenreich's claim that a natural "warlike instinct" does not exist. Although our student writer agrees with this statement, she believes, as her thesis states, that video games increase the possibility of a natural desire for war and violence. The paragraphs following this thesis statement provide evidence to support her claim.

Finding Sources

No matter what you are studying in college, you should know how to find sources and evaluate them. In today's electronic world, learning how to assess and use the resources available through the library's services is a basic survival skill.

Many of the sources you will use for your documented essays are available online, often through databases that your library subscribes to. In addition to online journals, magazines, and books, you might locate relevant information from electronic newsletters, discussion groups, bulletin boards, or email inquiries. It is important to remember that not all sources are equally accurate and reliable. You need to exercise your best judgment and may need to get your instructor's help in assessing the most useful online sources for your purposes.

Sources That Are Relevant, Reliable, and Recent

To find convincing supporting material, use the "3Rs" approach: your sources must always be Relevant, Reliable, and Recent. Here are some questions that will help you evaluate your sources in this regard:

The 3Rs: Relevant, Reliable, and Recent

Relevant

- Does the source focus on your subject?
- Does the source deal in depth with the topic?

Reliable

- What is the origin of the source?
- Is the author an expert in the field?
- Is the author biased?
- Does the source represent all sides of an issue?
- Are the author's claims well supported?

Recent

• Is the source current enough for your subject and your purpose?

Our student writer's thesis suggests that video games can affect people's attitudes toward war and violence. To convince her readers of her thesis, she consulted books, scientific and online journals, and general circulation publications. Here are some of her sources:

- Book: *Violent Video Game Effects on Children and Adolescents: Theory, Research, and Public Policy*
- Scientific journal: *Journal of Experimental Social Psychology*
- Online journal articles: *Brandweek*
- Online article: *Psychological Science Agenda*
- General circulation publications: *The Saturday Evening Post, Time* magazine

In these sources, our student writer found information that did a thorough job of supporting her thesis and fulfilled our "3R" criteria: Relevant, Reliable, and Recent.

Consulting Interdisciplinary Databases, Subject-Specific Indexes, and Electronic Journal Collections

Most instructors agree that students should use scholarly academic databases—such EBSCOhost, ProQuest's ABI/INFORM, and LexisNexis—that you can access through your library. These databases contain articles, conference papers, and reports from a variety of sources, many of which are academic journals that have undergone peer review. Articles that have been academically peer reviewed or subjected to reputable editorial scrutiny are more reliable than those that have not.

Regardless of where you obtain your information, you should watch for bias and inaccuracy.

The best places to begin searching for sources are interdisciplinary databases, subject-specific indexes, and electronic journal collections. You should have access to these services from home through your library's homepage or from a computer in your library. We will discuss each one briefly. You may need a reference librarian to help you find these for the first time.

Interdisciplinary Databases

Some online databases, such as EBSCO's Academic Search, provide access to full texts in a variety of subject areas. They could be described as "interdisciplinary databases." These databases direct you to a large number of books and journals on a wide range of subjects.

Subject-Specific Indexes

Many databases index and abstract materials for specific subject disciplines, such as psychology or law. Others may index news articles. For example, PsychINFO covers psychology, while EBSCO's ERIC is dedicated to education.

Electronic Journal Collections

Electronic journal collections are online databases where you can obtain complete journal articles directly from your computer. JSTOR, for example, provides you with back issues of core journals in the humanities, social sciences, and sciences.

Most databases have a "default search" that lets you explore multiple fields at once. You can also narrow searches by author, title, or subject. Most databases no longer require that you type in the Boolean operators (AND, OR, and NOT) manually. They provide multiple search boxes, normally separated by a default AND.

Accessing Sources

Once you type your topic into the search function of a database, index, or journal collection, the computer will display the number of articles and books it has found in a "results list."

Searching for Websites

When you use a search engine such as Google or Yahoo!, you will search millions of websites. Using the advanced search option in Google will allow you to narrow or expand your search. Most search engines will then begin helping you narrow your search and will provide a list of other possible topics. Here are some variations that our student writer explored while conducting her research.

Topic	**Other Possible Topics**
Video games and violence	*War in video games*
	Effects of media violence
	Media violence and adolescents
	Psychology of violence and war
	Aggression and military views

Evaluating Websites

Since anyone can put material online, you need to make sure you are not using biased or unreliable information in your academic papers. To use websites intelligently, follow these four guidelines.

1. Understand the URL addresses you consult. The endings of the URLs refer to different sources: *.com* stands for "commercial," *.edu* for "education," *.gov* for "government," and *.org* for "organization." Ensure that the sites you find are maintained and current.
2. Pay attention to the argument a site makes. Who is the author, and what is his or her purpose for entering information on the site? If you log on to a Martin Luther King, Jr. site and are inundated with racial slurs, chances are you've found a site that was created by a faction of the Ku Klux Klan. If the information does not fit the site or if the author has an obvious agenda, avoid the site altogether.
3. Make sure the site is providing fact and not opinion. For academic purposes, facts and statistics are generally more useful than opinions. If you are looking for a site that deals with crime in Canada, you will want to avoid the site that gives you paragraph after paragraph about how the Canadian government is soft on crime but fails to give you any specific information, or that provides statistics without sources.
4. Check that the site provides information about the other sides of the argument. The best sites provide all sides of an argument so they can, in turn, show why one side is more valid than the others. If you find a website that does not offer balanced information, consider it biased, and avoid it altogether.

The best way to determine whether the information you are using will be acceptable for your instructor is to rely principally on academic sources, such as published literature in the library databases, for the bulk of your research. There are, however, a number of "open source" academic websites, such as Google Scholar, where you can access articles that have been peer reviewed or refereed. Please note, however, that you still need to evaluate these sources to make sure their arguments are sound.

Avoiding Plagiarism

Plagiarism is using someone else's words or ideas as if they were your own. It comes from a Latin word meaning "kidnapper." Because it is dishonest, plagiarism is a serious offence in college and beyond. Among student writers, plagiarism usually takes one of three forms: (1) using words from another source without quotation marks; (2) using someone else's ideas in the form of a summary or paraphrase without citing your source; and (3) using someone else's essay as your own. When you work with outside sources, whether you are quoting, paraphrasing, or summarizing, you must give credit to the authors who wrote them.

If you don't cite your sources properly, your readers will think the words and ideas are yours when they actually came from someone else. When you steal material in this way in college, you can be dismissed from school. When you commit the same offence in the professional world, you can get fired or end up in court. So make sure you understand what plagiarism is as you move through this chapter.

Types of Material

A documented paper usually blends three types of material:

- Common knowledge, such as the places and dates of events (even if you had to look them up). If you are referring to historical events and other well-known facts, such as the effects of smoking, you do not have to cite a source. This material is called common knowledge because it can be found in a number of different sources.

  Example: Although they were around for decades before, video games reached blockbuster popularity during the 1980s with classics such as the *Legend of Zelda* and *Super Mario Brothers*, and they have been gaining in popularity ever since.

- Someone else's thoughts and observations. If you want to use someone's original words or ideas, you must give that person credit by revealing where you found this information. This process is called citing or documenting your sources. Since documented essays are developed around sources that support your position, citations are an essential ingredient!

Example: President Ronald Reagan once said about video games, "Many young people have developed incredible hand, eye, and brain coordination in playing these games. The Air Force believes these kids will be our outstanding pilots should they fly our jets."

- Your own thoughts and observations. These are conclusions that you draw from the sources you are reading.

  Example: While video games can be used for educational purposes, they often present glamorized pictures of violence and aggression to children, making these games a risky form of entertainment.

Of these three types of information, you must document or cite your exact source only for the second type. Negligence in citing your sources, whether purposeful or accidental, is plagiarism.

Acknowledging Sources

In addition to showing your reader where you got your material from, acknowledging your sources also gives you credit for the reading you have done and for your ability to synthesize and use sources to support your observations and conclusions.

Two specific forms of documentation can sometimes cause students unexpected problems. But if you heed the following warnings, you will avoid these stumbling blocks. First, when you paraphrase (or put another writer's ideas in your own words), you cannot use the author's words or sentence structure. You must also cite your source at the end of a paraphrase. Second, when you put an author's words in quotation marks, you must print the words you want to use exactly as they are in the original source.

In our student writer's paper, every source she uses is acknowledged at least twice: (1) in the paper directly after a quotation or idea and (2) at the end of the paper in a list. The first type of citation is known as an in-text citation, and the second is a list of works cited in the paper. These two types of documentation work together to provide readers with the exact details of the sources used.

At the note-taking stage, you should make sure that you have all the information on your sources you will need later to acknowledge them properly in your paper. Having to track down missing details when you prepare your lists of works cited can be frustrating and time consuming.

Direct Quotation, Paraphrase, and Summary

As you research, your notes will probably fall into one of four categories: (1) direct quotations from sources; (2) paraphrase—a restatement in your own words of someone else's ideas or observations; (3) summary—a condensed statement of someone else's thoughts or observations; or (4) a combination of these forms. Be sure to make a distinction in your notes between actual quotes and paraphrases or summaries. (Also, record the sources, including page and/or paragraph numbers, of all your quoted, summarized, and paraphrased material. See the section below on note taking for more tips on this).

This section explains the first three options to you. We will begin with an original source and show you how to acknowledge material from this source in different ways.

The following quotation is from "Violent Video Games: Myths, Facts, and Unanswered Questions" by Dr. Craig A. Anderson. It was published in the scientific journal *Psychological Science Agenda* in October 2003.

Original Source

"Cartoonish and fantasy violence is often perceived (incorrectly) by parents and public policy makers as safe even for children. However, experimental studies with college students have consistently found increased aggression after exposure to clearly unrealistic and fantasy violent video games. Indeed, at least one recent study found significant increases in aggression by college students after playing E-rated (suitable for everyone) violent video games" (Anderson, par. 11).

Direct Quotation

If you use a direct quotation from another source, you must put the exact material you want to use in quotation marks:

> Dr. Craig A. Anderson, in his article "Violent Video Games: Myths, Facts, and Unanswered Questions," responds to people who dismiss the threat of violence in children's video games: "Cartoonish

> and fantasy violence is often perceived (incorrectly) by parents and public policy makers as safe even for children. However, experimental studies with college students have consistently found increased aggression after exposure to clearly unrealistic and fantasy violent video games" (par. 11).

Direct Quotation with Some Words Omitted

If you want to leave something out of the quotation, use three dots (with spaces before and after each dot). Omitting words like this is known as ellipsis. Also, make sure that you place brackets [ ] around any words that you alter in the quotation.

> Dr. Craig A. Anderson, in his article "Violent Video Games: Myths, Facts, and Unanswered Questions," states, "Cartoonish and fantasy violence . . . [causes] increased aggression" (par. 11).

Paraphrase

When you paraphrase, you are restating the main ideas of a quotation in your own words. *Paraphrase* literally means "similar phrasing," so it is usually about the same length as the original. Paraphrasing is one of the most difficult skills to master in college, but one trick you can use is to read the material, put it aside, and write a sentence or two from memory. Then compare what you wrote with the original to make sure they are similar but not exactly the same. If you look at the source while you are trying to paraphrase it, you might inadvertently take phrases from the original, which would make you guilty of plagiarism.

Even though this information is in your own words, you still need to let your readers know where you found it. A paraphrase of our original source might look like this:

> Dr. Craig A. Anderson, in his article "Violent Video Games: Myths, Facts, and Unanswered Questions," addresses the common misperception that video games intended for children do not contain violent or aggressive behaviour. He cites scientific studies that show college students respond similarly to realistic and unrealistic violence in video games, leading researchers to believe that make-believe violence poses just as much threat as lifelike violence in the media (par. 11).

Summary

To summarize, state the author's main idea in your own words. A summary is much briefer than the original or a paraphrase. As with a paraphrase, you need to furnish the details of your original source. Here is a summary of our original source:

> In his article "Violent Video Games: Myths, Facts, and Unanswered Questions," Dr. Craig A. Anderson asserts that fantastical violence can be as harmful as realistic violence in video games.

When to Quote? When to Paraphrase?

A general rule is that you never want to have more than 10 percent of directly quoted information in your paper, which means 90 percent of the outside information you use in your essay should be paraphrased or summarized. To determine whether you should use a direct quotation, ask yourself if this is the best possible way to relay this information. If you can't phrase it any better than the original or if the author of the quotation is famous enough to give your argument credibility, then you should use a direct quotation. In most cases, however, you should try to put your research into your own words.

Staying Organized

Taking Notes on Sources

It is important to keep your sources separate from your own ideas in the research stage. As you gather information, consider keeping a journal, separate from your research, where you can record your own opinions, interpretations, and analyses in response to your reading. This is where you can track and develop your own ideas and theories, and clarify your thinking on an issue.

For your research, take a few moments to set up a system to collect information. Some people prefer to record their research on note cards. This method allows you to rearrange cards as you organize your ideas. Put only one idea on each note card.

Taking notes electronically is another option. Set up a new page or new document for each new source, using the headings suggested below.

Whatever your choice, the best time to start keeping track of the information for the citations in your paper is when you are taking notes. If you cannot tell your reader where you found the quotation, then you cannot use the material.

Listed here is all the information you will need later to cite a source in your paper:

For a book:
- Book title
- Author(s)
- Editor(s) if applicable
- City where published
- Publisher
- Year of publication
- Page(s) on which material appeared

For an article:
- Article title
- Author(s)
- Title of magazine, journal, newspaper
- Date of issue (magazine) or date (newspaper)
- Year/volume number (journal)
- Page(s) on which article appeared
- Database name (if found using a database)
- URL

For other online material:
- Article title
- Author(s)
- Sponsoring organization
- Website title
- Date of posting and date of access
- URL

The format in which you present this information will depend on the field of study. A good handbook will help you with the formats of the various documentation styles, which include Modern Language Association (MLA) style for the arts and humanities, American Psychological Association (APA) style for the social sciences, and *Chicago Manual of Style* (CMS) style for history, some sciences, and many other disciplines. Make sure you understand which documentation style your instructor wants you to use, because they are all slightly different. These styles are all explained in the online appendix Reference: Reading and Writing from Sources.

Our student writer used the MLA citation style. The Anderson essay in the MLA format would look like this:

Anderson, Craig. "Violent Video Games: Myths, Facts, and Unanswered Questions." *Psychological Science Agenda* 16.5 (2003): n. pag. Web. 28 May 2009.

Making a Working Outline

Before you begin your first draft, you might want to write an informal working outline to help check the range of your coverage and the order and development of your ideas. With an outline, you can readily see where you need more information, less information, or more reliable sources. Try to be flexible, however. This outline may change dramatically as your essay develops.

A good way to begin an outline is to write your tentative thesis statement at the top of a page and then list under that thesis the topics you have developed. Each topic should directly support your thesis statement. Leave room in your outline to add research material, subtopics, and details throughout the paper. This outline then becomes a guide for your writing. It will change and grow with every paragraph that you add to your paper.

Writing Documented Essays

Writing the first draft of a documented essay is your chance to discover new insights and important connections. This draft is your opportunity to demonstrate that you understand your topic and your sources on three increasingly difficult levels—literal, interpretive, and analytical; that you can organize your material effectively; that you can integrate your sources (in the form of summaries, paraphrases, or quotations) with your opinions; and that you can document (that is, cite) your sources.

To begin this process, look again at your thesis statement and your working outline, and adjust them to represent any new discoveries you have made as you researched your topic and wrote in your journal.

When you begin to draft your paper, write the sections of the essay that you feel most comfortable with first. Throughout the essay, feature your own point of view by integrating your own analysis into the summaries, paraphrases, and quotations from other sources. Remember that the primary reason for doing such an assignment is to let you demonstrate your ability to synthesize material, draw your own conclusions, and analyze your sources and your own reasoning.

Writing the Introduction

Construct an introduction that leads to your thesis statement. The introduction to a research paper is your chance to make a great first impression. Just like a firm handshake and a warm smile in a job interview, an essay's introduction should capture your readers' interest, set the tone for your essay, and state your specific purpose. Introductions often have a funnel effect. They typically begin with general information and then narrow the focus to your position on a particular issue. Regardless of your method, your introduction should "hook" your readers by grabbing their attention and letting them know what you are going to attempt to prove in your essay.

Some effective ways of capturing your audience's attention and giving necessary background information are to (1) use a quotation; (2) tell a story that relates to your topic; (3) provide a revealing fact, statistic, or definition; (4) offer an interesting comparison; or (5) ask an intriguing question. Be sure your introduction gives readers all the information they will need to follow your logic through the rest of your paper.

Our student writer's introduction starts out with a statement about the relationship of games and war. The paragraph then refers to the Ehrenreich essay and its claim about the "aggressive instinct." The last sentence of the first paragraph contains our student writer's thesis statement and ends the introduction.

Writing the Supporting Paragraphs

Develop as many supporting paragraphs, or body paragraphs, as you think are necessary to explain your thesis statement. Following the introductory paragraph, a research paper includes several body paragraphs that support and explain the essay's thesis statement. Each body paragraph covers a topic that is directly related to the thesis statement.

Supporting paragraphs, or body paragraphs, usually include a topic sentence, which is a general statement of the paragraph's contents, and examples or details that support the topic sentence.

To write your supporting paragraphs, follow your working outline and your note cards or research files. Make adjustments in your outline as you write so you can keep track of your ideas and make sure you are developing them in a logical fashion. The body of the paper and your outline should change and develop together with each sentence you draft.

After you write your body paragraphs, look at your thesis statement again to confirm that it introduces what you say in the rest of your paper. Your thesis statement should refer to all your topics, even if only indirectly, in the order you discuss them. It should also prepare your readers for the conclusions you are going to draw.

Our student writer's paper contains four body paragraphs, each making a separate point that is directly related to her thesis:

Paragraph	**Point**
2	*Although studies exist on either side of the controversy, most research shows that violent video games cause physiological changes, and these changes alter a player's attitude toward war and violence.*
3	*Authenticity in the realm of virtual warfare is highly sought after, contributing to the glamorized view many people have of war.*
4	*Video games remove the need for "transformation," enabling ordinary men and women to act upon their "aggressive instinct."*
5	*Many have criticized reports connecting video games and aggression [offering opposing viewpoints].*

In addition to including strong topic sentences, you should also use concluding sentences in your body paragraphs to help reinforce your thesis statement or build a transition to the next paragraph. Concluding sentences bring a paragraph to a close just like a conclusion brings an essay to a close, and well-crafted concluding sentences also focus your readers on the highlights of your argument.

Introducing Sources

Your sources must be seamlessly integrated into your paper. In other words, you should introduce them effectively while showing readers they are credible and provide valuable evidence to back up your argument.

When you use a source for the first time, always (1) introduce the author(s) using the full name(s); (2) give the title of the source (use quotes to enclose the titles of works inside larger works and italics or underlining for book titles); and (3) quote or paraphrase the information you need to build your argument. Here are some examples of good introductions of Daphnee Rentfrow's "S(t) imulating War: From Early Films to Military Games."

- Daphnee Rentfrow, in "S(t)imulating War: From Early Films to Military Games," explains that re-enacting war on-screen can possibly lead to actual war.
- One problem, asserts Daphnee Rentfrow in "S(t)imulating War: From Early Films to Military Games," is that re-enacting war on-screen can possibly lead to actual war.
- According to Daphnee Rentfrow in "S(t)imulating War: From Early Films to Military Games," re-enacting war on-screen can possibly lead to actual war.
- Re-enacting war on-screen can possibly lead to actual war, explains Daphnee Rentfrow in "S(t)imulating War: From Early Films to Military Games."

These model sentences are only a few options for introducing Rentfrow's ideas; you can probably think of many more. The main words in the titles are capitalized; commas and periods, as end punctuation, go inside the quotation marks. In addition, note that the verbs in these examples each express a slightly different meaning. Finally, you should refer to the author by last name only—"according to Rentfrow"—each subsequent time you use the source and mention the author.

Using Sources

Make sure you use your sources as evidence for your argument. The best way to do this is to tell your reader the significance of the direct quotations, paraphrases, or summaries that you use. Look, for example, at an excerpt from one of our student writer's paragraphs:

> Siobhan Morrissey cites trained law enforcement professionals when she says, "Officers raiding methamphetamine labs and gang hangouts often find violent video games left behind" (par. 9). Game players feel the adrenaline rush associated with violence and war in the comfort of their living rooms. As a result, "more young people have no compunction about opening fire on a man or woman in uniform" (Morrissey par. 8). In this situation, we see that war and violence are localized and normalized.

Notice how our student writer does not stop with her source's remarks. Instead, she shows the significance of her source by reminding readers that game players are becoming comfortable with their relationship to violence and to war.

If you simply provide a series of quotations and let them argue for you, you are not demonstrating your understanding of the quotations or showing how they fit into your argument. Make sure to use the quotations as support for your argument, rather than let them serve as the argument itself.

Documenting Sources

As you have already learned in this part of the text, you must document each source you use in your research paper with two types of citations that support each other: an in-text citation and an end-of-paper citation. Both types follow very strict guidelines based on the documentation style you use.

Documentation Format

As you document your sources, you should know that documentation styles vary from discipline to discipline. Ask your instructor about the particular documentation style he or she wants you to follow. Three of the major documentation styles are Modern Language Association (MLA), used in humanities courses; American Psychological Association (APA), used in social science courses; and *Chicago Manual of Style* (CMS), used in history, mathematics, and science classes. Even though documentation styles vary somewhat from one field to another, the basic concept is the same: You must give proper credit to other writers by acknowledging the sources of the summaries, paraphrases, and quotations that you use to support the ideas in your documented essay. Remember that you have two goals in any citation: (1) to acknowledge the author and (2) to help the reader locate the material. Once you grasp this basic concept and accept it, you will have no trouble avoiding plagiarism.

For a look at the differences among the three documentation styles, consult the online appendix.

Writing the Conclusion

In its most basic form, the concluding paragraph should summarize the main points of the essay and remind readers of the thesis statement.

The best conclusions expand on these two basic requirements and bring the essay to a close with one of these creative strategies: (1) ask a question that provokes thought on the part of the reader, (2) predict the future, (3) offer a solution to a problem, or (4) call the reader to action. Each of these options sends a specific message and creates a slightly different effect at the end of the paper. The most important responsibility of the last paragraph is to bring the essay to an effective close. It is the last information that readers see before they form their own opinions or take action.

Our student writer's conclusion opens with a restatement of the problem:

> War-based video games will not send people into war; they will, however, normalize the idea of war and amplify the instincts that propel men and women into combat.

At the end of her conclusion, she gives a solution and calls the reader to action:

> We must respond to this problem by recreating some distance between the average game-player and the actual battlefield. By concentrating less on authenticity and more on entertainment, players would have an easier time separating their fantasy from the dim reality of war. Also, continued research should work to identify degrees of aggressive behaviour in all levels of video games (from E—everyone to AO—adults only) in order to eliminate violence in games available to children and teens because they are the most eager to identify with the imaginary roles they play and the most susceptible to appropriating the "aggressive instinct."

Creating the Title

Your title is what readers see first in any paper. A title should suggest or sum up the subject, purpose, or focus of the essay. A good title should also catch the audience's attention and make them want to read your paper. Our student writer's title, "War-Based Video Games and Real-Life Violence," will catch most readers' attention because of its relevant subject matter and the rhythm of its words.

Revising and Editing a Documented Essay

Part of the process of writing any paper, including a documented essay, is revising and editing your work.

Revising

To revise your documented essay, you should play the role of your readers and impartially evaluate your argument and the sources you have used as evidence in that argument. To begin, revise your thesis to represent all the discoveries you made as you wrote your first draft. Then, look for problems in logic throughout the essay; you might even develop an outline at this point to help evaluate your reasoning:

- Are the essay's assertions clear? Are they adequately supported?
- Are other points of view recognized and examined?
- Does the organization of my paper further my assertions/argument?
- Have I removed irrelevant material?

Next, check your documentation style:

- Is my source material (either summarized, paraphrased, or quoted) presented fairly and accurately?
- Do I introduce the sources in my paper when appropriate?
- Are my sources in the proper format (MLA, APA, or another) according to my instructor's guidelines?

Then, proofread carefully. Finally, prepare your paper to be submitted to your instructor:

- Have I followed my instructor's guidelines for my title page, margins, page numbers, tables, and abstracts?
- Do I have an alphabetical list of my sources at the end of my essay?

For a closer look at how our student writer revised her essay, please see the online appendix.

Any additional guidance you may need as you write and revise your documented essays is provided on pages 34–39 of the Introduction.

Student Essay: Documentation at Work

The following student-written documented essay uses sources to support its observations and conclusions about the connection between video games and aggressive behaviour. First, the writer discusses the dilemma surrounding war-based video games. Then she goes on to show how video games can desensitize players and distort their perception of war. After recognizing and refuting some opposing views, this student writer ends her paper by asserting that changes need to be made to the current status of violent video games. Throughout the essay, the student writer carefully supports her main points with summaries, paraphrases, and quotations from other sources. Notice that she uses the MLA documentation style and closes the paper with an alphabetical list of works cited. Look also for her uses of different rhetorical modes, which are identified in the margins in brackets [ ].

Focused title

War-Based Video Games and Real-Life Violence

Background/ general information

[Examples]

Summary

Games and war have a longstanding relationship. Consider examples of popular board games such as Battleship and Chess, which emphasize strategy and elimination, or action figures such as G.I. Joe, who provide rugged representations of armed forces. While these forms of entertainment may hint at some aspect of combat, none can compare to the accurate and thrilling portrayal of war found in contemporary video games. In her essay "The Ecstasy of War," Barbara Ehrenreich discusses the history and the psychology surrounding war. Ehrenreich's main point is that the human "aggressive instinct" is not the primary force behind "the major wellspring of war" (8). She argues that while aggression may be a natural impulse of human beings, there are several reasons why it cannot be held responsible for the world's extensive history of warfare. But war-based video games seem to directly activate this natural aggressive impulse. In a community where violence is an integral part of entertainment, war-based video games normalize the "aggressive instinct" and create an illusion of war that becomes both desirable and natural.

Thesis statement

Common knowledge

[Cause/ Effect]

Writer's first point

[Cause/ Effect]

Quotation

In-text citation

Over the last forty years, media violence has become a highly debated issue. Although studies exist on either side of the controversy, most research shows that violent video games cause physiological changes, and these changes alter a player's attitude toward war and violence. In their study "The Effect of Video Game Violence on Physiological Desensitization to Real-Life Violence," experts Carnagey, Anderson, and Bushman find that, "playing a violent video game, even for just 20 min, can cause people to become less physiologically aroused by real violence" (494). If playing violent games can affect our perception of violence, then participating in games based on war can adjust our opinions—and instincts—surrounding war. Another study by Konijn, Bujvank, and Bushman finds that "media-related aggression" is related to "identification with violent characters" (1038). Researchers also assert, "Adolescents are especially likely to look for role models to identify with because they are in the process of developing their own identities" (Konijn, Bujvank, and Bushman 1038). War-based video games portray soldiers as killing machines: individuals on a murderous spree under the guise of national service. While this couldn't be farther from the reality of war, the games perpetuate this image, and as a result children and adolescents will choose to identify with the war-game version of soldiers. Some researchers have proven that violence, so prevalent in war-based video games, is problematic especially for adolescents. Whether or not people act on new thoughts of war, violence, and aggression is debatable; however, scientific evidence shows that physiological and psychological changes do occur—when people participate in violent, interactive games, their "aggressive instinct" surfaces.

[Cause/Effect] In-text citation In-text citation [Cause/Effect]

War-based video games are also controversial because of their lifelike quality. Authenticity in the realm of virtual warfare is highly sought after, contributing to the glamorized view many people have of war. One of the most accurate war-based video games is *America's Army*, a "government-sponsored video game" whose "primary mission is to recruit" (L. Grossman par. 2). Lev Grossman, in an article for *Time* entitled "The Army's Killer App," reports that between 2002 and 2005, "America's Army . . . signed up 4.6 million registered players, and it adds 100,000 new ones every month" (par. 3). Ironically, this ultra-realistic game does not depict death. In her article "S(t)imulating War: From Early Films to Military Games," Daphnee Rentfrow comments, "Whereas films [and other games] have staged death in war in an attempt to make themselves realistic . . . *America's Army* refuses this same representation in order to highlight the game's status as a game" (95). By emphasizing the fantastical nature of the game, *America's Army* provides a sharp contrast to other games that willingly and grotesquely depict death on the battlefield and glorify war. *The Call of Duty* series, for example, boasts an "uncensored edge to combat" on the Treyarch Games website. For Carnagey et al. the consequences for players of these war-based games are clear: "Individuals who play violent video games habituate or 'get used to' all the violence and eventually become physiologically numb to it" (495). While a natural "aggressive instinct" is not enough to

Writer's second point [Example] In-text citation (web-based source) In-text citation (web-based source) In-text citation [Comparison/Contrast] Example [Cause/Effect] In-text citation compel individuals to destroy others on its own, participation in violent, war-based games has the ability to motivate this milder impulse to more hostile thoughts and behaviour. Lieutenant Colonel Dave Grossman would agree with their assessment. In his article "We Are Training Our Kids to Kill," Grossman says plainly, "Children don't naturally kill. It is a learned skill. And they learn it . . . most pervasively, from violence as entertainment in television, the movies, and interactive video games" (65). Whether this behaviour is learned in a militaristic setting or in front of a television, it is still learned. He also points out that soldiers exercise caution and control by shooting only when absolutely necessary, as opposed to a game where the objective is to shoot (successfully) and to kill (72). Basically, the response of a trained professional and the response of an amateur gamer will differ greatly. While the games might seem authentic, and therefore desirable, they are not teaching the responsibility that is required by the roles players assume on the virtual battlefield. The seeming authenticity of war-based video games, coupled with the thrill and excitement associated with killing for amusement, fuels players' natural instincts for aggression and war.

[Cause/Effect]

In-text citation

[Comparison/Contrast]

In-text citation

Ehrenreich acknowledges that even without the "aggressive instinct," men and women have shown their ability to murder in cold blood in a multitude of environments. History shows, though, that they are only able to act on these impulses *after* undergoing a transformation. Video games remove the need for "transformation," enabling ordinary men and women to act upon their "aggressive instinct." Ehrenreich states, "There is a huge difference between a war and an ordinary fight. War not only departs from the normal; it inverts all that is moral and right" (12). She goes on to qualify this statement, stating that individuals will only participate in this behaviour "by entering what appears to be an 'altered state'—induced by drugs or lengthy drilling, and denoted by face paint or khakis" (12). Game players lack this "transformation" that apparently turns mere men into killing machines; they can act out violence in their natural state of being, sitting on their couch at home. Siobhan Morrissey cites trained law enforcement professionals when she says, "Officers raiding methamphetamine labs and gang hangouts often find violent video games left behind" (par. 9). Game players feel the adrenaline rush associated with war in the comfort of their living rooms. As a result, "more young people have no compunction about opening fire on a man or woman in uniform" (Morrissey par. 8). In this situation, we see that war and violence are localized

Writer's third point

[Comparison/Contrast]

In-text citation

In-text citation

In-text citation (web-based source)

In-text citation (web-based source)

and normalized. When adolescents play video games, they do not undergo months of training and drilling; their survival instincts are not tested; they do not wear ritual garments; and they do not depend on drugs or alcohol to transform them into trained warriors. Video games do away with the transformation and preparation that usually accompanies war, changing the "aggressive instinct" from innately unnatural, as Ehrenreich claims, to an ordinary impulse.

Acknowledging opposite side

Many have criticized reports connecting video games and aggression. They believe that most people can separate the fantasy from reality, and they choose to embrace the few scientific studies that minimize this correlation. Expert Craig Anderson addresses this in his article "Violent Video Games: Myths, Facts, and Unanswered Questions":

Indented quotation

> Some studies have yielded nonsignificant video game effects, just as some smoking studies failed to find a significant link to lung cancer. But when one combines all relevant empirical studies using meta-analytic techniques, five separate effects emerge with considerable consistency. Violent video games are significantly associated with increased aggressive behaviour, thoughts, and affect; increased physiological arousal; and decreased prosocial (helping) behaviour. (par. 4)

In-text citation (web-based source)

Others cite the Entertainment Software Review Board (ESRB), which rates games in a similar system as movies, as a successful remedy to the issue. Anderson, this time with colleagues Doug Gentile and Katherine Buckley, addresses the ineffectual nature of ratings in their book *Violent Video Game Effects on Children and Adolescents: Theory, Research, and Public Policy*. They expected to find that "participants who played one of the violent video games chose to punish their opponents with louder noise blasts than those who played the nonviolent video games" (Anderson, Gentile, and Buckley 66). The fact that, "even cartoonish violent video games" had a similar effect, however, was surprising. "People tend to believe that T-rated [teen] games are more violent than E-rated [everyone] games, but what seems to matter is whether the game includes aggression" on any level (66). Those desensitized to violence from video games will certainly respond similarly to war. War becomes a game in a completely interactive way, and players' instincts and impulses are significantly altered. Just as games may cultivate or encourage violence or drug abuse, they could also foster the "war gene" that Ehrenreich dismisses in her essay.

In-text citation

In-text citation

[Comparison/Contrast]

Conclusion

War-based video games will not send people into war; they will, however, normalize the idea of war and amplify the instincts that propel men and women into combat. The physiological and psychological changes inspired by war-based games, their authenticity, and their presence in everyday, normal lives help to make "war" accessible and even desirable. We must respond to this problem by recreating some distance between the average game-player and the actual battlefield. By concentrating less on authenticity and more on entertainment, players would have an easier time separating their fantasy from the dim reality of war. Also, continued research should work to identify degrees of aggressive behaviour in all levels of video games (from E–everyone to AO–adults only) in order to eliminate violence in games available to children and teens because they are the most eager to identify with the imaginary roles they play and the most susceptible to appropriating the "aggressive instinct."

Summary

[Cause/ Effect]

[Cause/ Effect]

Works Cited

List of sources used in paper: MLA Style

Alphabetical order

Anderson, Craig. "Violent Video Games: Myths, Facts, and Unanswered Questions." *Psychological Science Agenda* 16.5 (2003): n. pag. Web. 28 May 2009.

Anderson, Craig A., Douglas A. Gentile, and Katherine E. Buckley. *Violent Video Game Effects on Children and Adolescents: Theory, Research, and Public Policy*. Oxford University Press, 2007. Print.

Carnagey, Nicholas L., Craig A. Anderson, and Brad J. Bushman. "The Effect of Video Game Violence on Physiological Desensitization to Real-Life Violence." *Journal of Experimental Social Psychology 43* (2007): 489–496. EBSCO. Web. 25 May 2009.

Ehrenreich, Barbara. "The Ecstasy of War." *Blood Rites: Origins and History of the Passions of War.* New York: Henry Holt and Company, LLC, 1997: 7–12. Print.

Grossman, Lt. Col. Dave. "We Are Training Our Kids to Kill." *Saturday Evening Post* 271.4 (1999): 64–72. Print.

Grossman, Lev. "The Army's Killer App." *Time Magazine.* 21 Feb. 2005. Web. 26 May 2009.

Konijn, Elly A., Marije Nije Bujvank, and Brad J. Bushman. "I Wish I Were a Warrior: The Role of Wishful Identification in the Effects of Violent Video Games on Aggression in Adolescent Boys." *Developmental Psychology* 43.4 (2007): 1038–1044. Print.

Morrissey, Siobhan. "A Surge in Cop Killings." *Time Magazine.* 28 Sept. 2007. Web. 25 May 2009.

Rentfrow, Daphnee. "S(t)imulating War: From Early Films to Military Games." *Computer Games as a Sociocultural Phenomenon: Games Without Frontiers, War Without Tears.* Ed. Andreas Jahn-Sudmann and Ralf Stockmann. New York: Palgrave Macmillan, 2008: 87–96. Print.

Sutton, Ward. "Honey, Did You See This Silly Article on Video Games." *The Onion.* 43.13 (2007). Web. 25 May 2009.

Treyarch Games. Treyarch. 2008. Web. 31 May 2009.

WRITING DOCUMENTED ESSAYS IN REVIEW

Writing Documented Essays

Preparing to Write

✓ What is my purpose?
✓ Who is my audience?

Writing

✓ Do I have a thesis statement?
✓ Have I organized my material effectively?
✓ Have I avoided plagiarism and cited my sources correctly?
✓ Do I use the appropriate documentation style?

Rewriting

✓ Are the essay's assertions clear? Are they adequately supported?
✓ Are other points of view recognized and examined?
✓ Does the organization of my paper further my argument?
✓ Are my summaries, paraphrases, or quotations presented accurately?
✓ Do I introduce the sources in my paper when appropriate?
✓ Are my sources in the proper format (MLA, APA, or another)?
✓ Have I followed my instructor's guidelines for my title page, margins, page numbers, tables, and abstracts?
✓ Do I have an alphabetical list of sources at the end of my essay?

CHAPTER 11

ESSAYS ON THINKING, READING, AND WRITING

In each of the preceding chapters, we have examined a single rhetorical mode in order to focus attention on how writers use that pattern to organize their thoughts. In this final chapter, three essays on the topics of thinking, reading, and writing use a combination of rhetorical modes in each selection.

Our primary purpose in this text has been to show how thinking, reading, and writing work together as fine machinery to help all of us function as intelligent and productive human beings. Our introduction discusses the relationships among thinking, reading, and writing; the text itself illustrates the crucial interdependence of these skills; and this last chapter concludes the book by presenting essays on such related topics as passion for language, understanding the writing process, and jargon. These essays are intended for you to read and enjoy. Let your mind run freely through the material as you recall in a leisurely way what you have learned in this text. The essays bring together the theoretical framework of this text as they illustrate how thinking, reading, and writing inform each other and work interdependently to make meaning. And they integrate the rhetorical patterns in such a way that each essay is a blend of the various rhetorical modes discussed in the preceding chapters—a perfect summary of the topics and strategies you have been working with throughout this text.

MARGUERITE ANDERSEN

Passion for Language (2000)

Language is my passion. I have no patience for those who mumble, use empty phrases and fill words, lack energy, character and emotion in their speech. In my opinion, all of this can be remedied through good training and, above all, through an acquisition of knowledge coupled with attention to everyday experience, through reading, of course, which is the basis of my passion. In other words, I am interested in language performance based on competence, to use Chomsky's terms. 1

It sounds like an arrogant position, yet I do not like to perceive myself as being part of an elite. But language is what allows me to speak and to write, state my thoughts, my feelings and give form to my imagination. How could linguistic ability not be important to me? I possess three languages, English, French, and German. Why have I opted for French in my professional life, as a university teacher and as a writer? I believe it has to do with what the French call *le mot juste*, which must be used to express oneself clearly. I love searching for the right word; I read dictionaries while eating breakfast or sitting in the bathtub. But of course speech is not just a question of words. According to Wittgenstein the meaning of a word is linked to the way we use it in the language. 2

Then there is the question of truth, political or personal. Here again, I look for clarity. A simple analogy: I have never lived in a basement apartment. Maybe I was just lucky; my places have always been filled with light. I love to wake up in the morning feeling the sun on my face. I am one of those indoor plants that thrive when there is light. I am always searching for clarity; I love to hear it in people's speech, discover it in works of literature. 3

As a young woman, I wanted to become an actor. Today, I say to myself that I did not pursue that dream because it was not that intense. I don't know. Rather than speak the words of others, I maybe prefer to use my own words. With passion! 4

NATALIE GOLDBERG

The Rules of Writing Practice (1990)

For fifteen years now, at the beginning of every writing workshop, I have repeated the rules for writing practice. So, I will repeat them again here. And I want to say why I repeat them: Because they are the bottom line, the beginning of all writing, the foundation of learning to trust your own mind. Trusting your own mind is essential for writing. Words come out of the mind. 1

And I believe in these rules. Perhaps I'm a little fanatical about them. 2

A friend, teasing me, said, "You act as if they are the rules to live by, as though they apply to everything." 3

I smiled. "Okay, let's try it. Do they apply to sex?" 4

I stuck up my thumb for rule number one. "Keep your hand moving." I nodded yes. 5

Index finger, rule number two. "Be specific." I let out a yelp of glee. It was working. 6

Finger number three. "Lose control." It was clear that sex and writing were the same thing. 7

Then, number four. "Don't think," I said. Yes, for sex, too, I nodded. 8

I proved my point. My friend and I laughed. 9

Go ahead, try these rules for tennis, hang gliding, driving a car, making a grilled cheese sandwich, disciplining a dog or a snake. Okay. They might not always work. They work for writing. Try them. 10

1. *Keep your hand moving.* When you sit down to write, whether it's for ten minutes or an hour, once you begin, don't stop. If an atom bomb drops at your feet eight minutes after you have begun and you were going to write for ten minutes, don't budge. You'll go out writing. 11

What is the purpose of this? Most of the time when we write, we mix up the editor and creator. Imagine your writing hand as the creator and the other hand as the editor. Now bring your two hands together and lock your fingers. This is what happens when 12 we write. The writing hand wants to write about what she did Saturday night: "I drank whiskey straight all night and stared at a man's back across the bar. He was wearing a red T-shirt. I imagined him to have the face of Harry Belafonte. At three A.M., he finally turned my way and I spit into the ashtray when I saw him. He had the face of a wet mongrel who had lost his teeth." The writing hand is three words into writing this first sentence—"I drank whiskey . . . "—when the other hand clenches her fingers tighter and the writing hand can't budge. The editor says to the creator, "Now, that's not nice, the whiskey and stuff. Don't let people know that. I have a better idea: 'Last night, I had a nice cup of warmed milk and then went to bed at nine o'clock.' Write that. Go ahead. I'll loosen my grip so you can."

13 If you keep your creator hand moving, the editor can't catch up with it and lock it. It gets to write out what it wants. "Keep your hand moving" strengthens the creator and gives little space for the editor to jump in.

14 Keep your hand moving is the main structure for writing practice.

15 2. *Lose control.* Say what you want to say. Don't worry if it's correct, polite, appropriate. Just let it rip. Allen Ginsberg was getting a master's degree from Columbia University. Back then, they were doing rhymed verse. He had a lot of practice in formal meter, and so forth. One night, he went home and said to himself that he was going to write whatever he wanted and forget about formalities. The result was "Howl." We shouldn't forget how much practice in writing he had prior to this, but it is remarkable how I can tell students, "Okay, say what you want, go for it," and their writing takes a substantial turn toward authenticity.

16 3. *Be specific.* Not car, but Cadillac. Not fruit, but apple. Not bird, but wren. Not a codependent, neurotic man, but Harry, who runs to open the refrigerator for his wife, thinking she wants an apple, when she is headed for the gas stove to light her cigarette. Be careful of those pop-psychology labels. Get below the label and be specific to the person.

17 But don't chastise yourself as you are writing, "I'm an idiot; Natalie said to be specific and like a fool I wrote 'tree.'" Just gently note that you wrote "tree," drop to a deeper level, and next to "tree" write "sycamore." Be gentle with yourself. Don't give room for the hard grip of the editor.

4. *Don't think.* We usually live in the realm of second or third thoughts, thoughts on thoughts, rather than in the realm of first thoughts, the real way we flash on something. Stay with the first flash. Writing practice will help you contact first thoughts. Just practice and forget everything else. 18

Now here are some rules that don't necessarily apply to sex, though you can try to apply them to sex if you like. 19

5. *Don't worry about punctuation, spelling, grammar.* 20

6. *You are free to write the worst junk in America.* You can be more specific, if you like: the worst junk in Santa Fe; New York; Kalamazoo, Michigan; your city block; your pasture; your neighborhood restaurant; your family. Or you can get more cosmic: free to write the worst junk in the universe, galaxy, world, hemisphere, Sahara Desert. 21

7. *Go for the jugular.* If something scary comes up, go for it. That's where the energy is. Otherwise, you'll spend all your time writing around whatever makes you nervous. It will probably be abstract, bland writing because you're avoiding the truth. Hemingway said, "Write hard and clear about what hurts." Don't avoid it. It has all the energy. Don't worry, no one ever died of it. You might cry or laugh, but not die. 22

I am often asked, "Well, isn't there a time when we need to stop our hand moving? You know, to figure out what we want to say?" 23

It's better to figure out what you want to say in the actual act of writing. For a long time, I was very strict with myself about writing practice. I kept that hand moving no matter what. I wanted to learn to cut through to first thoughts. Sure, you can stop for a few moments, but it is a tricky business. It's good to stop if you want, look up and get a better picture of what you're writing about, but often I don't stay there. If I give myself a little gap, I'm off for an hour daydreaming. You have to learn your own rhythm, but make sure you do some focused, disciplined "keeping the hand moving" to learn about cutting through resistance. 24

If you learn writing practice well, it is a good foundation for all other writing. 25

When I was young, I played tennis. My arm wasn't very strong, and I was impatient. I was so eager to play, I held the racquet up higher on the grip than I was supposed to in order to compensate. Unfortunately, I got used to using the racquet this way. I was a fine 26 tennis player, but no matter how much I played, there was just so far I could improve, because I never mastered one of the important basics: the proper grip on the racquet.

27 I use this as an example for writing practice. Grow comfortable with it in its basic form before you begin to veer off into your own manner and style. Trust it. It is as basic as drinking water.

28 Sometimes an interviewer asks me, "So writing practice is old hat? Have you developed something new?"

29 And I say, "It would be like a Zen master teaching you meditation one year and the next year saying, 'Forget compassion. Standing on our head is what's in.'"

30 The old essentials are still necessary. Stay with them under all circumstances. It will make you stable—something unusual for a writer.

BENOIT VIROLE

Harry Potter's Cauldron: The Power of Myth and the Rebirth of the Sacred (2004)

In literary circles, the mention of Harry Potter is liable to annoy. Here's a work—we might as well call it that—antithetical to established literary values, sustained by clearly monetary interests, and which in a few short years has climbed to an astonishing peak of international glory and financial success. Those are the facts. But not content with putting in a single appearance, the success continues and is repeated with each instalment in a series whose rhythm is shrewdly orchestrated by a score combining complex lines blending writing, cinema, and the video game industry. 1

J.K. Rowling's uncommon success is often attributed to good marketing, to promotional campaigns, and even to the rise of mass cultural consumption. This explanation is not without substance. The existence of an industry driven by spin-offs should be enough to make us realize that Harry Potter's success is the result of a global marketing strategy designed to exploit to the lees the public's devotion to the adventures of the young wizard. Movie follows book at a measured pace. The book is just the first phase in a string of consumer goods that generate others in their turn. With their content tightly under the author's control, the movies tell the books' tales with remarkable fidelity. Harry Potter is also the first work that genuinely incorporates the new givens of the video game market. A ready-made closed world, well-defined units of time, well-defined places with their trappings differentiated like stage settings, gains and losses of power, the construction and collapse of alliances, projective identification with the principal characters, cliff-hangers pointing to the next product—all the structural elements of a video game are integrated into Rowling's very writing. Book, movie, and video game are the three facets of a single multimedia product limning what might be the objects of mass "culture" to come: composite objects launched into different consumer spaces. But it is remarkable that the root of this composite object is still a book. 2

There is certainly material here for an in-depth sociological analysis of Harry Potter's success. And yet an explanation by market strategy alone cannot explain that success, because many other products have been launched and maintained in the same way without ever producing a comparable phenomenon. Advertising, evolving market expectations, and changes due to the globalization of culture certainly play an important role, but they have only amplified something that's a very real literary success among young readers. Stewing in Rowling's magic cauldron is a unique recipe that has latched on to the spirit of our time. 3

Let me try to identify some of the ingredients in this mysterious recipe. Harry Potter is a young hero whose tragic past (the dramatic death of his parents) and singular destiny (Harry is unique: on his forehead he bears a mark of predestination) will allow young readers to identify with him since the readers are themselves locked in their own unconscious novels of origin. To live an exceptional life and to be the child of an extraordinary, but vanished, couple is a universal fantasy linked to the Oedipus complex and therefore constitutive of human nature. This is certainly a psychoanalytic theme common to many other literary works for young people, but J.K. Rowling embellishes it in an interesting way by writing Harry as a wizard who can conjure up miracles and who therefore enjoys a form of omnipotence that he has yet to learn to master. Harry's initiation, his apprenticeship in what is allowed and what is forbidden, is a second ingredient that reinforces the young (often pre-adolescent) reader's link to the hero, and all the more so because the initiation carries with it opportunities for transgression. This initiation into magic and the world of wizardry is thus a metaphor for initiation into the adult world. It is all the more interesting for being developed in the confines of an imaginary society, constructed by the author, with its own rules, an original and specific vocabulary, and set rituals that the reader—sometimes especially the adult reader—sees as a pastiche of actual social convention. The building of a society with its own rules and structures, essentially the construction of a virtual universe, is one of the major reasons for the fascination with J.K. Rowling's imaginative work. 4

But these few ingredients blended in our literary cauldron couldn't justify the success of Harry Potter if it weren't for a remarkable binding agent. Rowling's narrative style is the special catalyst that has turned the ingredients into a dish that is now almost universally consumed. Her style is direct, 5 stringing together short narrative sequences laid out in a determinate and clearly defined spatiotemporal sequence, but stripped of any really detailed description.(1) It's a stylistic method that can disconcert lovers of written language. Indeed many educators don't consider Harry Potter a genuine work of literature. And yet, there is something in this way of writing that's especially effective and perfectly adapted to the cognitive style of today's children, who have been raised on a constant flux of images and for whom quickness of mental picture-painting and focus on action are preferable to literal description and the complications of inner states.

In Harry Potter, form (i.e., literary expression) matches content. As in every myth, Harry's tale is one of an existential journey through a symbolic world. At bottom, Harry is seeking to re-establish the balance of an original position thrown off-kilter by his parents' murder, committed by the horrifying Lord Voldemort. The twists in his adventures are variations on a central theme: his confrontation with Voldemort as anti-hero, a confrontation whose outcome will be Harry's knowledge of his own origins. The quest is carried out in a universe marked by polar opposites (the wizard world versus the Muggle world, Hogwarts versus the Forbidden Forest, and so on). These places are points in a system and are thus defined in opposition to other points rather than by a yardstick of absolute value. This is why describing them ultimately matters fairly little and gives the young reader freedom from descriptions that would demand attentive effort. The same logic governs myths and fables. Places are first and foremost symbolic points where the action unfolds. In the same way, time is standardized into an immutable chronology of events. And so every volume corresponds to a school year and is painted onto the same temporal canvas: end of the summer holidays in the Muggle world, followed by exposition of the plot, followed by the trip to Hogwarts, the unfolding of the plot, the denouement, and finally a return to the Muggle world. The lack of variety in the framework brings dynamic action to the fore, but it is also connected to a standard schema that underpins the work as a whole. 6

Ever since Greimas, we've known that any tale can be described as the production of a kind of hidden entity, underlying the whole but never explicit, called narrative structure. This structure has generative properties. It produces elements of the tale that, when laid out end to end, make up the whole of a story. 7

Semioticians' work has shown that this narrative structure has the universal form of a square defined by four points. The first is an initial situation. It is generally a situation of balance and calm. In a great many myths, this situation is rendered as a state of culture in opposition to a state of nature. Then the situation undergoes a radical transformation that undermines it, either in the form of a privation or of an assault initiated from the polar opposite. In fairy tales, the initiating and traumatic event is often the kidnapping of the kingdom's princess, whom the hero must then deliver from captivity.

8 The task of restoring balance establishes the hero's constitution. Often introduced as poor and weak, he leaves the original position alone. He then accomplishes a variety of tasks to prove his worth and is aided by other characters or objects. At some point he crosses a geographical border and comes to an unknown and frightening place. He then confronts the anti-hero, the emissary of an antagonistic power, who either appears in the form of a monster or of a character of awesome power. Following an epic battle, the hero frequently defeats the anti-hero thanks to the help of a sidekick subjugated during one of the qualifying tasks. Defeat of the antagonistic power follows, and balance is restored. In fairy tales, for instance, the hero returns to the castle with the princess, marries her, ascends to the throne and has many children.

9 This structure corresponds to a mutual dynamic between archetypes that underpin our mental representations and make a tale intelligible to human minds. In psychoanalysis, the structure is seen as functioning as a symbol of conflict between unconscious representations crystallized around good (loving, salvational) and evil (sadistic, terrifying) forms, or imagos. Under the surface of every story we can, after many derivations and substitutions, discover the struggle between the good and the evil phantasmagoric things of the unconscious.

10 If we examine Harry's story as a whole, it is easy to recognize the elements of this structure. The initial position is the family nucleus of Harry with his two parents. The destabilizing catastrophe is Voldemort's initial attack. Harry then becomes the hero of the story. He takes on auxiliary help (Ron and Hermione), undergoes rites of passage (his apprenticeship in magic), crosses borders and enters forbidden spaces (the Forbidden Forest), and ends up in a duel with the anti-hero (Voldemort). This very same structure is repeated in every book. And so, the original

position corresponds to the beginning of the school year. Then Lord Voldemort launches a destabilizing initiative (a nefarious sign, the news that Sirius Black is out to kill Harry, and so on); then Harry is off to Hogwarts, experiences a variety of adventures that all culminate in a confrontation with an avatar of Lord Voldemort's, and finally Harry is victorious and returns to the original position, albeit a year older, wiser, and more skilful.

11 The magical recipe that has generated Harry Potter's magnetic attraction over readers' imaginations is born of the very small distance that separates the content of the stories, on the one hand, and their underlying structure, on the other. The same analysis can be applied to the profusion of characters who are the result of the choice to focus on action. It is better to create a new character or a new object endowed with specific intentional actions than it is to complicate a pre-existing character by ascribing to them multiple intentions that might eventually appear contradictory. The latter course would lead to supposedly boring elaboration and would slow the action down. Rowling's way of telling the tale, centred on a simplification of the framework and on a denial of her characters' inner lives to the exclusive benefit of dynamic action, should not be evaluated by pedagogical or literary standards.

12 In fact it is the result of a stylistic choice deliberately directed toward an approximation to generative structure. It's a choice that's in line with the general evolution of current modes of communication that privilege the immediate condensation of information (images) over complex discourse (written linear text). This is not contradicted by the ever-increasing length of the Harry Potter books. It is perfectly possible to keep readers' attention and even to get them to read substantial texts, as long as the text produces in them a collection of mental images that matches their mode of thought. And therein lies the magic of Rowling's style: her writing acknowledges universal constraints on the production of meaning. She has made use of the grand archetypal oppositions of every mythical tale by bending them to the service of a product adapted to the cognitive modes and imaginative needs of today's young readers.

13 What remains to be discussed is how a story featuring a young wizard's initiation in a school modelled on English institutions and describing a world organized along lines characteristic of Western society has managed to generate such intoxication in very diverse cultures, for whom the vicissitudes of life in an

English boarding school have no particular resonance. In a way, the great question is still that of the anthropological significance of Harry Potter's worldwide success. Going beyond rationalization in terms of effective marketing, beyond an analysis of the effective writing and content of the books, beyond the observation that children of a global culture need a universal coming-of-age story, we need to understand the pervasiveness of magic as the real anthropological key that Harry Potter turns.

14 It is certainly a magic that has faded into technical applications. The wizards' magic is, above all, functional. Action at a distance, communicating with the departed, telekinesis, changing the world: Harry's magic is definitely practical. But his magic is also what makes communication with the beyond possible, what makes the dead live, allows an understanding of the past and finally enables a reading of the meaning of the universe. This magic must also be limited, circumscribed within precise boundaries whose transgression is essentially sacrilege.

15 Yes, sacrilege indeed, because we are effectively witnessing a rebirth of representations of the sacred, a representation that runs through all of J.K. Rowling's work. The Muggle world and the magical world reproduce the fundamental cleavage between the profane and the sacred, between the secularized world of imbecilic commercial society (incarnated by the Dursley family) and a sacred world, which is certainly dangerous and ambivalent but where questions of meaning are not just central, but are also the only real questions. This is not the least paradoxical aspect of Harry Potter's success. This startling work, supported by the secular and profane flow of capitalist markets, offers a planet-wide secret vision of the sacred.

Note:

16 1. Mind you, this is only true of the book. The (very well-made) movies' charm owes much to the marvellous decor. In a way, the films are synopses of the books. The video game (by Electronic Arts) makes use of the movies' sets, making the books' narrative elements flesh—where the books are, in themselves, rather short on descriptive elements.

RYAN BIGGE

Speak English, Dammit: Why Has Jargon Become the Language of Business? (2000)

In his 1946 essay "Politics and the English Language," George Orwell wrote that language "becomes ugly and inaccurate because our thoughts are foolish, but the slovenliness of our language makes it easier for us to have foolish thoughts." Spent any time in the new economy crossword puzzle? Things are definitely doubleplusungood. 1

The language of business is fast becoming a kind of torture chamber for plain English. Clear, comprehensible words enter; horrifically disfigured and unrecognizable phrases stumble out: management bandwidth; acquisition lockdown; mind-share; stickiness; point of contact; vector; push back; tear down; granularity. Please somebody, stop them before they neologize again. 2

Business has always had buzzwords, and this isn't the first time diction or intention have been obscured by sloppy verbiage. In his 1978 book, *The Jargon of the Professions*, Kenneth Hudson noted that "Business is subject to two quite different linguistic pressures. On the one hand, there is the never-ending search for the new, even more arresting phrase . . . and on the other, the wish to tone words down, to make them less dangerous, less precise, less likely to blow up in the face of the person who uses them." This has never been truer than it is today: in 1978, business was still largely conducted in English; these days, it's done in a kind of impenetrable Esperanto. The worst examples of e-lingo combine what Hudson described, at once impressing people with their futurism ("vortal") while insulating the speaker from actually having an opinion that might later prove unpopular or incorrect. 3

Language is the filter through which we describe reality, but when it comes to dot-com-speak, unreality is the result. What do words like reskin or envisioneer really mean, beyond proving that the person saying them has found the time to skim through *Fast Company*? 4

The problem is less the existence of jargon, which can act as verbal shorthand between like-minded professionals, than the 5 proliferation of nonsense jargon, words that appear to have no clearly defined meaning. This inflated language strives to make the ordinary extraordinary, or, as Orwell put it, "give an appearance of solidity to pure wind." Both of which are good descriptors for the new economy, where an entire lexicon has emerged to help obscure the fact that most web-based enterprises are still in the widget business—sorry, "clicks-and-mortar." Sadly, Internet start-ups are often too harried trying to become the beneficiary of the IPO fairy to find the time to question their most cherished words and phrases.

Given an uncritiqued column inch, some writers are producing a mile of meaningless prose, best witnessed in the recent and buzz-ridden book, *Funky Business*. Swedish authors Jonas Ridderstrale and Kjell Nordstrom brag about their funky bald heads and black leather pants to reinforce their funky, revolutionary theories about business. To prove their rather intriguing theory that "talent makes capital dance," and in lieu of case studies and statistics, they create words like infomediaries, heart share, staminacs, prosumption, heterarchical and hyphenation. After reading about CDOs (chief destruction officers) or phrase after phrase like "funky leaders are creators of chaos as much as originators of order," one cannot help but recall Orwell's dystopic *Nineteen Eighty-Four*. Phrases like "war is peace," "freedom is slavery" and "ignorance is strength" require nearly the same mental gymnastics to unpack as the "funked up" assertion that "total innovation requires ignoring and listening to the customer." 6

Normally, when a business word or phrase crosses over into popular culture, it acts as a eulogy. But despite Edward Norton's world-weary "Do you want me to deprioritize my current reports until you advise of a status upgrade?" in *Fight Club*, and the occasional Dilbert pot-shot, e-lingo continues to thrive. The Jargon Watch column in *Wired* magazine ends up legitimizing the problem rather than ridiculing it. 7

Then again, maybe the Web is self-governing enough to solve the problems it generated. There are sites devoted to Lingo Bingo, e-lingo dictionaries (**www.polarisconsulting.com**) and the web economy bullshit generator (WEBG), provided by **www.dack.com**. The WEBG randomly combines the most common nonsense words to create uniquely meaningless phrases of unintentional hilarity: implement integrated niches; exploit granular eyeballs; streamline vector convergence. When a Java applet sounds as bleeding-edge as a real person, perhaps it's time to declare e-lingo, like Latin, a dead language. 8

CREDITS

Marguerite Andersen, "Passion for Language." Originally appeared in *Queen's Quarterly* 107.1 (Spring 2000), p. 59. Reprinted with permission of the author. • Anita Rau Badami, "My Canada." Copyright © 2002 by Anita Rau Badami. Originally published in *Canada in Reviews* by Imperial Oil. Reprinted by permission of the author. • Dakshana Bascarmurty, "My Parents Killed Santa (and Nobody Cared)." Originally published in *The Globe & Mail* (23 December 2010). Copyright © The Globe and Mail Inc. All Rights Reserved. • The Beatles, lyric from "I'll Follow the Sun."© 1964 Sony/ATV Music Publishing LLC. All rights administered by Sony/ATV Music Publishing LLC, 8 Music Square West, Nashville, TN 37203. All rights reserved. Used by permission. • Ryan Bigge, "Speak English, Dammit" from *National Post Business Magazine* (December 2000), p. 110. Reprinted by permission of the author. • Simon Black, "The Search for Mandela's Gun" from *Pound Magazine* 36 (December 2006) p. 28. www.poundmag.com/index/html. Copyright © Simon Black. Reprinted by permission of Simon Black. • Alex Boyd, "In Defence of Graffiti." Copyright © 2003 Alex Boyd. Reprinted by permission of the author. • Will Braun, "Seven Criteria for the Adoption of New Technology." Originally published in *Geez magazine* (Winter 2010). Copyright © Will Braun. Reprinted by permission of the author. • June Callwood, "Forgiveness" from *The Walrus Magazine*, July 2007. www.walrusmagazine.com/print/2007.06-forgiveness-story. Copyright © 2007 June Callwood. Reprinted by permission of the Estate of June Callwood. • Matt Cohen, "Zada's Hanukkah Legacy." Originally published in *Canadian Geographic* (Nov./Dec. 1995). Copyright © Stickland 2002 for the Matt Cohen estate. • Stanley Coren, "Dogs and Monsters." Originally appeared in *Saturday Night* (May 2000), pp. 18–19. Reprinted with permission of the author. • Christopher DeWolf, "Montrealers, Cherish Your Clotheslines" from *Spacing Magazine* (6 December 2007). Copyright © 2007 Christopher DeWolf. Reprinted by permission of Christopher DeWolf. • Brian Denis Egan, "The Role of Critical Thinking in Effective Decision Making," updated from the Global Knowledge Training LLC website. Copyright © 2011 Global Knowledge Training LLC. • Barbara Ehrenreich, "The Ecstasy of War" from *Blood Rites: Origins and History of the Passions of War*. Copyright © 1997 by Barbara Ehrenreich. Reprinted by permission of Henry Holt and Company, LLC. • Linda Elder, "Looking to the Future with a Critical Eye: A Message for High School Graduates." Copyright © 2004 Linda Elder and Foundation For Critical Thinking. www.criticalthinking.org. Used by permission of the copyright holders. • Joe Fiorito, "Night Shift on the Main" from *Tango on the Main*, published by Signature/Nuage Editions. Reprinted by permission. • Daniel Fricker and Lars Kushner, "Anti-Gay Bullying." Originally published in *Outlooks Magazine* (17 November 2010). Copyright © Daniel Fricker and Lars Kushner. Used by permission of the author. • Howard Gabennesch, "Critical Thinking: What Is It Good For?" Originally published in *Skeptical Inquirer* 30.2 (March/April 2006). Used by permission of the author. • Cynara Geissler, "Fat Acceptance." Originally published in *Geez magazine* (Summer 2010). Copyright © Cynara Geissler. Reprinted by permission of the author. • Alison Gillmor, "Repress Yourself" from *The Walrus Magazine* (March 2006). www.walrusmagazine.com/print/2006.03-culture-repress-yourself. Copyright © 2006 Alison Gillmor. Reprinted by permission of Alison Gillmor. • Malcolm Gladwell, "Is the Belgian Coca-Cola Hysteria the Real Thing?" Originally appeared in *The New Yorker* (July 1999). Reprinted by permission of the author. • Douglas Glover, "On Winning and Responsibility." Originally published on the *Global Brief* website (13 October 2010). Copyright © Douglas Glover. Reprinted by permission of the author. Douglas Glover is the Governor-General's Award-winning author of the novel *Elle*. • Natalie Goldberg, "The Rules of Writing Practice" from *Wild Mind: Living the Writer's Life*, copyright © 1990 by Natalie Goldberg. Used by permission of Bantam

Books, a division of Random House Inc. • Adam Goodheart, "How to Mummify a Pharaoh." First published in *Civilization Magazine*. Copyright © 1995 by Adam Goodheart, reprinted with permission of The Wylie Agency, LLC. • Adam Gopnik, "Shootings." Copyright © 2007 Conde Nast Publications. All rights reserved. Originally published in *The New Yorker* (April 2007). Reprinted by permission. • Jeannie Guy, "Newfoundland Cooking." Originally published in *Newfoundland Quarterly* 102.2 (Issue #433, 2009). Copyright © Jeannie Guy. Used by permission of the author. • Steven Heighton, "Elegy in Stone" from *The Admen Move on Lhasa*. Copyright © 1997. Reproduced with the permission of House of Anansi Press, Toronto. • Tomson Highway, "What a Certain Visionary Once Said." Copyright © 1992 by Tomson Highway. Reprinted with permission of the author. • Lawrence Hill, "Don't Call Me That Word." Essays on www.lawrencehill.com. September 2002. Reprinted with permission of the author. • Monte Hummel, "A Passion for the Environment: Two Accounts" from *Queen's Quarterly* 107.1 (Spring 2000), pp. 66–67. Reprinted with permission of the author. • Edith Iglauer, "Red Smile." Originally publishing in *GEIST* 77 (Summer 2010), pp. 19-20. Copyright © Edith Iglauer. Reprinted by permission of the author. • Sheema Khan, "Hijabs: Don't Kick Up a Fuss" (p. A21) from *The Globe & Mail* (27 February 2007). Copyright © 2007 Sheema Khan. Reprinted by permission of the author. • Stephen King, "Why We Crave Horror Movies." Reprinted With Permission. © Stephen King. All Rights Reserved. Originally appeared in *Playboy* (1982). • Barbara Kingsolver, "Life Without Go-Go Boots" from *High Tide in Tucson: Essays from Now or Never*, pp. 54–58. Copyright © 1995 by Barbara Kingsolver. Reprinted by permission of HarperCollins Publishers. • Naomi Klein, "Co-opting Dissent: How Multinationals Are 'Re-branding' for the Post-Seattle Era." Excerpted from *Fences and Windows: Dispatches from the Front Lines of the Globalization Debate*. Copyright © 2002 Naomi Klein. Reprinted by permission of Knopf Canada. • K'naan, "Between the Highs and the Lows, Life Happens." Originally published in *The Globe & Mail* (10 May 2010). Copyright © K'naan. Reprinted by permission of the author. • Jenn Lamothe, "Giving up the Fight" from *This I Believe*. Copyright © 2007 Canadian Broadcasting Corporation. Reprinted by permission of Canadian Broadcasting Corporation. • Evelyn Lau, "More and More," an excerpt from *Addicted: Notes From the Belly of the Beast*, edited by Lorna Crozier and Patrick Lane, published 2001 & 2006 by Greystone Books: an imprint of D&M Publishers Inc. Reprinted with permission from the publisher. • Daniel J. Levitin, "The Music of My Mind: A Neuroscientist Examines the Recipe for Listening Ecstasy" from *Scrapbook, Paste Magazine*, September 2006. Copyright © Daniel J. Levitin 2006, 2012. Reprinted by permission of the author. • Maureen Littlejohn, "You Are a Contract Painkiller." Originally published in *Equinox* (April/May 1997). Reprinted with permission of Maureen Littlejohn, feature writer, editor, and journalist. • Rafe Mair, "Raise the Driving Age" from *The Tyee* www.thetyee.ca/Views/2007/08/13/DrivingAge. Copyright © 2007 Rafe Mair. Reprinted by permission of the author. • Irshad Manji, "Status Anxiety? Consider Socrates and the Sewer Saviour." Originally published in *The Globe & Mail* (15 October 2010). Copyright © Irshad Manji. Reprinted by permission of the author. Irshad Manji is a professor of Leadership and Director of The Moral Courage Project at New York University. • Michael McKinley, "Opera Night in Canada." Originally appeared in *Saturday Night* (Dec. 2000), pp. 16–17. Reprinted with permission of the author. • Ryan McNutt, "The Music We Hate: Joanna Newsom." Originally published in *Maisonneuve* 36 (Summer 2010). Copyright © 2010 Ryan McNutt. Reprinted by permission of the author. • John Moore, "Sporting Life." Originally published in *Vancouver Review* 9 (Spring 2006). Copyright © John Moore. Used by permission of the author. • Lisa Moore, "Between the North Bridge and the King George IV Bridge." First published in *Eighteen Bridges* (Fall 2010), p. 62. Copyright © Lisa Moore. Reprinted by permission of the author. • Faith Moosang, "Nancy Drew Knows It's Hard." Originally published in *GEIST* 73 (Summer 2009), pp. 18–29. Copyright © Faith Moosang. Reprinted by permission of the author. • Peter Nicholson,

"Information-Rich and Attention-Poor." Originally published in *The Globe & Mail* (11 September 2009). Copyright © The Globe and Mail Inc. All Rights Reserved. • Lawrence Norton, "Facilitated Communication & The Power of Belief" from *Skeptic Magazine* www.skeptic.com (25 May 2006). Copyright © 2006 Skeptic Magazine. • Katrina Onstad, "John Lennon, Michael Jackson — Do Celebrities Die Anymore?" Originally published in The *Globe & Mail* (27 December 2010). Copyright © The Globe and Mail Inc. All Rights Reserved. • Stephen Osborne, "The Lost Art of Waving." First published in *GEIST* 46. © Stephen Osborne. Used by permission of the author. • Nick Paumgarten, "Master of Play." Originally published in *The New Yorker* (20 December 2010). © 2011 Nick Paumgarten. Used by permission of the author. Nick Paumgarten is a staff writer at *The New Yorker*. • Arlene Perly Rae, Irshad Manji, and Anna Porter, "A Call to Arms on Anti-Semitism." Reprinted by permission. • Jennie Punter, "Crime and Punishment in a Foreign Land." Originally published in *Queen's Quarterly* 177.3 (Fall 2010), pp. 380-391. Copyright © Jennie Punter. Reprinted by permission of the author. • Judy Rebick, "The Culture of Overwork" from *Elm Street* (Feb./Mar. 2001), p. 88. Reprinted with permission of the author and *Elm Street* magazine. • Laura Robinson, "Sports Breeds Real-Life Violence" from *Winnipeg Free Press* (17 May 2007), p. A14. Copyright © 2007 Laura Robinson. Reprinted by permission of the author. • Anik See, "Borderland" from *GEIST* 53 (Summer 2004). Copyright © 2007 Anik See. Reprinted by permission of Anik See. • Russell Smith, "Potty Mouthed and Proud of It" from *The Globe & Mail* (22 January 2004). Copyright © 2004 Russell Smith. Reprinted by permission of Russell Smith. • Janice Stein, "Whisper, Echo and Voice: Developing a National Voice" from "Great Canadian Questions." *The Dominion Institute*. www.greatquestions.com (1999). Reprinted with permission. • Drew Hayden Taylor, "Pretty Like a White Boy: The Adventures of a Blue-Eyed Ojibway" from *An Anthology of Native Canadian Literature in English*, Oxford University Press. First printed in *THIS Magazine* (August 1991). Copyright © Drew Hayden Taylor. • Jowi Taylor, "Beginning," an excerpt from *Six String Nation: 64 Pieces. 6 Strings. 1 Canada. 1 Guitar*, published 2009 by Douglas & McIntyre: an imprint of D&M Publishers Inc. Reprinted with permission from the publisher. • Dylan Thomas, line from "Do Not Go Gentle Into That Good Night." Copyright © David Higham Associates Ltd. • Lewis Thomas, "To Err is Human", copyright © 1976 by Lewis Thomas, from *THE MEDUSA AND THE SNAIL* by Lewis Thomas. Used by permission of Viking Penguin, a division of Penguin Group (USA) Inc. • Benoit Virole, "Harry Potter's Cauldron: The Power of Myth and the Rebirth of the Sacred" from *Queen's Quarterly* 111.3 (Fall 2004), p. 370. Copyright © 2004 Queen's Quarterly. Reprinted by permission of Queen's Quarterly. • Carmen Everest Wahl, "Gluten Intolerance: Why Are More People Suffering Than Ever Before?" Originally published in *edible Toronto* (Winter 2010/2011), pp. 8–9. Copyright © Carmen Everest Wahl. Used by permission of the author. • Aaron Wherry, "Violently Happy: Why the NHL Needs to Make Hockey Safe Again for Those Who Appreciate Bloodshed" from *Maisonneuve* (19 January 2007). Copyright © 2007 Maisonneuve Magazine. www.maisonneuve.org. Reprinted by permission of the author. • Barbara J. Wilson, abstract from the article "Media and Children's Aggression, Fear, and Altruism" from *The Future of Children*, a collaboration of The Woodrow Wilson School of Public and International Affairs at Princeton University and the Brookings Institution. • Jean Yoon, "Halmonee" from *Han Kut: Critical Art & Writing by Korean Canadian Women*, pp. 18–22. Copyright © 2007 Jean Yoon. Reprinted by permission of Jean Yoon.

INDEX OF AUTHORS AND TITLES

Andersen, Marguerite 519
"Anti-Gay Bullying" (Fricker, Kushner) 431

Badami, Anita Rau 139
Bascaramurty, Dakshana 200
"Beginning" from *Six String Nation* (Taylor, J.) 120
"Between the Highs and the Lows, Life Happens" (K'naan) 102
"Between the North Bridge and the King George IV Bridge" (Moore, L.) 79
Bigge, Ryan 530
Black, Simon 335
"Borderland" (See) 107
Boyd, Alex 256
Braun, Will 237

"Call to Arms on Anti-Semitism, A" (Perly Rae, Manji, Porter) 421
Callwood, June 318
Cohen, Matt 112
"Co-opting Dissent" (Klein) 164
Coren, Stanley 190
"Crime and Punishment in a Foreign Land" (Punter) 293
"Critical Thinking: What Is It Good For? (In Fact, What Is It?)" (Gabennesch) 12
"Culture of Overwork, The" (Rebick) 426

DeWolf, Christopher 289
"Dogs and Monsters" (Coren) 190
"Don't Call Me That Word" (Hill) 339

"Ecstasy of War, The" (Ehrenreich) 477
Egan, Brian Denis 9
Ehrenreich, Barbara 477
Elder, Linda 5
"Elegy in Stone" (Heighton) 94

"Facilitated Communication & the Power of Belief: How *Time* Magazine Got It Wrong" (Norton) 486
"Fat Acceptance: A Basic Primer" (Geissler) 330
Fiorito, Joe 73
"Forgiveness" (Callwood) 318
Fricker, Daniel 431

Gabennesch, Howard 12
Geissler, Cynara 330
Gillmor, Alison 226
"Giving Up the Fight" (Lamothe) 125
Gladwell, Malcolm 185
Glover, Douglas 325
"Gluten Intolerance: Why Are More People Suffering Than Ever Before?" (Wahl) 384
Goldberg, Natalie 520
Goodheart, Adam 212
Gopnik, Adam 457
Guy, Jeannie 391

"Halmonee" (Yoon) 59
"Harry Potter's Cauldron: The Power of Myth and the Rebirth of the Sacred" (Virole) 524
Heighton, Steven 94
Highway, Tomson 55
"Hijabs: Don't Kick Up a Fuss" (Khan) 448
Hill, Lawrence 339
"How to Mummify a Pharaoh" (Goodheart) 212
Hummel, Monte 274

Iglauer, Edith 67
"In Defense of Graffiti" (Boyd) 256
"Information-Rich and Attention-Poor" (Nicholson) 362
"Is the Belgian Coca-Cola Hysteria the Real Thing?" (Gladwell) 185

"John Lennon, Michael Jackson: Do Celebrities Die Anymore?" (Onstad) 152

Khan, Sheema 448
King, Stephen 356
Kingsolver, Barbara 157
Klein, Naomi 164
K'naan 102
Kushner, Lars 431

Lamothe, Jenn 125
Lau, Evelyn 397
Levitin, Daniel J. 250
"Life Without Go-Go Boots" (Kingsolver) 157
Littlejohn, Maureen 196

"Looking to the Future with a Critical Eye: A Message for High School Graduates" (Elder) 5
"Lost Art of Waving, The" (Osborne) 169

Mair, Rafe 452
Manji, Irshad 284, 421
"Master of Play" (Paumgarten) 205
McKinley, Michael 278
McNutt, Ryan 148
"Montrealers, Cherish Your Clotheslines" (DeWolf) 289
Moore, John 370
Moore, Lisa 79
Moosang, Faith 246
"More and More" (Lau) 397
"Music of My Mind: A Neuroscientist Examines the Recipe for Listening Ecstasy, The" (Levitin) 250
"Music We Hate: Joanna Newsom, The" (McNutt) 148
"My Canada" (Badami) 139
"My Parents Killed Santa (and Nobody Cared)" (Bascaramurty) 200

"Nancy Drew Knows It's Hard" (Moosang) 246
"Newfoundland Cooking" (Guy) 391
Nicholson, Peter 362
"Night Shift on the Main" (Fiorito) 73
Norton, Lawrence 486

"On Winning and Responsibility" (Glover) 325
Onstad, Katrina 152
Osborne, Stephen 169
"Opera Night in Canada" (McKinley) 278

"Passion for Language" (Andersen) 519
"Passion for the Environment: Two Accounts, A" (Hummel) 274
Paumgarten, Nick 205
Perly Rae, Arlene 421
Porter, Anna 421
"Potty-Mouthed and Proud of It" (Smith) 443
"Pretty Like a White Boy: The Adventures of a Blue-Eyed Ojibway" (Taylor, D.H.) 310
Punter, Jennie 293

"Raise the Driving Age" (Mair) 452
Rebick, Judy 426
"Red Smile" (Iglauer) 67
"Repress Yourself" (Gillmor) 226
Robinson, Laura 467
"Role of Critical Thinking in Effective Decision Making, The" (Egan) 9
"Rules of Writing Practice, The" (Goldberg) 520

"Search for Mandela's Gun, The" (Black) 335
See, Anik 107
"Seven Criteria for the Adoption of New Technology" (Braun) 237
"Shootings" (Gopnik) 457
Smith, Russell 443
"Speak English, Dammit: Why Has Jargon Become the Language of Business?" (Bigge) 530
"Sporting Life" (Moore, J.) 370
"Sports Breeds Real-Life Violence" (Robinson) 467
"Status Anxiety? Consider Socrates and the Sewer Saviour" (Manji) 284
Stein, Janice Gross 437

Taylor, Drew Hayden 310
Taylor, Jowi 120
Thomas, Lewis 17, 21
"To Err Is Human" (Thomas) 21

"Violently Happy: Why the NHL Needs to Make Hockey Safe Again for Those Who Appreciate Bloodshed" (Wherry) 463
Virole, Benoit 524

"What a Certain Visionary Once Said" (Highway) 55
Wahl, Carmen Everest 384
Wherry, Aaron 463
"Whisper, Echo and Voice" (Stein) 437
"Why We Crave Horror Movies" (King) 356

Yoon, Jean 59
"You Are a Contract Painkiller" (Littlejohn) 196

"Zada's Hanukkah Legacy" (Cohen) 112